In Memoriam

Tyntesfield and

The First World War

Written and compiled

By David J. Hogg

All rights reserved. No part of this book may be reproduced, stored or introduced into a retrieval system or transmitted in any form or by any means (electronic, mechanical, photocopying, recording or otherwise) without the prior permission of the author.

Copyright © David J. Hogg, 2012.

ISBN 978-0-9554457-4-3

Published by D. J. Hogg, 2012

Printed and bound by CPI Group (UK) Ltd, Croydon, CR0 4YY

CONTENTS

Acknowledgements... 4

Introduction.. 5

Chapter One – Halcyon Years.. 6

Chapter Two – The Diary of Anstice Katharine Gibbs............... 23

Chapter Three – Wedding at Tyntesfield...................................... 62

Chapter Four – Edwardian Tyntesfield...................................... 104

Chapter Five – The Great War.. 126

Chapter Six – The Armistice and Versailles........................... 392

Chapter Seven – Peace Returns... 418

Illustrations.. 429

Index.. 432

References... 449

Figure 1. Officers of the North Somerset Yeomanry in France, October 1914.

Acknowledgements

Anstice Katharine Gibbs' grand-daughter, Susanna Swallow, donated a collection of family correspondence to Tyntesfield, which included letters sent by Antony and Janet Gibbs' sons from South Africa during the Boer War and also letters sent from John Evelyn Gibbs when he was a prisoner of war in Germany during the First World War. At Windsor Castle, I located the Archive of the Reverend and Mrs. Arthur Stafford Crawley, which had been placed in the Archives of St. George's Chapel, Windsor by their daughter, Lady Goodman. Stafford Crawley was the Canon of St Georges Chapel and the King's Chaplain for George VI. Mrs. Crawley was Antony and Janet Gibbs' second daughter – Anstice Katharine Gibbs – Nancy. The archival collection includes letters from the Boer War and from the First World War written by her brothers, and Nancy's diaries. I should like to express my special thanks to Dr Clare Rider, the Archivist at St. George's Chapel, who gave her consent for me to use these letters and diaries, and to her very courteous and helpful assistants. Acknowledgement is due to the Dean and Canons of St. George's Chapel, Windsor.

From reading the letters at Windsor I gleaned that there was a War Diary written by Antony and Janet Gibbs' youngest son, Lancelot, who was always called Lags. Lancelot Merivale Gibbs' grandson – Giles Gibbs – very kindly sent me a typed copy of this diary, which forms the backbone of the story of the First World War. Jane Bennett, the grand daughter of Albinia Rose Gibbs, gave Tyntesfield her grandmother's photo albums and a small collection of letters written to her grandfather, Richard Bennett, from the Boer War. Albinia Rose was Antony and Janet Gibbs' eldest daughter, who sadly was crippled after a riding accident. Theresa Courtauld supplied a copy of her grandfather's "Some Memories of William Gibbs, 1877 to 1963". Further photographs came from Antony and Virginia Gibbs – Antony's grandmother was Janet Blanche Gibbs. Susanna Swallow also very kindly gave me access to Anstice Katharine's photo albums and her collection of press cuttings.

Thanks are also due to the volunteers who helped with the transcribing of the letters and diaries. These include Heather Bailey, Jo Delafaille, Margaret Lemon, Hilary Parker, Sue Price, Margaret Rowley and Joyce Schaffer. Margaret Wilcock helped with the Census Returns and the War Records of soldiers associated with the Gibbs family at Tyntesfield. Denis and Rachel Gibbs also gave me much encouragement and useful contacts when needed. Rachel Gibbs' Pedigree of the Family of Gibbs (1981) provided invaluable biographical and genealogical information. The National Trust at Tyntesfield gave me permission to include the letters, portraits and photographs in their collection.

David J. Hogg, 16th July 2012.

Introduction

In 1887 Antony Gibbs inherited Tyntesfield, which had been his mother's home since his father died in 1875. The story begins in this Victorian Gothic mansion which, after nearly three years of considerable renovation and extension by the architect Henry Woodyer from 1887 to 1890, sprung into life as the home of a large family with six boys and three girls enjoying all the delights of country house living in late Victorian and Edwardian England. Their parents – Antony and Janet Gibbs – had since their marriage in 1872 lived at Charlton House, high on the hill to the north of Tyntesfield, whence there were wonderful views overlooking the surrounding countryside and not far away over the Severn Estuary towards Wales. Their lives were filled with sports and amateur dramatics, with music and dancing, with horse riding and excursions by carriage or by train, and when country life palled, they were off to their home in London at 16 Hyde Park Gardens. In London they enjoyed the concerts and the theatre, the opera and the ballet, and on the southern side of Hyde Park were all the new Victorian Museums of Exhibition Road and of course the Albert Hall.

This idyll was interrupted by the Boer War in which three sons, George Abraham, William and John Evelyn took part, but mercifully they came home safely ready to resume the annual Cricket Week in July, the Grouse Season in the Scottish Highlands, the house parties all over England at the homes of friends and relations, and the gatherings of friends and family at Tyntesfield. After Antony died in 1907, the house became quieter with George Abraham Gibbs and his wife Victoria as the new owners, but still the younger children – Lancelot and Janet Blanche regarded Tyntesfield as their home. Seven years later their whole world was thrown into confusion with the outbreak of War in August 1914.

Photographs from members of the Gibbs' family have enabled us to envisage what their lives were like at the time, and letters from various family members helped to clarify these images. The photo albums of Albinia Rose, Anstice Katharine, and Janet Blanche Gibbs bring to life the extraordinary story of Tyntesfield before the Great War.

Lancelot Merivale Gibbs in a remarkable Diary, which began in August 1914 and ended in June 1919, recorded the events of that War. Luckily Lancelot's sister Anstice Katharine (always known as Nancy) also wrote a diary, and her Diaries for 1894, 1902 and 1903 together with many family letters were kept by her and are now safely preserved in the Archives of St. George's Chapel, Windsor. The letters from South Africa and from the Great War are of particular interest. These form a basis from which we are able to build up a picture of what life was like at the time, and to get an insight into the unimaginable conflict, which suddenly shattered all the illusions of Edwardian England.

Chapter One

Halcyon Years

In 1887 Antony Gibbs inherited Tyntesfield and the Gibbs' London home at 16, Hyde Park Gardens on the death of his mother, Matilda Blanche Gibbs on September 22nd 1887. He had been much involved in running the estate with two model farms at Charlton and Tyntesfield completed in 1882. On June 22nd 1872, Antony married Janet Louisa Merivale at the Church of St Michael's and All Angels in Paddington. This Church and the Vicarage had been built between 1860 and 1861 with the money given by his father. Rhode Hawkins was the architect[i].

Janet's family, the Merivales, came from Exeter and had known the Gibbs family for many years. Antony and Dorothea Gibbs were Merivale tenants when they lived at Cowley from 1803 to 1808. Janet's father, John Lewis Merivale, was a close friend of Anthony Trollope, whom he had known since school days at Sunbury and Harrow. His nephew Herman Charles Merivale described him as a convivial man with many friends and something of an eccentric, (*Bar, Stage and Platform, Herman Charles Merivale 1902, page 96*). He was Clerk in the Chancery Registrar's Office from 1841 until 1882 and then Senior Registrar of the Supreme Court from 1882 until he retired in 1885. He died on 14 December 1886. Two of Janet's uncles were very distiguished – Herman Merivale, a barrister, who was Professor of Political Economy at Oxford, Permanent Under-Secretary of State for the Colonies, and then from 1860 for the new India Office, and Charles Merivale, a founder of the Oxford and Cambridge Boat Race, a classical scholar and historian of the Roman Empire, and Dean of Ely Cathedral[ii].

John Lewis Merivale married Mary Ann Webster on 14th August 1849 in Aston, Warwickshire. They had five children; Janet Louisa 1850-1909, Reginald 1852-1937, Catherine 1853-1937, George Montague 1855-1931 and Laura Augusta 1856-1862. Sadly Mary died in Exeter on 5th October 1857 at the age of only 29. Then in 1859 John Lewis Merivale married Frances Rose Heath, the daughter of Baron John Benjamin Heath (1790-1879), who was his mother's first cousin. The family home was at 5, Norfolk Square[iii].

After their marriage, Antony and Janet Gibbs moved into the house at Charlton, which was to be their home until 1890. They had ten children, nine of whom survived into adulthood. They were:

1. George Abraham Gibbs born at Charlton 6th July 1873
2. Antony Hubert Gibbs born at Charlton 18th September 1874
3. Albinia Rose Gibbs born at 16 Hyde Park Gardens, 31st March 1876

4. William Gibbs born at 16, Hyde Park Gardens, 20th November 1877
5. John Evelyn Gibbs born at 16 Hyde Park Gardens, 22nd December 1879
6. Anstice Katharine Gibbs born at Charlton 12th September 1881
7. Louis Merivale Gibbs born at Charlton, 24th April 1883, died 1st May 1884
8. Eustace Lyle Gibbs born at Tyntesfield 10th March 1885
9. Janet Blanche Gibbs born at Charlton 15th May 1887
10. Lancelot Merivale Gibbs born at Charlton, 23rd December 1889.[iv]

When Antony inherited in 1887, he embarked upon an ambitious program spending £50,000 to make extensive changes to Tyntesfield. His architect was Henry Woodyer. This meant that during 1888 and 1889, the house was a building site. In 1890, when the work was completed, the family with nine children finally moved in to Tyntesfield.

William and Matilda Blanche Gibbs had three surviving children. The eldest, Dorothea, was born at 13, Hyde Park Street on 12th June 1840. She lived for many years at 77, Crystal Palace Park, Sydenham, where she died on September 20th 1914. She was known as Aunt Dolly. While well provided for by her parents, the greater part of the family fortune went firstly to Antony and then to Henry Martin who both became very wealthy men.[v] Antony purchased Barrow Court for his brother in 1881, and Henry Martin then restored the house, which he finally purchased from Antony in 1884. In 1887, Antony became the sole owner of Tyntesfield. Hence the two brothers had large houses and estates on opposite sides of the valley. The great wealth being created by the family firm of Antony Gibbs and Sons under the chairmanship of Henry Hucks Gibbs, the First Lord Aldenham, enhanced the prosperity of the Gibbs family.

A description of life at Charlton and Tyntesfield at the time is given by Antony and Janet's third son, William. He wrote in "Some Memories of William Gibbs 1877 to 1963",

"I was born at 16 Hyde Park Gardens but my earliest recollections are of Charlton. Nanny Sparks was in charge of me but soon gave place to Nanny Bailey. The former went to live in London and took a small stall in an indoor Arcade – I think in Lisson Grove. Lee was the butler, a very nice man, but he slipped up over another female servant, my mother's maid I think. He was succeeded by Pollard, who eventually married the cook, Lizzie. Our favourite maid was Liza. Page, the coachman had been in the 14th Hussars. Shipstone was head gardener.

I can just remember Father riding at home and with the Yeomanry. His troop had a large lunch in the hall and then drilled in the park.

The original Charlton was an Elizabethan house but was spoilt by alterations, especially by my father's additions in local stone, executed a short time before my Grandmother's death. This event caused our move to Tyntesfield. The setting of Charlton is charming. The view from the north front is to the Bristol Channel at Portishead.

Figure 2. Four of Antony and Janet's children at Charlton – Nancy, Eustace, Albinia and Blanche.

We all learnt to bicycle at Charlton. An expert from Willways in Bristol taught us. He also supplied the bicycles. Father stuck to his tricycle. We had a succession of ponies. They were too much for us as a rule and we were never given any proper riding instruction. I think we preferred a frosty winter when we could skate on the small shallow pond in the garden. Other amusements were indoor cricket in our bedroom passage. Georgie had a room to himself. Huie and I together next door. Rooms were in the old part of the house – I think ours was panelled. Miss Hughes the governess taught Georgie and Hughie. I was too young. Driving to Bristol station we passed her home in Coronation Road.

We used to hang about the stables a good deal and the carriage horses were great favourites. "Khars" was the "clipper that stood in the stall at the top". His name marked the period of Lord Roberts's Afghanistan march. There was always a donkey in a small paddock. Our earliest riding was done on it, sitting on a pannier.

Figure 3. Charlton House, North Somerset, now the Downs School.

Figure 4. Charlton Model Farm, now The Children's Hospice South West.

A cricket ground was made when Georgie and Hughie were old enough and matches were held. I was too young to play. Father was chairman of the North Somerset Conservative Association so when Mr. Llewellyn was elected he arrived at Nailsea station to stay at Charlton. Page put four horses in the break and the family met him and there was a triumphal drive. Grandmother also went to the station in her yellow barouche, which had a rumble behind containing two seats. Another child and I sat in the rumble. We came to the steep hill and the carriage was very heavy. Halfway up one of the two horses had a heart attack and fell down dead. It was a terrific thrill.

We were very fond of the Home Farm ¼ of a mile away and Mr. and Mrs. Lear, the bailiff and his wife, were family friends. The latter made the butter and made it of Devonshire cream. It must have been lovely butter. We ate a good deal of the cream before it was made into butter.

Figure 5. Pembroke Lodge School, near Bournemouth

In 1887 I went to Pembroke Lodge private school, just before we left Charlton. Georgie and Huie had already left the school.

At Charlton we had a French Governess whom we liked but eventually she had to be dismissed because she flirted with Tom Bennett. Everyone liked Tom and Mademoiselle liked him so much that she married him. They settled in Exeter and kept a tobacconist shop.

Sibby Nichols, widow of James Nichols the Tyntesfield bailiff, lived along the Charlton Drive and was often visited. Her husband was a cousin of Beverly Nichols and, like Mademoiselle, left under a cloud.

A bathing pool was constructed at Charlton with an island in the middle. There was a bridge from mainland to it and Father stood on this bridge and dangled us in the water below, teaching us to swim. It was rather a stagnant pool.

An early recollection is of meeting Father at Portbury station on his return from Spain, bringing a lovely sweetmeat.

The southern aspect from Charlton was lovely; a sunk fence (Ha Ha) and, beyond the Park with Indian deer.

We walked to Wraxall Church on Sunday with Father. The females went in the Landau. There were pews of the "loose box" variety and the oak arrangement of the pulpit and the clerk's seat below. All this was cleared away when Father restored the Church.

Our family vault was just outside the Chancel. In fact it is still there but my parents and brother are all buried outside. I don't like to see the Churchyard as it is today. It has been crammed with graves and obviously many who were not Wraxall people have been accommodated. The Vaughans were Parsons, father and then son.... Young Mrs. Vaughan was known as "butter" owing to her habit of speech joining her sentences with "but...er".

We had many horse carriages: the Landau for Mother and the Victoria if the weather was warm; her pony carriage with seat behind for the groom, drawn by Castor and Pollux; Father's Phaeton for 2 horses; the Wagonette, the Break, the Dog-Cart, the Brougham and the sledge. Except for the sledge every vehicle had 4 wheels. Two-wheeled carriages were considered dangerous in such hilly country.

Charlton garden was on the south side of the house. It was very nice except for the shrubbery, a gloomy place of mostly laurels, but useful to hide in when cousins came to stay whom we did not appreciate.

Both Father and Mother were shy people and our visitors were nearly always relations. The ones who came most were probably Aunt Catty and Uncle Reggie (Merivale).

Charlton is an Elizabethan house with a south front added in early Victorian days but it was presumably too small for our large family so Father, during the 1880s, built on a billiard room with bedrooms over it. Local stone was used and to our present ideas the addition is hideous.

After Grand Mother's death much alteration was done to Tyntesfield, the work continuing for about two years. Then we moved there for good and all.

Everyone dislikes Victorian Ecclesiastical Gothic architecture nowadays and I think what Father did to the house made it worse than it was before. The new long pillared dining room, which we children admired, was not successful. The pillars made it necessary for the dining table to be at the dark side of the room and too near the fireplace.

Altering the central staircase in the hall was a great mistake in my view. There was some idea of making it a "sitting hall" and it was so used in spite of there being seven other sitting rooms available. Draughts could not be prevented in the hall. However, Mr. Care the architect designed a dreadful oak divan where air could not penetrate.

The drawing room was never used in daytime because Grandmother had built a verandah in front of its windows. It ruined the room but the verandah was nice in summer.

Mr. Hardie, late Chaplain, continued to live in the house until a cottage was provided for him. He wore a cassock reaching to his toes every day and all day. Mr. Medley became Chaplain and looked after the library, liked by all. A house was built for him and he conducted Chapel Services every day.

There were 2 Services every week day in the Chapel. We boys attended before breakfast when we could "make it". In Winter Father wore his fur cloak in chapel. It had been his Father's and I have got it now."

Antony and Janet were frequent visitors to Tyntesfield and one of their children, Eustace Lyle Gibbs was actually born there. Although Antony managed the Model Farm, which was completed in 1882, the family continued to live at Charlton. When Henry Woodyer's extensive building work was completed in 1890, the family finally moved into Tyntesfield.

The boys went to Pembroke Lodge Preparatory School and then on to Eton College, while the girls were educated at home by a Governess. There was a French Mademoiselle and from 1890 a German Fraulein, Anna Schmincke, and at Tyntesfield there was a School Room, which later was to become Lady Wraxall's Bedroom. Albinia Rose Gibbs in her photo albums had several pictures of a notorious protest at Cambridge University staged by male undergraduates against the idea of women being able to graduate. It was obviously a theme she felt strongly about.

In 1897, a proposal was put before Cambridge University's Senate to grant full degrees to female graduates. Male students responded with outrage. The image below shows the scene in the market square on the day of the debate. An effigy of a woman on a bicycle was suspended out of the window of Bowes and Bowes Bookshop, whose building was opposite the Senate. Banners reading "No Gowns for Girtonites" and "Varsity for Men" flew alongside it. The lady cyclist in her rational costume was a readily recognised symbol of the new woman whose entrance into higher education the male students resented.

At the time of the protest, women were permitted to study at Cambridge, but were not granted full degrees. Newnham and Girton Colleges for women opened in the 1870s, and in 1881 women gained the right to sit for the Tripos examination. The 1897 ruling would have admitted women as full members of the university. The resolution did not, however, pass. Women studying at Cambridge University were not to receive the titles of full degrees until 1921, and even then it was without associated privileges[vi]. The photographs of this event in Albinia Rose Gibbs's albums suggest that the protests were a topic of some controversy in the family. As Antony Hubert Gibbs was the only boy to go to Cambridge, was this the source of these pictures?

Figure 6. Demonstration against Women's degrees at Cambridge in 1897.

While the daughters of Antony and Janet Gibbs family were educated at home by a governess, the boys went first to preparatory school and then off in succession to Eton College. These are the details of their education:

George Abraham	Eton College	1887-92
	Christchurch College Oxford	1892-97
Antony Hubert	Eton College	1888-92
	Trinity Hall Cambridge	1893-97
William	Eton College	1891-96
	Magdalen College Oxford	1896-99
John Evelyn	Eton College	1892-97
	Sandhurst	1898-99

Eustace	Eton College	1898-03
	Magdalen College Oxford	1903-06
Lancelot Merivale	Eton College	1902-08

Figure 7. House Group at Eton in 1891. No 1 = William Gibbs, No 2 = George Abraham Gibbs, No 3 = Antony Hubert Gibbs and No 4 = Richard Bennett.

From the photo albums of Albinia Rose Bennett, née Gibbs, Antony and Janet's eldest daughter we get a glimpse of life at Tyntesfield. Croquet was played on the lawn, horse riding, cycling, hunting and shooting, tennis and cricket were popular pastimes. Albinia's husband, Richard Bennett, who was at Eton with the three older Gibbs boys, was a very accomplished cricketer who played for Hampshire and the M.C.C. The whole family was mad about cricket and every summer there was a cricket week at Tyntesfield. Golf and billiards were also popular and there was swimming at a pool near Watercress Farm. At Belmont there was a racquets court where the boys could hone their game ready for coming matches at Eton.

Henry Martin Gibbs, Antony's younger brother, and his wife Emily Otter had nine children. They lived at Barrow Court on the opposite side of the valley to Tyntesfield. There were seven sons –

William Otter (born 19th September 1883), Noel Martin (born 25th December 1884), Francis (born 19th December 1885), Roland Vicary (born 16th March 1887), Guy Melvil (born 15th December 1889), Ralph Crawley Boevey (born 24th July 1891) and Lionel Cyril (born 15th February 1893). Hence there were always plenty of family cricketers available to play at Tyntesfield. Their first daughter – Matilda Blanche – was born on November 20th 1888 but sadly died on 14th January 1889. Mary Albinia, the only surviving daughter was born on 5th November 1894 and died on 15th September 1979. vii

In the evening at Tyntesfield there were amateur dramatics and dances, bridge and board games were played, and there was music and singing with playing of the harp and the piano. There was much socializing and family and friends frequently visited the house.

Figure 8. The Gibbs boys at the front entrance to Tyntesfield in order of age from left to right, George Abraham, Antony Hubert, William, John Evelyn, Eustace Lyle and Lancelot Merivale.

On August 12th every year, the whole family would travel up to Scotland for the beginning of the Grouse Season. Houses rented in Scotland included Glenfeshie, 1877, Lude House, 1892, Loch Kennard 1894, 1895, 1896 and 1898, Black Mount, 1880, and other years, Moncrieffe House, 1902, Thurso 1903, and Corrie Fergis, 1904.viii Some of the hunting trophies still hang in the Billiard Room at Tyntesfield. The family would go on walks through the highlands, visit neighbouring houses, entertain guests and even climb some of the local mountains. When the winters were very cold there was even skating on the pond at Belmont.

Figure 9. Horse riding at Tyntesfield in 1897 - left to right - Richard Bennett, George Abraham, Anstice Katharine, Albinia Rose and John Evelyn Gibbs.

Figure 10. Cycling at Tyntesfield in 1896 - left to right - Janet Blanche, Antony, Albinia Rose, Francis, AL, WC, Anstice Katharine, ECG, WHG, and Lancelot Merivale Gibbs.

The family members were great travellers and went to Chamonix and St. Moritz for the winter sports and in the summer to Paris, Pau in the Pyrenees, Florence, Venice and Rome. Antony in particular travelled far and wide visiting France and Germany, Spain and Portugal, Switzerland and Italy, Austria, Egypt and Russia in search of art and architecture.

Figure 11. Antony Gibbs - Photograph taken in Cairo.

There are large albums in the Oratory at Tyntesfield, which illustrate his travels. There are numerous photographs of works of art from the Louvre in Paris, the Prado in Madrid, the Uffizi in Florence and the Vatican Museum in Rome. In Spain he saw the Alhambra in Granada, the Mesquite in Cordoba, the Cathedral in Toledo and the Alcazar in Seville. In Italy he visited Pompeii a few years after the eruption of Vesuvius in 1872. He went to Naples, Paestum, Capri and Amalfi. He also visited Rome, Florence, Assisi, Venice and Milan. Sometimes his family accompanied him. The family firm – Antony Gibbs and Sons – installed electric light and power in the city of St. Petersburg in Russia.

This gave Antony an excellent opportunity to see the Russia of Nicholas and Alexandra.[ix]

Figure 12. The Suez Canal opened in 1869 photographed by Antony Gibbs.

Figure 13. The eruption of Vesuvius in 1872 just before Antony's visit.

Figure 14. Il Duomo - the cathedral - in Milan. Gothic architecture loved by William and Antony Gibbs.

Figure 15. Antony, Janet, George Abraham and Albinia Rose on holiday in Venice.

Antony and Janet's sons joined the Cadets at Eton and became very keen on the army. This led to their participation in the North Somerset Yeomanry and other regiments. Henry Hucks Gibbs' son, Alban married Lord Salisbury's niece on the 18th February 1873. Lord Salisbury and Arthur Balfour were witnesses. William Gibbs and his family attended the wedding service and reception at Bedgebury Park, which was very grand.[x] The Gibbs family developed a great enthusiasm for the Empire of which Lord Salisbury was so strong an advocate.

This enthusiasm was shared by Henry Martin's family at Barrow Court and two of his sons, Noel and Lionel, went to farm in Kenya. Henry Martin and Emily Gibbs' sons also went to Eton. Three went on to Magdalen College Oxford and one, Lionel, to Christchurch College Oxford.

William Otter	Eton College	1896-1901
	Sandhurst	1901-1902
Noel Martin	Eton College	1898-1899
	Radley College	1899-1902
Francis Antony	Eton College	1899-1904
	Magdalen College Oxford	1906-1909
Roland Vicary	Eton College	1900-1906
	Magdalen College Oxford	1906-1909
Guy Melvil	Eton College	1902-1908
	Cirencester Agricultural College	1909-1910
Ralph C.Boevey	Eton College	1904-1909
	Magdalen College Oxford	1910-1912
Lionel Cyril	Eton College	1906-1912
	Christ Church Oxford	1912-1913

William Otter Gibbs served with the Somerset Light Infantry in India at Mhow (1903-1906) and Rawal Pindi (1906-1912). He was then attached to the Egyptian Army from 1912 to 1914.

Lieutenant Noel Martin Gibbs went to British East Africa (Kenya) in 1906 and farmed at North Tabibbi, Naivasha and Nakuru. In September 1914 he enlisted in the East African Mounted Rifles and was in operations near Kisi on Lake Victoria and near Kilimanjaro. He was killed on the Ruhu River near Kahe Railway Station in German East Africa (Tanzania) on March 20th 1916.

Lieutenant Lionel Gibbs lost his left arm at Ypres on 13th May 1915. After the War he farmed in Kenya from 1920 to 1929, and founded the Kenya Coffee Company in London in 1921. The Gibbs family was to have many links with colonial Africa particularly with Kenya, Rhodesia and South Africa.[xi]

Figure 16. George Abraham Gibbs (front left of centre) with the Christchurch Beagles in 1895.

At Christchurch College Oxford George Abraham Gibbs was Master Of the Beagles and seems to have entered into the life of the university with some gusto. He also developed an enthusiasm for things military and joined the North Somerset Yeomanry in 1893.

Figure 17. George Abraham Gibbs (front row right) with the North Somerset Yeomanry.

Figure 18. Walking on the Mer de Glace, Chamonix, 1894.

Figure 19. Tyntesfield's Tilbury gig to take you to the Railway Station.

During the 1890s life at Tyntesfield was idyllic and luckily one of the children wrote a diary, which has survived. Anstice Katharine Gibbs's Diary for 1894 describes with childlike innocence what it was like to live at Tyntesfield and at 16 Hyde Park Gardens in London and to travel with the family.

Chapter Two

The Diary of Anstice Katharine Gibbs (Nancy) 1894

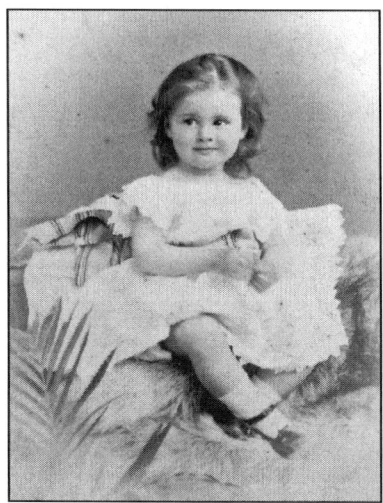 

Figure 20. Anstice Katharine Gibbs, known as Nancy.

I had my head washed in evening. Four gents went to the Emigration Ball in evening, three went as themselves, and Georgie in his uniform.

Jan 11th Poor Mary died. Jan 13th Poor Mary was buried. Albinia, Evelyn and Billy went to the funeral.
Jan 23rd Kathleen Spencer came. She was very unhappy at leaving home. From Jan 24th till February 1st
Kathleen is quite happy now.
Jan 27th Georgie had an accident out Hunting. He got kicked and rolled upon. But is luckily not badly hurt.
Dec 25th 1893 Xmas Day. Had a quantity of presents all very jolly ones.
Feb 13th 1894. I am giving up tea and have milk instead this Lent.
March 2nd I, Kathy and Eustace were upset in the donkey chase.
Aug 15th Arriving in Scotland
Aug 31st 1894 Went out with the shooters for the first time and sat in Mr. Bright's butt.
September 8th Went out with the shooters all day for a grouse drive.

These are my candles *(here is a drawing of two candlesticks with candles in them).* One is so big

Sat 10th Nov
Cyril Gurney was married in London to Miss Trotter

Anstice Katharine Gibbs born 12 September 1882
Died 8th January 1963. She was 12 in 1894

Her Mother
Janet Louisa Gibbs
Born 15th December 1850
Died 10th December 1909

Her Father
Antony Gibbs
Born December 10th 1841
Died April 24th 1907

January 1894
Monday 1st
Kathleen Spencer came. Violet, Albinia, Mr Leigh, Hughie and Georgie went to a ball at the Hills in Clevedon in evening. Cyril Daubeny came. Mary not so well in morning. Packed parcels for the poor in morning after which I sat in the Billiard Room reading Punch, till Kathy came. Spent most of the afternoon on the farm watching different things being done, such as see the horses pull enormous carts of manure out of the buildings, it was dreadfully hard work for them. Made an awful row in evening.
Tuesday 2nd
Seven of the party went out riding in afternoon. They meant to go out hunting, but couldn't because it was too hard and frosty. Spent the morning in trying on fancy dresses, because the Hills of Clevedon are going to give a children's fancy dress dance, I am going to be Amy Robsart, which is the same dress as Albinia wore two years ago here. The Cornishes asked me to go there and stay there for two nights, the 10th and 11th, the tenth is the Hills dance, the 11th is their own.
Wednesday 3rd
Skated in afternoon. Albinia and Violet went in to Clifton and bought me a new pair of skates. Cyril Daubeny and Violet acted Schraras in the evening.
Thursday 4th
Skated all day. Willy Gurney came in evening. Mary a little bit better. Was sent to bed just before Cyril and Violet acted. We had the Hot Air turned on, so there was a horrible smell in the house all day. Hilda and Edmund Evans came and skated.
Friday 5th
Dreadfully cold all day. Albinia went away to stay with Uncle Martin. Tobogganed in afternoon. Evelyn hurt his knee. Am going to sleep with Violet this evening. Had a preaching letter from Fraulein, asking me to

write her a nice little repentance letter. I have already written to her twice telling her how sorry I am I didn't give her her letter, so I don't see why I should write again. George Morehouse came and stayed. Mary a little bit better.

Figure 21. Albinia as Amy Robsart 1892.

Saturday 6th
Skated a little in morning. Went to the pantomime in afternoon, had a headache at the pantomime and coming back in fact have only just got rid of it. Mr. R. A. Ford came to dinner. Father and Georgie went to dine with the Eltons, Mother was going but she had a headache. The Edward Frys came and skated in morning, and Mr. and Mrs. Edwards in afternoon. Slept with Violet last night and am going to again tonight. Tara.

Sunday 7th
Too cold and slippery to go to Church so Mother gave us bible questions to answer and asked our catechism. Mary very much worse, thought she <u>couldn't</u> live in evening but she got a tiny bit better later on. Mother got a cold. Blanche got a cold. Slept with Violet last night and am going to tonight also. She is going away tomorrow.

Monday 8th
Violet went away, a gloom fell on the House when she was gone. Got a <u>bad</u> cold, so has Mother, Blanche and Mr Leigh. The boys tobogganed all day, ice is covered with water. Mary the same. Wrote to Albinia. Theatrical things returned from Hutton in evening. We all dressed up in them. Four boys, Father, Mr. Leigh and Cyril Daubeny went to a club dinner at Wraxall.

Tuesday 9th
Cyril Daubeny went away. Georgie and Billy went to a yeomanry ball at Clevedon, Georgie in his uniform. Hughie has got a <u>bad</u> cold. Mine is better, Mother's the same and the rest are <u>all</u> better. A party of seven (all gentlemen) went out for a ride in afternoon. Do <u>hope</u> I shall be allowed to go to Clevedon tomorrow night. How I <u>wish</u> I hadn't got a cold.

Wednesday 10th
Was <u>not</u> allowed to go to Clevedon <u>dreadfully</u> disappointed. Have telegraphed to the Cornishes asking them if I may go there tomorrow if my cold is better. Mary the same. Mother was in bed with her cold half the day. Father went down to Wraxall in evening. Georgie went away to stay somewhere. Had to write to Albinia telling her to come home on Friday instead of Saturday.
<u>Tararaboomdeay</u>

Thursday 11th
The greatest sorrow I have ever had happened today. Poor Mary died early in the morning. Mother took Billy, Evelyn, and I to see her after death she looked very peaceful but somehow she looked dreadful, I don't think I've ever cried so much as I did today. Of course I didn't go to the Cornishes. She is to be buried on Saturday and was put into her coffin tonight and carried into the Chapel. A party of gentlemen went for a ride.

Friday 12th
Made a cross of white flowers and maiden hair fern for Mary's grave. She is going to be buried tomorrow at Wraxall. Albinia came home. Very glad to see her again. Four gentlemen went out hunting. Was sent to bed <u>very</u> early. Got a letter from Fraulein. A <u>very</u> nice letter it was too.

Saturday 13th
Mary was buried in afternoon. Albinia, Billy and Evelyn went to the funeral. The servants all joined together and bought a most beautiful wreath. Walters made Mother a lovely cross. I made a cross and so did Eustace. The wreath that Blanche and Nana made was quite dead by this

morning. Mary's Brother came down from Aldershot early in the morning. We watched the procession start from the North Room window. Harry Brain (Mary's young man) went to the funeral. Georgie came home.

Sunday 14th
To wet to go to Church so had Chapel. Lancey was in bed half the day with a cold. Had a letter from Fraulein and Olive. We all tried to write poetry in evening. Played with Lancey the whole afternoon. Hughie was sitting in the hall so I threw a cushion on his head - his revenge was so strong that he almost broke my door open.

Monday 15th
A party went out riding. Billy was thrown and shaken a good deal. He was carried into a cottage where he remained for a long time. Mr Leigh went to fetch a doctor who said he mustn't ride home, so we sent a carriage for him. He looked very white and shaken when he arrived home, and has a <u>very</u> bad headache as he was thrown over the horses head on to his own, at least that's what I gathered from Albinia. Mother and Father were very anxious about him before he came home. Hughie went to Cambridge in the morning.

Tuesday 16th
Billy had to keep quiet all day. Georgie went to Clevedon for an artillery ball or something and is going to spend the night at the Court. Walked down to the parsonage with Evelyn, was caught in the rain went into the Wraxall Shop for shelter. Bought lots of peppermints which we ate coming home. Were <u>very</u> wet when we arrived home. Eric Spencer came to see Evelyn and asked him to go and play football one fine day.

Wednesday 17th
Lancey had his hair cut for the first time. He looks very funny. Went to see Rosa. Had a <u>bad</u> headache all day. Went for a long walk in afternoon. Mother, Albinia, Mr. Leigh and Evelyn went to a ball in Wraxall in evening.

Thursday 18th
Edmund and Hilda Evans came. Had a nice afternoon. Albinia drove into Clevedon to see Kathleen Elton. Billy and Evelyn drove into Clifton, and did not come back till seven. Mr. Leigh and Willy rode about the place. The whole party with the exception of Billy, Evelyn and myself went to the Madrigals in Bristol. I dressed two dolls for the schoolchildren today, there are a lot more to do by next Wednesday.

Friday 19th
Kathleen and Angela Elton came to lunch and tea. They all went out a drive in the pony cart in afternoon, there was not room for me, so as Albinia said they would go very slowly I thought I'd run but as they went as fast as the pony could trot I soon got so blown that I stopped and turned back. I dressed two or three dolls today. We danced in the evening

a little. The time is coming near to begin lessons again. Ugh how dreadful it seems to poor me.

Saturday 20th
Louie and Agnes Merivale came. They are going to stay for a fortnight. Three went for a ride. Billy and Evelyn went for a drive in the pony carriage up to Charlton, and brought down the lovely clock out of the Hall. It is put outside the nursery. Played Halma in evening with Evelyn and Aunt Cass (*Catherine Merivale*). The rest played whist.

Sunday 21st
Went to Church in morning and Chapel in evening. Went to the farm in the afternoon. Six of us said our catechism in the afternoon. Had a dull day altogether.

Monday 22nd
Fraulein came back. Will have to begin lessons tomorrow - worst luck. Aunt Cass and Mr. Leigh went away. Mother and Albinia went to sing at Bourton. It's a kind of society which go and practice once a week at the school. Evelyn made a coat for Bon the dog, he <u>did</u> look funny.

Tuesday 23rd
Kathleen Spencer came. She was <u>very</u> unhappy and cried a great deal. I went to Naish (Naish House, Wraxall, home of the Spencer family) and lunched there and then brought Kathy back. A party went out for a ride. Did a few lessons in morning. Am going to begin in real earnest tomorrow.

Wednesday 24th
Had a Christmas tree for the schoolchildren. I think they enjoyed it awfully. They had about five presents of sorts each. Fraulein, Albinia, Kathy and I went to have a drawing lesson in Clifton in morning. Kathy quite happy all day. Did a few lessons before going to Clifton, and before giving the presents to the children. Had a game of bear after tea.

Thursday 25th
Mother went away, so did Albinia, the poor boys and Ginger Gurney. Did lessons a good deal and fussed still more. Walked up to the Lodge to meet Mrs. Spencer but she didn't come, the only people from Naish were an ugly little *child* and an ugly butler and a nice little doggie who smelt. K. played the donkey ass.

Friday 26th
Mrs. Spencer came with Evie Spencer in the afternoon. We almost all of us wrote to Mother. Did very nice lessons. K. played the being brave. We all played bear in the evening.

Saturday 27th
Went to Naish in afternoon. Brought back one of Evie's dolls which we broke. Am going to write to Mrs. Spencer to tell her. Went for a walk in morning.

Sunday 28th
Went to Church in morning and Chapel in evening. Went to the farm in

afternoon. Louie felt sick in evening and had to leave the dinner table.
Monday 29ᵗʰ
Johnie Gibbs and Dick Bennet came. Dick played the fool and dictated the most foolish donkeyish letter that can be imagined. Did lessons. Went for a walk in the morning.
Tuesday 30ᵗʰ
Helen Gibbs, Mr. Leigh, and Mr. Olivier came. They all went to a ball at the Eltons in the evening. Made toffee in the afternoon as it rained. Mother came home to my great joy.
Wednesday 31ˢᵗ
Mr. Leigh, Dick Bennet and Mr. Olivier went away. Went in to Clifton for our drawing lesson. We left Kathleen to go and try on dresses and cetera with Mrs. Spencer. She came back in time for lessons in afternoon. Fraulein and I returned from Clifton alone and it <u>snowed</u> and <u>hailed</u> like old Jerimimah. Poor Henry (*the groom*) got white and wet. Mr. Olivier sang in the evening just before he went. Louie and Aggie were going away.

February 1894
Thursday 1ˢᵗ
Mother and Helen Gibbs went back to Ablington. Mother says she will perhaps bring back Georgie on Saturday as he is much better. He has had an accident out hunting. We were going for a drive with Albinia in afternoon but it rained. So we played billiards. Louie and Agnes went home to our satisfaction.
Friday 2ⁿᵈ
Went for a smelly walk in morning. K and I went for a drive in the single pony carriage in afternoon with Albinia. Was in Fraulein's <u>very</u> black books all day, and had to learn a piece of poetry for laughing when she was lecturing me. I couldn't help it because K looked at me in a very funny way.
Saturday 3ʳᵈ
Mother and Georgie came home. Georgie had to be carried upstairs and then he went to bed. Tony Gibbs came in evening, he's going to stop till Monday. Kathleen went up to Naish in afternoon and returned in evening. Albinia went to Clevedon. I went for a walk in the woods with Lancelot and Rosa. Mr. Edwards came to luncheon with his big dog. Almost had to learn a piece of poetry in morning for I don't recollect what.
Sunday 4ᵗʰ
Went to Church in morning and Chapel in evening. It rained in afternoon. Mr. Morehouse and Mr. R. A. Ford came to tea in the hall. Georgie was better and he came down to lunch. Eustace handed round the bag to our aisle in church this morning.
Monday 5ᵗʰ
Mr. Dickinson came. He and Mother and Albinia went to a ball in Clevedon.

We have heard from Eton saying Evelyn has had an accident. A boy has hit him with a Racquet by mistake and has given him two lovely black eyes and cut his nose. Had a headache most of the day.

Tuesday 6th

Shrove Tuesday

Mr. Dickinson went. Had pancakes for lunch. Had a headache all day and so had Kathleen. Albinia took Georgie out for a drive in the single pony carriage in the afternoon. Mother and Father went out to dinner in the evening. Was in Fraulein's black books half the day. Rosa went out to a little party at the innkeepers at Bourton, so Kathleen and I have to manage our own hairs and cetera.

Wednesday 7th

Went to Chapel morning and evening. Albinia, Fraulein and Kathleen went to Clifton for their drawing lesson. I was not quite well so I couldn't go. Lent has begun now so I shall always write in black ink.

Thursday 8th

Mother and Albinia went to Barton Place (*Merivale house near Exeter*). Kathy and I had headaches all day. The New School room maid came. Father went out with Georgie in afternoon. Mr. Ford came to dinner.

Friday 9th

Nasty day. Don't remember what we did.

Saturday 10th

Went up to Naish with Fraulein and Kathleen. Had a very nice afternoon although we were nearly blown away on the hill. Mother and Albinia came home bringing Aunt Rose and Aunt Catty (*Merivale*). Mr. and Mrs. Bovel came and so did Hugh Mallet. Forgot to write my diary last night so I wrote it tonight, that's why I've put such a little.

Sunday 11th

Church in morning, Chapel in evening, I went to both. Mr. Spencer and Mr. Murray-Anderson called in afternoon. K and I went down to the farm in the afternoon and brought up some cream for tea.

Here Nancy writes the letters of her name in a V shape

Monday 12th

Did lessons as usual. Kathy and I went for a run on the Warren in the morning instead of a stiff old walk. We were sent to bed horribly early. It was a lovely <u>day</u>.

Tuesday 13th

Went into Clifton for drawing lessons in afternoon. Did not go down to dinner because we think its <u>rot</u> to be sent to bed just before dessert. Mr. Matthews and Pierre Freman came to stay. Mr. Medley and Mr. Morehouse came to dine.

Wednesday 14th

Albinia went to Clevedon for a lecture on Astronomy. A certain Mr.

Knight came to dine. Mr. Medley is away so Mr. Knight takes the service. K and I began a House of bushes in the woods. We went for a run on the Warren instead of a smelly walk.

Thursday 15th
Mr. Somebody who is taking the services for tonight and tomorrow morning.* Did lessons as usual. Albinia went for a ride with Winifred Elton. We went for a walk in the woods in morning with Fraulein and Aunt Catty. Enjoyed it very much.
* Mr Somebody came to dine

Friday 16th
Did a good deal to our house. Made dolls clothes in Maillot's room, the time passed so quickly that we found ourselves at a quarter to 9 instead of a quarter to 8. We did not go down to dinner. We are going to be sent to bed early tomorrow night.

Saturday 17th
We were going to Weston but it rained so we couldn't go. Evie Spencer was coming but as it rained and she has a bad cold she didn't come. We weren't sent to bed at all early in fact we were sent rather late. Mr. and Mrs. Bovil went away. Am very sorry they're gone. Had a letter from Willy Gurney. Everybody was very shocked at it which I think absurd it was only a little bit vulgar.

Sunday 18th
Church in morning. Chapel in evening. Farm in afternoon. Aunt Catty and Albinia went to tea with the Downalls and then to Bourton Church. Mr. Medley (afterwards) came to dine.

Monday 19th
Have to be in bed by nine which has just struck. Albinia and Georgie and Blanche went to Clifton and Georgie got Lance a silver mug. He is Lancey's godfather.

Tuesday 20th
Went into Clifton for our drawing lesson by train. I drove the dogcart to Bourton. I think Fraulein was very nervous. Fraulein, Kathleen and I are going to stay a week at Weston tomorrow. Albinia went out hunting.

Wednesday 21st
Came to Weston. Met Mrs. Spencer and Evie. Walked about with them for a little time. Was awfully tired in the evening and I had a headache. Did lessons in the morning but had a half holiday in afternoon. We have got very comfortable lodgings. Kathy and I are going to sleep together. We've got an awfully nice sitting room.

Thursday 22nd
We were let off an hours lessons which was rather jolly. Mr. Spencer came down. I wrote to Mother. Olive came to see us; I and Kathy were out so Fraulein has asked her to lunch tomorrow.

Friday 23rd
Olive came to lunch. I had to stay in a little bit, so that when I got out I couldn't find Kathy anywhere. But I met her after a time. We went to tea at Mrs. Spencer; there was an awful gale in evening. We walked home at 9.30 in pouring rain.

Saturday 24th
Mrs. Spencer came to tea. All the children came down, with a few Evans added to their party. It was a lovely day.

Sunday 25th
It rained a great deal. But it cleared up about 4.30. So I and Fraulein went to tea with the Mordaunts and Church afterwards. Kathy went to spend the afternoon with Mrs. Spencer.

Monday 26th
Mother, Albinia and Eustace came down to tea. Had a half holiday. Mother bought K and I a book each. And told us we'd better stay till Wednesday to our great disgust. I felt rather homesick when Kathy and I saw Mother off which I suppose was rather silly.

Tuesday 27th
Lovely day. Milly Mordaunt came and asked us to go to a concert in evening. Fraulein accepted. I was awfully homesick in afternoon, and made Kathy just the same. I did feel bad afterwards, considering I shall see Mother tomorrow. We went to the concert and enjoyed it very much. Got home about 9.45.

Wednesday 28th
Started home early in morning at least at 9.30. We went straight to Clifton and had our lesson, after which we went to the station, got our luggage and drove home. Kathy had bad headache in evening. We were let off an hours lessons because Mother was so pleased with our drawings. Am <u>so</u> glad to get home.

March 1894
Thursday 1st
Rained all day. We played Battledore and shuttlecock in the morning. Mr. and Miss Dyke came to dine. We did lessons as usual.

Friday 2nd
Mother, Mrs. and Miss Kensington and Albinia went to Clifton. I, Kathleen and Eustace went out in the donkey cart. When we got to the hill just above the place where there is a new road being made, I said I thought I'd better drive as it was downhill. But Kathy said she could manage it so I ran on in front. I think the donkey must have wanted to come too because just as I got to the bottom I heard Kathy calling to me to stop the donkey. I jumped in and we both pulled hard, and just as it was beginning to stop we ran over a root at the side of the road and the cart upset we were all thrown out, Eustace bumped his head. I grazed my

hand, which hurts rather, but Kathy was only shaken. There were lots of men about, who picked up the donkey and cart.
Saturday 3rd
Evie Spencer came for the afternoon, and so did Edmund and Hilda Evans. My hand is a good deal swollen and looks very nasty, as it is continually watering. We at least I didn't have a very enjoyable afternoon.
Sunday 4th
Church in morning, Chapel in evening, went to both. Wrote to Mother and Evelyn and sent an envelope with a piece of paper inside with this inscription. MARCH HARE SMELLY AND HIGH. Lovely day.
Monday 5th
Mother came home. Albinia went out with Eustace in the pony-carriage and lunched with the Edwardses. Went for a run in the morning instead of a walk. My hand is a good deal better. I hope to leave off the rag tomorrow. Not a nice day nor a nasty one.
Tuesday 6th
Have heard some most awful news. Kathy and I are going to change our rooms. We are going to sleep together in one of the night nurseries. We shall move tomorrow and are going to have the children next door to us with a door between which we are not allowed to block up. Also we have heard Rosa is going to leave at Easter; am dreadfully sorry, cried a good deal. Albinia went out hunting. Father came home.
Wednesday 7th
Smelly change happened. Kathy and I have moved and so have Nana, Eustace, Rosa, Blanche and Lancelot. The men had awful trouble in moving cupboards and things. Am not at all pleased with the move.
Thursday 8th
Kathy went home to lunch. Fraulein and Eustace went to meet her. Some people came to luncheon. Mr. Lord came to dine.
Friday 9th
Beastly wet day, but still we went into Clifton for our drawing lesson. It was Mr. Medley's birthday and he came to dine and we all drank his health. I got a present for Eustace as it is his birthday tomorrow, he will be 9 years old.
Saturday 10th
Winifred Elton came to stay for a short time. It was Eustace's birthday. It was a fairly nice day. We had a whole holiday which was great fun.
Sunday 11th
Church in morning, Chapel in evening, attended both. Kathy was not quite well in evening so didn't go Chapel. Have heard some beastly news. Mother, three of the boys and Albinia and Father are going abroad perhaps in the Easter holidays, while Kathy and I work hard with Fraulein. So we shall only get about 17 days holidays.

Monday 12th
Beastly day. K and I took up some eatables to old Mrs Lot. Georgie went up to Naish in morning.

Tuesday 13th
Mr. Leigh and Hughie came. Mr. Leigh is I believe going to help Georgie read up for something. Winifred and Albinia had out their horses and jumped over hurdles in a field. Henry (the groom) then brought out the little brown mare and tried to make it jump while K and I were watching it didn't jump once but I believe they did make it jump after a time.

Wednesday 14th
Winifred and Albinia went to Clevedon for the day. Winifred went to the dentist and then they both went to a lecture on astronomy. In the evening at dinner the conversation was all on astronomy.

Thursday 15th
Hughie, Winifred, Mr. Leigh and Albinia all had out their horses in afternoon and jumped over hurdles, they also had a steeple chase, Hughie won, Albinia next then Winifred but Mr. Leigh's horse broke down just before the end and he walked it to the winning post. Mother went away for a night.

Friday 16th
Mother came home. Winifred went away. Mr. and Miss Heberden have come to stay a little while. Mother and Father went out to dine with the Edwardses. Hughie went up to London. Albinia went back with Winifred for a night.

Saturday 17th
Margaret Mackinnon came for lunch and tea. Kathy and I like her <u>awfully</u>. It was a beautiful day. The Daubenys came, they are going to stay till Monday. Stanley Gibbs also came and is staying till Monday. Mr. Leigh and Stanley jumped hurdles (on horses) in afternoon.

Sunday 18th
Palm Sunday
A most beautiful day. Very hot in morning. We went to Church and Chapel, and Mr Honeywell gave us a very objectionably long sermon, which was made worse by the sun on our backs. Heard from Billy.

Monday 19th
The entry for Monday is crossed out but reads as follows:
Albinia and Hughie went out hunting and haven't come back yet but I believe will return about 11 o'clock. They are having lunch and dinner at Langford with the Llewellyns. Broke up lessons this evening and K packed a lot in evening.

Tuesday 20th
Albinia and Hughie went out hunting, and I believe won't return until 11 o'clock, as they are lunching at Langford.

Wednesday 21st
Fraulein and Kathy went away so holidays have begun. Have been out from 8.35 till 5.48 p.m. today with only about an hour in the middle. Went out with the Beagles with Georgie and Eustace. We saw one or two hares but didn't ever get much of run. One of the hounds got caught in a trap and Georgie had to call a man to get it out with a strap. Missed Kathy very much in evening.

Thursday 22nd
The two boys, Billy and Evelyn came home. Cousin Vicary, Johnnie Gibbs and Willy Gurney came to stay. I heard from Georgie the Spencers had just gone down to Bourton with their Father and would be back soon so I went to meet them and drove a little way up the hill with them. The boys and Mr. Leigh rode in afternoon. Evelyn came off twice and Billy once.

Friday 23rd
Good Friday
Church in morning Chapel in evening as usual went to both. Nothing happened at all. I kept on thinking it was Sunday. Lovely day.

Saturday 24th
Lovely day. Played croquet in afternoon. Johnnie Gibbs went away. Have had an Easter card from Miss Stephaney and an Easter egg from Aunt Dora.

Sunday 25th
Easter Sunday
Lovely day. Saw the Spencers after Church. Chapel in evening as usual. Can't write any more because there is no paper.*

There are various mistakes and crossings out on the page for 24th and 25th March

Monday 26th
Bank Holiday
Saxham and Cousin Isabel Drury came to dine. A large party went out riding and jumping in a field in afternoon. We played croquet in morning and evening. The boys played cricket in evening. It was very hot in the day. Too hot.

Tuesday 27th
Cyril and Uncle Regie came to stay. Mr. G. T. Morehouse came to dine. Winifred and Bernard Elton came over to lunch and galloped and jumped in the field all the afternoon. All of our party and the Eltons put together made seven riding. It was a lovely day. We played tennis and croquet a good deal. Lent is over so I can write in red and purple ink.

Wednesday 28th
Very warm day. Played tennis in cotton shirt in morning with Cyril, Saxham and Willy Gurney. Went up to Naish for tea and lunch and had a very nice time of it. Mother and Father went out to a meeting in Clevedon

in the evening and dined with the Eltons. Albinia, Evelyn Heberden and Evelyn (Gibbs) went in to Clifton and got some tennis shoes, Nana also went in and got me shoes, gloves and stockings for the ball.

Thursday 29th
Albinia went away to stay a night at Hutton, and is bringing back two of the girls for our dance tomorrow night. The boys rode in afternoon. Evelyn was not quite well in evening. My dance frock came.

Friday 30th
Gave a dance in evening. Kept it up till three. Three Eltons, Mr. Wilson Fox, Stanley Gibbs, May Gibbs and Harry Mordaunt came for the night. I danced every dance except one, which I sat out with Evelyn. Mrs. Spencer came. I was very hoarse and I think I'm going to have a sore throat. I am going to sleep in the Rose Room because the children would wake me up in the morning early.

Saturday 31st
Got up about 11.30 and was not down till 11.50. Was most dreadfully tired and sleepy all day, and I lay down in the afternoon. All the people who came yesterday went away today. And so did the Heberdens. It was a lovely day again.

April 1894
Sunday 1st
Lovely day. Mother Father and all the rest except Georgie and the ones younger than me are going abroad tomorrow. I feel most frightfully miserable. I have a little sore throat. And so has Mother. Evelyn was not quite well in the evening. Didn't go to Church in morning.

Monday 2nd
A most extraordinary thing has happened. Evelyn has got the measles and Mother has to stop at home to nurse him and so has Billy because he has been sleeping with Evelyn and is almost sure to get it. Albinia, Father, Hughie and Mr. R A Ford have gone. I was not allowed to go to the Spencers. Mother and Billy are both very much disappointed. I don't know which to feel glad or sorry.

No entry for Tuesday

Wednesday 4th
Fraulein came back. Eustace is going to be in the schoolroom now and so will have breakfast in there with us at 8.30. I had a game of Racquets with Billy in the morning and we played billiards and tennis. I am one of Billy's only companions now, and so I am not going to do many lessons. Lovely day. Billy heard from Albinia but I don't know what she said.

Thursday 5th
Did lessons. I am always let out at 10.30 in the morning now because Billy has no one to play with. Evelyn is much better. Mr. Leigh, Georgie and Billy went into Clifton. Lovely day only a little bit too windy. Fraulein went up in the pony carriage to Naish and asked when Kathleen

can come back. Mrs. Spencer says Monday or Tuesday. Have made a mistake and have left out what I did on Tuesday and have put on Tuesday what happened on Wednesday.

Friday 6th
Went to the drawing lesson with Fraulein. Had a headache all day. Played Racquets in morning and billiards in evening. My new shirts came from D and F. They are much too pretty Mother says.

Saturday 7th
Half holiday. I heard from Albinia and I wrote to her a long letter. Georgie, Mr Leigh and Billy went for a long drive in the waggonette. I played croquet with Mother in morning. I won one game and she the other while Evelyn watched us from his window. Fairly nice day. Played Racquets with Billy in morning. This week has passed excessively quickly. I think too quickly.

Sunday 8th
Mr. Morehouse and Mr. Edwards came over in afternoon. Saw Kathleen, Mr. Spencer and Eric after Church. Kathy is coming back on Tuesday. Was late for breakfast. I haven't been down in time for breakfast for the last four mornings. I must get up earlier tomorrow. Mother heard from Father. Evelyn is better.

Monday 9th
Billy wasn't down till late as he didn't feel quite well so I did all my morning lessons, but was let off an hour in afternoon to play croquet with Billy. Went for a walk with B in the woods in evening. Had neuralgia at different times of the day.

Tuesday 10th
Kathleen came back in the morning. We played tennis a little. Am very glad to have K back again. Lancelot is not well so we are sleeping in the North Room. I expect L is going to have the measles.

Wednesday 11th
Eustace is not well he is very feverish. Lancelot is much better. Billy has got them now. Evelyn is much better.

Thursday 12th
It rained. Billy has got them rather badly. Kathy and I played tennis and croquet with Fraulein.

Friday 13th
Lovely day. We fussed about all day. Eustace and Lancelot have got the measles. Evelyn comes down now but is not allowed to go out.

Saturday 14th
Kathy went up to Naish. We had a telegram from Geneva saying that Albinia has got the measles but has got a good doctor. Mr. Morehouse came over and played croquet with me against Georgie and Mr. Leigh. Mr. M and I won but I'm afraid we all cheated.

Sunday 15th   Blanche's birthday

Kathy and Fraulein went to Church in morning, I staid at home as Mother thought I might take the infection. I go up to see Billy whenever I like, I think Mother wants me to get it.

Monday 16th

We all fussed. Evelyn went out for the first time. Eustace has got them very well. I trained a great deal. Blanche had two or three <u>nice</u> presents.

Tuesday 17th

Forget entirely what I did.

Wednesday 18th

Went up to Charlton in morning.

Thursday 19th

Went up to Charlton in afternoon in single pony carriage. Had a telegram telling Mother to send Evelyn over to Geneva with Pollard, Mother is going to ask the doctor.

Friday 20th

Went out in pony carriage in morning. Did lessons early, made cowslip balls and played tennis and croquet. The Dr. says Evelyn may go.

Saturday 21st

Eric Spencer came and played racquets and Kathy and I took him to tea. We all fussed together. Hughie came home last night and brought K and I two lovely handkerchiefs with Brussels lace round them. Mine were mauve and pink, K's were blue and yellow.

Sunday 22nd

Church in morning. Chapel in evening as usual. We didn't go to the farm in the afternoon because Edith Lear was not quite well. Forgot to put yesterday that Evelyn and Pollard started for London.

Monday 23rd

Wet all day. Fussed about the place. Kathy was going up to the White House but it was so wet that she is going tomorrow instead.

Tuesday 24th

Kathy went up to the White House to have her fusses tried on she came back in time for lessons. Blanche has got the measles.

Wednesday 25th

Kathy went to Bristol to meet her Mother and Eric. She brought me a penny bun and had her hair shampooed. Nana has actually broken out with the plague.

Thursday 26th and Friday 27th

Showery all day.

Saturday 28th

Lovely day. Meant to go to Charlton but it was so thundery that we stayed at home. Mr. Morehouse and Stanley came over and played cricket. Billy and Willy went to join Father, Albinia and Evelyn abroad.

Sunday 29th

Church and Chapel. Went down to the farm. Mr. Lear says he will get as

many birds eggs as he can for us by next Sunday.
Monday 30th
Heard from Evelyn. Mrs. Spencer, Eric and one of the schoolboys came over the boys played Racquets. It rained a good deal in the morning.

May 1894
Tuesday 1st
Lovely day. Played croquet a little. Did lessons. Blanche and Nana are both much better. Georgie went out in evening.
Wednesday 2nd
Entirely forget what I did.
Thursday 3rd
Whole holiday. Nice day, it didn't rain once. In the afternoon Mother, Fraulein, K and I went to the Bristol Cathedral, after that we went shopping. Mother got us some very pretty cups and saucers and three saltcellars in the shape of a tiny swan in white china and only cost 1d each. Then we went to tea with the Daubenys.
Friday 4th
Smelly old lessons began again. FORGET WHAT ELSE I DID.
Saturday 5th
Albinia, Father and Evelyn came home. We went up to watch a cricket match at Failand. Albinia has given me a dear little model of a Swiss house, Evelyn a stick top and Father a most <u>lovely</u> cuckoo clock. Evie Spencer was here all the afternoon playing with Kathy.
Sunday 6th
Mr. Lear gave us a lot of eggs, which we have blown. K and I both had bad headaches in evening. I had to go off Chapel with K because she felt so bad.
Monday 7th
Georgie and Mr. Leigh went to Bath. Evelyn and Albinia rode over to Clevedon and saw Winifred and Angella. Played croquet.
Tuesday 8th
Tuesday (in Nancy's hand)
Evelyn went back
[Tuesday 8th - Thursday 10th filled in as follows but crossed out - Nancy seems to have got in a muddle with the days!]
The choir people came in the evening and sang glees after which they all had supper. We played at croquet. All three children went to Weston with Mother and Albinia they are going to stay there a week.
Wednesday 9th
The choir came and sang glees to us in the evening after which they had supper. All the three children went to Weston with Mother and Albinia who returned in the evening.
Thursday 10th
Evelyn, Mother, Father and Albinia went away to Clyst St. George for two

nights. Rained a good deal.
Friday 11th
Mother, Father and Albinia came home. Mother went down to Weston in afternoon. We went into Clifton for our drawing lesson. It rained almost all day.
Saturday 12th
Fraulein and I went down to Weston to see the children. Kathleen and Mother went to Bath and I believe had a very nice time, they saw Georgie and Mr. Leigh. Albinia went to Clevedon and we went a little way with Stanley in the train. Lovely day. Miss Bright, the Woodwards, the Honey Wills, and a few other people came to dinner.
Sunday 13th Whit Sunday.
Nice day. Evie Spencer came back from Church with us and had lunch and tea. Mr. Morehouse came over in the afternoon and fussed.
Monday 14th
Albinia went out riding with Mr. Morehouse. Miss Woodward and a cousin came to lunch. We played croquet. The Home people came up. Albinia gave us a lot more birds eggs.
Tuesday 15th
Mr. Leigh and Georgie came back. Beastly day.
Wednesday 16th
Horrible day. Read and did lessons all day. Had peaches in the evening for the first time.
Thursday 17th
Georgie went to Weston. Mother, Albinia and Mr. Leigh all went to Weston to see the children in the afternoon. We played that awful game croquet a little.
Friday 18th *[crossed out]*
Saturday.
Have come down to Weston am going to stay till Monday. Saw Georgie and spoke to him. Went to bed 10 o'clock. Came down with Mrs. Hills and Hilda Evans.
Saturday 19th *(crossed out)* Sunday *(written in Nancy's hand)*
Did not go to Church but went to see the Yeomanry Church Parade in their helmets. Went to tea with Mordaunts and Georgie came too.
Sunday 20th *(crossed out)* Monday *(written in Nancy's hand)*
Came home with Mother and Uncle Reggie. Found K and Fraulein.
Monday 21st
Have got all wrong again with this diary.
Tuesday 22nd
Went to Weston to see the Military Tournament by the Yeomanry. The Eltons came with us but went back before the end. Kathy, Eustace and I came home alone. There is going to be a dance at Weston this evening and Albinia and Mother have stayed for it. The children came home.

Wednesday 23rd
Horrible day. Went into Clifton for our drawing lesson. Fraulein and Kathy played croquet.
Thursday 24th
Went up to Naish to see the Chapel opened. Stayed there most of the afternoon and played cricket a little. We are going up to London tomorrow.
Friday 25th
Came up to London. Left the children behind at Tyntesfield. They are coming here tomorrow. Very hot day. Kathy and I are sleeping in Albinia's room. Albinia, Mother and Father went out to dinner in *the* evening. We walked in the gardens in *the* evening.
Saturday 26th
Mother, Albinia and Eustace went down to Windsor. Fraulein, K and I went to the German Lieder in the afternoon it was very amusing.
Sunday 27th
Went to St. James' in morning. Cyril and Tony came in the afternoon. Willy came to dinner in evening and so did Uncle Reggie.
Monday 28th
Walked in the Kew Gardens in morning. Went out shopping in afternoon.
Tuesday 29th
Walked in the row in the morning and saw Albinia and Helen riding. Herr Dressel came and gave us a music lesson.
Wednesday 30th
Hughie came. Walked in the street in morning. Thundered and rained.
Thursday 31st
We had our hair cut and washed. A Church was burnt in evening and we watched it, it was a dreadful but lovely sight, it lighted up all the houses round. We thought it was a house being burnt but Nana and Maillot went out to see.

June 1894
Friday 1st
Herr Dressel came and gave us our music lesson. Went to see the church which was burnt last night. The roof is all burnt and the rafters look very weird and odd. We did not go down to dinner as seven people came.
Saturday 2nd
Have forgotten to write my diary and I quite forget what I did.
Sunday 3rd
Forget what I did.
Monday 4th
The boys came and we went to the Military Tournament with the Eltons.
Tuesday 5th
Jack Gibbs came. Herr Dressel came.
Wednesday 6th
Went to Madame Tussaudes with Jack.

Thursday 7th
Went to "Charlie's Aunt" in evening. Went to the swimming baths in morning.
Friday 8th
Herr Dressel came. Jack Gibbs went.
Saturday 9th
Went to see some children act in afternoon. Mother, Father and Albinia went out in evening.
Sunday 10th
Went to Children's Service. Walked in the Park in afternoon.
Monday 11th
Went to the bathing place, that's all.
Tuesday 12th
Herr Dressel came. I've got a cold. Mother, Albinia and Winifred went to Cambridge.
Wednesday 13th
Did not go out. Kathy fussed.
Thursday 14th
Mother, Albinia and Winifred came home. Lovely day. Went out in afternoon.
Friday 15th
Herr Dressel came. Kathy and Fraulein went to the swimming baths. I went out shopping with Mother.
Saturday 16th
Hughie came. Kathy went out with one of her aunts not a real one. I spent a beastly afternoon in garden, but had a nice evening with Mother as A and W went out.
Sunday 17th
9 people came to lunch and with 7 of our party it made too many and we had to clear out. I have miles of poetry to learn tomorrow.
Monday 18th
Went to have my frock tried on at Wolmershausen. Mother and Father went out to dinner and Albinia and Hughie went out after.
Tuesday 19th
Herr Dressel came. Mother, Father, Albinia and Hughie all went out in evening.
Wednesday 20th
Forget what I did.
Thursday 21st
Went to have my dress tried on. Kathy went to the bathing place with Fraulein. I have been asked to go and stay with Saxham tomorrow.
Friday 22nd
Herr Dressel came. Went to Saxham. Played cards in evening. Went to bed at 10 o'clock.

Saturday 23rd
Went over to see the Bells at Pendel Court. Had a very nice afternoon. Played cards. Bed.
Sunday 24th
Walked to Church which was 1¾ of a mile away. Read in the hay and played croquet in afternoon.
Monday 25th
Started early in morning with Saxham. A girl called May Crawley Boevey came to tea.
Tuesday 26th
Went to the bathing place early in morning. Herr Dressel came.
Wednesday 27th
Cousin Hettie, Miss Frair and Mr. Watman came to lunch. Walked in the garden in evening. Mother and Father went out to dine. All the rest went out to a theatre.
Thursday 28th
Went to the bathing place. Lancelot and Blanche went to the Crystal Palace. Georgie and Hughie went down to Barrow for the ball. Billy came up and went to the Dentist.
Friday 29th
Herr Dressel came in the morning. Saxham and C. Gertrude came to stay with us. Hughie came back and they all went to a play in the evening called "The Candidate".
Saturday 30th
Fraulein, K, Eustace and I went to the Crystal Palace for the afternoon. Aunt Dora gave us 5/- to spend each. Hughie has been playing the fool and has been writing in this diary, but I've rubbed his nonsense out.

July 1894
Sunday 1st
Went to the children's service. Mr. M. A. came in the afternoon and sat in the garden with us. It was beastly hot all day.
Monday 2nd
Went to Lords cricket ground and watched the cricket. Oxford is 338 all out.
Tuesday 3rd
Went to Lords in morning. Cambridge 226 all out. Came back to Tyntesfield. HURRAH. Violet Freeman came down with us.
Wednesday 4th
Kathy has gone home for a night. Cousin Willy Cobham came to stay. It was a lovely day all through.
Thursday 5th
Kathy came back.

Figure 22. George Abraham Gibbs' 21st Birthday - July 6th 1894.

Friday 6th
Georgie's birthday. He has come of age. He has a lot of lovely presents. Ours is a silver flask. The boys came to stay and lots of other people with Them. In the evening there was a large dinner given to the tenants, which lasted from 6.30 till 9 o'clock. Lots of people made speeches. After dinner there were splendid fireworks and at 10.30 a large bonfire.

Saturday 7th
We are to have holidays until Tuesday. In the afternoon there was a village fete to which about 14 hundred people came. There was a large lunch at two, which we did not go to. I went on the merry go round 1000s of times.

Sunday 8th
Church in morning. Chapel in evening. Kitchen Garden (where the fruit is) in the afternoon. Kathy went home for a night.

Monday 9th
We had a large ball in evening. I had splendid fun and danced a lot.

Tuesday 10th
Boys went away and so did several other people. I am very tired. I broke a statue of Aunt Alice. The Devonshire tenants came up.

Wednesday 11th
There was a servants' ball in evening. I stayed up till 12.30. It was a lovely day and Kathy and I played tennis. This is the last day of the festivities.

Thursday 12th
Mother, Father, Georgie, Hughie, Mr. Buxton, Helen, Violet and Albinia all went up for the Eton and Harrow match and had tea with the Downalls. The house seems BEASTLY solitary now everybody has gone.

Friday 13th
Went in for our drawing lesson and came back in rain. Played tennis in evening.

Saturday 14th
Evie Spencer came to lunch and tea. Mother and Father and the rest are coming back from London at 10.30 this evening. Beautiful day.

Sunday 15th
Church and Chapel as usual. Rather a nice day.

Monday 16th
Wet day. Dressed some tiny dolls for Kathy.

Tuesday 17th
Went into Clifton for our drawing lesson. Played tennis with Albinia and Kathy. A very windy day.

Wednesday 18th
There was a great gathering of the Primrose Leaguers. It was a beastly day. We had a half holiday. Georgie gave me a shilling to spend on the merry go round.

Thursday 19th
Aunt Rose and Aunt Cathy came. Albinia and Hughie went away. Showery day. I left out some tennis balls out last night so am not allowed to play for a fortnight.

Friday 20th
The two Miss Downalls brought up the little Cobham Gibbs to tea and we played with them all the evening. Georgie told me that Cyril Gurney is going to be married to Miss Trotter. It seems very odd somehow.

Saturday 21st
We all spent the afternoon at Barrow. Came home at 6.30 enjoyed it very much. Beautiful day.

Sunday 22nd
Beastly day. Took some flowers in the rain to Mrs. Lot. Heard from angry Hughie.

Monday 23rd
The Mothers of Bedminster came over and ran some races in the

afternoon. It rained a good deal. Mother, Albinia and Hughie came home.

Tuesday 24th
Rained buckets of water all day. A lot more Bedminster people came over in the rain. Cousin Herman (*Merivale*) and his wife came to stay.

Wednesday 25th
Lovely day. Hughie has had a raft made to go on the pond and we launched it today for the first time.

Thursday 26th
Cyril Daubeny came to stay. Albinia, Fraulein, K and I went down to the bathing place and had a swim. Four people went out to a ball at the Hingstons.

Friday 27th
Lots of people came to call in the afternoon. Went on the raft a lot.

Saturday 28th
Had a children's garden party in the afternoon. Phyllis Hill came to stay with us. Dick Bennett came and so did Cousin Mary and Mabel Daubeny.

Sunday 29th
Beastly day. Had Chapel in morning. That's all.

Monday 30th
Lovely day. Our holidays begin tomorrow. We had to play in the evening, which I hated. Cyril Gurney came to stay.

Tuesday 31st
Miss Bridges, Evelyn, Helen, Tony, Mr. Olivier, Mr. Watman and Mr. Studley came to stay and a lot of them went to a ball at Clevedon Hall. Kathy, Fraulein and Phyllis went away. Dick B. has failed for the army.

August 1894
Wednesday 1st
Mr. and Mrs. Smithmasters, Monica, Mrs. Egerton Leigh and Kid came. We played a match against Tom Llewellyn's team and beat them. Evie Spencer came down. TARARA/BOOM/DE/AY - I haven't fussed today.

Thursday 2nd
Mr. Galthorn brought an eleven and beat us. Billy and Evelyn came home. Mr. Cox and Mr. Egerton Leigh both came. Albinia sang in the evening.

Friday 3rd
We played Mr. Ford's team but it rained such a lot that it was a draw. Billy and Evelyn came home and so did Mr. Cox. Albinia sang in the evening.

Saturday 4th
We played Bourton and beat them. Dick Bennett and Mr. Morris went

away.

Sunday 5th
We went 20 to Church in the omnibus and all the rest walked. We went to the Racquet Court in afternoon and watched them play. We had awful fun in evening and I stayed up later than usual. It is Monica's birthday today.

Monday 6th
The match today is going to be finished tomorrow; the other side are 260 for 3 wickets which we shall never get. We danced in the evening and had rare old fun.

Tuesday 7th
We were well beaten in this last match. We had a lovely dance in the evening. I danced every dance and enjoyed myself awfully.

Wednesday 8th
Everybody except Mr. Leigh and Mr. Olivier went away today, even Mother and Albinia. We went up to Barrow to watch the cricket.

Thursday 9th
Mr. Leigh and R. Ernest Olivier went away. The 3 boys went into Bristol and stayed there all day. It was rather a nice day. I was very tired in the evening so went to bed early.

Friday 10th
Mother, Albinia, Mr. Olivier and Willy Gurney came back. Father and Hughie went up to Scotland and the boys went into Clifton.

Saturday 11th
Went to the Drurys in afternoon till five and then Mother and I went up to the cricket field on the hill. Mr. Olivier sang "Round the Town", and then after that some other rotten little song in the evening which sent me to bed very effectually.

Sunday 12th
Church and Chapel as usual. It rained a lot.

Monday 13th
Ethel Gibbs came. The boys went to Taunton. I and the squirts went to tea with Mr. Medley. Mother and the rest went up to Charlton to see Lady Hobhouse.

Tuesday 14th
Mr. Olivier went away in morning and Willy in afternoon. We started at 6.15 and found a very nice sleeping carriage.

Wednesday 15th
I slept a lot in the night and after driving up a steep hill of 5 miles we arrived at this house, which is a very nice one with a loch in front (*Loch Kennard*). Blanche is sleeping with me.

Thursday 16th
Spent the morning on the lake and picking heather. Mother, Ethel, Albinia and I went down to Aberfeldy and shopped after that we

went to see Sir Robert and Miss Menzies. There was a full moon in evening.

Friday 17th
I did an hour of working while Mother read aloud to me. I am going to do that all the time while we are up here. We played cricket a great deal and in the evening I went out on the loch with Evelyn while he fished.

Saturday 18th
Played cricket most of the morning until I went to Mother. In the afternoon we all went to the Island and cut down a big tree with meat choppers which with a penknife were the only tools we had, after that we had tea. Cousin Sophie Merivale came with a boy who is I believe a cousin of ours. I sat next to him at dinner and almost all the time I was thinking what to say to him so we hardly talked at all.

Sunday 19th
It rained a great deal. We had Church in the drawing room. I rowed in a race in afternoon. Went for a walk in evening.

Monday 20th
Saxham and his wife came. Had tea on the island.

Tuesday 21st
It rained all the morning. Went over to the island for a short time only. The gentlemen did not go out shooting because of the rain. The bag up to now is 366½ brace, which is very good.

Wednesday 22nd
The gentlemen went out shooting as usual and got 43 brace altogether. Albinia and Evelyn went out fishing at another loch and all the rest of us went to see the Moness Falls, which were very pretty, and we had lunch there. It didn't rain once all day for a wonder, but I suppose it will rain all tomorrow instead.

Thursday 23rd
Climbed the hill opposite to the house in the morning with Gertrude and lost her. I took about 20 minutes finding her again and I found that she had arrived at the bottom before me. I had to play in the evening. We went over to the island and dug a lot of earth away.

Friday 24th
Spent a lot of the morning on the island. Mother, Albinia and the rest of the ladies went a drive, and three of the boys went to Aberfeldy. Eustace and Bernard went for a long walk of 4 hours and made us all anxious.

Saturday 25th
We went out on the moor and lunched with the shooters, and then when we came home we had tea on the Island. Mr. Bright came and he and Father went out to sketch the house from the hill.

Figure 23. The Gibbs family on a walk from Loch Kennard.

Sunday 26th
Rather a cold day. Hughie photographed us in the morning after which we had Church. After lunch there came off the Loch Kennard Regatta which was rather a failure. I wrote to K. she hasn't written to me for months.

Monday 27th
There was a great divergence out of eight people, the first party were Saxham and Gertrude, Albinia , Billy and Evelyn who are going on an expedition to Skye and the second party Uncle Reggie and Cousin Sophie and Bernard. Mr. Hope Barton came to stay and we took him to the Island and had tea and after that he fished. I must say I am sorry Saxham and Gertrude have gone the house feels so empty.

Tuesday 28th
Mr. Bridgeman and Mr. Roberts came to stay. Didn't do much in morning. Mother and Ethel went to Aberfeldy in afternoon and Mother got me two casts. It was a bad day for shooting and they shot very little. If I don't hear from K. S. on Thursday or Friday I shall be very angry because I've written to her so many times these holidays and she has only written once what could be called a letter, the other was on a small piece of paper.

Wednesday 29th
It was a case of "Lazily Drowsily" with me all day. We had tea on the island. The gentlemen in two parties only got 25 brace which I think is the smallest bag.

Thursday 30th
Spent a lazy morning. Mother read to Ethel and I in the afternoon and we took our tea to the opposite shore and had it there. We took a long time starting back again because the boat stuck, so Ethel and I pushed it off and walked round and got home just after the boat. The boys and Albinia will be here soon, it is now 10.35 p.m.

Friday 31st
We went and had lunch with the gentlemen. We had a very good lunch and after that Ethel, Eustace and I went on with the shooters. Mr. Bright was very kind and offered to take me in his *boat*. It was a very bad day and they got very few birds but still I enjoyed it awfully. We were very wet indeed and I was sent to bed the minute we came out of dinner which was 10 o'clock.

September 1894
Saturday 1st
I've never spent such a lazy day up here before. Mother, Ethel and Albinia went to call on Lady Stewart of Grantully Castle in afternoon. Mr. Oliverson came. He came over to the Island where I and Eustace were as nobody was in so we called Albinia. I stayed up till 11 in the evening thinking that we were going to dance but we didn't. I spent most of the day in playing cricket and rowing.

Sunday 2nd
We had service in the drawing room as usual. It was a lovely morning and it really rained a very little in the afternoon. We had races as usual and for a wonder nobody quarrelled at all. I was very <u>tired</u> in evening so retired early (with apologies to Mr. Pooter).

Monday 3rd
Spent the morning in playing cricket of which I am getting very sick. Mother, Father, the two girls and little Blanche went for a long drive, but I not being very partial to drives, stayed at home. The shooters had a rotten day. I made a mistake last night. Mr Pooter's joke was that he retired, tired - but never mind now, I must go to bed quickly.

Tuesday 4th
Father, Billy and Evelyn went to Aberfeldy in the morning and got me some very pleasant brown stuff for a skirt. We had tea on the Island as usual and Mother and the girls went for a walk for which I was too lazy. Mr. Llewellyn came and made us all laugh awfully at dinner.

Wednesday 5th
Played cricket almost all the morning. Mother, Ethel, Albinia and

Betty went to a ball at Blair Atholl. They are going with Miss Menzies in a special train and are going to sleep at Aberfeldy. I was the only lady at dinner. Evelyn went to bed early.

Thursday 6th
The ball goers came home in the morning. I spent the morning knitting indoors. We had tea on the opposite shore.

Friday 7th
I found it a very cold day today. Ethel and Mr Bright went away to our great grief and sorrow. I sat and read most of the afternoon. All the gentlemen except Mr. Oliverson didn't go out shooting until the afternoon.

Saturday 8th
I went out the whole day with the shooters and enjoyed myself very much indeed. I was supposed to be tired in the evening but I wasn't. It was a very bad drive. Mr. Oliverson went away. Mother and the squirts went into Aberfeldy in the afternoon and I believe enjoyed themselves very much.

Sunday 9th
Spent most of the day reading and *ragging* in a boat. We had service in the morning. Mr. Llewellyn played the goat a great deal all day. It was the hottest day we have had here.

Monday 10th
Dawdled away most of the morning and rowed Albinia about when she fished and caught one ¼ of a pound in this (*picture of a boat here*). Mr. Latham came and then we all had tea on the Island. Billy shot 4 rabbits and a grouse.

Tuesday 11th
The lake was very rough in the morning and some of the people of this house poured oil upon the angry water but they failed to quell the stormy ocean. Albinia, Evelyn and I went into the city of Aberfeldy and I bought Kathie a silver brooch for a birthday present. Albinia gave me two books for my birthday present.

Wednesday 12th
It was my 13th birthday. We had lunch on the hill after which we walked up Grantully Hill and then in the evening before dinner we made a huge fire on the island and burnt up the trunk of the tree we burnt down. We danced and sang in the evening and just after dinner we had a bonfire on the shore of the lake in front of the house. I will put my presents in tomorrow.

Thursday 13th
We went an expedition to Loch Tay and enjoyed it very much. Mr. Llewellyn ragged dreadfully coming back. Mother and Father have given me a gold chain, Billy a gold pen, Albinia two nice books,

Eustace an inkpot, Blanchy some little books, Aunt D a book and a little case with nice sharp scissors in it and Mr. Latham two frames.

Friday 14th
I wrote 5 letters in the morning and I also played cricket and worked in the form of digging on the Island. In the afternoon and evening I did the same. They got 18 brace driving today. (*The following written in mirror writing*) Albinia and Evelyn caught five fish altogether.

Saturday 15th
Wrote two more letters, received one and rowed about in a boat in the morning. Father, Mr. Llewellyn and Evelyn went away at 9 a.m. I got up and saw them off. Albinia, Mr Latham Hughes and I walked into Aberfeldy in the afternoon, it is a matter of 3 miles uphill coming back so I was rather tired. I have got a little cold.

Sunday 16th
We had service in the morning and Georgie took the clergymans part. I wrote to M. MacKinnon. Spent the afternoon in reading and *rowing* about in the tub.

Monday 17th
Nothing interesting happened in the morning. Went a walk round the loch. Albinia went down to Aberfeldy to meet K. Elton

Tuesday 18th
We spent the morning in making little window blind things because the ground floor bedrooms are very public. Kathleen and Albinia have gone to Kenmare (it is now 10.30 p.m.) to meet Evelyn and Father, and have not returned yet. I did not go out for more than 5 minutes in the morning, all day.

Wednesday 19th
Stayed in most of the morning. Mother and a few other people went to a cattle show at Aberfeldy. I have finished Lancelot's first stocking.

Thursday 20th
Stayed in all the morning. Went out a long walk with Mother in afternoon. Kathleen and Albinia went out with the shooters all day. (*The next sentence is in Cyrillic script*) I hope you are quite well. (*The next sentence is in mirror writing*) My cold was much better today.

Friday 21st
Spent a lazy day, between making fires, fetching wood and splashing Kathleen. Beatrice and Mr. Graham came in the evening.

Saturday 22nd
Went out with the shooters all day. Beatrice went away early 9 a.m.

Sunday 23rd
We were all photographed by Hughie as usual. I fell into the lake up to my knees, and K. Elton did the same a little later on.

Figure 24. Antony Gibbs in his Deerstalker and the Gibbs family at Loch Kennard. 1896. From left to right – Anstice Katharine, Janet Louisa, Mrs. Llewellyn, Antony Gibbs, Albinia Rose, Winifred Elton, ----, George Abraham Gibbs. In the hammock Lancelot to the left and William to the right.

Monday 24th
We went for an expedition to Pitlochry and Killicrankie. Billy and Evelyn went back to school. It will be dull without them.

Tuesday 25th
We made curtains for the drawing room windows most of the day. The two girls and Georgie and Hughie went to a dance at Weem.

Wednesday 26th
Mother gave us some lessons to do in the morning. Although they were short I hate these Scotland lessons. Walked up on the hill with K.E. and Blanche to see the sunset.

Thursday 27th
Taught Blanche in the morning. Dug on the Island in afternoon and had tea there in evening. Are going a night expedition tomorrow.

Friday 28th
Went an expedition down Loch Tay to the Trossachs. We are going to spend the night here. Our party consists of Georgie and Hughie, Mother and Kathleen, Albinia and me.

Saturday 29th
Started at 11 and went down Loch Katrine, and then on to Loch Lomond, and arrived at Aberfeldy at a quarter to 10 very tired indeed.

Figure 25. Loch Kennard 1896. Left to right - Janet Blanche, Antony, Cyril Gurney, Janet Louisa, William, Albinia Rose, Margaret Evelyn Gurney, Cyril. Daubeny. Eustace Lyle, Anstice Katharine, Kathleen Elton, George Abraham, John Evelyn and Lancelot Merivale Gibbs.

Sunday 30th
Georgie read the service as Father is away. Went for a long walk in afternoon. Sang Hymns in evening.

October 1894
Monday 1st
Played and walked about with Lancelot all the morning. Sir Edmund and Lady (Elton) and Winifred and Ambrose Elton came in evening. Rather a nice day.

Tuesday 2nd
Went out with the shooters all day. Evelyn sent me a silver topped scent bottle for a birthday present.

Wednesday 3rd
Taught Blanche and translated French. We all made a huge fire on the Island. Lady Stewart came to call.

Thursday 4th
The girls went out grouse driving. Lady Elton, Mother, I and Blanche drove to Dunkeld and spent the day there. Wrote to Evelyn a very pleasant letter, which ought to please him exceedingly.

Friday 5th
Beastly day. Winifred and Albinia and Eustace walked to Aberfeldy. I walked round the loch with the rest of the ladies.

Saturday 6th
Horrid day again. Went a walk in the afternoon.

Sunday 7th
Beastly day. Went for a small walk in afternoon. Sang hymns in the evening.

Monday 8th
All the Elton family and Hughie went away. Mother and Albinia went down to Aberfeldy to shop. Rather a horrid day. Played Battledore and Shuttlecock with Winifred in morning but only kept up to 218.

Tuesday 9th
Went a walk in afternoon and taught Blanche her lessons. Played B and S with Mother and kept up to 8 hundred and 3 which was good. I think.

Wednesday 10th
Made a bonfire on the Island all day except when I was eating which was fairly often. Am going to leave this palace on Friday for Edinburgh and etc. etc.

Thursday 11th
Spent the morning indoors busy. Made our last bonfire on the Island. Don't feel at all inclined to go away tomorrow.

Friday 12th
Left Loch Kennard at 12.45 and arrived at Edinburgh in the evening. The children have gone down to Tyntesfield. We have lovely rooms.

Saturday 13th
Walked about Edinburgh and went to see Holyrood. Left for St. Andrews in evening.

Sunday 14th
Went to Church in morning. Went for walk in afternoon.

Monday 15th
Started for London at 8.15 a.m. and arrived at 8.45 p.m. Was very tired.

Tuesday 16th
Shopped in morning with Mother. Eustace and I travelled down alone to Tyntesfield and here we are again quite safe.

Wednesday 17th
Went up to Naish for lunch and came back at 3.20. Fraulein arrived at 3.30. We begin lessons tomorrow. Filthy things. Ugh ugh ugh!

Thursday 18th
Kathleen Alice Spencer came. Miss Caffin came and gave us a dancing lesson. Played bear.

Friday 19th
Went a fat walk in morning. Cooked in afternoon and fussed.
Saturday 20th
Went up to Naish for lunch and tea. Mother and Albinia came home and we all fussed together.
Sunday 21st
Church in the morning. Went down to the farm in afternoon, and chapel in evening.
Monday 22nd
Spent a dull day. The Liddles came in evening, and are going to stay for I don't know how long. Nana brought home our skirt dance dresses which was fussy of her.
Tuesday 23rd
Spent an uninteresting day. Miss D. Smith came. Albinia has got a cold and has got no voice.
Wednesday 24th
Rained a lot. Was too wet to go to Mr. Smith's so we made toffee.
Thursday 25th
Miss Caffin came and we had our first skirt dance lesson.
Friday 26th
Forget entirely what I did.
Saturday 27th
Three Cornishes and Evie Spencer came to lunch and tea. We played some fussy games.
Sunday 28th
Went to Church and Chapel. Showery day!! Wrote to Evelyn.
Monday 29th
Went for a fat walk in morning as usual. Fussed a lot.
Tuesday 30th
Rained all day without stopping once. Father and Albinia went to Wells to see the new Bishop enthroned. Had to learn 5 pieces of poetry in evening.
Wednesday 31st
Went into Clifton for our drawing lesson and came back in torrents of rain. Played Hide and Seek in afternoon. The new Bishop came for a night and we had a dinner party. K and I went down after dinner.

November 1894
Thursday 1st
Had our dancing lesson in morning. The Bishop went away after having consecrated the Church yard in the morning.
Friday 2nd
Rained a lot. Fussed a lot.

Saturday 3rd
Went our usual walk in morning. Fanny Crawley came for the afternoon.
Sunday 4th
Church and Chapel as usual. Went and sat on the haystacks with Spencer.
Monday 5th
The Liddells and Daubenys went away. Filthy day.
Tuesday 6th
Lovely day. Went for a walk in morning as usual. Eustace rode.
Wednesday 7th
Went into Clifton for our drawing lesson. Eustace went to Bath with Mr. Medley.
Thursday 8th
We had our drawing lesson. Beautiful day. Went to tea with Mr. Medley. W. Elton came to stay.
Friday 9th
Poured all day. Father went away. Albinia and Winifred went out with the Harriers and in spite of the rain had a very good day.
Saturday 10th
Mother and Albinia went up to London for Cyril's wedding. Aunt Dora and Aunt Cathy went away. K and I went up to Naish for lunch and tea. Fairly fine day. House very quiet and dull.
Sunday 11th
Went to Church and Chapel as always. It rained a trifle hard in afternoon. Father came back.
Monday 12th
Mother and Albinia came back again. They say that Cyril's wedding went off very well.
Tuesday 13th
Mr., Mrs. and Miss Warry, Cousin Arthur and Anne Crawley Boo, two more Crawley Boos and Mr. and Mrs. Wicks came here to stay.
Wednesday 14th
Beastly day. Couldn't go into Clifton because of rain.
Thursday 15th
Dancing lesson as usual. Lovely day. Went to see Bunduck's *baby*
Friday 16th
Nice day. Fussed about the place.
Saturday 17th
Went into Clifton for to see some theatricals, which we found very pleasant. Billy and Evelyn came back at about 10.30 p.m. driven from Eton by floods. Very pleasant. Hurrah.
Sunday 18th
Church and Chapel in the usual course. Farm and catechism also.

We were very naughty.

Monday 19th
Lovely day. Got into fearful trouble about last night and have been sent to bed early which is fat. Danced in evening. Mother and Albinia went down to Bourton.

Tuesday 20th
Forget what I did.

Wednesday 21st
Went into Clifton for our lesson on drawing.

Thursday 22nd
Had our dancing lesson given us.

Friday 23rd
Muggy day.

Saturday 24th
Everybody went away except Cilla Crawley Boevey. Mr. and Mrs. Bovill and Mr. Munro gone. We went into Clifton to see a sort of horse show. We brought Mr. Morehouse back.

Sunday 25th
Walked back from Church. Walked back from Charlton in afternoon. Chapel in evening.

Monday 26th
Cold day. Evelyn hurt his leg. Fraulein went up to Naish in evening.

Tuesday 27th
Cold day. Fraulein has a bad toe so she couldn't go for a walk. K and I went alone. Lots of people came so we had dinner with Father who is in bed with a cold.

Wednesday 28th
Kathleen and Fraulein went into Clifton. I have a little cold so couldn't go.

Thursday 29th
Dancing class as usual. I have a sore throat.

Friday 30th
K. went down to Bourton to meet her Mother.

December 1894

Saturday 1st
Everybody except Mr. Lee Warner went away including Albinia who has gone to stay with Cousin Martin to be Godmother to his little daughter. Eltons came in evening.

Sunday 2nd Advent Sunday.
Didn't go out all day. K has a bad sore throat.

Monday 3rd
The Eltons went away and Mr Lee Warner also. Went out with the beagles to get a hare but failed entirely. K had a toothache last night.

Tuesday 4th
Evelyn went away. Fairly nice day. Fussed about the place. New scarf.
Wednesday 5th
Went in for our drawing lesson. I found it very cold.
Thursday 6th
Dancing lesson as usual. Billy and Eustace went into Clifton.
Friday 7th
Fairly nice day. Went to some theatricals in evening which we enjoyed.
Saturday 8th
Nice day. Went to Clevedon Court in afternoon which I found pleasant.
Sunday 9th
Went to Church. Mother and Billy went up to London in evening.
Monday 10th
Mother came back in evening. Had a half holiday and went up to Naish.

(*Naish House was destroyed by fire on December 25th 1902.*)

Figure 26. Naish House, Wraxall.

Tuesday 11th
Did lessons. *(This is written in very large letters)*

Figure 27. Family group at the entrance to Tyntesfield. Left to right John Evelyn Gibbs, L.C., Charlotte Merivale, Anstice Katharine, William and George Abraham Gibbs, T.S.C., Antony Hubert and Albinia Rose Gibbs.
Front row – Janet Blanche and Eustace Lyle Gibbs.

Wednesday 12th
Albinia, Georgie and Hughie came back and brought pals with them. Kathy S came to stay. Went in for our drawing lesson.

Thursday 13th
Had our dancing lesson. *(This is written in very large letters)*

Friday 14th
Don't know what we did.

Saturday 15th
Dressed a doll in day. Went to a children's party in evening which was <u>fairly nice.</u>

Sunday 16th
Went to Church and Chapel. Went to see Cousin Marion to talk about the Operetta.

Monday 17th
Had a pleasant day.

Tuesday 18th
Fraulein, Eustace and Blanche and Miss Porter went up to see some

acting at Naish, which they enjoyed very much.

Wednesday 19th
Went into Clifton in morning for our drawing lesson. Went up to Naish in evening to see the boys act. It was very good.

Thursday 20th
Had our dancing lesson. Boys came home late in evening.

Friday 21st
Broke up in afternoon. K is not going till tomorrow. Went to a children's fancy dance in evening at the Schwabe's which we enjoyed awfully.

Saturday 22nd
Was down at 11. Fraulein and K went away. Went to see the beef given away at the farm. Cyril and his wife came to stay (Margaret Evelyn, née Trotter).

There are no further entries in the diary after 22nd December

Figure 28. The Family at Tyntesfield, 1894. Front row L to R – Fraulein, Nancy (Anstice Katharine), Albinia, Antony and Janet Gibbs. Behind Nancy & Albinia – Janet Blanche and in the back row Lancelot Merivale and John Evelyn Gibbs.

Chapter Three

Wedding at Tyntesfield

On the 20th and 21st of June 1897, Queen Victoria celebrated her Diamond Jubilee. Antony Gibbs at Tyntesfield erected an Orangery and laid out a Diamond Jubilee Garden to celebrate the occasion. There was a fete in the grounds, which included a fair ground roundabout. There was a cricket match and much celebration in the newly opened gardens.

The first of Antony and Janet's children to be married was their second son, Antony Hubert Gibbs who married Mary Mercy Llewellyn, the eldest daughter of the Somerset Member of Parliament, Evan Henry Llewellyn of Langford Court, Burrington, and his wife Mary Blanche. The wedding took place at Burrington on the 18th October 1899.

Albinia Rose Gibbs and Richard Alexander Bennett were very close friends and in 1899 they also became engaged to be married. Richard was born at Holdenhurst in Bournemouth on 12th December 1872. He was the elder son of the Rev. Alexander Sykes Bennett, Vicar of St. Stephen's Church, Bournemouth. He was in the same house as George Abraham, Antony Hubert and William Gibbs at Eton. He was an accomplished cricketer and played for Hampshire. A right-handed batsman

Figure 29. English batsmen waiting their turn at Staten Island, New York. Richard Bennett is to the left of the padded batsman.

Figure 30. Wedding of Richard Bennett and Albinia Rose Gibbs at Wraxall.

Figure 31. Guests at Tyntesfield for Richard and Albinia's wedding.

and wicket keeper, in September and October 1897 he toured with Plum Warner's team that played matches against Staten Island Club, New York, and the Mannheim, Belmont and Merion Clubs in Philadelphia. He was Captain of a team that toured the West Indies in 1901-1902. It was through her brothers that Richard met Albinia Rose who being born on the 31st March 1876 was younger than her fiancé.

The Wedding on Saturday December 2nd 1899 was at All Saints Church in Wraxall. An arch above the Wraxall Gate to Tyntesfield said "Farewell Miss Gibbs". When the bride returned to Tyntesfield, the greeting on the arch was "Welcome Mrs. Bennett"! Two of the bridesmaids were Albinia's sisters, Anstice Katharine and Janet Blanche (to the right in the photo). Other bridesmaids were her cousins, Alice Gurney (front right) and Mary Albinia Gibbs, Henry Martin and Emily Gibbs's only surviving daughter (front left). Richard Bennett's two sisters (to the left), Annie and Georgina, were also bridesmaids.

With the outbreak of the Boer War in South Africa, George Abraham Gibbs was soon en route to Cape Town. William Gibbs, who was off to Sandhurst for military training, and John Evelyn Gibbs followed later in 1901.

George Abraham Gibbs was commissioned as a Second Lieutenant in the North Somerset Yeomanry on 28th January 1893, and promoted to Captain on 25th December 1895. He served with the 48th Company of the 7th Battalion of the Imperial Yeomanry during the South African War. The Company acted as the bodyguard to the Commander in Chief, Lord Roberts. He was involved in operations in the Transvaal in May and June 1900, including actions near Johannesburg and Diamond Hill on 11th and 12th June. He was with Lord Roberts when the British paraded through Pretoria on June 5th 1900. He was awarded the Queen's South African Medal with the following bars: Johannesburg, Diamond Hill, Belfast, Cape Colony and Orange Free State. He was invalided home after a riding accident in July 1900.

William Gibbs was commissioned as 2nd Lieutenant in the 7th Hussars on 17th February 1900; he was promoted Lieutenant on 29th November 1900. In the South African War, he took part in operations in the Cape Colony (December 1901 to January 1902), in the Orange River Colony (January to March, and May 1902) and in the Transvaal (March to May 1902). He was awarded the Queen's South Africa Medal with 5 bars.

John Evelyn Gibbs was commissioned in the Coldstream Guards on 20th January 1900. He was promoted Lieutenant on 1st November 1901. He served in the South African War and took part in operations in the Cape Colony between July 1901 and 31st May 1902. He was awarded the Queen's South African Medal with three bars.

The best description available of their experiences in South Africa comes from the letters, which they wrote home, some of which have survived. Here are the letters, which have been preserved in family archives from George Abraham, John Evelyn and William Gibbs.

Figure 32. George Abraham Gibbs was in the Body Guard for Field Marshal Lord Roberts at the Entry into Pretoria on June 5th 1900.

Courts of Justice Hospital
Pretoria
North Somerset Imperial Yeomanry
Care of Field Marshall Lord Roberts Field Force
South Africa

July 5th 1900

My dear Dick,
    Here I am lying hors de combat laid low not by the bullet from the rifle of a savage Boer or from the ravages of fever but from the combination of dust and the body of a quadruped – to wit an English hunting horse. We had a so-called Paper Chase last Saturday (June 30th) at which there were certainly 80 starters, there was no paper in the affair at all but the course was a made one with the exception of the first two obstacles, which were two natural stone walls after which fences all very low and narrow built up with bricks mud and sandbags, the rendezvous was a quarter of a mile SW of the race course whither we made our way so as to arrive there at 3:00 p.m. All sorts of people were there including the Commander in Chief and Generals of sorts besides. I got near the

starter one Major Furse on the H Q Staff who was also riding himself and when there were a certain amount of the intending starters around him he said "Off" at the same time urging his steed to its best pace, and so off we went over the 1st wall across a bit of veldt and then down into a drift and up again keeping a regimental flag on our left and over a 2nd stone wall and then on again to the 3rd, on arriving at which the ten horses who were more of less in a bunch in front of me made such a dust that the part of the fence which was to be negotiated was invisible to myself and also to the really excellent bit of horse flesh I was bestriding, and so he for himself being happily in ignorance of the immediate presence of the obstacle galloped on full of confidence. I on the other hand having doubts about the safe continuance of our ride in which doubts I was not mistaken speedily finding myself lying on the veldt with the excellent animal on top of me, another horse landed right over us but with considerable cleverness placed his feet all round us just touching my finger to show what he had done, after a second or two I got clear and walked away a few yards and then lay down, luckily there were two or three doctors standing at the fence and they immediately administered to my wants sending for a stretcher and ambulance which after an hour arrived and I was brought along here where the head of this (the Irish Hospital) Sir William Thompson examined me and found that as far as breakages I had escaped with a broken rib, but I was naturally a bit knocked about as well, my ill-natured horse having kicked me in the back just above my hip bone which is still painful. Things are going on much as usual here, they have turned all the Hollanders out and all males not provided with passes over 16 years of age, these passes show that they have laid down their arms and have taken the oath. De Wet is still causing trouble and there are several columns down trying to round him up, all the Cavalry except the 1st Cavalry Brigade (Tony's brigade) have gone down south for that purpose having been rehorsed. Re Tony, he has seen a good bit of fighting and is like everyone else anxious to get home, I do not think entre nous that he is quite satisfied with his regiment which I am not altogether surprised at although there are some good chaps in it and the regiment has done some good work out here having seen I should think more service than any with perhaps the exception of the 12th and 9th. I heard from Arthur Watman two days ago from Senekal in the Orange River Colony. I do not expect he will ever get up here. I think it is a pity if he wants a commission not to apply now instead of waiting till the end and till he gets home as applications have been going in and are still, two of our men want them and will get them for certain. There are 5 other officers in this ward one a Colonel of the Essex, Wood by name, and the others Captains and Lieutenants, Crispin, Wyndham, Tamplin, and an Officer in the Argyle and Sutherland Highlanders our latest comrade and one like many others who has had fever. Pretoria is not a bad place, there are not many streets with shops but the houses where people of wealth live are quite good though small and are like the best sort of houses in the suburbs of Oxford but of course having only one storey. We played cricket on cocoanut matting on a sort of village green there is near our house but with our very limited number of men it has been difficult to get up many games, they have just started playing polo on the race course but I shall miss that now which is a pity as very few of the players have ever tried it before and none of the ponies but of course nearly all the countrybreds are of the polo pony stamp. There are a good many of Billy's regiment out here as you know and some of them like Haig and Porre have done well and are sure to get something at the close of the campaign also Charlie Rankin who is Rimmington's right hand man. The Yeomanry Officers of the 7th Imperial Yeomanry have been trying to get temporary billets in the Town and one man was given 500 keys and told to find which locks they belonged to in the Treasury and in other places in the Government Buildings, but Douglas McLean got into the Provost Marshall's office, which is much better. I hope that you have been getting some runs.

With best love to Albinia and yourself

Ever yours affectionately

George

Pretoria

June 10th 1900

My dear Dick

Many thanks for your letter, which I received at Kroonstad. As you see by the heading of this, I have safely reached Brother Boer's Capital and want to go no further. I have had quite enough and hanker after no more trekking. It is no country for a foot soldier. We are doing garrison duty here with the rest of the 14th Brigade and our General has been appointed Governor so I think we shall be left here in comparative peace. We are occupying the Staat Artillery Barracks. Most sumptuous. Electric Light. Hot and cold water to bathe. Pommery. Port and civilization in General. Each Staats Artillery Officer has a villa residence to himself and we are putting 4 officers or so into each of these houses. They evidently left in a great hurry. Letters, uniforms, rifles, ammunition etc. left all over the place. I hope the war will soon be over now but expect it will drag on for some time, especially if the Boers take to the Mountains. The day of our arrival here we were all drawn up to witness the meeting between Lord Roberts and Botha on a certain hill outside the town. Of course Botha never came but took the opportunity to leave in the last train for the East! Another example of Boerness. It is really too absurd to treat these hairy-heeled devils with the ordinary courtesies of civilized warfare. They only think and call us damned fools for our pains. The place swarms with released British prisoners of war. The officers are being tried in our Mess, which interferes with the luncheon arrangements. I have seen nothing of either George Gibbs or Watman but one very seldom meets anybody outside one's own brigade. When on the march we get up at 4, breakfast and march by 6 a.m. and often don't get into Camp until after dark so there is not much time for looking up people. We have had great luck in getting here without being left anywhere on the lines. We are very weak and I was much afraid that they might leave us for garrison duty somewhere short of this in consequence. I was always very keen to get here but as I say don't want to go any further. Please give my best respects to Mrs. Bennett and your people.

Yours ever

Hen(ry)

Did you see the Prince's horse win the Derby?

Johannesburg

26 January 1901

My dear Dick

Many thanks for your interesting quantum of news. I suppose you gave ADW the meeting at Crawley Towers on his return to the native soil. He was well out of Clements show on the Magaliesberg, although I fancy Clements did a pretty good get out, and slew a few Boers.

I am in hospital here with a touch of fever, which is an infernal nuisance; I was just going off as Galloper to Allenby who has got a Column consisting of Scots Greys, Carabineers, 14th Hussars, Scots Guards and Guns and Gordon is oft rather resigned on his own. This war will never finish, as far as I can see. The Boers have us one way, if they don't another. They have just taken a nice train load of 800 horses coming up.

I have been trekking in the Free State lately with Rimington's Tigers and the Cape Mounted Rifles. Whenever we did see any Boers we gave them a proper shelling. You mention that I ought to exchange into the 7th Hussars, but as a matter of fact, I am going to chuck it as soon as possible after the war, being far too old. All my Contemporaries are

Captains now.

This war has used not only the regular Army but every man in England of any irregular corps too, so that one makes no advantage of being out here, or of a little rapid promotion which everybody gets alike, so I shall be glad to see the back of it.

These damned Boers are not half so refined as the English labourer, nor are they half so clean, and the women are positively hideous, hence the morality of the war.

I have been dumped down in hospital among the enteric patients. They tell me smilingly not to mind its being catching.

I am so glad to hear your boy grows in stature and is fine of feature. I suppose you feel quite the proud father as you walk home o'nights to the paternal hearth.

Very sorry to hear about George Muirhouse's business, I thought that some alterations were coming in about the Sugar Bounties, which would make the concern pay.

At the Field Force Canteen, I chanced upon 4 cases of Cliquot '92 duty free 100/- per dozen so I snaffled the lot and we were not long in emptying the cases. You ought to bring out a fine assortment of wines and 5 star Brandy is much sought after out here. When in off trek the soldier will pay fabulous sums for a bottle of wine.

How are they all at Tyntesfield? I suppose George is not thinking of taking the field again out here? Is there any likelihood of Bill or Evy coming out? I have heard little of the doings of these famous two warriors lately.

The Scots Guards have been trekking with us lately. They walk well in the towns, they wear tight bands round the waist, are very select in their company, lunching generally all together and doing themselves nicely in the way of playing a good knife and fork.

I must stop now, so good-bye and hoping to meet soon when we will take a nice glass of wine together.

Give my love to Albinia and any others of the family you chance to see.

Yours ever

Antony Edmund Gibbs

Antony Edmund Gibbs was the fourth son of George Louis Monck Gibbs and Laura Beatrice, daughter of Sir Arthur Hallam Elton of Clevedon Court. He was a Second Lieutenant in the Royal East Kent Yeomanry Cavalry.

Graaff Reinet.
c.c.
(16 Hyde Park Gardens.)

Aug. 1st 1901.

My Dearest Nancy,
  Just a line. Enclosed are some photographs - results of my skill: with subject written behind not bad, but I can't find any very interesting subjects. Also a programme of Company now visiting the town: and my railway ticket from Nieuwpoort to here. The latter 2 only interesting to me, in time to come. If you will keep them all for me, against my coming home, I shall be very happy and obliged. All the news I have, I have sent to mother.
  Please thank very much for constant letters received, yourself, Georgie, Eustace, Blanche and Lags, and say I will answer them as soon as I can.
  Have just heard the bugles in the distance playing the 'Last Post' over the grave of a man who died of excessive drink two days since: rather dispiriting so must stop.

Love to all.

Your loving brother Evelyn

Will send Jane some more photographs next week if possible.

Judicial Palace
Graaff Reinet

August 8th 1901

My dearest Nancy
  This is the Coronation Eve, and I am just going to bed. Your last from Broke (*Broke Hall near Ipswich*) was cheery if somewhat ungrammatical: however I understood all, so it did not matter. Stafford and two Curate friends as the only men of the party sounds very cheerful. I am glad to hear they were so genial. The fact that Edward VII will be crowned tomorrow is no doubt an important if unusual one, but it is entirely eclipsed by the fact that I shall be up at 7.15, having left my bed about 6.30 a.m.
  When I tell you that there is a dance now in progress and that I am not going, you may be puzzled: but when I go on to say that I only know

Figure 33, John Evelyn Gibbs at Tyntesfield in the battle uniform of the Coldstream Guards with Lancelot behind playing at soldiers.

two ladies, both of whom are wonderfully uninteresting and exceedingly stiff in the joints and very heavy in the toes, you will I surmise cease to wonder. Tomorrow I shall be employed in many different capacities. 1st as a layman at a Thanksgiving service, 2nd as an officer on a Grand Parade, 3rd as a Polo player, 4th as a listener at a concert and 5th, several times, as a hungry and thirsty man at his meals: and all, with the exceptions of the 3rd and 5th, because Edward is being made a real king.

I did not know Richard of Andover was to be married on August 6th, or I would have cabled congratulations; but I should be infinitely indebted if you would forward the enclosed letter of congratulations to him at his new Rectory wherever it may be ------

I am to return to the 3rd Battalion under Mr. Beckwith I find after all, so shall have to go to that most poisonous of places, Aldershot, when I return to England, with a very heavy, large and emphasized accent on the 'when'.

Beatrice's addenda to your last letter showed signs of considerable haste.

You might mention to her that she should not hurry when writing; one is apt to miss-spell words when in any way hustled or pressed for time. Love to all

Goodbye dear child

Your loving brother Evelyn

Oudeberg
(Pronounced Oodeburg)

Thursday August 15th 1901

My dearest Nancy

Yes as you say we have all the fun here now or rather some do I don't. There are four or five columns trekking about the Colony trying to drive the Burghers northwards, but some how the wily Boer manages to slip past them and still roams about the place snapping up small bodies of troops. These columns generally consist of about one Squadron of cavalry and one gun, sometimes two guns. Here (about twelve miles from Graaff Reinet) we continually hear reports of Boers at farms round about, but although we have a patrol of Yeomanry out every day we never see any Boers, they keep very dark and are mostly in bodies of 60 to 100. However we'll catch them soon. A fellow called 'Barber' in the 3rd Imperial Yeomanry caught one nicely the other day. He was out with a patrol and saw four Boers. They galloped after them, the Boers of course split up and Barber, on a racing pony, galloped after. The Boer stopped shot at him finding he could not escape, but Barber let drive at him twice with a revolver, so brother Boer held up his arms and surrendered. They turned out to be Boer despatch riders.

This Barber is what in books is called a regular 'fire eater' and fears nothing from mere man and a very good fellow to boot (at least so his boot maker says). I am sorry to hear from Albinia that you and she are subjects for mirth for having sent me delicious food stuffs but you can tell these merrymakers that delicacies are always most acceptable (especially here) and I also quote from the old proverb 'she laughs longest who laughs last' so I shall hope to find you both still in fits of laughter when I return.

I am very glad to hear you had so many dances in London. I hope your ball at 16 Hyde Park Gardens was a rollicking success and also that the dance at Tyntesfield (I suppose you had one) was equally enjoyed and that no one overstepped the limits etc. Talking of limits, the 'Diary' which some kind friend sent me, is enjoyed out here by young and old alike.

The Colonel says he knows it by heart and several others have had a hearty laugh at the inhabitants of Birchfield Terrace.

I hope your new dog is good and nice and not savage. You must have enjoyed your visit to Yatton station just the place for a hot afternoon. I hope to be there shortly after Christmas, booted and spurred with a bevy of first class horses stamping with impatience at Bicester in charge of Donelly. I am sorry Bill did not sell 'Nap', but I expect he would be lucky if he got £20 for him.

We live very well out here plenty of nice food and drink but water is very scarce and my bath is always of muddy water brought with great trouble by my old and trusted dependant 'Blizzard' who is in excellent health and looks.

I am sending some more photographs and the man who printed them has only got this horrible mauve paper so they are not very distinct and some are uninteresting. I am going to try and get a photograph of and also a shot at, some of these monkeys, mostly great big Baboons I saw the other day. Amongst very many other letters, I had a rather amusing letter from Walter R. last mail. He was acting as a Judge Marshall at the time.

A cup of tea at 11.00 a.m. seems to be the fashion in the country, almost as bad for one as tea at 11.00 p.m. in Billy's room at Tyntesfield. I hope Katie, Minnie and Gerald were all well and that the shooting there was good. No more news.

Ever your loving brother Evelyn

Return to Nancy

GRAAFF REINET CLUB

Aug 30th 1901

My Dearest Nancy

I am so awfully sorry to hear that you got measles just at the beginning of the cricket week. Your letter announcing the fact was most temperate considering the circumstances. Well I am afraid this letter will arrive after Sept 12th but never the less perhaps you will receive my heartiest congratulations and wishes for many happy returns for you of that happy date.

I am sending you by this mail a present (nothing less) of a few (thirteen to be accurate) ostrich feathers, chosen by an expert and said to be very good of their kind. The four long feathers will have to be straightened out again by some expert in dressing feathers, and will be quite nice and long.

Also I am sending back on another dozen photographs of great value and fair interest. Pretty good our doing so well against the S. Stragglers, who must have been a very strong team.

I am very sorry to hear poor Blanche C. M. is so ill, I hope she is well again by now. I had a most amazing letter from Bill Beckwith last mail, which made me laugh no little.

Today I Have been out to shoot pigeons, but having missed many, I ended by shooting a poor little dove (which abound here) and brought it back in triumph, as they are very good to eat.

I hope you enjoyed yourself at Invergeldie, and that Pitchroy is nice. I suppose Mrs. Boyle has paid a visit there by now. She certainly is well read (in D of H). We had a great polo match yesterday, 4 juniors versus 4 seniors, but were badly beat, 4 goals to 0. I expected to win.

I am so glad to hear Willie has got into Sandhurst: an excellent thing for him.

Yes. Let them all have a photo of me, blow the expense as I can quite understand the immense pleasure it must be to have one on the drawing room piano (grand or college).

I think it is beginning to get hot here, but thank goodness the nights continue very cold at times I like cold nights and hot days. Sorry to hear of <u>Empress</u> Fred's death, a pity.

No news of moving from here or returning home, I want to do one or the other. King, I hear, is getting a <u>bit bustled</u> about in the 1st Battalion, which should do him great good.

Love to all,

Your loving brother Evelyn.

3rd BATTALION, THE.QUEEN'S REGIMENT,
De Aar.

October 17th 1901

My Dear Nancy

I am afraid it is some time since I wrote to you last but just lately I have been rather scrambled over my mails, dashing here and rushing there absolutely ad te libitum (*at your pleasure*). The reason you did not get my letters the week of September 10 must have been because the ship was late. I wrote as you will see by my letter to Mother, I am on my way to a dull spot called Britstown, 30 miles from here on a railway. We have laid in enormous stores so as to live well, even if it is desperate dull, and drown all cares in Champagne and Paté de foie gras. These staff officers and people here are maddening, they cannot tell us when we are to start, it may be today and may be tomorrow.

I have really got no news. I enjoyed being on the Armoured Train, but don't enjoy being here. I have got three spools being developed but the old ass of a man at Graaff Reinet has apparently lost one and not finished the others but I have asked one Pryce Jones to keep haggling at him to send them on to me, and I will then send them on to you. Rather curious that proclamation by Mr. Llewellyn. I hope Mother got it and that you will keep it for me.

Of course you know Miss Long. I don't! And should like a likeness, if you by any chance you happen to Kodakize her.

I hear reports of 3 more officers coming out, I wonder who they will be, and if old Gilly will make a bid to get out again. I hope so. Frightfully hot and dusty here, in fact horrible. This is merely a huge camp with few troops, but lots of Remounts and stores etc. I was very sorry to leave Graaff Reinet and its polo, tennis, cricket, billiards and charming society. Best love

Your loving brother

Evelyn.

Britstown C. C.

Sunday October 27 1901

My dearest child
Delighted to hear the few ostrich feathers will come in useful for trimming your 'at. They are rather choice of their sort I am told and if I am able, but don't mention for fear of acute disappointment, I shall get a few to send to Via as a slight token of my appreciation of her quite excellent choice. You must persuade Mother, Georgie or Billy to let you see their letters from me as I am almost unable to write any more. About my Christmas Basket of good cheer. The cake should be of the very best Xmas pattern covered thickly with Almond icing and much sugar and in fact made as rich and unwholesome as possible as we have quite made up our minds to overeat ourselves on that day of days, all days excelling. I have asked Billy to choose the Liqueurs I put in for and the Pate de Fois Gras only wants ordering: if you do this, you will thus ease Mother of a lot of bother which should be and I hope is your great aim and ambition. Talking of cakes, I have received two most excellent results from your orders at Cobbetts, and hope for a continuance of your great favours and

for which very many thanks. Papers also roll up continually now.

I suppose you will add another dress to your already overstocked wardrobe with Georgie's wedding. Oh, so lucky and what will the colour be and I hope it will fit.

The enclosed photographs are excellent please give them a front seat in my books.

Two more printed lots are looking for me somewhere in the country too, so next week I hope to have them to send you.

No more news

Your loving brother Evelyn

Britstown (Regimental Logo)

November 10th 1901

My dearest Nancy

Fancy you a bridesmaid dressed up in a Louis XVII Coat of green Moire and green velvet hat, quite a little picture (for Phil May of course I mean) and I hope you will be able to persuade some brave photographer to make it (if Mr. Philip May won't) and send me a copy.

By the time you get this I suppose it will be all over, but I can't stop without saying that of course the Bride looked lovely in a gown of 'Crepe de Chine' and beautiful 'Tulle' veil and shoes to match. The exact date has not yet been disclosed to me, but I hope to be able to send a cable to reach the house to meet the happy pair when they return from the Church to refresh on a little cold mutton, with parsley over the place where it had been cut before. I hope to meet Billy at De Aar when the 7th Hussars come up country, if I can learn the date of his arrival at Cape Town. I ought to be sending some more photographs by this mail, but the wicked man has not returned them.

I again conducted Divine Service this morning, with no little success. Mr. Medley could not have done it better. I got a lady to perform on the Harmonium too which enlivened it a bit.

Just off to afternoon tea with the Doctor's wife, Mrs. Hopkins by name, and who is Irish and dull, but not quite so dull as her husband.

No news really, though I compiled no less than 7 runs in Each innings in a match against the Town yesterday, and also gave three cheers for King Edward VII on his birthday.

Your loving brother

Evelyn

Britstown

November 16th 1901

My dearest Nancy,

I have just had an interview with a Dutchman, which has made me feel rather poorly. He wanted me to pay for some fowls and ducks I got from him for our consumption. Most unreasonable man and as he did not understand English, I was able to call him all sorts of nice names, which I redoubled when he began to spit (pardon the coarse word) on the floor of our Dining Room, a habit which all Dutchmen have and most unpleasant!

To get exercise in this town, I have now begun to learn to work Indian clubs, which is quite amusing and excellent exercise. I shall come home a young Hercules I expect and also ready to take on young Stadward at club swinging.

Did I tell you that I had a most excellent letter from Lear about a month ago, will you thank him for it and say it was most welcome containing as it did, so much news of Tyntesfield.

The flies are getting awful here now as Summer draws on: they are at their worst about January and February so poor Billy will just come in for them.

What bad luck him just coming out before Georgie's wedding. Who will be the Best man now?

Huie very kindly sent me a very nice photograph of Mercy and Elaine but hope it is not a flattering likeness of Elaine, but plain children grow up pretty I'm told

I hope by the time you get this you will have sent off a photograph of Via for me to see. I expect I shall recognise her face, but can't bring it to mind at all now. I see the 26th is to be the happy date - Has anyone heard anything of Cyril Daubeny? I suppose he can't be going home till this old war ends.

I have written to Bill Beckworth to say that if my horse is not wanted at home, he can have it to hunt if he likes. If you think it will be useful at home, tell him he can't have it, he will quite understand. Someone should teach Lags to spell Gymnasium; he spells it "Jiminasioum", not quite correctly.

If Father or Mother would care to present me with a gift, say for December 22nd, you might suggest that a suitcase, the same size as Billy's and same pattern, would be very nice. My present one is too small and won't go under a railway carriage seat, but its fittings would do for the new bag as they are excellent.

No news of the war. The Doctor's wife gave a picnic yesterday which was terrible; and it was terrible one meets all the shop people at them. She said to me one day "I suppose you found it very hard when you first came out here to make friends with the shopkeepers and their wives; I know I did." I said it "had been a little difficult at first," but of course no self respecting person ever does take any notice of the brutes. All Dutch are horrid and never will meet the people.

"Yama" looks a nice little dog

I am sending you a lot of photographs, some not bad, you will observe I figure a good deal myself in them.

Glad to hear there is a chance of Walters going. (I am gardener here). We have about 8 fig trees and 3 vines growing in the garden and do hope to enjoy fruit for and between every meal. Well love to all

Ever your loving brother Evelyn

Dielfontein Hospital

December 9th 1901

My dearest little one,

A happy, bright, merry, lucky and jolly New Year to you. By skillful reckoning, I find I have not the slightest idea when you will get this, but it should be during 1902.

It is no good my describing this palace to you as you will see it in my letter to Mother, if maybe you turn up before 10.00 a.m. for breakfast on the eventful day of its arrival. Suffice it that I am thoroughly comfortable, doing nothing but just waiting till the 'Yaller Jaundice' shall leave me white again. The 'Sisters' are all charming I believe, I have met two up to now, both most excellent ladies. My Doctor is, I hear, an exceedingly clever man and certainly gives me that impression: though a little unfortunate in his name, which is 'Black'.

One of the officers in the next ward to me is a quaint old fish: he is a Quarter Master in some Yeomanry. He came out here with four sons, of whom one is since dead. When he came down here to hospital, he asked his Colonel if he might bring his youngest son (16 years) with him. The youth is a trumpeter in the same Yeomanry: he was allowed to do so : so he left his servant and brought his son down in his place: so now we are in the quaint position that we hobnob with the father while Mr Blizard and the other servants hobnob with his son. Quaint! - One Ferneaux who was our Supply Officer at Graaff Reinet slept here one night on his way home to England; he has had a very bad go of Enteritis for three months. A very nice fellow whom I was very glad to see before he went home. He was travelling in the Hospital train and took me over it, they are most beautifully comfortable. I am sending you another view of Britstown taken by Versturme Bunbury (of Bath) the militia officer we had there.

I am rather sorry for the Queen of Holland, it seems hard she should have a husband who insults her and then wounds all those who stick up for her: though I daresay she richly deserved it if he boxed her ears.

Weather very hot and will be hotter - I hope to return to Graaff Reinet when I leave here as I expect my place will be filled at Britstown.

No more news. Love to any and all. I hope Mr. Slugs got the very Lowther Areadish whip I sent him; it is a Kaffir production.

Your loving brother

Evelyn

Figure 34. William Gibbs at Tyntesfield in the battle uniform of the 7th Hussars.

CAVALRY, ARTILLERY AND
OVERSEA COLONIAL DEPOT.
GREEN POINT
SOUTH AFRICA

Dec. 21.1901

My Dearest Nancy,
Here we are at Cape Town. We arrived yesterday. The horses were very fit. This is a sort of depot mess. The food is very bad, but we have got rooms to sleep in. We probably stay here till Monday. This is on the outskirts of Cape Town, Green Point, but it isn't very green. We were very glad to see the last of the Templemore. Last night we went down and dined at the Mount Nelson Hotel. It was very nice. There is a band there and we met a lot of fellows we knew which was very nice. Haig joins us

off French's staff.

On Monday we go to Stellenbosch for a few days. Then, when the horses are fit, to Colesburg, where we shall probably be a column by ourselves; at least we hope so. The Colonel is not fit, I am sorry to say, but I hope he won't be bad long; he has got neuralgia in a nerve of the leg.

I am very fit, though the sun has rather caught my face when I shave. I don't expect I shall be able to do much photographing. I have used up the first spool. The climate seems very pleasant here; but I can imagine that marching will be very hot. We are just by where they kept all the Boers prisoners with the patent flash light and electric alarm signal for the sentry to use.

I must see about storing the things not to be taken up country today.

I heard several chaps saying that the war should be getting near the end now and that Kitchener keeps saying so.

Well goodbye my dear Nancy and the best of love to all.

Your loving brother

William Gibbs

Deelfontein

January 5 1902

My dearest Nancy,

How charmingly kind of Emma Buckingham to paint a calendar for me, of course it will be very jolly to hang up in a tent. No! On second thoughts I think I will keep it in a box as one wants to forget the date and not be constantly reminded how long exactly one has been in this desert land. Sorry to hear you had not been photographed in bridesmaids clothes by December 13, so awkward with Christmas so near, you might want to have the blouse made up as a smart New Year overcoat or riding habit - Talking of presents I was much gratified and slightly amused to receive a letter from Messrs. Stohwasser (of gaiter fame) to say they were sending me a present of a few cigars: I have only had three pairs of Khaki breeches and a few odds and ends from them in my life. However neither their cigars nor Emma's Calendar have turned up yet. I have written to thank Stohwasser in advance but I think I had better wait till I get Emma's Calendar before I write to her.

Your loving brother

Evelyn

Deelfontein

January 13 1902

My dearest Nancy,
   For most of my news see more of today to Mother. First please expect one packet 5 inches by 4 inches, containing photographs taken by yours truly and one lone packet 9 inches by 1 inch containing two photographs of the Armoured Train and Crew taken by a professor of Beaufort West.
   Your last letter was from Stratton Firs, when it was freezing and you had two horses there, a great nuisance for you.
   Hatherop Castle seems a comfortable house from your description. An electric clock sounds quaint, has he got any worked by steam or by windmills but perhaps you mean clocks lit up by Electric 'lit'. Capital fun it must be if Aunt Blanche cooos the whole time, but two young hearts etc. I hope your ink sketch does not flatter the child, if so it must be almost ugly. You seem to be having a merry party for January dances. My love to Beckwith and sister Jilly, Beatrice, Cicely W., A. Ord, A.A.G.B., Margo Cru and the rest. It seems funny to think that the time I get home Willy will be in the army and last time I saw him he seemed quite a little boy at Eton. I can quite believe Noel would be better for a slight application of boot so very precocious. I went up to De Aar yesterday to see Billy once more before he starts. He was very fit and glad to be leaving De Aar. I do hope he will have a good time, he will see the country anyhow.
   I shall leave hospital next Sunday or Monday unless anything unforeseen occurs, as I am now quite fit enough to go out.
   I have cut out a pleasing picture of Via from Country Life. How sick they must be of seeing their pictures and names in the papers. Not many of the family to write to now, George in Egypt, Billy here and Albinia in the West Indies. The photograph Billy took of me, which you will find among the rest, makes me look frightfully ill, I ain't like that really, t'was the wind as did it.
   No more news.
               Your loving brother Evelyn

Britstown

January 26 1902

My dearest Nan,
   With this you will find quite a quantity of photographs. The small

one of Mick, he sent himself. Via told me he was a great friend of hers and he is of mine too: boys together in fact and at Eton and Sandhurst.

We are living in very poor style just now, as we have no stores, but directly I arrived and took over the food management I ordered large supplies, which should arrive in a day or so. I feel capable of running the Carleton Restaurant now. I have taken up the duties of 'Parson' again too and we have beautiful services, much better singing than St. George's Windsor; the collections too are better than at first, several times one 1/-.

Exercise is the difficulty, it's so frightfully hot in the daytime and 'orrible dark o' nights.

I am very glad you liked Miss Beckwith, quite a good egg I thought and a bit of a sportswoman too. I hope Beatrice and Cicely etc. all behaved themselves nice, and enjoyed the dance grand. Faute de mieux, we have had to call out the Town Guard here to fill the Forts round the town, as the militia detachment were taken off on convoy duty for a fortnight.

It is rather fun, because it annoys them frightfully. They are only called out in Emergencies and this is one. They said it hindered the trade in their stores them having to be away, so to prevent that, all shops are now shut at 2.00 pm, so they are caught that way too.

The Battalion is now split up
2 Companies and Head Quarters at Graaff Reinet
1 Company at Britstown
1 Company at Blauwater (siding on Graaff Reinet line)
1 Company at Aberdeen (on Port Elizabeth's line)
3 Companies at Nieuwpoort

So if you look at the map, you will see we are spread all over the country of Cape Colony

I heard from Beckwith last mail but one, full of fun at going to Tyntesfield, and saying the 3rd Battalion goes to Windsor in April, if we are not back by then. Have got to call on the Doctor's wife today, rather a bore.

I told you in my letter about a month ago how fond I am of Walter Riddell, but like me, you know, he is much too young to think of such things. If I were you I should try and forget all about it if you can, that is what I am doing for myself. I really believe it is the best way.

Goodbye Nancy and best love

Your loving brother

Evelyn

What shall I give up in Lent? 'Writing letters' or 'Alcohol' or 'Neither'?

Britstown

February 2 1902

My dearest Nancy,

    I can spare time for more than a line or so. Very many thanks for the cake from Cobbetts, which was excellent and had a great reception. By the bye, will you have turned off, what I fancy you ordered to be turned on, i.e. the Eastmans - weekly - supply - of - one - Kodak - film tap as I have now got a stock of about 14 and can't use them here.

    Yes, Quorn is a very nice house, and does George Farnham great credit. Why did you not have Eric Spencer stripped of his Embroidered Waistcoat then turned out and the Waistcoat burnt? It must have been what he expected to have done to him. Beatrice seems to have got over her former fear of Cicely W. Don't you remember your young girls Tea fight in London, how frightened she said she was of Cicely. Anyhow altogether your party seems to have been a grand success. Ralph Webber still keeps up his weekly flow of fun in letters. He is quite splendid at writing letters and more regular than my watch.

    Frightfully hot and no rain, otherwise fairly happy here thank you! I have asked Bill Beckwith to have my horse sold when he has done with him. No more news.

        Goodbye dear child, with love to all

        Your loving brother Evelyn

Wynburg

Feb. 2. 1902.

My dearest Nancy,

    You seem to have had a merry party for the fun after Xmas. I hope Bill B's hand is progressing.

    It is rotten luck for Ralph D. to have to go back to India.

    So Jessy Rideout is in bad odour again. However we had fine sport with the tame partridges in October.

    I am afraid my photo snapping has been neglected lately. I see Roddy Brownlow came out with the Rifle Brigade the other day.

    So Miss Christobel has found another young man very soon. She certainly was not worth Evelyn bothering himself about, and he certainly has quite forgotten her. Now he will see she was no good. Claud Serscold was at Eton with me but I don't know him. I think Mother has met his fat sister.

Very many thanks for the papers and films which arrive duly. I am accumulating the film a little at present, so perhaps if you told them to send them less often, it would be enough.

Our horses have been out grazing this morning, and just now they came stampeding back into camp, (sketch of camp shelter drawn here).

The above is a picture of our shelter and chairs, which we use for meals. The drawing is not very good or accurate.

This is my tent d'abris..... (sketch of tent with word "green" on it). They are very good and roll up very small. We are just going to have lunch (1.30) consisting of

Tea and Nestles milk.
Fried mutton and tongue
(Mutton killed yesterday)
Jam and potted meat.

We have got an Indian cook who is very good, but he nearly struck yesterday as we had such a fearful long day, although all he did was to drive on the Cape Cart 16 miles mostly in the dark. We had to walk nearly all the way, while we had been out all day from 7 o'clock at this farm and patrolling round it.

The sentences of Courts Martial are read out on parade. This morning after church the prisoner was brought out and his Sentence read – 2 years hard and to be discharged with infamy from the Service. This was for saying he wouldn't when told to do something.

No more news.

Your ever loving brother.

William Gibbs

I have also sent a copy of the Great Paper to Beatrice Crawley, as it is the kind of nonsense, which seems to amuse her.

Saturday February 8th 1902

At Britstown

My dearest little one,
There is fun at the top of this letter almost a joke but not quite luckily. Mr. Button Webber must have enjoyed the better part of the family writing their letters in his room, I noticed he did not write himself. Sorry to hear Margaret Chester Master gets more foolish as she grows more old, it ought to be just the reverse. I am sending Mother two copies of a delightful paper which we (I wrote very little) have brought out 'for one week only'. Graham wrote all of it really, one or two of the

advertisements are real, being those of Store Keepers in the Town. Keep one copy for me if you can as I shall like to laugh at it in future years. I have not got any photographs this week, but hope to send some next week or the week after.

Billy has been on trek for nearly a fortnight, I have not heard from him yet as to how he likes it. I heard last from him at Wynburg (ORC) just two days before he started. It is warm at nights now, which is nice on trek, and very hot during the day, which is not so nice. Excuse me a minute the post has come and I needs must read it. Right, a few local letters, a magazine from Cyril Gurney and long and nice letter from Uncle George who says he hopes to be going home for a lttle soon. He says he supposes Billy and I will be close enough to meet occasionally, I am afraid not!

A convoy came through yesterday, having had a very unsuccessful fight against Conroy's Commando just this side of Prieska (which is 90 miles S.W. of here), however they only lost one man killed. Don't forget to stop the Kodak Company sending me weekly spools.
Best love to all.

                Your loving brother Evelyn

Thebus

March 9 1902

My dearest child,
    Your extraordinary kindness in writing to me every week is only equaled by my marvelous thoughtfulness in doing the same by you as frequently so you see we are both quite 'fresh eggs'.

I really can't write at any great length today as I have told Mother all my news and that is not much.

Being on the railway line we are able to look well after our appetites, in fact as I sit I see a row of bottles labelled Benedictine, Cherry Brandy - Sloe Gin - Old Port, and Whisky. However that won't interest you so much as me.

I am sending you a few more photographs today to be inserted in The book or books; they will be of great value shortly these books and of great National interest, especially the many of myself.

Tell mother that I had a letter from Sister Westbrook, delighted with her kindness in writing and her presents of a cake etc.

Really can't write no more. Read mine to Mother. Love

                Your loving brother Evelyn

Thebus

March 16th 1902

My dearest Nan,
    Capital fun for Hugo Mallett being engaged to Miss Fry. Surely it can't be our old friend Ruth, she's so plain, but of course Hugo is not beautiful; however if they really love each other, what does it matter.
    No fun here - I had a chat with my old friend Charles Grahamstown yesterday, met him in Steynsburg Station. Rather quaint, in course of conversation, he said "Yes, I often think of the good Tyntesfield pheasants,' so I said, "Yes they are nice and high aren't they". I meant they were nice and high to shoot, but it has since struck me that he meant "to eat": he must have thought my taste rather curious.
    We have been intending to go and shoot Guinea Fowl the last week, but we have been so busy digging sangars (fortifications)) and it has rained so hard the last three days that we have been unable to go.
    I hope that you went to Hagley, rather dull perhaps during Lent, but otherwise pleasant I imagine.
    We have just purchased a Dutch Bible to learn the language from. Unluckily we have only got an English New Testament between us. However a Roman Catholic Army Chaplain passed through the other day and stayed the night, so we turned him on to translate for us, but we only learnt one word thoroughly and that was from the 'Miracle of a Man Possessed', so now we have written to Port Elizabeth for books of sentences etc.
    Please make my room smart and tidy (I believe I've changed into the one next door) and put some everlasting flowers in it, as, being an optimist, I quite think I shall be back by next November or December.
    By the time you get this, the Scholdras will be with you again and you will be all assembled I hope.

Love to all

Your loving brother Evelyn

Thebus

23rd March 1902

My dearest Nan,
    Again many thanks for your flow of letters, which are like the Thames. I have told Mother all the news and the rest is rubbish. Don't

quite understand now, but I may when the next mail comes in, whether Eustace is going to Pau with you or not. No good cadging for invites to Down Ampney after Easter is it? Surely all the hunting will be over, and I should have thought a week or so at Pau or Biarritz very nice. Bit of nice fun staying with the Miss Tyndalls for a couple of days almost as good as a Wraxall Ball. Yes I should go to the Parrs in April, nice fresh air and close to Folkstone. You may safely scream with delight at the idea of our being home by Edward Rex's first Jubilee but don't waste your valuable time screaming at the idea of the Coronation. Tain't possible! My polo ponies seem to be an everlasting form of amusement. Dear little Pikky would be too, if he could. If I can I shall bring him back, but I'm afraid it will be difficult. He isn't much of a leaper but is toppers to ride and plays polo in a slow old-fashioned sort of way

We are shortly to have an addition here, our 'Frederick' of the Royal Fusiliers who was at Eton and Sandhurst with me, is coming: he is a great friend of mine so it is altogether a good arrangement. Then we shall be Graham, Frederick, Saunderson (Maud Ll's Brother) and I.

Much colder for the last week. It is about September now in England, just beginning of autumn. Bit more rain too!

Mick Hodgson (vide photographs) came through two days ago, he is Via's first cousin. He is now at Steynsburg, so I hope to see him again often. Just come off Crabbes' Column, which he has been trekking with for over a year. Well, no more news dear child

Love to all

Your loving brother

Evelyn.

Mark the 2 pages of solid better writing.

Thebus,

Easter Day, 30th March 1902

My dearest N.

Many thanks for yours from Hagley, from your account of your doings there, Lent does not seem to have interfered with sport much, though it may have done so with novel reading during Morning Prayers. Most unlucky for poor me not being able to go to Church on this Great day, but it could not be and I had to content myself with riding round my Battalion Headquarters and getting their monstrous and never differing reports. Graham is away unluckily and I am in sole charge which gives me a good deal to do but I am not dull as there are two Royal Fusiliers officers here.

A few photographs are enclosed and a few more will follow next mail. Yes, Billy told me he did not think he would be able to take his Kodak on trek, as they are trekking very light, so that accounts for his not sending home any results. By now you will have Georgie and Via and Albinia and Dick with you again and many stories of travel will be passing around. I had a letter from Albinia at Trinidad last Mail, saying that as she heard such good reports of the war, she hoped I should be home before her, dear child. She was very optimistic, but t' won't be for a bit yet says O! (*O'Grady*)

                Your loving brother

                Evelyn

Schoombie

Saturday April 3rd 1902

My dearest little Nancy,

What a clever gal not to be ill at all crossing the Channel; and also how exquisitely grand to be able to write from the Folkestone Hotel where you seem to have been staying a deux (as we say here) with Miss Maudina Goodenough: bit of nice fun for you. Why ride pore Billy's charger when you have a charming mustard horse as it is, as for auld Blanche, I have written to Gilly that as he is coming out, he had better send four ponies to Tyntesfield, and let Blanche ride one of them and turn out the remainder. He doesn't seem to think he will sail before the summer. After all we have always had the ponies at home and you have all been able to ride them, it is only fair old Father F. should have a look in as they are all half or even more belonging to Gilly.

Eustace does not seem to have cared much about the young Gooden or Phelips, but enjoyed the ball at the Clifton Club nonetheless. If you hear of our returning in the autumn please buy 18 hunters (good) for me and 3 hacks and 2 ponies and traps, and house and stables at Brackley: so that I can hunt quite once a fortnight for certain.

Hope you got the photographs last week; I shall have some of this place soon. I have got an Indian Cooley here to look after my transport. I must get him to make me a curry; I suppose he can, although I hate curry horse nor anything.

I shall be quite alone after Monday and I expect it will be dull, but work, work, that is what I love! --- a little of. Send me 1,000,000's and 1,000,000's of papers and books and 1,000,000's of good things and

1,000,000's of bottles of liqueurs and 1,000,000's of letters: in fact 1,000,000's of everything good. Love to all

Your loving brother Evelyn.

Thebus

April 6 1902

My dearest Nancy,

    By now I suppose you are home again, having, I hope, enjoyed Pau and Biarritz to the full and made some friends out of all the people who, according to the papers, are staying there. I heard from Cyril Gurney last mail that you had asked Evie to go abroad with you, but Cyril said they were too busy with their estate at Bognor or Cromer or wherever it is, to go away just then. I hope you and Blanche did not disgrace yourselves crossing to Boulogne, by being publicly ill on the deck, but were able, like my friend Arthur Roberts in 'HMS Irresponsible' to gain the side before too late.

    Well, here at Thebus, everything is as usual, our men still out in Sangars. Boers who are supposed to, but never do, try to cross - occasional news (always very late) of our doings in other parts of the Continent - and the weekly seven days pleasant anticipation of our English mail, occasionally varied by a letter from Billy or other friends fighting.

    Thirteen Boers crossed this line about 30 miles east of our Section and on the Grenadiers Section, their horses stampeded and they took off their boots in order to cross quietly and were only detected after they had crossed and were slinking away up a Donga on the far side and none of them were even hit; and so it goes on.

    I am glad to hear Lord Methuen is going on well and I hope will recover and go home and mind you give him a hearty cheer if you see him, as he has done extraordinary well and for a man of his age to have trekked steadily for two and a half years is no mean performance.

    We found a covey of partridges the other day and now go slow and now we go out daily to try and find the rest, but no success hitherto.

    I have got a new gun from Cape Town hammerless etc. for £15, not so bad, so I can join again, my other gun fell to pieces. I wish Winter would begin it is frightfully hot again today and lately we have had a lot of rain in fact a lot too much to be pleasant.

    No more news. Love to all

Ever your loving brother
Evelyn

Thebus

13. 04. 02   Embossed coat of arms

My dearest Nancy,

It is not really Sunday the 13th at all, that's only my fun, it is really Friday the 11th, but it will leave on the 13th, and sail on the 16th from Cape Town.

I am glad to hear you and Blanche were good on your first crossing to Boulogne, but nothing will make me believe you were equally good on the return journey, that cannot have happened! Well, your first letters from Pau arrived today. Pau seems to be a good place, with lots of nice scenery, and so nice for you to be able to keep up your riding, on donkeys, as I believe they sometimes trot. Be careful about going into mountains, or you may be compelled to emulate Miss Stone, and pay all your year's allowance and all you can borrow from trusting friends to get away again. Never trust a Brigand!! But all this will I fear, arrive too late to be of use, and for all I know you may be a prisoner in the Pyrenees now, but I trust not.

I had a letter from Mrs. Bond this week, very pleased with and amused by the 'Britstown Bugle', which I sent to her. Rather amusing, she says Algy recognised several of my Witticisms, and they were all Grahams and none mine!

Hot weather again and flies 'Ugh! Go away! Brute I haf you, now you shall die-e'. This is the way one must talk to Dutch flies, in what you might call 'Theatrical English.'

From Huie this mail I hear George and Via have got to Rome and that 'Shannon Lass' won the National and my old friend 'Manifesto' third, marvelous horse, almost as wonderful as Tikky.

At last our poor unhappy men have returned to their Battalion houses, as the party of Boers, who they were supposed to catch, crossed where the authorities had forgotten to put men out. To show you what fun picking up men at Blockhouses and putting them down at others is, I may tell you that yesterday the Train started at 4 a.m. from Stormberg (about 40 miles from here) and got here at 7 p.m., and I expect is still going, as it has to put out men for the next 50 miles, fun for the Engine Driver and the Guard.

Maybe the last batch of photographs will come to me in time to send by this mail, and maybe not. I have still got seven spools left. I cabled Bill Beckwith for a new sporting rifle, and he has just cabled to say it is on this Mail S.S., which is very good of him. I heard form Gilly last week, in the middle of a fortnight's hunting, out every day, Sundays excepted, very nice for him, he is very clever at getting mounts from other people.

No more news except that Maud Ll's brother is suffering as usual from insomnia, and as a result of that, melancholia, and for the last 14 days has nearly driven us mad by never saying a word and looking miserable, so much so, that when he suddenly dashed off to shoot by himself yesterday, we made sure it was a case of Susaneide, but he returned safe.

Your loving brother

Evelyn

Thebus

April 29th 1902

My dearest Nancy,
   Just a line cos I haven't got time for more, cos I'm busy, cos I'm moving, cos I'm told to. By this mail you will receive a pleasing number of photographs, don't trouble to put each photograph of the BH's in the Book, only the First, Second and Third prizes.
   I have also put in the film of the photographs of Frederick, Tikky and Grouse. Will you send the film to same good man, and have it enlarged and put in a frame and put in my room at Tyntesfield.
   I'm going to Schoombie, to Schoombie to Schoombie (etc. etc. etc. to the tune of Hi! Ho the Keel Ro!) and am annoyed, cos I've got to go alone, and I lonesomity: but I'm going to take some Benedictine, and shall try and be happy with a bottle under my pillow.
   Winter has come, hurrah, hurrah (etc. etc. etc. to the tune of the Campbells are coming.)
   No more news

Your loving brother

Evelyn

Schoombie

11.5.1902

My dearest Nancy
   As I sit in 'Castle Gibbs,' at Schoombie, I see before me two delightful photographs, which I enclose. Wonderful pictures one showing

a party of 'fine' old English sportsmen (and a Dutchman) as they appeared after a Buck hunt. Some say we look more like a party of Boers with stolen khaki, but don't you believe it, we look ourselves and that's the highest praise possible in my opinion. I had a most amazing letter from Ralph Webber this week, giving a description of his visit to Roehampton at Brin's invitation and his dinner there. He says he talked to Cousin Mary all the time at dinner and that afterwards she said to him that one of her daughters had told her that he (Ralph) had been most amusing, but that she had not heard a word; so he said at the top of his voice 'Whistle'. 'That's all right, you did not miss much;' which he says, though he said it moSt. Politely, did not seem to have been quite the right thing to say.

He also tells me that the only tunes he ever hears are 'The Honeysuckle and the Bee' and 'Goodbye Dolly Grey', neither of which have permeated to Schoombie yet. At last after many attempts, I shot a Buck yesterday and am so pleased that I am going to send home the head to be put just exactly on the place where my eye first looks on waking in the morning in my room at Tyntesfield. It is a dull day! It may rain soon, very soon! I may get wet! I may not! It may not rain! That's all about the weather! Mr Billiam Beckwith very kindly got me a Sporting Rifle and sent it out, it took 16 days to go about 70,000 miles, and has taken 28 days, up to now, to go about 500 miles from Cape Town and has not arrived yet! Aunt Catty (*Merivale*) sent me 5 delightful woolen comforters for the men this mail, really most useful and 4 books last week! When I am very dull I tell myself Billy's story about 'The Brigands were gathered round the fire' etc. and I find it occupies just exactly as much time as I want to fill up.

Love to all

Your loving brother

Evelyn

Henning

May 31st 1902

My dearest Nancy

Kind Cousin Mary Daubeny is just a little incorrect; and as you say, you post for South Africa in ample time, you posted on May 9th, it sailed May 10th, got to Cape Town May 27th and here May 31st, so that's all right and keep writing, the more the merrier!

We went out for a shoot 3 days ago, and all thought it was to be at 'Blesbuck', but the farmer said he only had 2 blesbuck left to be shot, as they are Royal Game and he only gets a permission to shoot 20 a year. He has got a herd of about 500, and they are the only ones in the Colony. They are magnificent deer, as big as a Donkey and dark bay in colour, with splendid heads. Pole-Gell got one and the farmer the other. I tried very hard to shoot one by mistake, but missed the brute. We each got a Springbok which are quite common, but very good to eat and some have very good heads. We have got enough venison to last some time.

    I lost the Springbok horns I said I would send home, but afterwards got a beautiful head and horns. Unluckily I kept the head too long and it went bad, but I have got the horns. A Springbok is about as big as the deer in Ashton Park. There are many and other sorts - 'Raebok' who live in the mountains, 'Stembok' which live on the veldt and are about as big as a rather small Roedeer etc. etc. etc.

    The Great Rebel Drive has not begun yet, but we are quite ready for them and I keep my loaders in constant practice. I am only practising for their coming, there will be no going away shots as we shan't let them cross here. I was sorry to hear Cyril Daubeny was taken, I only hope it was not his fault, as it goes against one terribly that sort of thing, allowing oneself to be surrounded and taken. I heard from Billy three days ago, having 3 days leave and well earned rest at Johannesburg. 'Malan' is mortally wounded and in our hands so that's all right! Rumours of peace being signed in Transvaal and Orange Colonies, but not confirmed.

    Love to all London.

                    Your loving brother,

                          Evelyn

Letter from E to N and a good one too

Rosmead

June 9th 1902 and Sunday

My dearest Nancy,
    Herewith a short note from your dear and now peaceful brother, in another envelope please find 12 photographs, one of which is of the above-mentioned well-known and renowned soldier.

    I have got nothing to tell you, except to write and say I have nothing to tell you! I mean, I have nothing to say except to say that I have nothing to say, except what I have just said and shall say in this essay.

    So now that's all right! - About coming home, I don't know when I shall come home (see letter from E to his Mother) about news out here. I can't say (see E's last letter to his Mother)

Well now there, who would have thought that I should nearly fill a page with that, but I have, eh!

I can't write, cos I've nuffin to write.

My mouth, eyes, nose and ears are full of dust, and the eyes, nose, ears and mouth of 'Grouse' are ditto, and the noses, eyes, ears and mouths of everyone must be ditto.

No more Knews.

Love to all

Your loving brother

Evelyn

No 16 Hospital   Monogram
of Elandsfontein
7th Hussars

June 14th 1902

My dearest Nancy,

Perhaps you will be going to Ascot tomorrow - who knows? I have been taking a lot of photographs at Heidelberg. The twisting business behind the chimaera is stiff. Our base is at Elandsfontein so I get our officer at the base in to see me, Hermon, also the Bags! fellow.

There is a funny old sort of quartermaster in here who jaws about Rhodes in Kimberley and he thinks Rhodes did himself tophole all the time up at his 'Sanatorium', but he himself eat donkeys, mules and horses. I have not received this week's mail yet. Tony was well and happy when I saw him. Allenby is applying to go home, also for Tony to do likewise.

Greville and Kelly arrived or are just going to arrive with the Regiment. The former from Inje where he has been with Lord Northcote.

Guernsey is coming from St. Helena, so we shall be chockerblock with orcifers (*officers*).

You seem to have been having some very agreeable ball dances. Is there going to be a cricket week this year?

Ever you loving brother

Billy

Palais Depetia
Graaff Reinet

July 3rd 1902

My dearest child,
    Please note the high sounding and aristocratic name of the House I live in: so called because the members of the Military Court who tried, and condemned to death by shooting, so many Rebels, lived here, however there are no ghosts and very little clanking of chains and mysterious shutting of doors goes on at nights. It really is no good my writing letters now as I have got absolutely no news for you except that I am well and hope you are the same etc.etc.etc. Poor old George, I am so sorry Via had been so seedy for both their sakes.
    Divine Providence has intervened and ordained that it was absurd for H.M. to think of being crowned unless he had his trusty friend to help him, so he was just made ill and the Coronation put off till we get back See?
    I've got a cold in my dose, which annoys me more than a little. Polo tomorrow! It seems years since I played in fact not since yesterday afternoon but we live for Polo days now as there is nothing else to do worth doing.
    I am going to try to get leave to go and see brother Billy very soon and think I ought to manage it all right.
    I believe Otterbourne in Northumberland is a good place, but I should prefer to go to Scotland on my return at the end of August, please! (Pause for 10 mins. here). No! I absolutely can't think of anymore to say, so I shan't say it. Did Beeeeeetrice ever get the Britstown Bode on her return from Germany?

Love

Your loving brother Evelyn

Palais de Justice
Graaff Reinet
(monogram)

July 10th 1902

My dearest little one,
    Your last effaced contained a most mad but I could not say interesting account your tea party to you favoured friends, and the

strawberries and cream did not agree with some of the Guests but these same people do not know when to stop or remember the old proverb about Feasting.

For other news please see other letters to other people and in other envelopes and to other parts of the world.

Give my love to Uncle George etc. if you see them.

Your loving brother

Evelyn

N.B. No! Don't much care about mixed bathing. But I like my hot bath of mornings.

Palais de Justice!
Graaff Reinet.

August 14th 1902

My dearest Nancy

This week I send you a few photographs of the Battalion and officers etc., which had better either go in my big red photo book or be mounted and framed. Also if I can remember, I will send the American edition of the "Ruthless Rhymes", to be well looked after and returned to me on my return home.

Rather afraid we shan't be able to play today at polo as it has been raining which will be a terrible thing as one has only got polo to look forward to all the week.

(We did though and it was awful!!)

I have just started agitating to be allowed to go away and see a little more of South Africa. I only wait for Colonel's decision, Yea or Nay.

I imagined the Shooters on Tuesday sitting in the Drawing Room at Loch Kennard dead beat after a hard days walking, and am waiting for the letters which ought to come today, to know whether Father's got Loch Kennard or not.

Coronation Day here was a great success. A parade in the morning, followed by laying of a foundation stone for a new Town Hall. We entertained many so called loyalists to lunch and dinner, great polo in the afternoon. Our house was certainly the most noticeable in the Town. I never saw colours arranged so as to clash so much as ours were. Yellow, Light Blue and pink on a dark red ground. Splendid!

Well: I must run away and lunch, and will finish after the mail has come in. Mail not coming 'till tomorrow. Be patient.

August 15th

Mail in. I still don't know whether you are at Loch Kennard. Photographs enclosed not so bad.

I am sure Graham would prefer a set of pearl shirt studs to any amount of magazines. "Go the whole hog" if you go at all. Always glad of any new books personally don't bother about Graham, he gets books, send him the old magazines and me the books. Arrange a dance at Tyntesfield when I return and I'll get him to come.

Love to all, goodbye dear child.

Your loving brother

Evelyn

Graaff Reinet
August 22nd 1902

My dearest Nancy

I send you this week a few photographs taken by others. It is practically arranged now that I can go away and see the country, and the Colonel has telegraphed the General for a fortnight's leave.

We are going a small party, the Colonel, Captains Pereira and Harry Gell and myself. We want to go to Port Elizabeth, ship to Durban, thence to Colenso, Ladysmith etc., thence to Pretoria, Johannesburg and Bloemfontein and then round to Modden River and go over the Battlefields and then on to Kimberley and thence home. It will be a lot of travelling, but one will see most of South Africa that way Natal, Transvaal, Orange River Country and a little more of the Colony itself.

We are now only waiting for the Colonel to decide what he wants to do and where he wants to go. When I applied to go I had no idea it would be a general thing like this but it is pleasanter this way.

My book must be nearly entirely composed of photographs of Tikky and myself, especially the latter ones that I've sent, however I can't think of any better subjects to fill any gentleman's book, and I shall present it to the Nation, when I go the way of all men.

Must go and shoot clay pigeons now and will resume later, by when I shall have my English meal? I heard the train whistle just now - mail in. I am so sorry to hear about poor Via, I had no idea that she was so ill. I am cabling to Georgie for the latest bulletin, and sincerely trust it will be good. Poor old boy, as you say, he has been most unlucky, who deserves such good luck. I am sorry to hear Loch Kennard has been taken but hope Father manages to get a place somewhere.

Your last letter came from Southampton, just about to meet Billy. The worst has befallen us, as you must see by my letter to Mother, as I have not got room to express my indignation at out treatment.

Goodbye dear child and don't get Hooping Cough

Your loving brother

Evelyn

Royal Coat of Arms
By Special appointment

PO Box 343
Heath's Hotel
(William Heath Proprietor)
Johannesburg

September 7th 1902

My dearest Nancy

By the time you get this, I hope I shall be nearly home. We got a wire at Durban telling us that we must return immediately as the Battalion was ordered to embark about the 15th of the month. I wrote to Mother from the ship and posted it at Durban, but I think this will go by the same mail. As I told her, we embarked at Port Elizabeth for Durban on Saturday last, and went up to East London on the 'Briton'. We had 9000 tons of cargo to put off at East London, but as we got there Sunday, we were waiting for Monday to unship it. On Monday morning a terrific gale got up, and we as near as possible were wrecked. One anchor suddenly began to drag and trying to get the anchor in we were nearly blown on to rocks. We did get among the first line of breakers even, and three huge seas came right across the decks. Just in time they decided to let the anchor run out and so lost it, and by backing with one screw and going full steam ahead with the other they just got clear in time. Everyone on shore thought we were done for, and there were men rushing about the beach with life lines etc. and the rocket brigade turned out. We then steamed out to sea and then up to Durban. It was frightfully rough all day, and I stayed in bed with the usual sea complaint. Next day it was a little better and we got opposite Durban Tuesday morning. It was too rough to land us Tuesday or Wednesday, and we just got off on Thursday though crossing the Bar was very rough and only just safe. At Port Elizabeth sixteen ships and three brigs were wrecked and sixty lives were lost. We walked about Durban all Thursday afternoon and went to the Theatre in the evening. It is a very nice town, quite the most up to date place I have seen out here. The Zulu rickshaws are splendid things and we drove about in them everywhere. On Friday we got the wire recalling us and rushed off to see if we could go back on the Briton to Port Elizabeth. The last passenger tug had gone off and then we tried to hire one but by the time we got down to the Docks the sea had got up again and the Port Captain would not let anything cross the Bar. Then we caught the 4 o'clock train for here but owing to a mistake made by the Staff Officer at Durban in our tickets, our servants and luggage missed the train. When we got to Pietermaritzburg (which is the seat of the Natal Government) we got out and waited 'till our servants arrived in a slower train called the 'Kaffirs Mail'. We came on in that, and passed through all Buller's fighting places by day and saw Colenso and Ladysmith and then Majuba Hill and Laing's Nek from the train.

(*Colenso, 15th December 1899, and Ladysmith, 30th October 1899, were defeats for General Sir Redvers Buller, but at Laing's Nek, 6th to 12th June 1900, he was victorious against the Boer Army. Majuba Hill was a victory for the Boers in the First South African War on 27th February 1881.*)

We got here early this morning (5 a.m.) and leave again tonight by the 9.30 p.m. mail and hope to reach Graaff Reinet on Wednesday night. Tommy Coke left here last night, which is bad luck. I hope to run across Bob here, but fear it is rather hopeless in such a scattered place as this. It was most interesting coming up through Natal and the Railway is excellent. I wish I could have just gone up to Pretoria but I haven't time.

If we do sail on the 15th we ought to be home about the 6th of October so just keep an eye open in case the Boat comes round and lands us at Clevedon.

I will send a cutting or so, showing how nearly I became a shipwrecked mariner on the East Coast very thrilling I can assure you!

Love to all

Your loving brother Evelyn

On September 30th 1902, Anstice Katharine Gibbs wrote to her fiancé, Stafford Crawley, from Moncrieffe House in Scotland, "I heard for the last time from Evelyn yesterday, he had a great escape from being shipwrecked in a storm 3 weeks ago, so much so that he wrote quite seriously about it and they had a thanks giving Service on board. He lands next Tuesday from the Mohawk."

So on Tuesday 7th October, John Evelyn Gibbs was expected to land back in England. That day Anstice Katharine wrote from Montcrieffe in

Scotland, "Evelyn landed last night, I wonder when we shall see him?"

Figure 35. The ocean liner, which brought William Gibbs home.

On October 16th, Anstice Katharine (always called Nancy) wrote from 16 Hyde Park Gardens to Stafford Crawley, "What a day, I'm just down. 1 o'clock, so many visitors again made me late, two up from Eton, Huie, Evelyn, sisters and Mother all making plans in my room. I'm stacks better but my head is like a sack of bricks, so heavy. All right for next Saturday probably. Tonight 15 of us go out, rather fun."

So for the family the War in South Africa was over and everyone had come home in one piece. Peace had been made with the Boers at the

Treaty of Vereeniging on May 31st 1902 and the British forces were gradually repatriated.

It had been thought that George Abraham Gibbs encountered Walter (Toby) Long in South Africa, and thus he was introduced to his sister Via de Burgh Long. This is exceedingly unlikely since as soon as Toby arrived he was assigned to General French to join the force going to the relief of Kimberley, which was being besieged by the Boers. Before reaching Kimberley he was seriously injured and in due course hospitalized in that town as soon as it was relieved. Cecil Rhodes was in Kimberley at the time. The letter, which follows, is to Toby's father, Walter Long, a Member of Parliament and leading Conservative Privy Councillor, from Lieutenant General Lord Methuen who commanded the First Infantry Division.[xii]

Kimberley

23rd February 1900

My Dear Walter,
I have been to your boy in hospital twice and Sir W. MacCormack spoke to me about him today, and I thought you might like to hear what he said. The wound has severed two nerves, and is one that may cause some anxiety. There is no danger of losing the arm, but it may lose feeling, and it is early days to form an opinion. It is a case that will require further careful treatment when he reaches home. I asked if he meant he might have to give up soldiering, but he could not give a decided answer, but thought with careful treatment and good health now he would recover. I thought you might like to know the truth, and I have made out the case rather worse than Sir. W. McC. told me. I was afraid when I asked for the name, the doctor would say Long. It is the best hospital I have seen in or out of England.

Yours ever

Methuen

I am bound for Mafeking with a very useful force tonight.

Lord Methuen lived in Corsham Court, Wiltshire, not far from Walter Long's home at Rood Ashton. Walter Long was Conservative Member of Parliament for Liverpool West Derby from 1893 to 1900 and then for Bristol South from 1900 to 1906. Hence George and Via would have met socially through mutual friends, the Conservative Party and the local landed gentry.

Figure 36. George (centre rear) and Via (seated 2nd from left) at a party.

Figure 37. The Wedding of Victoria De Burgh Long and George Abraham Gibbs.

Figure 38. George and Via at Milton Lodge, Dorset.

George Abraham Gibbs married Victoria de Burgh Long, the eldest daughter of the Right Honorable Walter Hume Long P.C. of Rood Ashton and Lady Dorothy Blanche Long, who was the 4th daughter of Richard Edmund St Lawrence Boyle, the 9th Earl of Cork and Orrery, and Lady Emily Charlotte de Burgh. George and Via Gibbs were married at All Saints Church, Ennismore Gardens on Tuesday November 26th 1901.[xiii]

The honeymoon was spent at Marston House, the Earl of Cork's Somerset residence. They then went on an adventurous journey to Egypt and the Sudan, travelling along the railway from Wadi Halfa to Abu Hamed, built by Kitchener's army during the two years before the Battle of Omdurman in 1898, and thence to Khartoum, the city where General Gordon had been killed by the followers of the Madhi in January 1885.[xiv]

When they returned, they set up home at 13 Hertford Street, Mayfair, and for a country residence took Milton Lodge near Gillingham in Dorset.

Chapter Four

Edwardian Tyntesfield

Figure 39. Fancy dress in the Conservatory at Tyntesfield.

The return of the boys from South Africa saw the family re-united again even though the three eldest children had all married and left the fold. Antony Hubert and Mary Mercy set up home at Clyst St George in Devon. He was always called Huie and she was known as Mercy. In letters and diaries they are referred to by these names. Albinia Rose and her husband Richard Bennett set up home at Thornbury Park to the North of Bristol. However the whole family gathered together regularly at Tyntesfield. Such a gathering can be seen in the photograph above when there was a fancy dress party possibly referred to by Nancy (Anstice Katharine) in the following Diary entry:

Tuesday 6th January 1903
Down very late. Men all went out shooting (Charlton). Blowy rainy day. We drove up in brake but failed to find guns who lunched at Moat House Farm. Dined at 7 o'clock or rather 7.30. Drove in 2 busses and landau to Napier Miles. Albinia as Mme de Valois, Mildred as Circassian or Bavarian Bohemian, Maud as Merveilleuse, F. Beckwith as Watteau, G.

Grandmother, self as Mrs. Antony Gibbs looked thin! Stafford as a Puritan. Danced and sat out a good deal with a Puritan who slept on my shoulder in the landau coming home. Dance very good.

Figure 40. Wedding of the Rev. Arthur Stafford Crawley and Anstice Katharine Gibbs at Tyntesfield on June 16th 1903. The bridesmaids left to right are Miss Katherine Spencer, Miss A.Pringle, Katherina Gibbs, Janet Blanche Gibbs, Beatrice Crawley, Alice Gurney, Miss Goodden, and Mary Gibbs.

On the afternoon of Tuesday June 16th 1903, the Rev. Arthur Stafford Crawley, son of the late George Baden Crawley, and of Mrs Pringle of Broke Hall, Suffolk, married Anstice Katharine Gibbs at All Saints Church in Wraxall. The Service was conducted at the outset by the Rev. John Medley (Chaplain at Tyntesfield) and then later by the Rev. Henry Vaughan (Rector of Wraxall) but the actual betrothal was performed by Cosmo Lang (Bishop of Stepney), who was later Archbishop of Canterbury. In his address he said that he and the bridegroom had worked together as great friends, and he hoped that the worries and anxieties, naturally attendant on the life of a clergyman and his wife, would not affect the peaceful happiness of their own home life. The hymns were "Thine for ever God of love", and "O perfect love, all human love transcending".

Along the drive from Tyntesfield were lines of flags, and at the Wraxall Lodge was a pretty arch bearing the words on the side nearest the house, "Farewell Miss Gibbs", and on the reverse side, "Welcome Mrs.

Crawley". Spanning the Wraxall Road wras a horseshoe arch bearing the words "The best of luck" on one side, and "Every Happiness" on the other. Near the Battle Axes was an arch saying "A Happy Future".

There were eight bridesmaids, Janet Blanche Gibbs (sister of the bride), Beatrice Crawley (sister of the groom), Katherina Gibbs, Mary Gibbs and Alice Gurney (cousins of the bride), Miss A.Pringle (cousin of the groom), Miss Goodden and Miss Katherine Spencer. Mr Ronald Monkton MacDonald of Largie was the best man. The wedding reception was at Tyntesfield and the event was celebrated by a holiday in the village. The couple left later for a honeymoon in Scotland.[xv] After two years as a Curate at St Luke's Church in Chelsea, Stafford (as he was always called) was appointed to be Vicar of Benenden in Kent where he remained for five delightful years.

Now there were only five children remaining at Tyntesfield – William, John Evelyn, Eustace, Janet Blanche and Lancelot. The whole family would gather together for Christmas, Easter, and Cricket Week every summer. Richard Bennett would bring cricketing friends and the whole week was devoted to the sport. The family still went on holiday together and there are photographs of curling, tobogganing, skiing and skating in St. Moritz, of a visit to Luzerne in Switzerland, and in February and March 1906 of an extended holiday to Florence, Rome, Naples and Venice. William, Albinia Rose and John Evelyn were photographed on the terrace of Bertolini's in Naples. They visited Pau, in the French Pyrenees, a favourite destination since William and Matilda Blanche Gibbs' days at Tyntesfield.[xvi]

Figure 41. Cricket Week 1904. Richard Bennett and Eustace Lyle Gibbs batting.

Figure 42, Cricket Week, Tyntesfield 1905.

Figure 43. Croquet at Tyntesfield.

Figure 44. Fancy Dress in the Library, Christmas 1905. This photograph reflects the values and attitudes of the age.

Figure 45. Tyntesfield Cricketers - Front Row - centre George Abraham Gibbs far right Richard Bennett – Back Row from Left – Antony Hubert (2), John Evelyn (4), Eustace Lyle (5) and William Gibbs (6).

Figure 46, Winter Sports at St. Moritz, Switzerland, 1902. Anstice Katharine (Nancy) and Janet Blanche Gibbs.

The family of course visited other families in their country seats. This is revealed by Janet Blache Gibbs' photo album and scrap book for the years 1905 to 1907. The houses visited include Melksham House (January 10th 1905), Shaw Hill, Melksham in Wiltshire (January 12th 1905), Pytte in Devon (July 1905), Millichope Park near Bridgenorth in Shropshire (July 1905), Port Elliot House in Cornwall, Dove Leys in Staffordshire, the home of Sir Arthur Heywood, Armadale Castle on the isle of Skye (August 1905), Sutton Veny near Warminster (December 1905), Ravensworth Castle near Gateshead, Tulloch Castle in Oxfordshire, Frilsham House in Berkshire (January 9th to 11th 1906 for the Craven Club Hunt Ball), Down Ampney House near Cirencester (January 26th 1906 for the Vale of White Horse Hunt Ball), Addington Manor in Buckinghamshire, Kilberry in Argyleshire and Chequers Court rented by the Clutterbuck family, ancestral home of the Russells in Buckinghamshire (December 1905, 18th December 1906, and January 31st 1907), and Clevedon Court (January 14th 1907). They also visited the Rev. and Mrs. Stafford Crawley at Benenden Vicarage in Kent.[xvii]

Grandchildren were born and before Janet Gibbs died in November 1909, there were six grandsons and four granddaughters. With the location and date of their birth these were:

Antony Hubert and Mary Mercy Gibbs's children:
Elaine Blanche	Burrington	17 Jan. 1901
Elizabeth Mercy	Hyde Park Gardens	13 Jan. 1905
Evan Llewellyn	Pytte, Clyst St George	17 May 1906
Antony	Pytte, Clyst St George	26 Oct. 1909

Richard and Albinia Bennett's children:
Alexander George	Tyntesfield	7 Sept. 1900
Anstice Jessie	Wickwar	31 Aug. 1905
Peter Richard	Wickwar	26 Feb. 1908

Rev. A. Stafford and Anstice Katharine Crawley's children:
Cosmo Stafford	Chelsea	27 May 1904
Janet Inez	Benenden	21 May 1906
Aidan Merivale	Benenden	10 Apr. 1908

More children were to be born after their grandmother's death, who sadly would never know their Gibbs' grandparents. These included Richard, the second Lord Wraxall and Eustace the third Lord Wraxall.

Figure 47. Janet, Cosmo and Aidan Crawley - Gibbs Grandchildren.

Antony Gibbs died on April 24th 1907 and was buried at Wraxall on April 29th. His Obituary from "Outlook" of May 18th 1907, entitled "Antony Gibbs In Memoriam", said:

"On April 29, in the parish of Wraxall, and in the lovely churchyard which surrounds one of the most beautiful churches in England – a church restored by his munificence in memory of his mother twelve years ago – was laid to rest the body of Antony Gibbs of Tyntesfield, Somerset. Antony Gibbs was the eldest son of William Gibbs, whose name will ever

Figure 48. Antony Gibbs in old age.

be associated with Keble College, Oxford, as the donor of its beautiful chapel. When he succeeded his father, Antony nobly followed in his footsteps, for the Hall and Library of that college, given by him jointly with his brother, Henry Martin Gibbs, who survives him, are by no means solitary proof of his liberality; indeed it is only those most closely connected with him who will ever know how great and varied that liberality was. In 1872 he married Janet Louisa, eldest daughter of John Lewis Merivale, Senior Registrar in Chancery, the eldest son of which marriage is George Abraham Gibbs, Member of Parliament for Bristol West. A strong Conservative, Antony Gibbs always took a wide view of our Imperial Responsibilities, and was intensely keen for the growth of a truer patriotism throughout the country. In 1887, on the death of his mother, he succeeded to his father's estate of Tyntesfield. Two years later he took up residence there, and will long be remembered as the best and most considerate of landlords. Though as a large-minded Conservative and a loyal Churchman and promoter of all good and useful work in the County of Somerset and elsewhere, he will be remembered by most men who knew him best for that singular gentleness and humility of character, which, in spite of large wealth, induced him to avoid ostentation and shrink from public gaze. As President of the North Somerset Conservative Association he always spoke wisely and to the point. A true lover of all that is best and healthiest in sport, he discountenanced the vices which often degrade it; he was a good rider in his earlier days and an excellent shot to the last. His genial qualities made him the tenderest of husbands, the gentlest of fathers, the most lovable of men, whilst his home was a centre of boundless hospitality, presided over by the most courteous of hosts."

The Pedigree of Gibbs gives an informed description of Antony Gibbs many attributes. He was born at his parents' home 13, Hyde Park Street on 10th December 1841 and baptised at St John's Paddington on 11th January 1842. He was educated at Radley College (1855 to 1857) and Exeter College, Oxford where he matriculated in 1862, was awarded a B.A degree in 1867 and an M.A in 1869. He studied Law entering the Inner Temple in 1865. Apart from Tyntesfield, Antony also succeeded to his father's other properties in Somerset and Devon. He bought Barrow Court in 1881 from John Henry Blagrave and sold it to his brother Henry Martin in 1884. He also purchased Barton Place near Exeter, the ancestral home of his wife's family, the Merivales, in 1874, when her family were in financial difficulty.

Antony Gibbs was Patron of the parishes of Clyst St George, Exwick, Stowe the Nine Churches, St Michael's Paddington, North Newton and Otterborne, which were all in his father's gift. He also bought the livings of Alphington in Devon and Flax Bourton in Somerset. He was a Member of the Council of Radley College from 1890 to 1897. He and his brother, Henry Martin, gave to Keble College in memory of their father the side of the Main Quadrangle of the College which embraces the Hall, the Library, Common Rooms and Kitchen. Wraxall Church was restored at his cost with Sir Arthur Blomfield as architect in 1893.

Antony Gibbs joined the North Somerset Yeomanry Cavalry as a Coronet on 3rd January 1871. He was commissioned as a Captain in October 1881, and as a Major in 1886. He retired in 1893. He was Justice of the Peace for Somerset from 1867 to 1907. He served on the Highway Board and the Board of Guardians. He was High Sheriff for Somerset in 1888, and Deputy Lieutenant from 1889 to 1907. For a great many years he was President of the North Somerset Conservative Association. He was also on Bristol Diocesan Committees for the promotion of Church

Matters, and was a Life Governor of Bristol General Hospital. His London home, in which his parents resided for many years, was 16, Hyde Park Gardens from 1887 until his death in 1907.

In the General Election of February 1906, the Liberals led by the Henry Campbell Bannerman won by a large majority with 397 Members of Parliament as opposed to 156 Conservatives, 82 Irish Parliamentary and 29 Labour members. It was therefore quite an achievement for Antony's son, George Abraham Gibbs, to be elected Member of Parliament for Bristol West, defeating the Liberal candidate with a slender majority of 365 votes. George and Via took a house in Clifton in the winters of 1904 and 1905 to get into the closest contact with his constituency. In London in 1906 they moved to a new address at 35 Wilton Crescent, Belgravia, which was to be their home until 1911. The lease on his father's house at Hyde Park Gardens was relinquished in 1907.

George Abraham was now kept very busy in London and less time was spent at Tyntesfield. However the hunting, shooting, tennis, cricket, croquet, socializing and partying continued and house parties welcomed social, political and family friends and relatives. George even kept a pack of Beagles. Via Gibbs was well known in Wraxall and loved by everyone. A woman from the village said, "We always felt we could rely on her, and she always understood." Her chauffeur said when she died, "I don't feel I have lost a mistress. I feel I have lost a friend." One of the lady gardeners said, "I would do anything for Mrs. Gibbs."

George and Via travelled extensively. On December 30th 1901, they set out on a long journey through France to Genoa and thence by ship to Egypt. After a fortnight in Cairo, they went on to Luxor, Aswan, Shellal, Wadi Halfa and Khartoum. They returned via Italy, visiting Naples, Pompeii, Rome, Florence, Venice and Milan. Passing through Switzerland, they stopped for a while in Lucerne. In November 1903, they sailed for India meaning to go round the World, but the outbreak of the Russo-Japanese War prevented them from carrying out this plan. They spent five delightful months in India going to all the chief cities and to Ceylon, and as far north as Sandak Phu in the Himalayas, 12,000 feet up, where they saw the sun rise on Mount Everest. In Hyderabad, they visited the Nizam and rode on one of his elephants. George took the opportunity to hunt black buck in Jaipur. From there they journeyed to Agra to see the Taj Mahal. They returned to England in April 1904.

Describing Via's life at Tyntesfield, Madeline Alston wrote, "The library at Tyntesfield where Via so often liked to sit in the evenings, is a magnificent room with an open timber roof and many treasures, and everywhere in the house there are valuable pictures. Via and her husband made a great many improvements and alterations in the house when they first went to live there. Via's eye for colour and love of brightness saved Tyntesfield from the oppressive gloom that so often characterizes big houses. She liked, too, big fires and soft carpets and a general air of warmth and comfort."

Figure 49. Via Gibbs on one of the Nizam of Hyderabad's elephants, 1904.

On September 5th 1911, Via gave birth to a little son, George Antony, who tragically died a few hours after he was born. Later that year she went with her husband on a tour of Canada, going from New York to Vancouver. They enjoyed the trip so much that in 1912 they went again, going this time from Quebec to Vancouver, and travelling to some of the wilder parts. It was then that she shot the moose, whose head hangs in the Billiard Room at Tyntesfield.[xviii] On 17th September 1913, Via gave birth to a little girl, Doreen, who brought much happiness to the family. George and Via's last journey abroad was in the spring of 1914, when they went to Madrid.[xix]

In September 1907, John Evelyn Gibbs arrived in Bombay, having been appointed Aide de Camp to Earl Minto, the Viceroy and Governor General of India. He remained in India until June 1910 when the Viceroy retired. Serving in India at the same time was his first cousin, Captain William Otter Gibbs of the 10th Prince of Wales Own Hussars. From 1906 to 1912, he was stationed at Rawal Pindi. Robert Tyndall Gibbs, second son of John Lomax Gibbs, was in the Indian Telegraph Service in Burmah from 1886 to 1887 and in India from 1886 to 1914.[xx]

Evelyn, as he was always known, travelled extensively with the Viceroy on his official visits to the Governors and Princes of India. His letters home give us a glimpse of life in Raj during Edwardian times.

Figure 50. John Evelyn Gibbs as A.D.C. to the Viceroy of India.

Viceregal Lodge, Simla (headed notepaper)
Viceroy's Camp India

Sept. 23rd 1909

My dearest Nan,
 Very little of interest as usual has happened. Last Friday was an enormous ball given by the Freemasons, at which some of the Knights of Malta and of Rouge Croix wear such beautiful robes that I have very nearly determined to become a Mason, in spite of everything.

Lady Minto has been out at a place called Chail, the Patiala Hill Station, for a cricket match, Simla won. I have been in and out to Mashobra to the very nice house the Viceroy has got out there. It's perfectly beautiful out there in the mornings, one can see the snows all round and a glorious freshness blows straight, I suppose, from them. Now the rains have stopped it is quite charming weather and gets better every day as it gets colder. Lady Minto, Lady Eileen and Francis Scott have gone out in the hills for a week's camping, absolute peace is what they have gone for and they won't get anything else, as there is very little chance of shooting out there.

I was to have gone too and we should have stayed on for another few days after Lady Minto had gone and been joined by the other two girls, but my exam coming next Monday has stopped me going so the whole thing has been given up except for these first few days.

I shall have finished my exam by the next time I write and I hope to be able to announce a satisfactory end to the beastly thing.

I heard from Violet Crawley that Gusty (Eustace Crawley, Stafford's brother) had got a huge stag, called a "Barak Sing" - and that she is going home early next year and he, for 3 months later on. He wants me to go and stay with them but I don't see how I can get leave. Goodbye.

Love to Stafford and all

Your loving Evelyn

India
Oct 14th 1909

Dearest Nan

Again I have left it till very late to start my letters and the result is that I have only got a very few minutes to do it in.

My pony Poniard won another race at Dehra Dun the other day but managed to get disqualified in another. Another pony called "Pathfinder" got a 2nd and a 3rd which was very creditable in good company.

His Excellency and three staff went out into camp for 3 days last week and got a lot of shooting. Her Excellency, Victor Brooke and Lady Eileen went out to Mashobra to stay a few days and I went out too for a couple of nights.

Charlie and Hilda Young went away yesterday at the end of his leave. They have been out in Camp for a month and Hilda looked the picture of good health when they came back. I like them both very much, and I wish I could like Bertie and his wife half as much, I think they are both terrible particularly she.

We get bad Polo 3 days a week and one gets exercise from it but a poor enjoyment as it is so very bad. Must stop.

In greatest possible haste, and wrong paper.

Love to Stafford and all.

Your loving

Evelyn

Viceregal Lodge,
Simla.

Oct. 21st 1909

Dearest Nancy

On Friday last I went down to Agra to meet Lady Antrim, who came up there straight from the ship. We spent 3 days there and it was really very interesting, though of course I had seen all the sights before. I had a horrible journey there, leaving here at 12 o'clock on Friday I got to Agra at 2 o'clock on Saturday afternoon. Lady Antrim arrived at 5.00 and we went straight off to see the Taj. We had the Circuit House and servants had been sent down from here, as none of the Hotels are open yet. Next day we started at 8.30 in a Motor that Scindia had lent and went to see the Fort, we explored that very thoroughly and then went to the great shop, Ganeshi Lall, who has all the nicest embroideries and Indian things. It is very nice going round with someone who has not seen India before if they are appreciative and I really enjoyed it. In the afternoon we went to Sikandra to see Akbar's Tomb which is very fine, and which I had not seen before. Then to what I think the finest thing in India, the Tomb of one Itmad-ud-Doula, the most perfect little building in the world I should think. That night after dinner we went for a drive in the Car, which was very nice as the temperature was exactly right. Next day we started again at 8.30 and motored the 24 miles to Fatehpur-Sikri, the wonderful city which Akbar built and left, with the Mother of Pearl Tomb of the Priest of Akbar. We got back again at Noon and rested till 3.30 when we went off for one more look at the Taj and then to the Station and came back here. We had a Motor to bring us up the Hill to Simla, which is a charming way of coming up, the road is frightfully twisty and we took 4 hours to do the 57 miles, but the scenery is magnificent especially now with the Snows on the distant Hills, and one sees so much better out of a Motor. As Lady Antrim kept saying one can never realize the magnificence till one has seen it, however much one may have heard of it before. We got here Monday and my time has been spent since then in getting ready to start on Tour. My next letter will be written from the Tour and will contain a little more news I hope. Glad the necklet pleases!! It cost £10,000 (*probably rupees*) exactly. I knocked off the odd pence for ready money!

Love to Stafford,

Your loving Evelyn.

P.T.O.
The Heather mixture stones are very rare. Yours are the only ones extant. They are called (a Hindustani word) "HETHRMXTAR LUVUTVEDE", and are only known to exist in one mine (now closed) on the top of the recently discovered Trans Himalayan Mountains.

Viceroy's Camp India
Lansdowne Palace,
Alwar, Rajputana.

Oct. 27th 1909

My dearest Nan,
Here we arrived yesterday from Simla, having come direct. Last Friday was held the last of the present day Legislative Councils at Simla, next time it meets there it will be the new and enormously enlarged Council, a good many people came to see it. On Saturday we played another of those horrible Hockey matches, we were beaten again and I have quite come to the conclusion that I am too old for that sort of fun.

Sunday I went to say a lot of Goodbyes to people who are going home, many of whom I shall probably never see again which lent a sadness to it.

On Monday we left Simla and drove down the hill in carriages. Owing to our huge party there were not enough Landaus to go round and I had to come down in an invention of prehistoric times called a "Phaeton Tonga", the most abominable vehicle I ever went in, the result was that I arrived at Kalka feeling like death and full of dust. We travelled in the broad gauge State train as far as Delhi, where we changed into the narrow ditto. There we found Rudolf Jelf just arrived from England and very fit. Again owing to a large number I was given an ordinary carriage, very comfortable though, and we went along very slow all night so as to arrive here at 8.30 a.m. Public arrival, which means that we are met by every Official in the place, and the Maharajah in full dress. This Maharajah's full dress is very plain but very effective too. He is a Rajput and a very well educated and clever man, but not a very good one. It is a small State but rich, and he does things on a very grand scale. His Palace, called Lansdowne, is wonderfully situated on a high rock and stands beautifully, approached by a road winding its way up round and round the rock. He has been to England and was so struck by the way our gardens are laid out with grass that he has initiated it here, with excellent results, it is the most English garden I have seen in India. He has got two Tigers in the garden with just a moat round them 30 feet broad, so that one sees them very well and naturally.

We began the day after breakfast in the usual way of the Maharajah's people calling to ask after His Excellency's health and then a visit in state of the Maharajah to His Excellency, and a return ditto of His Excellency to the Maharajah. Then in the afternoon H.E. opened a new Hospital that the Maharajah has built, and then we went round the place in Motors. He breeds a lot of horses here, they are let to go wild on the plains and only come in to be fed. They sound a bugle and open some gates and in come all the horses as fast as they can and have to jump 4 walls as they come, it was a very pretty sight. Then we went to the Elephant stables, all the Elephants painted all over their heads and trunks and salaaming by holding up the trunks with a fan in it. All the country round here is flat except for one short range just outside the city, on which is the old fort, and directly under it and connecting is the old Palace. There we went for a State Banquet last night. A wonderful old place with all sorts of fine things in it and a marvellous collection of Armour. We drove all through the city to get to it and the whole route was lit up by coloured and white flares.

A speech each by H.E. and the Mahrajah, both good, and some native music after not so good. All the party came to it and all the European people in Alwar. This morning at 7.30 a.m. H.E. inspected the Imperial Service troops of the State, they are the troops the Maharajahs keep up for the Government and are officered by Natives and inspected by English Officers. These were not so good as some I have seen in other States. He has the usual lot of Motors, they consist of a 60 Napier, 40 Daimler, 30 Siddeley and a White Steam Car.

His Excellency and all the ladies are living in the Palace, while the Staff and guests are in camp at the foot of the rock. A garden party this evening and we leave here at 10.30 p.m. for Jaipur, where we arrive at 8.30 a.m. tomorrow morning.

It is indistinct isn't it! But it's worth a few hours worrying out. I made so many jokes in my last letter to you that I'm clean out of witticisms now.

Love to Stafford and all

Your loving Evelyn

The Residency, Udaipur.
Rajputans.
Viceroy's Camp, India.

November 3rd 1909.

My dearest Nan,
    We arrived at Jaipur on Thursday last. The drive through the place to the Residency where we stayed was most impressive. The Maharajah met us at the station and all his chief nobles. Jaipur is one of the old-fashioned States where things are much as they were. The city is laid out in great broad streets, quite straight and all parallel. It was done 140 years ago by Jai Singh when he left Amber to found this new city. The best account of all these places we are seeing now is in R. Kipling's "From Sea to Sea". The Maharajah is a conservative old boy who does not like modern innovations.

    I had two mornings Pig-sticking there and got a pig each day but though big they were not good fighting pig. His Excellency shot a Tiger. Four of us went over to Amber one evening to see it, a most wonderful place, the most beautiful I have seen in India I think. The Palace standing on the side of the Hill and one looks down on this deserted City, nothing is moving though from that distance it looks as if people would appear at any minute. The Palace itself has some most wonderful work in Marble and one Gateway in particular is magnificent. The Jaipur mural is the famous work of the place and is very pretty. I shot two Black buck the last day there. We left Saturday. On Sunday at 9.30 a.m. we got to Chitar, a famous old Rajput Fort, which we went over. There is not very much to see there, the chief things being, two splendid Obelisks all carved, and a wonderful carved ceiling in an old Jain temple The interest of the place is in the fact that it has been besieged so often, and on 9 occasions when the defenders found they could not hold out any longer all the women, 3000, committed Johur, and the men issued out to die on the swords of the enemy. Johur is shutting themselves up and being voluntarily suffocated rather than be taken by men who were not Rajputs. We left Chitar at 2.00 p.m. and arrived here at 5.00. Received by the Maharana, the proudest and most blue-blooded man in India probably. The great pride of the Udaipur family is that they never gave one of their daughters to the Moghuls even when they had been conquered, most of the other Rajput (Hindu) families did, and it is still a very great honour for an Udaipur Princess to marry even into another ruling Rajput family. The Maharana is a fine looking old man, even more conservative than Jaipur.

    The Lakes are the chief feature of this place and are quite beautiful, with the white palaces built on the edges and on the islands. Tonight after the Banquet they are to be illuminated and it will be a glorious sight. The

Native Chief knows better than anyone how to do it then. He is an old fashioned man in many ways, for instance one day we went up and saw fights in a deep pit, specially made for it, between a wild Pig and two black bears, it was most amusing, if horrible, as the pig with the bravery of his race went for the Bears each in turn and rolled them over time after time. Then the bears were let out and a Lion let in. The pig went straight for him, but the lion lay down and though the pig bit his toe he refused to move, so the pig went off and had a bathe in a trough quite happy. A degrading sport but amusing for once.

We have two glorious moonlight nights and have been out on the Lake, and it really was charming. This is the only quiet time we are going to have on this tour so we are making the best of it. The worst of it all is that at each place we go to the Resident thinks it correct to have an enormous party to meet the Viceroy, so quite wrong if he only knew the Viceroy. The heat is very great in the middle of the day, but the nights are cool. We are just a month too early for Rajputana really, but it would have been much worse to have gone to the South at this time. We go next to Gwalior. This is one of the places you will have to see when you come to India - perfectly lovely. By the Bye when do you propose coming? I hear Cavan and Inez are coming next year.

Love to Staff and all and Godchild.

Your loving Evelyn.

The Earl of Cavan was Nancy's brother-in-law married to her husband's sister, Inez Crawley.

Lal Kothi Camp.
Bhopal. C.I.
VICEROY'S CAMP, INDIA.

Nov. 11th 1909.

My dearest Nan,
The last day I wrote was just before the Banquet and Fireworks at Udaipur. The Lake was lit up everywhere, all the islands were outlined and on the sides of the Lake the houses were outlined, the whole thing most beautifully done and the prettiest illuminations I have ever seen. After that we watched a Bhil dance; the Bhils are the Aborigines of that part and are a practically wild race still; there dance is very dull, much what imagines a witch-doctor's dance in Central Africa to have been. We stayed an extra day at Udaipur because our visit to Ajmer had to be abandoned on account of the Plague there, and left it on Friday. We had a

long journey, changing back onto the broad gauge at Agra on Saturday morning and arrived at Gwalior at 2.50 p.m. on Saturday. The Maharajah and all his attendants met us and we drove in State to the Palace. He had made a tremendous reception and we went a very circuitous route to the Palace so that he might show off a great many of his troops. We had a Banquet that night which was as dull as usual. Next day we went to the English Church for which a Parson had been imported for the occasion. In the afternoon we went up to see his Fort, which is very old, with some very old Temples on it said to date about AD 800. Next morning was a Review of his Troops, he had nearly 5000 men on Parade, and they all looked very smart and workmanlike, but I believe the men are not good material there really.

After that there was news in of a Tigress and two full grown cubs in a beat, so off went a Regiment in a special train to the place nearest the beat; then we got into Motors and lunch was sent on in other Motors 17 miles. When we got there we had lunch at once and then had the beat. All the Tiger got out without being fired at; the Jungle was so thick that one could not see more than 20 yards in front of one. I was on an Elephant with 2 others, one of whom had never seen a Tiger even beaten for though he has been in India about 12 years, that brings it home to one how very fortunately one is placed by being on this Staff.

We left Gwalior on Monday night and arrived here at 8.30 a.m. next day. This is a Mohammedan State, next in importance of such States to Hyderabad. It is the only State in India ruled by a woman, the Begum. Our camp here is quite the nicest we have had; everything done just as well as is possible for it to be. We had the usual visits and return visits, and in the afternoon we took part in a Gymkhana, for which we were supplied with ponies, but won nothing. This morning we played them at Polo at 7.30 and won, great fun, very good ponies and a nice ground, and back to breakfast at 9.30. Since that I have spent a peaceful morning writing. We leave here for Baroda tomorrow evening.

It is very hard Tour for the Viceroy, as at every place there is a Banquet, and every Banquet means a speech to say nothing of upsetting his inside. The Native servants love these Tours as they are given free, by the Chief of each State all the food they can possibly eat, and they take away enough to last them till they come to the next place.

Lady A. Carrington and Miss Howard left us at Gwalior and are going to see the Races at Lucknow and, I hope, the sights too; they will rejoin us at Calcutta.

I hope Mother will go to you. I'm sure it's good for her to have as much change as possible. I am sorry you find her more helpless. No! I daresay babies are glorious fun, but they are such expensive luxuries, and you have got a "Quiver full" now - more would be a crowd. I've had an attack of Liver, very unpleasant, but not to be wondered at considering we eat enormously perforce, train a lot and get no exercise. Kutano cured it!!

Your loving Evelyn.

On 10th December 1909 Janet Louisa Gibbs died at 104, Eaton Square, Belgravia. Sadly Evelyn was in India when he heard of the death of his mother.

The next day her daughter, Anstice Katharine, wrote the following letter to her husband, Stafford Crawley:

104, Eaton Square

11th December 1909

My Darling One,

Georgie would like a short service on Monday Evening late. I did not go into particulars, but I think just evensong would be best darling, and on Tuesday morning we should like a Celebration and I have written to ask Mr. Vaughan about it, so it will be all right. Sweetheart don't reproach yourself about last night. I was rather broken down and wanted you to say a prayer with me so much, but it is probably better for me to wrestle with it alone. I should only have missed you more tonight. I read those very nice prayers this morning in the book you left. They are coming to put the lid of the coffin on this evening. One cannot bear to think of her shut up. I love going into the room so it seems just as if she were still there, and Oh I do miss her so terribly now. Already I am realizing it so much more today and long to hear her speak. No more now as we are off in the motor.

Your very loving

Nancy

Kiss the children.

The following day she wrote again from 104, Eaton Square

12th December 1909

My Darling One,

Evensong is to be as near 7 o'clock as possible tomorrow evening. You will arrive at Tyntesfield before that and so be all right. Will you read the lesson you spoke to me about and another? An organist and some choir boys are coming from Bristol for it. Four of us went out early to be at St Peter's this morning, and at 11 o'clock Lags (*Lancelot Merivale Gibbs*) and I went to dear old St Luke's and now this evening four or five of us go to Westminster Abbey and have dinner late. I spent the afternoon talking to Georgie and writing.

Poor Blanche is not at all well and I think will stay on a little at Tyntesfield. Billy might be going out to India to see Evelyn. If he goes he starts on Friday. I wish rather I could go with him. Lancy and Blanche are to meet Eustace at Barcelona on Boxing Day. If Blanche can't go I shall almost feel bound to go with Lancy myself, but it would be very hard to be away for Christmas, and in writing this I feel a selfish pig.

A lot of letters came yesterday, mine the least interesting perhaps, because none of my friends knew mother well. Tell nurse to write to Tyntesfield on Tuesday or Wednesday. A post card will do. How are my pets, I do hope well? I shall be so glad to have you with me again darling.

Ever your own very loving

Nancy

The funeral service on 14th December 1909 was at Wraxall where Janet Louisa Gibbs was laid to rest in the family vault next to her husband, Antony.

In 1908 Eustace Lyle Gibbs started work with Antony Gibbs and Sons firstly in London and then in 1909 at Iquique in Chile. In 1913, he moved to the American branch of the family firm in New York. Lancelot Merivale Gibbs joined the Army as Second Lieutenant in the Somerset Light Infantry in 1908 and in December 1910 transferred to the Coldstream Guards.

On June 22nd 1911, Captain John Evelyn Gibbs served as Acting Aide de Camp to Field Marshal Lord Kitchener at the Coronation of King George V. A month later on July 22nd 1911, William Gibbs married Ruby Mabel, the youngest daughter of Henry Arthur Brassey M.P. of Preston Hall, Kent. The wedding took place at St Paul's Church in Knightsbridge. In 1911 too, George Abraham Gibbs and his wife, Via, moved into a new London residence at 22, Belgrave Square, one of the most fashionable addresses in Belgravia. Their life focused more and more on London and Tyntesfield as their country house seemed almost empty.[xxi]

On 28th June 1914, Archduke Franz Ferdinand of Austria, heir presumptive to Austro-Hungarian throne, and his wife Sophie, Duchess of Hohenberg, were shot dead in Sarajevo by Gavrilo Princip, one of a group of Bosnian Serb Assassins. When its demands were not met, Austria declared War on Serbia. In response Russia declared War on Austria, and then Germany declared War on Russia.

Figure 51. George Abraham Gibbs (front left) and Geoffrey Glynn (front centre) at North Somerset Infantry Camp in 1910.

Figure 52. North Somerset Infantry, Frome, 1913. Seated George Abraham Gibbs centre and Antony Hubert Gibbs 3rd from right with Eustace Lyle Gibbs standing at the end right.

Chapter Five

The Great War

On August 3rd 1914, Germany declared War against France. Great Britain sent an ultimatum demanding that the German Army should not pass through neutral Belgium. German forces rejecting the ultimatum immediately crossed the Belgian border and so, on Tuesday 4th August, Britain declared war against Germany. The Declaration of War stunned the nation and signaled the end of an era. At the time people thought that the War would be over by Christmas. Despite the lessons of the Boer War, no one could conceive the horrors of industrialized warfare.

It was particularly hard for Anna Schminke, who had been with the Gibbs' family at Charlton and Tyntesfield for 25 years, to come to terms with the coming conflict. The following extraordinary letter from Germany shows how hard it was for German nationals who had lived in England to accept the reality of war. Queen Victoria and Prince Albert were German. The Kaiser was Queen Victoria's grandson. George V, the Kaiser's first cousin had married a German princess – May of Teck. It seemed impossible that Britain should be at war with Germany. This is the letter of September 1914, which Anna sent to Anstice Katharine Gibbs (*always known as Nancy*).

Bad Wildungen
September 15th 1914

P.S. Don't you know anybody in a neutral country through whom you could send me a letter?

Darling Nancy

For 25 years I wrote to you in time for your birthday! Alas! That it was impossible this year. As for the Marzipan-Torte I might as well have tried to send it to the moon. However there seems to be a chance to get a letter through to you, so I take it to tell you a little of our doings. Your newspapers are very badly informed - or were so till shortly. Here is the truth. We make war in the most humane way possible. In Longwy (Longouin) they have found a machine to make Dum-Dum bullets and thousands of them ready packed for use. <u>We</u> do not make use of them. In Belgium the people have tortured the wounded on the battlefields, have murdered by hundreds the sleeping soldiers quartered upon them. Unspeakable cruelties have been committed by women and children, yes children. We make no war upon citizens, but when they shoot from windows and hedges, it is quite justified to raise the town or village to the ground. In Cassel there is a wounded soldier whose eyes were put out by a girl, and a cousin of my sister-in-law was shot dead by a franc tireur. I should think the Belgian authorities now see what a mistake they made not to allow the German troops to pass quietly through their land, which was all we wanted to. The Belgians are the scum of humanity (at any rate the "Wallonen" are) and I don't think they will ever become pleasant compatriots.

The French are quite different and it is a thousand pities that France has again been persuaded to measure herself against us. She will be beaten again and worse than in 1870. There is a battle going on on the Marne and we are hourly expecting the bells of victory to ring. The forts of Paris, however strong they are, will fall to our 42 Diameter cannons. Poor France! East Russia is free from Russians and Hindenburg announced a great victory yesterday and 30,000 unwounded prisoners. In spite of their millions we are not afraid of the Russians. They are quite demoralized. Oh! that noble and free England should be their ally! Times have indeed changed under Asquith and Grey. I wish they were both at the bottom of the sea! Yesterday we heard of the loss of the Kreuzer "Hela". Thank the Lord, we are allowed to know the worst as well as the best. Germany has raised warfare to a Science. Abroad and at home the military apparatus works miraculously. All party strife has ceased. We all work for the Nation. The Students who do not go to the war help the peasants to bring in the harvest. Old Professors take the musket and drill recruits. We women look after the wives and children of the soldiers - and the wounded in the Hospitals. We have several hundreds of wounded soldiers here - two have died…and try to make up for the tremendous strain they have had: long marches by night and fighting by day. We have already over 20,000 prisoners to feed and to house till the war be over. When will that be?!?!

I am anxious about your brother Billy. Is he with his regiment in France? They never mentioned any other troops by name but the Seaforth Highlanders. The London Illustrated News has not come since the middle of July. You may imagine my feelings when I heard that England had declared war. I was quite ill for a day or two!

Give my love to Blanche, Albinia and Lancelot. I am so glad that dear Lancelot's regiment cannot be sent out.

Ever

Your loving

Anna Schmincke.

Figure 53. Captain Eustace Lyle Gibbs, Commanding Officer with B Squadron, North Somerset Yeomanry, Christmas 1914.

One of the first members of the family to cross the Channel to France was Lancelot Merivale Gibbs of the Coldstream Guards. He wrote an extraordinary Diary of the First World War, which is presented here interleaved with letters from the Western Front. There are also letters from Gallipoli, where William Gibbs and Jack Merivale served. Indeed Jack died in this conflict. John Evelyn Gibbs was taken a Prisoner of War at Gheluvelt on 29th October 1914, and spent the War in Officers' Prisoner of War Camps at Stralsund, Heidelberg, Holzminden and Freiberg. Some of his letters survive and are also included.

The first letter is from Lancelot Merivale Gibbs, known as Lags.

22 B Regiment S.W.
Thursday 19th August 1914

Darling Nancy,

At last after many changes I am off tonight about 4.30 a.m. with my 100 men and about 10 Tons of luggage, and I expect shall have a proper time getting all this across.

Well! Good bye old Nancy and God bless you.

Your loving

Lags

DIARY OF

LANCELOT MERIVALE GIBBS

SECOND BATTALION

COLDSTREAM GUARDS.

FOURTH GUARDS BRIGADE.

1914

August 21st. Left Wellington Barracks about 3:30 for "Nine Elms". Blanche (*sister*), Via (*sister-in-law*), and George (*brother*) came and saw me off. Left Southampton about 2:30 p.m. after a 4 hour wait. Very crowded on board. I get fairly good cabin with Arthur Hay. Very smooth. Saw very little of any excitement while crossing. Got to LE HAVRE at about midnight.

August 22nd. Started unloading at once, about 12,000 kits. Great fuss on the Quay which was very badly managed, men got strolling all over the town. Eventually about 12 noon we marched out through LE HAVRE, where we got a good welcome, women giving men apples and children getting their "numerals" for souvenirs. Very hard march to camp where we arrived dead beat, there being a long hill to finish the 7 miles to it. Several men falling out. Equally bad management at camp. Eventually we got into our tents, and with the few things we had with us, and some tea some Boy Scouts brought us (after a very funny conversation between these boys Arthur Smith, Drill Sergeant Grey, and self). We had a meal and so to bed on the ground.

August 23rd. Had a bit of a sleep, then had to take 40 men and go down into LE HAVRE to pile Black bags. Found absolute chaos there at first. Got going after a bit. Very hot. Men dismissed at 12:30. Self and two others went to quite good café near Station and had jolly good luncheon. Arthur S. brought down next party and so I was not wanted. Got an old cab, fetched Irish Guards mess box and went back to camp. Got cheered by some French girls en route, who did nothing but shout "Good Night". Went over to First Battalion and saw 'Gazeke'. Arthur Hay produced eggs and rolls for dinner, also some Brandy and Soda from mess box, and so slept very heavily!! Wrote postcard to G.A.E.

August 24th. Slept somewhat late for "camp life". Collected the few eggs we had bought the night before and with some very thick bacon and milkless tea of the men's we got a good feed. Remained in camp while others went and foraged in LE HAVRE. Hill very hot, tents got like ovens about mid-day. Water turned off and so we had to be very careful. Washing being the first thing to be missed. Got 3 days of growth off my face with some hot water Scott produced. "Barbon" suddenly had to take a fatigue party to LE HAVRE at 7:30 and was there all night loading provisions on trains. Found a Service going on under a haystack and so joined in. Found out afterwards it s Weslyan.

August 25th. Took the men for a short run in the morning and then returned for further sleep. After luncheon Arthur Smith and I went down to LE HAVRE by train to relieve Arthur Hay at "Hangar Coton" (ie. loading provisions). This took a long time to find and made me very hot. After we had loaded 500 Biscuit Boxes an A.S.C. Major came and said it was all wrong as it "looked so bad", however we ignored him. Had a very funny ride in Bus which we thought was a public one, which turned out to he anything but. Also took us miles somewhere, but got back to hear we had to move at once. Trouble, bustle ensued, packing, hammering and shouting, we eventually left at 11:30; I left one man behind. Got to the Station at 12:30 a.m. and had to wait 4 hours. We then had to pack 40 men a truck and off we went - where we didn't know.

August 26th. About 6 a.m. the train stopped at ROUEN, where the men got out and had a wash by the line also some very strong coffee and gin mixed. In and on again at 8 a.m. and we rolled in to AMIENS at about mid-day. Glittering staff to meet us but they knew little. Eventually we moved off about 2 hours later for about 3 miles to a bivouac. We were now nearly 3 Divisions, lots of details, a stubble field was our lot, which was most unpleasant for the bare feet. After a short time Arthur Hay and I went down into the town, bought several things and also had a very good high tea. To return about 7 p.m. laden with eggs etc: for dinner. Fine night luckily.

August 27th. Route march ordered, but as it was raining it was cancelled. So about 12 we made another sortée to the town, A.H., "Barbon", and self, then to the "Hôtel de Rhin" for a jolly good 'Sock'. We returned to hear we were moving very shortly. Later we got the order that some German Cavalry were within 14 miles and so we had to put out Picquets and stand to arms. Raining hard. I may spend worse, but to date I have never had a worse night. We lit a fire among my lot and I collected them and sat with them, and got several of the men to sing and we joined in with the Chorus. About 10:30 we lay down, the officers together round a very low fire. Self with a Burberry, fleece lining and woolley, lying on wet grass, raining about and cold as the North Pole. Thus we shivered until 5, when I got-up and walked about.

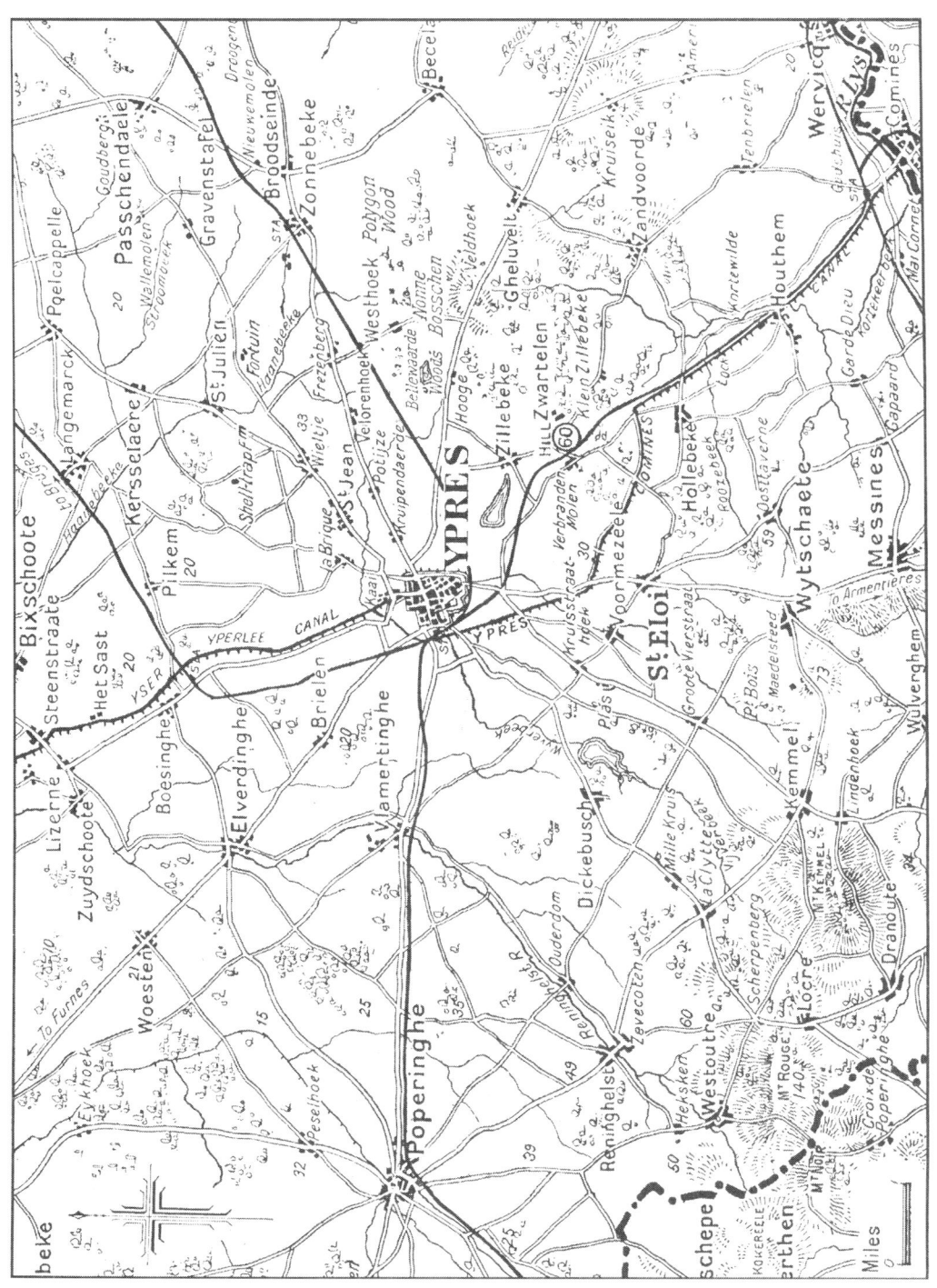

Figure 54. This map of the Ypres region at the time of the First World War shows many of the places referred to in the Diary and Letters.

August 28th. At last about 3 we got the order to move, and pushed down to the Station loading up. The train as full as before, we sat down very sleepy, no breakfast and no chance of food as far as we could see except for 4 dog biscuits I had collected. About 2:30 the train drew up at ROUEN and a moth-eaten "dug up" Captain came up and pushed us off to quite a good camp on the hill about 3 miles from ROUEN. We pushed off at once to the town for a bath and dinner. Sir Savile Crossley lent A.H. and self his room and we had a jolly good bath and shave. After a jolly good dinner and some "Château Latour 98"!! we managed to persuade 2 frightful looking bounders in some "Gamage Khaki" uniform with a Rolls Royce to drive us up thinking we were on the Staff. They said they had just come from the "front", but by their description I don't think they had been nearer than 100 miles from it. Bed very sleepy and just a little drunk at 11:30 p.m.!

August 29th. Arthur S made us some buttered eggs for breakfast and we got some milkless tea. Then a washing clothes parade much needed, and my bed was aired, also much needed. Changed my drawers for Scott to wash (lucky Scott!!) and made out a pay sheet (incidentally wrong but I hope to adjust it) and then with great difficulty said the men who doubted the accuracy of their payments made one franc out of it somehow. Then went down to town to buy provisions and dine. An early bed.

August 30th. Up fairly early and had a short bayonet parade. After that we started for a route march led by Arthur S. This was a terrible affair it being 100°F in the shade and some awful hills. One Irishman and one Grenadier fainted. 2 Coldstream Battalions had about 6 fall out. Got back having lost about a stone. Went down to Hospital and found Dick Rowley and Whitbread wounded. They told us of the other casualties in the 3rd Battalion, which were all from one Company. Had to get back early – scare about moving.

August 31st. Reveillé at 4:30 a.m. luckily we kept our tents as we didn't move off until after 12 mid-day. Terrible scramble at Station, lot of linesmen getting out into Pub and drinking. Eventually we found a train and got in, there being no one to tell us. The heat in the carriage was awful. The train stopped at every station and all the troops got out. We spent most of the time trying to find out where we were going, and not even the engine driver knew. Luckily we brought a good box of food with us as we were 14 hours on the train. At some station a woman came and forced a bottle into my hand, which turned out to be sherry, rather good but very sweet. Had to go to sleep about 8 p.m. as there was no light in the carriage.

September 1st. LE MANS. Got here about 9:30 a.m. very dirty, hot and tired. Not much waiting about at station. We were then taken up to the

French Mobilization Barracks and were squashed into a big barn. After a good deal of fussing Officers were into big rooms where they kept the spare harness. 10% of the men were allowed out and these were treated not wisely but too well by the French soldiers and in consequence 2 officers patrols had to go out. Had a very good bath and then an excellent dinner at a tiny French Restaurant (where the Lady who waited on me would insist on kissing me).

September 2nd. Slept late and on getting up found it hotter than usual. Nothing doing. Went and collected provisions in the town. 10:30 took a party down to bathe, had great difficulty to get them all into the bath water. Met Lionel Tennyson and others after dinner. Great crowd of men in town with a good many drunks.

Letter to Via Gibbs
2nd September, 1914.

This is a sort of small Aldershot of the French Army, and they have put us in the mobilization rooms and barns. The Officers are in the harness part, which is really quite comfortable, as one can hang one's wardrobe on the saddle racks to air. We had a proper journey down here from Rouen - fourteen hours in the hottest train I have ever been in. We took some food in the shape of sardines, bread etc. - otherwise get nothing - and very little water. You would laugh to see our mess, which we carry from place to place: six of us. Each day one of us buys sardines, eggs and melons (Canteloupe): the latter are very cheap (F1.50) also peaches in galore. We then return piled with parcels and eat: everything off the same plate: sardines first as a rule, and the melon with a dash of sardine oil! If we are on the move the plates etc. do not get washed, and you get a peach on a three year old sardine plate. Last night we went to a tiny restaurant here, and got a most splendid dinner. The only thing that marred the evening was that the somewhat rotound waitress would insist on kissing me on handing the soup!

I shall be very glad when we join up with the Battalion, as we now get jostled about, and fed when they think of it, although I must say that they are feeding them very well, as, of course, all our (Officers') food is the same and cooked by the men. So far, we have got little news. I saw two of the third Battalion at Rouen who had been slightly wounded; and they told me that the 2nd and 3rd Battalions were all right; but the third had one Company in it rather badly knocked about. We never know where we are going. When we left Rouen on Sunday we asked the Engine Driver all the way down, and he never seemed to know (or had orders not to say). It is very odd, and splendid, to see the way these French soldiers mix with ours. Last night in the town nearly every other man I saw was with a French soldier, and seemed to spend the whole evening with him.

It seems that the conversation must be somewhat limited! They treat them rather too well at the restaurants: at least, last night a good many would have done better to stick to water.

I got my second bath yesterday, which was a relief. One certainly gets very used to a dry rub off every morning, and begins to rather resent a bath!

I have hardly met anyone I know yet; but perhaps this is not surprising, as we have been shifting about so.

Well, Via! I hope all your Red Cross arrangements have been going on well. I have not seen a proper English paper at all since I left, except the Continental "Daily Mail".

Yours affectionately

L A N C E L OT

September 3rd. Brigade went off for a Route March.

September 4th. Arrived COULOMMIERS about 9:30 a.m. and found Taylor waiting for me. Men bivouaced in the line and made tea. Meanwhile I went up to the First Battalion, then billeted in the town, and Evelyn and others. All of them very cheery. After a drink I returned and found Brigade details waiting for orders, we did until 7:30 p.m., when we started off under Bernard Gordon Lennox, and walked about 8 miles in the dark. Found Battalion bivouaced at LA CELLE. Had something hot to eat and got some cocoa, and bedded down about 12 a.m. – my first experience of straw. Reveille at 4:30 a.m., and started to march, still retreating. Went on until 10:30, when we got a halt for four hours. Being my first march, I found the heat very trying and my feet got rather sore. On again for about four hours, after about 3 kms to FONTENAY and bivouaced in an orchard, fruit in the shape of apples and pears, very plentiful. The men came along very well, but have got rather despondent at always going the wrong way. Posted to No.4 Company. Bed about 8 p.m. in straw in next field to Company.

September 6th. Reveillé at 4:30 a.m., and then a bit of await. Then at last we turned to go forward, having heard the Germans had got a fright about Berlin, and were retiring and rushing troops back. We got to a village about 3 miles back, where we dug ourselves in. We had not got to wait long before their guns began to sweep round and we saw the shells getting slowly round to us. However our own guns got to work and silenced them a bit. One of the shells of own guns made a premature burst and three bits missed me by about 2 yards and one man by ½ foot. When things quietened down we went back and had luncheon at the mess-cart. Towards evening we went onto a village about 3 miles on and bivouaced

– de Winton (3rd Battalion) and Britton (lst Battalion) killed during the day. Tolly, Muller and Stuart wounded. Took me for out posts; had to go about a mile ahead with about 2 lots of sentries. Got back for dinner, was then awake most of the night as had no coat; saw nothing. Coldest night on record. This was TOUQUIN, only about 5 miles on from the last night.

September 7th. Battalion left about 9:30. I was made Transport Officer and got a horse. Transport Brigade came along very slowly. Going down one small road the mess wagon got into a ditch, and we took about ½ hour to get it out. Meanwhile Artillery were longing to pass, and expressed themselves strongly to me. Luckily Cubitt was in charge of the train. Eventually got in about 5:30 p.m. at ST. SIMEON, and found everyone very anxious for the food. Got lots of straw, and made a good bed with Verelst and so kept warm. The Battalion had a bit of fun in the village on the way through. Came across several very nasty sights as one passed them in cold blood.

September 8th. Reveillé 5:30 a.m. Found myself in charge of the train today; had great difficulty collecting it. Then we had to turn off the road the Brigade had taken. As the Third Division came up, went through REBAIS and then all lst line transport turned off the road and parted. Waited about 4 or 5 hours, and having got no orders went on. Got well cursed by Davies (6th Brigade) for blocking the road but kept on. After crossing the bridge at LA TRETOIRE we halted for about 3 hours. I went on and eventually found the Brigade at BOITRON, from there it took me over 3 hours to get up the last 2 miles. Got in the way of a 60 pounder Battery and got well cursed by the Major. Got in at 8:30 p.m., very dark, and with great difficulty. Found the Battalion had had great fun during the day; captured 11 horses; 3 machine guns; 3 other carts, besides many trophies. Got to bed very tired about 10:30. Casualties Giant; Trotter; Jackson; Corbett; and Charles Monk wounded.

September 9th. Reveillé at 4:30 bit forward. Then was no hurry as no orders received. Got the German horses fitted to their harness, and sort our very lame and sore horses off in the German carts to Headquarters. Greys and "20th" passed our bivouac. Left about 1:30 p.m. and had a very gentle walk crossing the famous 'MARNE' and through CHARLY (VILLIERS-SUR-MARNE) about 1 mile the other side, bivouacing on the side of a bad hill. Very little straw. I got in with Dick and Bewicke and kept fairly warm.

September 10th. Up again at 4:30, no water to be got so we gave washing a miss. Stood by some time as First and Second Divisions moving on same road; - result - an awful block for over two hours. Got off eventually about 7, raining like ****! and felt very depressed. About 5 miles on I met Bache Hay who was full of spirits having just captured about 30 Ulans; marched along about 100 yards with him. Got up short of CHEVILLON and had a bit to eat about 2:30 p.m. Found they had just had a good fight where we halted (Fifth Brigade) and captured 250 prisoners, few of ours killed. The Germans having had about 250 casualties as well. Moved on from this hill, after watching a German column pass across our front about 6 miles off – but unfortunately "Cow Guns" could not get up in time – to a bivouac about 3 miles where we got lots of straw and had a good meal.

[Ref: German Column. Hear afterwards that the 18 pounders got within 2,000yds, and now it ceases to exist!]

September 11th. Reveillé 3:30 a.m., had to have breakfast in the dark which I hate. Still very wet after yesterday's rain. Needless to say we did not move off until 9 a.m. Took over transport again as Harry Pane gone to 3rd battalion, and got quite a nice looking German horse. Moved slowly along for some time, being too far behind to hear much. Uneventful day as transport was all up with Battalion. About 2:30 p.m. we came in for the worst storm I have been in for years, got absolutely soaked. Result – we got billeted in OUICHY LE CHÂTEAU. Got the transport into the market square and then found a deserted house. Scott got a huge fire going in the sitting room, while I dried my clothes before it. Went down to a meal in very odd costume with French Sabots on. Slept well on a mattress and bed.

September 12th. Was called at 3:30 and got into a so called bath, then heard I had got another 1½ hours sleep, so went back. Rained as we went off about 7, and continued doing so most of the day. Had no halt for a meal, only got a bit of cheese from a farm, otherwise no food. About 3 or 4 miles from our billet it simply poured until we got into COUVRELLE. Then I had to wait until the remainder of the first line came in, as it had been split up today ½ with the Battalion and ½ with Brigade. Nowhere to put anything: got most of the cookers into a square. Then 4 'Coat' wagons got up a road and had to be turned round (each had a team of 6) – result I got to our meal about 9:30 absolutely soaked. Slept (6 of us) in a wee room on the floor of a cottage. Had no change, however very sleepy. Worst day and night I have had so far. Almost chaos in the town, as streets very small and transport and cavalry coming in by every road.

September 13th. Still raining a bit but we were cheered up by the arrival of the mail, the first for about a fortnight. I got postcard from Cissie (Beckwith Smith), a shirt and socks plus a pair of trousers. Got the first line off fairly easily up a very bad hill on the top of which our line was halted for about 3 hours. I managed to get dry a bit in the sun, and got a bit to eat with David B. and Trousers. We suddenly had to rush on the S.A.A. carts down a hill into a village (CYS) by a stream, over which the Germans had blown up the bridge. I got up in the firing line with

Headquarters and waited about 2 or 3 hours and watched our advance up to and over the river, having got across on planks we were told to come back and billet in CYS where we got a very good shop. Trousers, SQM (*Senior Quarter Master*) and self got a room and 'hogged it some'. Got some red wine off the good lady, who was delighted to get us in, having had her shop well pillaged by the Germans the day before. [We always have a fight on a Sunday somehow, even if the other 6 days are quiet.]

September 14th. Got off about 6 a.m., raining as hard as ever. One horse had to be chucked out, and most of them lost shoes. However we got off somehow. We then trekked down one side of the Canal to a pontoon bridge the R.E. had made, and we then got the Battalion over, also the SA and water carts. Came to a village SOUPIR where we got heavily shelled. The Battalion split up and I remained in the village with the SAA carts. Little Man came in wounded, so I got him a few things, also Charles Guthrie and Harcourt-Vernon. The Battalion was in reserve most of the day and so no ammunition required. Got very little news. The Germans seem to have been holding the hill with a large force (9 Battalions). Shell after shell of shrapnel kept bursting just about us in the village of SOUPIR. We must have given the Germans hell by their wounded. Poor old Dick L. got two, one in the head and one in the heart, in the afternoon. Bartlelott wounded and about 20 men. In the 3rd Battalion David B. and Percy W. killed. Took the SAA Carts with difficulty back to first line, and went up to Headquarters of the Battalion and got some dinner. It was an awful day. Men being brought in all day and night to the church, school and anywhere else. All the villagers terrified, but very kind to us about giving food. I got back down to the first line about 11:30 p.m., and bedded down in a little straw with my British Warm.

September 15th. Went up to breakfast at Headquarters again, and took them up provisions. Found they had been fairly quiet in the night on the right (battle outposts with 2 companies, 2nd Battalion in reserve). First Division on right then 60th Battalion; 2 GG; 2 CG; I G; and 3 CG and so on up to the Third Army. Brought my SAA carts back to their old place. Went off and saw to the burying dear old Dick in the R.C. Cemetry half way up the hill. Heard Roger Bentinck got wounded by a shell early in the morning. Got an egg, bread, margarine; also coffee and tea and potatoes from a kind woman. Sat and waited for about 4 hours and then had orders to send cookers to various places. Went up myself and found ½ the Battalion in the same place, resting, the other ½ being in the trenches. One shell of our own guns had just burst in the middle and got two men. Otherwise no damage by the Germans. Wasted some time for dinner. Meanwhile it rained hard, as the other two companies did not come in, I went off and had my hot 'Bully' and 'Spuds'. Also good dish of bread and marmalade, well soaked by the rain. While going back two shrapnel bursts over my head, breaking all the branches all round. Got back to my kind lady who had prepared a bed and talked for about ½ hour drinking coffee and a prune liqueur. Bed at 9 still at SOUPIR. Saw Willy Gibbs (10th Hussars) also Frank Crossley (9th Lancers) and Pat Armstrong during the day.

September 16th. Got up very late about 6:30 and found a most delicious omelette waiting with bread and red wine (however I managed to exchange wine for coffee). Went the round of the transport. The Battalion then came back into billet by ½ battalion. I went foraging for the mess; result 6 chickens, 9 eggs, and lots of milk, also I got a most delicious pot of honey from the Curé. Cakes B died in the night, so I took down limber and buried him in the Cemetery. Got another shirt and socks from Hilditch & Key. Firing began again (rifle) – small scare from Grenadier Guards that we were being attacked but found untrue. Shrapnel has now continually burst round and in the village for 3 days. I have had to keep all the horses up against a wall. Had a slight alarm about 2 that we were being attacked, however it blew over. The Companies (1&2) went out to relieve 3&4 from the trenches about 5:30 under a heavy shell fire which was being badly directed by the enemy. Trousers, SQM, Alan and self then went down to Madame Bourson's Château, and 'S' and I sat with Hugo Gough (Irish Guards) for about 15 hours; found him very uncomfortable but getting on having had his left arm taken off at midday. Little rifle fire started in the wood about 8 for a short time, but soon stopped. Had an enlarged dinner having bought 8 litres of milk and 9 chickens during the day. Returned to my old billet.

Letter to George Abraham Gibbs
16th September 1914

Dearest George,
    Many thanks for your letter of the 2nd September, which was very acceptable, being the first (bar one from Billy) I have had. It seemed funny opening your letter during one of the biggest battle modern times. We have had quite a hard time lately; but most people seem fairly well on it. I fear we have suffered as a Regiment as regards officers; personally I am fairly safe, as I have taken over duties of Transport Officer. Two days ago I saw Willy Gibbs, who was very well and had lately seen Evelyn, of whom I had not heard for a week or so. Today I got two consignments from Fortnum & Mason which were very acceptable as the G's have looted these villages very much. After you have finished with such things as "Sketch", "Tatler", they would be very nice out here; also a small consignment of writing paper and envelopes occasionally. Blanche has been really managing sending things, but as I have only one envelope, I

am writing it here. We have had for the last days a rest, and are all the better for it.

    Letters, I fear, are not very interesting to you, as no news may be put. I have got quite a nice German horse to ride, captured by Gillie Follett's Company

Your loving brother

Lancelot

September 17th. Rose about 6. Meanwhile Madame made us another omelette and coffee. Got some more breakfast up at the school. Raining hard as usual. Went a round of the horses, and then went to the Château and saw Gough. Found him more conscious; got him a few things. Rather a scare on the left, and so both reserve companies dashed out, but soon returned wet through. Got them a hot meal. They (3&4) eventually went off relieving 1&2 about 5:30. Meanwhile SQM and self went foraging and got a good supply of milk and chicken. The two companies got in a bit earlier and reported that Trousers had got well into about 50 Germans advancing on the left, otherwise doing nothing. Got off to bed about 9. Found the women still over dinner and had to talk to them for ½ hour or so. I got the bed and SQM took the floor. (Mattress on floor).

17th September 1914

Darling Nancy

    Many thanks for your letter and papers which were very acceptable being the first I have had at all so far. It seemed funny opening them hearing this great battle going on the whole time. It seems that our army has done very well and especially my brigade. The Regiment has lost a few officers I am afraid but the remainder are all very cheery also the men. Our casualties may have been rather heavy but nothing to be compared with the German losses.

    We had some hard trekking to start off with but now we have just had a good rest. I have been made Transport Officer and so get a horse, which is good, a rather nicely bred German one captured by Gillie Follett's Company, also I am much safer! As I have to keep behind and look after the horses. I have been billeted lately here (I can't say where!) with a charming lady who always has a splendid cup of coffee and a good omelette for me in the morning. Only this continually talking French to her is rather trying to the brain! I forgot to mention in a letter to Georgie but if you have any "Bromo" to spare occasionally you might send me some – only I should like a more compact parcel than the ordinary Bromo one.

No more news. Good luck and God bless you and Stafford.

Your loving brother

Lags

September 18th. Hogged it a bit and found everything much quieter. Germans seem to have run short of ammunition or 'summot'. Went down to the Château and had a further look round. Found Bartlelott there and much better for being moved from that beastly church, which now has nothing but the Germans wounded and the most awful smell imaginable. Had one of Number 2's Pack horses shot in the trenches. Now we are one short, however have requisitioned for another at once. Ordered milk and eggs as far as possible. Had a long argument with a man for oats and eventually got them cheap by saying I would take the army away from SOUPIR and leave it to the Germans!! Foraged as usual and got rather too much. Headquarter party had dinner first and others came in about 7:45 very wet and tired. Had some Champagne for them (very cheap 4 francs a bottle!) Got off to bed early, hoped for the second line which never turned up.

Headquarters, 4th Guards,
From Earl of Cavan
Commander of the Fourth Guards Brigade
Friday 18th September 1914

Very exciting start. Left our overnight (bivouac) with 18 officers about six this morning and had a peaceful trek of 3½ or 4 miles to 2nd Division Head Quarters. Saw General Monro and he gave us coffee and marmalade and sent us off - after explaining to me the situation. All went well until we got about 14 miles from a Château when we were passed by a squadron of remounts and a high explosion shell burst just at the tail of the column and the whole of the remounts stampeded. Poor Francis Scott was knocked over by the horses but is pretty well, and my big cob wanted to off it but I managed to get clear. White, my man, was riding another and leading another one behind me, the led horse was hit and fell over, White's horse was covered with blood - but all's well. I have now just come back from going all round our position. It is rather gruesome to see German dead still lying out in front where they attacked the day before I got here. The trouble is the big shells, they are most alarming to everybody and the German gunners are very clever indeed at suddenly picking out a section of the trenches and fairly smothering them. They never stop and their waste of ammunition must be frightful. As I write shells are bursting all along the high ground in front. I am very well and find all very cheerful but they've had a hellish time and the losses in officers are terrible. If only the Russian story was true! It must make them go back to the Rhine. I'm quite satisfied about holding on here we want reserves badly – and if the enemy broke through anywhere we should have to go back quick.

Food good enough and I hope to get the Cobbett box tonight but we never can tell. Send us all the cheering news you can especially about the Russians in Austria and Germany, so much depends on them.

Cavan

September 19th. Had the omelette and coffee as usual. Took eggs and milk to Bartlelott and Gough. Saw Cavan who had just arrived. Looked round horses and found all pretty well except the two wounded ones. Got a few parcels, socks from Albinia, handkerchiefs from Mr. Barker J. and socks from Hilditch & Key. Shelling started again a bit after luncheon: did not seem very much at first but later on there was a good deal of rifle fire, so remaining two companies (3&4) got ready about 3:30 and eventually were sent out to the left about 5 o'clock. Sim, Doctor and self remained (Doctor being Sinclaire just returned). Later on Battalion Headquarters had to follow and later again (after dark) I had to go to Brigade Headquarters and got orders from them (Cavan now) to take 1st line to CHAVONNE. Awful scramble to get mess cart way, but with help of tool cart this was done. Also I had to give my horse to a S.A. cart on account of the one which got shot, and I took the German horse which is a pig. Eventually we got there (about 2 miles), successfully evading two barricades en route. I stayed in an evacuated house which smelt rather but had a good food store for the dinner. Got to bed drenched, but well fed!

September 20th. Supplies arriving made a good noise during the night but never woke me! Went round with the Sergeant Major for billets. This was not easy as the XIth, Bays, and 5th Dragoon Guards had got there first. However we got them and returned to an enormous luncheon at the house. Rained the whole morning without stopping; found the bridge over the river Aisne to CYS in good order now after our taking it the other day. Shelling continued very heavily the whole morning. Went up to "Troclydite" Mansion and saw Colonel, arranged about billets when 6 Platoons came down. Got into our farm and found it very fairly comfortable. S and self got a room.

September 21st. Very little doing in the morning, raining as usual. Had 3 casualties during the night from a patrol that got in front of our own line. Slept till luncheon. Firing started a bit after luncheon, but slept through it. Got sent for by Brigade Headquarters after dinner. Cycled there getting challenged the whole way and when I got there, drenched through, I was not wanted. Got back about 10. My turn to sleep in the bed!

September 22nd. Very little doing during the night. Had a good look round horses and sent up fresh supplies to the "Troclydite" Mansion. Lots of parcels and letters arrived. Mess almost overdone now with provisions. Nice day for change, and so Sim and self rode to CYS, St. Mard, then back to SOUPIR foraging with some success. Result 5 Kilos of Honey, 4 bottles of milk, 14 eggs, and 5 loaves of bread which we brought back sticking out of our pockets. We then had a dinner also bully à la Ritz, due to a stove I had brought up in the morning and built.

September 23rd. Lovely day again, everything beginning to dry again now. Our artillery making a good noise and more or less silencing the Germans, very little happening in the trenches. Rode down to CYS and got some butter and milk. Had suet for lunch a friche (*abandoned land*) ox having been killed in the morning! Rode into VAILLY, got about 4 shrapnel pretty close on the way there and so we cleared off the road. Found the town a wreck from high explosives. Got lots of eggs and milk on the way home. Very quiet night.

Headquarters, 4th Brigade

23rd September 1914

      We are told that there is a chance of letters going straight home by a messenger today, so you may get this before all my other letters. I have not heard from you yet as letters take 14 days ordinarily. Well we are still clinging on and German trenches are only 500 to 800 yards in front of us. If you expose yourself you get shot at and shelled at once. My Head Quarters are very comfy and we feed well, but I shall be glad when we can make a push forward. Guernsey is buried in the cemetery here (I may not say the place but will keep it in my diary) (SOUPIRS near LAON) with Banbury, Arthur Hay, Berners (who lived opposite Broke Hall) and Lockwood. Guernsey was killed by a German who lay down pretending to be dead. He was caught all right. His ring and locket were sent down to the Record Base to the Sergeant of the Irish Guards, and if she has not got them Lady Guernsey should write to him addressed O. R. Sergeant, Irish Guards, Base Record Office, Expeditionary Force, or even better to the Irish Guards Orderly Room at Buckingham Gate and get them to do it. Lancelot Gibbs is all right in the 2nd Coldstreams under me, but Evelyn is not in my Brigade, but I know he was fit and well on the 21st. The very heavy shelling seems to be lessening and I hope the enemy are getting frightened. Don't forget that what we want most are Candles, Matches, Soap Tablets, Tinned milk; and I want 2 Khaki flannel shirts and a safety razor with a dozen blades. The one in the hold-all won't cut butter. Everything else is excellent. A few good cigars would be a great luxury.

                                          Cavan

September 24th. They started shelling village a bit, but no harm done. Lovely day again. Slept in the morning. Rode over to CYS and SOUPIR collecting eggs and wine with Sim. Shelled again in the afternoon. Sergeant Major, Cook Johnson, getting rather badly hit, also a Corporal otherwise no damage.

September 25th. Managed to get hold of rain-tub and so got a bath, of which I was badly in need. A few shells came over about 5:30 a.m. and rather disturbed my sleep, but no damage. 7th Brigade made an attack during the night. Also Grenadiers on our left made maximum demonstration but not much result. Foraged as usual.

September 26th. Got 3 of our horses hit by one of our own shells, and had to shoot two. Foraged as usual.

September 27th. Rumour we were moving; everything got ready, and then cancelled. Talked to Jock Ainsworth (XIth) for some time. Foraged for some time in the afternoon. Very little shelling. All well.

September 28th. Went up to trenches and watched Corporal Brown and Dodgson bring in wounded man from in front. Very fine act as under fire the whole time. Colonel came to see horses. Foraged in the morning with Trousers and went to SOUPIR after luncheon. Saw Brigadier (Cavan) for a few minutes. Tried 3 horses for C.O. Got 3 x 26th Sunday Papers with good news on flanks – all seems to be going well. Shelled a bit in the evening.

September 29th. Section sent out to try and find a sniper in a wood North of SOUPIR. Foraged as usual on C.O's horse, without a very large result. Wright (Quartermaster) turned up with 50 eggs (which afterwards turned out to be very *good* cooking!). Got two shells (coal-boxes) within 15 yards of me in CYS, obviously aimed, a third came but I was behind a wall by that time – horse very frightened. Conducted 2 Gendarmes round and arrested one man.

September 30th. Took party of 50 into SOUPIR for Early Service. Party proved too big and so only Officers could go up. Trousers and self rode into VAILLY and found shops open again, and so managed to get a supply of writing paper & C. Got a few eggs and a bunch of grapes.

October 1st. All Transport inspected by General Munro at SOUPIR at 9:30 a.m. He just looked quickly at them and approved quietly to Brigadier. Foraged and got 37 eggs and a few fly-papers, otherwise no excitement. Several Continental (Daily Mail) papers arrived and gave us cheery news.

October 2nd. Got up about 6:30 a.m. and with Trousers marched a party of about 60 in to SOUPIR for a Service (H.C.). The number proved far more than the clergyman had expected and so only Officers could communicate. Went into VAILLY with Trousers and found many more shops open. Spent a lot of money without much result. Alan D. and self went for a ride in the evening to 3rd Battalion Coldstream Guards. But found no one in.

October 3rd. Went to church at11:30, short hymn service. Foraged with Darwin and got given small plate of strawberries from one farm. Alan D and self went a short ride via SOUPIR. Had another short service at 6:30 p.m. with about 2 Candles, rather impressive, as men sang loudly and shells burst most of the time.

October 4th. Got up rather later being Sunday and gave exercise a miss. A bit of bit of firing went on in night but nothing much came of it. The Engineers improved the trenches by making a good wire entanglement in front during the night. Also they made several communication trenches. Eggs getting scarce I find. A very quiet Sunday for us. Shells flew a bit about 5:30 but no damage.

October 5th. Exercise as usual. Took chargers up through ST. MARD towards COURCELLES to vary the monotony. Got in about 7 a.m. Got very large consignment of parcels and letters which occupied most of the morning. Pro's platoon rather caught out when coming down in the evening from one shrapnel, one killed and 4 wounded. Went to Church at 6:30 p.m., rather nice service with only altar candles alight.

October 5th 1914

Darling Nancy,
    Many thanks for your small present enclosed in your letter. I used a bit this morning and it was a great luxury You will know by then time you get this where we are by the people who have come back wounded, also by my diary if Blanche will forward it to you or a copy of it.

    We are still in the same place entrenched and are quite ready to go forward. We are not so far advanced as the Times of the 25th September says.

    I wonder if you have heard much of the Greys. I saw them once but not since, this was some time ago and then most of the people I knew were wounded or away except Toby Long.

    I wish Stafford could come out and get specially attached to the 4th Guards Brigade – it would be very nice to have him here. At last we have got a Chaplain (with No. 4 Field Ambulance) but for the first fortnight here we did not have one at all. So we got a service a day and sometimes two, in the local Roman Catholic Church.

    This morning we had a regular Xmas parcel post nearly everyone getting something and "yours truly" six, why I do not quite know as we have had a post in (and out) every day now for three weeks.

Poor old Gillie is getting terribly sick of this war and gets very depressed at times otherwise most people are fairly cheery. I think he writes rather pessimistic letters to Lady Mildred which is rather hard on her.

Must now go and see my Transport horses after their exercise from 5.30 to 7, which I attend rather reluctantly. Good'bye old Nancy and God bless you all until we return.

Your loving brother

Lags

October 6th. Still larger consignment of parcels arrived for me, and a lot of things I had written for from SOUPIR also something from Blanche (Sister) and Cissie (Beckwith-Smith). Drove out in Brewers cart for supplies with a very slow horse. On the way back had to stop in CYS for ¾ hour as shells were coming so heavily over the CYS-CHAVONNE road. Then made horse canter by shouting and stamping on the floor until we get over AISNE when shells started again, so again we had to keep under until they stopped. One proper 'Black Maria' burst just short of the river. Got in about 5:30 p.m.

October 7th. Slipped while coming up steps during the night, and pulled nail on big toe right back to the quick, hurt a bit. Not much sleep and so gave exercise a miss. Hobbled about during the morning. Lots of shells about all going wide. Drove out again with moderate success with supplies. got in without danger. Fellow in the Grenadiers got hit by 5 shrapnel bullets but none of them broke the skin. Beautiful day, hot as anything. Turkey for dinner!

October 8th. Gave exercise a miss, toe as excuse! Had a very funny drive into SOUPIR, taking Pro to hospital. P-J sat in bottom of the cart beating the horse while I drove. Went and saw graves in the cemetery and found them much improved. Found Colonel Feilding at lunch. Drove round with man in afternoon obtaining 4 dozen eggs. Enemy's heavy guns got at CYS, but were short of our guns – some rare explosions. Wrote several letters which just caught post.

October 9th. Up again at 5:30 a.m. went above ST. MARD in wood to avoid being seen. Found so many parcels for me that I gave up any idea of going out during the morning. Foraged again as usual in mess cart – no excitement. Alan insisted on my coming for a walk with him to SOUPIR and back; very dark and got repeatedly challenged by "'alt, 'oo are yer ?" which frightened us rather. Large dinner during which P-J got rather ragged. Had one of the cigars that had just turned up for me. Paddy B-N (Beaumont-Nesbitt) came in in the morning.

October 10th. 5:30. Exercise. Transport very late. Numerous parcels, among them a Kodak which I started on at once and took the TROCLYDITE MANSION, and C. Ympkin, Bewick and self drove out in afternoon with moderate success. Very little shelling; village not shelled at all during the day; our guns were only fairly offensive too. Yes, I agree. Everything one gives up <u>does</u> in some way help on the whole cause.

10th October 1914

Dearest Georgie,

    Very many thanks for your letter and very acceptable presents, which arrived this morning. The only kind of present one can send in return is the enclosed. It is the fuse setting and of High Explosive (i.e. the nose). These are rather rare things to find as a rule, as they go off in the ground and get buried, making a hole big enough for one to stand in. This one evidently struck a tree about 2 foot thick and 30 or 40 feet high which it cut clean down; the nose cap falling on the ground.

    I expect your papers the last few days have been very uninteresting as regards the centre, as we have simply done nothing. In fact, for the last three days we have only sat and watched the Germans in their trenches: so there is nothing for the papers to put. Everything is improving perfectly enormously out here now in many of the Posts, which now go to England in five days; also we get one in and one out every day: also a large parcel post (personally I have had some 32 parcels in the last three days!). Enormous quantities of food for the men, and very excellent it always is, also several large presents from kind people to the troops from England.

    It is starting to get very cold in the early mornings here, especially near the river about 5:30, when I go exercising. I go out double my size with clothes on.

    We feel very safe now should we have any more scraps in the near future, first with Cavan as Brigadier, who everybody acknowledges is perfectly excellent, and Pereira, (our Colonel) has already proved himself to be very sound too. Some even go as far as to say they think that that is one of the reasons the Second Battalion has had so few losses; but I think that we have also been lucky when it has been our turn to lead the Brigade, which comes every 12th day for 3 days when on the move.

    There are still a good many farmers' wives left in the farms round here, with about one old man of 60 to every 3 farms. All have been very much looted by Germans, but are recovering now, and are very good to the men with their milk and eggs. It is most amusing to see them carrying on conversations each in their own language, but the odd thing is that they seem to understand each other perfectly. The only thing they don't appreciate is their potatoes being taken, which I can quite understand; and so the Colonel has made a small collection for the Battalion, and will give it to the mayor when we leave here.

Once again many thanks for your presents.

Your loving brother

Lancelot

It is very sad about poor George Brook. I only saw him about 3 days before he was hit. It was an absolute chance shell miles from anything it was aimed at – 3 came at once, one hitting him and two wide.

Coldstream Guards
Blenheim Barracks,
Aldershot
(Headed notepaper not location)
October 10th 1914

Darling Nan

I have 3 unanswered letters from you, for which thank you very much also for your enclosures, most useful always.

Ref. Russians – I can tell you nothing – all the same rumours reached us here and seemed most authentic, but the Heads all deny it here and at home and we have seen no signs of them yet – of course if all their ammunition really went down in the Oceanic it would cramp their style a bit, till they got more. So we know absolutely nothing more than you do of the Russian enterprise.

Just got a letter from Lags dated September 30th so his takes much longer than yours I have of October 3rd – and he can't be many miles away from here, though I don't know exactly.

Yes it is a long battle – more like a siege – we are motionless on both sides really.

I get weekly supplies from Fortnum and Masons and as Mails arrive nearly every night now we are doing pretty well – but the country is entirely denuded of the producers of milk, butter and eggs and such like. So if you are passing the York store any time and have ½ crown to spare, send me a tin of milk or butter, they make such a difference to a meal.

I have not seen Eustace G. for a long time – he was very fit then – but the 12th have not been near us. I have seen Willy and Joe – I have heard no details of the latter's wounds.

The Walker you mentioned used to be at Mr Davies – contemporary of Huie's – I saw his name as wounded in the paper.

St Aidans sounded charming and I hope it did you all good. Now to get away from war news would be the best rest for you all I expect.

We could hear the Germans singing last night their National Anthem. I thought I heard cheers first and then the singing – I expect it was the arrival of the C. P. or some Prince or the announcement of some fictitious victory. The wind was our way and it was most distinct – about 7.00 pm.

I hear Georgie hopes to get command of a Reserve Regiment of Somerset Yeomanry – I hope he will – then we shall be all at it.

We are down to 10 officers now, which is very short, 1/8 in fact. It is getting very cold at nights – but we are very lucky in having the most lovely weather just now.

Letters are most welcome and you have all been very good about writing – and Blanche works hard at sending me my many wants.

The money subscribed to charities and organisations at home is astonishing – what a rich country it is – there must have been 6 million given since war began and more probably.

I am very fit thank God – a slight abscess on a tooth and a wasp sting have been my worst and both are gone now.

My own belief is that it must be a short war, home for Xmas sort of thing – let us hope so. My love to Staff and all

Your very loving brother

Evelyn

October 11th. Being Sunday, no exercise. Went to the church at 11:30. After lunch Paddy B-N and self went to VAILLY. Had a very funny drive there trying to make old transport horse trot. Got some wine from Felix Potin, then tried to cross river to come back by 'safe' side, however guard stopped us and Paddy had to run back and get a "Laissez Passé" from the Brigade Major. First news of our departure, but kept very quiet.

October 12th. Everyone fussing and talking in whispers about going, although all the villagers knew as well as we did all about it. Got all the transport harnessed up ready. No sign of any French to relieve us by 5 p.m. things looked blue. About 6 p.m. we heard from Brigade Headquarters that Grenadiers only would be relieved. Companies changed late, and night as usual.

Letter from Captain Evelyn Gibbs to Mr. George A. Gibbs, M.P.

October 12th.

Dearest Georgie,

I have only been able to send you a post-card lately, owing to scarcity of envelopes: but today this excellent pad arrived from Exeter (from Uncle Reggie) and a supply of envelopes too. Very many thanks for arranging it, and I thought I had written long ago to say I did get the money from Cox & Co: and it was certainly the best method. As a matter of fact, we can't use money at all practically – just every now and again one can pay, in a billet, for something one has taken, or been supplied with – but very often they will not accept payment – for potatoes for instance – and sometimes there is no one to pay. About where we are now there is nothing to buy – one cannot get eggs, or milk or butter. I have had one egg or one pat of butter during the last month, and no milk for ages. The Germans took practically everything and destroyed the rest: and the remainder is snapped up – (more than four quarters equal one here!). I think the Regiments in Reserve may manage to get some things sometimes – but up in the Trenches, Oh!

We are having the most perfect weather just now, the last three weeks have been sunny and bright, and a bit of frost every night – but everyone has a great coat and one blanket now, so it is all right. "Comforts" too are arriving from home, and the men get a good bit of tobacco and some matches and clothing and socks. If you are asked what men (of all Regiments) want, I don't think you can do better than recommend cigarette papers, mufflers, woollies, warm gloves. Practically everything else is a Government Issue, and they are beginning to send up a good supply of Government stuff now. It is impossible for the men to carry much more than they have already. Of course, delicacies of food they can always do with.

We take cover directly any shelling begins, so we spend very little time outside. The German aeroplanes give ranges to their guns by dropping out smoke balls when they are directly above a trench or body of troops – a very cunning plan – and the guns take the angle. It is a certainty if one sees the smoke ball drop that one will get some shells over very soon after – and very accurately too. I suppose we do something of the same sort to them.

I should not be surprised if we either make our 1st and 3rd Battalions into one Battalion, or practically do so by sending the Headquarters of one home, or to the L. of C. I am afraid three Battalions at war strength was really more than we could have ever maintained with the great loss of Officers we have suffered, and were bound to suffer I suppose. Whatever we do will be at once I expect.

Will you thank Via very much for her letter. She and the S. & G. F.A. are evidently doing most splendid work. Tell her I am glad the Cavalry appreciate us and what we do, as we are all talking of the splendid work the Cavalry have done. Their day has by no means passed, as some wiseacres said before the war. We all heard the Russian rumour, but have heard or seen no more confirmation of it than you at home.

Blanche is doing good work among the men's wives, which the

men appreciate very much. Washing is a difficulty now – but I get a shave and semi-wash every other day – a hot bath would do a lot of good though.

My love to Via and Doreen and all.

Your loving brother

Evelyn

October 13th. Went down to transport about 10 a.m. and found two French Companies who had just come up. Showed the Commander the way to SOUPIR. One Lieutenant came up, we gave him a 'blow-out'. Went foraging before lunch and returned with 3 fowls. Commander, three French Lieutenants, and Francis Scott came to lunch which ran out after a bit. Some very odd conversations went on and almost a continual buzz of "um's and er's" from those less acquainted with the language. Had to forage again after lunch as French Officers eat so much. Guy and Sim came too. Madame Genty obliged with a couple of fowls. Hurried dinner at 5:30. We then got ready to go. A very dark night, but with the help of an electric torch I got all the 1st line turned round facing CYS. At 7:30 p.m. the Battalion came down and we followed. First incident was one SAA got one wheel over side of the bridge, through jibbing, however this was soon put right without damage. The ST. MARD hill then proved too much for the French cart we had commandeered and so I had to send back an SAA cart to help it, which meant dropping men at all crossroads to show them the way. We then proceeded slowly but without incident to PRESLES, where I parked the 1st line in a field and myself in a barn for about 4 hours sleep, having got in about 12. Rather interesting to note the 3rd Battalion Coldstream were the last English troops to leave the trenches on the AISNE.

October 14th. Called at 4:30 a.m. after which Trousers, Darwin and self went down to the station at FISMES to load the 1st line. Found Grenadiers just going. Only just enough trucks, horse went fairly easily, wagons had to be lifted on in most cases. Eventually we got off about 10 o'clock, horses very tightly packed, but all the better for this. I got into a carriage with Colonel, Tony, Alan, and P-J. About 12:30 we felt hungry and so got some food in from next door, through the window. A very messy affair. After a cigar, sleep till 5 and some cold tea. We heard that we were going to halt at AMIENS but we did not. A fair night only. During the afternoon two horses got fairly down in their box and we had to almost slide them out onto the very low platform. Another box was quickly procured and 4 of them put onto the front part of the train. Again at St Denis (PARIS) another got down and somehow got right under the legs of the other 4 horses opposite him. This box had to be taken off and left for the next train.

October 15th. We thought we were going to get ½ hour at CALAIS, and so we had arranged for tea for the men, also an issue of rations. However when everyone was well out of the train, it slowly moved out and left between 500 - 600 men behind, also some 21 Officers. Colonel, Tony, Sim, and self went on. There was a splendid bustle at HAZEBROUCK where we detrained. Luckily the others were only ¾ hour after us. It took about 2 hours to get the old horses and wagons out and then sorted up. We then had to get half up first and come back for the remainder. Remaining 8 horses were walked from ST. OMER about 12 miles by Trousers. The transport yard was a slaughter yard in which a beast is killed every half hour. Headquarters billets excellent, room each nearly, and bath with Geyser. Water smelt a bit but had a good bath. Opened up the drawing room and had a rare dinner.

October 16th. Moved the transport into a field as the slaughter yard smelt so. Found all sorts of things in the town and bought for the mess until I ran out of money. After lunch I took the horses out for a bit of exercise. Some French Cavalry came through (going the wrong way!) to a man we gave a cheer. Lots of troops of sorts in the town, including 3rd Army Headquarters. The Brigadier was coming to dinner, but as it was his 50th birthday, his staff prepared a "Birthday Dinner" for him. However we got a very good one. Got the order to be ready to move at 6 a.m., which rather put a damper on us.

October 17th. Had to be ready to move at 7 a.m., which we did. Got the transport off with difficulty on account of having lost some cooker harness the day before which we supplemented with some drag-ropes. After about the 2nd halt I went on and bought butter, and at this moment one of the SAA carts took the opportunity to fall into the ditch. It was luckily extracted before I returned by Trousers. We got into BOESCHEPE (*West of Ypres, south of Poperinghe*) about midday and found some moderate billets. I put the transport in a field. Very little news from the Front, but we heard that the 3rd and 4th Army were there and so we felt fairly safe. Heard distant guns. Number 1 sent out one Platoon as outpost taking Stobby L-B. Guy S-S (Shaw-Stewart), and self took a walk round. Came across Munro (IInd Division) and he told us a bit before spinning off in his Rolls Royce. Found these French people very hard to understand as they talk a sort of Belgian/German/French. Not much to be got as this small village had 4th Guards Brigade also Divisional Cavalry in it (XVth Hussars). Hobbled around as walking on the march made the toe swell up. Headquarters billet small and so Trousers and self found a very clean one over a shop (outside our area incidentally but no matter). Got a bit of hay, paid for 100 kilos but fancy

Sergeant Doël got about 300 kilos onto the cart. The wine shop for our dining was not very savoury, but had some excellent beer with the result that I slept very well.

October 18th. Unfortunately I did not know the day, and so missed the Early Service in the school. Lots of parcels again and a letter from Cissie telling me Merton (Beckwith-Smith) was wounded. I also saw in Divisional Orders that he had got a DSO, which is splendid. Went to Church in an upstair loft place at 11:00. New Chaplain not so interesting as Fleming. Stamped letters hard up to 12 o'clock, also sent off my second film. After lunch Guy, Trousers, and self had some success with the eggs and returned with some 163, not all quite poachable! Found a Skittle yard in which we made a stump cricket place with the help of a very moderate ball. Got quite a good game. Some difficulty in making some man understand I wanted 7 chickens, as they talk such a Flemish sort of French. However they turned up and the washer up (Facey) pulled their heads off, which had the desired effect but was a primitive way of doing it.

October 19th. Had another jolly good night in my sheets. Lovely day and so took the transport horses out for an hour. Guy S-S came too, mounted on 'Fritz'. Our pub, where we have all meals, terribly hot at luncheon. After lunch Byng, Humphrey (de Trafford), Pro and self went foraging to a farm just beyond the outpost, got about (what they called) "vieux oeufs", also two bottles of cream. Met Budget and Bewicke cycling, carrying 10 live chickens between them in sacks. Had a sort of game of bowls in the skittle ally. A most enormous mail, 20 bags. Personally I got 8 parcels and letters from Via (Sister-in-Law), Ethel Gibbs, Margaret English, and Cissie B-S. I staggered back to my billets and Scott came and put a few into the valise.

October 20th. Heard Sergeant Major's voice outside my window at 5 a.m., still quite dark. Orders to move in an hour's time. Great scramble, luckily my saddle-bags had arrived the night before and so Scott put most of my things into these. Got a bit of breakfast at 5:45 a.m., then dashed down to transport. Brigade moved off 2nd Battalion finding advance guard of 2 Companies, Vanguard, and 2 Companies with Brigadier. Transport Brigade (and always will be now) under Eric Gough (Irish Guards), so we did not move for ¾ hour. Not very cold for a wonder. Got going alright for about 7 or 8 miles, when our 4 year old cart horse in an SAA cart riding horse slipped up on the pavé roads and got cast under the cart. This caused a delay of ¼ hour, however no damage. As we neared YPRES, guns *could* clearly be heard. We were halted inside this town, and heard rumours of the Warwicks having taken the knock the day before. A few minutes later little Willy Gibbs (*William Otter Gibbs*) passed through looking very well, making his way to join his Regiment.

Had a short talk but he had to hurry on. Then Edward Tennant who had just alighted having been out on a bomb throwing expedition. Eventually moved on about 3 p.m. and found Battalion in billet. Just as I got the cookers up they were pulled out and made to go on about 2 miles, and take up a position at ST. JULIAAN, 2 miles N.E. of YPRES. Went on, about 7 or 8 p.m. and got a scramble of a dinner at a farm. Heard rifle fire the whole time just in front of the Warwicks. Had to take the whole lot back to a road ½ mile back in the dark, and leave them on the road, while the Battalion took up battle outposts. Dr. and I found a floor in a cottage for night, but continual firing kept one awake. Night not very cold but raining a bit.

October 21st. Message to take cookers up at 4:45 a.m. Found everyone very cold having had to sleep in the roots. Got breakfast in the dark with difficulty, as we could not light a fire. Went back as soon as it got light. Shelling started about 6:30 a.m., but not very near us. Most of the Blues and 2nd Lancers passed us. The 2nd Lancers having got rather a hard knock the day before. Took lst line back to crossroad 2 miles back. Harry C. and self foraged and found eggs in a deserted farm. Got the woman at H' Cabaret to make us an omelette and coffee for which she charged us 5 francs for 4 of us. Was having a shave in the front room of the Inn when suddenly Wynn L.C. walked in having come up attached to the 60th. Had a long talk to him until the 6th Brigade had to go on. Walked over to 'Cow Guns' and watched them fire for a bit. Several armoured motors passed us with maxims in them. No message for cookers by dark and so prepared to stay night there. Heard Charles Monck killed and Colonel Feilding wounded. Got message at 8 to take cookers up. Some way off but got there then found we were only 400 yards from *the* German trenches. Colonel did not think it safe for me to stay there and so I went back to where I was last night. Met Wright and 2nd line halfway back; great difficulty in passing them. Bedded down in cottage again.

October 22nd. Cookers went up about 5:30 a.m. Found Battalion had had to fall Back during the night as 22nd Brigade had suddenly done so on their right for no apparent reason. Divided Transport up than came up myself, and Sim and I dug ourselves in with a communication tunnel in between, which took me till 3 o'clock. Grant returned to the Battalion, cheery as ever. Dinner in the dark with a very low fire as we are so close to the German trenches - curried bully and cheese. Got down to it about 8 as waited to see cookers off to get supplies. Could not get to sleep for some time as found the tunnel made an awful draught, though read for a bit. Eventually slept till 7 a.m.

October 23rd. Very quiet during the night, but jolly cold even in our bug-hutch. Had a jolly good shave and wash in a farm. Went round and saw horses. Still in the same place for the last 3 nights – North of ST. JEAN and about ½ mile North East of WIELTJE. Shelling became rather heavy and so had to move cookers and mess cart in rather a hurry back to crossroads at WIELTJE where I stayed all day. Lunched with Harry C. and Pritchard at 3rd Battalion expense. Lots of French troops turned up in the afternoon. I suppose to attack. Enormous mail – 35 bags for this Battalion alone. Wrote some seven letters. Got in to a small cottage with Staff Sergeants and waited for orders. At 11 o'clock had some cocoa and lay down.

North of Hazebrouck

23rd October 1914

Darling Nancy

    We have pushed on a bit since we arrived at the above place and are now well at it again. Yesterday I had to take a wretched little German prisoner back to Brigade Head Quarters, he was in quite a good German regiment and was only 16 having been in nearly a year, so they are evidently taking them very young.

    Yesterday I saw little Willy Gibbs at Banon who was riding along to join his regiment, which he said were somewhere on the left – rather vague I thought but he quite expected to find them. Up to date he has been with the 18th Hussars, but now the tenth have come out. Very soon after that I was having a quiet shave in a wayside pub in the front room when Wynn Llewellyn came in, he is attached to the 60th. He brought a certain amount of news. I spent most of yesterday making myself an enormous trench to sleep in. One Taylor and self arranged to dig ours fairly close and have a communicating tunnel in between. I started thinking it was an hour's job, but it took six before it was really good. It wasn't really so good to sleep in as we thought as there was a tremendous draught through the tunnel.

    This morning I got me boots off for the first time for 3 days and also had a shave. Scott arranged it in a farm. ½ an hour after we left it was hit by a German shell and burnt. Think their shells must have something extra in them as lately they have been burning a lot of houses.

    I am safely back with my transport away from danger! Our ginger cake arrived and was very good, also several other things from York.

    Cavan is perfectly splendid and always very calm and collected.

Love to all.

Your loving brother

Lancelot

October 24th. At 5:00 a.m. cycle orderly came with orders for 1st line to go to the Battalion. It is now over 24 hours since they have seen the cookers. Started off in the dark, very cold and my horse very fresh, were taken long way round but eventually came to them at ZILLEBEKE (near YPRES) about 7:00 a.m. Terrible scramble. 3rd Division Cavalry Headquarters, also 1st Army Corps Headquarters, also 4th Brigade in the same village. Just had breakfast and were dishing out shirts, when they said the Germans had got into the wood nearby. "Fuss and bustle as there never was". Eventually got the transport out somehow and along the village whole street packed with motors and carts going in every direction. Men running after them and stuffing things in. Got my carts clear and only hit two motors! Scare very soon quieted down and got transport parked on YPRES-MENIN road and waited. Meanwhile Battalion went up into wood however the Germans had retired long before, routed by some cavalry. Heard Tony Markham had got badly hit in the head and Bewicke Copley slightly in the shoulder, the day before. Came up to Battalion in a field near EKSTERNEST about 4 p.m. Good deal of shelling all around but not near us. Arranged billets in some very dirty farms. Some straw was put in the bar of the local pub and 10 of us slept there. Heard later that Tony M. had died of his wounds.

October 25th. Woke up very cold about 2 a.m. and found I was sleeping under a window, however could not shut it and so dossed down again. Got a 'lick over' only and went down to breakfast in the dark in a field. Lovely sun about 8:30 a.m. got back to a field ¼ mile East of EKSTERNEST in HOGE where we stayed most of the day. Just arranging a nice bed for myself when order came to go up to Battalions. Found they had been in reserve most of the day. Bad road horses had to struggle to get up as only a sand track. Raining hard when I got up about 8:30 p.m. Brigadier allowed us into Headquarters for our dinner. After which I spent the most miserable night I have ever spent. Men were down a side road sleeping in the ditch. While Colonel, Alan D, Trousers, Sim and self got a bench along a wall and sat up against it the whole night with our heads on the next man's shoulder. Rain off the roof dripped straight on us plus the ordinary rain soaked us right through and for most of the night. The bullets that were going high over the firing line, some 400 yards on, whistled round us. However only one man hit. In spite of this we managed to keep very cheery.

October 26th. Before light I collected the cookers and water carts and moved off back to the field we were in yesterday. This sand road now a perfect 'quagmire'. As I got out onto the main YPRES road who should come past but the lst Battalion. Got hold of Evelyn (GIBBS) and rode about ½ mile with him. Found him very well but his Battalion had suffered terribly. Only 10 Officers left at all and only 80 men in Evelyn's

Company. They went on up to GHELUVELT and so I went back to the old field. Lit fires and got a hit dry, managed to get a sort of shave. Younger, with lst Division Cyclist Company came up later and we talked for about an hour while he waited for orders. Whole day driblets of 7th Division, which has been so hammered for the last few days, came past us making for their Battalions. Very unfortunate incident happened in the evening. British Airmen flew over throwing out aiming marks for our artillery and for some reason one Regiment, said to be Highland Light Infantry, but I am not sure, thought he was a German and fired on him. There can have been little excuse since as he was flying over his own people he was flying very low. The second volley fired his petrol tank and down it came, both men being killed and the machine burnt. A rumour came out that it was Germans flying under English Colours, but this was not so. About 5 p.m. we moved up to Battalion, which by now had got into trenches in the firing line. Very little damage during day. Budget Lloyd got slight wound in the head. A scratch dinner in the dark, then got a very shallow trench run up for me and got in. About ½ hour later very heavy fire started, bullets whistling over at about 50 a minute. We replied a bit. I thought they were probably going to try and rush our trenches with the bayonet but nothing happened and after ½ hour of it all was quiet, and except for an occasional shot nothing more happened. It was this night I have since discovered that the Scots Guards (20th Brigade) got so badly cut up, losing upwards of 300 – 400 killed and wounded. The Germans had evidently had to go back rather hurriedly from our trenches as the whole way up on the path there were dead bodies of Germans, so there must be many more in the wood.

October 27th. Woke up at about 4:30 a.m. very cold and cramped as my trench is not long enough. Breakfast was brought up in the dark and with difficulty we ate it. I got away about 5:30 a.m. and took the cookers back again to the old field which is now about a mile back – found a better road. Met Francis G-L (Gore-Langton) with 1st Battalion Transport, who told me Murray had been killed and Warde-Aldam wounded leaving them 8 officers only. Got some more sleep in the morning and waited about. Came upon rather a bad sight in the afternoon just as we were going up again. Scots Guards (20th Brigade Battalion) having been relieved out of the firing line calling the roll of the Battalion, which I heard came to under 300 (1,020 being war strength). 2nd Battalion still in same trenches which they had improved (all except mine!). Sat down to dinner in the dark when suddenly the firing started, everyone scrambled for their trenches, jammy bread in one hand, cocoa in the other, which lasted about 20 minutes, with the same result as the night before, i.e. no-one touched. We then resumed our meal everyone roaring with laughter at what had happened. Firing continued more or less the whole night, no damage.

Tuesday 27 October 1914

Dearest Nancy

Just a hasty scrawl to tell you that the N.S.Y. go out on the 30th inst. - i.e. Friday. I enclose a letter from Lags.

We are getting new rifles and clothes for the men in two days and there will be a frightful hurroosh I expect. We only heard at 6.30 this morning

I don't suppose I shall have much time for writing so this had better be goodbye. Give my best love to Staff and the chicks. I am very glad that I caught a glimpse of you and it was very lucky.

Good bye old girl

Your loving Eustace

October 28th. Breakfasted in the light, slept a bit better as kept my legs warm with my motor-bicycling trousers. Got off about 7 a.m. and got back safely. Paid Francis G-L a visit and heard 1st Battalion and Evelyn all safe. Very cold again but soon got a good fug-up in our bug hutch. Shelling continued very heavily most of the day but did not reach us. German aeroplane flew over and gave some ranging marks. Got heavily shot at but no result. Simply overwhelmed with parcels getting some 22, however they were quickly disposed of as a good many were presents to the men. Had a pretty fair wash during the afternoon, having missed it for some 5 days. Order to go up came very late and we did not leave here until 5:30 p.m. already very cold. Got up and fed Battalion as usual. Heard an attack was likely and so took horses to a place of safety. In so doing I found a very good bug hutch in a ditch built by R.F.A., which I slept in and kept very warm – best night I have had for weeks.

October 28th 1914

Letter to Nancy

We have not moved on much during the last few days and have had a fairish battle round here. However Evelyn and I are well and happy. I saw him two days ago for ten minutes, they are quite near us now – his division. I had a letter from Stafford this morning he seems very anxious to come out and says that if our chaplain is sick but of course we have not got one of our own, they are a corps of their own attached to the Ambulance.

from Lags

This is the only one I have had for ages. Evelyn and a lot were taken prisoners last Friday, all wounded slightly they think. We shall now have to wait patiently.

October 29th. Woke up at 4:30 a.m.; went down with cookers and so to the trenches. Very white frost, a proper cold. Found no attack had been made. Suppose the Germans funked it. However later they attacked the first Brigade, which was successful for a short time but they were quickly counter-attacked. "Black Maria" dropped into Brigade ammunition reserve, killing about 5 men and wounding 6 others. One man of mine got his arm blown quite off, poor fellow. 'Winley' a pioneer. I am afraid he may die. Asked all 1st Battalion I met if they knew anything of Evelyn, but they were all too scared to know anything. Stood up on the road waiting and asking. Eventually a machine-gun sergeant told me Number 3 had been surrounded and were fighting hack to back, Evelyn in the middle. I then went to 1st Brigade Headquarters and saw a message he had written at 7:40 a.m. to say he was surrounded (attack started at 5:30 a.m.) After taking cookers up, I rode on ahead back into the advance Hospital. Simply pouring with rain. No sign of Evelyn. Then on back into YPRES to the main Hospital and looked all round it. Found Francis Gore-Langton, who being Transport Officer, knew nothing except what he had heard. Eventually got back to my hut soaked, tired and very depressed.

October 30th. After breakfast I again went on to the road, but few Coldstreamers were now passing. Heard from Sergeant Harris (1st Coldstream Guards Cycle Company) that all 1st Battalion were collecting up the road by the Château. I quickly went up there, where I found Boyd (Quarter Master) who told me that as far as he knew at present, he was <u>the only officer of the 1st Battalion left.</u> This news was awful yesterday I did hope there were 5 of them. Went to 1st Brigade again who knew nothing of anyone except Boyd and 80 men. Heard from a Corporal of Evelyn's Company that they had been surrounded, and the last he saw of Evelyn, he was standing with about 11 men round him trying to fight their way out. The 1st Grenadiers having retired from their right, so letting the Germans get in behind. No news by the time I took cookers up. Found Nobby Legge had been killed by a shrapnel shell. He had just got out of his trench to give an order, and got hit right through the head. Dinner rather cold by the time I got it up there. Found them all rather depressed. Got away about 7:30 p.m.

October 31st. Let the cookers up alone. Got on the road but found no more news. Made Nobby's things into a parcel and sent them off to Lady Victoria. Things not going very well. Eventually at about midday we heard that they had broken through at GHELUVELT. Great consternation. Got horses in very quickly and onto the road, found they were going 3 deep towards YPRES. When we got as far as the railway crossing at HALTE found things had quieted down, and so pulled out on the left. Found Grenadiers and Irish Guards there who had been detached from us 2 days before. About 3 or 4 o'clock the crowd ceased and so I sent up to Colonel and got the order to move up to old place about 5:30 p.m. Everyone thought we were mad going up that road, but we got up without any shelling. Found them all rather excited, but managed to calm them down.

November 1st. Let cookers go up alone and hoped to get a bit of sleep, but had a bad toothache and so got little. Guns came into our field and so we moved into wood behind the Château. Met little Willy who had just come in, walked about with him most of the morning. Grant H came down very badly wounded in the head. Got him into Cavalry Ambulance and sent him in to YPRES. After lunch we got heavily shelled and several artillery men got hit. Made ourselves a very indifferent bug hutch. Then moved higher up the field; no casualties. Found going up to Battalion no joke now. Ist Brigade have brought their line of trenches back to "Six cross-roads". Bullets whistling uncomfortably near us. Went round N.E. side of wood as German snipers around the old way. Very deep and heavy road. About a mile's walk to Battalion Headquarters when we did get there.

November 2nd. Had a wretched night as had to share a very small bed with Archie Trotter who had just returned to his Battalion. Started up at 2:45 a.m. so as to do it all in the dark. Got away without incident. Found Château grounds too hot for us and so moved down towards YPRES. Spent most of the morning making a bug hutch. Got about ½ hour's sleep in the afternoon. Heard that enemy had broken through on our ½ right, but were pushed back again. Things evidently not going too well. Lot of wounded coming down all day. Started to go up about 5:30 p.m. but shelling too heavy; heard lots of rumours about Germans breaking through but none true. Got away; up about 7 p.m.; back about 11 p.m. Just got to sleep when there was a cry that the enemy were coming down the road: dashed out and harnessed up; then found it was an excited Corporal. Stopped in road for a bit with A. Provost and pushed people back. Got no bed.

November 3rd. Went up again at 2:30 a.m. Some of the Companies very late with breakfast. Did not get away until 6:30 and tried to find FREZENBERG. Great difficulty as we had to dodge the shells as well. Got into one field then had to shift, had a few words with a French Corporal (each in our own tongue!) Eventually stopped in the field much to the Corporal's disgust. Had a pretty fair sleep as this field was comparatively quiet. We were right in the midst of the French Cavalry, who were stopping behind hedges and in barns. Some very fine uniforms among them. Had a talk to one officer who wanted to know all about our cookers, the French Army not having anything of the kind. Started back stopping at EKSTERNEST on the way to drop kit for supplies and thence up to Battalion. Found poor Graves-Sawle had been killed in much the same way as Nobby Legge was by shrapnel (Lt. Nigel Legge-Bourke). Went up to and had dinner with No: 3. Had not seen Humphrey and Pro for a very long time. They had a great story of how the Germans got up within 8 feet of their trench and cut some wire during the night before. Colonel asked me to take a day off in YPRES, but I declined. Went back for supplies and found Rooke there with a draft of 80 men. Brought him up and we shared a dug-out we found.

November 4th. Came down fairly well in dark, but they plunked a few shells at us near EKSTERNEST. Got some straw under the hedge and made up a bit for my two hours sleep during the night. Got a bit of a wash and shave and felt much cleaner although rather cold! One of our No.1 cooks did my eggs and bacon for me. Except that he made full use of his fingers, he did it well. Met one Boril (Gunner and friend of Little Willy's) who seemed rather depressed about the position, but think he is wrong, as we have heard two French Army Corps are coming up. Almost continuous gun-fire all along the line at about 50 a minute the whole day. Started to rain hard which made it miserable. Found Nos: 1 and 4 Companies in reserve and having dinner in a house. Colonel Westmacott (Commanding 5th Brigade) came to dine. Other wretched devils had to go back to the trenches. I stayed in the house and let the cookers draw supplies on their own.

Ypres

4th November 1914

Darling Nancy,

    I am afraid by now you will have seen in the paper that Evelyn is "missing". Personally I feel <u>quite</u> confident that he is all right. I heard from quite a sensible man in his company that the last he saw of him was that he was <u>slightly</u> wounded but still standing up, his company quite surrounded and about 100 to 150 of them were just afterwards taken prisoner. From the accounts our Army Doctor, who was captured and got away, gives of the way they treat our wounded, I feel sure he will be quite all right again. It has just started to rain which makes sleeping out very unpleasant, however we cannot complain much of the weather as up to date we have had very little wet.

    Your presents arrive very regular, as a matter o' fact without seeming ungrateful I am afraid I don't like ginger, and so those excellent finger cakes I am afraid are rather wasted on me. - I hope we shall push on from this place (Ypres) very shortly, as the French will probably give them a bit of a knock, at least we hope so.

Ever your loving brother,

Lags.

November 5th. Rare bit of sleep for once from about 9:30 p.m. to 5 a.m. Roads in a most awful state as French guns use same road as I do. Met French Gunner lieutenant who had lost his gun, could not help him much as he would talk so fast. Scott had got a bit of a bug hutch for me out of straw. A Buzzard Cake and a few things from Cissie came which was splendid as had no lunch. Also a 6ft waterproof bag from Blanche, which I think I shall sleep in, instead of Evelyn's waterproof sheet which is very heavy. Sun came out so I dried my boots. Scott prepared me a splendid meal with some potatoes he 'pinched' out of a farm close by. Could get no news. Met 150 men from lst Battalion who had come to join on to us under Sergeant Parkin (no officers). Took them up to Sergeant-Major. Dined up in the trenches. Everyone much the same; the official report gave good news, so I hope we may push on. I think the Germans find the "Contemptible Little Army" a hard nut to crack, as in their orders they expected to be in YPRES by 30th October, and they are now a week late and no nearer. Found 2nd Battalion 60th Rifles back at 5th Brigade Headquarters ready to support us. They were reduced to 86 men and 7 Officers (Wynn Ll. with them before he was wounded). Slight alarm about mid-night but it quieted down and we got to sleep.

November 6th. Pitt called me at 4:30 a.m. and gave me some porridge and eggs, sausages and bacon. Very cold out and strong white frost. Got back to our field at FREZENBERG about 7 a.m. Went to sleep again for a bit and then opened some papers sent me by Ruby (Gibbs). Scott made mean excellent lunch with the help of Fortnum & Mason - Grouse, Paté de Foie gras, jam and coffee. We certainly never lack food; men included who still get done excellently and plentifully. Wrote letters after lunch. Glorious day and quite warm. Nothing much happened. A good deal of rifle and gunfire on right somewhere beyond HOGE I should think. Went up without incident at 5:30 p.m.

November 7th. Slept the night in a trench in the wood by Sergeant Major, as "Black Maria" had hit mess house yesterday and unfortunately killed both Grey and Facey, absolutely blown to hits. Took mess cart back with me to FREZENBERG, much colder. Good deal of firing today by ZONNEBEKE. Armoured train (English) went up and had a few rounds. Cubitt came and had some luncheon, which consisted of 2 pigeons shot by someone on the Transport with a gun he had "found"! Started for

Battalion at 5 p.m. but had to stop about a mile on as firing heavy. Got on about 5 hour later when bullets ceased to fly. Road getting very heavy and full of holes made by "Black Marias".

November 8th. Slept in a splendid 'dug-out' made for Sinclair our (M.O.) which he did not want. Pitt woke me about 5 a.m. and I got something to drink. Perfectly beastly day, cold and wet, misty. Got all cookers back by 7 a.m. including lst Battalion one, who are now attached to us, so putting the whole Regiment in one line under Pinto. Talked to a French Artillery Commodore, but he seemed to know surprisingly little, or else I could not understand all he said. Passed a day full of sleep in my straw bug-hutch as built by a French Guard and used by them at night. Dug myself a chair and table in the ground. Also worked hard at a dug-out which I completed just in time. Off we go again but only got about ¾ mile this time when there was a heavy attack on the right. Stopped for ½ hour and then got on up. On the way through the wood I found one of the pack-horses had fallen off a wooden bridge into the stream upside down, about 6 Dixies of tea waiting to pass up to men in the trenches (this was about 300 yards behind trenches), just at this moment a hellish rifle fire broke out. So made all the men lie down and crawled down to the horse and held him still, after about 10 minutes it quieted down, so I got men across to their Companies. Found this horse had been there some time and the men were trying to pull him out by his tail! 6 men and a rope round his neck soon got him out, and I got up to my dinner in the trenches. Found Alan D had gone sick with a sort of rheumatism otherwise all well. Quieter night except for an attack obviously made some way to our left. Slept with Cubitt in Sinclair's dug-out again.

8th November 1914

Darling Nancy,
 We are still in much the same place as when last I wrote near Ypres. For the moment we have left Cavan, as the Brigade has divided up but I expect very shortly we shall get back.
 I wonder if Old York and Hasty are doing much this year and if you have any Canadian horse billeted on you, you can take out. Good things arrive from Collins of York and frequently for which many thanks.
 We hope very shortly now to get a move on from this place from one side or other. I wonder if you would like to send me something that is a cholera belt or tummy band made by Dr Jäegar. I don't know what my size is but I am fairly flat. Love to all

Your loving

Lags

November 9th. Nothing much happened.

November 10th. Had SAA cart horses and chargers exercised from 3:30 to 4:45 a.m., beastly cold day. Found my horse (Evelyn's} a bit lame, think he must have strained his tendons a bit in the dark. Found my dugout a great blessing today as there was a bitter wind. Opened about 5 parcels of Evelyn's. Walked down to 1st Division Headquarters but got no news. Everyone seems to think the war will be over by Christmas which is good. washed my feet in a barn! Very heavy firing on the left and fairly heavy on the right, our wood seems fairly quiet. Had a letter from Margaret English and from Nancy (*sister*) – who is very good and writes about twice a week. No letter from Blanche for over a week!!

November 11th. Still very wet in the morning from having fallen into a small brook about 9 p.m. last night. Came down a new way with the mess cart, shorter but a worse road. Shells were bursting everywhere. I then saw some stragglers coming down the road and found they were Camerons and Black watch. Apparently the Germans had broken through on the right by the HOSE-GHELUVELT road and had got right onto the heights. Got all ready to move and stopped everyone I saw. Gunners got very excited. However about an hour later (3 p.m.) things seemed to have quieted down, but I had to keep on the move. At about 5 p.m. Harry C and self walked over to No. 9 Battery Headquarters who said it was pretty quiet now, so off we started. 4 shrapnel seem to burst right over us at EKSTERNEST but did no damage. Darkest night I have ever been out on, but driver drove very well – no accidents occurred. Found Battalion fairly cheery with a good intelligence summary.

12th November 1914

Darling Nancy

    11 pairs of socks and one pair of mitts to hand for which many thanks. I have kept one pair and given the rest to my Transport men of which there are 40, I pair between 4, as Scott did not require any more. Hurrah! S has just brought me a bucket with holes all round and full of red hot charcoal which he has put at the door of my dug out bed, set up about four feet under ground and sit there all day having fixed up boxes let into the sides for shelves. Come what may in the way of shrapnel shells and I am safe then! Too dark to write more.

                  Your loving lags

Thank Stafford for his letter.

November 12th. 3 months since Battalion left Windsor and might be 3 years. Down again and safely bedded down, when brutes started to shell road just by us. Then French Battery choose field next door to us to take up a position. Had to move horses back one field, but left everything else. Started to dig another underground place so as to communicate with Cubitt's and mine. Wrote to Mercy (sister-in-law), Blanche, also Thompson and Fortnum & Mason. Soon got tired of digging. Started to rain about 4:30 p.m. and continued doing so until we got up to the Battalion. Walking through the wood one was up to one's ankles in mud the whole way. Found Pro Leigh-Bennett had been slightly wounded by one of the hand grenades the Germans had thrown, also an R. E. Officer. Talked to Sinclair over a cup of cocoa until about 10 or 11 o'clock, and then got into his dug-out as usual.

November 13th. Night pretty quiet. I did not wake until 6 a.m.. Went down feeling in a very had temper as had got a bit of a chill: vented it on one or two. Started to rain so got into my dug-out and put the coal bucket in the doorway and wrote letters. Stayed there most of the day and got dripped on. Got a notice that 5 horses were coming to us, which brings us up to strength. Road up now a perfect river. Got up fairly quietly on the whole. Heard French had driven Germans back ¾ mile on our left. Our dining-room leaked terribly and Gilly would keep putting the butter under it. Did not waste much time, our position exactly the same. They had been fairly heavily shelled. Gunners lost 40 horses but no men. Our casualties about the same as usual 6 - 8. Dug-out very wet but slept alright.

November 14th. Stayed up to see horses, had breakfast with Sinclair. Poor old Brocklehurst came in wounded for the second time this war, shot through the ankle, not very bad. Rode off back about 9:30 a.m., still raining hard, had a few shrapnel pretty close just before I got into EKSTERNEST, which made me trot otherwise quiet. Spent most of the day in a house occupied by the French Artillery Commandant. Went off after dark, still raining hard: roads in a very bad state. Got held up by French Infantry and 2 Batteries, but managed to charge past them much to their annoyance. Mess cart got stuck in a shell hole and nearly run down by an English Battery. Tried lead horse in it, but it did nothing but turn round and look at the shaft horse.

November 15th. Snowing hard when I got up. Looked round horses, had to go back by different road as EKSTERNEST under heavy shrapnel fire. Found a lot of dead horses on the road, the effect of last night's shelling. Passed French 'Place de Secours' (Red Cross), which seemed very full. Kept indoors most of the day, as got dysentery a bit and very cold. Heard likelihood of leaving for a rest. About 5:30 p.m. in rain we started off, had to break into some French Infantry and got through in bits. 3rd Battalion mess cart turned right over by windmill at FREZENBERG, got it back with difficulty. Water cart got into a ditch, pulled out by Artillery horses. 2nd Battalion mess cart broke trace catch on the hill, fixed up with halter, and then it got into a shell hole. Man-handled out and eventually got all up. Water cart went to fill and got turned over, got it back about 3 a.m.; other one went to fill at farm close by got hit by shell: lead horse killed, shell case went through the cart, man and other horse not touched.

Sunday November 15th 1914

My dearest Nan

Many thanks for your letter also for the Bromo-Seltzer. It is a capital plan and please send some whenever you should write.

Well here we are right in the thick of it. We took 12 hours on the sea passage, then two nights in a barn, then 24 hours in a train, one night in some French cavalry barracks. Then we marched three days up to where we are now. Our first march was very unpleasant - as we did not get in till about 10 at night. A pitch-dark night and raining most of the time. These Belgian roads are in a terrible state - the pavé along the middle slopes down to each side then at each side is a regular quagmire. One of our waggons upset. I believe we passed through the place where Lags is. Eventually we got up the day before yesterday to the very thick of it. We were shelled going along a road and then tied our horses up in a field which we were told would be our permanent headquarters. The fun began pretty soon with shells from the big German siege guns. One landed in a field where A squadron horses were and Ernest was knocked over by the concussion - unhurt however. Then one landed just outside our field and another one just in the hedge of our field when one of our lads was knocked down by a rock thrown up. He was more frightened than hurt. Then just as it got dark we were suddenly told that we had to move out on foot as the Germans were attacking strongly. We sloshed out in the mud for about 3 miles, waited about for a bit and were then told we were not wanted. Coming back the road was a mass of soldiery of French, Belgian and English and the rear troop of our squadron lost touch and got separated – I was behind and did not know it for a bit – however got them back alright. We then put the men into their billets in two houses and went into ours in a small château. We were told that they usually stop shelling the town at night but this night they did not. I forgot to say that just before moving off that night on foot we all formed up whilst more ammunition was dealt out. We had not moved off more than a few minutes when a shell pitched just where our squadron had been. It was a wonderful escape as it would have got us all. Well to continue, Lionel, Guy, Ralph and I were to have slept upstairs but after one or two shells had whistled over the house we elected to sleep in the cellar – a tiny place where we all got in somehow – Lionel with his head on my tummy.

Another shell pitched in the garden and then one twenty yards from the house right in line with it. This smashed every window in the house and several bits of shell buried themselves in the wall. We then got orders (2.30 a.m.) to get saddled up and move out. We got ready and then waited until just before dawn all half asleep and making a meal off burgundy (found in the cellar) and bread and jam. Everybody was and had been for some time pretty frightened and several had been cut with glass.

I am bound to say that those big shells are most terrifying as they make a noise like a small clap of thunder and make a hole 20 feet deep and 25 feet in diameter, a ready made duck pond every time. We got off at dawn and joined the rest of our brigade in a small railway cutting. However about midday they started on us with shrapnel and we had to move back to where we are now. I can't see what use cavalry are in this battle and I think that when more infantry come up we shall go back a bit. There has been almost incessant cannonading for three days and even here the windows were rattling all the time.

Tonight we are to have our first experience in the trenches for 48 hours. We move up as near as we can on horses and then go on foot. Several people have told us that our first experience has been a pretty hot one and we are very lucky. Certainly we all owned that we were very frightened. This is the first moment I have had for writing and I must stop in a moment. It has rained on and off for the last week and today all the men are soaked and we shall get to the trenches very wet. It has turned very cold today and has been snowing so we are not looking forward to the next two nights. Our poor horses have had an awful time and will not last long at this rate.

I have not written to Blanche as she will hear of me from Huie and Guy but would you send this to Albinia or anyone who would care to see it. Huie and I were much relieved to hear that Evelyn is probably a prisoner.

We have had one lot of letters and papers and know very little of what is going on, but believe we have an awful lot of Germans against us here and that the fighting is fiercest here.

Good bye

Your loving Brother

Eustace

November 16th. After breakfast went round horses. Shell case passed my head about a yard off, and so I came in for a bit as a lot were falling round and about. Stayed up at wood ready to go off. Two more came and killed 5 horses and one other which killed a sixth and damaged the water cart. Lot of French troops turned up in a vague sort of way. Rumours of our going for rest seem to be coming true. No orders for our destination but ordered to go to ZILLEBEKE for night. I took all transport off at 8 p.m. First a SAA cart got stuck 100 yards off. This took 3 hour to get out. 10 yards on a water cart went sideways into a "Black-Maria" hole. While trying to get that out rest went on wrong way, stumbled after them and put them right. Eventually got to field to fill up and found Ambulance having moved with French supply wagons which stopped us parking. Gave justice in favour of Britain and so on. Got to ZILLEBEKE about 12:30 a.m., sleeting hard.

November 17th. Found orders for Battalion to take up reserve trenches and no sign of rest. Waited about until 4:30 a.m. and went to Brigade office (4th Guards Brigade) again. Told to go to crossroads at HALTE and give them breakfast there. Went then and waited while it got light. Heavily shelled but no Battalion. Eventually about 9 a.m. got orders to go back to ZILLEBEKE to them; got there. Shells simply flew about. Men got into trenches. Colonel told me to take Alan's place as Adjutant until he came back. Much warmer with sun. Seldom had so many shells round us, but none came into us at all. One Corporal got hit by shrapnel. Suddenly found our Battalion was in support to North Somerset Yeomanry. Tried to go up to trenches but found it was too dangerous, bullets everywhere. Saw their Doctor also Longridge. Gillie's Company went up later and got into Eustace's (Gibbs) trenches. H-E-G-R-L Gibbs' all well. (Hubert, Eustace, Guy, Ralph and Lionel). Felt very weary as no bed last night. Got into my straw about 9 after a huge dinner (first for 3 weeks). Sergeant-Major came with note about 11 p.m., had to go out and get grave digging party for 2nd Grenadiers Guards officers. More orders about 12:30 and then I got to sleep. (*Guy, Ralph and Lionel Gibbs were sons of Henry Martin Gibbs younget son of William Gibbs of Tyntesfield*).

November 18th. White frost and very cold. Colonel and self walked round Companies and made several suggestions. Came in and gingered up fire in house, not very much doing. One Straker came in and played and sang to us most excellently, really quite cheered us up. About 5 p.m. we got our orders to go for rest, so we started to make great preparations. Got off going into trenches as 3rd Battalion doing it. Got to bed early.

November 18th 1914:

Antony Hubert Gibbs to his sister Nancy (Anstice Katharine).
North Somerset Yeomanry in the Trenches.

We have spent two days and a night here now, and it is now the second day. We hope to be relieved this evening – death seems very close all the time. The shells are horrid. The men are behaving very well, but it is trying them very high. Bates was hit by a sniper on the cheekbone yesterday, but I hear not badly. We are doing the work of Infantry, which we were never trained for. I sent Cowell back with the horses. He keeps in very good spirits. I have not washed for a week – it has rained nearly all the time and the mud is awful. It is very cold at nights, water drips all the time, so this letter will be rather a smudge.

We hear no news and have no idea how things are going on. We heard of Lord Roberts' death at St. Omer – I suppose it was heart failure.

We got back to our billets last night about 1.30 a.m. The Regiment has no doubt covered itself with glory – we lost 22 killed, 39 wounded – of this number B Squadron lost 16 killed and 18 wounded, amongst the killed are poor Fred Liebert and Jack Davy, both killed instantaneously, Corporal Thomas who cut my hair, one of the Dickinsons and young Glass. The wounded include Sergeant Watte badly in the foot, Seymour in the neck, not bad, Bates slightly in the chin, Bailward in the head, the Doctor thinks not seriously, young Barstow hit twice, but walked back all right. He was knocked out by a shrapnel in the head, but got well enough to help carry another man and got hit by a maxi just above the right wrist while doing so.

However, he came in quite cheerfully to be dressed, and was very brave. Davenport hit slightly in the back, but still cheerful and walked to the ambulance. Lancelot was quite close last night, Eustace saw Gilly Follett. I wish we could have seen Lags – he was galloper for Cavan, and was sent to tell the Coldstreams to come and support us. They had the misfortune to lose two officers and 7 men just behind us. I was with our reserve all the time and moved up to the support towards the end, when the First Lifeguards came up, shortly to be followed by the Coldstreams. We are now told that we move back 15 miles tomorrow for a week to refit. I hope we do because I am sure the regiment wants a rest to recover a bit. I should not like to take them into the trenches for a bit, as a great number of them are very shaken.

Our Brigadier came this morning and addressed us in very complimentary terms, which I am sure we deserved. I hear the other regiments were very complimentary to us yesterday. It was a very severe attack, and the fact that we repulsed it, speaks for itself, but between ourselves I think it was trying us a bit too high.

Some of the Germans who advanced to within 20 yards of the trenches staggered along with their hands over their faces so Eustace tells me. Eustace and the three boys did splendidly. Yesterday was much the most severe, and B Squadron were in the front trenches, they all say they hope never to see such a day again, and can't imagine how they survived. The 3rd Dragoon Guards who are on our left lost very heavily, and we kept on moving to the left of the trench to help them. Ernest English went up with some of A. Squadron in the afternoon to reinforce them and behaved very well. C Squadron did not have so much to do, being reserve to the 10th Hussars, both days, and had two wounded only. The Brigadier said this morning that we are not likely to have such a severe trial again as the last two days. The shelling was frightful and very few regiments have had such an introduction to fighting as we have. The big shells which were poured on us when we first arrived here, or rather in the town, where we spent our first night, 11 falling amongst us in the twelve hours we were there, but hurting nobody, so the whole brigade moved three miles out to this farm. We got our second consignment of letters and parcels this morning. Please send me a mackintosh – I lost mine yesterday, also a thin sou'wester hat.

I don't think the Germans are going to push us back here, but any good news encourages everyone very much. They are burying poor Fred and Jack today. The Colonel and several others have gone in this morning to Ypres for the service, so I am left in charge. I got six of your letters this morning, also a Fortnum and Mason parcel, 2 shirts, socks, cigarettes, tobacco, matches, a folding lamp, most useful – we should like more candles, Peel's boots, the Turnicot, the Iodine, cigarette lighter, a tin of food from Tyntesfield and the Mentholated tin.

Cowell was very glad to see me back. It snowed this morning and there was ice on the pond.

We hear this morning of a great sea fight, in which we have come off best – if it is true it ought to help matters a lot. You cannot imagine how dirty I am, I hope to get a basin to wash in this afternoon – all the water is filthy and the farmhouse also. We sleep in a barn on straw, very draughty.

The German spies are everywhere and we keep on catching them. Kiss the children, I will write to them soon.

Huie

November 19th. Only disturbed once during the night; got up about 7. Found a strong black frost. Walked round Companies with Colonel. Found poor old woman who had been killed about a week ago and left on the ground. They suddenly got our range with their small guns, and put about 20 into our farm and around the trenches, however no one touched. Colonel and self took cover in a trench. Sat in our dug-out for a bit and then we returned one by one like rabbits. After lunch Colonel and self went down to Brigade Headquarters and got our orders to relieve Herts. Territorials. This we did at 7 p.m. in a heavy snow storm. Luckily Colonel did not want me so I had a warm night, Gillie and I bedded down in straw.

November 20th. Gillie woke me up when he went off to meet the French officers to show them the trenches. I got up at 8. Sat round the fire most of the morning, ground all covered with snow. Got orders about the officers leave and sent it on up to the Colonel. Gillie returned about 3 having been driven about with a French Colonel. Colonel sent back list of leave, self to have second week. Had dinner about 6. Very cold, waited for a long time, eventually at about 10:30 p.m. Colonel and some men came having had to withdraw these men before the French arrived as they had far fewer number to cover the trenches! About 12:30 we were ready and moved off slowly. Roads covered with ice.

November 21st. I got warmer as we walked along. About 8 miles on we got blocked by other troops. Moved on slowly for about an hour, then we got blocked by transport from about 4 - 5 a.m., the coldest hour I have ever spent. Eventually about 5:30 a.m. we got to OUDERDOM, where we found the first line with breakfast ready for us. An hour later we started off the 1st line with us and managed to cut in, in front of some Ambulances. We got the Battalion along but the transport got cut off. The whole way along we came across SAA carts, G. S. wagons, and which simply could not move for the ice. We got to METEREN about 11:30 a.m., Towers-Clark had found us quite good billets, but the men were most awfully crowded. The whole of the rest of the day we went round trying to expand our area and getting the horses in. Also numerous messages arrived up to mid-night. Got to bed about 9 p.m., done to a turn.

November 22nd. Up about 8:00 and went to Holy Communion at 4th Brigade Headquarters, very few people there. Sat in our improvised Orderly room most of the morning writing. Went to Church again at 11:30 a.m. in village Roman Catholic Church, done by 4th Field Ambulance Chaplain. Still very cold and a hard frost.

November 23rd. Had Commanding Officer's orders at 9:30 a.m., very little for them. Colonel went round billets directly after them. We then walked about ½ mile out to No: 4 who had moved to a farm. After luncheon I chartered Sergeant Sutherland's bicycle and went to try and find the North Somerset Yeomanry at LA COURONNE, got there about 3 p.m., and went all over the country asking at every Headquarters I could see. Eventually, at a quarter to 6, I came up to Eustace, Guy, Ralph, and Lionel (all Gibbs) in a farm. Huie (also Gibbs – *Antony Hubert*) turned up very soon after. They were very well and cheery having had an awful two days in the trenches. Started off back about 6:15 p.m., bright moon and very frosty. Got into dinner about 7:30 p.m. Found Wilfred Smith dining.

November 24th. After orders Colonel went on route march, I stayed and wrote. Lots of messages kept pouring in, eventually was in all afternoon. Colonels Ponsonby and Feilding came to dine, and so we had all 3 Colonels of the Coldstreams in a line rather a record on active service.

November 25th. Very little of importance happened. I started to go and see North Somerset Yeomanry, but met Huie and Eustace in VIEUX BERQUIN so turned round and brought them back to tea at METEREN. Paddy Beaumont-Nesbitt came to dine, also Crawley de Crespigny, most amusing dinner.

November 26th. Gave billets a miss. Found my old German horse very bad with mange, fear I shall have to shoot him. Walked into BAILLEUL with Byng H. found little to buy. Carried a heavy tin of paraffin back and then found there was an issue of it. Dined with Grenadiers, found China (?), Edward Tennant and Prince of Wales there. Stayed till 10:30 p.m. Very amusing dinner, China had thrilling stories of fights in the air.

November 27th. Had to shoot my old horse, very sad about it. Much less cold and roads filthy as all thawed. Rode into BAILLEUL with Sim and bought lots of grapes to take to England. Jimmy Horlick came to dinner, got to bed early.

November 28th. Woke up early and felt as if I was going home from a Private School for the Summer Holidays. Very little happened all day. About 9 p.m. the others returned off leave and as soon as I had handed over to Trousers; Sim, Fatty, Rooke, and self dashed round to the 3rd Battalion Coldstream Guards and stepped lightly into the Rolls Royce and went off. They went at breakneck speed and were continuously stopped by sentries.

November 29th. Got to BOULOGNE about 3:30 a.m., had some tea from some ladies who were on the station and as there was nowhere else to sleep we got down to it in the cabins of the ship we were going in. Rough crossing about 11:30 a.m. (saw Bella Young just before starting). English carriages seemed very comfortable. Huie, Mercy, and Uncle Reggie met me at Victoria. Went back to Church at Chester Square. Blanche, George. Via, Eustace, Nancy and Albinia came up for dinner – talked long.

November 30th. We all shopped very hard, went round in a car hired by Blanche. Got back to tea, 15 of us dined at Prince's and went on to Hippodrome and a play. Eustace, Willy, and self went out to "400" for an hour or so and thence to bed.

December 1st. Up rather late. Huie and Eustace had to go off at 1 p.m., we all went and saw them off; great crowd going by that train. Blanche and self, also Margot (Gibbs) went off shopping. Went and saw Dentist. He hurt a bit. Saw Alan D. also Lockwoods. Then Albinia, Mercy, Margot, Uncle Reggie and self dined and went to play.

December 2nd. Dentist again, also Doctor. Got through the day mostly shopping. Spent evening in doing Mess Bills, which I did not complete.

December 3rd. Lunched with Arch Bishop (*Cosmo Lang*). Had a wire saying I had got an extra day. Did a lot of telephoning about party for tonight. Blanche rather late dressing, so I took the hired car on to Berkeley and party turned up consisting of Amy (Coats) and Doris Gordon-Lennox, Rupert and Mrs. Clutterbuck, Margot, Cissie, Miss Somers Cocks, Paddy Beaumont-Nesbitt, Eric Mackenzie, Budget Lloyd, George Lane, Dermot Brown. Had a large box at Palace; then men section went on to "400"; thence "Acorn"; and then to bed about 3:30 a.m.

December 4th. Somewhat sticky mouth. Went to Dentist and then Doctor, who made awful prescriptions and diets. Albinia, Mercy, Margot, Uncle Reggie, Mr. Coxe and self dined and went to play.

December 5th. Went and saw Ralph off at 1 p.m. Aunt Emmy and Mary returned to luncheon. Albinia and self went and saw Cousin Edith and Vicary (*Henry Hucks Gibbs' children*), who seemed very pleased to see us. Blanche and self dined with Paddy B-Nesbitt, and his sister, then tried every theatre in London – no good.

December 6th. Up very late, dressed in a hurry and collected my things. George came up and we all went to the station and I caught the 1 p.m. train; large crowd. Crossing fair. We then got into a horrible Motor Bus after a large tea. This took 5 hours, and shook and jolted something terrific. I luckily had bought 3 bottles of champagne and some sandwiches, which we devoured getting back to METEREN about 12:30 a.m.

December 7th. Found everything much as usual; had a lot of writing to do and so did not go out. My inside not right yet.

7th December 1914

Darling Nancy,

A scrawl to say I got across safely, not sick on the boat but nearly so in the 5 hours we had in a very stuffy motor bus and got here about 12 midnight, Sunday.

Today we had a great game of football ("socker") 2nd Battalion Coldstream and any other officers in Meterin, and beat them 3-2. We were all nearly "pewking"! The Colonel was very efficient in goal.

No sign of a move at present. I hope there's no hurry as we are very comfy here.

Your loving

Lags.

I had a very happy week thanks to you all coming up.

December 8th. Went round billets with Colonel and then copied out a long list of recommendations for him, which took till tea. Then wrote 12 letters.

December 9th. Went down to see some hand grenades thrown, but we missed the way and so missed them. Played a hard game of football (association) 2nd Battalion versus any other officers in METEREN. We won 3-2. With a good hot bath I went to bed.

December 10th. Spent a very quiet day and refused any inducement to play football again. Still doing my cure. Battalion slowly getting refitted.

December 11th. Colonel and self went and inspected all Companies and went round billets. Dined with Little Man Vaughan (Major George Edmund Vaughan) at his house.

December 12th. Quiet morning. Rode into BAILLEUL with Byng and Humphrey and bought several things. Spent most of the evening writing and searching in King's Regulations for a committee of adjustment, which I found among Regimental Debts Act.

Kriegsgefangerensendung
Lt. Offiziergefangerenlager
Heidelberg
Baden
December 12th 1914

To Blanche

    A short letter to tell you we are moving from here (Stralsund) and going to Heidelberg. I do not know what our exact address will be but I should think the above would be enough till I can write you from there.

    We move on 14th I think – in 3 parties all to different places. I go to Heidelberg with Krook (Black Watch) and Joliffe (Scots Guards) with me – the others go 2 to each of the other two places.

    My Russian friend and teacher Leonide Sokoloff, also come to Heidelberg so I hope to continue my Russian lessons there.

    Aunt Cath writes she is sending me a cushion – I am glad it is not potted meat – a cushion is very kind. Cigarettes, one lot have turned up – most welcome.

    It has not been cold here the last 3 weeks but we have rapid changes wet the last two days. Albinia's cake was excellent.

    I think socks and books are all I want now. I received today some books from Berlin which the Censor Baron von Haiking kindly got for me so am well supplied at present.

    As you will understand news from here is practically nil – I am very well and getting rather too fat from inaction.

You may add to the list which contains boiled mutton and sweet omelette, pork – I do not much like it.

I hear Huie and Lags were both to be at home – how splendid for you and all – I do hope you had a real good re-union while they were there.

Tell me news of everyone when you write. All my letters have been most kind as to my behaviour on 29 October – too kind – it ended disastrously – whatever. A small bible and prayer book I should like – my prayer book I lost alas on 29th – the one I had in S. Africa – perhaps I may get it sometime. I valued it very highly. My love to all. Keep a good feast. Mercy and all. Happy Xmas and better New Year. Had letters from Tollemache, W. Riddell, and F. Cokayne, but cannot answer all – will you tell them.

Your loving

Evelyn

12th December 1914

Darling Nancy

A nice bit of "bumph" from you this morning – we are still here in Meteren.

I rode into Baillent today and bought several cosmetics which are about the only things they sell. Very few people have been through here this week. Rumours of us leaving here, but I don't attach much to them at present. The old Navy seems to be waking up well doesn't it?

I see a "Loveband" in the paper of the West Yorks is killed. I am afraid this must be Molly Loveband's son, isn't it. He was a nice fellow I remember him during our month up there 2 years ago.

Your loving brother

Lags

Note our new censor stamp.

December 13th. Very wet and beastly out so did not go except just round billets. Had to take Summary of Court Martial and so missed Church. After lunch I bicycled over to North Somerset Yeomanry and saw Huie and Eustace. Horrible ride, head wind and skidded like mad. Found them both well, they were preparing for a move and so very busy. Had tea, Brigadier General Bulkeley Johnson and Prince Arthur of Connaught came in. Ride back I did a bit quicker, but ran into one or two people as had no light. Arrived very hot.

December 14th. Had to be up a bit earlier as after 9 a.m. we had to be ready to move at 2 hours notice. Colonel went round billets but no route march. I started at 9:30 taking Summaries of Evidence. Went to Court Martial at 12, finished at 4 p.m., after that I spent till 6 promulgating them.

December 15th. No move yet. Raining hard and very cold. Everyone rather fussed. Heard English–French had got one lot of trenches, think we shan't move today.

December 16th. Did not move. Heard that these trenches taken yesterday had been lost and that the Gordons and Royal Scots had lost rather heavily, nothing done. Went for a route march with No. 2 walked up to a windmill where anti-aircraft Company is of 3rd Battalion Coldstream Guards and talked to Archie Trotter.

December 17th. Cold but no rain. Started my strict diet to try and get rid of my inside trouble. Very dull food when all these Christmas food things are arriving. Fred Beaumont-Nesbitt came to dine and we discussed last summer very thoroughly.

December 18th. Raining like --! Wrote some 20 'active service' postcards for Christmas. Brigadier came round our billets, and complimented us on them. My chilblains are coming up a bit, rubbed spirits of wine on them for want of something to do.

December 18th

My Dearest Nancy

Many thanks for letters and very welcome parcels. The last parcel of shortbread came in extraordinarily handy as we started off one morning before it was light and I stuffed the whole tin into my haversack. It was all I had to eat until about 6 p.m. that night except some chocolate, and Huie and I rather appreciated it very much.

We moved up to just behind our big guns and all our division (six regiments of cavalry) waited about, shivering all day. We then picketed our horses and all slept in enormous glass grape and peach houses for two nights and my word! The ground was hard. Eventually we all trekked back here again to our old billets without firing a shot. It was interesting watching the guns working and the Germans did not seem to reply in our direction. Ralph Bramwell and I are now in a small cottage, which is fairly snug. Bramwell is 2nd in command of the 15th Hussars but as his regiment is split up he was out of a job and now commands our squadron. Quite a nice fellow about 45 years old and I am very glad to have him. Is Stafford any nearer getting out here?

Things seem to be at rather a deadlock out in this quarter, and I don't know what is going to happen. The Germans are very strongly entrenched and so are we.

I have made a beautiful W.C. in out-house, out of a biscuit tin (large one) a plank which the carpenter made for me and a lot of bricks. The tin is now ¼ full of Condys Fluid and ready for use.

Guy and Huie are in a farm about ¾ mile from here. They have our French speaking cook with them as neither of them can string 3 words of French together.

Lags came over a week ago and he, Huie, Glyn, Col. Berkely Johnson and Prince Arthur of Connaught and I all had a nice cup of tea together.

Best wishes for New Year to you all

Your loving Brother

Eustace

I have not written to Albinia lately – will you let her have this.

December 19th. Had to stand by at 2 hours notice but nothing happened. Watched a football match in afternoon. Very cold and muddy. Very glad I'm not playing. Paddy B-N came to dine and we gossiped late after dinner.

December 20th. Glorious day, went to Church at 11:30 a.m. very large attendance. Brigadier read the Lessons. Lots of people came through during the day.

December 21st. Put on an hour's notice and so nothing doing all day. Had to take a Summary on Culverwell and attend the Court Martial most of the day. Went for a walk with Paddy B-N in evening. Later we got news we had to start at 7 a.m. Went to bed early.

December 22nd. Up by 6 a.m. Went round to the Brigade office for orders, breakfasted and off we went, fairly good day. Hertfordshires led then the 2nd Coldstream Guards. Kept going until 11 a.m. when we had ½ hour halt for watering; again at 1 p.m. we had 2 hours for luncheon. Then on. We stopped a long time outside BÉTHUNE and at last we got into Girls School, not a bad billet, rather cold. Took an awful long time getting in as 3rd Battalion had to come in too, and 1st Battalion had been there. Men slept in long rooms, officers in dormitory. Very cold night.

December 23rd. Slept very badly as was so cold. Lot of orders came in during the night. Breakfasted at 7 and got off about 8, marched out N.E. from BÉTHUNE, went about 6 miles and then halted. Brigadier had Commanding Officers up and told us that 2nd Grenadiers and 2nd Coldstream were for the trenches. We waited for about 3 hours in a field, then went up to take over from Sussex, Northampton's and King's Royal Rifles. Very difficult trenches to take over. Grenadiers had very bad ones on the right; up to their knees in water. But we were better on the left. Only one ammunition trench to each side, and so it took all night to do it.

December 24th. Slept very little during night. Gilly's Company only got into their trenches about 7 a.m. Very trying day especially for Grenadiers as their trenches were so bad and they had bombs thrown all day. They had to come back out of two of them. Our Companies were not too happy but we held on all right. We changed our Headquarters to a house away from the Grenadiers.

December 25th. Freezing like mad and very cold. MacGregor and self slept in room with the Colonel next door. Not a good Christmas. Grenadiers got 3 officers killed. Colonel went round trenches and I went with him. Found trenches not at all good. Crawled along them, had to run across the road, found Bury (Grenadiers) who had just had to come back out of an advance trench, several men badly wounded. Got back safely. In the evening the Colonel ricked his back somehow and had to go and lie down. Eventually he stayed in bed as his back got worse. We had about 15 casualties during the day. Our trenches considerably improved. We had to take on a bit more line and then managed to relieve ourselves; two Companies in the firing line, one in the supporting trenches, and one in the billets. Colonel a bit easier through hot water bottles.

December 26th. Woke up very cold and had great difficulty in getting my boots on again. Breakfasted rather late. Everything quite white with frost. Companies had a very quiet night in trenches. Colonel decided to go home as his back no better. Poor Alan Tritton was hit in the head and killed. Lots of orders came in but nothing very much doing. All quiet up to luncheon time. Colonel went off to 4th Field Ambulance on a stretcher. Everyone very sad at his going but I expect he will get well all the sooner. Still quite quiet, about 5 p.m. MacGregor went round the trenches in the evening. Gunner with French Mortar Gun attached to us. Had a little practice with the smaller trench mortar, 3 more smaller trench mortar, 3 more gunners attached to work it. Very cold but got a bit warmed up by dinner: few casualties, mostly snipers and head wounds. Byng, Burn, Gilly, and Humphrey in to dinner. Got down to it by about 10 p.m.

December 27th. Woken up at 12:10 a.m. with message from Brigade Headquarters saying attack expected at 12:15 a.m from information of a German deserter. MacGregor and self went to telephone to let Nos;1 & 4 know but could not get telephone to work. Then tried to message to Nos:2 & 3 but orderlies could not be found. Eventually telephone all right, but time 12:45 a.m. and so too late, and so no one was informed. Got to bed again at 1 a.m. and slept late. Raining hard again, went round trenches for MacGregor. Very wet and dirty. Arranged with Ympkin where to put Trench Mortar and came back by 3rd Battalion communication trench, which was rather deeper than ours, but wetter in spite of small hurdles put down. My fur coat had to be washed after this. Took a Summary on Corporal in No:3 most of the afternoon. Everything pretty quiet except some bombing in the left trenches, about 8 casualties. Rather warmer.

December 28th. A real good night. No messages until about 7:30 a.m. Had breakfast about 9 a.m. Much warmer and very quiet in front. Several Artillery officers came in and discussed what houses and places they would demolish for us. A very quiet day nothing happened. Rained a bit in the afternoon and some Royal Engineer officers came and discussed how to drain the trenches and fussed generally, hope to get our trenches much better. Heard Colonel P. had not got further than the 4th Ambulance and so hope he will soon be back. No casualties by 5 p.m. and only one after. Gilly came down to dinner very depressed, but was bucked up by a very good dinner, mostly made of the things Via had sent me.

December 29th. Slept even better and again not disturbed. Not raining but hear the trenches were as bad as ever. Irish Guards had advanced a bit on our left and we shall shortly convene to it. General turned up to see Trench Howitzer and condemned it, thank goodness! MacBride went round trenches and came back very muddy. Heard from Colonel again, still not gone home. R.E are further improving communication trenches. Few casualties in morning, mostly from supporting trenches. Very quiet all afternoon.

29th December 1914

Darling Nancy

Your enclosures in your last two letters came most conveniently, as it was very short at that moment, however "Bethune" has now supplemented. I have not had a letter from the Archbishop yet but no doubt it will come. Very kind of him to worry to answer, I thought perhaps he might like to hear from the "front". We are back in the Trenches, brutes they were when we first took them over, however, these last 5 days we have managed to improve them. Personally I am very lucky as I am doing Adjutant and the Colonel and I live in a windowless and holey roofed house, very cold but drier than the trenches.

He (Pereira) unfortunately wricked his back two days ago and has had to go into hospital, however I hope very shortly he will be back.

One, Major MacGregor, is taking his place. I am longing for Pinto to return.

We don't know how long we are going to stay in but hope not for more than another week, and then a short rest again.

Lots of things arrived from Collings two days ago for which so many thanks, what a terrible lot I must be costing you.

Good luck for 1915

Your loving brother

Lancelot

Cavan is very well.

December 30th. Raining still and rather colder. Gillie F. got hit about 11 a.m., sent down for Sinclair (M.O) waited to hear how had he was. Luckily not dangerous, through calf of left leg from High Explosive. Got him off in the evening. Budget Loyd came up with Jerry Brabazon who showed him the way up. All very quiet, except for some bombs which they threw. Our casualties 1 killed and 8 wounded. Our Artillery got into them once or twice.

December 31st. Budget, Trousers, and self slept very confidential in straw for two. Trenches worse than ever if anything on account of rain during night. No: 4 did a bit of a sap forward. Bombs started to come over, so guns got on to them. One shell dropped short and did a little damage to 3rd Battalion. Archie Trotter got hit in the head, and while being brought down, died. Dreadful all the best people being killed. After dinner a lot of firing on right somewhere in 1st Division, heard afterwards it was a German attack. Got to bed about 11:30 p.m. and waited up in case any attack came on us, this being the first night that we had 2 Companies in billets and only 1½ Companies in the firing line.

1915

January 1st. Happy New Year! Woke about ¼ to 10. Had rather a cold breakfast an account of fire having to be put out because of smoke. Our relief that we heard so much about looks rather 'blue', as they are now keeping 5th Brigade for 1st Division. One man killed, and one mortally wounded in night. News that 4 our of men got the D.C.M.

January 2nd. Rose moderately early very excited with the idea of our relief. Lot of the King's Liverpool Regiment came up to look round and generally arrange for taking over our line. Very little happened during the day. No. 1 had a few casualties. About 3 o'clock they suddenly started to shell the "brewery" and knocked over 'Rumbold' (Grenadier) but did not hurt him. 4 out of the 10 shells actually hit it, otherwise no damage done. Relief took place without any mishap and we marched to LOCON getting there about 10 p.m.

January 3rd. Took it out a bit as nothing doing. Lots of reports and papers came in. Had to arrange for men to go and have baths in LOCON. Raining as usual. Went with Humphrey to reconnoitre a road towards firing line, took cyclists with us. Think they were more muddled when they got hack than when they started, as we went the wrong way so often. My '65' Brandy arrived, so we opened it for dinner.

January 4th. Had a celebration in a barn having up fixed a box and two candles stuck in tobacco tins; about 50 men came from ½ the Battalion. After lunch Colonel returned not quite fit but much better, also O.R.Sergeant Webb, which is good. Rained hard but went for a very quick walk with Rooke. Had letters from Cissie and the Arch Bishop, they were not in quite the same style!

4th January 1915

Darling Nancy

I have just had a very nice letter from the Arch Bishop. It took me some time to read it but when I did it was good. You were so kind as to send me a tummy-warmer before, I wonder if you could repeat that gift as the one I have on has done its share and soon when I take it off I fear it may run off! We are back in very comfy billets after some very bad trenches.

We managed with great difficulty to get one Christmas celebration today doing it in two halves in a straw-barn with a box with a blanket over it and two candles stuck on tobacco tins. It seemed very odd having it in such a place. Mr Fleming, our Chaplain, brought a few things with him in a haversack including 'white-wine'! I should think about 80 came from the Battalion.

Raining hard. Periera, the Colonel has just returned to us, which is splendid.

Love to all.

Your loving brother

Lags

January 5th. Had orders at 10 a.m. Went round No: 2 billets after luncheon. Colonel and self drove into BÉTHUNE and I took Summary on Bytheway and Upton in No: 4 Field Ambulance – self-inflicted. Farmer's cart quite comfortable, bicycled into 4th Brigade in evening to find out if they can be tried (No!). Lawrence (3rd Coldstream Guards) came to dinner. "Cordon Rouge" and "Heidsick" was produced followed by a disastrous evening for me in "Vingt-et-Un", bed at 10:30 p.m.

January 6th. General Horne came round to see all Battalions, just came into the mess. Colonel and self went round to 4th Brigade and got all particulars about our move. Bicycled into BÉTHUNE and got my hair cut.

North Somerset.Yeomanry.
January 6th 1915

My dearest Nancy
    Thank you very much for your letters and parcels of very welcome little delicacies, which come in very well indeed for tea. One so often has someone from another regiment or Squadron in to take a mug of tea.
    We are all still leading the same dull uneventful life but have had a hard weeks work this week practising new forms of attack etc. Our Squadron leader has gone home on a weeks leave so I am in charge again for a week.
    Last week we all went in in turn to Hazebrouck to learn how to throw bombs and hand grenades. They only have hand made bombs so far, but I should think they are very effective. You light the fuse and just have time to aim and throw them – rather alarming!
    The guns have been booming away merrily most of this week but I don't know what has been going on.
    Where is it you say Staff is going? Could you let me know whereabouts it is?
    Afraid I have never let you know about "hand and water" so I don't get it now and should be very glad of an occasional number.
    I wonder whether Staff will be able to get up here to see us. He could probably get the loan of a motor.
    Quite a nice morning for a change but it is bound to rain sometime before dark – it <u>always</u> does. I am giving the men an afternoon off today and shall probably play football with them.
    I suppose Cosmo has gone back to school by now.

Love to all

Your loving

Eustace

January 7th. Orders at 9 a.m. the Colonel drove off in farmer's small cart in pouring rain to 5th Brigade at RICHEBOURG ST VAAST to get the dispositions of their trenches. Met Colonel Geoffrey F. then, and we all conferred with the Glasgow Highlanders whose trenches we take over.

Back for lunch. Spent afternoon getting my pocket-book up to date as Record and Officers Roster. Wrote to Blanche. More "Vingt-et-Un", started with 1 fr, borrowed 5 frs, and finished with 335 frs. Orders to move.

January 8th. Lots of fuss and bustle and eventually off at 10 a.m. walked via LOCON and LA COUTURE about 5 miles to RICHEBOURG St VAAST found Sim waiting for us. Billets fair but very dirty. Our house fairly good but almost windowless. Raining as usual. Colonel and self walked round. Rather a smell in No: 2's billet, eventually traced to a dead dog in the yard. Father Wagget came to stay for 2 or 3 days. We are in reserve to 3rd Battalion, who are in trenches.

January 9th. Woken up at 1 a.m. by Jerry Brabazon who wanted our machine gun up before light. Luckily Trousers lived in room opposite and so saved me getting out of bed. Sent 200 men and 5 officers to dig a redoubt; very cold and raining. They could not do much as it was too wet. Lost at "21".

January 10th. Fine for once. Had to be ready to move at 5 hour's notice from 1:30 a.m. Large mail at 4 p.m., we came to relieve 3rd Battalion in the trenches. Colonel and self walked up to "Rue de Bois" and looked at line in a very dim light. Budget and Fatty (2 & 3) took over the line. 4 in Battalion Headquarters and No. 1 behind. Very wet taking over but completed without a casualty.

January 11th. Woke very late and found Colonel had been round trenches alone. Spent a very quiet day. Artillery Captain came in about midday saying he noticed more Germans in their trenches than usual, but think this was due to very heavy shelling we gave them yesterday. Made us rather uneasy but nothing happened. 1 casualty otherwise relief went off well.

January 12th. Woke early and at 6 a.m. Colonel and I went round the Companies in the RUE de BOIS, all going well. Fine day for once, arranged bombs a bit during morning, also tried to work a dog we found over a field, but found too many bullets coming over. Looked for shell cases with Trousers and found one. Relieved by 3rd Battalion at 4:30 p.m. and strolled back to RICHEBOURG to find a good mail.

January 13th. Went round companies in rain, found some billets rather dirty. Brigadier had a conference at 4:30 p.m. when we were told that we were leaving and going back to our old place near RUE DE L'EPINETTE.

January 14th. Orders early, then Colonel and self walked over to Battalion Headquarters near Brewery and found out 'Kings' Liverpool's dispositions and back by another road. Went round to Brigade

Headquarters to try and get one new line shortened (unsuccessful!). Long game of "vingt-et-un". Lost.

January 15th. Made an enlargement to a map amidst a great deal of comment. Moved off about 1:30 p.m. 1 & 4 Company, and 2 & 3 Companies later. Colonel went up and took over from "Kings" Colonel. Nos: 1 & 4 went into billets, while 2 & 3 held the trenches with posts from right to left respectively. We settled in in an 'Estaminet' inhabited by an old couple that much resented our arrival. Colonel, McBride and self lived in a cottage next door. Very high gale blowing.

January 16th. Had to get up at about 4 a.m. and shut the door which had blown open. After breakfast Colonel and self walked up and down road for exercise and discussed drainage. Folkes (R.E. Major) came in and gave us a few hints. Got to bed about 9 p.m. A message in about 10 p.m. About 11:30 p.m. Rowland Corbett came in and asked for a bed, so he dossed down with me and took most of the bed. He was looking for the 3rd Battalion.

January 17th. Colonel and self went up to Brewery and looked round with the Brigadier. Looked through Gunners telescope, but could not see any Germans. Walked up and down with Humphrey in the afternoon and gossiped. Colonel and self went round the posts and saw Pro, Byng and Rooke, all quiet; trench blown in during day and killed 2, and wounded 3, not very badly. Went to bed early as room was so hot.

Kriegsgefangenensendung
Offizier-Gefangenlager,
Heidelberg,
Baden.

January 17th

To Blanche,
    I don't know the address for the enclosed letter to Mrs. G. Stewart. Will you ring up Mrs. C. Baring, at 35, Gloucester Place and ask her? She is sure to know, I think. I am so dreadfully sorry for poor little Mrs. G. S. and their two small children. His father was killed in Egypt.
    In answer to your letter, I have still no news of any of the six officers missing the same day as me – and I want to hear what happened to Leslie Hamilton, from you, as no one has ever mentioned him yet. I fear the six were all killed that day.
    The Censor here tells me that though we may only write two letters a week, we may receive what are written to us – he knows English very well, and so there is no difficulty. Will you tell Via this,

and also thank her for her letter of December 19th – also Lags, December 14th – Cyril Daubeny, December 22nd – Cyril Gurney, December 16th – and for their parcels which they have sent, not yet arrived.

Two books from Bath, G., I expect and thank: one was "Grossmith". I last saw any of the six missing two nights before, i.e. on October 27th, and heard nothing of them after that. Will you tell Cox and Co. I have received their remittances (and letters) of December 24th and January 1st, and that your signature is my receipt for them?

A pity that "Priest", turned out at Tyntesfield, is not up for Eustace to have hunted, if he got home. I hope "Coleman" is well.

Pitman, who was servant to poor Freddy Pollock, was also a prisoner. I forget if I mentioned his name.

I think you seem to have got all my things home – except those on my pony, where also was my sword. We cannot buy cigarettes at the canteen any more, so I am the more anxious to receive them from home. Luckily, Krook has just got 200 sent him. If Isherwood's give out, send any other brand.

I read a lot, and have still got a good many left to read, so have the others. Vicary told me to ask him for anything I could want, and I wrote and said books. If it is he who sends them to me from Hatchard's, will you thank him very much for me? Nancy's German Grammar, and Uncle Reggie's dominoes have arrived. It is very mild here - always is, I believe – and we have had a lot of rain lately.

Heidelberg is some way off, so one cannot see the beauties of the place, though the hills in front would be very pretty in summer, I should think. I think I asked you before to send my field-boots – the old ones from my kit – and I should like a pair of those stockings which slip on and look like putties, khaki.

Well done, our covert at Whissenthorpe! A good fox, two hours over the cream of the country, no doubt. I hope "Kells" got Miss Eglantine there.

I am very fit, and have ceased to get fat, I am glad to say, though fatter than before, I expect.

Will you congratulate Cyril and Marjorie on their daughter for me – also our new captains, Tolly and Francis G. L.?

We play at Patience – but I soon get tired of them, I find, and get back to my books.

From Evelyn

January 18th. Called at 5:30 a.m. went up to trenches with Colonel. Washed and shaved on return. Started to snow hard and continued to do so all the morning. Walked down to Brigade Headquarters with Crawley (de Crespigny) and had to run all the way back as it started to pour. After lunch 2 & 3 Companies were relieved by 3rd Battalion Coldstream Guards being Companies in reserve. We waited about for a long time. Eventually about 6 p.m. Nos: 1 & 4 got back and we all marched over to PONT TOURNANT, getting there about 7:30 p.m. and finding our billets very bad and small.

January 19th. Snow beginning to clear off a bit; walked round billets which took us up to luncheon time as they were so scattered. Everything very quiet, went for a walk with Sim. Lost heavily at 'vingt-et-un' in the evening.

January 20th. Nothing doing. Irish Guards had unfortunate accident while practising bomb throwing. Keeting killed and about 12 wounded by a premature explosion. We moved off about 2:30 p.m. as a Battalion to our old billets other side of LACON. Road for ¼ mile ½ ft under water. Our old farm Lady delighted to have us back.

January 21st. Orders rather earlier after which Colonel and self walked down to Brigade Headquarters for a Conference of about an hour. In afternoon Colonel MacBride and I rode over to ESSARS and other places to see new position. Rained hard the whole time.

January 22nd. Frost which made roads dry a bit; went round billets. Took two Summaries during afternoon, after which Pro and self walked to Command Paymaster in LOCON and drew about 10,000frs to pay Battalion with. Met Paddy B-N and other Grenadiers then, found Paddy rather seedy. Had a good bank with Colonel at 'vingt-et-un'. Eventually lost most of it and retired to bed at 2 a.m. Battalion in waiting and ready to move at 25 minutes notice for 24 hours.

January 23rd. Sharp frost. Colonel, McBride and self went round and saw Companies drilling, mud hard enough to walk on. Floods considerably decreased. No one could go far as Battalion in waiting. Had to take a short walk to digest my lunch, and so forced Trousers to come out much against his will. "Little Man" and Feilding came into tea. Had long letters from Amy, Nancy, and Blanche.

23rd January 1915

Darling Nancy,
    Another splendid parcel arrived from you. You ask for a suggestion to improve which seems almost impossible, but perhaps some of the following: Candles are <u>always</u> good. Matches, 2½ inch Bryant and May's are better than 4¼ ones. Shortcake has been much appreciated. Soap squares are not much good to one as the Mess have a supply, nor is chocolate now-a-days, but anything like Carlsbad plums, or like the ones

Bill Rannie used to send at Christmas are very nice. Enough of food!

I forgot exactly to where Stafford is going out, it was somewhere near, Boulogne wasn't it. Perhaps I may seem him in the near future if any more leave comes in February.

I wonder what is the general opinion of these air raids made by Germany. I suppose it helps recruiting considerably and seems to do very little damage at very great risk to themselves.

There is perfectly extraordinary little news from here, we go in and out of trenches at intervals, they are very wet but we have very easy reliefs. They are sending us on some more officers now, which is a good thing.

I am very well, this wet is knocking up some of the more rheumaticy.

I expect Cavan writes very interesting letters home as he sees all the leading people of the fighting world.

Ever your loving brother,

Lags

January 24th. Fleming arrived about 11:15 a.m. and we had a short service in a barn for ½ the Battalion, very poor attendance, Jock played the hymns on the concertina. After tea Byng, Ympkin and self walked into BÉTHUNE to try and send a wire, but found it impossible. Sinclair (RAMC) left in the morning and one Dyas came instead.

Kriegsgefangenensendung
Offizier-Gefangenlager,
Heidelberg,
Baden.
Sunday, January 24th

For Blanche.

First, will you somehow acknowledge for me letters from: - Billy, December 28, and say I did get his most excellent coat – C. Vicary, January 2, a most charming letter, his account of L's school being most encouraging, and I hope it will go on improving, also for the book; not yet arrived – Albinia's, two letters of December 8 and 30; the books, cake and chocolate arrived, not the second lot of books – Cyril Daubeny, December 24; both letters arrived, the cake not yet – E. Tollemache, December 31, and his most exciting account of some football matches, which I much appreciate, particularly glad to hear the Monckton Wanderers, my old team, have done so well in their games – Walter Riddlell, December 31, his nice, cheerful letter – Lady Crooke Lawless,

December 25, from British Red Cross Hospital, Netley, and hope to hear again from her whenever she can write – Mr. Stone for his most interesting and amusing letter of December 22, from Tyntesfield – I hope young Pope will get his commission – and say how very much I appreciate his kind thought of writing, and hope he will do so again – Mrs. Wavell, 7, Egerton Gardens; I can't tell her how delighted I am to hear of her son (Gazeka) being in hospital. I felt very hopeless about him before – Roger Ford, December 9th, his usual cheer, so good for those shut up like I am – Nancy, January 5th, her plums and caviare have not turned up yet, and I rather think that things sent direct get here quickest. The parcel of shirts, etc., sent by you have not arrived yet, whereas I got yesterday the box of cigarettes you posted at Knightsbridge on January 6th, which is quick.

I also got your letter from John P., and also a letter direct from him – both so kind I feel almost ashamed of ever have written despondently about that day – the answers are too kind.

Will you tell Nancy that the only Riddell I know (besides Walter R.) is rather a rascal. He used to be in the army, but afterwards went out to East Africa to trade. If it is I should advise dropping his acquaintance, quite an undesirable, I believe.

There seems almost a fatality against my receiving a new shirt. I have borrowed one from Jolliffe now. I think Mr. Gaston is very slow though he may be very sure, that is yet to be seen.

Cigarettes and tobacco are most welcome. An Indian native officer has arrived, wounded in the leg two months ago. Being a Mohamedan, it is difficult to feed him, but he is doing very well. Luckily for him, he speaks a little English, which is unusual for native officers.

Cousin Vicary's letter was very kind. Will you tell him how nice I thought it – especially that I should be the cause of, what he calls, a "Vicarious" pride to him?

I wrote to John P. last mail. My plan is to send one letter per week to you or one of the family, and the other letter to answer one of the many I receive.

A list of missing officers, from the War Office, was shown to us the other day to ask if we could help in giving information about them. I saw there the names of Hugh Grosvenor, Grenville Smith, W. Blake, Harry Crichton, and others whom I knew less well. Don't ever hesitate to tell me the names of anyone I know to whom anything happens. It is so much better to know now, than to learn afterwards of a great number suddenly – besides, I might make such awful mistakes when writing to people.

Last week we had some snow – not very much – but it was cold and bright, now the thaw has come, and it is mild again. We keep quite warm here – in fact, the Russians like their rooms too hot, being so accustomed to it in Russia.

    Cyril D. tells me he cracked some jokes with you when you had a bad throat. I hope that is well by now.

    Best love and luck, Blanchie, to you and Mercy, and all, wherever they are.

From Evelyn

We all three felt satisfied now that people we know did their best on October 29th, but you will understand one wanted comforting – it seemed so awful.

January 25th. Very much hurried over dressing as orders came in to he ready to move at once. We got off about 10 a.m. meeting the Brigadier outside his Headquarters. We found the 1st and 3rd Brigades had been attacked round GIVENCHY and forward posts pushed in. Cavan and Grenadiers and 3rd Battalion Coldstreams went on, leaving 2nd Coldstream Guards, Irish Guards, and Hertfordshires under our Colonel. So he and self took our abode in Brigade Headquarters and waited all day. Several Staff officers came in giving us news of the sinking of the "BLUCHER". About 5 p.m. orders to return to billets came. I was left at Brigade Headquarters to take messages. Hampden also stayed. We waited until 8 p.m. and the Brigadier returned. Had dinner and bed at home. Orders came in late.

January 26th. Breakfast at 4:30 a.m., and off we went to ESSARS, getting there at ¼ to 7. Looked round for Headquarters which we got in small and rather smelly estaminet. This we sat in all day long, having a wire to Brigade Headquarters, as nothing happened we started for home about 4 p.m. and got in just after dark.

January 27th. Kept at short notice to move all day and so could not go far. Day cold as sharp frost during night.

January 28th. Had to go down to ESSARS again being there by 7 a.m. again. Battalion was increased yesterday by Ashley, Carter-Wood, Pinto and Pratt (late Drill Sergeant). Very cold and roads like ice. Found a new and cleaner 'Estaminet'. Little Man came in and talked to us, as 3rd Battalion were there with us. Started for home about 1 p.m. as all quiet about GIVENCHY. Had two cases for Field General Court Martial at 2:30 p.m. under Seymour at our Headquarters. Still at 20 minutes notice.

January 29th. Hoped to have a quiet breakfast, but no! Orders to move at once, and off about 10 a.m. Feeling like nothing on earth, but got off and walked down to a wood where we stopped. Very cold and I steadily felt worse. About 12 noon we were ordered home at the same time Dyas took my temperature and finding it over 100! I had to go with him into

BÉTHUNE and into the 3rd Field Ambulance (4th not being there). Went to ward which was ½ for officers and got into bed. Mostly sick! Then a few wounded Privates. Had dinner and felt better.

January 30th. Woke often in the night, got a wash and shave about 8:30 a.m. Several more wounded brought in; two bad abdominal cases! Had the thickest and coldest bit of bacon whatever was for breakfast. Wiled away the day thinking of my next meal. Sat up a bit in the evening and wrote letters.

January 31st. My washing arrangements somewhat disturbed by the Sister coming and having breakfast in the washing place, however I finished and returned. Most of the cases evacuated except officers. After luncheon Rooke came in with much the same complaint as self. He was much annoyed as they would give him so little to eat. Lot of people evacuated about 8 p.m.

February 1st. Passed fit to go out. So got dressed by 12 noon and went out and lunched at 'Hôtel de Paris'. Went and talked to Tom Bevan and Jack Hughes in No: 4 Field Hospital officers house. Went down looking for billets, eventually found them nearly outside BÉTHUNE . 1st line just arrived at 3:30 p.m. Walked back and got valise from Hospital. Battalion turned up about 10 p.m., found they had been heavily attacked in morning but No: 4 had made a very good counter attack near CUINCHY and had made good the trenches they had been bombed out of in the morning. Also got about 100 yards more. Losses about 50 also Carter-Wood killed. While relieving in the evening poor Fatty Northland was killed. ST NICHOLAS College, BÉTHUNE .

February 2nd. Everyone very late. I was up at 10 a.m.. Raining hard, wrote letters all morning and made up returns. Birkbeck and self went out in evening and went round the bomb factory, most interesting place. Sim and Pro went off to bed with colds, otherwise fairly cheery dinner.

February 3rd. Nothing doing during morning, arranged about relief and sent various messages. Sim went off to Hospital about 3 o'clock. 1st Company went up to CUINCHY. Colonel and self went with No: 3, some 5 mile walk. Called at 4th Brigade Headquarters. Had to wait about ¼ hour, as Generals Haking and Herne were there. Eventually got up. Relief completed without casualties. Our Headquarters in a cellar. Very dirty; cooked up a bit of dinner. McBride and Ympkin came back off leave.

February 4th. Up pretty early. Scott cooked the breakfast. Had to open the windows an awful smell. Certain amount of bombing but not much damage. Companies in trenches spending all their time burying. Body of Mills (1st Battalion) found. Splendid day but hardly went out all day.

February 5th. Colonel pushed me up about 8 a.m., went round the trenches with him about 11. Found they were pretty good. Walked back via No: 1 in billets. Casualties for day two only, all very quiet. 3rd Battalion started to come about 4:30 p.m. We got away about 6:00, Colonel. McBride and self walking straight back to our billets.

5th Feb 1915

Darling Nancy,
    The enclosed may interest you and even Inez if she happens to be with you. It is the Brigadier watching some shells bursting, the others are on his right Horlick. 3rd Coldstream and his left Colonel Fielding and beyond him Ipswich also 3rd Coldstream. The other is one of our boys in trenches somewhere.
    At last we are having a short spell of fine weather. I found a tree just outside our house beginning to sprout in fact. Nothing doing much out here.
                      Your loving

                          Lags.

February 6th. Everyone very late up. Colonel and self went down into BÉTHUNE and had a haircut, also saw Sim in Hospital. Everybody had to be back between 2 – 3 p.m. as 3rd Battalion Coldstream were going to rush Brick-Stacks in front of CUINCHY. Most successful about 20 Germans captured and new line held, about 30 casualties including poor Tommy Musgrave (Irish Guards) killed and Cotterell-Dormer (3rd Coldstream) mortally wounded. Walked into BÉTHUNE again with Byng and Trousers just before dinner.

February 7th. Had to go to 4th Field Ambulance to take 3 Summaries. Saw Steven Burton who had been slightly wounded by a shell. He told me 3rd Battalion had taken 2 machine guns. Colonel, McBride and self started up about 3 p.m. About a mile from Brigade Headquarters very heavy shelling started. Colonel sent me back to hurry Companies to Brigade Headquarters. While coming up with No: 3 a 'Black Maria' landed 15 yards from Company and on road just as we had passed. Waited about 1 hour at Brigade Headquarters, and then went slowly on up. Found 3rd Battalion very tired, but very pleased with themselves. Everything quieted down considerably. Colonel spent night up near "Culvert", while McBride and self stayed at Battalion Headquarters.

February 8th. Woke up to find everything very quiet. Colonel came back for breakfast and told us no casualties. Personally had very bad night messages coming in most of time. Had letter from Eustace and A. Wrote several letters in evening but forgot to post them. Went round the trenches with MacGregor in afternoon, found we had very good line now. Deserted German trenches full of clothing, rifles, bayonets etc. Got a saw-bayonet. Found all very quiet. Wounded German out in front of our barbed wire so Byng after much difficulty got another German to come out of his trench and fetch him in, amongst cheers from our men. The German on reaching his own trench shouted out, "Thank you very much, you are sportsmen". Several artillery blokes came in and passed time of day. About 11 p.m. heavy firing over French side by Germans, our guns got to work, after about ¼ hour it quieted down, but we could not find out what it all was, as our telephone took the opportunity of ceasing work and the bullets too thick to send man up the line. Some more firing about 12, then all quiet.

February 9th. Raining a bit, helped Scott cook the breakfast and consequently broke most of the eggs. Brigadier turned up about 9:30 a.m., but he had not much news. Colonel got back soon after. Very quiet day only one casualty, wounded, up to 5 p.m. I stayed in the cellar. Wrote to Blanche via Parkin, but it did not go. Colonel, McBride and self walked back to our old billets in St. Nicholas School, and found there was a bottle of champagne in the mess.

February 10th. Latish up. Went up to 4th Field Ambulance and took 3 Summaries. Walked through with Colonel and again in evening with Byng and Trousers. Battalion Concert. .

February 11th. Went round billets and moved back to CUINCHY via Brigade Headquarters about 3 p.m. Found everything pretty quiet up there, luckily we went up by communication trench as heavy fire opened as we crossed open ground and we heard the bullets over our heads.

February 12th. Stayed in the cellar all day and felt very gammy by the evening. Brigadier came in, cheery as ever but no news. Colonel came back and had to lie down as he was rather seedy. McBride slept up at Bridge.

12th February 1915

Darling Nancy,
    Parcels in galore arrived from Messrs Collins including soap "Vanolia", just at a psychological moment, as my piece of "Honey" was getting thin.
    Things seem much as usual; I hope the rumours of great victories in the Eastern theatre are true, also of food shortage among the "Huns". I think they must have had pretty useful casualties in the East. We have had a pretty fair bag round these parts lately.
    During our short spells in the trenches, Scott cooks for the Head

Quarters' Officers and very good he is becoming! That includes the Colonel, Major MacGregor, Towers, Clark and self.

Many thanks for Evelyn's letter. I hope for his sake especially that the war finishes soon. I thought that he had no other English and am delighted to hear Krook and Joliffe are there although the latter is rather a dull dog.

Very glad to see Cloche Bell is a prisoner, we all heard out here that he was killed.

I wonder how Stafford likes Wimereux and if he will go on anywhere from there.

Your loving

Lags

February 12th 1915

My dearest Nancy

I am writing to you all to tell you how it happened as far as I can gather from those who were present.

We heard yesterday that one of the Gibbs's was badly wounded and our cyclist returned today and told me it was Eustace. He was shot through the head by a chance shot which went through another man's head first at 7.30 yesterday morning, he was taken to Ypres hospital by our Ambulance and died at 1 pm without recovering consciousness, so he did not suffer at all. Lionel came back to tell me all about it today as he saw it happen. He was buried in the Churchyard close to several friends. He was there only about 10 days ago taking photographs for Mrs Liebert and Mrs Davey.

He has been so splendid out here all the time and I have been so proud of him and I shall miss him more than I can say.

The Division will be relieved tomorrow evening and returns here early on Sunday. They have had very few casualties.

The shells coming into Ypres seem to have been the most dangerous. I have so many letters to write. Thank you for Evelyn's.

I hope Stafford will find us.

Your loving brother A.H. Gibbs

February 13th. Quiet night. Colonel rather better, but not right, however he insisted on going round. Vivian came up and gave us a few bits of news and several Gunners came in. Rained a bit. Colonel and self got relieved about 6:30 p.m., and walked off down "Hertford Street" (a new communication trench). Did not stay long at Brigade Headquarters. Had a cup of soup from motor soup kitchen en route.

BISHOPTHORPE.
YORK.

February 13th 1915

My poor dear Nancy

Just a chat line to tell you how much I am thinking of you all now that this sorrow has come so specially near. I know how much you have dreaded this news, and how brave you have been, but even so it must be terribly hard. May God come very very close to you, and help you to bear up for the sake of the others, and give you that comfort and strength, which we all long may be yours and yet are powerless to convey. So it is dear old Eustace who I used to know so well in the Oxford days, may God accept the offering of his life, and grant him perfect rest, and perfect peace. God bless you all and comfort you as He alone can.

Yours very affectionately

Edward Gibbs

P.S. Don't bother to answer this, give them all my love.

The Rev. Edward Gibbs was George Louis Manck Gibbs grandson, Chaplain to the Archbishop of York and to the First Battalion of the Grenadier Guards. He was killed at Boisleux le Mont on 29th March 1918 and is buried in the War Cemetery there.[xxii]

February 14th. Just going off to Church at the theatre when wire came that we must be prepared as French were making an attack. This we heard later was entirely successful, and as it rained no one wanted to go out.

February 15th. Went round billets with Colonel. Saw George's notice in Morning Post about Eustace being killed in action. Do not know quite what to think of it. Called in at Brigade Headquarters on way up. Brigadier very sorry to hear about Eustace. Heard French attack not so successful as we hoped.

February 16th. Remained in cellar all day. Had Blanche's letter saying Geoffrey Glynn had wired George about Eustace. Very quiet day. Wilfred Smith came in for short time, also Jack Trefusis in the evening.

February 17th. Woke up with heavy cold. Spent most of the day feeding. Very quiet, certain amount of shelling, as French made three set bombardments. Only 3 men slightly wounded, very good day. Walked quickly home and got back about 8:30 p.m. to our new billets and champagne. Very good house with electric light and 2 big rooms. Josh played piano and Bonvalot violin up to ¼ to 1 a.m.

February 18th. Late up and had to rush off to orders, breakfast after and Court Martial on Sergeant Dixon at 11:30 a.m. Walked down town with Colonel and saw Town Commandant about Tobacco Factory, and again with Budget. Very cheery dinner. Took a bank at Roulette and made about £20 – mostly off Birkbeck! Bed about 1 a.m.

February 19th. Managed to get some breakfast before orders. Went round billets with Colonel, nothing much doing. We started off at 3:30 p.m. called in at 4th Brigade and on up via "Hertford Street". Found 3rd Battalion in very good spirits and after a good deal of talk they went off. Colonel went up to trenches for night as usual.

February 20th. Very quiet morning, went out with small party and collected doors etc. for trenches. Looked round graves. Went round trenches with Colonel and saw everyone, also the mine head which Sim showed me. Stopped with Pro some time in cellar as it came on to rain 'cats and dogs'. Pudding Lane full of water, also Coldstream Lane, "Love Lane" not quite finished. Looked at "Old Kent Road' (Grenadier Communication trench). Suddenly about 5 p.m. "***K", (signal for attack on Hollow) came down the telephone hard, all jumped up, wired it on to Brigade, guns started within 2½ minutes at 18 rounds per ½ minute, McB rushed up to trenches, Colonel and I stayed back. However it all proved a signaler's mistake, but very satisfactory to know guns are so ready. Irish Guards and Hertfordshires all had orders to stand by within 5 minutes also. Still raining and trenches filling visibly.

February 21st. Fine but thick mist. Trenches in very bad state. Got pumps to work and sent up lots of sand-bags. Brigadier came up during the morning. Went down road, as 'Hertford Street" so bad, with Colonel. Back to our billets and piano.

February 22nd. Not much for orders, walked in town after. Got the bath-house for the men going, and washed ¼ of the Battalion. Wrote letters most of the day. "Dotty" and Bonvalot played most of the evening. Took the bank again at Roulette and lost what I had won last time, (about £20).

February 23rd. Straker and Eric Greer came in and played most of the morning. Great excitement over leave, which eventually did not come off for Humphrey and self (25th Feb.). President Grant and Ilchester came to lunch and brought 2 dozen Port with them. Used President Grant's car to go to Division to find out about leave. Colonel Feilding and Jimmy H. came in 'en route' for leave. Walked up, Colonel feeling bad, self fairly bad, and McBride 'off colour', so all rather silent. Leave for 25th February confirmed. Colonel went to bed, also self soon after arrival.

February 24th. Colonel still bad and so M.O. called and he was sent off to hospital in BÉTHUNE much against his will, he has only got 'flue'. Snowed a bit after lunch, which turned to rain.

February 25th. Very little doing all the morning. Humphrey and self started off for leave about 12 noon. Rode back and caught 3:39 p.m. to St. Omer, changed and went on to BOULOGNE, arriving about 9 p.m. Had dinner with Rudolph de Trafford and Gill. Slept crossing, very calm.

February 26th. Arrived in London at 8:30 a.m. Nancy met me at Victoria. Went back to Belgrave Square and found Mercy; shopped; Uncle came to dinner at Belgrave Square.

February 27th. Dashed round all day. Saw Gilly F., John Wynne-Finch and his wife came to a play with me in the evening. Got back about 12 and found George and Via had arrived. Went down to Sandown in afternoon.

February 28th. Talked all morning. Went and saw Vicary and Edith in evening. Billy (Gibbs) arrived after dinner. Church at St Michael's, Chester Square.

February 29th. Bought Blanche a wedding present in morning. Paddy Beaumont-Nesbitt, lunched with me at Bachelors. Dined Merton, Cissie, Guy S-S (Shaw-Stewart), Amy and Doris Gordon-Lennox, and Mrs. Becky.

March 2nd. Had lunch party of 8 Ladies, Merton and self at the Ritz. Blanche and Willy arrived during afternoon. Had tea with Blanche at Bachelors. Via arranged Theatre and we went to "Man who stayed at home".

March 3rd. Up rather late; did last of shopping and saw Beckwith-Smiths; had photograph taken at Speich – very/fairly good. Caught 8 p.m. train at Victoria. Blanche, Nancy, and Willy came and saw me off. Stafford (Crawley) met me at BOULOGNE and we had supper at Bella Young's Hotel.

March 4th. Missed changing at St. Omer, but managed it at HAZEBROUCK and got to BÉTHUNE about 12 noon. Found Battalion resting in same billets (135 Rue de Lille).

March 5th. Had few people to dinner. Large Coldstream Concert at Theatre, great success.

March 6th. Court Martial in morning. Irish Guards boxing in evening, otherwise we do nothing.

March 7th. Went to the Service at the theatre. Walked in afternoon to get me fat down!

March 8th. Several people came to dinner. Gambled a bit at Roulette. (I won £150!). Huie suddenly turned up in morning. I had to finish off a Court Martial and then we walked about the town until 4:30 p.m. when he had to come back. He looked very well and cheery.

March 9th. Rode out early with Matheson and Arthur Smith to GIVENCHY and went all round their trenches. Very dirty and wet. Orders came in very late in evening and had to make arrangements for an early start.

9th March 1915

Darling Nancy

Being of a Jewish turn of mind the enclosed I may be able to realise on in about 50 years when the Prince is King! It may amuse to see it and if you'll keep it we'll make a bit on it together when the opportunity occurs!!

Many thanks for your letter. Nothing doing here. Oh Yes! Huie came over yesterday. Splendid of him, and stayed the whole day. Looked very well.

Your loving

Lags.

HEAD-QUARTERS
2nd Division.
March 9th 1915

Dear Gibbs

As I told you yesterday the Queen has sent me some waterproof aprons, with instructions to send 25 to each Battalion of the 8th Guards Brigade. I therefore send you 25 for the Battalion Coldstream Guards.

I don't know if they are practical knowing alas nothing about trench work; but I think they are meant to be "sat on" in wet weather. They are for the use of the officers first and then anyone else you may think fit to issue them to. Anyhow the Queen hopes they may be useful.

I remain

Yours very sincerely

Edward (Prince of Wales)

March 10th. Breakfast at 5:15 a.m. and we marched to a spot on the Canal. Bombardment of German trenches due at 7:30 a.m., which began absolutely on the stroke the whole way up the line, about 400 guns making the most awful noise. Poor old Huns! Then at 8:05 they were to rush the trenches. 6th Brigade in front of us and Indians on the left. They were most awfully successful all along and by NEUVE CHAPELLE. The South Staffords unfortunately got rather in front in our attack and met a machine gun in the Orchard. They got up twice but each time had to go back. The Indians and 8th Division got some 450 prisoners. The attack was on a very large scale and extended very far up the line. We waited all day by the Canal, very cold and rather damp. Colonel Feilding was in command of the Brigade, Cavan being on leave. A heavy bombardment was kept up all day, but nothing like the ½ hour from 7:30 – 8 o'clock which must have broken in nearly all the German trenches. About 5 p.m. we were told we could return to our billets in BÉTHUNE. The Irish Guards taking over some trenches, while the 3rd Battalion billeted close behind. On the way back the Armoured train with the 4.7 passed the transport on the tow-path and made one of our cookers go into the Canal, the horses having to be shot. Otherwise no damage. Bed about 11 p.m. very tired.

March 10th 1915

My dearest Nancy

Many thanks for food from the man at York. I think it all arrived but he packs things so badly that everything was loose, a box of turtle soup was tied on outside by the postman. The news seems pretty good all round.

We are making use of Stafford to bring home some purchases we have made and have sent them to Bella Young at Boulogne. I can't remember Stafford's hospital or I would write to him. I went down and spent 4½ hours with Lancelot on Monday. He seemed very well and cheerful I thought. It took me about an hour by train.

With love to all

Your loving brother

A. H. Gibbs

March 11th. Breakfast 4 a.m. Started 5 to 5, and marched to much the same place only other side of Canal. Found R.E. had got the cookers out of the Canal with very little damage. Not much "Gunning", went to Brigade Headquarters. General Feilding still in command. He told us Generals were very pleased with yesterday's show and that everything seemed quiet now. Waited about until about 1 o'clock, when we got orders to go to billets at QUESNOY. 'Monkey' B (?) went on and arranged about them. Very few and very dirty, so we put two Companies in Railway trucks which were in a siding on Canal. Owners of Headquarters House very grumpy, but Bonvalot pacified them a bit. Colonel and self slept in a small and rather dirty cottage.

March 12th. Very disturbed night, messages at 1 a.m., 5 and 6, last being to send officers to reconnoitre position in case of an advance, so had to get up and arrange. News of yesterday's doings came in. Meerut Division took 200 more prisoners, bringing total up to about 1,100. Went round billets. Lot of gunfire went on all day, so we had to keep at short notice. News came in in the evening that 7th Division had done very well and "broken" the line and the Cavalry had been called up and big things were expected. A little 'vingt et un' after dinner! Firbank (of Langford) came to lunch.

March 13th. A real good night with no messages. Colonel and several others went off see position to take over tonight. Message came in that the Indian Corps estimated 2,000 dead in front of them, so German casualties in these parts must be over 6,000, otherwise quiet. We walked up to PONT FIXE about 4 o'clock. Brigadier told us on the way German casualties must now reach 10,000 counting prisoners. Took over from 3rd Battalion. Two Companies in front and two Companies in reserve. Good place for mess and to sleep in. Good deal of bombarding on left, all quiet with us. Budget and Pro in front trenches for 48 hours.

March 14th. Quiet night, MacGregor went round them early. Lovely day. Walked round village which is far less desolate than CUINCHY was. Brigadier came round with Crawley, no fresh news. Nothing more happening on left at present. Ashley returned yesterday from 3 days in Hospital. Leese left with 3rd Battalion with a sprained ankle he has had for 5 days. Had 3 casualties only all slightly wounded. Colonel and self went up to trenches about 5 p.m., and walked round whole front. Parts very wet, over knee in mud, but we are draining towards Canal. Waited in advanced main line till dusk and then walked over land to outpost platoons (3 of them) isolated in front. Their trenches very good but must be most uncomfortable, having no connection with each other or back. However communication trench should soon be finished. Got back about 7:30 p.m. very wet and dirty.

March 15th. Very quiet night. Few shells came into PONT FIXE in morning but did no damage; fancy they are searching for guns, our guns answered presumably with some effect as enemy stopped. Brigadier came round also Staff-Captain from 1st Army Corps to see Lock. We now have to take height of water above and below once daily so as to keep enough for the barges below. 3rd Battalion started to arrive soon after 4 p.m. Battalion took a long time to arrive at LE QUESNOY as front trenches relieved late on account of burst of fire; No: 4 got back at 10 p.m.

March 16th. Colonel and self went round billets which are very far apart taking 1½ hours to do 2 Companies, the others we left as we were so tired. Several fellows rode into BÉTHUNE and buying parties allowed in by Companies. Very quiet afternoon. Heard that attack on ST ELOI and counter-attack cost us a good deal, and the Germans a good deal more. Humphrey de T went to Hospital with "Jaundice".

March 17th. Colonel went down to Brigade Headquarters at 11:30 a.m., went round billets of 1 & 2. Also the platoon of No: 3 that got burnt out last night, damage :- one barn, about 23 kits and rifles, 2 Cows dead and 6 injured, all men all right. Held a board on it but no-one admitted lighting a match. Heard a lot of shelling in direction of CUINCHY and GIVENCHY. Companies started going about 3 p.m. Nos: 1 & 2 to front line, 3 & 4 to PONT FIXE. Colonel, MacGregor, and self got up about 4:30 p.m. Everything pretty quiet now, but 3rd Battalion reported heavy shelling most of the day with "Fizz-Bang" gun and a 9.2", however only two casualties. MacG went round after relief and Colonel after dinner.

March 18th. (Slept very badly). Lot of firing North of us about 12 and 1:00 a.m., also machine gun. Seven fairly big shells put into PONT FIXE about 3:00 a.m., no damage. Party of No: 4 got rather caught returning to their trench at sunrise, getting 3 wounded. Quiet morning Brigadier came round, not much news; hear our casualties at NEUVE CHAPELLE rather bigger than originally given out. Had 1 killed, and 5 wounded (one died) in 24 hours. I am afraid they realize that we are being more active than the Battalion we took over from, and so shell and fire considerably more. Sent up about 60 "Cheveux de Frises" wire entanglement for 'East Anglian' R.E. Company to put out, but they did not do it at all well.

18th March 1915

Darling Nancy

    Great things have been happening round these parts lately, which did <u>not</u> involve us I'm glad to say.

    The casualties were pretty heavy on both sides but the advantage was ours, we have re-enforcements to put in which the Germans have to draw from other parts of their line.

    Cavan has just been in here looking much better than when I last saw him, he brought cheering news of the authorities!

    Confidence is great successes shortly. There is really very little news from here, very often the first we see of anything that has happened, is in the 'Times' of the day before. We stick in these trenches, which have been held I believe for over 4 months, in and out every 2 days.

Love to the family and you

Your loving

Lags

March 19th. About ¼ to 2 a.m. nine fair sized shells came over, but mostly dropped in rear of PONT FIXE. Good deal of work got through in trenches, mostly filling in old trenches. Trench East of SPOIL BANK too wet to do much with. Communication trenches to right and left of line complete. Colonel and self went up tonight to see Nos: 1 & 3. Got Byng out of his cellar and walked through SPOIL BANK, to trench alongside Canal right up to front line by WILLOW ROAD. Germans about 300 yards off. Thick lines of wire in front of them and several barricades on Tow path, ground in front very wet. Walked back via Tow path and through 'DISTILLERY'. 3rd Battalion got up at about 4:30 p.m. Still snowing a bit, got to LE QUESNOY at about 6 p.m.

March 20th. Some shelling in the distance. Very short orders (C.O.'s). The draft of 98 men and one officer (E. St. L. Bonvalet) arrived about 12 noon, bringing our total strength up to 944. Went through employed men with Colonel and Sergeant Major, finding we have about 120, but are unable to reduce it. After lunch Sim and self rode over to see 1st Battalion at LE TOURET, found Merton, Tolly, Colonel P, Claud Willoughby. Dermot Brown there besides many I did not know. They were more cheery than I had seen them since they came out. Merton was doing Adjutant. Stopped till about 5:30 p.m. Then took Robert Walker back with us, he having joined the 1st Battalion in error.

March 21st. Holy Communion 8:30 a.m. in Headquarters. I got there just in time, very small attendance. Colonel went off to his service so MacG took the Parade Service which we had in a field. R.E. and Gunners also came, not a very satisfactory one, conducted by Father Waggett. Most lovely day. We all sat on steps of mess. New order that all cameras are to be sent home, and so everyone finishing off their films taking groups. Got up to PONT FIXE again about 4:30 p.m., found 3rd Battalion had been heavily shelled with little damage, Nos: 3 & 4 Companies in front trenches. Trenches much improved. Hope to use my new Periscope sent me by Cousin Vicary.

March 22nd. About 1 a.m. we made a small demonstration with fire and machine gun. Just after Birkbeck came rushing to say Byng had been wounded. They had hauled more than carried him through the trench and than had to run along tow path as this fusillade was coming off. Wound nasty but not dangerous at present, in at nose, and out at jaw-bone via or round cheek-bone. Otherwise quiet night. Byng sent off to BÉTHUNE. Grenadiers captured 6' 6" Hun weighing 17 stone, wounded. Some aeroplanes over followed by about 10 shells, two going through house opposite. Colonel and self went round trenches first up to right. "Bayswater" far less wet, and water running into Canal hard. Choose sites for dug outs in SPOIL BANK. Went right up left side along "Cambridge Terrace" up to GIVENCHY, through but very very sticky still. Afternoon very quiet. Freddy Marshall (Grenadier Guards) killed by a stray bullet. Played piano until about 11 p.m.

March 23rd. 1:30 a.m. Sergeant Major came in to say signalling could be seen and so Colonel and self took party and went to house, surrounded it, and searched it, but nothing there. Nearly got shot by one man on meeting round a corner and he thinking I was the spy escaping. Left front trench got a bit shelled in the morning, but the armoured train stopped it. Late relief tonight on account of Brigade, the Huns having got the time of our relief at 5 p.m., and always shell then. Got back here after 8 p.m., and some did not get in till nearly 10 p.m. Birkbeck went to Hospital during the day with slight flue.

23rd March 1915

Excuse envelope but I have run out
temporarily and this I borrowed

Darling Nancy

I am afraid there have been a good many casualties lately but mostly with the other Divisions and I knew very few except Hulse (Scots Guards) who was at Wanen Hill with me.

I rather think the Germans have lost their initiative in these parts and have been concentrating their efforts against the French – Prympsyl will make them think a bit too.

I think there is almost a unanimous opinion out here about racing i.e. that what good would it do anyone out here if it did stop? None! And on the other hand it would knock breeding etc. out if it stopped. I think it is a very good solution that they should make Ascot and Epsom plain race meetings for racing only this year and not social gatherings. Also I am sure anyone back wounded would want to go. Although I do think that it is that class of man, the jockey, small trainer and bookies that do not realize the war and merely look on it as a bore and loss of trade.

Poor Byng Hopwood got wounded yesterday, through the nose, and out at the jaw, nasty but not dangerous.

It was at night and his company were working above ground. He was rather splendid as he would not allow those who came to help him to do so before they had first got all the men back under cover, also he would not leave the dressing-station until he had seen his Company Sergeant Major to arrange about their breakfasts.

We had a Parade Service last Sunday out in the open. Last night the Colonel and I had a hunt for spies, we thought we had been regular 'Sherlock Holmes' and took a party down to a certain house, which proved blank. There were a good many amusing incidents men coming round corners and meeting someone else with an "Ah", like the detective in a play who catches the wrong man. I walked into a sandbag barricade and apologised profusely to it thinking it was a man, which amused the Colonel awfully.

I wrote to Cousin Vicary asking him to order me a periscope before Blanche came back to London, which he insisted on giving me. It is a very high class one with prismatic sight etc (at £9!!)

The Grenadiers made a prize prisoner 2 nights ago, a German Sergeant Major, 6 foot 6" and 17 stone. He said they were all warned that whenever caught by the British they were shot and was awfully surprised at being taken to a Dressing Station and then sent on in a Motor Ambulance.

He also could not understand us living in the houses we were which gave us a splendid opening. They told him German shells never burst and those that did always went into the Canal (not strictly true! but lowered his opinion of his own Artillery!).

Ever your loving

Lags

March 24th. Raining a bit. Colonel and self took nearly two hours going round billets. After luncheon Trousers and self rode over to the 1st Battalion, found Colonel P, Merton, Tolly etc. They were just moving off to LOCON. Saw Birkbeck in Hospital, went into Transport on way back, found them in excellent form. Took Summary on MacFadyen. Wrote several letters, John S. and Georgie.

March 25th. Raining like the Devil. Shudder to think what the trenches will be like. Made out orders for relief which is much later than usual. Field General Court Martial on MacFadyen; MacB. President, rather long. Becky and Dermot Brown came over to tea from their 'resting place'. Moved off about 5 p.m. Found 3rd Battalion had had a very quiet time without any casualties. We left Pro behind under this new system of giving the Junior Officers the Command, also about 10 NCO's were left. Trousers hurt his knee a bit, but not much damage.

March 26th. Colonel started on his rounds with Brigadier up to right trenches, coming back to Battalion Headquarters and picking me up. We went up by 'Orchard Street' which was in excellent condition, up to 'Oxford & Cambridge Terrace', through the Grenadiers to 'Duck's Bill', where we used our periscopes at the Hun's trenches which were 40-50 yards off. I tried to "ring the plate" on a German iron loop-hole, but could not hit it. They shelled us a good deal with "Jack Johnson's" doing very little damage, otherwise a quiet day. Casualties 1 killed 2 wounded.

March 27th. A real cold night, freezing still about 8 a.m., however as long as it is fine it will dry up. Man in No: 4 got hit by stray bullet otherwise no damage. A platoon of the Post Office Rifles came up under "Seedy" and Micky Lawrence. I took latter round DUCK'S BILL as he was very anxious to see some 'dead Germans', a gruesome task. Relief completed earlier and we all got to dinner at LE QUESNOY by 8 p.m.

March 28th. We could not get a service of any kind until 2 p.m., which was a bad time and consequently I fear a very small attendance. MacGregor and self rode over to 1st Battalion who were at LOCON, finding Merton, Colonel, and Steele, and others out, stayed to tea and home via BÉTHUNE.

March 29th. Up early to promulgate a Court Martial at ¼ to 8 on account of the Battalion going to the Baths at BÉTHUNE. 5 new telephones arrived from Polly Lambton, a real good present to the Battalion. We are now independent of the Government instruments. Back to the trenches without incident: finding a 'Post Office' Captain and Subaltern also a platoon to stop with us the night.

March 30th. Colonel went off earlier than usual with our Brigadier, also Brigadier of 47th Brigade, so I went up later with another platoon of 'Post Office' rifles who had come to work for the day. Then I went round to right forward trench following up telephone wires, found it was being bombed, also found on my return I had been following up the wrong wire! An extra quiet day. 2 men wounded and Walker to Hospital.

March 31st. Think Germans must be having Easter festivities as so quiet. One casualty. Went round to left post with Pro. Got away about 5:30 and back to find no mail.

April 1st. Got caught once by the Colonel due to the date! After luncheon went for a ride with MacBride to BÉTHUNE and then on to HINGES and back across fields. Large mail no news.

2nd Battalionn Coldstream Guards
4th Guards Brigade
British Expeditionary Force

1st April 1915

Darling Nancy,
    "Sir R. Walker Bout", didn't care much about the trenches and has now gone home sick. How sick we don't know. But I hope they will very soon send him out again as I think this life is doing him a world of good.

As you are so kind as to 'Cummerbunds' I have two now, one always on and the other at the wash, but one has shrunk so it is only fit for Pavlova or other such advert for "CB"s. I have got it on now but would welcome an ordinary rather thinner man's size.

Nothing much happening here.

Your loving

Lags.

Am going to hear the Bishop of London at Béthune tomorrow, 2nd Friday.

April 2nd. Went into BÉTHUNE where Bishop of London had a Service in the Theatre, excellent sermon, rode home via fields with Trousers. Received orders about harassing Germans and various other methods. Relieved about 5:30, before which General Vesey Dawson came in and saw us. Went out to look round with Sergeant Major about 9:30 p.m. but did not see much. Good many bullets flying around.

April 2nd 1915
Good Friday.

My dearest Nancy,
　　Many thanks for the cake, gelantine and drops. As they are Terry's drops I suppose it was you who sent 3 tins to Col. Glyn about a month ago. He did not know who they were from.
　　I enclose Lags letters. We have not done anything remarkable lately and life is a bit slow, but what would you *expect* in Lent. We have had a service this evening at 5 and on Easter day we have an 8 o'clock celebration and a 9 o'clock morning service.
　　The Bishop of London was nearby yesterday and had a service for the Life Guards and Blues. He probably visits the regiments of his Diocese. He has gone to a dangerous spot today but I think things are quiet as we didn't hear much going on. I hear from B. Young who has moved to Dunkerque where he will see more of what is going on. No doubt Stafford knew he had gone there. I have not heard if Edward has taken Stafford's place, (*as Chaplain to the Archbishop of York*). I must celebrate Easter by having a bath.

Your loving brother

Antony Hubert Gibbs

April 3rd. At daybreak (4:30 a.m.) a heavy fire was opened by us, with some shelling but the Germans did not make much reply. I went up to the Bridge to see if I could see anything, but it was not light enough. This went on fairly continuously and then just after 5 a.m. the British mine at CUINCHY was blown up, making very little noise but a great deal of smoke. Very few Germans were said to be there. A very quiet morning followed. After lunch Colonel and self went round B-3, now held by Post Office Rifles, and which we take over shortly. Some very indifferent trenches. Had tea there. I went back and talked to Micky and Seedy Lawrence for about ½ hour. Raining hard but so far one section has stood it well.

April 4th. Easter Day, and consequently a very quiet one. Went up to right hand forward post after lunch and fired a few rounds which started the "Fizz-Bang", so perhaps I did some damage. Relief as usual.

April 5th. Raining hard. Had to cancel open air service, which was the Easter Service. Had Holy Communion in No: 1's billet. After service I rode over to 5th Brigade Headquarters and lunched with "Mr. P" and his General (Chichester), and after we rode into BÉTHUNE and had haircut.

April 6th. Orders as usual at 10 a.m. then Colonel and self went round Nos:1 & 2 Companies' billets. Companies did 1 hour's drill. Brigadier came in, no news. Started off for B-3 section about 3:30 p.m. Took over from Post Office Rifles fairly easily. Very bad section and wants a great deal of work. Good Headquarters billets with piano.

April 7th. A good deal of firing on right about 1 a.m., which turned out to be a German, mine exploding in the French lines which did no good. Got up about 8 a.m., went round trenches and made a map which took some time. No:3 up on right in SCOTTISH trench and No:4 on left in NEW CUT, the other two Companies in billets. Put the map on a clean bit of paper which took whole afternoon. Very quiet day. I had a snipe or so from No:3 into the backs of some Germans in the front of 5th Brigade at 2,200yds. Went round with Colonel after dinner.

April 8th. MacB did orders at 10 a.m., went round again with Colonel in afternoon. Brushworks out from Grouse-butts getting on well; these are being put up on account of the shortage in Sand-bags. Arranged for relief which took place in evening. No:2 relieving No:3 in SCOTTISH Trench and No:1- 4 in NEW CUT. Went round billets which are fairly good but still very dirty. The 15th London Battalion attached to us with about 6 Officers and 2 Platoons.

April 9th. Raining and cold. Everything very quiet, went round with Colonel. "Civil Service" rifles have 2 Platoons attached to us.

April 10th. Started to dig dug-out in garden of our house. A quick round with Colonel. Guy S-S turned up about 5 p.m. with 75 men. Nos:2 & 4 went up to trenches. No:4 to SCOTTISH Trenches. 2 more Platoons from "Civil Service" Rifles, an odd lot they are.

April 11th. Rained a bit but made practically no difference to the trenches. Hurdles across our front now and nearly wired up, 50 yards more filling in to do. 1 casualty in the night, Bonner No:3, very slight – quiet day. About 9 p.m. we arranged to fire on a German working party. The trench Howitzer started it and 'Monkey' continued with his gun. Again at 12 and again at 3 a.m. "Some frightfulness"!

April 12th. General Pole Carew came round. Colonel and self met him at "WHITE HOUSE" (right of B-3). He seemed delighted to see the old Battalion which he had commanded in 1898. One more Platoon of 15th London Battalion for instruction.

April 13th. Brigadier De Haviland (of Eton) and Gort came round. Also orders for relief. The 3rd Battalion Coldstream Guards got up about 3:15 p.m. (the 1st Company). "Little Man" and Piccolo Feilding having come up on in front, I took them up to NEW CUT and SCOTTISH trench. We moved off about 4 p.m. but had to change the route of the Battalion as the Germans started to shell it. Came into billets in the Girl's School, BÉTHUNE, Headquarters in 15 RUE DE LILLE. Champagne to celebrate the night of coming out for 4 days rest.

April 14th. Two cigars after dinner caused awful trouble in my inside. Even 2 cups of tea in bed would not assuage my thirst, soda-water for breakfast! Somewhat lengthy orders. After lunch Colonel and self went through Promotions. Sim and self then rode over to RICHEBOURG to see 1st Battalion, but found them in trenches and so came away quickly!

Offiziergefangenenlagen
Heidelberg
Baden

April 14th 1915

My darling Nance
    Your turn I think! Very many and much, much happier returns of tomorrow to Blanchie. First letters from:
Gilly F 29/3, many thanks for sad list, many shocks but I prefer to know. Tell him to give Milly my love and I hope she is getting stronger.
Miss Eglantine Hanbury 29/3, so fond of her to write, and it was a kindness to me for her to have ridden my "Kells".
Lady Crooke Lawless, 4/4

Aunt C, 31/3 her presents have arrived, a cushion etc.
Willy Otter Gibbs, my brother-in-law, 21/3, tell him to keep fit.
Janet Crawley, no date (her mother's fault!) a very nice letter.
Eileen Scott, now with Francis at Cannes, so glad Francis is getting well slowly. Lancelot, 17/3, delighted to hear from him, quite time he was confirmed as Adjutant. Miss Lucia White, 27/3, Hermione would perhaps thank her for me, very nice of her to write.
Evie Gurney, Easter day, her letter most welcome and my love to her Cyril, Alice, John etc. and blessings.
Blanchies of 27/3 and yours of 77th (?) both arrived today, the months appear to seem even longer to you than they do here, but 77th is too exaggerated!?
Parcels from George and Via 18 – 22 and 25 March and 1 other.
From Mrs W. Gibbs mostly Blanche I think and one or two from Ruby, of March 20th, 26th (3); Fortnum & Mason 2 of 27/3, Harrods 29/3.
Mrs Tollemache 4/3, your good self 23/3, Gilly F 25/3, Dunhill 22/3 and 2 more London no date no name.

    Mrs Dorothy Ryder sends 1 a fortnight, as I thought 1 a week too much, but it is a very good idea. Please tell Cox & Co to send me £5 a month in future. We are well supplied with food now. Will you ask Blanche to find out about my pony mare at J. Hunter & Co., Aston Magna, Moreton in Marsh. She ought to have foaled by now if she was going to, also J. H. might like to be paid. Also Blanche might pay as many bills as she likes.

    Two days ago poor Joliffe was suddenly ordered off to go to Rastadt to a prison and since it has appeared in the papers that for every man or officer of German Submarines left in naval Detention Barracks in England, one British officer will be put in prison here. One is quite ready if that is considered war here.

    Will you tell Cox & Co that J. has gone to Rastadt and also tell his sister at 27 Lowndes Square, Mrs Wyndham. Poor fellow, it is hard for him, altogether 39 officers have been thus treated, from all the various prisoners camps.

    I am so very sorry to hear of Mick and Maureen Hodgson being killed, and send Via all my sympathy. Mick I was so very fond of, he had been a great friend at Eton and ever since, though lately I have seen so little of him. Very glad to hear of Tom Gurney, D.S.O. and a Major – tell Mrs. Tom if you see her how pleased I am. I know she and Mrs Clitheroe will be prouder than ever.

    I expect Staff have some very interesting experiences. Everyone writes delighted with Lags. He is evidently doing very splendidly. I am so glad and not at all surprised.

    Perhaps a little packet containing 1 or 2 (not more) suits of thin pyjamas might be sent to me – those I have are very thick. Except for

Joliffe leaving here nothing unusual has happened. With the pyjamas I should like a pair of those flannel khaki trousers, these I did mention before also. Of books I have enough and some good woman of Heidelberg has also sent in 40 English books so we shall not lack reading matter.

I am now giving English lessons to a French Colonel Walton – he and another Colonel Raymond are both charming people. Also 2 Russians, Sipiagin and Zogovski who talked a bit before. For myself, I confine my attention to French and have considerably improved in talking I think and I read it too.

The weather has at last cleared up after a fortnights rain and wet. Blanche's cigars arrived 3 days ago! I have had a letter or so from friends in America and R. de Rothschild sent me another parcel. I suppose poor dear Eustace's things in New York are being all sent back – or sold there. He had several ponies, 2 of which certainly he paid big prices for in England. 250 for each I think. Then his car and etc. He must have had a great many things altogether.

Blanche writes very content with marriage. I wonder if it is really worth giving up all the freedom of bachelordom to be sat on by a wife! What do you think? Remain the bachelor uncle, who takes Janet to plays etc. or lives a fearful life (as bachelors are always supposed to do), or settle down with all pomp and dullness in Cheltenham?

Tell Blanche that I'll have Whissenthorpe if it comes into the market reasonably cheap. I don't so much fancy Peake's house now. Also I think poor Geoffrey Stewart's house Winwick Manor might suit if Mrs. Stewart wishes to sell Pytchley.

I walk a lot here (blue pencil through two lines). But I am very fit thank Heaven – as long as one is well it is easier to be patient.

Now bless you all and thank everyone for their letters and parcels. You are all much too good to me, but don't stop being so!

Your very loving

Evelyn

April 15th. Good Gazette including my appointment as Adjutant! Dated March 16th 1915. Went round billets. About 3 p.m. Battalion paraded in Girls School Yard, about 950 on Parade. We then marched to LE QUESNOY for two days before going in again. Landlady furious at our return and made a terrible scene, but we in got all the same.

April 16th. Lovely day and very quiet. Several people came in to see us. After lunch T-Clark, "Monkey", Guy S-S, and self rode over to 1st

Battalion at LOCON after some jumping practice in a paddock by Transport. Found Merton, Colonel Julian Steele and had tea.

April 17th. Uneventful morning. Battalion started about 2 p.m. for trenches but were held up for short time owing to PONT FIXE being shelled. Got up to B-1 section about 4 p.m. relieving Hertfordshires. Found it very much the same. Nos: 4 & 3 in front on right and left. We stay this time for a four days tour. Self made a temporary Captain in today's Gazette.

April 18th. A good deal of firing during the night. Lovely day. Took a short walk with Colonel round back parts of trenches. Some shelling by our Siege with very little effect. Matheson and Longtail (Junior) came over from 3rd Battalion and passed 'time of day'. No casualties.

April 19th. Early during the night a good deal of machine gun fire, more for "frightfulness" than effect. Battery came up to do some demonstration firing, which broke most of our windows by the noise, but results good; went over to 3rd Battalion with Colonel to B-3 and then right round whole of B section. Germans blew up a mine in front of GIVENCHY hoping to blow in our mine. Total damage, candles blown out! and men continued working. Some of their own parapet blown down. Put in for 36 hours leave to go to BOULOGNE to see Blanche on 26th, who comes over to see Willy (*William Otter Gibbs whom she married on February 23rd 1915 at St Michael's Church Paddington*).

April 20th. Colonel slept up in Lock house. Some shelling in morning but no damage. Went round our line in afternoon. Nos: 2 and 3 front posts nearly connected up now. Colonel and self 'ran' across and then down BAKER STREET home. Beautiful day. Had a good bank at Roulette!

2nd Battalionn Coldstream Guards
4th Guards Brigade
British Expeditionary Force

20th April 1915.

Darling Nancy,

I have just put in for 36 hours leave and go down to Boulogne to see Blanche when she is there. I hope to get there night 26th April and leave next night. Cavan has forwarded it so I hope all will be well. Pity Stafford isn't still at Wimereux then you might have come over and we could have bonded together, us 4. The poor old Huns tried to mine a trench not far up from ours but made a hopeless 'beafsteak', only getting about 40 yards from their own parapet. It did no harm except to shake down some of their own parapet. So I'm afraid that fellow won't get an "iron cross".

One of their aeroplanes tried to come over this afternoon and was greeted by 4 of our aircraft guns who concentrated on it. I have never seen one turn so quick.

Your loving brother,

Lags.

April 21st. Dug a bit on the trench round PONT FIXE. Few shells over but small ones. Slight change of roster, we got 3 days out now. Several American Military Attaches came round trenches with Brind 2nd Division. Were relieved by 3rd Battalion Coldstream Guards and marched to LE QUESNOY to same billets.

April 22nd. Orders and billets as usual. Rode Mules and Transport horses all afternoon. Mules bucked well, many heavy falls.

April 23rd. Very stiff after riding mules barebacked. Moved into BÉTHUNE at 3:30 p.m. to École des Jeunes Filles. Headquarters at 15 Rue de Lille. Had large dinner party: Little Man, Francis Longueville, Cubitt, Arthur Smith, Colonel Feilding. Good evening! and some damage to furniture.

April 24th. Hair cut in BÉTHUNE. Met Little Man who looked pale! Paraded in Girls School at 2 p.m. and marched via South Bank of Canal to LE PRÉOL. Battalion about 970 strong. Billets fair but very scattered. Slight reverse up North to French but most of the ground regained. Germans did it with asphyxiating gases. Wilkinson turned up from Base and posted to No: 3 Company. Dyas (M.O) left us and Woodyatt takes his place.

April 25th. Church Parade at 10:30 a.m. Quite a good Service. Weslyan Minister turned up about 11:30 a.m., I had unfortunately forgotten to order his Parade. He seemed rather annoyed! A short game of stump cricket in a field and then into B-1 GIVENCHY again. Nos: 4 on right and 3 on left. Sent all the children Field Service Post Cards. Line almost same as we last left it. No casualties while taking over. A little shelling in the evening. Colonel slept in Lock house.

April 26th. Heard reverse to French rather bigger than we thought but about ¾ retaken. Manchesters had success somewhere just South of YPRES. Went round with Colonel after lunch. Very heavy shelling in B-2 (GIVENCHY Village) with 6 inches I should think, but heard afterwards no damage. Colonel Feilding thought he saw that German wire was cut near DUCK'S BILL, so I wired this up to M.G. about midnight.

2nd Battalionn Coldstream Guards
4th Guards Brigade
British Expeditionary Force

26th April 1915

Darling Nancy
    Yours of the 22nd April come through pretty quick. The questions in order!
    Yes! I'm bound to say it was more of a surprise to me than anyone and never realized they had got down so far. I shall have to make the best of it while I am out here, as, as soon as I get back it will be cancelled I fear. I am afraid Aunt Cathy has missed it!
    I had remembered the old maxim about casting clouts and have had to stick to it more from necessity than otherwise as I have only written to Blanche about 4 days ago to purchase thinner. Those I wear now <u>can</u> stand up by themselves!
    What brutes the Germans were up North with their 'consfixicating' gases. The French had to go back about four miles, I believe, but have regained three.

Your loving

Lags

    Writing somewhat indifferent due to having cut the top of my index finger off, or nearly so.
    Yes! Thank you so much for Tiptree, they came. I thanked Albinia thinking it was her as she sent some just before.

April 27th. Less shelling. Went round about 11 a.m. German shelling left of DUCK'S BILL with 18 pounders (or equivalent), very accurate. Geoffrey Feilding got a Brigade which leaves Matheson in command of 3rd Battalion. French slowly advancing up North. Canadians also doing well. Our front is very quiet. 13 men (details) came up from Base. Heard a lot of Motor and Wagon Transport moving North in rear of German lines. Two German aeroplanes came over during the day.

April 28th. Real hot day. Sat out and read, went round trenches once, Nos: 1 & 2 in front. Nearly all front posts joined, about 10 yards more to do between Nos: 1 & 2. Relieved by Hertfordshires rather late owing to a relief the day before being shelled. Got back to LE QUESNOY about ¼ to 9 p.m.

April 29th. Usual routine in the morning. Rode over to 12 Battalion, who were at OBLINGHEM, found them very short of Officers. Tolly having gone on staff. Claud W (?) away. Becky 3rd in command. A successful bank after dinner.

April 30th. Too hot to sit in the sun. Battalion going down by l00's to Baths in BÉTHUNE, also arranged a bathing Picquet on the Canal. Guy S-S, Budget, Ashley, and self rode over to dine with 1st Battalion. Very cheery dinner, got back about midnight.

May 1st. Companies did an hours drill. Colonel and self round 3 & 4's billets. We relieved Hertfordshires in B-l section, also not leaving LE QUESNOY until 5 p.m. No news except that the YPRES show was a very bad one. Trenches much the same.

May 2nd. Quiet night. Service in the Distillery by Fleming. Went up to trenches in afternoon taking Gage and Smith who had just arrived up, Haynes having arrived yesterday. BAKER STREET much improved being lower. Nos: 1 & 2 in front right and left. A new bomb thrower, not very good except for very short distances. Did a lot of typing.

May 3rd. A few shells towards PONT FIXE otherwise a quiet day. Went up to left side. Relieved by Hertfordshires in the evening, came back through wood by LE PRÉOL as Canal bank being shelled.

May 4th. Round 3 & 4 billets. Very hot. Rode round Transport jumps with Guy S-S and Ympkin.

May 5th. Message to say not going into GIVENCHY. Had an awful fright, Colonel went off to 1st Division to take over 2nd Brigade, but luckily he was not wanted and so he returned by about 10 a.m. Made many arrangements about change of position.

2nd Battalionn Coldstream Guards
4th Guards Brigade
British Expeditionary Force

2nd May 1915

Darling Nancy
    A 'uge parcel from you arrived today with dried fruits, cake etc. I have given the fruits + receipt to one chef and asked him to make the delicious dish.
    I enclose a German bullet which fell round these parts, for your eldest unmarried daughter for a 4th Sunday after Easter present. Fleming conducted an 'odd' service today in a barn <u>just</u> behind the firing line, at times the singing was almost drowned by guns (<u>mostly</u> ours). His text was "Fed-up" or words to that effect. He is an excellent preacher for soldiers.

One Gaythorne-Hardy of 60th (or R. Brigade) is Adjutant of Herts Territorial Regiment which is in the Brigade. We relieve them and often, and he often speaks of you in glowing terms of affection (Don't let Stafford see this!!).

As to guns lost at Ypres I don't know at all who has them now.

It was a badly managed show and there should not have been such heavy losses even after the French had gone back in that 'almost' disgraceful way.

I had dinner with the 1st Battalion Coldstream Guards two days ago. They are again very badly off for officers due to sickness. Mostly some have gone on Staff jobs. They are as near Béthune as we are now.

Your loving

Lags

May 6th. No drill as moving off to CUINCHY early. Very hot and thundery. Colonel to command Section and so MacGregor has taken over Battalion. Took over from the Worcesters (Major Lambton) found trenches in very good order. No: 3 took over Brickstacks and No: 4 Hollow, No: 1 Pudding Lane, and No: 2 Glasgow Street.

May 7th. Quiet night. MacB. went round late last night and early this morning, while I slept. Hot but more wind not Easterly! Some shelling over the French South of us. Crater of mine blown up by Germans 2 days ago, bombed a bit by No: 3 Company. Some anti-asphyxiating stuff arrived which Drill Sergeant Higgins, self and others mixed up till 2 a.m. and sent up. Casualties 2 killed and 2 wounded.

May 8th. Some big 'Jack Johnsons' came into CUINCHY but did no harm. Went down and saw Sim and Little Man at Section Headquarters. French pretty active down South. No: 1 moves into Brickstack, and No: 2 into Hollow.

May 9th. A quiet day, orders received as to an attack to be made tomorrow. We were to make a demonstration of firing. Some more anti-asphyxiating gas soda turned up which was mixed.

May 10th. Bombardment started early but we could see very little. Some big shells came over and fell West of one road. We had various reports all day. The first being that the 4th Corps at ARMENTIÈRES had got to the 3rd line of German trenches. This was true but the first two lines were still full of Germans, and the 60th and Lincolns had to cut their way back. Very quiet in our front.

May 11th. We heard that the 1st Brigade had had a very bad time, and that the Black Watch and Camerons had lost heavily with no result, which goes to show that the Germans have still got their best troops in front of us. French doing very well down by NOTRE DAME de LORETTE. They took 3,000 prisoners, 32 machine guns, 11 big guns, and had walked over any amount of dead. MacGregor not very well so I went round trenches in evening. Just as Budget and I were going up Pudding Lane they started shelling right down it, wounding 3 fellows, most uncomfortable!

May 12th. Were relieved evening by Welsh Regiment – funny lot. 3rd Brigade, they had been badly cut up 3 days before losing 11 Officers. Got away about 6:30 p.m. Then most memorable thing in the Regiment's annals happened. The 3rd Battalion had selected LE PRÉOL to have tea in – so had we. So we met. Not only that but the 1st Battalion were actually billeted there. Some 65 Officers of the Coldstream in a village of about 15 houses. It was not for long however as the 3rd Battalion moved on in about ½ hour and the 2nd Battalion about 1½ hours later. We moved on to PONT TOURNANT LOCON under the Colonel once more.

May 13th. Very crowded in billets but we were luckier than the Irish and Grenadiers, of whom half were bivouacing. Orders as usual and a quiet but cold and rainy morning. After lunch Colonel and self rode over to RICHEBOURG and looked at roads and mastworks. Very heavy bombardment going on. At one time we got in front of two batteries, who were firing battery, firing over our heads. A very wet afternoon's ride. Fildes came to us from 3rd Battalion in exchange for Menzies an M.G. Officer.

2nd Battalionn Coldstream Guards
4th Guards Brigade
British Expeditionary Force

13th May 1915

Darling Nancy

Our gallant 'Allies', the French, have been doing very well lately haven't they. 'Carency' and the Lights of 'Notre Dame de Lorette today.

I am afraid the British advance was not so 'marked'! As we are "in status quo". The Black Watch and Camerons having lost considerably, also the Welsh Regiment, Welsh Fusiliers T., and the Gloucestershires, however I'm glad to say our 1st Battalion were right out of it. A thing happened yesterday which hasn't happened before this war which was the 1st, 2nd and 3rd Battalions all met on the road, the 1st Battalion being billeted in the Village and the 2nd and 3rd Battalions had stopped to have teas in it.

So far this fighting has not involved us at all and I don't much think it will.

Raining hard today

Your loving Lags

May 14th. No news of a move yet. All men's greatcoats and blankets given in, also Officers kits and valises considerably lightened. French appear to have got on well at NOTRE DAME de LORETTE but no exact news. Attack by 5th & 6th Brigade put off.

May 15th. Fine at last. Companies went for a route march. Colonel and self waited for news. Same orders as last night. Attack to come off this time, and so early to bed.

May 16th. Breakfast 3:15 a.m. and ready to move (towards the Rhine!). 5th & 6th Brigade attacked at 11:30 p.m. last night and got in opposite RICHEBOURG. However by 5 a.m. they had only got the bit opposite "Cinder Track". 5th Brigade failed also Indians. VIth Division got their first line of trenches near FESTUBERT.

May 17th. One of the saddest days since we have been out here, the Colonel went off to take over the 85th Brigade. MacGregor takes over command and Leigh-Bennett 2nd in command. Attack made by 5th & 6th Brigades again and only a partial success. Some prisoners came through.

May 17th 1915
1 p.m. From the Earl of Cavan, Nancy's brother in law, to his wife, Inez.

Fighting in progress and so far all going well. About 600 or 700 of our men and our Division has advanced some 1500 yards and is advancing as I write, but it's slow and hard work. We have caused enemy to bring reinforcements all the way from Sedan. My Brigade awaiting orders any moment to relieve those in front. Shells falling all over village where I write. Perier got a Brigade great loss. Julian Steele will get his Batallion. Got a bit of a cold but am well.

Dearest love.

K. (Viscount Kilcoursie)

May 18th. Breakfast 4:30 a.m., fine at last. Quiet morning. Grenadiers and Irish Guards take over some trenches with Hertfordshires in support, we remain where we are.

May 18th 1915 – From the Earl of Cavan, Commander of the 4th Guards Brigade to his wife, Inez.

Battle was going well, 5 officers 541 men captured, but weather by bad luck has prevented us continuing this morning. We were ordered to advance yesterday about 3.p.m. into the first line and I took up the Grenadiers and Irish. Herts in support and 2nd & 3rd Coldstreams in reserve. The going was awful and shelling very heavy, but we were pretty busy and at night we got up to the first line, but it was pitch dark, raining hard, and at 3 a.m. when I went round the points it was thick mist and hopeless weather for gunners. The actual result so far is that we have taken a line as it were stretching from Ayot to Wheatampstead and of a depth of about from a line drawn through Lamer to a line drawn through Bride Hall, like this, see?

Germans are very tired and have only been able to bring up few reinforcements........... New attack just beginning.

Figure 55. Frederick Rudolph Lambart, the Tenth Earl of Cavan.

May 19th. Irish Guards had very heavy casualties and lost 17 Officers, only 2 killed; also Colonel W. Smith, 2 Grenadiers killed. MacGregor and self went up to Brigade Office and then round Hertfordshires trenches from whom we take over. MacGregor, Verelst, and Towers-Clark went over again in afternoon. Leigh-Bennett brought Battalion. Got to "CHOCOLATE MENIER CORNER" about 8:30 p.m. just getting dark and shelling subsiding. No: 1 Verelst in front line made by Irish. No: 2 in old German trench, 3 and 4 in old British salient trench. German trenches as dirty as they always are. MacGregor. Leigh-Bennett and self slept in dug out.

May 19th 1915 – Cavan to Inez

Yours of Sunday and Monday arrived this Wednesday morning in a tornado of shells. Gort's servant hit and the tiles of our dirty hovel rattling around. Our attack yesterday could not reach its objective. We gained about 300 yards in open country under awful machine gun fire. Irish Guards had 350 casualties, 15 officers, Grenadiers 70 casualties, 4 officers. Barrington Kenneth killed, charming fellow who was going to fly over to our garden party 3 years ago. Wilfred Smith very bad and must die I'm afraid. Young Lang and Creed wounded. We stuck to our ground and dug it in and now hold it with Herts and Grenadiers. Two Coldstream Battalions come forward to night and I hope we may get a bit forward in the dark. I can never describe the battlefield. I walked over it in the early mist at 4 a.m. this morning. Masses of dead Germans, rifles kit, bombs in hundreds. Am bringing up all I can, but it is difficult for parties to work owing to shells. The sights are appalling but I find I can bear them. Oh! They are shelling our billets, bang, bang, whizz, - no peace at all.

Delighted you are at B. M. Hotel with your friends, much nicer for you. Am sending you a German bayonet knot, just as a trophy of this big battle. We shall get them really going if we press hard enough, as they are really short of reserves, but they must be pressed at many places, and not only by the great 1st Army. There are other moves in the offing, and I think the 2nd division must have a few days to refit and make good its losses. Our pals, the 5th and 6th Brigades, have lost heavily, but we are forward, all to the thanks to Cavalry.

Haste. Love. K.

May 20th. Woke fairly early. Shelling fairly continuous until 12:30 p.m., when they fairly put them all round us, but luckily very few in. About 1:30 p.m. it subsided again during this Pro got it very slightly in the hand, and so he walked on down to the Dressing Station. During whole afternoon they kept up a fairly continuous shelling. We were relieved by part of the Highland Territorial Division, 5th Gordons. We arranged a somewhat elaborate system of relief which took rather a long time, but eventually by about 11 p.m. MacGregor and self got away and stopped at LES GLAUMES where Battalion were collecting, and where we found champagne and Quails waiting for us. After a wait we continued.

May 21st. Arriving at our billets in OBLINGHEM about 3:30 a.m. Along lie in and breakfast about 12 noon! Slept most of afternoon.

May 21st 1915 Friday – Cavan to Inez.

Breathe more freely my beloved girl for I and my Brigade, less about 1000 casualties are now 5 miles behind Bethune to right and get drafts for a few days before we go forward again. I am in MONT EVENTE (near LAPUCHOY) Château and I got here at 2 a.m., 11 miles from firing line in car very kindly lent by General Horne, which I was thankful for, as I was as sick as a cat at 4 a.m. the morning before after sniffing bad shells all day.

Took a fine dose of castor oil in brandy and am as clear and fresh as a daisy this morning after sleeping till 9.15. It is now a most exciting battle. You see for the moment we are through the great German lines and the fighting is looser, though of course we have to dig in as one cannot live a minute for the shells after one has gained a bit of ground. In the 3 days fighting our casualties are Irish about 380, Grenadiers 120, Herts 110, 2/Coldstreams 20, 3/Coldstreams 30, and some 25 officers, about 700 all told, but a quarter of what it would have been if I had not stopped them on Wednesday afternoon.

There is a Private 2717 E. NEALE among the Herts killed, but I don't know if the Station Master's son or not, as it is a fairly common name in the regiment. If it is please give him my sincere sympathy and say the Battalion behaved magnificently. The shelling yesterday was as bad as Ypres, though the actual shells are not quite so destructive. Our officer and 2 men were hit at my Head Quarters, and I was almost blinded by one fellow that burst 20 feet from my right ear. We can hear the guns today as hard at it as ever. I was anxious as we had to hand over to a quite new Territorial Division, who had never seen a fight and the relief was very tricky work. However I waited till all was finished and as I say got here in a car at 2 a.m. I'm off to Béthune now to see the Corps Commander, probably about future operations. It is too delightful to be among trees and woods and no smell of dead. We buried over 130 Germans and got a complete kit for the Prince of Wales who says, "Father bagged all his collection when he got home last time".

I will write again when I have seen the General. Poor Wilfred was buried in our little cemetery we made in December when we were on this battleground. A dear little Service punctured by shells.

K.

May 22nd. General cleaning up and quiet day. Looked over our casualties for the 24 hours in at RUE de BOIS, which were 2 killed and 11 wounded, which was good considering we must have had about 5,000 shells over us.

May 23rd. Church Parade in a field by Fleming and Holy Communion after. Very hot; after lunch Pro, Sim, and self rode oven to "Bois des Dames" a topping ride right through the woods, gorse all out, a brilliant yellow. Julian Steele arrived in evening from 1st Battalion to take over command. Also Druce Bentinck, Senhouse and Brotherton (Quartermaster).

May 24th. Walked round Companies with C.O., Companies were doing drill. Went to BÉTHUNE with Towers-Clark and had my hair cut very short. Came back and dined with Little Man, 3rd Battalion, a very cheery evening. Inspected by General Horne and well buttered.

May 25th. On 5 minutes notice in morning but cancelled about lunch time. About 4:15 p.m. we got an order from 2nd Division to move at once to LE PRÉOL. Great bustle and fuss but we got off about 5 p.m., only leaving 3 Officers and 20 men absent. Halted in BÉTHUNE and then up South bank of Canal where we met Jerry Brabazon who showed us a field to bivouac in. 47th London Division doing an attack. 4 guns fired just over our heads all night and so not much sleep. Very warm night.

May 26th. Breakfast at 3:30 a.m. Heard attack had done fairly well. Quite the hottest day we have had. Not even the woods were properly cool. Gunning ceased a bit, slept and dripped alternatively most of day. Men bathed in Canal much to the amusement of German prisoners who passed and expected us to be cowering in dug outs.

May 27th. Quieter night so we all slept more. 47th London Division consolidated their position, but they have been very much hammered. Brigadier came round but had no news for us except that we probably stay here. Played stump cricket most of the evening. Ramsay got kicked on the foot by the C.O.'s charger and had to go into Hospital. Our Baggage wagon came up and so for the first time during the war I slept in my bivouac tent. Felt very sorry for the men who only have their mackintoshes. Cold evening.

May 28th. Did not get up until 7 a.m. Slept so well. Everything still very quiet. Went into a cottage and shaved and bathed. Got orders to move at 1p.m. Quite a good day for marching; moved back to LAPUGNOY about 6 miles West of BÉTHUNE. Men went well, only two falling out. We remain at 2 hours notice to move. Shaw-Stewart took over Transport in Ramsay's absence. Billets fair, men on stone floors in places. Applied for straw.

May 29th. Companies spent morning cleaning up. Large lot of papers to do in Orderly room. Managed to get some straw for Nos: 2 & 3 Companies. Prince of Wales came in for short time, no news. Went for ride in evening alone.

2nd Battalion Coldstream Guards,
4th Guards Brigade.
British Expeditionary Force.

29th May, 1915 – to George Abraham Gibbs.

Dearest Georgie.
      I think the battle round "Festubert" has somewhat subsided now. We had the most exciting and unpleasant and lucky 24 hours than I have had since I have been out here. We took over a bit of the line that had just been captured from the Germans. They did not feel like counter-attacking; but just shelled us for the whole 24 hours we were in, as hard as they could. I should think they must have put out between 4000 and 5,000, as I counted 94 in one minute when they coming rather quicker than usual. However, they nearly all went over or short; and those that did get the trench invariably got it in a place where no one was. Our losses were 2 killed and 11 wounded.
      Now we have come a long way back into billets, further than we have been since December 21st (about 7 miles) and can only just hear the guns. But I'm afraid it is for a very short time. What really stopped the rushes round Festubert were Machine Guns very cleverly hidden in the trenches, which the Germans brought up as soon as an attack was made. While the Artillery Bombardment was going on they would keep them down in the bottom of the trench where they couldn't be hit; otherwise I fancy the front German trenches were very lightly held.
      Yesterday the Germans sent a kite over to the British trenches near GIVENCHY with a note attached, in which was written the following:- "We are too strong to retire, we have not enough men to attack, we are too proud to ask for peace, but we want peace and to go home". So, they seem rather sick of it.
      Weather out here lovely. We slept in a field last 3 nights.

Your loving brother

Lancelot

Plate One. Lord Roberts of Kandahar, who led the British Army to Victory in the Boer War. A Portrait by Robertson at Tyntesfield, January 1901.

Plate Two. 22 Belgrave Square, George Abraham Gibbs' London home from 1911 to 1928, where Via was hostess until her death in 1920.

Plate Three. Via, Victoria de Burgh Gibbs by Albert Henry Collins, 1908.

Plate Four. The Grave of Captain Eusatce Lyle Gibbs in the Town Cemetery at Ypres. He died on 11th February 1915. Flowers and photograph by the Author, 2008.

Plate Five. Captain Eustace Lyle Gibbs by Albert Henry Collins, a posthumous portrait.

Eustace Lyle Gibbs was born at Tyntesfield on 10th March 1885. He was baptized on 12th April 1885 at Wraxall Parish Church. He was educated at Eton College from 1898 to 1903, and then studied at Magdalen College Oxford where he distinguished himself on the Cricket Field. In 1906 he was commissioned as a Second Lieutenant in the North Somerset Yeomanry, being promoted Lieutenant in 1909 and Captain in 1914.

He entered Antony Gibbs and Sons in London in 1908, and from 1909 to 1913 he worked for Antony Gibbs in Chile. He was appointed manager in Chile in 1911. In 1913 he was transferred to New York where he worked as Second in Charge of the American branch of Antony Gibbs until he returned to Britain in August 1914.

Plate Six. Eustace Lyle Gibbs as a boy by William Blake Richmond.

Captain Eustace Lyle Gibbs served in France and Belgium from October 1914 until his death at Ypres on February 11th 1915. He was buried in the Town Cemetery at Ypres, which lies East of the Menin Gate. He is commemorated on the War Memorials at All Saints Wraxall, Eton College, Magdalen College Oxford and Wells Cathedral.

May 30th. Church Parade at 9:45 a.m. by Reverend Lushington, who has just come to 4th Brigade. MacGregor had a letter to say Colonel Pinto was wounded, but not bad luckily. Monkey, Shaw Stewart, Senhouse, Trousers, A. H. Smith, Ashley and self went for a ride in 'Bois des Dames', got separated and joined up other side by means of "View Holloa's" to each other. We then pushed our horses over some Cavalry School jumps which several French Dragoons put up for us. Orders to be ready to move at 4:30 a.m. tomorrow, which means breakfast at 8 a.m., which I hate! Fancy French peasants in wood thought that the war had been too much for the seven officers shooting and riding through the wood! Got orders at about 7 p.m. that we had to start at 4:30 a.m. 31st. Wrote out orders hurriedly, C.O. being out. Got to bed early.

May 31st. Battalion got off soon after 4:15 a.m. and passed 'Starting Point' within 15 seconds of scheduled time!! Marched as Brigade with 3 Battalions, i.e. 3rd Battalion, us and Hertfordshires. Got into NŒUX LES MINES soon after 7 a.m. Billets very crowded and took some time getting. Soon after arrival the Germans began to shell the place, putting 10 right into the town killing one woman and wounding one civilian butcher. This soon stopped and we had a very quiet afternoon. Two Companies had to move their billets giving up room to the Grenadiers who were in the shelled quarter of the town. They got settled eventually. The mess was particularly lucky here, getting the "Mairie", which easily accommodated the 26 officers, which the Battalion now boasts of.

2nd Battalionn Coldstream Guards
4th Guards Brigade
British Expeditionary Force

31st May 1915

Darling Nancy

    I may get a lot of these. Would you like to deal with them? If so, I will send them to you as they come also the vote paper as I am not very well up in the Clerical Financial Stability.

    We had an early start to come to the place we are now in, which is South of where we were. Breakfast 3.15 etc., which I never did enjoy! I have now got Julian Steele as Commanding Officer. He is nice but fussy and has several coils of reddish tape about him otherwise good I think. We are still enjoying times of rest.

Your loving Lags

GALLIPOLI

May and June 1915

There follow some letters from John Merivale, the son of George Montague Merivale, Janet Louisa's brother. John (Jack) was Antony and Janet Gibbs' nephew. George was a partner in Gibbs, Bright and Company, Australia from 1883 to 1924.

John Merivale's first letter is written off the Dardanelles in the Prize of War – S.S. Lutzow – to his mother, Mrs George Merivale in Australia.

19th May 1915

My dear Mother,

We left Maadi on Saturday as per schedule and got on board this boat, an ex Hamburg-Amerika Liner of 9000 tons, on Sunday morning. We spent practically all Sunday at Alexandria leaving at 6 p.m. There are no less than 2600 men on board so it is rather crowded as you may imagine, and the washing arrangements etc. are indescribably filthy. The aforesaid crowd consists of the 5th, 6th, 7th, and 10th L. H. Regiments, all dismounted, a squadron of the 4th, and some A. S. C. men. We had a two days uneventful trip but a sharp look out was kept for submarines and the boats had each its armed guard. I was in charge of one with six men the first night. This was a very necessary precaution as there is only sufficient accommodation in them for 600 men. We had no naval escort whatever, so I suppose things are pretty safe.

We got here at seven yesterday evening and lay among a lot of other transports and men of war a few miles off land. The men of war had just commenced to fire on some hill in the distance and kept it up till dark. From the heavy rumble I should think the "Lizzy" as they call her was joining in too and the Turks got an awful gruelling. Then at 10:30 p.m. they started again and fairly shook the earth. The sound was terrible. Searchlights were flashing everywhere and every now and then a star shell would go up and light up everything. Amongst it all there was the continuous rattle of musketry and machine guns sounding very much like a motor with a silencer off.

Of course we can watch the fighting on both sides as it were. The ships inside and those firing across the peninsula. This morning all was quiet for a while. I don't know how long they kept it up last night as I went to sleep listening to it, and then an aeroplane started out to see what damage had been done. The Turks started firing at her and it was pretty to watch the fleecy white smoke balls as the shells burst beneath her. She was much too high for them and only one went anywhere near her. Since then the bombardment has started again and I can hear the rumble of guns as I write.

We are told that another fort was silenced last night. What our job will be no one seems to know except that we have to go another 15 miles up towards the Narrows and land tonight. Tomorrow I understand there is some position they want us to take. Apparently the Turks on the Gallipoli Peninsula are now hemmed in on 3 sides by the British Australians and French and pretty well surrounded so that their plight can be none too good. They say we have only another seven miles to advance and they must chuck up the sponge. However history tells us that the Turks never fight better than when they have their backs against a wall.

I must stop now to get this away. It will be posted at Malta by some one on board this ship. She is taking wounded there, as all the Alexandria Hospitals are full. Will try and get another letter through shortly or a post card.

One thing that seems strange to me is the casual way this transport came up and anchored well within range of the Turkish guns. We have had no shells near us so far so I suppose they know what they are doing. Our only excitement this morning was being rammed by an empty French ship.

Anzac 31/5/15.

Dear Mater,

We are out of paper again. I am reduced to the back of an A.F. There is not much news since I wrote last, as it is only two days ago. We got a lot of Reinforcements today. They look a good lot and will soon be tested. I am enclosing a letter we got from General Birdwood before the show started. You may have seen it but a copy of the original may be better. I am kept pretty busy now and have been trying to get a few minutes to write, and now it is ten minutes to closing time, and I have only just started. I got a letter from Uncle Burtie this week and some papers and a letter from Monty. Please thank them. Tell Nina that her friend Howard is now a Lance Corporal a very good chap too. I enlisted him in Sydney and took a fancy to him then. As for news here there's none. All the ships are gone and there are only a few trawlers and T.B.Ds. in and a transport comes over with stores or troops occasionally. They say that the scare here is nothing to that in the Sea of Marmora, which is welcome news to us. The troops are in good heart and longing for another scrap. We dig all day and night to keep ourselves amused and succeed pretty well too. It is funny the Turks seem to find it very interesting too from the amount they are doing. But they have been very quiet lately. They must be thinking hard. Great excitement, 3 Destroyers just chasing a Submarine but she has beaten them and goodness knows where she is now. An Aeroplane has just gone up so they may see her yet. I will let you know in my next letter how they got on.

Yours ever

John

Please thank Grandma for her letter I loved getting it.

Gallipoli Peninsula.
31st May 1915
John (Jack) Merivale to his father

My dear Father,
After ten days in the Trenches am still sound and whole. I transferred to the Machine gun section after we arrived as likely to prove more exciting, but so far it has proved exactly the opposite, as the squadron has had a severe gruelling, rather hard luck for their first experience, especially as they are acting as Infantry when their whole training has been a cavalry one.

Shell fire is what they have suffered from most and shrapnel is most demoralising, striking down as it does. The only thing is to lie down and hope for the best. We had forty shells over us the other morning in as many minutes, but one soon gets used to it. At the commencement of the bombardment I was lying asleep with two others in the communication trench after all night duty with the guns. I had just woken up when three shells hit the parapet above us in quick succession and covered us with sandbags and dirt; we left hurriedly for safer quarters and on returning later to rescue my blankets found them buried in bags and dirt and pieces of shell lying on top. The spirits of the infantry are amazing. They have been here five weeks now and suffered as of course you will have heard terribly at first on landing. They have a great contempt for the enemy who they say can't stand the bayonet and who is flogged to the attack by the German Officers. They lost 3000 killed and 4000 wounded in an attack just before we arrived. The infantry described it as better than a wallaby drive and shot them down in droves. Yesterday they mined a portion of our trenches on the extreme left furthest from us and tried to rush us. Our artillery tore them to bits however and the infantry advancing seized and held a portion of their trenches, since then they have been ominously quiet and no doubt they have some fresh surprise to spring on us. The enemy trenches are only 70 yards away from us just here and 200 yards at furthest.

Being quite close to the sea and a hill overlooking our historic landing, we can watch the naval side of the question too. The hill slopes very steeply to the waters edge and how our infantry ever got ashore is a mystery which they themselves can't explain in the face of the awful fire the enemy poured on them.

But to return to the navy we saw the "Albion" go ashore close by the other day and the forts poured a hail of shot upon her. She replied spiritedly and apparently did not suffer at all from the enemy's fire. She finally got off and steamed triumphantly away. A few days later we saw the "Triumph" torpedoed and sunk also fairly close in shore. She kept firing to the last, and we heard only lost 50 men. It is splendid also watching the aeroplanes out scouting; they are generally surrounded by little clouds of white smoke, shrapnel from the enemy, but so far have been untouched. An enemy 'plane came over the other day and dropped a bomb, it made a terrific row but did not do much damage.

Young Pattrick has been hit in the head by a piece of shrapnel but not badly hurt I think. Moffatt has also been hit by a bullet but how seriously I have not heard. Every Officer in the squadron has been hit except our Major Charley. The snipers are our worst enemy and show great cunning. However we hope to go forward some day and reach our goal viz: - Constantinople.

One gets quite used to sleeping in one's boots, bandolier and bayonet every night and sleeping anywhere in the trenches where one can get room. Washing is the great trouble but I have managed to get a bath in the sea every second day, shave, brush my teeth and wash my face and hands, but others don't seem to be so lucky. The enemy have an unpleasant habit of shelling the beach at odd times which makes it exciting dodging the shrapnel and bullets.

This country reminds me very much of Marouba as it slopes to the beach with the same kind of scrub but better soil.

Everyone as soon as he arrives burrows into the side of the hill and makes a dug out for protection against shell fire. It is rather funny to see the dash for cover on the arrival of a bit one, just like a lot of rabbits making for their burrows.

The weather is getting much warmer though it is still chilly at 3 a.m. when we generally get roused out if not on duty with the guns, which means no sleep at all.

We are getting much better food here and have arranged for our own cook, which means much as we can't get our meals outside as we used to at Maadi.

I am however trying to arrange with Mary to send me tobacco and some chocolate from England as tobacco is very hard to get here.

Love to all

Your affectionate son,

Jack.

Figure 56. Jack Merivale as a boy.

Anzac
10/6/15.

Dear Mater,
 The last few days have passed quietly. The enemy are still digging and saving ammunition and we are doing much the same although the latter is not so important. The Major comes back on Tuesday. He is still pretty weak and only came out of hospital on Friday. Magee came back yesterday. He is not well but will pick up here all right. The Turks are up to all kinds of things. They have put a gun on Cape Nebruisi which may be a bit troublesome until it is blown off. They have dug a tunnel through a hill and we are expecting to hear from them any time now. They bang away and never do very much damage so we are not much worried about it.
 Our Artillery are doing fairly well. They fired 12 shots the other day and two Turks died, laughing they say. They are very handicapped.

They are compelled to go to only 2 or 3 places and are shelled out of them consistently. All the men are well and cheerful and are anxious to get at it again.

There seems to be less news this mail than before or perhaps it is because I have only just got up. I have to write a report before 6 a.m. daily on the previous operations. I have just got this done and am waiting for breakfast – 6.30 a.m.

Give my love to everyone at home. I was expecting a mail last Tuesday but it has not come yet. They say at Lemnos that they have more important things than mails to send along, but they will probably be sent on soon. There is a story told about the Queen Elizabeth. She fired a 15 shrapnel at a Battalion of Turks which they caught sight of. After the dust and smoke cleared away one of the sailors on the fighting top, after examining with his telescope said to his mate "By cripes Bill, there is one of the Blighters crawling away"!

Rather a silly thing has happened. Our censor stamp that we have been using for 5 weeks now has been cancelled I am afraid, so if you have not got any letters for some time you will know why.

Yours ever,

JOHN

Anzac
4th Battalion
4/6/15.

Dear Mater,

We are still in the same place and doing much the same thing as we have been doing for the last month. The digging still continues. The improvement of the trenched is an unending job especially as the clay soil dries and cracks. The enemy have not stopped digging since we have been here. They say some more are coming down here. They started by sea, but decided in a hurry that it would probably be much healthier on land owing to the submarines so they were popped ashore at Constantinople and have hoofed it all the way. The chase was in progress when I had to close my last letter. It did not come to anything unfortunately but it was quite exciting while it lasted. I don't think it can be as easy to see them from an aeroplane as they say it is. It is really very hard to think of any news to tell you although there is plenty I would like to. I have worn out my breeches, my spare ones are in my valise which has been returned to Alexandria, and I can't get an issue pair to fit so I have written to Cairo for a pair, and am hoping against hope that they will arrive in time. A web equipment seat will not be comfortable although it may keep the draught out. It is really very inconvenient not having a valise but we manage very well indeed considering. I had my first wash the other day for five weeks and have not had to hold my head up so much since. A new and interesting pastime has been started in the trenches. It is called - spotting – and is played as follows. Any number of competitors can play in fact as many as possible are encouraged to do so. Each competitor stands opposite his dugout – in support trenches – and at the word go each takes off his shirt and sits down. The first to catch 50 has the privilege of sleeping alone for a bit. It causes much amusement and is a very restful pastime.

The work keeps crowding on and now I have an office staff of 2 clerks and a draughtsman and they are kept busy. My R. S. M. is no good I am afraid, and it just about doubles my work. I fought against it as long as I could but he was thrust on me. They say the mail is in, so I will probably hear from home today. Everyone is awfully good writing to me, and I look forward to getting them very much.

I saw George Onslow and Tom Rutledge this week; both are well and like their job. They had most of the hard work done for them before they came.

JOHN.

Gallipoli Peninsula.
16 June 1915.

My dear Mother,
I was very glad to get your letters Nos. 16 and 17 two days ago, also Father's, Angel's and Rose's. The previous one I had from you here was No. 15 and that is all I have had during the month I have been here. The mails are naturally very erratic and generally come in a bunch after a good interval. Glad you liked the shawls. Also got your R.P. cable of 22nd May, the day before yesterday, and replied at once that I had been here a month and was well, but it has to go by post to Cairo, so am afraid it will take some time reaching you if you ever get it all.

Have also heard from Mary and Uncle Reggie who seems to have developed a sudden interest in me. He says he would like to send me something, and wants to know what I would like.

As it may interest you, I will give you an account of what we do every day here. I have, as you already know, transferred to the Machine Gun Section, and we really form an independent unit. There is no doubt one has a more interesting time than with the troops, and I like it very much. The Section is really split into halves, one having day off and on, but all sleep in the trenches at night. Today for instance I am on duty, and of course cannot leave for meals so those off wait on us, bringing food and water etc, and we do the same for them tomorrow. Our extra gear is kept in dugouts outside where we cook etc., but we always have our great coats, blankets etc. with us. Washing is one great difficulty but I generally manage a swim in the sea on my off day when I go down for wood, water, and doing the general fatigues of the camp. I also get a shave and wash my face and hands in a quart of water on that day, and that's all the washing I can manage, and this is more than the majority manage. One soon gets accustomed to being in a continually dirty and dusty condition and also to sleeping in one's uniform and boots. Practically all the men have unwelcome guests in their clothes, but so far I have managed to escape this, though they say it is inevitable to become "Chatty" as it is locally termed.

The Section has an excellent cook and we are certainly well fed, but miss green vegetables a good deal, as is evidenced by sores and cuts never healing properly. It is a trouble much the same as one gets in Queensland "The Barcos". They give us however to eat ships biscuits, tinned meat, corned beef generally, onions or desiccated vegetables, cheese, bacon or ham, tea, a pint there times a day, 1lb tin of jam, always plum, between four men daily, and now we are getting bread three times a week instead of the hard biscuits. We also get a weekly issue of 1 box matches, 1 oz of tobacco and 4 packets cigarettes each. We are soon to have a canteen I hear and this will be very welcome. The things most unobtainable at present are tobacco, matches and notepaper, and the substitutes being used for the latter are most amusing – cardboard the back of a letter just received or any scrap of paper obtainable. I have written to Mary for some tobacco and chocolates and am expecting Aunt C. to send me another notebook as my stock has been very low.

We used to get an issue of rum occasionally, but they have knocked it off lately, as I suppose they don't consider the strain at present is severe enough on us.

I suffered mostly from lack of sleep at first, one gets two hours one night and six the next night alternately, but you generally make it up in the day time and I now sleep at any time and in any position or place quite comfortably.

The tactics adopted here are Fabian on both sides and things are pretty monotonous. Until the papers arrived with your letters we had absolutely nothing to ready, which made things worse. I got the Sunday Times, Bulletin, a Sydney Mail from Father, and the Australasian, but the Sun has never turned up yet. The enemy livened things up yesterday by throwing about a dozen 8" shells at us, they each weigh about 200 lbs but mostly fail to burst, but they certainly succeeded in waking us for the moment, though the damage was infinitesimal. But we chiefly get fired at with shrapnel from 12 to 15 pounders to which our artillery replies. Sniping at each other cutting the sand bags or breaking periscopes with bullets on the opposing parapets seems the most popular amusement between the men of both sides. All the observing by day is done by periscopes, just two pieces of looking glass on two parallel sticks, which stick up over the parapet and this lessen the risk of one getting a bullet; at night of course the port holes are opened up to look through and one does one hour on and two off the whole time one is in the trenches.

Will you tell Captain MacArthur that his nephew, Alan Carnes, was wounded in the forearm the night before last. The bullet caught him in the fleshy part and did not touch the bone. He lost a good deal of blood however, and is to go to Alexandria to convalesce. I don't fancy it is very serious however, and he should recover rapidly.

I don't know whether I told you that poor young Patrick afterwards died from the effects of his wound. The blow apparently fractured his skull. Moffat too has gone to Alexandria with a cut over the eye from a bullet.

Socks and shirts periodically are what I shall chiefly need for the future I think, as washing is practically impossible, and also some thin drawers shorts. They are much more comfortable than breeches and don't collect the dirt and grit like the others do. Our kit bags of course have been left behind and we only have here what we stand in practically. I doubt if we ever see them again.

The latest news of the horses from Maadi is fairly good, though there has been "flue" amongst them and the heat has been very great.

The one thing we have been blessed here with is fine weather and bright sun. Fairly hot at midday, the nights are beautifully cool and sometimes cold. The flies however are atrocious and in the trenches there is no getting away from them. I think the dead who lay for days outside here after the last attack just before we came, without being buried and smelt abominably, must have brought them. However they are buried now I am glad to say.

I don't understand Mary's movements at all. I thought she was to return in the "Medina", but in her last letter she says she is not doing this, but does not give any alternative plan.

Would you tell Cousin Maud that I have been unable to see Max he must be somewhere at the opposite end of the line to where we are and as it is five miles long I have never yet had time to go along and find him.

Glad to hear the ponies are doing so well, but fodder is at awful rates I see by the papers, so they are much better out if the winter is good.

Love to everybody,

Your affectionate son,

JACK.

Second Lieutenant John Laidley Merivale of the 4th Battalion Australian Infantry, Son of George Montague and Emily Jane Merivale of 37, Pitt Street, Sydney, New South Wales was killed between the 6th and the 9th August 1915 at Gallipoli and is buried in the Lone Pine Cemetery, Anzac.

June 1st. The whole morning was devoted to cleaning up. The French having left the place filthy. The C.O., MacGregor and self went round billets which took many different forms, deserted houses, barns. stables. and lean-to sheds. No shells came in to spoil an otherwise lovely hot day. The 4th Brigade being so concentrated one met many officers of the other Battalions, especially the Grenadiers whom we have not been near for some time. A great deal of French Transport and ambulances galore. The chief item of interest of the day being that I was inoculated with 15,000,000 "little fellers". News that the French have taken AMBIAN ST NAZAIN also 1,200 prisoners. Ramsey returned from Hospital, also Leese from LAPUGNOY where we had left him yesterday with 30 inoculated men too seedy to move.

June 2nd. A very hot day. Battalion continued cleaning up the streets. I was inoculated in the evening, and so kept quiet.

June 3rd. Battalion went for a six mile route march in the early morning. I had breakfast in bed, but got up for orders. Quiet day. I spent most of it in my room so as to keep quiet.

June 4th. Quiet all night again. 4 Captains and self went up to trenches near MAZINGARBE and looked round, trenches fair, very quiet place. Great 4th of June dinner in evening, to which Brigadier General Cavan and Lambton came + 53 others. John Ponsonby sent telegram to King, of congratulations on Birthday from 3 Battalions of Coldstream in France, to which he sent a very nice answer.

June 5th. Everyone rather late for breakfast in consequence of late night. Went over to lunch with 1st Battalion, found Becky and John P and all the others. Found them rather depressed.

June 6th. Brigade Parade Service in field, very hot. Captains of Companies went forward to see bit of line near VERMELLES, which we now take over instead of the bit looked at on 4th June. We paraded about 8:30 p.m. and moved to VERMELLES (about 4 miles) and then up a very long communication trench relieving the 20th London Battalion. Trenches good. Relief completed 1 a.m.; no casualties.

June 7th. Woke about 7 a.m. Headquarters dug outs as made by the French excellent. C.O. – Telephones – and self separate. Mine was about 24ft x 4ft with a mattress in it, table and every convenience. Very hot day. Brigadier came round about 10 a.m. but had little news. All trenches have French names which the men pronounce in some very odd ways. Went round trenches in evening; found right Company had most palatial dug out, also left Company. Got back about 7:30 p.m., we dined in the open. No casualties.

2nd Battalion Coldstream Guards,
4th Guards Brigade.
British Expeditionary Force

7th June 1915

Darling Nancy

Still more lovely cakes, lolly drops etc. keep arriving. Thank you so much.

We have moved up now near Vermelles into some excellent trenches that the French made some time ago. Very quiet.

I have seldom seen such palatial dugouts, I have got one about 24' x 4' x 3ft. high, so I sleep one end and write the other. The Village having been reduced to ruins they have brought up beds and furniture and furnished the 'dugouts'.

I hope you saw the mention of the Gibbs' in the Times of 5 June under reference to '4th of June' at Eton.

Scott has just send a palatial lunch which I now indulge in + 5 others and then a short sleep to digest and then I go round and cheer up (or depress) the officers who are with their Companies!!

Your loving

Lags

June 8th. Hotter than ever. Brigadier and Divisional GOC came round inspecting and 'prospecting'! Captains of 3rd Battalion came round and looked at line. Started to thunder about 1p.m. Germans put few rounds but did no damage. 3rd Battalion arrived about 10:30 p.m. and took over from us. C.O and self got off about 12:30 and rode on to SAILLY LABOURSE where we were billeted.

June 9th. Last Company not having got in much before 2:30 a.m., réveillé was late, and C.O did his orders at 11:30 a.m. The Mess Steward not having returned, having gone off when we were at NŒUX LES MINES in a temper, Sergeant King late of the 2nd Line Transport was made Mess Sergeant. A great many papers and orders occupied most of the afternoon. Our mess was in a big school-room, very uncomfortable but commodious.

June 10th. C.O went round the Grenadier trenches leaving MacGregor to do orders. I had a parade of Headquarters and practised the masks. Very hot muggy day again. Started off at 7 p.m. to move by a new route which Senhouse had reconnoitred, awful communication trench; got in eventually about 10:00, relief went fairly quickly. It began to fairly pour with rain just as we got in and continued most of the night. No casualties during relief.

June 11th. Towers-Clark came to me about 6 a.m. to show him the new dining room dug out, so I got up. A good many visitors in gunners etc: also O.C's Irish and Grenadiers owing to change over which is coming off in 3 days time. Some shelling in evening but otherwise quiet, one casualty in No:1 Company, man hit by stray bullet through shoulder and top part of lung, bad I'm afraid. Went round in evening, found Crawley and Copper Seymour with Leigh-Bennett.

June 12th. Some shells during morning. Went over to Grenadier Headquarters in Z: 2 with Bill Bailey and looked round, also to No: 2, upon which they put six all down reserve trench. Trousers and self cowered in a corner for a bit! Relieved by Irish Guards, who got up in very good time so we got to billets by 10:30 p.m. Found that SAILLY LABOURSE had been shelled a bit during the day, but no damage done.

June 13th. Brigadier gave Grenadiers and ourselves a 'Pow-wow" at 10:30 a.m. in our school-room, reading us a bit from the "Round Table". most interesting. He also said that we must keep up our habit of annoying the 'Huns' on all occasions and he hoped shortly we would be in the attack! Got our orders for relieving 3rd Battalion in "Z: 2" section this evening. We moved off about 5:30 p.m. and got up quite successfully, they had just been bombarding CAMBRIN before we arrived. No: 1 was in front on right, No: 2 on left, No: 3 right reserve, and No: 4 left reserve.

June 15th. Jerry Brabazon came round very worried about an emergency ammunition depot he was forming, and so I spent the morning finding out about it, and wired him that all was correct. Went and saw all Companies in evening, found them mostly asleep. Watched a gunner bombing the Huns from the left end of trenches, but as he twice running forgot to take the safety pin out I moved off before there was a premature explosion, which however there wasn't. Spent most of the night trying to roof in two large dug outs, the biggest of which subsided just as we had finished, and as it was getting light we had to give it up and get back into the trenches.

June 16th. Two casualties from shells in No: 3, one bad I'm afraid. Stretcher-bearers as usual bound his leg into two splints most excellently. A great deal of noise over FESTUBERT way; the 4th Corps trying again to get on, having failed yesterday. 3rd Battalion arrived very punctually at

6:30 p.m. and so we moved off back to SAILLY LABOURSE. Ramsey having forgotten to order dinner we didn't get much.

2nd Battalionn Coldstream Guards
4th Guards Brigade
British Expeditionary Force

June 16th, 1915

Darling Nancy,
    As you may or may not know Maurice Ponsonby is now attached to the 4th Guards Brigade together with one Lushington.
    He came up to our trenches this afternoon and made himself known to Graham Steele and self. Our conversation consisted mostly of lice and fleas of which he seemed very well informed! He is at present doing the trench part and Lushington the Billets.
    He (M.P.) lives in a well shelled village and I think rather likes coming up here as it is safer!
    Love to my God-daughter and wish her many happy returns of the day.

                    Your loving

                    Lags

P.S. Reference as to what I said about Graham Steele being rather wrapped in Red tape, this was a very first impression and I find now it is not at all the case.

June 17th. Spent the morning in the Orderly Room, also prosecuted in Court Martial on Lance Corporal Charlish for drunkenness. He said he had only "come over queer"! Rode into BÉTHUNE and bought wallpaper for my dug out (48ft. very chaste @ ½d the lot!). At dinner Brigadier wired to us that poor old Jerry Brabazon had been killed by a shell; a real good fellow, and one of the last 4th Guards Brigade Staff. He used to be in the Battalion and used very often to come round the trenches.

June 18th. 8 of us went to Jerry's funeral at CAMBRIN Church at 9 a.m. to find the Divisional General, Brigadier, and all the Staff there. After a quiet day in billets, we started for the trenches about 5:30 p.m. We took over without any casualties. Several Companies had patrols and covering parties out. About 11:30 p.m. No: 2 were changing their parties over and Oscar Senhouse was arranging the relief when he somewhat lost his way in the long grass and ran into a German patrol of two men. These men threw bombs at him and ran away. One of these must have landed right under him. Towers-Clark managed to drag him into the front trench. An orderly came to me for the Doctor, when we got there (Dr. & self) we found him terribly knocked about, and he died about ¼ hour after without gaining conscience. A real loss to the Battalion, although only out here one month everybody got to like him enormously.

June 19th. Poor Oscar was buried in CAMBRIN churchyard at 10 a.m. Towers-Clark going to the funeral conducted by Lushington. A few shells from the "Fizz Bang" gun, but no damage. We continued two dug outs at Headquarters, also the front line on the right was connected up and deepened.

June 20th. The French seem to be firing a lot down South, but no news. Russians still retiring. After a quiet day the 3rd Battalion got up about 7:00 p.m. and we returned to SAILLY.

June 21st. The usual routine in billets. I went for a ride into BÉTHUNE and saw John Wynne-Finch (1st Battalion).

June 22nd. A wet morning, otherwise a day without incident. We relieved the 3rd Battalion arriving about 6:30 p.m. The C.O. (Julian Steele) went off in the morning on seven days leave. No: 1 was on right, and No: 2 on left. Bruce B. came as 2nd in command for this tour of duty in the trenches.

June 23rd. One man got hit in the night, but not very bad. Brigadier came in with great news of leave for 3 officers and 10 men, at the time also relief by another Brigade on Saturday, which means we do not come in again. Spent most of the day sending in names for leave:- officers, Leigh-Bennett, Verelst, Birbeck. Dined with No: 2 Company.

June 24th. Very quiet night and morning. In afternoon 6th Brigade (on our left) blew up two mines which seemed to annoy the Huns, and so for 2 or 3 hours they "Fizz Banged" us, killing one man and wounding another – rather unpleasant. Relieved about 7:30 p.m. by 3rd Battalion and went off.

2nd Battalionn Coldstream Guards
4th Guards Brigade
British Expeditionary Force

June 24th 1915

Darling Nancy

    I hear Leave is in the air so in about fortnight or three weeks I may be about again for 3 or 4 days. Will you be busy then?

    Maurice Ponsonby came to tea in the trenches today.

Your loving Lags

June 25th. Very dull morning which eventually turned into a thunderstorm. Everything seems very quiet to our front except the French who pound on. Took no excercise. Heard details of relief which takes place tomorrow.

June 26th. Spent most of the morning getting out orders for moving into "Orphanage" BÉTHUNE. Taylor to go into billet for Battalion, and Shaw-Stewart to hand over to a Brigade of the 9th Division (Kitchener's Army). About 2 p.m. all orders cancelled, and we stay on here, 3rd Battalion does another day in trenches!

June 27th. Leave came out late last night. 10 men and 3 officers (Leigh-Bennett, Birbeck, and Verelst) go off today, former for 5 days and latter for 8 days. Church Parade at 10:30 a.m. by Lushington. Grenadiers sent a few under Crawley De Crespigny. Taylor went off billeting and Ashley handed over our billets to Liverpools (2nd Brigade 1st Division). Raining most of the day. We left SAILLY LABOURSE about 8:15 p.m. and marched to FOUQUIÈRES via BÉTHUNE. Sim had found a splendid Château for the mess, and 7 officers to sleep in.

June 28th. Walked about garden till 11:30 a.m., when we left and marched to VENDIN (just North of BÉTHUNE). Billets fair, men rather crowded. Very hot, played stump cricket in evening.

2nd Battalion Coldstream Guards,
4th Guards Brigade.
British Expeditionary Force

June 28th 1915

Darling Nancy

At last I fear we really lose Cavan as he has been given the Northumbrian Division. We had seen it coming for a very long time. He came today and bade us farewell, making a most touching speech, as he alone can, and shook everyone by the fist and departed – the best Brigadier that ever commanded a Brigade and loved and respected personally, as well as for his Military genius by all down to the latest enlisted cook. He was always to be seen walking round the trenches.

He is replaced by Geoffrey Feilding who commanded the 3rd Battalion of the Coldstream for the first 8 months of the war, and a very capable fellow too. I am very glad a Coldstreamer should take his place. A cake and 3 wee tins arrived today for which many thanks.

Your loving brother

Lags

June 29th. A quiet morning cleaning up, rode over to NŒUX LES MINES with Sim and Budget.

June 30th. Julian Steele returned to Battalion. Had Adjutant's parade for Nos: 3 and 4 Companies at 8:30 a.m. Nos: 1 and 2 went to Swimming Baths.

July 1st. Too wet for parade, rode into BÉTHUNE in evening and dined with Little Man Vaughan.

July 2nd. Another Adjutant's parade of Nos: 1 and 2 Companies, very hot, spent most of the the day in Orderly room. C.O. went round with Medical Officer arranging to clean out most other "muck heaps" in the farmyards. We played 4th Field Ambulance at cricket in evening with some success. Most awfully dangerous pitch, no casualties.

July 3rd. Did absolutely nothing. John Wynne-Finch (who has come to this Battalion from the 1st) and self went for a walk in evening.

July 4th. Commanding officer had to go round trenches and so MacB took Church conducted by Lushington. Budget and self rode into BÉTHUNE late and dined at Hôtel de France.

July 5th. Spent most of morning packing up, moved off about 2 p.m. via BÉTHUNE to CAMBRIN and took over trenches just South of LA BASSEE road from 60th (K.R.R.), Jelf was their C.O. Not a very nice line, Germans so close and they bomb so much. Nos: 1, 2 and 3 Companies in firing line, No: 4 in support. Trousers returned from his week as acting Brigade Major. Not at all a quiet night, mostly bombing and rifle grenades.

July 6th. No: 1 Company had 6 casualties last night from one bomb, which landed among a dozen men. Nearly all day this continued, mostly on No: 3 who were on the left and had the crater of an old mine in front of them, the Germans only being 20 yards away. Trench Mortars worried them a bit; we also got guns to work but shrapnel is no good and they are not allowed to use high explosive. The Germans shelled us a bit with high explosive. No: 3 had 5 casualties, and No: 1 – two more, making 3 killed. Went round Companies and watched 'Minenwerfers' coming over, they mostly went wide. Messages came in all day. Bombs running very short, and when we ask for "Mills" bombs they say they are too expensive, they also keep rubbing it in that rifle grenades cost £1 each. The Germans don't seem to mind the cost!

July 7th. A quieter night but No.1 had 5 more casualties and No: 3 had 2 only one really bad. Everyone wiring wildly for bombs, which still are scarce, lots of trench mortar ammunition but no powder (just like them!}. During the night we pushed so many bombs over and got the guns to shoot quite a lot, so that we had a quiet morning. I went round Companies after lunch and found No: 2 Company had had an unlucky rifle grenade into them, killing one man and wounding 4 others including Sergeant Lavington, luckily most of them slightly. About 5 p.m. they suddenly started shelling CAMBRIN with great big ones, and must have sent over about 40 all round the houses there, also several "Fizz bangs" over our trenches. Relieved by 3rd Battalion about 8 p.m., they were rather delayed by the shelling. Several of our Guides went wrong also which delayed matters. Got back to BEUVRY about 9 p.m. into quite a nice big house.

July 8th. Two Court Martials in morning otherwise uneventful day. Sat in garden most of the day.

2nd Battalion Coldstream Guards,
4th Guards Brigade.
British Expeditionary Force.

July 8th 1915

Darling Nancy

Some more shortbread and soap arrived from you today. Thank you so much. Perhaps as you say, a change from shortbread might be nice. Leave I fear is rather postponed but I hope I get it at the end of the month.

If it is a week, as it should be, I thought of going to Tyntesfield for the weekend of it. No news from here, it rains a bit, otherwise hot.

Your loving brother

Lags

July 9th. Ralph Bingham came to luncheon on his way to join 3rd Battalion. Started up about 3:30 p.m. to relieve 3rd Battalion in some trenches near CAMBRIN. Colonel had to go to a conference at Brigade Headquarters and so Druce Bentinck and self took Battalion up. Took over from John Campbell. Fairly quiet, but still very few bombs in our line.

July 10th. Had one man killed in the night and 2 wounded. Budget Lloyd went off on leave. Later Medical Officer came and took my temperature and made me go into Hospital, as I had been rather seedy for last two days. Taylor took Adjutantcy. Went to "Harley Street" Dressing Station, thence by Ambulance to BEUVRY, then by another motor Ambulance to BÉTHUNE and 2 hours later by another Ambulance to Château near CHOCQUES called No: 1 Clearing Hospital, where I was put into the officers ward.

July 11th. Kept in bed all day on milk.

July 12th. Got up about 10 a.m. and walked about, found I was very weak still. Ipswich (3rd Battalion) came in in the evening suffering from 'shock'. Marsham went out having been shot through his left eye, otherwise his brain not touched. Went to bed early.

July 13th. Didn't get up till after luncheon as did not feel so well. A quiet and warm day. A very bad place for insects. Ipswich still here as no Hospital train today. Got up about 3 p.m. and spent a quiet day.

July 14th. They got us up at 6 a.m. for some reason, however once up I did not mind, felt much better. Ipswich went off. Could not find my Doctor all day and so arranged with Staff Sergeant to go out tomorrow. Evans (late Captain Oxford Cricket XI and now 'observer' in Flying Corps] came in 'sick'.

No. 1 Clearing Hospital

July 14th – 15th 1915

Darling Nancy,
    If Tyntesfield is not too far, why not come there. What I thought of doing if it comes in all right was to go to Tyntesfield for a Saturday – Tuesday and spend the rest in London. I am in here (see address) for a few days as I found I was paying too frequent visits to "Aunt Cathy" for convenience sake and so came in here for a diet and hope to go out tomorrow having been 4 days in here.
    It is in an awfully nice old 1715 French Château and is really very comfortable with a garden about as big as Charlton in which I have been sitting today. I should think my leave ought to come on in about a fortnight's time from now.

Your loving

Lags

July 15th. Got a car about 9:30 a.m. and was driven to 1st Line Transport near BEUVRY where I stayed. Lunched with Little Man Vaughan in BEUVRY before they went up to relieve the 2nd Battalion. Walked out in evening to meet Colonel riding back. Dinner about 9 p.m.

July 16th. Lot of writing in Orderly room, which took all morning. Rained whole of afternoon, too wet for a ride, so John W-F and self went for a walk round LE QUESNOY and back. Rooke took the bank (and my money!) at Roulette after dinner, but we did not keep it up very late.

July 17th. Still raining. Went and interviewed lady in 'Estaminet' about drunk man in No: 3 who had struck her. However she refused to give evidence for a Field General Court Martial. Had short game of stump cricket in garden. Moved off to relieve 3rd Battalion about 5 p.m. from BEUVRY. Relief completed about 8 p.m. Battalion Headquarters in WOBURN ABBEY. Most palatial with a dug out in each room. MacGregor's Luncheon/Tea basket used for first time, a really clean meal at last. MacGregor went to Hospital with a high temperature. No: 1 on right, No: 2 left, No: 3 in QUINCHY support, and No: 4 back. Everything quiet. Some funk 'holes' started at Headquarters. Two bursts of firing by Siege battery on German working party in "B1" section GIVENCHY at 10 p.m. and 11:30 p.m., but not many rounds. A very dark night and consequently many flares going up. Germans turned on about 4 machine guns hard on first few rounds of guns.

July 18th. Quiet night, one man hit himself with 'Very Light' and two men slightly wounded, otherwise nothing. Nice warm day: continued dug outs round Battalion Headquarters. Went round trenches about 3:30 p.m., stayed some time with No: 1 Company, all very cheery. Germans started putting six inchers down trench as I walked back also they put some back at our guns. Got back and found Colonel very agitated, thinking I had got caught. After about ½ hour's shelling all was quiet again and no casualties at all.

July 19th. Very quiet night followed by very quiet morning. Brigadier came up and went round with Colonel. Brigadier General Corkran (who has just taken over 5th Brigade) came round. After lunch Budget returned; went round trenches and found most people half asleep; Leese got hit by brick splinters from bullet near his head not very bad but went to Hospital. Relieved by 3rd Battalion at about 7:30 p.m.

July 20th. A quiet day in billets at BEUVRY. In evening 'Father' Smith, Monkey Shaw, Merton, and self dined at Hôtel de France at BÉTHUNE. When I got back I found leave had been altered again and I go tomorrow.

July 21st. Woken up about 3 a.m. by Drill Sergeant Higgins to say Sergeant Major had fallen out of window when walking in his sleep. Went round and found him in awful state of hysteria, with help of Medical Officer we got him off to Hospital about 4 a.m. Returned to bed and got up about 9 a.m. Had lot to arrange in the Orderly Room. Handed over to John Wynne-Finch and rode into FOUQUEREUIL to catch 2:30 p.m. Scott having walked on ahead. Had to wait about an hour, when train started and went straight to BOULOGNE. Had slight difficulty in getting Scott on but managed it. Fair crossing.

July 22nd. Got to Victoria 3 a.m., went to Belgrave Square. Via woke up and greeted me. Slept till 1 p.m. Went to Theatre.

July 23rd. Shopped – Theatre with Blanche and Willie – supper with Trousers.

July 24th. Shopped – Started for Tyntesfield in Hotchkiss, broke down several times, got there 11 p.m.

July 25th. Party; Cyril, Evie and Alice Gurney, Uncle Reggie, Nancy, Hughie and Mercy, and Elaine, George and Via, and self. Church. Rained most of the day. Drove to Pill with George in evening in "Bewick".

July 26th. Raining. Went to Barrow for tea, whole family there, including Dorothy Houldsworth (Ralph's).

July 27th. Went up by 12 o'clock train. Billy, Ruby, Albinia and Dick turned up. Large family party at Berkeley and then on to Hippodrome.

July 28th. Shopped – Lunch Windsor – Party consisting of Blanche, Maisie Wynne-Finch, Madie Macdonell, Chattie, Cissie Beckwith-Smith, Annabelle S-C, Little Man Vaughan, Sim, Harry Cubitt, and Joe Lane: to Empire from Ritz and on to Savoy.

July 29th. Went to Regimental Orderly Room, lunched in. Caught the 5:40 p.m. at Victoria. George, Via, Nancy, Cissie, and Uncle Reggie came and saw me off. Very crowded train; very calm crossing.

July 30th. Very crowded train to FOUQUEREUIL, where I got at about 6 a.m. Found my horse waiting. Rode to GORRE where Guy S-S was with 1st line Transport. Breakfast and shave and up to the trenches near LE PLANTIN by 11 a.m. Very quiet trenches, mostly breastworks. Nos: 3 & 4 in front, 1 support and 2 reserve. Took over Adjutantcy from 'Ympkin'. These trenches are those taken from the Germans from 9th May onwards and so were rather interesting. Rained a bit otherwise a very quiet day. Great many sandbags used.

July 31st. Brigadier came round and talked for a short time. A few German shells came over about midday but fell in open field doing no harm. Went round after luncheon and saw everyone. German trenches about 400 yards off, but come in much closer by craters on GIVENCHY. Hertfordshires came in rather late and took over very quickly, we returned to big house in LE QUESNOY.

August 1st. Maurice Ponsonby came and gave a voluntary service, which was not very well attended. After tea Towers-Clark and self rode into BÉTHUNE.

August 2nd. Raining hard. Orderly Room Sergeant Webb returned and so I went through things with him. Took a Summary of Evidence after lunch. Started up for the trenches about 8:30 p.m., still raining. Mine blown up in front of GIVENCHY, which made Germans rather jumpy and so there were rather a lot of bullets flying about as we came up, however no casualties. Relieved Hertfordshires in LE PLANTIN.

August 3rd. Divisional GOC came round at 8 a.m., which necessitated me rising early. An extra quiet day. Spent some of the day with Budget Lloyd and No: 3 Company. Rained at intervals. Our servants had a fire and most of the Lunch/Tea Basket got burnt, however luckily most of the fittings escaped. Went out with small party burying a wire in the open after dark, but so wet we came in at 11 p.m. and left it. Pitch black night and lots of German flares.

August 4th. Fine at last. Very little work done. No: 1 made up parapet on the right in sap leading to "Dead Man's" trench. Another National disaster – One of the servants slipped when bringing up our stores last night and broke all the wine bottles. Germans put up a white flag opposite No: 2 Company's sap. It was greeted with bombs. Think it must be meant for a guide for artillery, eventually it was shot down. Hertfordshires arrived about 8:30 p.m. and we got back to LE QUESNOY without incident.

August 5th. A court martial in the morning on Cattermole. Rode into BÉTHUNE about 4:30 p.m. with Sim and and 'Father' Smith. Went round the Transport jumps on way back.

August 6th. A long Gazette of temporary rank in paper including Sim and Marsham. Rained most of morning. A party including Colonel went down to Transport jumps. Relieved Hertfordshires in "B3" LE PLANTIN. Went via "Windy Corner" as Brigade of IXth Division were using "Estaminet Corner. No casualties.

August 7th. A quiet night inspite of mines that were blown up in GIVENCHY section. Some new wire to be done, which was finished almost down No:4 communication trench.

August 8th. New trench from Lee's keep to support line got on with during night, also more wiring in front. Two patrols went out, one of which found the white flag, which Germans put up 4 days ago. Relieved by Hertfordshires in evening. Some bullets flying about as we went out along the road. No casualties for 48 hours.

August 9th. Hot day. Drums having come they had a practice. South Irish Horse lent us 4 horses, which we pushed round the jumps in the evening. Byng and Dermot Brown came to dinner.

August 10th. Woke up with Heavy thirst after last night's champagne. Went round all billets with Colonel. Got very hot and thirsty, it took up about 1½ hours. South Irish Horse lent us 10 horses which we pushed round jumps till after 4 p.m., getting hotter and thirstier than before! Relieved Hertfordshires in "B3". No casualties, very warm night, had a long drink on arrival! Irish Guards had some "frightfulness" on hand which was eventually put off.

August 11th. A very hot and quiet night. Guns fired a good deal during the morning. Ammunition evidently coming through easier now. Trousers came round about bombs etc. and found me asleep, it being very quiet and hot. Two German aeroplanes came over about 4:30 p.m., one got turned back by our anti-aircraft guns, the other got through. Several of our aeroplanes went up later. Patrol of No: 1 went out without getting much information.

August 12th. Quiet morning. Went round putting up notice boards most of the morning. Brigadier came round in afternoon, but he had no news. Some bodies were found in disused trench, which we had to burn with petrol. Made a big smoke but Germans didn't seem to notice it. Sergeant Milward and Corporal Slade (No: 3 Company) went out on patrol up to German wire, met 5 Germans on way back, threw a bomb at them and fired but Germans ran away.

August 13th. A great of deal German and English kit collected from old trenches and sent back. Started to fill up LE PLANTIN keep with stores and small garrison. Hertfordshires got up about 8:30 p.m., one of the quietest nights for relief. Got back to LE QUESNOY about 10:30 p.m.

August 14th. Pioneers went up to CUINCHY Cemetery to put up new crosses on Northland's, Mills and Carter-Wood's graves, unfortunately one of them got slightly wounded doing it. South Irish Horse sent 6 horses in afternoon, which kept us going up till 6 p.m. Little Man Vaughan came into tea. Made out Leave Roster for next 5 days.

August 15th. Rained at intervals. Had Church Parade with Drums and Flutes. Flutes not a great success in Chants as they did not notice the "pointing" and so one had to get the words in pretty quick. Bentinck, Gage and Wilkinson went off on leave. We left LE QUESNOY at 3 p.m. and marched through BÉTHUNE with drums playing which caused a great sensation. Arrived at VENDIN-LES-BÉTHUNE about 4. Billets as before, my room very bare. French Chef arrives from PARIS for Officers Mess.

August 16th. Thunderstorm in morning. Very long Court Martial which took up to 4 p.m. Went in to dine at Paon d'Or. Farewell dinner to BÉTHUNE, 12 of us got up by Smith ("Father") and Sim.

August 17th. Route march for Companies. 4th Brigade officers photographed on steps of Theatre BÉTHUNE in the rain. Rained most of the day.

August 18th. Packed up all day.

August 19th. We had the most splendid 'send off' imaginable from 2nd Division. We left about 8 a.m. and small parties from every single unit in lm Division were lined up on BÉTHUNE - CHOCQUES road and cheered us as we passed. General Horne and staff and Divisional Band were also there. We then marched via CHOCQUES-LILLERS to MOLINGHEM where we arrived about 1 p.m., about a 12 mile march. They came along very well only two men falling out, who had good excuse for doing so.

August 20th. March resumed again at 8:30 a.m. We joined rest of Brigade at LAMBRES and very soon after that spot we passed General Sir Douglas Haig and his staff who had come down to see us. Rather a hot day, but not dusty. We got into RENESCURE about 12:30 p.m. Shaw and self rode down to Greys who were in WARDRECQUES but no one in. George Rodney and Crawley De Crespigny came to dinner. Mess was in a very nice old Château.

August 21st. Started off about 9 a.m. and joined Brigade in ARQUES, we then marched past Sir John French in ST. OMER. He had about 150 of his staff round him, all the streets being cleared for us. Thence on to MOULLE about 5 miles West of it, getting in at 1 p.m. Billets fair but on top of a hill. My own billet splendid, sheets on bed and all the luxuries.

August 22nd. Maurice Ponsonby came and gave us a service at 10 a.m., also Brigadier Cavan and Cuthbert Headlam, his ADC, came and saw us. Lovely day.

August 23rd. Walked round billets. Rode into ST. OMER alone in afternoon to get my hair cut, met A. H. Smith and had tea there.

August 24th. Started off about 8 a.m. and marched to OUVE WIRQUIN. Marched as Brigade to LUMBRES [Divisional Headquarters Guards] and then on by ourselves. Passed 4th Battalion (Pioneers). Bathed in evening. Glass and another came to dine.

August 25th. Marched off about 8:30 a.m. to VERCHOCQ, almost 9 miles. Passed Leicester Yeomanry and 2nd Life Guards. Billets very nice in valley with stream.

August 26th. Cleaned up all day. Sim and self bathed in evening.

August 27th. Played 4th Field Ambulance at cricket and beat them.

August 28th. Bathed before breakfast with Grubby (Gage). Sim went down to BERCK-PLAGE and hired a car for he and I to drive.

August 29th. Went off to lunch with 1st Battalion at LUMBRES. Pro, Sim, Baynes and self got there very late; Arthur Egerton, Dermot B, and Byng there.

August 30th. Had morning parade of Nos:1 & 2 Companies. Drove over to see Willie and Xth Royal Hussars, found him but could not stop. Played Polo in evening.

August 31st. Drove to MONTRIEUL and changed car for another 10HP Bayard as old one went so badly. Druce, Pro, Verelst and self took on 2nd Life Guards. F. Penn, Euan, Beaumont, and Speed at Polo. We beat them 6 - 3.

September 1st. Divisional Field day. We left VERCHOCQ at 7 a.m. and marched to THIEMBRONNE where we joined Brigade. Thence to DRIONVILLE where we met Cavan. We hid in a wood (from aircraft!) for 1 hour and then marched to the river Aa, had dinner and marched home in pouring rain.

September 2nd. Rained most of day and so nothing done. Sim and Pro took car over to 1st Battalion at LUMBRES.

September 3rd. Still raining. Took car over to FRUGES and tried hard to hire another but no luck. Lost our way coming home.

September 4th. Had parade of Nos: 1 & 2 Companies and did little Battalion drill. Played Polo in evening.

September 5th. Had Church at 12 noon by Maurice Ponsonby. After lunch Sim, Guy S-S and self took car to MONTRIEUL as man claimed his magneto back. Went on to BERCK PLAGE, where we had to leave car. Spent from 4:30 p.m. till 8 trying to get another. Eventually got a man with "Le Matin" written all over him to drive us back. Got to VERCHOCQ by 11 p.m.

September 6th. Colonel MacGregor and Leigh-Bennett having gone on leave Saturday Bentinck in command. Great muddle over Courts Martial, eventually Druce had to sit on one. One of our men (Naughton) got found "not guilty". Played Polo in evening.

September 7th. Started on Small Field day between Nos: 1 & 3 Companies, but was not a great success. Baynes and Hugh Burn off leave. Boxing in No.1 in evening. Willie came over and saw me and stayed to tea. Lloyd and Verelst went off on leave on special boat. Rode out and looked at ground for tomorrow. Judged Boxing in No: 1 Company.

September 8th. Field day between Nos: 1 , 2 and 4 Companies versus No: 3, which took the morning. Commanding Officer 's orders at 2 p.m. Kept time at Boxing. We played Polo at 5 p.m. Cavendish and Cunningham came over from Grenadiers. Sim went off on leave. Leaving us with a very young lot of officers. Drums played up at Château and the Lady of the house was perfectly delighted.

September 9th. Cleaned up most of the morning in billets. I had to go to Court Martial at 1st Irish Guards in THIEMBRONNE. Battalion marched off at 3:30 p.m. I met them in FAUQUEMBERGUES. We got to the new billets – fair. Smith (A.H), Fildes, Bulteel, and Bonvalot went off to Brigade Headquarters for a course on the "Lewis Gun".

September 10th. We paraded at 7:30 a.m. and Nos: 2 & 4 Companies went together and 1 & 3 Companies and dug a 17th line. Not very deep but quite enough to go on if it had to be taken up in a hurry and gone on with at night. Stopped at 12 noon and on again at 1:30 - 5 p.m., then back to billets.

September 11th. Companies went down independently about 7:30 a.m. I stayed behind to take a Summary of Evidence. Very hot day. Went down later on to lunch with Nos: 3 & 1 in a farm. Rode back about 6 p.m. Put in for self and Ramsay to go on leave.

September 12th. Started to march back to VERCHOCQ about 7:30 a.m. and got in just before it began to get hot. Stafford and Cuthbert Headlam came over about 4 p.m. and we walked down the stream. Leave came in about 7 p.m. Ramsay got a car from No: 4 Field Ambulance and went into ST. OMER and got there about 10 p.m. wandered about the town trying to get a car, but failed.

September 13th. Got onto the Post Van at 6:30 a.m. and caught the 10:30 a.m. boat. London at 3:30 p.m. No one there, washed and shaved. Blanche arrived about 5 p.m. and we went to the Alhambra in the evening.

September 14th. Late up: shopped. Guy and Margot dined at Bath Club. Went to Gerald de Maurier's piece. Supper Thomas A-Robartes.

September 15th. Via and George came up, also Nancy. Lunched Berkeley and shopped again buying a motor bicycle. Dined Carlton and went to Empire. Supper with Sim and Roger Cook.

September 16th. Spent most of day wiring to Billy. Eventually he wired saying he couldn't come up, and so Nancy and self dashed down to Saxmundham, getting there about 10 p.m. Albinia came to London for ½ hour.

September 17th. Talked to Billy all morning, then drove into Ipswich (30 miles) and caught 1:30 p.m. train, saw Mic-Lawrence on way. Blanche and self caught 8 p.m. train to Inverness.

September 18th. Had to change at Perth at 5:30 a.m., and got to Aberarder about 12 noon. Cissie, Annabelle, Mrs. Becky and self went out walking for Grouse and Snipe in afternoon. Got 2 Grouse and 1 Snipe and 1 Lark.

September 19th. Drove about in Cissie's car in afternoon. Hills looking lovely. Stayed out on Hill till about 7 p.m.

September 20th. Started about 9 a.m. and shot on "Ruthven" side. Frank Sopper, Stewart, and 3 others came. Got in 3 drives before lunch and got 55 brace – I shot very badly. Caught 4 p.m. train at Inverness, large crowd Annabelle, Mrs. Becky and Cissie came and saw us off. Dined at Perth.

September 21st. Got in about 10 a.m. Changed into uniform and saw about bicycle. George, Via, Huie, Mercy, Blanche and self lunched at Berkeley. I caught 5:40 p.m. Victoria, got bicycle on. Boat very crowded. Life belts on. Ramsay and I and Chick (1st Guards Brigade Supply Officer) slept at Hôtel du Louvre.

September 22nd. Got a pass and rode bicycle off with some difficulty and got to VERCHOCQ about 2 p.m., found Battalion getting ready to move. We marched about 6 p.m. Scott took bicycle on. We billeted in DENNEBRŒUCQ for night. Fair billets.

September 23rd. Stafford came to lunch. We marched again at 6 p.m. via COYECOUES, a steep hill and wet march to NEDONCHEL (Herman Fontaine) getting there late, tired and very wet. Billets crowded.

September 24th. Spent most of day getting dry. Several lots of orders came in, but eventually we had orders to move early next day.

2nd Battalion, Coldstream Guards
British Expeditionary Force.

September 24th 1915

Darling Nancy,
    I have seen quite a lot of your old man since I have been back. I took him round to try and show him some of the Grenadiers who are in his "Parish" but found most of them out. He then came and rode with this Battalion which we were marching. He had a most indifferent waterproof that got wet through before starting, but didn't seem to mind.
    I had an adventurous ride back to the Battalion on my Motor Bicycle; having a severe skid in Boulogne which nearly did it in. Now I have put an Orderly onto it who knows almost as little as I do.
    I had a very good week in England thanks to all of you who came up to see me.

Your loving

Lags

September 25th. Left about 5 a.m. and marched as a Brigade. I think one of the wettest and most unpleasant marches I have had. We got to AUCHEL about 9 a.m., and the men got into bad billets. Here we waited until about 1 p.m. and on again, raining harder than ever. We kept going on all right for first 10 miles and then we got into a long column, at one place we halted by side of road for 3 hours, rain fairly beating down. We then moved on in jerks and stops until we got into NŒUX LES MINES about 10 p.m.; very scattered and bad billets. All men very tired as we had done about 20 miles. Had to go to bed as we were as no kit brought up.

September 26th. Got a mess in an estaminet. Spent most of morning trying to pick up news. French had done very well and British well South of LA BASSEE road. North of it no gains. Stafford held a street corner Service for about ½ hour. Orders came in at 12 noon and we moved off at 1 p.m. This Battalion leading the Brigade, which in its turn was leading the Division, so we were first 'for it'. We halted outside VERMELLES and moved forward in small 'bits' through VERMELLES and up past LE RUTOIRE to old British line in support to 21st Division. By this time it was quite dark and the Division in front seemed in a terrible muddle. Brigades so congested that they didn't know where any of their Battalions were. Men walking in every direction and kit lying thick in every trench. We got orders to move up to old German front trench (present British 2nd trench). We went and looked at it and found it full of men of all Battalions of 21st Division, who didn't know where their Battalions were. Eventually about 8 p.m. we got orders to take over front line trenches, which was really a great relief as we should then feel safer. This we did all night and just got settled down before dawn. Nos: 1 & 4 in front, 2 just behind, and 4 behind again.

September 27th. Got down to sleep about 8 a.m. "beat to the world" and very wet. We went on improving these very bad trenches, continued shelling the Germans, but they didn't answer much. Tried to get in touch with the Germans but found they had retired very far. A great deal more kit left by 21st Division in these trenches. This attack was a very high trial to them but I should feel very safe behind them. Sited a new line to start on, which was started after dark by Nos: 1 & 4 Companies helped by No: 2 Company. Battalion had 18 casualties during the day including Company Sergeant Major (acting Drill Sergeant) Robson very badly wounded, who died later on, a very great loss to the Battalion.

September 28th. A quieter morning. During night 2nd Guards Brigade had come in on our right, which makes us safer also 3rd Coldstream on our left. In afternoon 2nd Guards Brigade made an attack from "Chalk Pit on Puits 14 bis" which was not a great success owing to German guns getting on to them and their supports in the Pit, also coming under heavy machine gun fire from the right, no progress made. We deepened our front line. Grenadiers moved up closer behind us. Also some of 4th Battalion Coldstream Guards came up to help dig, but not much could be done as it simply poured all night. Our dug out leaked badly. Casualties for day 7. Very good news from French in CHAMPAGNE, 20,000 prisoners and 40 guns. Attacks on CUINCHY and GIVENCHY have not progressed at all.

September 29th. Woke up very wet, dug out having leaked badly. Hear 1st Coldstream lost rather heavily yesterday. Raining still. Bombardment somewhat lessened over us. Hugh Burn went over to try and get connection with 2nd Guards Brigade, by 3 p.m. he had not returned. We got very nervous that he must have been killed. Sergeant Gough went after him. He eventually returned about midnight much scared by the shells.

September 30th. Colonel went off to a Brigade Conference, and returned with good news that we were going to be relieved. A quiet day. Sergeant Gough not yet returned, which is serious. About 7:30 the Colonel, Adjutant, and 2nd in command of the 11th Battalion Middlesex, 36th Brigade (New Army) turned up and said his Battalion were following him. This however was not the case as his Battalion had lost their way in the rain. However they all went to bed and so I spent most of the time up to 12 mid-night going to the "Lone Tree" and bringing up platoons. Eventually we got out and got to fair billets at MAZINGARBE by 4 a.m.

October 1st. Slept till 11 a.m., very tired. Went round billets with Bentinck after lunch. Stafford came to tea and we took a walk. Shaw and self dined with Harry Cubitt (3rd Battalion).

From Capt. John Eveleyn Gibbs to Mrs. Crawley (Nancy)

October 1st 1915

"I got today your letter of Sept. 20th. Your own 'snap' is good only too much reminds of 'Miss Silk Stockings of the Frivolity Theatre at the wheel of her 90 h.p. Humber' and Molly's is not good enough. I had a letter from Uncle George today of the 3rd August in which he says that as I recommend Molly staying in England I must find her a rich parti, as it is expensive living in England. I am sorry to hear she is leaving here, though I can so understand her feelings. Give her my love, and every good message to those at Sydney, especially Uncle George who I thought was particularly charming when he was at home.

Your 'Snap' of the children are added to the Gallery on my wall which is nearly all children. People who come in say I must have a dozen wives at home for so numerous a progeny.

Stafford's leaving you was very precipitous, but I know how pleased he will be. To think of Willie (*William Otter Gibbs*) as Lieutenant Colonel is certainly surprising. He came to Sandhurst a year after me, but he deserves it with his two wounds etc. Best love to him and Mrs. Colonel.

Looking forward to your photograph: but shall not put it up if it is not like you, I still remember your face.

Merci of 16th September. I can only tell Mrs. Wynne that on October 27th; I met and shook hands with her poor son about 11 p.m. in a dark room under a fairly heavy under fire. He and Allison and Watts Russell had just arrived….. He was appointed to No. 1 Company with Hargreaves Brown and I never saw him again. I think he must have been killed in the trench with Hargraves Brown. I just remember he looked tall and young and seemed surprised when I bustled in (having been summoned there by poor Leslie Hamilton) and shook hands all round, and at once started talking about changing our position.

I heard from Davenport, Huie gave him my address. Letters from Billie of 29th August and 19th September. I wrote a line to Ruby on Sunday week last. I cannot say how much I hope he will have a good time when he goes.

Elaine 16$^{th.}$ September. Betty 9$^{th.}$ September, both very nice letters. Albinia of September 11th. I suppose she will stay with you all in turn in London. The plum pudding arrived today quite well.

Walter Riddel, September 12th, a Captain and so am I – brave and so am I – and so on like St. Paul. Many thanks to him and tell him to stay where he is.

Charles King September 8th, many thanks for excellent cake. Via Price Jones September 9th, and such a nice letter too good for this very ordinary person. I am so glad she has got Harry there, long may he stay, but it is terrible about Alan being so entirely crippled by rheumatism, I am sorry. Best love to Guy when he returns, and if he has a minute I should love a letter from him, and an interesting one.

I wish I could have been Giant Hardy's best man as he asked me.

Mrs. Bassett of the Manor House Petersham, 14th September, awfully nice of her to write, and I hope she will do it again often. Blanche met her at dinner once with me when she was Miss Sturges, and she talks of going to see Blanche soon. A very nice girl she was, and is and her husband is an old friend of Indian days. I am wondering if he has been with his old chief lately, till he got his present job.

Also through her my love to Lady Birdie i.e. Lady Birdwood. Blanche will I expect know her, as she has evidently enquired after me once or twice. Ask Blanche to tell her I well remember the dinner when she and Blanche met.

The 'Vida' bread always arrives green now from Via, and I don't really think it is any more good sending bread from England. That which comes from Switzerland is very good, though sometimes Evie Gurney's Dijon loaves arrive good.

I have written today to Cousin Vicary also an extra letter as he made enquiries through a German Colonel for me. The 'Colynos' and shaving powder have arrived.

In case of accident I mention again that I ask sometime to be sent me medium and best quality underclothes, and pyjamas and Blanche says she is sending my rug.

Well au revoir. Keep good hearts all of you. It is an awful time but there must come an end.

My best love to all.

Evelyn.

From Lord Cavan.
October. 1st, 1915

"Mails seem to have gone to the devil, but we got rather spoilt at Tumbres, so never mind. Of course I cannot buck about my own Division officially but I can only say that some French officers and 2 or 3 Generals who saw the advance of the 3rd Brigade under the most awful shell fire on the 27th, all say it was the finest sight the world has ever known. God, how I love them. I don't think our losses are quite as heavy as I feared. I am rather worried by my signallers who are bad. All Kitchener's army have not trained of course. I gave an harangue to twenty Motor cycle Dispatch Riders this morning and told them they must consider it a matter of personal honour to deliver dispatches. Five times we found our orders not received and <u>no</u> word from the Dispatch Rider that they had not delivered them. Of course this would soon mean chaos. The losses of officers I simply cannot think of, it must be and there is an end of it".

October 2nd. Very busy day with Summaries and writing up papers diaries. Stafford came round and arranged a service. Colonel went off to Brigade Conference. Harry Cubitt and Francis Longueville came to dinner.

October 2nd, Lord Cavan to Inez

"Pushing on" is what we all want to do, but it cost the army fifty one thousand casualties already, and now it is all "huggered up" and wired up again. My lot at peace until Sunday night, and next week no doubt more big things will happen.

The Commander in Chief came here this morning and said charming things to my Brigadiers and groups of men, they deserve it all. I expect this battle will go on for another fortnight also, and then settle down to trenches for the winter, and I hope to get a bit of leave again about November or December but of course we may press the Bosches back and seven prisoners taken last night in the Hohenzollern dugout all belonged to seven different regiments so they are nicely mixed up, and there feeding and supply must be chaotic. We shall all keep on pressing all we can, but men must be given sleep sometimes.

Flemming tells me that Stafford did splendidly all through the last fighting in Vermelles, and that Ponsonby was magnificent. Truly I am well served in all my departments.

Cavan

October 2nd 1915

Dearest Nancy
Just one scribble to tell you Stafford did splendid work with the wounded all through our last fight. God keep him. I knew he would do well.

We are resting now and go forward again Sunday night.

Yours with love

Lord Cavan

October 3rd. Colonel, Pro and all other Company Commanders went up to see new line. Stafford Crawley held voluntary service at 11 a.m. Colonel etc. returned back about 3 p.m. to say that poor old Pro Leigh-Bennett had been killed while going round. A great loss to the 2nd Battalion. We also heard Petre had died of wounds. Started off for new trenches East of VERMELLES about 6 p.m. Had a most unpleasant walk up to them. I got hit by a shell but so slight that it really only bruised. Relieved the 1st K.R.R. (King's Royal Rifles) in some very nasty trenches, which had been partially blown in during day by a German attack. Finished relief about 11 p.m. Had my shoulder "Dressed"! Druce went round the trenches after K.R.R. had gone. Everything seemed fairly quiet.

October 3rd, Lord Cavan to Inez

"Tonight we go into the line. Fielding's Brigade on the left, Heyworth's on right, Ponsonby in reserve. I go up to a Château much knocked about but with excellent cellars. Moyelle just behind Vermelle, with a good dugout further forward, to which all telephone wires are already run and in which Cuthbert is arranging to put a stove tonight. Enemy reinforcements have arrived but we have taken prisoners of only ten weeks training so they must be short of trained men.

This next week will be a strenuous and hard one, but God grant successful in that we may push back the enemy. The French are still hard at it in Champagne and will be hard at it, on our right at Viney directly so of course we must go on. But wire! The curse of fox hunting and the curse of this war, and it grows up by miles in a night.

October 4th. Some shelling during night but no damage. A great deal of rifle fire on our left about 5:00 – 7:00 a.m., which we took to be an attack on the HOHENZOLLERN redoubt. Brigadier came round the trenches and arranged several things between us and the 3rd Battalion on our left. Got Pro's body down during night also dug out one Benthall in the 1st K.R.R. who had been killed yesterday. A fairly quiet morning trenches improving but are still very shallow and dangerous. I hope within 3 or 4 days we shall get the upper hand of the "Bosches" here and make the Quarries untenable. Gunners are good and have lots of ammunition. Bombs for us are good and plentiful. "Kiddies" got rather heavily shelled. I think the Germans meant attacking but were put off by our guns. Quiet night.

October 5th. The "Kiddies" again got very shelled also; thought they were going to be attacked. However nothing much happened. Stafford came up to luncheon. Relieved by 1st Battalion Irish Guards. Started at 8:00 p.m. and last Company got into VERMELLES at 2:30 a.m. 5 Company of Irish Guards having got lost. Drill Sergeant (acting Sergeant Major) Higgins wounded last night.

October 6th. Breakfast at 10 a.m., and did little all morning. Had to supply a few fatigue parties for digging and carrying. Druce, Sim, and I went down and had a look at Pro's grave in British Soldiers Cemetery VERMELLES. A little shelling in the evening otherwise quiet. No casualties.

October 6th, Lord Cavan to Inez

"About casualties. Officially the day's casualties are collected by Brigades and sent to us by wire next morning. It is almost impossible to say who is dead wounded and missing till the roll is called, and bodies in this awful war cannot be picked up till dark, and not always then. We wire the names of officers and numbers of men to the Adjutant General at base. He wires them daily to War Office but with one million men you must make allowances for blocks on the wire and delays of official news. Remember I only tell you of one small division and the War Office has to deal with 40 or 50 Divisions. Stafford and Lancelot quite all right at 10:00 a.m. this morning.

Whacking big shells falling now in and around Noyelles, which we have just left, a lot of rifle fire too, must go to the telephone and ask about it………. All right nothing awful.

October 7th. A few fatigues had to be supplied in the morning. Quartermaster Sergeant and Orderly Room Sergeant Webb went off to take over War Office appointment, leaving Sergeant King in Orderly Room. Gilly Follett turned up about 4:30 p.m. just as we were starting for the trenches. Relieved Irish Guards in same bit of line as they took over from us. Went up along communication trench but whole Battalion got in by 9:00 p.m. Quite a quiet night, trenches not much improved.

October 7th, Lord Cavan to Inez

I suppose it was those damned gas shells but I had a cracking headache after I had finished my yesterday's letter, made worse by a long stuffy conference at army Head Quarters so soup and a potato in bed. Awful four hours and then sleep, and now much better. Even here they chucked some small shells this morning into the garden, but no harm done. I cannot help thinking that if Germany sends a big force against Serbia, they really won't be able to stand the strain in men. Russia, Serbia, France, all taking their daily toll of thousands. Even Prussian numbers must be reduced in time. I hear we had no difficulty in taking two Divisions away from the Dardanelles unscathed, and putting them over to Salonica fine work.
Later: Feeling better, but crack Grenadier snipers got four brace of Germans yesterday.

October 8th. Worked hard on recesses but no wood had come up and so it was impossible to do much. About 12 noon the Germans began a very heavy bombardment, which was mostly concentrated on our second line and round about Battalion Headquarters, this continued for 4 hours mostly small shells but a 5" came over about every other minute. Communication with Brigade was cut, also with artillery, but the latter replied well. Intercommunication made very difficult by trenches being blown in. About 4 p.m. the Germans made three bombing attacks, the one on the 2nd Battalion was mostly on No: 3 Company. They kept them off for some time, then the two front bombers got killed and they nearly got a footing, however a rush with fresh bombs was made and they were quickly pushed out. They then got into their own sap head which had been blown in behind them and so were caught and "played with"! After a good deal of firing things quieted down a bit. During this time all communication by wire with Companies had been cut, but Sergeant Finch ran out some new wire and got one man wounded in the proceeding. Just at dark a good deal of shooting started again but came to nothing the gunners having got communication again and kept up a fairly heavy bombardment.

The 3rd Battalion on our left got it even harder than we did, being attacked down several sapheads. They took several prisoners who said that our guns had fairly got into the Germans waiting behind the attack, and they had only attacked today because they thought the Guards had been relieved. So I expect they are feeling rather sore. Got to bed about 10:00 p.m. feeling very tired. Night quite quiet and not many messages.

October 8th, Lord Cavan to Inez

Whew! What a day! Went up to Head Quarters of 1st Brigade at 11 o'clock terrific bombardment of our trenches and Vermelles, was imprisoned in the Dugout until one, when in a lull we made a bolt down the trenches to a wall, where we had left the car, got away all right then at 5 o'clock Germans made a terrific attack with bombs aerial torpedoes after bombardment all day, so far 6:00 p.m.

We are holding our own. Taken some prisoners and a bit of German trench. Have sent up two Companies and 500 more bombs, and trust we can finish this off.

It is pitch dark but guns still roaring. Thank God I can trust my men to fight it out. These are very anxious days and the strain is great.

Men are dug in and comfy, well fed and go up tonight full of good cheer and hearty. God bless them, and I think we have got everything ready for them, bombs, sandbags, tools, trench mortars and all the engines of destruction. You cannot conceive the difficulties of a relief trench, all knocked about by shells, many choked with kit and rifles and dead, though all these are being collected by large Cavalry working parties. We sent away 4 long loads of rifles mostly those of wounded men, but many of them hurled away in the panic by the 21st and 24th Divisions. Might be all right next time they were very highly tried. General Wing was killed yesterday, I handed over to him.

11 p.m. – "May God be praised and all His heavenly host. After a really terrific bomb fight we have maintained, lost, and entirely regained all our ground, and a wee bit more, and Germans have suffered very heavily from machine guns and artillery fire. Now I am going to bed and hope to sleep, but brain is active all the time.

October 9th. An extra quiet morning. Some 12 Divisional officers came round line. Whole day continued quiet which goes to show that the Germans had a good knock yesterday. During yesterday's action poor little E. St. L. Bonvalet got mortally wounded in the head by a bullet and was carried back to the Dressing station in the evening. The Irish Guards came up and relieved us about 6:30 p.m. and we moved on back to the support trenches, the men being rather tired. Just before dark we were shelled but not very heavily, most of them 'appeared' to be directed against our Headquarters dug out but they did not hit it. No: 1 had a "Minen Werfer" into their Company which caused some 10 casualties. During the night there were a good many fatigues mostly carrying bombs and sandbags up.

Morning of the 9th, Lord Cavan to Inez.

All satisfactory, all our ground consolidated. Our Casualties about 100. Three officers wounded, none badly. Germans lost at least five times as many. 2nd and 3rd Coldstreams, 2nd Irish, and 3rd Grenadiers, all fought well and valiantly. We used over 9000 bombs. French lost a wee bit of ground on our right, but beat off, four frontal attacks against Loos, and Germans lost very heavily. Fog, and comparative calm today.

2nd Battalion Coldstream Guards
British Expeditionary Force.

October 9th 1915.

Darling Nancy,

Tous va bien ici. I expect your better half had somewhat to do these last few days as the "Huns" did a heavy attack yesterday on us and those round us, and got a good deal more than they bargained for. Those who were taken prisoner said, "They thought the Guards had been relieved" and so were rather surprised. We got 4 of them "boxed up" in one of their own sapheads the trench behind having been blown in, and I believe the men opposite played with them like cat and mice. I believe K was very pleased with what happened as I fancy they really meant business and we fairly upset their plan (by "we" I mean the Brigade).

I hear Molly is off back. Where will she go as I will write her a letter of "good byes"? I'm afraid I have seen very little of her and feel I ought to have taken more trouble the summer of 1914 but of course did not realise this would happen (the war).

Ever your loving

Lags.

October 10th. A quieter morning, Desmond F-G rang up about 12 noon to say poor Monty Gore Langton had been killed about the same spot as Leigh-Bennett was. A heavy fatigue to make a communication trench, which took the whole night. Luckily no casualties as we were working above ground most of the time.

October 10th, Lord Cavan to Inez

Our casualties yesterday, were 190 and five officers, but we killed over 600 Germans. Four men won the battle, by bombing, and I have determined to get the V.C. for one of them, and three D.C.Ms for the others. We shall be ready now in a few days for another good push on. Oh that all the Divisions were equally good. I am very very hopeful now about the future because I am positive, even German numbers cannot stand the enormous drain that Serbia, France and Russia will put upon her. I trust that Ferdinand will be assassinated. Drat him!

But no rest and cannot be until 1st Army fulfils its' task. I see "Land and Water" has me among the great men. What ho! But I beat the Germans yesterday.

Just read my Psalms and Lessons like your mother, as I cannot go to Church. It is such a lovely evening. Makes one feel homesick, but still I am as I said yesterday, far more hopeful of a really fine finish next year, than I have ever been. I suppose in the last three days, at least ten thousand Germans have been laid out within an area of three miles of me. It is very horrible and 19 of my officers, 7 killed and 12 wounded, since the big battle and 526 men, who have covered themselves with glory. What a Command it is. Don't be nervous at next big push, it is not our turn and we shall be just behind.

October 11th. The hoped for relief postponed a night, but we stay where we are. In the afternoon Colonel Madden and Father Gwynne were brought down, the former with leg broken, and the latter I'm afraid done for, hit all over the back and spine. They had at last got a shell right into that dug out we left. We kept them at our Headquarters until dark and sent them down across country as the trenches were too narrow for stretchers. Stafford called in but did not stay.

Oct. 11th, Lord Cavan to Inez

Another tough fight last night by the 2nd Grenadiers in my old Brigade who bombed out of a very nasty corner which worried us much and resisted. The devil of a counter stroke at 4:00 a.m. Our old Battalion are masters of the Bosches, and they know it.

Not so the new Battalion yet, only long experience can teach them. We have not had such a hard fight since Ypres in November, but the great difference is that we now have a vast superiority in big guns.

The loss of Captain Gore Langton, is awful to us, such a very very glorious fighter and gallant soul. The noise and din is incessant, and unceasing night and day, and I have to be careful in picking my time for going up to B.H.Q. There was a fine air fight this morning in full view of us, and the German was brought down unhurt, and the two officers captured, and a good machine to us. Their "control" was cut by our air machine guns.

Angus Hamilton's death is very fine, and there are many gallant and great hearts now at rest with God, and what could one ask for more. Yes, all Bob's Division did very well right through, not a word except of praise have I heard. Do contradict armchair critics at home who talk about bad Staff work, and so on. This battle so far has been admirably run, and bravely fought, and if asses at home think it could have been done better, let them come and try. It is terrific work. In time we shall so reduce the German numbers, that they must go to shorter lines, but only by Pluck, Perseverence, Patience and Preparation. Some notes I have written on the fight of last week and use of bombs, have been circulated to the Army. What a clever man you'll say, but someone must act as teacher, as some of our leaders are still nervous of Stillen Bosche, and so don't follow the dictates of common sense.

I saw Staff this morning, looking well and very hearty, and I hope he will be able to dine with me on the first night after we come out of trenches. My one fear is the Division, which relieves us, will lose some vital point, which we have taken and kept. It is purely a matter of individual bravery and physical strength and bomb throwing. Keep a good heart.I would not change places with the German opposite us for thousands a year. He must be having an awful time. 5 inch, 8 inch, 12 inch, and 15 inch all over him. Their bombing attack defeated, but left twelve dead in five yards last night.

October 12th. Berks and Essex (Kitchener's Army) officers trooped up to go round our lines but I don't think they learnt much as we did not really know them. Orders for relief came about 11:00 a.m. and we pushed out about 5:00 p.m., very glad to be 'shot' of some of the beastliest trenches I have been in. A halt en route for teas and then on across country to VERQUIN where we arrived about 7:30 p.m. to find fairly good billets.

October 12th, Lord Cavan to Inez

Anxious day because my Division is gradually being removed, and as I am responsible for safety of line till relief is complete it means I have to issue orders to new troops and relieving Divisions. The Germans evidently thought the relief was done at 5:00 p.m. for they attacked heavily after bombardment, but they were sold because my own men were still there, and beat them off. Well I shan't be happy till I hear my men are all out. I hear that it is possible that more Divisions including some from here may be sent to Salonica. God Help us if it is so. I cannot believe it. Will nobody tell the Government that such a dispersal of Forces spells disaster.

Here we are just getting the upper hand, and it should be so clear to any soldier that the Germans know they are at a disadvantage east and west, and only seek the Serbian distraction to draw troops away from the decisive point. If they would wriggle all the troops out of the Dardanelles I would not mind, and it would be a splendid excuse of a bad hole.

Stafford is dining here tonight and is thankful for a good meal and a few quiet hours. Father Gwyn, the R.C. Chaplain to the Irish Guards, died last night of shell wounds. Such a good fellow. After tomorrow I shall be free of care and I trust for 24 hours, but we never know, anyhow all my men will be asleep I hope all day and all night too. For ten days now they have kept after the Hun and had no rest.

October 13th. A very good night. The whole morning was spent in making up Promotions, which included the Sergeant Major and two Drill Sergeants. After tea I rode the motor bicycle over to Headquarters 2nd Guards Brigade and had dinner. John Ponsonby in very good form. Guy Baring, Byng, Hopwood, Merton, and Boy Brooke were also there.

October 13th 1915, Lord Cavan to Inez

A fierce conflict is raging for the possession of Hohenzollern by the 46th Division. We are not yet engaged. The reports are good and bad, but I hope they have gained something. They started grandly but soon got checked and while some brave souls have gone on, others have not. Meanwhile the 4th Corps on the right who had a simpler task, have gained their objective.

Later: The result as far as one can make out is that we have gained three bits out of their enemy line at H. which was taken, was being evacuated at dark. My criticism is that the schemers are too ambitious. If the 46th had been told to take the H. only I think they would have done it, but they aimed at more and got neither. I think we could take H. by bombing."

October 14th. A lovely morning with lots to do. Still at 2 hours notice to move. Willie Otter Gibbs came over to lunch and got let in for a concert by the Guards Division Supply Train to which Generals Haking and Douglas Haig came. Willie stayed to tea. Byng and Humphrey de T came over from 15 Battalion to dinner.

October 15th. Misty morning and I think a move shortly; which came and we left at 3:30 p.m. and had a very slow march with continual stops to VERMELLES where we arrived about 8:00 p.m. Very little cover but a few walls to lie under.

October 16th. Cleaned up the whole morning. Very little German shelling. Gilly and I walked round to see 3rd Battalion. No news. Enemy artillery a little more active in the evening.

2nd Battalion Coldstream Guards,
British Expeditionary Force.
October 16th 1915.

Darling Nancy,
 Sickening about your London House. Most unfortunate about Staff. Our beast of a Commanding Officer says he thinks our Mess is rather over-crowded already, it is, but I should have thought he could manage it.
 I thought at one time you had a house near Blanche already settled.
 Things have quietened down very "considerable" here which makes life healthier.
 I saw Willie Otter Gibbs the other day. He looked the picture of health and was doing Policing duties round these parts.
 Stafford has just been in about tomorrow Services and returns to tea.
Your loving

Lags.

Goodbye to Molly if she hasn't gone.

October 17th. About 4:30 a.m., our guns started a heavy bombardment of the HOHENZOLLERN redoubt, then later the 2nd and 3rd Guards Brigade did a bombing attack up 2 or 3 sap heads. Stafford had a service in a roofless house. This was just over in time as they started shelling the place. In the afternoon the Irish Guards came and took over our billets and we moved back to SAILLY LABOURSE, better billets and safer.

October 18th. Spent most of the day in the Orderly room. Went in on the motor bicycle to BÉTHUNE and had tooth stopped. Men cleaned themselves and their billets most of the day.

October 19th. Colonel went up to look over line we take over. Companies went up in two lots. Colonel, Gilly and self started at 4 p.m. and started up "Gordon Alley" communication trench. About ½ way up we got blocked and Germans started a heavy bombardment, most unpleasant but did not do much damage. Six casualties. Took over from Ally Cator and 2nd Scots Guards.

October 20th. Morning fairly quiet, after lunch Gilly and self went round, trenches quite fairly good, No: 1 on right all fairly quiet, No: 2 on left have 3 bombing posts running into "Big Willie" and other trenches of the HOHENZOLLERN redoubt. About 3:30 p.m. they started putting over those Aerial Torpedoes into No: 2's lines. Sim who was at Battalion Headquarters at the time went back to his Company to see if there had been any damage. On the way one fell quite close to him and a piece went into his head, killing him at once. We got his body back after dark to VERMELLES that night. A very great loss to the Battalion, as he had done over 14 months without a break with the Battalion in France. A still greater loss to his brother officers, being universally loved by all and a very true friend on all occasions especially to me.

October 21st. Arranged with Stafford Crawley to bury poor Sim in VERMELLES cemetery at 11:00 a.m. A much quieter day. Irish Guards arrived about 5:00 p.m. Rather a congestion while relieving but we got back to our VERMELLES bivouacs about 7:00 p.m. Colonel and self met a man with a sprained ankle which took some time to get to the No: 4 Field Ambulance. Dug outs quite good. Clean straw and a small mess for Headquarters. Companies had their own.

October 22nd. Slept late. No room for much writing or orders. Gilly, self and Verelst went and looked at Château where French originally took VERMELLES by mining, afterwards. Afterwards to Sim's grave in the British cemetery. Dinner with Nos: 1 and 2 Companies in evening, a fairly cheery dinner. Very frosty night with bright moon.

October 23rd. Cold but dry. Orders at 10:00 a.m. Board of Adjustment on poor Sim's effects at 11:00 a.m. A good many papers to sign. Some artillery activity over our heads during the morning in the direction of LABASSÉE-BÉTHUNE road and a few 'fat' ones in VERMELLES that did no harm. Relieved Irish Guards, relief completed before 7:00 p.m. Colonel and I got rather blocked, but by running over-ground for 50 yards we got on. Took over from Alexander who has got the 1st Battalion Irish Guards temporally.

2nd Battalion Coldstream Guards,
British Expeditionary Force.

23rd October 1915

Darling Nancy

I have passed your complete letter onto Stafford when I met him in Vermelles yesterday. I am afraid Uncle George is very upset over Jack.

It is somewhat late to write to Molly now but I will do so to Sydney when I have more time.

I think you should concentrate your efforts on Stafford with food as I am rather better placed than he is poor fellow.

Gilly F. has returned full of spirits and is very keen on getting news from anyone he meets, which are mostly rumours.

Servia (Serbia) does not look very bright at present does it, but I can't help thinking something will turn up shortly to turn the tide or put an end in view.

Weather still good, long may it remain so.

Your loving

Lags

October 24th. Most of the new trenches dug through, line beginning to look quite good. A very quiet day. Artillery communication bad: complaints sent in.

October 25th. Raining hard and continued to do so most of the day. Very cold, could not get warm. Result both sides were rather quiet. CRA came round and cleared up situation of Artillery. They appear to be giving the 'Bosch' a very heavy shelling night and day. The relieving Company Commanders came and looked round our lines. Trenches got very sticky by night time.

October 26th. Sun and wind which dried up the trenches splendidly. More activity on both sides. A most unlucky shell into our 'back' headquarters in VERMELLES which knocked out the Police Sergeant and 2 others. Believed by 35th Brigade, 5th Berkshires who started coming in about 3 p.m. We got clear about 5 p.m. had teas en route and got to HESDIGNEUL about 8 p.m. Billets fair.

October 27th. Most of the day spent in cleaning up for the King's inspection tomorrow. Raining and cold. Stafford arrived to stay for a fortnight.

October 28th. We paraded about 10:30 a.m. and marched for 2 hours en route for LILLERS. Half way there we heard that the King had had a fall from his horse and that it was off. We returned wet and disappointed. Gilly and self went round to Brigade Headquarters and passed 'time of day'.

October 29th. Sunny at last. Got seven men off on leave. Message to say King not very bad. Rode Motor Bicycle into BÉTHUNE, very bad roads.

October 30th. Cleaned up billets and practiced throwing bombs. C.O. went off on leave, also seven others including Ashley. Rode into BÉTHUNE with Verelst and brought out small "Zebra" car. Dined at Divisional (Guards) Headquarters with Cuthbert Headlam. Dull dinner.

October 31st. Large Service of 2nd and 3rd Battalions Coldstream Guards with Grenadier Band. Cold and rather wet. Budget Lloyd and self went over in small car to see 1st Battalion Coldstream at ST HILAIRE. Found most of them on leave. Gilly and self dined with John Campbell at 3rd Battalion Headquarters.

November 1st. Leave increased to 12 men and 1 Officer per day.

November 2nd. Leave decreased to 9 men, one Officer every other day. Went out in 'wee' car. 6 HP. 'Zebra' hired from BÉTHUNE. Gilly and Self. Lunched with Byng and 1st Battalion Coldstream, also went on to 4th Battalion and saw Edwards.

November 3rd. Had to cancel a Battalion parade owing to wet. Had a great Battalion Concert in evening. 15 of the Grenadier Band and several other artistes. Great success.

November 4th. Battalion parade in a fog! Rode over to some jumps. Jack Gibbs and young Winn came over to lunch. Stafford and self drove over to "ESTRÉE-BLANCHE" to dine with Willie and Jack Gibbs. Lamp would not work and so we had to stay night in make shift billets.

November 5th. Called at 5:00 a.m. Got off about 6:30 a.m. Very nice morning and not very cold. Got back about 8:00 a.m. and I got on parade at 8:30 a.m. Drove car into BÉTHUNE. Early bed.

November 6th. Went up with another large party to jumps. Tried Lewis Guns and "Sniperscopes" on small range in afternoon. Had a very rowdy dinner.

November 7th. Service at 9:45 a.m. for ½ Battalion with Grenadier Band. Very cold affair. Played 3rd Battallion Coldstream at Eton Football and got beaten 9 points to 3. Harry Cubitt and Francis Longueville to dinner. Billets improved a bit during our stay here and washing arrangements installed as billet property.

November 8th. Commanding Officer returned off leave and Gilly got away as such! Budget did orders. Went into Dentist at LILLERS. Played polo near VAUDRICOURT with 3rd Battalion and Stuart Wortley. Rode into BÉTHUNE and arranged about car which Gage broke yesterday.

November 9th. Colonel did C.O.'s orders; spent most of morning writing. After lunch we played polo again, rather wet and slippery but good exercise. Wrote orders for move tomorrow. A gusty beastly day.

November 10th. Moved off at 8:30 a.m. Colonel MacGregor commanding the Brigade temporarily. Cold and rather wet. We went nearly into CHOCQUES, then half right to HINGES, thence to CALONNE where we found poor John Hugh Smith tearing his hair there being one Division, 2 R.A Brigades, and Guards Divisional Train already in billets then. Eventually we went along the road to the MERVILLE side of CALONNE and got in very scattered, No: 4 being nearly 2 miles from No: 1.

November 11th. Still a beastly day and so wrote most of it. Rode into ST. VENANT with Leese and Gage and inspected Expeditionary Force

Canteen Branch. Billets are fairly good here in CALONNE. Leese goes on leave.

November 12th. After lunch Verelst. Bentinck, Shaw-Stewart, and self rode over to 1st Battalion in LA GORGUE, and went to quite a good concert helped by Grenadier Band. After to dinner with Humphrey de T, and so to home, night fine and fairly warm.

November 13th. Very little for orders. Mess accounts audited and found to be very high. Humphrey de T. came over for lunch, he, Guy S-S and self rode into MERVILLE, very wet and cold. Battalion employed mostly in "resting" and cleaning up.

November 14th. Stafford returned from his "jolly" to PARIS in time to give us two services. About 2 p.m. Battalion paraded and marched through MERVILLE to billets just N.E of it taking over from the 2nd Battalion Scots Guards. Very good billets and not very scattered. An excellent mess. Bonvalot produced a piano from the town in the evening. Still very cold.

November 15th. Cleaned up and football most of the day. After lunch I rode motor bicycle down to LOCON to see Cyril Daubeny but found he had gone on a course. Ran into a team of 4 Mules also one motor Ambulance on way back otherwise no incident. Watson Smyth returned off leave, which was most unfortunate as it showed that he had never got my letter extending leave to 10 days.

November 16th. Went round billets with Commanding Officer. Very good they are, 3 & 2 Companies being in 6 almost finished houses, 1 & 4 in big barns and lots of straw. Stafford and self went for a ride but returned hurriedly owing to hail storm; he gave a small cinematograph show in evening and I managed gramophone. Most successful and very well attended by the men in spite of rain. Stafford dined after, and Bonvalot, Stafford, and self played violin duets till about 11 o'clock. Worse! Wilkinson returned off leave as he had not got my letter extending it.

November 17th. Colonel and self attended gas demonstration in morning and walked through it with helmets on, not much effect but gas stuck to ones clothes for some time. Also 100 men from Battalion walked through it. Proper hail storm on way back.

November 18th. Companies played intra Platoon matches at football most of the morning. Colonel, Bunny Crawford, Arthur Smith and self went round line of trenches we take up. Very quiet part. 1st Battalion there. Byng H. took Colonel, Bunny and Arthur round, while Guy Baring and Humphrey de T. showed me the supports and Battalion Headquarters. Big concert by Grenadier Band in Cinema Hall MERVILLE. Quite good and well attended.

November 19th. Football most of the day. I spent most of the day writing. Janson went off on leave. Stafford had an evening service.

November 20th. Packed most of morning, paraded after lunch and marched by rather round about way to PONT DU HEM South of LA GORGUE. The Third Coldstream went in and we took over from the First Coldstream (2nd Brigade). Very cold and bad billets.

November 21st. Made arrangements about taking over and went up about 5:00 p.m. and marched up over ground up railway, very bad road and some stray bullets. Very bad Headquarters and frightfully cold. Line wet but otherwise fair. No line of approach to it - 1; 2; 3 in front and 4 in support. 3 casualties.

November 22nd. Spent most of the day getting warm: everything frozen hard. A good many callers. Gilly and I went round line in afternoon. A thick mist came on which enabled us to get back over ground and so saved a long walk round. The rations came up on the trollies and so saved a lot of labour.

November 23rd. Went up to Druce early and walked round his bit of the line. Some letters written. The Third Coldstream came up about 5:00 p.m., raining hard. We got back without any casualties.

November 24th. Got my things more or less in order and handed over to Gilly F. and left the Battalion about 3:00 p.m. and rode to LA GORGUE had tea at 2nd Brigade Headquarters and Merton. About 5:00 p.m. I clambered onto a motor bus and drove to LILLERS, where a train left at 11:30 p.m. Got in and to sleep, about 5 in carriage.

November 25th. In train all day and rather unpleasant Canadian who drank whisky most of the way. Got to LE HAVRE about 7:00 p.m. Got on board and had to wait till 1:00 a.m. to go off.

November 26th. We then had to slow up off the Isle or Wight due to fog and into Waterloo about ¼ to 12 a.m. So I altered all leave papers of Guards Division on one day. Nancy came round. She and Ruby and self went to dine at the Carlton and on to a play.

November 27th. Shopped and to a play in the evening. Albinia staying at 22, Belgrave Square. George came up for night.

November 28th. Too late for Church. Huie and Mercy up for weekend. Lunch with Ruby and dine with Uncle Reggie.

November 29th. Blanche and self lunched and then caught 4:20 p.m. to Melton. Very cold but hope to hunt.

November 30th. Went to meet at Loddington. Too hard to hunt; very angry; drove to Leicester and back to London; dinner and a play.

December 1st. Shopped and down by 4:15 p.m. to Bath. Stayed with Huie and Mercy.

December 2nd. Went to Tyntesfield and shot round outside cover: 30 Pheasants. Dined with Becky Smith's at Carlton and a play.

December 3rd. Wired round to get people for party. Dinner at Carlton of 14, to Palace and then on to Princes, and several more came on and we danced up to 2:00 a.m. Great fun and everyone in great form.

December 4th. Caught the 8:00 a.m. train to Oakham and drove to Munro's, raining hard. Met at Somerby. Very bad day only one run from Wymondon Ruffs. Back to London and quiet dinner with Margery Daubeny, Blanche and self in Bachelors.

December 5th. Staying with Blanche at 6, Evelyn Gardens. Lunched at Ritz. Tea with Violet Hammersley, and dinner at Trocadero.

December 6th. Shopped continuously. George; Via; Blanche; Nancy; Stafford; Ruby and self dined and went to "Shell out".

December 7th. Dashed round with Via and did last shopping. Lunched at the Berkeley and caught 4:00 p.m. train at Waterloo and got to Southampton at 7:00 p.m. Some difficulty in getting sidecar on board. Got made Adjutant of Ship and so got a cabin. Shared dinner with Twist, a Major in 13th Hussars.

December 8th. Got to LE HAVRE at 5:30 a.m. Great difficulty in getting the sidecar off and had to leave it for M.F.Officer to send on. Walked 1¼ miles to station in town and so into the train, 3 in Carriage.

Headquarters
Guards Division
December 8th 1915

Dearest Cosmo

    Here's something for Xmas for you from the Front. I hope you saw your father while he was at home. He came back today. How's the football going? We are busy tickling up the Germans here. Making great holes in their parapets across the roads and then not letting them mend them.

Your very affectionate uncle
Cavan

December 9th. Got to LILLERS at 5:30 a.m. Went with Peel (Post Office Rifles) and had breakfast, got back to station. Got a car on a bit of the way. Waited till 4:30 p.m. and got on again. Back to Battalion about 5.00 p.m. and greeted with "You're late off leave" but wasn't!

December 10th. Tried to catch up with correspondence that had come in. Went up to trenches and relieved 3rd Coldstream. Very good place for Battalion Headquarters. Trenches all breastworks and overland relief. All Companies in front line. Some 16 Royal Welsh Fusiliers attached to us. 1 Company, also 2nd in Command, which made us very pushed for room.

December 11th. Not up very early. Colonel and Gilly out most of the morning, so I had to stay in. Went up to Post in the evening. Some petrol got in our food, otherwise very comfortable.

December 12th. Went up to other posts. Very quiet night and only one casualty. Relieved by 3rd Coldstream and back to LAVENTIE.

December 13th. Took Janson down to Orderly Room to hand over as I go temporarily as Staff Captain to 1st Guards Brigade tomorrow. In Orderly Room all day.

December 14th. Had to go up to Brigade early, very frightened. Found Gort, Brigadier, and all their Generals, still got a bad leg from bomb accident; remained there all day. Gort going off. Late bed.

December 15th. Started fairly early after getting to bed at 2:45 a.m. as Grenadiers had a small raiding party going into German trench. This party went up it for short way, eventually coming on a post, two of which they knocked on the head with life preservers and one they got as a prisoner, the others ran away and opened fire so they had to come away with their prisoner, one man unfortunately being killed. Wrote reports most of the morning. General Haking also Cavan came in. Prince of Wales in evening for short time. Early to bed. Lieutenant Colonel Jeffreys commanding Brigade while General Feilding in England for fortnight to have treatment.

December 15th 1915

My Dear Nancy

Just seen Lancelot and told him he must never go on leave again for fear of clashing with Stafford!! It was bad luck and eczema only that brought it about. So glad you had a happy time – but I can't say I think Stafford looks well. He gets so deadly white.

Don't let folks be gloomy. The gloom in Germany is deeper and we really are top dog here.

The 2nd Grenadiers and the 2nd Coldstreams had a raid last night, and caught a Hun and killed two. They would have brought them all in but one made such a noise he had to be quieted to save our own men.

Happy Xmas to you all – so glad the kids were all made happy. I shall look forward to my Calendar.

Very affectionately

Cavan

December 16th. Cavan came at 10:00 a.m. and congratulated patrols of two nights ago. Philip Hunlock and Murray to lunch. Brigadier General 'Jack' Seely came in for short time. Prince of Wales in the afternoon but did not stop long. A very quiet day. A good many messages and Division often ringing up. George Lane and Gwynn to dinner also Brigade Major of a Welsh Brigade attached to us.

December 17th. I was left alone in Headquarters. Divisional General came in and asked several questions. Luckily I knew the answers to all. Raining hard. After lunch I went round bomb stores and met a good many people. Had tea with 3rd Coldstream, found Trousers fussing about Company of Welsh Fusiliers who were late carrying up the gas cylinders. Had another tea with 2nd Coldstream. Had to rush back to Brigade Headquarters to send in evening report. Had another tea. Gas cylinder fatigue finished about 12 midnight.

December 18th. Great difficulty fitting in Gas cylinder fatigue to night relief. Also another Battalion of Welsh Fusiliers attached to us. Trousers went to meet them, very cold. Most of the Welsh turned up, few had got lost! After lunch I took T's motor bicycle and met some cadets at 3 p.m., disposed of them and called in on Merton on my return. Brigadier out to dinner.

December 19th. Huns much more active than usual. They shelled LAVENTIE and the trenches, only damage one French soldier home on leave – killed. General Haking came in also General Hayworth (3rd Guards Brigade). After lunch I rode T's motor bicycle down to try and find Stafford re burying a 2nd Grenadier. Got ready for relief. John Campbell and George Lane for dinner.

December 20th. A good deal of fussing about the relief. I went off on Trousers bicycle and got to LA GORGUE. Saw Battalions there, went on towards MERVILLE, had a skid and footboards came off. So took bicycle back to LA GORGUE on trolley. Got into my sidecar and started off again. Again about half way sidecar broke down and we *then* repaired it and got to MERVILLE. Got Chick (Supply officer) to take me back to LAVENTIE. Handed over to Warner Staff Captain 3rd Guards Brigade and had to walk back to LA GORGUE. Very hungry for dinner, being my first meal since breakfast.

December 21st. During the night Colonel Tempest-Hicks arrived to be attached to us (a very old man) at 2:30 a.m., so I had to turn out and give him my bed. Arranged baths, rooms for Christmas dinners, billet improvements etc. most of the morning. Went round to 2nd Coldstream after luncheon. Got motor bicycle back. Budget Lloyd and Guy S-S came to dinner. Brigadier out to dinner.

December 22nd. Rather late up. A good deal of telephoning and argument about the wood for improving billets. Had to go down and see issue of stores to Battalions from XIth Corps dump, as Corps Labour Department refused to let them go. Edwin Brassey came round after luncheon and I took him down to 2nd Battalion Coldstream to whom he is attached for a month for instruction as Second-in-Command. Rang up Cyril Daubeny in the evening and arranged for Colonel Tempest-Hicks to catch 1:45 a.m. train tomorrow to BOULOGNE.

December 23rd. A fine day for my birthday! In spite of all the hints at breakfast that all the shops were open, no one volunteered a present! Maurice Ponsonby back from fetching the Cinematograph. In most of the day. Went to tea with 2nd Coldstream. Very little work to do.

December 24th. Fine at last. Had to dash out and stop No: 1 Company Coldstream bombing as they were too close to LA GORGUE. Went round Battalion dinners with Gilly and glass of beer at each. Very big dinners with nearly all they would get in England. Rode over to 2nd Guards Brigade with Maurice Ponsonby, had tea and talked to Merton. Not much to hand over. Gilly came to dine also Jack Whitaker.

December 25th. Stafford took an Early Service in Concert Hall. Large Parade Service, which I could not go to. Cavan said "Goodbye" to 2nd Coldstream on his appointment to the IVth Corps. Went to ESTAIRES with Philips (Signal Officer Worcesters) and Delevalt (Interpreter to Brigade) and had tea. Trousers and self dined with 2nd Coldstream. An enormous and rowdy dinner, very much decorated room. Trousers and self managed to slip away at 11 p.m. and left them playing football on the lawn.

December 26th. Spent most of the morning fussing about relieving 2nd Guards Brigade. Went over to new billets also Brigade Headquarters, found them rather worried as Xmas day being so quiet both sides got up and buried the dead lying out in front. Back to luncheon and over again about 3:30 p.m. Huge mess-up over the 15th Royal Welsh Fusiliers attached. All their trench tools and rations went wrong. All their own fault too. These attached Battalions are an awful nuisance as they are so helpless. Eventually got in and settled about 7 p.m. Wind wrong otherwise we thought of giving the Germans some "pepper" (gas), and so to bed.

December 27th. A high wind but fine. All progress. Stores etc. reports late and so spent most of the morning on the telephone. Mining officer came in awfully pleased with himself having struck a German mine. I tried to show how pleased I was, but gave it away by holding his mining map upside down and mistaking a shell crater for a gallery! Philips added to my worries about the reports by disconnecting the telephone without telling me. The Supply officer came in in an awful 'stew' wanting to know what he was to do with 750 rations he had drawn. The only thing I could think to say was "eat them", this he didn't appreciate having had his Xmas dinner the night before! He then told me they were for the "Swabs" which I did not realize till afterwards was the name for the South Wales Borderers (SWB)! Wrote most of the afternoon. Went round on Trousers' motor bicycle to see the 'said' rations, which turned out to be short in bacon and jam! Meant to go up to bomb store but it was being shelled and so I pretended I had never thought of going there. Bicycle ran out of petrol about 2 miles from home. Luckily Prince of Wales came along so I stopped him and got him to get some out of his tank; it was a slow business as we only had a cup borrowed from a cottage.

December 28th. Colonel and Trousers went round trenches. General Cavan came in and we went and looked at surrounding country from top of a house. Trousers out the whole of the afternoon, so I was in. Dined with 4th Coldstream (Pioneers) in evening.

December 29th. Colonel went round early so as to be back before bombardment. Bombardment started at 10:00 a.m and continued up to 11:00 a.m., breaking up the front German trenches well. A small bombardment at 2:00 p.m. for the benefit of a cinematograph man who was taking result from front trenches. Nothing much happened from bombardment. Quiet dinner.

December 30th. A fine quiet day. Headquarters of one Battalion got rather shelled, but no damage done.

December 31st. We shelled several points of enemy's line which brought some retaliation. We waited up to see New Year in. At 11 p.m. Germans opened heavy rifle fire (Berlin time was 1 Hour ahead). This did no damage. We gave them a shell or so at 12:01 a.m. Phillips having retired to bed at 10 p.m., Trousers and I went and wished him 'Happy New Year" at 12:15 a.m.!

1916

January 1st. Raining hard and everything bad again. Went down to drying room and baths in afternoon. Tea-ed with 2nd Coldstream. Went to dine at Headquarters 2nd Guards Brigade with Becky. General J. Ponsonby out to dinner. Cheery evening.

January 2nd. Raining. Corps Commander (Haking) came to luncheon, also Paddy Beaumont-Nesbitt (his ADC). After luncheon I went down to M. G. Company. Colonel Ruthven came in to see General Feilding, who has been given the Guards Division. George Lane came in for half an hour. Some shells over Winchester Horse, otherwise quiet. Wind wrong for 'Thermos' flasks.

January 3rd. Car came at 10:00 a.m. and Delavault and self went billeting first round PONT DU HEM and then on to CALONNE to take over billets from 114th Brigade. Went round with their interpreter. Lunched at Brigade Headquarters and then back to "Cockshie" house and LAVENTIE. SWB's sent fatigue parties to take Thermos flasks out of the line.

January 4th. Lt. Colonel Ruthven came round and went up to line with Lt. Colonel Jeffreys. Billy Darell came in. A good deal of discussion over "Mention in Dispatches" list. Fine at last. Two lots of officers and NCO's from 114th (Welsh) Brigade came up in buses. Both buses got lost and separated. One went right up to Winchester House in daylight but was soon turned back, the occupants not being at all happy about the shells which dropped very handy to it. The other pushed its occupants out at BELLE CROIX (about 2½ miles back) in the rain with their kits. I rode out to try and collect them but missed the lot. The two Colonels turned up about 7 and one at 8. The first had been to a lecture and the second had got off at LA GORGUE to "have tea" and walked on. He refused to go into the trenches as it was "so wet", and I think was looking for a "Hotel". We got rid of him. Staff Captain of that Brigade attached to us. Remainder of "Thermos Flasks" taken out by 2nd Coldstream.

January 5th. 2nd Coldstream and 1st Irish moved out of their billets which were taken over by 10th and 15th Welsh about 12 noon. Jerry Ruthven came over and went up line. I rode Trousers' motor bicycle over to CALONNE and just got there as 2nd Coldstream got into billets. Billets fair. Went round to Irish Guards. Found their billets very dirty. Got back after dark having run into a very portly gunner en route (but he was very soft!). Asked more questions by the Staff Captain 114th Brigade attached!

January 6th. Spent most of morning writing progress report. Trousers and Colonel went up to trenches. About 12:00 John Campbell rang up furiously saying Winchester House was being heavily shelled. I got gunners to retaliate, but I fancy they got several direct hits on the House before they stopped. Large lot of people came in and asked conundrums, but I managed to dispose of them all satisfactorily. Went down to drying room and arranged a relief. 10th Welsh and 15th Welsh relieve 2nd Grenadiers and 3rd Coldstream respectively, fairly satisfactorily.

January 7th. After some work in "Cockshie" House went off on motor bicycle to new billets round CALONNE. Brigade Headquarters followed. 2nd Grenadiers relieved by 13th Welsh Regiment and 3rd Coldstream by 14th Welsh, and marched to billets between CALONNE and ROBECQ – rained considerably.

January 8th. Colonel Jeffreys went round billets with Trousers all day. I stayed in office. Dined 2nd Coldstream in evening.

January 9th. A great day. Brigadier General G. E. Pereira arrived and took over command of the Brigade.

January 10th. General P. went round billets (Headquarters) with Trousers most of the day. Colonel Darell gave very interesting lecture on "Supply of an Army in the field". General P. and Trousers dined with 2nd Coldstream.

January 11th. Went over to LES LAURIERS with Delavault and looked round billets of 56th Infantry Brigade from whom we take over. Billets scattered but fair.

January 12th. Brigade started to move off about 10:30 a.m. I went off on motor bicycle but got a puncture and had to have it repaired. Brigade well on the road so I got a boat and took bicycle across canal, nearly losing it in the canal as it ran down the bank into the boat and knocked the Ferryman over. Billets fair and Battalions happy by about 4:30 p.m. Gort arrived back by about 12 noon and so just before tea, I returned to 2nd Coldstream and resumed my duties as Adjutant.

January 13th. Gilly and self rode round billets and finished about 12 noon. After lunch I got orders to return to the Brigade as Gort and Trousers had got to go to England for H.M's Investiture. To Brigade Headquarters by tea.

January 14th. Rode with Brigadier to Headquarters 2nd Coldstream and went round their billets. Brigadier went out after lunch, I worried over returns. Gilly and Byng Hopwood to dinner and talked over many "old days".

January 15th. Went round billets of 1st Irish with General, found them very scattered but good. Stayed in most of the afternoon. Darell came in otherwise no visitors. General went to see John Ponsonby.

January 16th. General went off to Church in MERVILLE. We lunched with 2nd Coldstream. General Ponsonby came also Green (1st Battalion). Otherwise nothing doing all day. Stafford held a small service at Brigade Headquarters about 7 p.m. and came into dinner after.

January 17th. General went off about 9:30 a.m. for a big Court Martial at Divisional Headquarters. Rained most of the day. Orders re: move on the 23rd received. Gort got back from 5 p.m. with a large basket of fish. Dined with 2nd Coldstream.

January 18th. General and Gort went to 3rd Coldstream billets. Raining hard. Delavault and self rode into MERVILLE and met Humphrey de T and Guy S-S. Very wet. Gilly came in to tea. Boy Brooke and Mar Jeffreys called. Former has got 3rd Grenadiers and latter the 58th Infantry Brigade; 19th Division.

January 19th. General and Gort went out, lovely day nothing much doing. Went down to range in FORÊT DE NIEPPE where the Lewis Guns are fired. Corps Commanders came round and looked at our Brigade Bath which is putting through about 800 men per day with clean clothing. After lunch General and I went for a ride in FORÊT DE NIEPPE, which is just west of LES LAURIERS. This has been a good deal cut down for stakes and wood for the trenches. Each Division having its' own square plot. Found 3rd Coldstream playing 1st Coldstream at Eton football. I was roped in to referee, however after about 10 minutes, I gave a very doubtful decision and left hurriedly. Gilly and Druce came in in the evening to ask about some Courts Martials. Gort returned with them to dine with 2nd Coldstream, we had a quiet dinner.

January 20th. Lovely day. Brigadier went over to Guards Division. Gort to Headquarters 115th Brigade at LAVENTIE, so I sat out in garden in sun. After lunch Brigadier and self walked round Irish Guards, 3rd Coldstream, 1st Coldstream to tea and so home.

January 21st. Brigadier and Gort out all morning. Brigadier and self went for a walk through FORÊT DE NIEPPE jumping ditches etc. Rode down to 3rd Coldstream to dinner, walked back after.

January 22nd. A fine day at last. Rode off after lunch with O'Brien (B.B.O.) via Divisional Headquarters to LAVENTIE to see Staff Captain of 115th Brigade. He seemed to know very little. Shelling the village so we came back by the LA BASSÉE road, went into 2nd Guards Brigade Headquarters for tea, found Becky, General John P., Boy Brooke, and Guy Darell there, and so home about 8 miles. Phillips returned.

January 23rd. 2nd Coldstream and 1st Irish marched to PONT DU HEM and RIEZ BAILLEUL and took over billets from 2 Battalions of 115th Infantry Brigade in billets. I remained at LES LAURIERS most of the day. Brigadier and Gort dined with Headquarters IIIrd Corps.

January 24th. Brigadier, Gort and self started off in car at 9:30 a.m. for LAVENTIE. On arrival they went round right sector. I went to ROUGE CROIX to take over trench boots and found 360. Back to Headquarters 2nd Coldstream and then home by horse. Lunched with 3rd Coldstream at LE SART (Near MERVILLE) and back to LES LAURIERS. Maurice Ponsonby back from leave. Leger Glyn came in to tea.

January 25th. Got on the move about 9:30 a.m. I rode Motor Bicycle; Brigadier and Gort rode over on horses. Bicycle punctured in MERVILLE. Had it repaired at Motor Ambulance Convoy and so via LA GORGUE where I took a proper toss. Took over from 115th Brigade at Cockshie House LAVENTIE. Commanding Officer of R.A. right group came in also 2 mining officers. Brigadier and Gort went round Battalion Headquarters. I rode down to ROUGE CROIX and found some more boots. 'Bosche' seemed to rather resent our straff which took place about 3 p.m. and shelled several roads round PONT DU HEM with little effect.

January 26th. A good deal of machine gun fire during night at 11 p.m. and 1:00 a.m. We sprang a mine about 8:30 a.m. and guns shelled 'Bosche' front trenches. Remainder of day very quiet. A Major C. G. Frost of the 1/7th Middlesex wandered about Irish Guards line looking for a grave of a brother officer, result was he got badly hit in the head. Divisional General came in after lunch and told us of several "straffes" there were going to be the next day (Kaiser's birthday). Prince of Wales and Claud H. came in about tea time and stayed about an hour. Heard that result of "springing" our mine was most satisfactory, almost certain one of the German Galleries split up. George Lane and Colonel Skeffington-Smyth came to dinner. Trousers returned.

January 27th. Our guns opened very actively about 2 a.m. for about 10 minutes, very little retaliation, otherwise a quiet night. Machine guns and Lewis guns traversed the German parapets and roads running at right angles from trenches most of the night, in case any reliefs or re-inforcements were coming up. Brigadier and Gort went off to 2nd Grenadiers in right sector. I returned to the 2nd Battalion and took over from Janson. Stayed in the Orderly Room most of the day. Rupert Clutterbuck came in to tea also Walter Legge.

January 28th. Janson went on leave. Court Martial in the morning otherwise remained in orderly room. Stafford came in. Relieved 3rd Coldstream in left sector (Winchester House). A quiet relief; Nos: 1 on right; 2 centre; 4 left; and 3 in Posts. Relief completed by 6 p.m.

January 29th. A very clear day and so movement had to be restricted. We stayed in the house until about 11 a.m., when some shells began to fall somewhere to the left and so we retired to dug out. Line considerably drier. After lunch Gilly, the Medical Officer and self went round. Not a very good afternoon for sniping, 2 victims claimed by one Company. While wiring in front of No: 2 Company about 8 p.m., 2nd Lieutenant Heywood and Corporal Clarke got hit, former by bullet, latter by bomb, both slight.

January 30th. A quiet night, cold and foggy morning. CRA (Commander Royal Artillery) of right group came round. A very quiet day owing to fog, we stayed in house all day. Three men wounded. Relieved by 3rd Coldstream and got back to billets at PONT DU HEM without casualties.

January 31st. Fog cleared and a good deal more activity with shells on both sides. Otherwise nothing of interest happened. Dined with Nos: 1 and 2 Companies.

February 1st. Sounds of a heavy bombardment somewhere South. Much colder and an East wind. Relieved 3rd Coldstream Nos: 1; 2; 3 in firing line, No: 4 in support and holding posts. Relieved without casualties although about 1 dozen shells came over during the relief.

February 2nd. A cold but quiet day. "Father" Smith took out a patrol on the right of line but did not get up to the wire. Gilly and self went round in afternoon, found Major Harrison (attached from School of Instruction Dublin University) with No: 3. Water gone down considerably, so much so that dead rats are smelling rather. Telephone to one Battery rather unsatisfactory. We got O.C. right group out of bed last night about 12 midnight. Fergusson returned off leave, but didn't come up to trenches.

February 3rd. A hardish frost during night and one man hit. "Father" Smith took his patrol out again to see the Germans wire for the "Torpedo", found it very strong. Brigadier came round and took Colonel up to line where they met "Pa" Hayworth (Temporary Divisional Commander) and General Feilding (Temporary Corps Commander). 3rd Coldstream arrived about 5:30 p.m. and we left having had two more casualties, both slight. Back to billets. champagne and bed.

February 4th. Correspondence seems to increase more and more each time we come out. A "Young officers cross country ride" conducted by Druce Bentinck, consisting of Edwin Brassey; Fergusson; Hugh B; Hartley; Ympkin and self spent most of the afternoon beating the horses over small brooks. Vian and Ronny arrived to join Battalion. Phillips (Brigade Signals Officer) and Trousers to dinner, a somewhat rowdy affair which ended in the loss of one of my five slippers and the capture of Trousers cap in lieu, some damage to the room.

February 5th. A very long Court Martial held at Headquarters 2nd Grenadiers, one case of ours, Budget and Fergusson members. Relieve 3rd Coldstream (I hope) for last time in this sector. Relief ½ hour later. "A.61" Huns were being shelled near RUGBY ROAD. No damage but it kept us standing under a house while 8" x 5" shells dropped about 300 yards off. Battalion got in safely, no casualties. Nos: 2; 3; 4 in front line Posts.

February 6th. Rather more shelling activity. Gilly and self went round trenches after lunch. We watch Germans shelling Verelst and Edmonstone as they walked across a field – one got within 20 yards of them ! A few shells near Winchester House during dinner.

February 7th. General swabbing with a view to relief. Leese came down and took over Adjutant. I went out about 2:30 p.m. I think they must have seen me as they put 2 Fizz bangs down at me, nearest was about 20 yards off. Also one or two larger size at LA FLINQUE cross roads about the time I should have got there (but I had taken to the fields, so they were "selled"). Passed 1st Battalion who were coming out with Coldstream Band. Found "Father" Smith installed in the billets, also Spinney who had just arrived. Had dinner and about 11 p.m. O'Brien (Irish Guards) and self went to LA GORGUE station to catch 1:45 a.m. for leave.

February 8th. Got to BOULOGNE about 9:30 a.m., had breakfast at Louvre Hôtel. Boat left about 12 noon. Got to Victoria about 5:00 p.m. Dined with Ruby, Blanche, and Albinia at Ruby's house.

February 9th. Spent going round London. Play in evening.

February 10th. Continued shopping. Play with Little Man and others.

February 11th. Shopped. Went down to Glynde (*bourne*) by 5:30 p.m. with Cissie.

February 12th. Shot snipe most of morning – got 2! Cissie and I went over to see George and Via at Uckfield. Went round Camp. Got back to Glynde found Amy, Doris, and Pru Sergisson-Brooke had arrived. Had a very cheery evening.

February 13th. Gave Church a miss. Went to Brighton in small car instead. Back to lunch and a long walk down in Park.

February 14th. Amy and Doris left in morning. Cissie and I went out hunting. Bad day, rode Dublin. Up to London.

February 15th. Caught 9:30 a.m. to Leicester. Found no hunting so dashed back. Blanche, Uncle Reggie and I dined together.

February 16th. Shopped. Dined with Joe Lane and supper with Little Man.

February 17th. Caught 8:00 a.m. to Manton. Quite a fairly good day with Cottesmore. Dashed back and had dinner party at Carlton of Nancy, Amy, Doris, and Cissie, George Dawson-Damer, Mark Tennant and Victor Walrond. Play and danced at Savoy after. Went on to 'Moncey' St Germans' dance at Princes. Bed at 4 a.m.

February 18th. Shopped hard. Dined George, Via, Nancy. and self. Had large lunch with Uncle Reggie first. Supper party Eric Ednam and "others".

February 19th. Caught 9:15 a.m. at Victoria. Found George Riviera on board, shared his cabin (he paid). ½ day at BOULOGNE. Train about 7:30 p.m.

February 20th. Got to POPERINGHE at 3:30 a.m. Slept at Mr.Talbot's Officers Rest House. Hun aeroplanes dropped bombs in morning. Met by my horse and got to Battalion about 11 a.m. Found them in the coldest tents and huts I have ever been in – Shivered.

February 21st. Shivered more. Spent most of the day in Orderly Room.

February 22nd. Snow and freezing hard. Went for cross country ride when it had cleared off. Dinner in coats.

February 23rd. More snow and frost. Had early parade but had to go in after ¼ hour. Had great snowball fight after lunch which made me warm for the first time. Dinner in fur coats and stoves between our legs.

February 24th. A little drier but snow very hard. Preparing to go off tomorrow. Orders did not come in until after 6 p.m. Spent most of the day waiting for orders, which came in in driblets.

February 25th. Up by about 7:00 a.m. Froze hard in the night. Transport started to get out of the field at 5:30 a.m. and were still at it at 8:00 a.m. Battalion started off in direction of WATOU at 9:30 a.m., after marching about 4 miles we came on poor Shaw with 3 horses down on the road and one cooker in the ditch. I stopped behind with him. We got through STEENVOORDE and nearly caught up the Battalion. However about 3 miles short of CASSEL more hills came and the old thing started, horses coming down on all sides. On arrival in CASSEL itself it started to snow, so 2 more horses fell down. Going down to station out of town, one pair in an Ammunition Cart were quite done, so we took them out and Shaw, Maurice Ponsonby, Wilks and self dragged it last 1½ miles. Men took boxes of SAA and tobogganed down the hill on them. A quick omelette and coffee, and the train started at ¼ to 5 p.m. Got to Calais at 8 p.m. Gilly, self, and 3 Companies marched on to camp, about 3 miles, leaving Colonel, Shaw etc. to bring out Transport. Got to bed after unloading at ¼ to 4 a.m. in a tent full of snow, after the worst march I have yet had out here.

February 26th. Very cold camp, about 3 miles from sea on North side of CALAIS. (No: 6 'Rest' Camp). Spent most of the day cleaning up. Went into CALAIS at 5 p.m. in train. Hair cut, bath, and large dinner of fourteen 2nd Battalion and ten 3rd Battalion at Hôtel Continental. Went round town after but nearly everything shut up. Had to walk out.

February 27th. Brigadier came into Camp. Companies trained, but ground not very good. 3rd Coldstream lines are next to ours and 2nd Grenadiers beyond them. Druce, Grubby, Hugo, and self went for a ride on sands in afternoon.

February 28th. Training cold most of the snow gone leaving an unpleasant black slush. Started to rain in afternoon during a parade.

February 29th. Typed nearly all day on the lists for Honours and Rewards. Parade at 1:45 cancelled. Dined in.

March 1st. In Camp. Fine day. Dined in CALAIS.

March 2nd. Went round some jumps Grenadiers had put up. Parade at 1:45 p.m. Into CALAIS for dinner at Hôtel Continental.

March 3rd. Battalion Parade at 8:30 a.m. Over jumps after lunch and so into CALAIS. Large Coldstream dinner at Hôtel Continental. 28 Coldstreamers and 3 guests. Most successful. Got a motor back. Bad bombing accident 1st Irish, Desmond FitzGerald killed.

March 4th. Parade ordered at 8:30 a.m., but Commanding Officer cancelled it at 8:00 a.m. Merton arrived to look round Camp. Budget, Shaw, Grubby, and Self dined with him in CALAIS.

March 5th. Cleaned up all day. Funeral of Desmond Fitzgerald in CALAIS Cemetery at 3:00 p.m. but we could not get there. Paraded at 3:00 p.m., marched to station. Transport having gone on 2 hours ahead. Drums played most of the way. Got into CASSEL at 8:30 p.m. Snowing hard. An 8 mile walk to WORMHOUT; bad march as men tired. John Hugh Smith rather messed up the Guides and so the Battalion took some time getting there. Got coffee and omelette on arrival about 12 midnight. Got to bed at 3 a.m. very tired.

March 6th. Ground well covered with snow. Breakfast at 11 a.m. Battalion very much scattered, but billets said to be good. Nos: 1 & 4 close to Headquarters; 3 next: and 2 (Edwin B's Company) some way off. Druce and I rode over to ZEGERS-CAPPEL and arranged about jumping competition for 8th.

March 7th. Very cold, still snowing. Companies spent most of the day cleaning up. Gilly and self dined at Guards Division Headquarters. We arrived ¼ hour late for dinner as car never turned up. Large party. Rupert,

Bulgey Thorne, Esmee Elliot, Alston, and self played Roulette till about 11 p.m.

March 8th. Snow fairly thick. About 12 noon Shaw, Verelst, Druce, and self went over to ZEGERS-CAPPEL and had a very large lunch with the Guards Division R.A. After watching judging of gun teams etc. About 3:00 p.m. Chargers came on. I think we had 8 entries. Budget got within the last 4, but failed to get a prize. Bulgey Thorne (1) Trousers (2) and O'Rorke (3). Jumping field rather heavy. My horse got over all except the open ditch which he wouldn't face. Very large entry, Druce Bentinck (on Tony Markham's Chestnut) (1), O'Rorke (vet to 2nd Life Guards) (2), and Perry (2nd Life Guards) (3). And so home. Dined with No: 2 Company. Edwin inoculated and so in bed. Two fellows in 2nd Life Guards there. Got away 11:30 p.m.

March 9th. Snow still thick on ground. Companies did bombing with snowballs. Verelst, Guy, and self rode in afternoon. Cold but fine.

March 10th. Training during morning. Coldstream Band played at 11:30 a.m. and 2:30 p.m. Rogan came to tea after.

March 11th. 10 French officers came round about 12 noon to see Battalion training. A selection of every sort was going on in field opposite Battalion Headquarters. They came into Mess and drank Port. They appeared "much impressed" and so I hope they were. Battalion Concert in evening. I accompanied Spinney in "Two Eyes of Grey", also Stafford on the violin, without much success but managed not to break down. Advanced operation orders for move arrived.

March 12th. Voluntary Service in School. I played "Groan Box" for Stafford. A real Sunday, no training, orders, or parades. Quite peaceful spring day. Went for a ride with Budget to LEDRINGHEM, lunched and dined with Budget (No: 3 Company).

March 13th. Hotter than ever, more operation orders arrived, started with orders for the Battalion. Rode with Guy S-S in afternoon. Tea with Edwin B., also had dinner there afterwards.

March 14th. Lovely day. Bombing competition in morning. Lecture on Gas in afternoon at Headquarters 3rd Coldstream, rode back to WORMHOUT found Band playing. Stafford and I played after dinner for 2 hours.

March 15th. Breakfast at 5:45 a.m. (just light). Left WORMHOUT at 7:15 a.m. Irish Guards Drums played us as far as HERZEELE. Battalion marched via HOUTKERQUE to WATOU. Here transport was diverted owing to bad "Pavée" on main POPERINGHE road. Met A. J. H. Smith about 2 miles west of POPERINGHE and turned into Camp "M", marching in file down floor-boards as road too deep, to Huts and Tents.

Fair Camp. Officers mess in house. Good day for marching. Battalion did the 11 miles in almost exactly 4 hours. Transport turned up about 2 p.m. having been via L'ABEELE (on STEENVOORDE road) and POPERINGHE, where Gilly met it. Slept for 2 hours in afternoon. Lovely evening. Lewis guns and snipers practised on small range behind mess. Retired early as had slight go of 'Flu'.

March 16th. Companies could not do much in Camp. Billeting party went off at 2 p.m. We went off at 7 p.m., marching via POPERINGHE to Camp about 3 miles East of it. Got in about 9 p.m. Camp in wood Huts rather better than last one.

March 17th. Got up very late. Brigadier came round, no news. Day mostly spent in Gas drill. Walked into POPERINGHE. Very warm and fine. Billeting party went on.

March 18th. Getting ready to move tonight. Brigadier came round no news. French doing well at VERDUN. Wrote orders for move this evening. Battalion paraded at 7 p.m. and marched to railway siding, after a wait of ½ hour the train turned up, and we got in and moved very slowly up. We got out at a small embankment and silently marched off in driblets in the moonlight. We walked for ¾ hour during which time there were few shells. Dug outs we got to were fair, not very big nor quite enough. Companies were distributed up by 12 midnight. My dug out leaked rather but just missed the 'bed'.

March 19th. A lovely day. Considerable work required on Canal Bank to get boards etc. put straight. YPRES shelled fairly heavily.

March 20th. Canal Bank heavily shelled, including 3 unlucky ones which caused 8 casualties, including killing Sergeant Luck (No: 4), a splendid fellow who had been out the whole war. Relieved the 3rd Coldstream in trenches round WIELTJE and ST. JAN, a nasty walk up, the road being considerably shelled at intervals. A moderate line with bad communications and little sign of work from the last Brigade. No: 1 went right front; No: 2 left; No: 3 right support; and No: 4 left support, which included a platoon on the Canal Bank, another in LA BRIQUE. Rather a long relief but got through without much difficulty, 3rd Battalion rather sorry to leave as Canal Bank was so unpleasant.

March 21st. Continued shelling all day directed to a great degree at ST. JAN, Colonel went round in afternoon. Right front Company almost cut off by day. No casualties.

March 22nd. Much too clear a day with result that we were shelled regularly one per half hour, but only shrapnel and a few 'woolly Bears' or H.E. Shrapnel. Very glad to be relieved which turned up in good time.

March 23rd. A dull day and consequently quiet for us. Hardly moved out at all.

March 24th. Some shelling but mostly over us onto the road. Poor Gage went for leave last night having lost his Mother, Wilkinson goes tonight. Colonel, who had not been well for some time, broke down in nerve, and so goes home to England tomorrow. The Command devolves onto Gilly Follet. We walked up together about 9 p.m., very fast as the road had been shelled.

March 25th. Gilly out most of the day going round, he does not spare himself at all. Budget Lloyd in right front trench had part of his trench blown in, also Oakman wounded rather badly in the abdomen. Gilly and I walked up after dark – a most unpleasant walk. I took 3 heavy falls, one on the road when a machine gun started! Back to our hut about 3 a.m.

March 26th. One of the most unpleasant days I have yet had out here. From 8:45 a.m. – 12:15 p.m. the Germans shelled our houses with 8.5" Naval Gun firing at an average of 1 per 3 minutes, in between these they fired high explosive shrapnel and 5.4". One big one fell 4 yards off our door where Anderson (RAMC) and self were standing. In the afternoon they put some on No: 2 Company. Casualties for 48 hours were 9 killed and wounded. Manton (Battalion Headquarters linesman} killed. Great loss. Our guns limited with ammunition and so could do little for us. 3rd Battalion arrived rather late in consequence and it took some time to relieve owing to the shell holes in the road and a very dark and wet night.

March 27th. Gilly and I got to bed at 3:00 a.m. At 3:30 a.m. there was a tremendous bombardment just South of YPRES which made us think the Germans had broken through. However when I woke up (at 11:l5 a.m!) we heard the Canadians had attacked and taken 2 lines of trenches. Very considerable shelling all day. Dined with Brigadier.

March 28th. A quieter morning, about 1:15 a.m. last night they put about 30 x 5.4" onto the Canal Bank, but not very near us (nearer Grenadiers!). About 10 a.m. Stafford and I went up to Cemetery at corner of MENIN-ZONNEBEKE road and found Eustace's grave rather knocked about. About 9 p.m. we moved off from Canal Bank up to ST. JAN.

March 29th. A fairly quiet night. Brigadier came up about 8:30 a.m. and went up on 'Garden Street' with Gilly. Some shelling during the day, retaliation by one of our guns very bad and inadequate. Evening brought considerably more shelling from the Huns. Gilly went round and I lay by the telephone.

March 30th. <u>The</u> worst day we have had for a very long time. About 6:15 a.m. No: 1 Company rang up for retaliation as the "S 8a" line was being shelled. This was got but not very effectively. This shelling became more and more intense up to about 12 noon. During this time all wires to right front Company and right support platoons (Edwin Brassey and Baynes respectively) were cut. At 12 noon it died down until 1:15 p.m. when it started heavier than ever mostly on Baynes and ST. JAN. Our guns got to work a bit, but it was impossible to leave our Headquarters to see what was happening. Heavy guns short of ammunition and what there is does not go off, as I hear it is old stuff. Hardly a single German round failed to explode. At 3:05 p.m. the intense shelling stopped and by the help of the 10th KRR on our left we heard that no attack had been made. About 6:30 p.m. the Gunner Observing Officer came and reported that the right front Company had had about 50 shells a minute at them from 1:05 a.m. – 3:05 p.m. and so we got very nervous about Edwin and sent up a platoon of No: 4 Company to support him. Luckily we found out later that most of the shells had gone over him and that Baynes' platoon of No: 4 got most of them. Intermittent shelling continued until 8:30 p.m. About 9:45 p.m. the 3rd Coldstream arrived to relieve us after one of the worst shelling I have yet been under since I came to France from 8", 5.4", and 4" mixed with a good percentage of Fizz Bangs. Casualties 4 killed (including Drill Sergeant Woyen), 19 wounded, and 11 suffering from shock (including Battalion Sergeant Major). Very light considering what we had been through. Very tired we got to bed about 1:00 a.m.

March 31st. About 8 a.m. I was somewhat 'rudely' woken up by some big shells dropping close by. After watching 2 x 8" drop into the Canal. I went to Gilly, and as we were in the line of fire, we padded up the towpath in pyjamas and slippers and went into No: 3 Company. Only just in time as it turned out as an 8" dropped onto the kitchen and Orderly Room catching poor Jackson (Gilly's servant) and Simpson (Officers mess cook) inside. Everything was blown to bits and they weren't got out till the evening. We got meals with Companies finishing with dinner at Brigade Headquarters. In the evening all Companies found 100 men to dig on Canal defences.

April 1st. Quiet morning except for some Fizz Bangs and shrapnel over the Canal. A lovely day. The men spent the day sunning themselves. Lunch with No: 2 Company. Gilly made temporary Lt. Colonel. A new Medical Officer, Montgomerie, arrived in the afternoon. About 7:30 p.m. the Germans became unpleasantly active and shrapnelled the road with "salvos" of six. Gilly and I started off about 9:15 p.m. and did the 2 miles in 20 minutes. One Company got rather caught between "Dead End" and "Hell Fire" corner having 3 men slightly hit, and another platoon had a man hit at "Suicide Corner". Relief complete about 1:30 p.m. Shelling continued un-interruptedly during whole night.

April 2nd. A 'Draining' Officer of 3rd Guards Brigade arrived at 3:45 a.m. and Gilly took him a short way up the line. Colonel Murray Threipland,

Aldridge, and one of the 1st Battalion Welsh Guards arrived about 5:30 a.m., Gilly again took them all round except right front Company. Companies were placed. Right front No: 4, left front No: 3. right support No: 2, left support No: 1. A most beautiful day, wind slightly from N.E. and brilliant sun all day. A very quiet day. "Suicide" corner shelled at intervals. About 5 "salvos" of 6 went over to "Hell Fire" corner in evening. Casualties 5 including Sergeant Hollyhead hit as he was going on leave. Also 2 horses. Edmonstone and Gage off leave. Got out orders for relief by 5:30 p.m.

April 3rd. A very quiet night, followed by a glorious day and quiet. Most of the day spent in cleaning line so as to help relief. About 7 p.m. guides were sent down to rail head to meet 1st Battalion Welsh Guards, and about 10:15 p.m. Colonel Murray Threipland and Adjutant arrived, the Battalion very close behind him. A very good and quick relief and fairly quiet walk down, several "salvos" of 6 shrapnel at "Hell Fire" corner, but they were in between Companies. Battalion got to rail head at 12:15 a.m. (4th).

April 4th. Train came in about 1:30 a.m. and we 'silently' entrained moving off in about 10 minutes. Train went much faster on return journey. Some shells into VLAMERTINGE as we passed, but they didn't hit the train. Got to POPERINGHE about 2:00 a.m. and into billets about 3:30 a.m. very tired.

April 5th. Had to be up by 9 a.m. and then Verelst and self dashed off to 20th Division Headquarters for Court Martial (General) on 2 officers. Verelst as a member and self as Prosecutor. Officers being Lt. Hall, RGA and Captain Boyd, Royal Scots (brother of Miss Doris Boyd). Cases lasted till 12:30 p.m. Billets pretty good, mess in Château. Day spent in sleep and cleaning by the men. About 9 of us went to the "Fancies" at 6 p.m., a very good show indeed run by 6 fellows of the 6th Division.

April 6th. Fine but cold. Companies cleaned up most of the morning. Went to hear Coldstream Band in Cinema Hall at 3 p.m.; large crowd. Spent most of afternoon looking for chairs and china for a dinner party in 3 days time. Most of mess out to Dinner. Worked after Dinner.

April 7th. Cold and fine. Companies trained. Massed drums of Brigade played in Square from 5:00 – 5:30 p.m. Dined at small Estaminet on BOESCHEPE road. Good dinner and crowded room. Kit Cator was dining there, being in Hospital with "flue" for 3 days.

April 8th. Checked Company books all day up to 7:30 p.m. Large Dinner party of 25 including – Cavan; General Feilding (GOC Division); Darell (AA and QMG Division); J. Campbell (Temporary GOC 1st Guards Brigade): McCalmont (Commanding 1st Irish Guards); Gort (Brigade Major); Bullough; Cubitt: and Longueville (3rd Coldstream); also Joe

Legh (ADC to Corps Commander). Coldstream Band played during dinner. Great success.

April 9th. Checked till 11 a.m. Parade Service in Cinema Hall by Maurice Ponsonby and Coldstream Band. Lt General Cavan and others came. Checked books after dinner. Rode in forest nearby.

April 10th. Nos: 3 & 4 did a small tactical exercise in the morning, Colonel umpired. Went to "Fancies" in evening. Very good show. Rupert Clutterbuck came to lunch.

April 11th. Cleaned up most of day and moved off in the evening marching as a Battalion to Camp "A". Had a most unpleasant march owing to a big gun (naval), which was shelling the road out of POPERINGHE. We broke up into platoons and got in without casualties.

April 12th. Rained whole day and it came through most of the huts, so we stopped in.

April 13th. Draft of Berkeley and Brocklebank and posted to Nos: 1 & 4 Companies. A wire came in saying all leave stopped and those on leave to return by 18th and so several officers had to be recalled including - Lloyd, A. J. H. Smith, Lease, and about 6 men. A confidential letter arrived detailing me to go to the Division for a fortnight's training in the "Q" branch and afterwards to go to the 1st Guards Brigade as Staff Captain. A very sad day after 20 months with the Battalion and 16 months Adjutant. Colonel (GBSF) came with me to POPERINGHE, we had a great 'send off' from Camp from some of the other officers. Spent the evening in "Q" branch with Lt. Colonel W. Darell (AA & QMS), Alston (DAA & QMG). Harmon Hodge (DAQMG), looking at papers.

April 14th. Spent whole day in 'Q' office doing nothing in particular except looking at papers. Went to Cinema for ½ hour in evening.

April 15th. Went over to CASSEL with Grigg (GSO 3) and saw Cuthbert Headlam who is GSO 3 Intelligence Second Army. Looked round all his maps etc. Office in afternoon.

April 16th. Church in Cinema Hall, Coldstream Band and Bishop of Khartoum (Chaplain General) to preach. Lunched with Mickey Lawrence (1st Battalion Coldstream). Drove out with Alston to new Divisional Headquarters and walked on to 4th Battalion Coldstream (Pioneers), listened to Band and so home. Dined at Headquarters 2nd Guards Brigade. Huge dinner party given by General Ponsonby and Merton, Coldstream Band played and we danced after dinner.

April 17th. Raining and so spent most of the day in the office. Large draft of officers and 90 men for 2nd Battalion Coldstream arrived. My night for officer on watch. So I hope nothing exciting happens.

April 17th 1916   Offiziergefangenenlager   Heidelberg

Darling Nance
       You will have been surprised to get a postcard from me with a good deal scratched out. It was for this reason:- I asked for and obtained permission to have a sort of gable tent and wrote to you at once for it – however then the Commandant came to the conclusion that if I had it, so many more might also demand it, which would be impossible, which I quite see, and so it was scratched out and sent as you received it, and I was informed. The tennis marker is on its way I had a letter from the A. E. Company at Rotterdam 2 days ago saying it had left there. I received yours of March 29th – the change in the parcels has not been apparent yet as they have not arrived, but a box from the A. E. Company sent by "Mrs W.O.G." (William Otter Gibbs) is on its way, I hear by their postcard. I feel sure that the supplies will be enough, but parcels have been late lately – today 17th just arrived, sheets (only 2, not 4) sponge, ties, cigars, Cake (Evie G), parcel Morels, B, olives, biscuits also – all arrived since I finished letters. Sorry to hear Staff has been sacrilegious with his plush armchair – these padres are always the worst! I hear rumours of his having an idea of remaining an Army Chaplain, I can't help feeling he would regret it immensely after – I believe a living would do him much better especially a harder one. An Army Chaplain has a constantly changing 'parish' and even if he stays the troops change constantly, and the Army Chaplains change, pretty often too, their places. It's an unsatisfactory job in peace time I should think. Regiments move, changing stations – soldiers only stay soldiers a certain time and then disappear. Altogether I advise him strongly against it, he would be wasted there and you would hate it. It is very very sad about Noel he too had been away so long and so much from home, (*He was killed in German East Africa on March 20th*) Aunt E (Emily) and Uncle H (Henry Martin) must be very upset and Willy and Albinia naturally too very much. Give me all your news of your children when you write I love hearing about them. How is Gettuan after his stay in London – much better I expect. Now I must begin to acknowledge parcels and letters:
from Via on 8/3 three parcels all good and nothing broken
8/3 Also box of Tiptree jam, I have already told Albinia to countermand my countermand and asked her to continue it.
8/3 Cigars from Benson & Hedges.
8/3 Edinburg Cake from Evie G. I think I have asked her to discontinue a cake – if she would send bread instead, delightful!
10/3 A parcel from Mrs P (your pal) in Switzerland.
8/3 2 pairs of socks from Mrs Serocold (what ancient history that recalls doesn't it!) 25A N. Audley St., Letters, Huie from 28/3. Yes I am delighted to give Uncle Reggie whatever is useful. What a brute is Upton,

I hope he won't be about again for some time.

Elaine 26/3 whose letter gave me the first news of poor Noel's death.

Mrs Wynne-Finch of 27/3, delighted for her letter (Elgin Lodge, Windsor) and to hear of John and others. Would <u>she</u> tell John, as his wife to write to me – and would John, as Adjutant, tell Major Vaughan to immediately write to me, unless Major Vaughan has any scruples about writing to prisoners of War! In which case he must write and say so! And I hope she too will write again.

Winifred Paisley 20/3 who had lately seen you. Didn't Eileen Browne marry Ned Grosvenor, Winifred talks of her as Eileen Browne still? Tell Winifred that I have built 100s of castles (in the air), if even one, only, could be realized afterwards.

Uncle R 21/3, yes, I want a life of Chatham which would take one to the end, Lord Rowberg's only goes ½ way. Yes I wish I fenced, but I could not do it here in any case. Get photograph in his Special Constable Kit!

Philip Coxe 30/3 good stories and poem. So glad he is so much better.

Also of 31/3 I quite agree. I find it hard to write to Uncle H even after Noel's death. Xander in tails is truely growing up.

George 30/3 I answered by postcard – I hope he is well again.

That's the lot.

It is about 8.30 p.m. I am just going down to another room to talk and drink chocolate and imagine it is whiskey and soda – funny habits, prisoners! I am very well – tennis has begun, but the last few days have been too cold and wet, snow on the hills even last night. Best love my darling Nan and to you all – don't let Staff become an Army Chaplain, I know he would regret it. I wish had news for you, but how can I? Write much. Write often to

Your very loving brother

Evelyn

April 18th. Very quiet night. Signaller sense if he should repeat "all quiet" to 20th or 6th Division, not knowing I said "both". Spent the morning from 7:30 a.m. going round the Divisional Train with Johns (ASC). Went to refilling point but did not stay long as it was raining. Back to office after lunch. Went to Cinema with Mickey Lawrence to hear Coldstream Band play some of their "Paris Programme". Dined with Humphrey de Trafford. General Hayworth and Charles Greville back off leave. Stayed night with Division.

April 19th. Raining. Lunch with Humphrey de T. and found large crowd there. Tea with Merton B-S at 2nd Guards Brigade. Rather a heavy bombardment on left of Divisional line at about ¼ to 8 p.m. 'S.O.S.' came through and red lights went up. I was dining out with Lloyd, A. J. H. Smith, De Trafford, S-Stewart, etc. and got in about 9:30 p.m. Bomb lorry and all cars standing by. Huns bombarded WIELTJE (2nd Battalion Scots Guards) for 2 hours and then made a small raiding attack of about 50 men. They were got at at once and only stayed in the trench 5 minutes, leaving 7 dead on our wire, and we got 2 prisoners. The Artillery got a good barrage on behind them, which the others had to go back through and so many more casualties should have occurred. Ours were between 50 and 60 including 4 officers – slight.

April 20th. "G" staff very tired after a sleepless night. Relief was carried out all right but was not completed till late. 1st & 2nd Brigades now in (Right and Left). 3rd Coldstream also relieved 2nd Battalion. Everything very quiet again. About 8 p.m. Eric Avery (Guards Division Supply Column) picked me up and took me to WORMHOUT where I dined and stayed with them.

April 21st. Went round Workshops after breakfast and saw lorries and cars being overhauled, after lunch I was shown our books and general working system. We came back to POPERINGHE about 4 p.m. Went and saw Ponting's pictures of Arctic Expedition. Good deal doing in "Q" office but not much that affected me.

April 22nd. Just after I got down to the office, I had to dash back and pack my valise. Order having come through that Towers-Clark was to go to Machine Gun School Grantham, and so I am made Staff Captain 1st Guards Brigade. Drove down with General (Feilding) stopped at 6th Division Headquarters, found that their attack (counter) had been successful with about 100 casualties. Came on up to Ramparts in YPRES where 1st Guards Brigade Headquarters are. Found General Pereira, Gort, Phillips (Signals), Maurice Ponsonby (Chaplain), and Towers-Clark. Took over from Towers-Clark and spent rest of the day looking through papers. Very quiet afternoon few shells over in evening. Casualties nil.

April 23rd. Brigadier and Gort went out very early, also Phillips down his telephone wires. A very quiet night. Lovely day ground dried up a bit, very unlike usual Easter Sundays I have spent. A few small Services were held. Casualties in Brigade nil again. A quiet evening. Davidson (GSO 2) came in for tea.

April 24th. Went off on motor bicycle to POPERINGHE about 8 a.m. YPRES getting shelled a bit. Got to refilling point about 8:30 a.m., found carts had not gone. Went to 3rd Brigade Headquarters and found Ballantyne-Dykes (Staff Captain) went back by car and found YPRES still being rather heavily shelled. Afternoon quiet, evening Canadians on our right began being very active, I think avenging 22nd April 1915, but no news in. We shelled a good deal. Irish Guards had bad luck last night having an officer (Lt. T. K. Walker) and 4 men killed also 6 wounded, spoiling the Brigade's record having had 'nil' for last 3 days.

April 25th. Fine and clear morning, consequently YPRES shelled somewhat. M. Ponsonby went on leave. Divisional General came to a Brigade Conference at Brigade Headquarters at 11 a.m. Germans put some big shells in the Ramparts about 4:30 p.m., but did no harm.

Head Quarters
1st Guards Brigade
British Expeditionary Force.

25th April 1916

Darling Nancy

    I have now moved to the above address permanently and am "Staff Captain" of this Brigade.
    About that Bronze plate you are having made for dear old Eustace's grave, it really ought to come out soon as we may be leaving this part before <u>very</u> long. Maurice Ponsonby is on leave now. Would it be ready for him to bring back with him? I have told him about it and he says he certainly will. I propose going up there with a spade tomorrow and tidy up a bit if it is quiet.
    I suppose you are just off back to Yorkshire.

               Your loving brother

                      Lags

April 26th. Got up at 5:00 a.m. and went up to Cemetery at fork roads MENIN road and POTIJZE road where Eustace is buried. Did up his grave for about ¾ hour. Returned to bed for 2 hours at 10:00 a.m. Brigadier and self went round 2nd Grenadier billets in town. Very hot-morning. After tea Brigadier and self went and called on 9th Canadian Brigade on our right. Found them in long tunnel and not so comfortable as we are. Chanders (1st Black watch) Brigade Major who knows Evelyn. Germans started a heavy bombardment on our right at 6:45 p.m. Casualties last night 3 including poor Vian (Coldstreamer) who was with Machine Gun Company, a very nice boy, wounded badly through lung. German bombardment continued almost without ceasing. About 11 p.m. Guards Division rang up to say Germans had attacked in two places, one at 'Alma Wood', and another elsewhere, they had been thoroughly repulsed at 'Alma Wood' and they thought the Huns had taken the knock at the other as well.

April 27th. Everything quieted down by the morning. The day spent in cleaning up. I came out to see the billets in POPERINGHE about 12 noon. Brigadier and Gort arrived about 11:30 p.m. A quiet relief.

April 28th. Very warm day. A good deal of firing going on South of YPRES. Brigadier, Gort, Phillips, and self went to 'Fancies', a very good show.

April 29th. Some German aeroplanes came and dropped bombs on the town about 4 a.m., no damage. Went off to refilling point but got stopped half way as they were now shelling it and so came back. Spent most of the day indoors – too hot.

April 30th. More bombs about 4 a.m., one falling about 50 yards from our Headquarters. But Lewis Guns got onto them and drove them off. Went to Early Service, also played Hymns at 2nd Coldstream Service at 9 a.m. Germans made a Gas attack about WIJTSCHATE but did no good against Canadians. Dined with Little Man Vaughan, large dinner party.

May 1st. Went to refilling point at 8:00 a.m. Germans shelling POPERINGHE Station but not going very near it at us. Brigadier and self went round all First Line Transports, very warm morning. Dined with Bunny Crawford and 3rd Coldstream.

May 2nd. Went down to refilling point. Still very hot, Brigadier went round Brigade Headquarters Transport. VLAMERTINGE being shelled a bit, but otherwise a quiet day. Orders were got out for relief of 2nd Guards Brigade. Guy Shaw-Stewart and self got a car from Division and motored to HAZEBROUCK. Caught 8:25 p.m. to BOULOGNE arriving at 12:15 a.m.

May 3rd. Boat went at 11:30 a.m. Fog in Channel, Folkestone about 1:15 p.m. and in to London 4:30 p.m. Blanche met me on Station, and so to Belgrave Square where we found Via in bed. Dinner Carlton and so home.

May 4th. Shopped etc.

May 5th. Went down to Glynde, found family and Annabelle there.

May 6th. Motored over to Brighton. Fitzroy came to stay.

May 7th. Church and afterwards to Eastbourne.

May 8th. Rode – very windy – motored over to Seaford. Amy and Doris came.

May 9th. To London early. Went to see Inch Coxe.

May 10th. Dined with Judge Baynes and Bobby Pratt Barlow.

May 11th. Nancy and Albinia came up. Dinner with Uncle Reggie.

May 12th. Had large dinner party of 15 at Carlton – onto Alhambra, and dance of Coats at Cavendish Hotel.

Assuit, Egypt
May 12th 1916

My dearest Nancy,

I hope Stafford is keeping well. Very glad he and Lags found Eustace's grave all right.

I suppose you are still in London, if so you are probably running the sending of parcels of food etc. to Evelyn.

Ruby will always give a hand gladly to help in packing parcels or ordering things. Evelyn is so absolutely dependent on stuff of all sorts from home; - food, books etc. I am very remiss in writing to him I am afraid.

I hear Cavan is optimistic about the war. When does he think it will end?

We are safe and comfortable here at Assuit in a nice house; but it is rather hot. We are off to Assouan this evening to inspect negro troops, (Egyptian) and view the country.

The charge of the Dorset Yeomanry was a very brave affair indeed, and had an excellent moral effect on the Senussi. They had just come under my General's command.

I suppose you won't be in London all the summer, but will return to Bishopthorpe. Ruby does not know where to go and I don't quite know what to advise.

I hope Blanche and her offspring are still doing well. So sorry to hear Albinia is to be troubled again.

Hope Cosmo is strong now. I will send him a Post Card.

We have flowers and trees in abundance here, parrots, hoo-poos and doves, also banana and apricot trees in the garden, just getting ripe.

Best love to you and yours,

From your loving

Billy.

May 13th. Georgie and Dick came up. Nancy went off to York.

May 14th. Left Victoria at 8:30 a.m. Spent whole day at Folkestone. Boat left at 8:15 p.m. Had to stay night at Hôtel "Folkestone" BOULOGNE.

May 15th. Stewart Richardson turned up, walked about BOULOGNE. Train left at 7:30 p.m., great squash.

May 16th. POPERINGHE at 4 a.m. slept at Talbot House. Town bombed about 5 a.m., no harm. Went to No: 4 Field Ambulance and got car on up to YPRES at 2 p.m. Found Brigade in left sector in Ramparts, quite good Headquarters.

May 17th. Went round the two Battalion Headquarters in afternoon, very hot but fairly quiet. Nothing much doing, some shelling of roads in evening.

May 18th. Packed up and handed over; left YPRES on motor bicycle about 12:30 p.m.: went and saw Eustace's grave early and saw new cross which Stafford had put up. Lunched Divisional Headquarters and rode on to ST. OMER, about 30 miles and round billets. Stewart Richardson killed, very sad as he was only married last week.

May 19th. Slept in Hotel Commerce. Went to Town Major and round billets in his car. Found 2nd Coldstream billets at ST. MARTIN already taken, so after some talking with 2nd Army we had to find others at ARQUES. 3rd Coldstream and 2nd Grenadiers arrived during day. Dined with 3rd Coldstream.

May 20th. Alston arrived LONGUENESS about 11 a.m. and said ARQUES no good for 2nd Coldstream and they must go on to LONGUENESS and so spent whole morning finding them very bad billets. 1st Irish and 2nd Coldstream arrived, also Brigade headquarters about 8 p.m.

May 21st. Rode out with Brigadier to training ground about 10 a.m. Very hot, back via 2nd Grenadier, 2nd Coldstream, and 1st Irish Headquarters. A very fine Château we have got with a bath and other modern conveniences. John Campbell, M. McCalmont, Bunny C., and one other to dinner.

May 22nd. Rode out to training ground and marked out trenches with stakes. Gilly, Little Man, Crawley de C, Napoleon V, Guffin Heywood to dinner.

May 23rd. Went out to training ground where 3rd Coldstream, and 2nd Coldstream were digging. Trenches about ¼ finished. Played Tennis with No: 1 Company 2nd Coldstream. In evening Verelst and Bentinck came to dinner.

May 24th. 2nd Grenadiers. 3rd Coldstream, and 1st Irish digging trenches, getting quite deep. Marked out some more communication trenches. Went round Machine Gun's billets. Rained a bit. Major General came over to tea.

May 25th. Raining hard until about 11:00 a.m. Brigadier and self walked into ST. OMER before lunch. Massed drums of Brigade played at Cadet School BLENDECQUES at 4:30 p.m. Brigadier and self motored over to 2nd Coldstream who had just moved to QUELMES and then on to BLENDECQUES, not a very large audience. Weather cleared up for whole day. Practice trenches were continued on by Battalions.

May 26th. Two buses left Brigade Headquarters at 10:30 a.m. with Brigadier; CO's Battalions; 2nd in Command; and 3 Company Commanders per Battalion also for HESDIN GHQ. "Stokes" Mortar School run by Ivor Rose. They had large demonstration of 2 Batteries of Mortars, a mine went up and small infantry attack followed. Long journey 2½ hours each way. Massed Drums of Brigade played in ST. OMER AT 6:30 p.m.

May 27th. Went up to practice trenches. Battalions finishing off. Went on to the Second Coldstream Brigade Conference at 4 p.m., discussed many details of the Brigade. Played polo on Flying Ground after and took heavy fall, but no damage. Bed early feeling very stiif.

May 28th. Very quiet day. Did not leave Brigade Headquarters as feeling very stiff from fall. (Also had toothache!).

May 29th. Bombing demonstration under O'Brian at 10 a.m. General Feilding came over also General Cockran (GOC 3rd Guards Brigade) and Guffin Heywood – very successful. 2nd Grenadiers and 3rd Coldstream using practice trenches for assaulting. Went into ST. OMER and hired car in evening; returned and had 2 Chukka's at polo.

May 30th. Raining hard, put off going out for ¾ hour. Rode up to trenches and watched Irish Guards do a practice assault. Wire not quite cut enough, also rather slippy. Brigadier and self rode into ST. OMER after tea and listened to Massed Drums playing in Square – played much better.

May 31st. 75th Field Company Royal Engineers joined Brigade and billeted in LONGUENESS also 1st Guards T. M. Battery rejoined M. G. Company in TATINGHEM. 3rd Coldstream and 2nd Grenadiers using practice trenches in morning. Lunched with 2nd Coldstream, large party including St Germans (of Greys). Small tactical exercise for M. G. Company in afternoon. Clark-Jervoise commanding M. G. Company fell on his head in the road and got slight concussion. I took him back to 2nd Grenadiers and eventually to No: 4 Field Ambulance. Played 2 Chukka's polo with 3rd Coldstream.

June 1st. Picked up Fox, commanding 75th Company Royal Engineers, and went on up to practice trenches, remained for morning. After lunch Gort and General Codrington turned up, the latter having come out on a "Cooks Tour". More polo in evening, played 5 Chukka's. About six 2nd Coldstream and six 3rd Coldstream came down – very good fun.

June 2nd. Very little to do now Gort has returned. Drums played in ST. OMER at 6 p.m.

Offiziergefangenenlagen
Heidelberg

June 2nd 1916

Darling Nancy

I think perhaps a little reorganization of parcels might be advantageous. So, I am sending you the following with that view. Perhaps Blanche who orders for me, and Via and Ruby who send me, very kindly, regular parcels, would have a look at this list, and then if Via and Ruby would send one or other of those things marked. Always, putting it in whatever they are sending. I would ask Blanche to arrange for the C. S. Stores to send strictly according to this list, and to send once a week. As before the things from outside could go to the C. S. S. to be put in the box, such as cigarettes, tobacco.

Always. Butter (Dominion Dairy Co.) – Coffee – China Tea – Sugar in some (any) form – Ideal milk.

Once a week. Tongue or tinned meat – Cross and Blackwells tinned meat – pudding – Tin fruit – Cream – Tinned fruit pudding – Soup Squares – Sliced bacon – Marquis chocolate – Jam or Marmalade – Cake.

Once a fortnight. Quaker oats, Hunters and Hardy Ham – Mustard and salt – Tin Vegetables – Bath Oliver Biscuits long tin – 300 cigarettes – 1 tin Shaving Soap – 1 cake soap - 1 tube tooth paste.

Once a month. Bromes Tobacco (Cigarette holder, tubes, wads).

Occasionally. A bottle of Port – a Cheddar cheese.

None of this means in any way to interfere with others, e.g. Via's biscuits etc., Albinia's fruit cakes, or to stop the occasional luxury of sweets etc. If the C. S. Stores could be told to follow exactly what I have written, I could always be sure of what to expect. Some people naturally get less and I can help more.

Perhaps Via would again arrange the port and cheese. We are very often short of the 'always' list especially butter. This all, not in anyway to dictate to anyone but the C. S. Stores.

The Commission to determine the British exchange to go to Switzerland was here 2 days ago, some will go soon to Constance for their final medical board there. I should very much like to go but good health is not one of the reasons for going, whereas bad health from any cause, wounds etc., is. I really think it is time that length of time in prison should count.

(Sir Arthur Lawley and the Prince Maximilian, the Grand Duke of Baden negotiated this exchange of wounded prisoners through the Red Cross at a meeting in Luzerne on May 9th 1916. In 1927, Sir Arthur's daughter Ursula married George Abraham Gibbs).

I have been out 3 times for the 'walk on parade' – a very pretty country and it does one good to get out.

I like it as long as we keep in the woods and unfrequented places.

Tennis is going well, but we had a lull of 3 weeks owing to awful weather, incessant rain. I think Lord Kitchener's death is the saddest possible thing and its manner.

But he had led a fine life and died in the moment of fame and hard unluckiness (sic). I have just read his Sudan campaign by Stevens, and one sees him again in reading it.

I write to acknowledge parcels:

Arrived 5/6 from Alfred in Anjou bread and 2 packets from Ruby.

Another 2 cases by A. E. Company, 1 from Via, and 1 from Lags very well addressed

Also four boxes of biscuits from ----, the best sort to send. And usual lagers.

On 14/6, – C. S. Stores Case and 2 Vada bread.

On the 19/6, 1 parcel from Ruby – 500 cigarettes.

Blanchie, 1 of books not yet crossed.

Parcel Hemmings of 19/5 – very glad to get news of him and of Draper and hope he will write again.

Ethel Gibbs 21/5 - very many thanks.

Jack Gibbs 18/5 – when staying with you, it is I and not he who must be introduced to the wife of Gladys Cooper's husband after the war, such are for soldiers not clergymen, because Jack's too old!

Your own nice self 18/5 – very glad your dual party succeeds. Shall be very glad indeed to have a photograph of all the children. I can't quite place Hugh Abbot Smith, but he is obviously a man of sound sense because W. Finch wrote to me of the dinner too. The idea is silly that letters don't matter as long as parcels arrive, it is quite the contrary, one copes without letters, and without parcels when one takes up a hole in the belt.

Elaine 15/5 – I hope she flutters her eyelashes every evening, like the girl in her story.

Blanchie 21/5 – St Cross must have been a regular bear garden with so many children. I look forward to seeing a photograph of No. 7 of my nephews. I hope Willy will stay head of the lot this time, young as he is. Yes, between either it may suit; any old thing would at this moment.

Albinia 23/5 – Alexander must chuckle P. Lode and Peter will soon be able to, lucky boys. What hardships we had!!

Mrs Wynne-Finch – very many thanks and do it again. I do hope the German measles were not bad and that she will keep her John – he was cold when I last saw him about 24.8.14.

Billy 7/5 – at Assuit – will be warm there. He talks of being an old Veteran of cricket; not so old! I hope he will stay where he is and become something very high soon.

Charles King 25/5 – very surprised to hear of J. Brand and Rosabelle Nansham, it seems so short a time, but it is not really.

You see by the dates, that letters are taking a long time to come, I don't know why. My room companions (1 of the 2) McLang, the Canadian, is going to Constance, and may pass for Switzerland; he has had a bad rheumatism in the sciatic nerve, I shall be sorry to lose him.

Letter from Elaine 31/5 – just come.

I still read a good deal and talk French as much as I can, but seem to have got to a point that it is hard to advance from, and am also more lazy as time crawls on. I've just had a cold, the first for about a year, and alas my old enemy malaria put up his head for a minute but I slipped some quinine into him and he sank again, but he is a hard dyer.

Best love my darling Nan and bless you all. My love and thanks to all for letters and parcels.

Ever your loving

Evelyn

Give my love to the Archbishop (*Cosmo Lang, Archbishop of York*), I suppose he's hard at work always. To 'every week' add tinned chickens to be rehotted and other birds likewise. Also Pâté de Foie Gras, alternating with something.

June 3rd. Generals Codrington and Feilding came over and watched Companies in attack in morning, also demonstration by our T.M. Battery. Large Boxing entertainment by 1st Irish. Sergeant Voyles fighting and beating an ex-champion in 16th Lancers. Good game polo. Large "4th June" Eton dinner in ST. OMER. About 45 in Brigade, got back about 11:30 p.m.

June 4th. Service in field by Irish Guards. 2nd Battalion Coldstream Sports in afternoon. Large attendance of Grey's, 16th Lancers, and 5th Lancers officers, most amusing afternoon.

June 5th. Raining and not much doing. Orders for move on 7th arrived. Played polo.

June 6th. Went off in a car we got from DDT Northern and billeted with Thompson and Monquet. Brigade in scattered billets North of HAZEBROUCK.

June 7th. Early start. Got car from the Division and dashed first to STAPLE where 2nd Coldstream were to be and then on round. Brigade turned up about 2 p.m. Spent most afternoon looking for Mails. Brigadier went on leave for 10 days.

June 8th. On again from STE MARIE CAPPEL where Brigade Headquarters are, on motor bicycle to ST. JANSTER BIEZEN just

West of POPERINGHE for Brigade Headquarters. Battalions in Camps K-L-M-N. Bicycle punctured as I got in. Hot march for troops.

June 9th. Large quantity of working parties required, nearly 1,100 men per day. Wrote most of day. Raining.

June 10th. Party of NCOs going to Canadians went wrong. Budget Lloyd rang up from Division about them. Guffin and Davidson to lunch. Good news from Russia, 62,000 Austrians taken. Rode out to play polo but none going on. Some "gunning" could be heard, but otherwise fairly quiet. Colonel Campbell went off to "Blue Seal" dinner at HORMHOUT with Gilly and Crawley de C.

June 11th. Acting Brigadier and Gort went up to trenches and so I stayed in. Raining hard. Went round Camps in afternoon and tea with 2nd Coldstream, also dinner. Further good news from Russia. Canadians got heavily attacked at HOGE and lost front line trenches.

June 12th. Russians taken still more prisoners and Canadians stand firm. Raining.

June 13th. Orders issued about relief. 2nd Coldstream and 1st Irish go up first and take over from 18th Infantry Brigade and part of 16th Infantry Brigade. Brigade has been finding for last 6 days nearly 1,100 men a day on fatigue. Burying cables, unloading ammunition and stores. These parties are continually going wrong, not being met by guides and buses not arriving.

June 14th. Went down to refilling point at WATOU at 7 a.m. Potatoes have been short but were all right today. Raining. Went up to Brigade Headquarters of 180 Infantry Brigade on Canal Bank and saw Staff Captain about taking over. Quarters small and rather dirty. Bicycle broke down on way back, but luckily well out of shell area. Meet party of 2nd Guards Brigade on road. 1st Scots and 1st Coldstream who were going up to relieve Canadians near HOGE, having been rushed up in buses, Canadians having re-taken most of what they lost. Put bicycle on lorry and got to POPERINGHE, thence pushed it home about 2 miles.

June 15th. Went to refilling point, back and caught car at 9:30 a.m. and up to Brigade Headquarters on Canal Bank, went round depots of bombs, SAA and rations. Got back about 2 p.m.

June 16th. Spent most of the morning packing up. Went off about 11:30 a.m. rode bicycle up via VLAMERTINGE, BRIELEN to Brigade Headquarters on Canal Bank. Lunched with 2nd Coldstream, after took a guide of the 11th Essex and went round right sector, up 'Skipton' road, 'Nile' covered trench E.27.28, back via 'Skipton' post. Very wet and bad communication trenches. Headquarters arrived about 11 p.m. and took over about 2:30 a.m.

June 17th. Fussed around finding out where things were. Ground on East side of Canal much swept by machine guns, 7 fellows hit during night. Some shelling but no harm. Montgomerie (21 Coldstream) killed. Stafford came in in evening.

June 18th. R.E.Material causes some difficulty here as it comes up on truck on " Ypres Express" and then comes on down loop line to our trolly line dumps, which it was very late doing last night. Went down to YPRES to meet it and brought them on up.

Assuit,
Egypt,

June 18th 1916.

My dearest Nancy,

    I hope Stafford is fit and well in France, and that you and your bairns are ditto.

    I hope Evelyn's parcels go out to him regularly; I always have rather misgivings as to how he will fare and later on, when food really gets scarce in Germany. It seems that even now they depend very much on their food which is sent them.

    It is pretty hot here, but I stand it very well. Just off to Cairo to go to a dentist. It is a bit cooler there.

    Hoskyn, the parson of Sheffield is our pastor. You and Staff know him. A nice little man with spectacles.

    The war news these last 2 days has been good - What with the Russians beating the Austrians, and our capture of Gillibecke.

    I was hoping that Lags might have got something in the birthday list of honours; a military cross or something.

    You were 'some party' down at Bournemouth.

    I was glad Ruby is settled and is going to Copse Hill - she worried so until she was settled.

    You must visit her there. It is a little lonely there perhaps, but very nice country.

    So long Nancy.

Your loving brother

Billy.

<u>Has</u> Evelyn's address <u>altered?</u> What is the number of his Stube (room)?

June 19th. Some shelling in field West of us and some on Coldstream Battalions; about 12 casualties. Brigadier got back last night, all the better for his leave. Large fatigue parties from Battalion deepening trenches etc. machine gun fire rather worse but not many casualties from it.

June 20th. Went up to right Battalion line in morning and looked at 'Lancaster Farm' at dump, very wet still all round back by 'Hugh Burn' and 2nd Coldstream down 'Cöln Valley'. Had a very heavy cold and so early to bed with hot whisky. Casualties 16.

June 21st. A nasty shell just over our Headquarters last night wounded the sentry. Cavan came and saw us, I was the only person in, also Guffin H. and Grigg, but not much news except that the War is going very well! Some more shelling on North end of Canal Bank. Brigade casualties 15.

June 22nd. Fairly quiet day. Went down to refilling point at 7:15 a.m. and then on to Transport of Brigade. Found them in very comfortable place. Met Humphrey de T, they had had fairly quiet time in HOGE, where they had relieved Canadians for a week. Davidson (GSO. 2 Guards Division) came to luncheon. Went down to dumps at 10 p.m., rather a muddle about trucks, 3 out of 6 only coming down from 'Asylum' (YPRES) and so other 3 had to go back to POPERINGHE full.

June 23rd. General J.Ponsonby, Guy Rasche, and Staff Officer from IVth Corps went round trenches, large luncheon party. Went to 2nd and 3rd Coldstream in afternoon. Arthur Hope (3rd Coldstream) wounded in face, not very bad. Rained and some thunder. Cassy joined.

June 24th. Moderate bombardment of German trenches started at 9 a.m. Some retaliation on North end of Canal and two bridges badly damaged. Few casualties including Sergeant Heywood. Brigade Headquarters Signal Master. 16 Casualties for Brigade. Shelling (by us) continued all day. At night they turned on to the main road and cross roads by GELUVELD and ST. JULIAAN

June 25th. Very little happened during night, machine gun fire being rather less than usual. Major General and others came round and inspected right bit of our line. Considerable shelling in evening near 'Reigersburg Farm'. Heavy bombardment by 20th Division over WELTJE followed by a raid which was entirely successful and some prisoners got. Quiet night.

June 26th. Left Company of 2nd Coldstream bombed during night without ill effects. Casualties 8. Gort left for GHQ.

June 27th. A bombardment with wire cutting of about 2,500 shrapnel and 600 High Explosive and 500 'Heavies'. This brought some retaliation on Canal Bank and right Battalion (1st Irish). German Officer supposed to have been shot and 2 other Germans.

Head Quarters,
1st Guards Brigade,
British Expeditionary Force.

June 27th 1916

Darling Nancy

The climatic conditions prevailing here are most inclement! or in other words it does nothing but pour every day now, and the milk goes bad every morning which is most disheartening to one who runs a mess as I do – very bad for trenches too. I had a letter from Billy not long ago but without a great deal of news.

Stafford only lives about 150 yards from me, I believe, in a very good dugout, he says he really finds it better to live on his own and be independent of everything. One Gort, the Brigade Major here, was to have gone off on another job today and a new one was coming but for some reason it fell through and so he returned.

I think you got a fair price for your car considering the times. I have also just sold mine (18/22 HP Hotchkiss) and got £350 for it with 22 months garaging thrown in which I think was very lucky.

Much love to you all

Your loving brother

Lags

Had a comic letter from Aunt C. yesterday telling me Hand had got a cold and had not got up for breakfast.

June 28th. More casualties during night. Brigadier and self went round right sector, very wet and muddy. Brigadier lost one boot at one place. Very quiet but raining. Casualties 33 including 2 Officers. Pusch (Irish Guards) killed and Spinney (2nd Coldstream) wounded badly. Relief by 2nd Guards Brigade. Small parties coming up all day. General Ponsonby and Guy Rasch arrived about 11 p.m. and took over. We left at 1:00 a.m. and got to Camp "D" about 1:30 a.m.

June 29th. Most of day spent in cleaning up. General and I went over to Battalion Headquarters of 2nd and 3rd Coldstream. Rained in evening.

June 30th. Brigadier and self went round all Brigade Transports. Raining hard. Cleaned in afternoon and Scots Guards Band played in "E" Camp. Dined 2nd Coldstream.

July 1st. Considerable bombardment going on South but nothing very near the Camps. A few shells at gun on railway but not very near it. A fine day at last. Dined with 3rd Coldstream.

July 2nd. Went to 2nd Coldstream Service at 9:45 a.m. Scots Guards Band played. Brigadier and self rode over to 4th Battalion Coldstream after luncheon, the Major General (Feilding) having first lunched with us. Colonels Campbell and McCalmont dined also Harry Cubitt and Bill Bailie (1st Irish Guards).

July 3rd. Went round 1st Irish Camp. Corps Commander (Cavan) came in for a few moments, very optimistic about 4th Army "push" down South. Rode motor bicycle up to 3rd Guards Brigade lunched; arranged relief and just got away as bombardment was starting. Chick Greenwood (ASC's), Gilly, Rupert, and Father Brown to dinner.

July 4th. Cloudy morning turning into very heavy rain and thunder in afternoon. Brigade Conference of Commanding Officers and 2nd's in Command. Brigadier discussed several points of the new bit of line to be taken over from 3rd Guards Brigade, just North of YPRES. Beckwith-Smith turned up at 5:30 p.m. to take over duties of Brigade Major. Major General came over and discussed the promotion of Special Reserve Officers in the Coldstream who have taken Regular Commissions. Phillips returned off leave. Showed Merton papers most of evening.

July 5th. Rained most of morning. Went over to ST SIXTE with Brigadier in afternoon to Divisional Headquarters. Dined with 2nd Coldstream.

July 6th. Good news from SOMME. Right of British advance and French seem to be going on although left held up. About 5,000 prisoners. Played polo in afternoon, large Coldstream gathering with some Gunners. 3rd Coldstream and 2nd Grenadiers went up to take over Reserve Battalion billets and dug outs after dinner.

July 7th. A quiet morning. General and Merton went up to Division Conference at 3rd Guards Brigade on Canal. 2nd Coldstream and 1st Irish go up to the Bank. About 9 p.m. we motored up to relieve them, (3rd Guards Brigade). Very quiet relief 2nd Grenadiers on right; 3rd Coldstream on left.

July 8th. 3rd Coldstream "minenwerfered" about 5 a.m., otherwise quiet night. Various RE and Right Group Commanders came in. 3rd Coldstream "minenwerfered" again about 3 p.m. Heavy retaliation put over which eventually stopped it. Wilmott-Sitwell very badly wounded and died in the Dressing Station. Quiet evening until about 11 p.m. when heavy bombardment opened South East of YPRES and lasted two hours, the sky being lit with shells. This turned out to be the Canadians making an unsuccessful attempt to get back a strong point near HOGE.

July 9th. Brigadier and Merton went round. Major General came round also two Officers from the Corps and asked conundrums, to which I "found" answers. Otherwise quiet. Good news from Russia.

July 10th. A much quieter day, a few casualties. Some bombing occurred during night on left of left Battalions. About 10:30 p.m. the 59th Infantry Brigade on our right carried out a minor enterprise on some German trenches East South East of WELTJE. It was not altogether a success. About 70 men took part from 10th and 11th Rifle Brigade. Gas was let off for 5 minutes and then a heavy artillery barrage. They got into the German trenches but got no prisoners. It caused a good deal of retaliation especially on the roads.

July 11th. Brigadier and self went up to left and saw John Campbell, then across to 2nd Grenadiers. Crawley de Crespigny came along with us up 'Threadneedle Street' to his right reserve Company. Brigadier and self returned via LA BRIQUE, met General Evans (CRA to Guards Division) and brought him back to luncheon. Wire to say all Regiments had to find 1 Officer and 20 men for big review in PARIS to take place on 14th. Harry Cubitt took Coldstream party, also Jonah Bailey for Grenadiers. Stafford came in for some food in evening.

July 12th. A quiet night except for one burst of shrapnel during relief but no damage. Some shelling of other parts of the sector during day to which our guns gave ample retaliation. Young Christie 1st Irish killed during night of 11th/12th.

July 13th. Got up at 5:45 a.m. and went off on bicycle to refilling point and after round 1st Line Transports with Shaw-Stewart. A fairly continuous bombardment kept up by the Germans most of the day. A patrol went out from Irish Guards during night which ran up against a German one, some firing but no casualties.

July 14th. Went round right sector with Brigadier also one Lt. Colonel James who had come up from War Office. We went down top end of "X" line, then up to front by 'Threadneedle Street' and 'Euston Road', nearly up to ones knees in parts in mud and water. Colonel James not very fit and so got very tired. We had a good look at "Canadian Dug Outs" and back by "La Belle Alliance". Gilly Follet, Major General, Grubby Gapes, and Colonel James to luncheon. Brigadier lunching with 2nd Guards Brigade (General John Ponsonby). A large patrol from 1st Irish left 'Cavan Trench' about 10:40 p.m.

July 15th. About 1:00 a.m., Gunners began to get a bit anxious about the patrol. At 2:00 a.m., Gordon (1st Irish) rang to say patrol had returned complete. They had come across a few Germans who ran when they saw them. Brigadier and Merton went round back lines. Very dull and slack day. Spent evening digging a small garden, got very hot which necessitated a bath. Francis Longueville came to dinner to celebrate getting his Military Cross for the way he held 'Morteldje Estaminet' the other night.

July 16th. Quiet night. Brigadier and Merton went round left sector. Merton and I went to a Service of Stafford's in a small dug out at 7 p.m., latter stayed to dinner.

July 17th. Brigadier and self went up to right sector: picked up Crawley de Crespigny at 'Irish Farm' and so on up 'Liverpool Street' to 'Cavan Trench': very hot and stuffy walk. Trenches considerably drier, very quiet walk. Back via 3rd Coldstream at 'La Belle Alliance', found Bunny C in. Pain (Divisional Signals Officer) came to luncheon. Gilly Follet and Fox (R.E.) to dinner. Huns sent over few "Minenwerfers" (about 6) to which we replied with about 300 shells of all sorts, the "Minenwerfers" stopped! Poor old Gilly Follet wounded about midnight, in the arm, a very "gentlemanly" wound.

July 18th. B.G. – G.S. IVth Corps and C.E. of Corps (Gaythorne-Hardy and Wilson) came round at 6 a.m. Merton took them up to left sector. Muggy day and quiet. Party from Review at PARIS returned after a most splendid 4 days from their accounts! Colonel McCalmont (1st Irish) came to dinner.

July 19th. "Minenwerfer" started on 3rd Coldstream about 2:30 a.m. I got on telephone and got retaliation and it stopped. Donald Campbell (3rd Coldstream) was killed during the night. Very sad as he was such a nice little fellow and only 19 years old. Fine and hot at last. Brigadier and self went up to Battalion Headquarters in line and on up 'Liverpool Street' to Right Battalion front line. Much drier and very quiet. Conference of Corps Commander, Prince of Wales, Major General, and all Brigadiers at our Headquarters. A very quiet afternoon. Relief of both Battalions in evening. A dummy raid by the 3rd Guards Brigade during night consisting of a heavy bombardment for half an hour, then 5 minutes quiet, and then a heavy go on Shrapnel on front German trenches. Patrols were then going out to find out the damage done.

July 20th. Grigg (Brigade Major 2nd Guards Brigade) came up and went on round with Merton, Brigadier and self. Went round Battalion Headquarters of Battalions in the line. Very hot morning. Major General and Grubby came round after lunch, after which I lay on my bed and – well meant to read! A fine and quiet evening, two people to dinner.

July 21st. Brigadier and Merton went up to MORTELDJE. A very quiet day. Major General called in, in afternoon.

July 22nd. Brigadier and self went round dug outs on Canal Bank. Heavy Scotch mist: good deal less shelling; several Corps Officers came round.

Brigadier of 18th Infantry Brigade (on our right) called on *our* Brigadier.

July 23rd. Davidson and Colonel Turner (GSO 1st & 2nd Army) came round our trenches. Brigadier took Major General round our trenches. Becky and Barny went round together and General went round in evening. Orders received that 4th Division relieve us 25th – 28th and we go back to WORMHOUT (for a very short time I expect!).

July 24th. Large number of Generals round, including Corps Comander and General Billy Lambton. Had started early to go to refilling point but bicycle broke down so pushed it back. Fine but muggy most of the day.

Head Quarters,
1st Guards Brigade,
British Expeditionary Force.

July 24 1916

Darling Nancy
     Your better half honoured us at dinner last night. He is becoming rather like Mr Medley, not in figure but in one habit and that of dining on Sunday evenings after service. (He's done it twice!! which is good)
     Fine here at last, very pleasant this morning when I stepped lightly onto my motor wheels at 6.47 a.m., but not so pleasant when at 7.20 a.m. it broke down on a road very much in view of the Bosche and I had to push it back about a mile, very hot and cross, luckily our bombing Officer here loves tinkering and knows a good bit so that saves my getting my hands dirty. I hear Wynn Llewellyn got rather a nasty wound in the hand.
     Gilly Follett got a very slight one in the arm. Eric Gurney's cousin Donald Campbell was killed the other day, such a very nice boy of just 20, in the 3rd Battalion Coldstream. You remember his father has been missing from the 1st Battalion Coldstream since January 25th 1915 – otherwise we have got on very well lately. Love to the Chicks

                Your loving brother

                     Lags

July 25th. Went off about 8 a.m. on bicycle, went to PROVEN and saw billets and then on to HOUTKERQUE and HERZEELE. Found 12th Infantry Brigade in HOUTKERQUE, one Hawkins (General's ADC) took me round Battalion Headquarters. Got back to Canal Bank about 1 p.m., found they had been shelling it a bit. Quiet afternoon.

July 26th. Went off again down to HOUTKERQUE and HERZEELE. Lunched with 12th Infantry Brigade and Hawkins took me round 2nd West Riding and 1st Essex Headquarters. Saw few billeting parties. Got back to Canal about 6 p.m. found 2 Battalions had been altered and were going to POPERINGHE. To bed at 11:30 p.m.

July 27th. Woken up at 2:30 a.m. by Bunny Crawford to say the party of Officers from relieving Battalion had not turned up. So rang up Battalion at TROTS TOURS through Gunners. A busy day for all. Went off on motor bicycle at 8:00 a.m. and billeted 2 Battalions and Brigade Headquarters in POPERINGHE. Rode over to HERZEELE and arranged Bath and clean clothes for 2nd Grenadiers and 3rd Coldstream and Machine Gun Company. Roads very crowded with R. E. Companies and Guns galore changing over. Dined at Officers Club in POPERINGHE. Brigadier and Merton turned up about 1 a.m. having had a very quiet relief. 1st Irish Guards train arrived in POPERINGHE about 1 a.m. and 2nd Coldstream about 2:30 a.m.

July 28th. Everyone very late up. Brigadier and self went round billets and Battalion Headquarters. Played polo in afternoon, three very good Chukka's. Heavy bombardment going on over trenches we have just left. (Poor old 10th Infantry Brigade!). Dinner party of 9 in evening. Went and played the piano with No: 1 Company 2nd Coldstream after dinner for 2 hours. Casualties for last tour in trenches of just over 3 weeks for Brigade:- 3 Officers killed – 6 Officers wounded; 18 Other Ranks killed – 150 Other Ranks wounded.

July 29th. Several lots of orders received during last few days, but things fairly well settled now I think. I left Brigade Headquarters about 10 p.m. with Thompson and interpreter, for entraining station PROVEN. 3rd Battalion Coldstream train left at 12 midnight. A great squash due to billeting parties from all Battalions, Company of R. E. and Field Ambulance coming too. A very uncomfortable 6½ hour journey brought us to ST. POL.

July 30th. Battalion detrained and had teas, which the billeting parties took first and two Motor Buses (leaving 43 for the Battalion) and went on to BOUQUEMAISON (4 miles North of DOULLENS). Battalions billeted: 3rd Coldstream; 1st Irish; 75 Company R.E.; No: 3 Company Divisional Train; No: 4 Field Ambulance: and Brigade Headquarters in BOUQUEMAISON, and 2nd Grenadiers; 2nd Coldstream: Machine Gun Company; at NEUVILLETTE. Very hot and dusty. Battalions continued arriving until 8 p.m. Billets bad, small and dirty.

July 31st. Except for the stream of motors, lorries and transport up and down the road, a quiet day. Very hot and dusty.

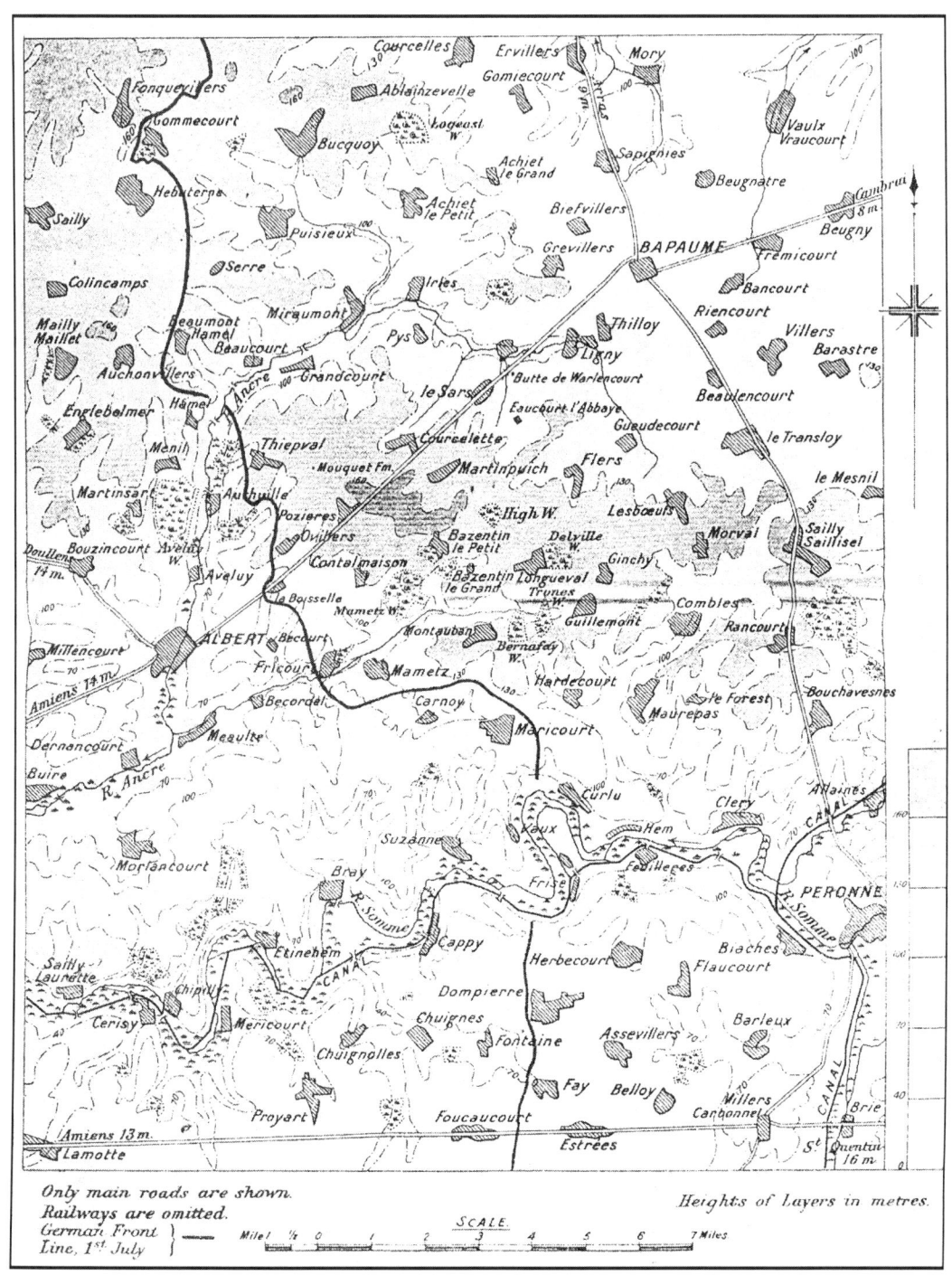

Figure 57. The Somme where Captain Lancelot Merivale Gibbs' Brigade moved at the end of July 1916.

THE SOMME

August 1st. The Brigade marched to new billets at SARTON and VAUCHELLES. Passing the starting point at 6:35 a.m. I started off on the motor bicycle which broke down after ½ mile, leaving it for O'Brien to mend. I took a bicycle; finding this too hot after 100 yards, I took a horse which after 3 miles seemed too slow. A motor lorry then took me 6 miles, but as it was turning off our road, I seized a Dispatch Rider round the waist, sat on the carrier of his bicycle for the last 3 miles to SARTON. After arranging billets for 2nd Grenadiers: 2nd Coldstream; No: 4 Field Ambulance: and 750 Company, I borrowed a motor bicycle and half way to VAUCHELLES took on an open drain in the road which landed me about 10 yards further on with bicycle on top of me. Our own dispatch rider happened to pass and so bleeding freely I continued and spent most of the morning in a First Aid dressing station. The Brigade got in about mid-day and some of the dirtiest billets in France with no Officers billets. However 30 Tents were procured.

August 2nd. Very hot and little to do. Heard that we shall be staying on here for a few days. All Officers of 1st Irish and 3rd Coldstream now bivouacing out with tents handy in case it rains.

August 3rd. Brigadier, Merton, and O'Brien went off to special 'P' smoke bomb demonstration about 8:30 a.m. Very hot and nothing doing. About 100 men, reinforcements, arrived for various Battalions in motor buses about 1 p.m. Brigadier did not return before 6:45 p.m. Rode over to 2nd Coldstream after tea. Lot of writing to be done, to bed about 1:15 a.m.

Offiziergefangenenlagen
Heidelberg
August 3rd 1916

My darling Nancy

I will start by acknowledging all the letters I have received. Would you please forward where necessary? Walter Riddell May 12th at Herts. Regiment, Bangalore – delighted to hear of him personally and glad to hear he is where he is. Sounds wonderful but no-one can have ever said he is nearly as good a Collector as me. He must not listen to obvious flattery that he is beloved by all that I can believe were mostly believed as a habit of his – it is his irresistible comic air I suppose! Blanche's July 12th I can't decipher. Nancy has canteen work at 6 - 9 Albany Place. Yes near to my old home, but the early mornings must be a terrible trial to her? My love to Martin and Will. I used to know Hardwicke slightly if it is he who married a Miss Parker. Yes Drummer Whiskies was frightful but since then all lots of things from me become possible. Also Blakely etc. already acknowledged I think. Have I mentioned that the

Meerschaum Lags says he sent me has not turned up. Elaine and J. Evans School – trunks and luxurious swimming bag and all sorts of goods
Billy of 17/6, 21/6 and 1/7 – he wants to know if I get his letters, so will Ruby tell him I do and ask if he gets mine. It was very reminiscent seeing his Turf Club Cairo writing paper again. (By the bye is my membership of the Turf Club Cairo paid up? George let me know I had been elected). I hope that Dentist was a good one. I hope he will visit the Wheadons there sometime and he will get news of us all. All fully. The home-dairymaid-made cream cheese sounds delicious and I look forward to it.
Here post arrives well always and anxious days in Landau were well filled.
I hear Eton beat Harrow – Harrow beat Winchester – and Winchester beat Eton. Curious who is top?
Lags 6/7, wrote to him on 1/8 a postcard. Very sorry he did not get that job. Via of June 5th and 2 of June 25th, stupidly I did not notice the dates last time I wrote I said I think only got the second half of her June 25th letter whereas I really had the first half all the time. It is very interesting. I had wanted to know the whole history. It is obvious no one is to be believed except Upton; and that we have both lost a little consulting. I might be able to help with some explanations when I get home, but it is not very likely. George's June 30. Surprised to hear that Crape could buy a house like Gosfield Park after one only wears a smallish band on the arm. Sir George Arthur would know all about my car. I hope Elaine won a prize at their sports. I hear Wyman is wounded again, not badly I hope.
Aunt Catty, July 6th, who says that Mrs Percy Vere Turner says that Hobb's children are 'superior'. Who is Mrs P. V. T?
My best congratulations to Miss Emily Walsh on her approaching nuptials with Rev. Hamilton. Who is Miss E. W. and Rev H?? Dear Aunt C, but I take as much interest as I can in these strangers?
Parcels from Via by mails on 20/7, 2 on 25/7 and 2 on 31/7.
Albinia from 21/7 and 31/7.
Ruby via Mails 3 on 21/7.
J. Caters of Bath, on 22/7 and 31/7
C.S. Stores by H.E. Company cases arrived, 2 on 18/7 and 2 on 27/7 and 1 book on 31/7.
Charles King a cake on 26/7.
Cigars on 31/7 – very many and best thanks to all senders.
Letter from P. H. Coxe just arrived – tell him that his stories puzzle my French as I have not yet got hold of enough slang!! but I like to practice.

About 70 British still here but about 45 expect to go on very soon to Switzerland, on exchange, some ill and some wounded. It is very nice seeing them en passant, and one gets new news. A representative of the American Embassy was here lately to ask if we had any suggestions etc. I hear that Eileen Scott (Elliot as was) had a daughter lately. It is all a forgotten history now. I have bought a cheap sprung bed, my old bones lie uneasily on a wooden one, though I had managed it for nearly 2 years. Best love dearest Nance and to all yours. I am very well all the fitter for tennis. Write to me often and may we meet soon.

Ever your loving Evelyn

August 4th. Not so hot. Band played in afternoon in this village. Gort came to dine, but not much news. Cold during dinner.

August 5th. Brigadier went round transports of Brigade with O'Rorke and self. Lunched with 2nd Coldstream. Rather a black day, everyone getting into trouble and Becky and I loosing things at intervals. Dined 1st Irish Guards.

August 6th. Parade Service at 11 a.m. by A. S. Crawley with Irish Guards Band. Lt. Colonel Ogsdon from 1st Corps came and took a Summary of Evidence on Lascelles (Viscount) 2nd Battalion Grenadiers for writing stuff in a letter contrary to the Censor regulations. Dined with 3rd Battalion Coldstream.

August 7th. Brigadier and Merton rode round Battalions; cooler day. About 5 p.m. Commander-in-Chief rode up to Brigade Headquarters. Brigadier and Merton were out, so I had to give him all the information he required, however he 'shook hands' and went off in about 5 minutes. Brigadier and Merton returned about 6:30 p.m. from looking over the ground the Division will eventually take over. Orders came in for Thompson to go to Reserve Army Headquarters.

August 8th. Got the spray baths going by the help of two water carts. Played polo for the 1st Battalion Coldstream versus 2nd Battalion, sides:- Byng H, Humphrey de T, Digby, and self, versus Bunny C, Druce B, Ympkin V, and Edwin B. Quite an amusing game in a clover field with a small football. Orders for move received. Thompson left for Reserve Army Headquarters.

August 9th. A busy morning up to 12:15 p.m., when H.M.the King with Prince and about 6 others arrived and stayed about ¾ hour; shook hands with us all twice! and went on down to the Irish Guards and then to 3rd Coldstream. He then went on to lunch with Cavan at the Corps. After lunch Brigadier, Merton, and self motored up to VITERMONT (71st Brigade). Brigadier and Merton went round line, which we take over from 3rd Worcesters (Beresford Gibbs' Battalion) in BERTRANCOURT. Back about 8 p.m.

August 10th. Rode over to SARTON with Brigadier and came back across the fields. 3rd Coldstream and 2nd Grenadiers left for

BERTRANCOURT about 5 p.m. Beresford Gibbs came to dinner also Gort.

August 11th. Two French Staff Officers came over with Gort to watch the Brigade march past. They 'appeared' very impressed. Brigade Headquarters moved off about 2 p.m. Brigadier, Merton, and self motored up to VITERMONT, which is close to ENGLEBELMER. Very quiet relief which was completed by 4 p.m. Very good dug outs for Brigade Headquarters and delightfully quiet spot.

August 12th. St Grouse's day. The crack of the rifle was heard quite early on the moor! A very quiet spot we live in. Major General called in afternoon also an R.E. who is managing a Gas attack on our left. Great dinner party, it being the anniversary of the 2nd year since 2nd Battalion Coldstream left Windsor. Party:- General Pereira; Hopwood; De Trafford; Lloyd; Shaw-Stewart; Verelst; and self with Becky Smith as Guest. They stayed until after 12 midnight. Luckily Gas attack off.

August 13th. Brigadier and Merton went off about 9 a.m. After lunch Bunny and self walked down to 1st Irish and borrowed two horses, rode over to BERTRANCOURT and saw 2nd Battalion. Coldstream. Guffin Heywood came over and told us about being relieved by 71st Brigade tomorrow. Spent most of night writing orders etc. and telephoning hard for lorries etc. Fox (R.E.) came to dinner.

August 14th. Went on to LOUVENCOURT where I arrived 7:30 a.m., arranged billets. Brigadier did not get back till 4 p.m. having handed over to 71st Brigade again. They were very angry at going back again so soon. Our typewriter got smashed on way down, so got a car out of the Division, Barny and I went into AMIENS (about 25 miles) had a very good dinner, bought a Remington @ £22 and got back about 11:30 p.m.

August 15th. Rained most of day. Brigadier dined out.

August 16th. Two Battalions in LOUVENCOURT started off for line about 11 a.m. to take over from 61st Brigade in front of COURCELLES. Brigadier, Merton, and self rode up about 2:30 p.m. A long relief but complete by 6:00 p.m. 3rd Coldstream in COUIN, 2nd Grenadiers in COURCELLES with Brigade Headquarters. Fairly quiet relief.

August 17th. Brigadier and Merton went up to line. Major General came in and asked conundrums. Casey and I rode up to COLINCAMPS and stayed there while it fairly pelted. Dined with 2nd Battalion Grenadiers.

August 18th. Left for Division at 9:15 a.m. General Court Martial on Lord Lascelles, 2nd Battalion Grenadier Guards, who wrote in a letter contrary to Censor regulations. John Ponsonby President, members – Boy Brooke, Bulgey Thorne, George Lane, Colonel Bethell. A very funny trial which lasted all day and then wasn't finished as Censor had not turned up. I was 1st Witness and Castlerosse prosecutor. A very quiet day and few casualties. Ralph Bingham and Desmond Abel-Smith to dinner.

August 19th. Court Martial continued in morning up to about 12 noon. After lunch rode down to AUTHUILLE to see billets and tents etc. for Brigade taking over tomorrow. Came back with Staff Captain of 6th Infantry Brigade (Watley of Hertfordshire Regiment). A very quiet day and few casualties. Crawley de Crespigny and Lascelles came to dinner.

August 20th. The second anniversary of my coming to France. Came down to BOIS WARNIMONT and looked round billets. All Brigade in about 8 p.m. A few casualties.

August 21st. Day spent in cleaning up the wood. Polo with the small football from 3:30 p.m. – 6:00 p.m. Bunny Crawford and George Lane to dine.

August 22nd. Got a car in the morning and went billeting in BEAUVAL with Castlerosse. Brigade easily billeted. Remainder of day spent in cleaning up. Band played during dinner, Major General, John Campbell, and McCalmont to dine.

August 23rd. Brigade and 75th Field Company and No: 4 Field Ambulance marched off at 8 a.m. At 10 a.m. Alston picked me up in car, after picking up John Dyer (Staff Captain 2nd Guards Brigade) and Dykes (Staff Captain 3rd Guards Brigade). We got to FLESSELLES about 3 p.m. where I was dropped. Village rather full but with the help of MONTONVILLERS, I got Brigade in. Stayed in Château of Marquis de Savigny at FLESSELLES. Very kind old couple.

August 24th. Called at 7 a.m. by Madame La Marquise's maid and met billeting parties at 8:30 a.m. Brigade arrived between 11 a.m. and 12 noon. Afternoon spent mostly in sleep. Massed drums played at 6:30 p.m. along main road. "Little Man" and O'Keiffe to dinner.

August 25th. Went off at 9 a.m. with Cook Alston and 2 others, billeting. Stopped in AMIENS en route to buy food. Got to MÉAULTE about 12 noon found parties already there having bicycled the 22 miles. Town very dirty, dusty and lots of traffic. Brigade came by "Tactical Train" (i.e. troops only no transport) from CANAPLES, on two trains. Transport got in about 8:30 p.m. having come by road. 2nd Grenadiers and 1st Irish got in about 9:00 p.m., the two Coldstream Battalions about 11:30 p.m. Brigade Headquarters house infested with rats and flies.

August 26th. Rained most of the day, nothing much doing.

August 27th. Rained and thundered nearly all day. Brigadier and I went over to ALBERT to see the figure of The Blessed Virgin Mary hanging from the top of the Church.

August 28th. Village getting in an awful state of slush and mud. Got a lift in a car to AMIENS and bought hard for half an hour, piled the car up and got back to MÉAULTE about 7:45 p.m. Dinner party consisting of Prince of Wales, Ralph Bingham, Ympkin, Verelst, and "Jonah" Baily, and General G. Pereira.

August 29th. Rained harder than I have seen it do for years, but luckily my "Cording" proved up to it. Rode over to Division with Brigadier; Battalions training and bombing.

August 30th. More rain. Went to refilling point also baths at 5:00 a.m. Continued to rain all day and so did not go out at all.

August 31st. Aeroplane test with Infantry. 3rd Battalion Coldstream did an assault of supposed trenches while contact aeroplane was flying over them, on reaching objective they lit flares upon which the aeroplane wrote a message and dropped it on Brigade Headquarters. Battalion Headquarters also had a green panel to signal the aeroplane with. This only worked fairly well, rest was a great success. Brigadier and self after lunch, went to censor a film on Divisional Cinema on SOMME Battle. Clearing up at last. 2nd Grenadiers went off up to CARNOY to dig.

September 1st. Fine and roads drying up well. Brigadier, Becky, and Commanding Officers went off at 9 a.m. to have a look at Battle Front from a high hill. One Officer went off on leave to PARIS.

September 2nd. Rained. Day of little incident. Played polo in evening near transport lines. Bewicke Copley who had just joined 1st Battalion came and played.

September 3rd. Brigade Church Parade attended by Major General. Sermon by Deputy Chaplain General (Glyn, Bishop of Khartoum). After lunch Lease, Burn, Edmonstone, and self motored into AMIENS, had a most amusing afternoon. Second big attack on this front. quite successful, GUILLEMONT taken (by Brigadier General George Pereira's Brigade) and consolidated. French got on well South of us. GINCHY remains to be taken. Dined with Verelst. No: 1 Company, 2nd Coldstream. 2nd Grenadiers returned from digging.

September 4th. Fine, more or less. 2nd Coldstream were going to do a demonstration attack but they were driven in by a heavy shower. Further attack made on "Falfemont Farm" by 5th Division, but unsuccessful. Further successes made on either side. Short game of polo in evening; started to rain again.

September 5th. Brigadier and Merton went round to training ground morning and afternoon. General Rawlinson (GOC 4th Army) came to see us. News came in that French had got right on and we had done well. Be ready to move.

September 6th. Kept rather on "Tender Hooks" until about midday when they took off the notice we were at to move. Training as usual, and some polo in the evening.

September 7th. News that we are to move on 9th and probably go in 10th. Arranged to store great coats and other surplus kit of Brigade. Went to dine in AMIENS with Prince of Wales, W.R. Baily, and Merton B-S, in Prince of Wales car. Very good dinner after which we danced. We sang loudly on the way home in the car, getting back about 1 a.m.

September 8th. Brigade Field-day. Got up at 6:30 a.m. feeling like nothing on earth. A fair success and got in about 12 noon. Rest of the day spent in recovering from last night! Stafford returned.

September 9th. Orders came in for us to move to CARNOY tomorrow, so most of the morning spent in fussing. Brigadier and Merton went up the line. After lunch Castlerosse and self rode over to CARNOY, saw the Town Mayor (a most incompetent fellow).

September 10th. O'Brien and self left about 7:30 a.m. and went over to CARNOY, and arranged with difficulty the bivouacs for the Brigade. 2nd Coldstream and 3rd Coldstream in dug outs and trench shelters, other two Battalions in the open. Brigade left MÉAULTE about 10:00 a.m. and got to hill near CARNOY where dinners were taken. Brigade got in about 3:00 p.m. finding everything very dirty. A quiet evening, a few shells over which killed one man. Brigade Headquarters in "Brick Ally" also very dirty and stuffy.

September 11th. Brigadier and self went round all Battalions. At about 4:00 p.m. Divisional Conference which Brigadier and self went to, they discussed future operations at some length. Had a Brigade conference at 6:00 p.m. by which time Merton had returned from the trenches. Spent most of the evening and ½ night trying to make the 'Roneo', which had just come, work, but with only moderate success as most had to be pencilled in afterwards.

September 12th. I went off about 12 noon up to 3rd Brigade Headquarters in BERNAFAY WOOD and on from there to our new Headquarters. Made several arrangements and then home. I have never seen such a sight as the country is up here, littered with debris of all sorts, petrol cans, rifles, ammunition. In one place the road is metalled with "detonated" Mills bombs. Returned for tea and then up again for a fatigue party of water carriers. 2nd Grenadiers took over front line from 3rd Guards Brigade, just East and North East of GINCHY. Bad trenches and much shelled. Our guns kept up a very heavy barrage the whole time; guns are so thick that they are almost axle to axle. 9" Howitzers, 6" Howitzers, 60 pounders, 18 pounders, and many others who fire about 5 shells a minute each every 24 hours. Relief complete by 12 midnight,

1st Irish are in BERNAFAY and TRONES WOOD also machine gun Company, 2nd and 3rd Coldstream remain at CARNOY until the day.

September 13th. Brigadier, Barny, and self went up to WATERLOT FARM and our new Brigade Headquarters at 4:30 a.m. and looked round. Attack by 6th Division at 6:00 a.m. invoked rather a barrage on TRONES WOOD and so we returned, and 'got down to it' for 2 hours. A somewhat strenuous day then ensued collecting petrol tins and arranging for rations. Started to rain and so had to have lunch in acme of discomfort, writing with one hand, eating with another and beating the typewriter with a 3rd in a dug out 20ft down about 4 yards by 3 yards (there are few things more annoying than hearing a typewriter being beaten in a confined space when you are trying to think!). Everyone asking for about 1,000 petrol tins of water when only 500 are available, also asking for rations from every side. About 4 p.m. I walked up to advanced Brigade Report Centre with Tisdall of 1st Battalion Irish Guards who is going to take up 2nd Battalion Grenadiers' rations, l,700 of them to be dumped. A barrage of about 20 shells a minute falling about the line I was going to, and so I gave it a wide berth and went up to 2nd Grenadier Headquarters instead. Noise of falling and bursting shells mixed with our guns going makes one quite deaf. The whole ground for about 30 acres has not had a square inch where a shell has not pitched, and everywhere there are 'duds' and arms and legs! The amount of equipment, ammunition, and dead bodies is too awful except that most dead are German. In my 'wildest' moment I never could have imagined a valley of about 30 acres to equal it. 2nd Battalion Grenadiers have had a bad time, luckily their casualties have only been about 10. An unpleasant barrage was put on their Reserve Trenches. Stafford turned up for dinner having spent last night in the open (his other alternative being sharing a dug out with a corpse!). 2nd Battalion Grenadiers make a small attack to straighten out the line for the big show.

September 14th. Attack a very fair success but rather costly owing to a machine gun in a sunken road. Morning spent in getting up water bombs and ammunition which was mostly done by 1st Irish Guards. In evening the 2nd and 3rd Battalion Coldstream moved up and took up the front line which was about 500 yards East and North East of GINCHY. The 2nd Battalion Grenadiers and 1st Battalion Irish Guards came up into a position of assembly and we moved Brigade Headquarters up West of GUILLEMONT. A 'murky' night if ever there was one, we took it in turns to lie down. Night was fine with a splendid moon. All the men were in excellent spirits and seemed all out for a good go at the Huns. 1,700 "Iron" rations were taken up to 2nd Grenadiers to complete them, also everyone had a good 'tot ' of Rum. Order of battle for the Division left to right: 3rd Coldstream; 2nd Coldstream; 1st Coldstream; 3rd Grenadiers, which brought the whole Regiment in line.

September 15th. Attack of the Guards Division forming part of the IVth Corps on the front running North and South of "LES BŒUFS". The two Coldstream Battalions "popped the parapet" at 6:20 a.m. After advancing for a very short distance they came under very heavy machine gun fire from right and left flanks, these guns not having been touched by our shelling. Here about 75% of their casualties occurred. 3 "Tanks", or sort of travelling forts with six machine guns and two six pounders on board proceeded the attack by ½ hour doing very little good as two of them stuck and one came back. About 11 a.m. we heard from John Campbell that they had got to 3rd Objective which afterwards proved to be only the 2nd. Later a pigeon message came from 2nd Battalion Grenadiers asking for "bombs" for Green line (2nd Objective). Several people came in and reported on Coldstream Battalions but all reports were quite different, and so we could not place them at all. Some bombs were sent up to 2nd Battalion Grenadiers by a Company of Pioneer (Coldstream) Battalion, who had a nasty job to get them up, having to go through the heavy barrage which was being kept up on the GINCHY ridge, they had 16 casualties. In the afternoon another Battalion was required to reinforce the two Coldstream Battalions who had been fairly well located, so I got a party from the 1st Battalion Grenadiers who carried ammunition and we filed up across the GINCHY ridge down and up the other side until we came to the 2nd Battalion Scots Guards in shell holes. I explained their orders to them. Left the ammunition and the party returned. I went on up to the "Green" line Objective occupied by the 2nd Battalion Grenadiers and others. The trench was so full of German dead that I had to walk outside. I could not get down to the Headquarters of the 2nd Grenadiers, but found out from an R.E. Officer where the Germans were massing for a counter attack and so made off home to get the guns onto it, which they did in about an hour. Night came on and we had to start getting rations up to the Battalions, which eventually we did by about 10 p.m., including Rum. Orders came in later that the 3rd Guards Brigade would attack through us in the morning, which we got out to the Battalions with difficulty.

September 16th. Night was spent with about ½ hour's sleep as many messages came in, we gave up our Headquarters to the 3rd Guards Brigade and went back to Dummy Trench at about 8:30 a.m. We began to realize that the 2nd Coldstream and Irish Guards Battalions were considerably North of what we thought, almost facing FLERS. Several small counter attacks were easily driven off during the day. About 5 p.m. Becky went off to go round and soon after orders came in for the 20th Division to relieve the Guards Division, so I went out and made such arrangements as were possible, came back and the Brigadier and I wrote orders. The right (2nd Grenadiers) was to be relieved by the 20th Division, which was easy but the left was to be relieved by a unit of 14th

Division. By 10:30 p.m. they had not told us who the "unit" were and so we telephoned wildly. This did not have much avail and so about 2 a.m. Merton went up and got the nearest Brigade of that Division to send someone. Meanwhile I went off and prepared tea and a meal for the men when they came out.

September 17th. It was a heart rending sight to see them come out, first the 2nd Battalion Grenadiers, some of their men were so tired they fell on the road as they marched up. Then the 2nd Battalion Coldstream which was worse as they only had two Officers left out of the 17 they took in. The 3rd Battalion had about 4 Officers, and the Irish about 7. We got into camp at the "Citadel" at about 9:30 a.m. Most awfully tired and tried to work and arrange things but I had to go to bed for a short time. Rest of day spent resting.

CASUALTIES.

	OFFICERS.				OTHER RANKS.			
	Killed	Wounded	Died of wounds	Total	Killed	Wounded	Died of wounds	Total
Second Grenadiers	1	10	3	14	79	220	38	337
Second Coldstream	4	9	2	15	67	245	128	440
Third Coldstream	3	8	0	11	36	270	90	396
First Irish	3	10	0	13	26	153	155	334
Brigade MG Coy.	1	4	0	5	19	58	10	87
T.M. Battery	0	1	0	1	4	6	0	10
Brigade H.Q.	0	0	0	0	3	9	0	12
				TOTAL: 59				TOTAL: 1,616

TOTAL FOR BRIGADE: 1675

The 2nd Battalion Coldstream Guards Officers being:-
Killed and died of wounds: Stan; Edmonstone; Fergusson; Burn; Butler.
The 3rd Battalion Coldstream Guards Officers being:-
Vaughan; Tufnell; Cubitt.

TOTAL SINCE SEPTEMBER 10th:-   59 OFFICERS.
                                                     1,785 OTHER RANKS.

September 18th. Nothing very much was done, the men sleeping late. The Brigadier went round Battalions Headquarters. A large Service in the evening for 1st and 2nd Guards Brigades. The 3rd Battalion Coldstream lost among others 'Little Man' Vaughan, Cubitt (*Capt. Henry Archibald Cubitt*), and C. E. Tufnell (*Capt. Charles Edward Tufnell*) killed, the 1st Battalion Coldstream had 9 Officers killed including Guy Baring (*Lt. Colonel The Hon. Guy Victor Baring*), and Micky Lawrence (*Capt. Michael Charles Lawrence*). The 15th September is truly one of the worst of the war for me for loss of friends. Brigadier and Merton dined out.

September 19th. Rained most of the day and most unpleasant. We worked all day nearly getting Honours and Rewards through. General John Ponsonby and Grigg dined.

September 20th. Orders to move into line just West of LES BŒUFS took most of the morning. Willie and Jack Gibbs came to luncheon both very well. Went on up to 60th Infantry Brigade Headquarters and looked round. Brigadier General Leslie Butler (late Irish Guards) gave up dinner. Took guides down to West edge of TRONES WOOD about 9:30 p.m. and got them off with two Coldstream Battalions. Brigade Headquarters very bad.

September 21st. We all slept in a row on the floor very close together. Relief complete about 6 a.m. At 9 a.m. the Brigadier and Merton went up to the line. At about 11 a.m. numerous Generals and Staff Officers arrived to take over a bit of our line. As I knew nothing about it I Could not help them much. Brigadier and Merton returned about 12 noon and got on with things. Right bit of our line taken over by 16th and 18th Infantry Brigade. Relief took a very long time as different units were relieving bits of Companies.

September 22nd. Fine and sun, so hopes of it drying up a bit as at present carts can hardly get up and guns cannot get their ammunition in sufficient quantities. Brigadier and self went up to line to see two Coldstream Battalions, finding them both fairly happy. We walked round and also had a look at the ground they advanced over on the 15th September and marvelled that any troops could have got across such a place, a quiet afternoon and very dark night. Rations went up on pack ponies.

September 23rd. Some shelling on front line during night, but not much damage. Some shelling around us most of the day but not very near. General Cavan and Prince of Wales came in about 11 a.m. Very cheery but not a great deal of news. The coming attack he thinks will be a great success. Two more dug outs being now ready we live in greater comfort, both are proof against rain but not much else. Brigadier and Barny went up to line. Afternoon I went round 2nd Grenadiers and 1st Irish also the salvage party who have collected about 200 rifles and same amount of equipment. Several Hun aeroplanes over, which were considerably shot at. One of ours was brought down during the day. Have sent up nearly 200 Tins of water and 90 boxes of rations [i.e. for 1,800 men) to advanced dump. Have collected a few souvenirs such as a rifle and about 20 shell fuse caps. Shelling continued rather heavily on front and support lines during evening and night.

September 24th. Merton and Barnard went off up about 5 a.m. to see some communication trench which 3rd Battalion Coldstream had been working on during the night, got rather straffed. Brigadier and self went up at 9 a.m. Very misty and most unpleasant walk as Huns shelling freely but we got to John Campbell's Headquarters without getting any very near us. They had a good deal of shelling throughout the night. Returned safely, had to fall flat twice. Major General and Guffin came in but no news. Sent up 100 tins more water also numbers of bombs and about 20 Trench boards. One man in Brigade went on leave. 2nd Grenadiers and 1st Irish relieved the 2nd Coldstream on right and 3rd Coldstream on left respectively. Moving off from TRONES AND BERNAFAY WOODS about 8:30 p.m. Guides were picked up at Brigade Headquarters. Men seemed in good heart for the 'morrow', each Battalion having been made up to about 500 strong. Gerald Barry came down with a "cushy" wound in the chest about 6 p.m. Night very dark but fairly quiet. Orders kept pouring in.

September 25th. A fine and sunny morning, our guns doing considerable shooting without much reply from the Huns except for several high shrapnel over TRONES WOOD and some "crumps" on WATERLOT FARM. Report came down about 9 a.m. that front was quiet but it is very clear for assembling, as Battalions are so thick in the trenches. The 2nd Grenadiers on right, 1st Irish on the left, the 2nd Coldstream Battalions being just behind. Some shelling during the morning caused several casualties. There are 3 Objectives, the 3rd being a line about 100 yards East, running North and South of LES BŒUFS. The guns by us shot normally up to 12:30 p.m., when an Officer got up in front of each Battery at "zero" hour (12:35 p.m.) the whole valley simply shook with the vibration of about 200 guns belting forth shells as fast as they could be put in, guns of every size. The Grenadiers and Irish went forward finding the first Objective fairly thickly held. The Irish got in well on the left also the left of the Grenadiers, unfortunately, the right of the Grenadiers (near "sunken road") came on 3 lines of wire uncut, this caused considerable Officer casualties and some men, including Parnell, Irving, and Arbuthnot killed. Half an hour was spent in consolidation, and onto a line just west of LES BŒUFS, here no opposition was met and the Battalions just walked in, about ¼ hour's consolidation, and on through Village to the last Objective, a few isolated Germans *in the* Village and on East side who were soon mopped up, a line was taken up and Battalions started digging in the open. No Germans in front, men walk about quite unmolested, barrage on LES BŒUFS slackened considerably. As we had a message back by 3:30 p.m. that last line held, I started up with an orderly to see the new line. A considerable barrage of big shells on our old front and support line and so we kept in the trench until we had got to get out. Got right into LES BŒUFS about 4:30 p.m. finding all 4 Commanding Officers in sunken road on West edge of LES BŒUFS. All seemed in very good heart, John Campbell rather worried as Coldstream Battalions very tired after their 6 days and they had got already 2 Companies in front line, remainder being in LES BŒUFS. Tools required and water later. Also our guns are not keeping the barrage sufficiently far in front, result several shells fell short and caused some casualties. I got back to Brigade Headquarters and gave in the full report which on the whole was satisfactory. Got back very hot and rather weary. Many congratulatory telegrams received. All Brigade Mules sent off with rations and they eventually got there somewhat late. A heavy barrage put up on LES BŒUFS but did very little damage. Most satisfactory day and on the whole, casualties slight, those of 2nd Grenadiers being heaviest. Brigade on our right (18th Infantry Brigade) got on equally well taking and holding MORVAL. Brigade on our left on first Objective which was in front of GUEUDECOURT. Two Companies from 2nd Guards Brigade sent up to form a defensive flank facing North, however so little opposition behind that it doesn't effect us much. It appears a grand opportunity for Cavalry, but one doesn't know the general situation.

September 26th. A quiet night, Merton went off up to LES BŒUFS at 5:00 a.m. I had a somewhat disturbed night owing to messages arriving every half hour. Situation still very good, a few Germans seem to be coming back in front of us, but our men can still stand about in the open. All Battalions connected up with us by telephone and they seem happy. News came in at 9:30 a.m. that we were going to be relieved by 2nd Guards Brigade, received with cheers as all very tired. Huns tried to make a counter attack North of us but just as first wave was in the open and second one was getting out, our Artillery got into them and they flew in disorder going in every direction. 3rd Guards Brigade very pleased and telephoned wildly for the Cavalry, parties of which did eventually go up into GUEUDECOURT. Our front remained fairly calm except for a heavy barrage they kept putting into LES BŒUFS. News that the French were through COMBLES. About lunch time a wire came in to say the 2nd Battalion Coldstream had had a bad bomb accident, and poor old Hal Verelst was killed, also Francis Clark and one MacGregor (*Lt. John Atholl MacGregor*). The worst bit of news for two days as up to today Verelst had been with the 2nd Battalion continuously, having never missed a single day's Company duty since August 12th 1914. Quite a record in the Army here, last real friend in any of the 4 Battalions out here. Germans kept on showing themselves which gave our artillery good targets. Our patrols pushed out well in front of LES BŒUFS, meeting very little if any opposition. Some Cavalry tried to get out in front of the 3rd Guards Brigade, i.e. South of GUEUDECOURT but did not succeed as it was too open. On several occasions counter attacks were supposed to be developing, but I think really the Hun was so rattled they were running about all over the place. About 7:30 p.m. the 2nd Guards Brigade turned up to relieve us and we got out quietly and home by 2 a.m.

September 27th. Slept rather late after only arriving at 4 a.m. After luncheon Brigadier and self went up to the Division and found out that 1st Irish and 2nd Grenadiers had got to move and so we went on to them and told them. They move to 7th (Guards) Entrenching Battalion Camp. About 5 p.m. we had orders that 2nd and 3rd Coldstream had to move just East of MÉAULTE, most uncomfortable march as it was in a thunderstorm and the ground was very slippery. Gilly Follett and Byng Pakenham to dine.

September 28th. Brigade Headquarters moved over to 3rd Coldstream Camp at 10:30 a.m. Passed a lot of dead horses, which had been killed in the night by German aeroplanes dropping bombs. Day warm and drying up. Irish Guards Band played in the Camp about 5 p.m. Machine Gun Company moved over on relief by 2nd Guards Brigade Company to Camp occupied by the 2nd Grenadiers. More rain in the evening.

September 29th. Went off early with Cook Alston to new billeting area and selected villages. Dined and slept in AMIENS.

September 30th. Returned early to find Brigade moved to just South of MÉAULTE. Moved over to MORLANCOURT about 2 p.m.

October 1st. Borrowed Prince of Wales' car and took Barny and Stafford and went over to DROMESNIL, where brigade Headquarters will be, about 50 miles. Went round area and also went down to see Transport on the road. Brigade came over in French motor buses and got in about 7 p.m.

October 2nd. Very wet. Hired a 12 h.p. Panhard in HORNOY, which broke down twice.

October 3rd. Some rain and little training. Car going rather better. Stafford got a Military Cross.

October 4th. Brigadier went round billets in car. Took Merton to Station ABBÉVILLE which went most awfully well.

October 5th. Rained considerably, Brigadier and self went round with Major General and inspected all Battalions making a speech to each. All looked very fine and marched off well.

October 6th. Brigadier went over to Divisional Headquarters to meet Army Commander Rawlinson. Rained in evening.

October 7th. Brigadier and self went to Irish Guards. Father Lane Fox came to lunch. Brigadier and I motored into ABBÉVILLE for afternoon. Tea'ed with Hermione Coke. Several breakdowns on way home, first the lights went out, then we ran out of petrol.

October 8th. Rather a wet Church. Spent most of the day preparing for the Dinner which took place at 8 p.m. 61 Officers of all departments of Guards Division came. Really a great success, they consumed 43 bottles of champagne and they eventually left about 11:30 p.m. or 12 midnight, "well oiled"!

October 9th. Somewhat "gummy" after last night's revels. Rode over to the Division with Brigadier. Spent most of the afternoon wrestling with the accounts of the dinner. Took General and Bunny Crawfurd over to dine with 3rd Coldstream at Selincourt Château. After dinner we went into the drawing room and sang with the Ladies of the house until about 10:30 p.m. Driving home without incident.

October 10th. Brigadier, A.D.V.S., and self went round Transports of Brigade in car. All horses looking very well. Afternoon we rode over to Selincourt Château and listened to the Band, having tea with the same Ladies. Heard that we don't move before 17th, which was received with cheers.

October 11th. Brigadier and self rode round. Dined with John Campbell in evening. Did not go into Ladies of the Château afterwards.

October 12th. Brigadier and self rode round Brigade area. Motored into ABBÉVILLE with Castlerosse and Mitchell (Veterinary Officer) and chose a new pony for myself. Got back about 7 p.m.

October 13th. Brigadier and self rode to HORNOY and back. Brigadier, Lane Fox, and self motored over to Rambures Château, about 16 miles. Lovely place. Got back about 5 p.m. One Hervey, Irish Guards arrived and dined. Barry took Ralph Bingham to Station in car to go on leave.

October 14th. Brigadier and self rode round Grenadiers, Irish, and Coldstream on Stafford's Grey. Brigadier went for a walk with George Lane. I shot at rabbits in the garden with my revolver, getting one. John Campbell and Jimmy Coats to dine.

October 15th. A cold Church Parade in Château grounds with rather a long sermon from Stafford. Rained most of the afternoon. Brigadier, Barny, and self took a quick walk just before tea. Fed my new pony with carrots. Brigadier and self went over and dined at Selincourt Château and talked to owners afterwards.

DUE TO A FIRE AT THE "CITADEL" THE ORIGINAL DIARY WAS BURNT.
OCTOBER 16th TO DECEMBER 1st REWRITTEN FROM MEMORY.

October 16th. Went on leave from ABBÉVILLE. Stayed at BOULOGNE the night.

October 17th. Crossed about 2 p.m. Quite calm. Met Georgie on platform at Victoria. Went to Belgrave Square.

October 18th to 31st. Spent mostly in London except for Friday to Monday at Thornbury and Tyntesfield. Billy arriving for last two days.

November 1st. Arrived back at DROMESNIL finding John Campbell commanding Brigade, Brigadier being on leave.

November 2nd. Inspection of Guards Division by the Duke of Connaught. A cold performance, but very fine sight. After the review we marched past in "fours" and so home. Lady Murray, Amy Gordon-Lennox and 3 other Ladies doing V.A.D. work at LE TRÉPORT came to lunch after.

November 3rd. Ordinary work in billets. Becky and I dined with John Campbell at Selincourt and celebrated his getting the 'V.C.' by drinking brandy out of "THE" horn after.

November 4th – 7th. Spent in a quiet life, varied by riding out after hares in the afternoon and killing about 2 a day, and with small dinners at night.

November 8th. Brigadier returned. Becky and I rode over and watched some French Battalion training.

November 9th. Day spent in arranging to go off the next day.

November 10th. The whole Brigade moved in French Buses to the CITADEL, near BRAY. Brigadier, Merton, and self going in car, lunching at AMIENS en route.

November 11th. A filthy Camp very cold and mud quite indescribable. With great difficulty we got our kit up at all.

November 12th. Very heavy firing opened some way North of us about 6:30 a.m., which eventually turned out to be the Canadians taking BEAUMONT HAMEL and about 4,000 prisoners. Brigadier and Merton went up to Battalion Headquarters, it not being possible to go further as one has to go across country. A fairly quiet day. Casualties about 6.

November 15th. Very cold. Brigadier and Merton went up towards line and returned early. I left for Camps about 12 noon. Saw A and B and got to 8th Division Headquarters about 1:30 p.m., having got twice stuck in the mud. Lunched with Cyril Daubeny, who was cheery and well. Looked round "H" Camps. 1st Coldstream (who are now attached to our group) just come in, in 2nd Grenadiers' place. A good Camp but not much room. Got back about 6 p.m. after losing my way badly once. Dug outs very cold and stores not much good.

November 16th. Very cold but fine. Division rang up to know if the General would allow me to go to the 25th Brigade as Brigade Major, which was answered in the affirmative. Whitaker and I went up to Battalion Headquarters in the line and found them both (2nd Coldstream, and 1st Irish) very uncomfortable. Spent the afternoon trying to keep warm. Sent up a lot of "Duck Boards" (footboards for trenches) on Mules and Trench Mortar Battery to "Needle Dump". Also some "Very" lights etc. for small operation that is coming off.

November 21st. Went down to Sandpits to arrange camps. Found that 4th Grenadiers and 2nd Scots Guards had gone to Brigade Headquarters billets and had a few words in turning them out. Came down to MÉAULTE to see 2nd Coldstream and 2nd Grenadiers. Spent a very cold night as my hut was a perfect wind trap.

November 22nd. Brigadier and Merton arrived about 12 noon and wrote a strong protest to 3rd Guards Brigade on these other two Battalions taking all the beds and tables from Brigade Headquarters. Brigadier and self walked round Headquarters of Battalions. At 6 p.m. (less Red Tabs and Blue Band!) I went down and took over Command of 2nd Battalion Coldstream Guards from Jimmy Coats who was the Adjutant. Found I really only know 4 Officers and names of about 6 others.

November 23rd. Went round billets in morning. After lunch Merton, Jonah Bailey, Prince of Wales, and self went into AMIENS in the Prince's car. Got there about 5 p.m., went round the shops buying all sorts of parcels. The Prince insisted on carrying most of them. Dined at Golbert's Restaurant, had a very big dinner, the Gendarmes came and turned us out at 11 p.m., (we were then dancing in one of the small rooms, after a few words of "encouragement" to the Chefs) we went off getting back to MÉAULT at 1:30 a.m.

November 24th. Had my orders at 10:30 a.m., after, going up to the Brigade Headquarters for a conference at 11:30 a.m. Lunched there and after we had a conference of Coldstream Commanding Officers to discuss the dating of certain Officers Commissions.

November 25th. Raining hard. Brigadier came round billets of Battalion at 10:30 a.m. Continued raining all day. Had a conference of Company Commanders at 2 p.m. Went for a walk with Jimmy Coats.

December 2nd. Froze hard during the night. Went round billets and rode off to 2nd Guards Brigade Headquarters in 'Citadel' to get news, but gathered none. Lunched at 1st Guards Brigade Headquarters. Had conference with Company Commanders most of the afternoon. A quick walk with Medical Officer and wrote most of the evening. Preparing for moving off to COMBLES the next day.

December 3rd. Marched off at 9 a.m., Companies at 200 yards interval and eventually got up to COMBLES, having had dinners en route and a slight difference of opinion with one of the Military Police.

December 4th. Spent in COMBLES area which is not a very salubrious spot. Had to find some fatigue parties.

December 5th. Went up to SAILLY-SAILLISEL Château and had lunch with the Colonel of the 160th Regiment and very nice fellow with a big staff. Fixed up about relief and came down with McCalmont.

December 6th. Jimmy Coats and one Officer per Company went up very early to the Château and stayed the day. The Battalion moved up about 6:00 p.m. from BOIS DE LA HAIE with a French guide per platoon. A very quiet relief completed at about 10:00 p.m. The French Colonel however stayed until about 6:30 a.m. Brigadier General Lord H. Seymour Commanding the right group came round the front line with me. We found it very disconnected but fair. Nos: 3 & 4 in front line No: 2 support and No: 1 in reserve.

December 7th. French left one Officer per Company for extra 24 hours. Went up again by day to line and made arrangements for No: 1 Company to take over from No: 1 Company of 2nd Battalion Scots Guards on our left and No: 4 to come back in reserve. This was completed by 10 p.m. I went up round new bit and found it bad and much undercut.

December 8th. Byng Hopwood came up and made arrangements as to relief. They got up about 6 p.m. and the relief was carried out very quietly and complete by 10 p.m. Casualties 1 Other Rank slightly wounded. Battalion marched back to MALTZHORN Camp (near TRONES WOOD) all being in by about 1:30 a.m.

December 9th. Paraded again at 10 a.m. and got very crowded train from TRONES WOOD siding to the Plateau, getting in about 12:30 p.m. Afternoon spent in sleep.

December 10th. Wet day and so very little done.

December 11th. Battalion paraded at 11.30 a.m. and marched up to the COMBLES area, having dinners on arrival. One unlucky shell into the last platoon of No: 1 Company which killed 7 and wounded 9 others.

December 12th. Heavy fatigues for Battalion in rain. We moved off at 4:00 p.m. to relieve the 3rd Battalion. Some shelling at SAILLY which caught one or two, but not many. Relief complete by 9:30 p.m. I went round finding trenches in most awful state, really almost untenable. I got in about 3 a.m.

December 13th. Went round Reserve Company trenches. They were wet and bad. Château got shelled till 12 noon, but no damage. Brigadier (Seymour) came up as far as Support Company, but could take him no further owing to bad communication trenches. Went round right Company at night and got sniped at.

December 14th. Went round Left front Company at 6 a.m. Very quiet but could not stay long owing to light coming on. Steven Burton and 1st Battalion came up about 6 p.m. Château very heavily shelled at 7 p.m., but very little damage. Men in dreadful state of fatigue and bad feet, and last lot got in about 4 a.m.

December 15th. Had to parade at 10 a.m. again to catch the train to TRONES WOOD. I have seldom seen great coats so wet, dirty, and heavy. By 10:45 a.m. we were all on and travelled down with 3rd Battalion Grenadiers. Train takes 20 minutes and is a cold journey in open coal trucks. Got in about 12 noon with a somewhat depleted Battalion, there being many cases of feet (*Trench Foot*), and some of absolute physical exhaustion. After examination by Medical Officer we sent 5 cases to Hospital and kept 40 for treatment, which is really very creditable. Everyone was still very weary, and consequently bed saw most people about 9 p.m.

December 16th. Battalion starting to look a little better, but as drying room is not yet going, great coats have not got a chance. Rifles and smoke helmets were the only things looked at. Arthur Hope from 3rd Battalion living with us.

December 17th. Battalion did a few fatigues in camp, parading at 3 p.m. and entraining at the Plateau. Raining hard when we got to TRONES WOOD siding. Walked to COMBLES where Battalion was billeted: two Companies in COMBLES trench; one in COMBLES Station dug-outs: and one in BOIS DE LA HAIE. Went in and saw Brigadier (Pereira) who had just taken over Command of right group sector and lived in the Catacombs.

December 18th. Fatigue for whole Battalion in the morning, mostly carrying R.E. Material to front line. Men had dinners at BOIS DE LA HAIE. Relieved 3rd Coldstream and installed in SAILLY-SAILLISEL by 7:30 p.m.

December 19th. A quiet and frosty night had greatly improved the trenches and dried them up. No: 3 Company was on the left and No: 4 Company on the right. Holding of the front line being a succession of posts.

December 20th. A further frost had greatly improved the going and walking about on the top during the night was quite easy. The 1st Battalion Coldstream arrived about 5 p.m. and relief was complete by about 7 p.m. Companies got out very quickly and left very few stragglers. All the Battalion was at TRONES WOOD siding by 10:30 p.m. and ready to start by that hour. Unfortunately the engine did not arrive until 12 midnight and we all got very cold waiting. The 2nd Battalion Scots Guards came down with us. Got into BRONFAY Camp by 1:30 a.m. and to bed.

December 21st. Battalion up by about 11:30 a.m. The frost had turned to rain, which will make all the trenches fall in. Day spent in brushing up.

December 22nd. Rain again and so little to do. Battalion had to do a short fatigue. "Judge" Baynes dined with us.

December 23rd. Not a very pleasant Birthday. Battalion paraded at 12 noon. Went by train from Plateau to TRONES. A wet march to COMBLES. New Battalion Headquarters in a cellar, which will be good, but at present there is no fire and very draughty, which was not pleasant as we were all feeling very ill with a sort of flue, and I had Neuralgia as well. Battalion distributed; Nos: 3 & 4 COMBLES trench; No: 1 BOIS DE LA HAIE; No: 2 in a work up by the Intermediate Line, with two sections in another Strong Point. Very wet, an unpleasant night.

December 24th. Two Companies on fatigue carrying and digging. Battalion relieved the 3rd Coldstream, taking over very bad trenches on account of the rain. All in by 6:45 p.m.

December 25th. Christmas Day. I started round the trenches at 3:15 a.m. when it was raining hard, found them very wet but liveable. Very quiet. Remained in front trench for "Stand To" in case there should be any "Fraternizing", but no sign of it. Communication trench up barely passable. Rain and cold most of the day. Our guns did two short bombardments which brought very little retaliation.

December 26th. Another wet night, which meant bailing continuously and a few men actually standing in water. 1st Coldstream arrived and we were away by 5:50 p.m. R. Bewicke-Copley was killed on December 20th, very sad – a great friend of mine. (Captain Redvers Lionel Calverley Bewicke-Copley).

December 27th. Having got Battalion to TRONES WOOD by 10 p.m., we got the train off at once and we were in by 12 midnight. A very wet lot, but got a change of jackets and trousers for the worst. Battalion bathed during afternoon and got a change of underclothing. "Judge" Baynes and Sutton Nelthorpe to dinner and we had an "Xmas Dinner".

December 28th. Stafford came up and we had one Christmas Service with Welsh Guards Band. After lunch Welsh Guards Band played from 3:00 to 5:00 p.m. Not a very large attendance of men. Fine and frosty. We found 400 men to work on the roads and Camp, in improving it. Greatcoats of men still very wet and muddy.

December 29th. Caught 6 p.m. train at Plateau with some difficulty as no one was about who knew anything about it. A somewhat unpleasant walk from TRONES WOOD to COMBLES as they put 5 x 5.9" shells just over us – LEUZE WOOD, however no casualties.

December 30th. Two Companies on carrying fatigue. Relieved 3rd Coldstream about 7 p.m., quiet and quick relief, Nos: 3 & 4 in front line, 2 in support, and 1 in reserve. Martyn from No: 1 had to go to No: 4 as Thompson went sick and there were only two Officers. Since we have been out it has rained considerably and the trenches are in an awful state, falling in, and in 2 or 3 places almost knee high in water where the men stand. I think the German trenches must be nearly as bad as they are so wonderfully quiet, not sniping at all.

December 31st. Our Artillery carried out a small bombardment which brought some retaliation on the Château and on the Reserve line. Luckily I had taken the precaution to thin out to half the Reserve line and brought 40 men into the Château, result – not a single casualty all day. Companies carried on with wiring after dark, and doing whatever they could to their trenches. About 11 p.m. a very frightened German wandered into our line trying to find his own, and we took him prisoner. He had been in Hospital and had been sent up to join his Regiment. He was a very poor specimen belonging to the King William of Wurtemburg's Regiment. Laing at Battalion Headquarters interrogated him. He was very wet and hated war. So we fed him and he went to sleep.

1917

January 1ˢᵗ. Germans made no demonstration at 11 p.m. (Their New Year). I was in front line for "Stand To" 6:15 a.m. – 7:15 a.m., but nothing happened. General George Jeffries, the new Brigadier replacing General "Pinto" came in to see us. "Pinto" left about 3 days previous amid the most profound regret of everyone. He goes in Command of the 2nd Division. Seldom was a Brigadier more liked and absolutely trusted as he was. Relieved by 1st Battalion Coldstream about 7 p.m., very quiet, completed by 9 p.m. and we walked down to TRONES WOOD. Companies came in well and the train started at 11:30 p.m. The 2nd Battalion Scots Guards (Commended by Jack Stirling) were on board too. Got into BONFRAY Camp (15) by about 1 a.m.

January 2ⁿᵈ. Slept almost till lunch time, after that day spent in preparing to go off to MÉAULTE tomorrow, and right back for 3 weeks on the 11th.

January 3ʳᵈ. Paraded at 10:15 a.m. and marched 500 yards between Companies to MÉAULTE took over billets in main street. Not very good and rather small. I retired to bed with a severe chill in my inside. Terrible bad news was sprung upon us, our rest is put off and we go into the worst bit of the line again on the 9th. Everyone very depressed and now fussing to get the Men's dinners put on the 6th, so as to get them over, but it will be a great rush.

January 4ᵗʰ. Got up at 11:30 a.m. feeling somewhat better. Conference at Brigade Headquarters. Tried to clean up the billets and streets a bit.

January 5ᵗʰ. Got many kind letters of congratulations for my Military Cross. Companies did training in billets.

January 6ᵗʰ. Battalion had Christmas Dinners, which included Pork and vegetables, 2 Pints of Beer a man and Plum Puddings. They lasted till about 3 or 4 p.m. Dined at Brigade Headquarters.

January 7ᵗʰ. Another Conference at 2 p.m., dealing with the coming situation, and also training for the Brigade during the time we are in rest.

January 8ᵗʰ. Longueville, "Judge" Baynes, Acland-Hood, and self rode over to the Citadel to attend a lecture given by a gas expert from General Headquarters. Rather interesting, a sticky ride, my pony taking one heavy fall and depositing me on my back.

January 9ᵗʰ. Rain stopped a Battalion parade, but Companies did some drill. Rode over to VILLE to look at new billets with Grubby Gage.

Concert given this Battalion by Troupe of 3rd Coldstream.

January 10th. Most of the morning spent in packing up. Battalion paraded at 3 p.m. and marched at 500 yards between Companies to VILLE. No: 4 and half No: 3 still being at the Citadel, it left Nos: 1 & 2 and ½ No:3 to march only. Brigadier met Battalion and watched it march past.

January 11th. Commanding Officer's orders at 9 a.m. and then 6 of us rode off to No: 9 Squadron R.F.A. and were shown round all the machines. We were to be taken up after lunch, but as it was snowing this was put off. Lecture by Brigadier at 3 p.m. on trench fighting and bombing.

January 12th. Brigadier inspected billets at 10 a.m. making many suggestions as to the improvement of them. Rained at intervals throughout the morning.

January 13th. Improved billets. Drill etc.

January 14th. Drill and General instruction. Rode up to BRIQUETERIE and saw our 100 Other Ranks and 2 officers. They are fairly comfortable but have strenuous fatigues. Got back on a lorry.

January 15th. Drill, hard frost which improved the ground for drill.

January 16th. Brigadier paid a surprise visit to our billets and was rather disappointed with amount of work done. Rode over to MÉRICOURT to look at rifle range.

January 17th. Snow had fallen quite thick during the night and was 5 foot deep making all drill and outside work impossible. Went into AMIENS in R.F.C. car and dined there.

January 18th. Snow somewhat disappeared by rain but everything very slushy. Bunny Crawford came over, after returning from 30 days leave.

January 19th. Ordinary Training.

January 20th. Training in morning. After lunch went in a "Tender" to AMIENS with O'Brien and Baynes and Stafford. Dined and returned. Very cold.

January 21st. Brigadier came round billets.

January 22nd. Had a Battalion Parade at 9 a.m. Got a Tender at 11 a.m. and with Baynes we got to AMIENS; lunched Godbers; caught 3:18 p.m. train to PARIS arriving 5:30 p.m. Got 2 rooms, bathroom etc. at the Edouard VII. Dined at Café de Paris.

January 23rd. Lunched "Henry" with Castlerosse. Dined at Maxim's. Very good dinner and amusing place. Went on to Olympia.

January 24th. Lunched Ritz. Very few people there. Saw Ralph Lambton also Geoffrey Glynn. Dined Paillard's and on to Concert Moyler. Quite a good show. Budget Lloyd had joined us by this time.

January 25th. Caught the 10:05 a.m. train to AMIENS. Bitterly cold. Lunched at the Savoy Restaurant and got a car through Rudolph de Trafford. Found Battalion at BILLON Camp near MARICOURT. Everything freezing at about 12° below freezing point.

January 26th. Have never known cold to touch this. Men cannot be kept standing more than 5 minutes. Training taking place mostly in the huts. Braziers are lit everywhere and parties sent out to "find"! wood. Battalion well off for room. Officers rather crowded as Machine Gun Company and T. M. Battery have to come in as well.

January 27th. Everything inside the huts freezing, including wine and soda water which frequently break their bottles. Billon Camp is right on top of everything. Training continued in huts. Lewis Guns being fired in the valley near by. Brigadier came over at 2:30 p.m. and went through the Orders written by this Battalion on a scheme which he proclaimed quite good.

January 28th. A Voluntary Service in the Guards Division Soldiers Club Hut at 11:15 a.m., which was very well attended including, the Brigadier. After, the Brigadier and self went round the transport and some billets. Still very cold. Brigadier came and interviewed two men for Commissions, casting one of the candidates who was not quite up to the mark.

On January 28th Brigadier General Walter Long C.M.G., D.S.O. of the Second Dragoons (Royal Scots Greys) commanding the 56th Infantry Brigade, 19th Division was killed in action. He was killed by a hostile shell while inspecting the front line trenches near the junction of "Yankee Street" and "The Red Line" in front of Hebuterne village near Arras. He was 37 years old. He had been invested as a Companion of the Order of St Michael and St George and was decorated with the award of the Order of St Stanislaus of Russia (Second Class with swords). His sister, Victoria de Burgh Gibbs, her husband George Abraham Gibbs M.P., and all the family were devastated at the news. He was buried in Couin British Cemetery.

January 29th. Cold about the same. Training as usual. Brigadier came round and noticed several points.

January 30th. Companies trained on assaults and extended order. Snow most of afternoon.

January 31st. Company Commanders and self started off about 10 a.m. for PRIEZ FARM to reconnoitre routes to the trenches. Got a lift on

DECAVILLE Railway for short way. Got there by 12 midday. Went up as far as Intermediate Line. Lunched with 3rd Coldstream. After lunch man picking in doorway of our hut struck a German bomb which went off wounding two R.E., most unpleasant, it covered us with dust. Got a car out of the Division to bring us back to Billon Farm. Snow had made roads very slippery and bad, but we got back safely.

Figure 58. Brigadier General Walter Long, Victoria Gibbs' brother - Toby.

February 1st. Cold as ever. Training continued.

February 2nd. Training.

February 3rd. Specially good trenches North East of Billon Wood allotted to us and used by Nos: 1 & 2 & 4 Companies. Brigadier came over and watched them.

February 4th. Service by Stafford at 9:45 a.m. He started early and so was late. Spent day keeping warm.

February 5th. Ordinary training. Preparing for move tomorrow. Ralph Bingham and 'Judge' Baynes came in to dinner. Budget Lloyd came in afterwards.

February 6th. Had breakfast at 7:30 a.m., very cold morning. Battalion paraded at 8:30 a.m. and marched @ 500 yards interval between Companies to PRIEZ FARM. East of MAUREPAS to relieve the 1st Battalion Irish Guards in immediate support of Front line held by 3rd Guards Brigade. 5 fatigue parties of about 20 men taken over. Quiet and somewhat misty.

February 7th. Went with Brigadier General Corkran and Guffin Heywood up to right Battalion Headquarters, then struck across country to left Battalion Headquarters on the PÉRONNE road. It was wonderful to see the thickness of the ice where a shell had landed in an old shell hole, sometimes quite a foot thick. Lunched with Norman Orr Ewing and Kit Cator, of the 2nd Battalion Scots Guards, left Battalion and had a look at the Support line. Got back to PRIEZ FARM about 4 p.m.

February 8th. Attack by 17th Division in SAILLISEL at 7:30 a.m., most successful getting their objective and about 62 Prisoners. Enemy shelled PRIEZ all day with 5.9"s, mostly at Guns in ravine behind. Some going very close to Battalion Cookers, but not actually hitting them.

February 9th. A quiet, sunny but cold day. Went down to No: 1 Company at MAUREPAS.

February 10th. Some shells over but wide of us. Moved Cookers up to a safer spot.

February 11th. Advanced party from 2nd Battalion Irish Guards having arrived, Battalion marched to MAUREPAS Ravine to new billets. Route chosen across country, however the path had several 5.9"s on to it, and so the road was selected. Then 5 or 6 x 4.2"s got direct hits on the road, and so eventually all Companies went across country. Battalion rather squashed in "Nissen" huts but all the warmer for it.

February 12th. Frost looked like breaking. Companies drilled most of the morning.

February 13th. Roads getting quite muddy. Two Companies taken by the

Sergeant Major and Drill Sergeant for an hour. I started to go up to Left Battalion Headquarters, but owing to heavy bombardment by our guns, was advised not to (I took this advice!). Phillips, (The Divisional Signals Officer), and Barny O'Brien to dinner.

February 14th. Froze again during night. Men had their feet done by new method, and relieved 3rd Coldstream in evening, very quiet.

February 15th. Frost still holding and line easy to go round. We hold 11 posts in front line. 5 in Support and 2 Companies in Reserve round Battalion Headquarters. A quiet day.

February 16th. Not much work can be done yet although it does not freeze so hard. Relief of front 2 Companies by 2 in Reserve and Front line divided into 2 halves, each front Company having 2 platoons in front and 2 in Support.

February 17th. I went down about 11 a.m. to Brigade Headquarters to go on leave, and Bunny Crawford took Battalion. Unfortunately I met the Major General who would not allow me to go, so back I went into the line.

February 18th. Relieved by 3rd Coldstream, very quiet. Back in MAUREPAS Camp by 10:30 p.m. Casualties 3 men wounded during whole tour. Big explosion at Plateau.

February 19th. Day spent in cleaning. Heavy thaw set in and mud reappearing.

February 20th. Some drill, but mud very sticky.

February 21st. Training in camp due to rain.

February 22nd. Stephen Burton having turned up, he and I took the Battalion up to trenches to relieve 3rd Coldstream. Very quiet, I returned with Bunny.

February 23rd. Geoffrey Holmesdale arrived with a car at 9:00 a.m. and he and I proceeded to AMIENS to go on leave. Got to BOULOGNE about 5:00 p.m. and went to Hôtel de Paris.

February 24th. Very calm. Crossed at 11 a.m. and in London by 3 p.m. Nancy rolled up from York about 6 p.m. Really feel I am "on leave" at last.

No Diary February 25th to November 23rd.

During this time Lancelot M. Gibbs went on a Month's Leave.

Then he was listed as sick in Regimental Records.

6 Sheet Street.
WINDSOR.

26th July 1917

Dearest Nancy

I saw Captain Fox, Scots Guards last night who escaped from Schwarmstadt about 4 weeks ago and he told me the following.

1. Evelyn is very well and seems happy with several friends. He takes a good deal of exercise and is allowed out 4 times a week on "parole".
2. Schwarmstadt is not nearly such a good place as Crefeld as there are no Tennis courts or Fives etc.
3. Washing arrangements are bad, there being only several pumps in the yard and no basins which entails their going out and standing under the cold water and pumping it over them.
4. They have to wait in long "queues" for parcels, pay and anything that is being given out.
5. Evelyn has 4 in his mess counting a Petty Officer who is their cook which he say he does very well.
6. They rely almost entirely on English parcels. The German food being only soup twice a day and coffee about 3 or 4 times a day.
7. It is very important to vary the food which goes out from here as much as possible as they get sick of the same things very quickly.
8. Food should now go much further as there are no Russian or French prisoners to feed from the English parcels.
9. To think the Germans <u>do not take</u> things out of the parcels.

The Commandant is rather full of his own importance but the German orderlies are good and kind.

Your loving

Lags

September 9th 1917
Offiziergefangenenlagen, Schwarmstadt,
Hanover.

Darling Nance

I hope this will prove to be, as I had hoped the last would be, the last letter from this country – as far as we can judge everything seemed to be settled some time ago and only patience was required before we (old ones) should be off to Holland – nothing more has transpired either way since, so I imagine it to be imminent, anyway I pray so, as even tethers have an end. I have a great many excellent, though somewhat belated, letters to acknowledge and will begin at once.

Your own of July 29 – I got Walter R's of June 22 shortly after.

Worsley and Evans (inseparable) and P Boyle are all here, I know each slightly, all very nice – also G. Smith – the last and I have met re your and his brothers letters – he is better but still affected bronchially a good bit. I wonder if Staff is staying at home now, <u>he</u> will find it hard I expect though we all know he has done a splendid bit – if he goes off again I hope you will come a bit further South and out of that climate of York.

Georgie – July 8 – very glad to hear of my ponies. I am wondering if the 3 year old might not come to Heidelberg for me to try my practice hand on as a breaker in, but don't expect at all that it is possible, funny how they all differ, the 3 youngsters.

Craig is well and sends his love.

Via July 8 – I don't think you will now ever get my first to Georgie, he must have got lost, I declare. Parcels arrived in great quantities lately but what gallons of milk! – Isn't there a mistake somehow, it causes for C S Stores and Cobbett's, masses of it. A bathing pool would be very nice where the old Conservatory was, a pretty one to act as a garden pond to, it seems to be readymade nearly from all accounts. Oh! the guilt of 1864 what a lot there was! Terrible. It is most splendid that all the Annesleys have got that money – they do indeed deserve it – for old Jack too could have made a great use of it. Caryl and Will going well I hear.

Blanche June 23 and July 23 – List of subs to Eton then has not arrived but there is one here I believe and I'll get hold of that. I asked Lags to send a set for me equal to his own. Yes it is indeed lucky you are so honest, what a good thing is a good upbringing – we will have an audit dinner one day, ale and all and I'll pay.

Huie July 20 – give my love to Ralph Webber, he and I have drifted far apart, but I have always a warm corner for him for old sake's sake and so on.

Elaine June 1st, July 1st and 30th, and 2 additions by Mercy. Her governess sounds to be having an amusing time.

Albinia July 17 – I should so like to go with her to Eton as a proud brother – last time we were there together it was so different, I hoped she would have "decent" clothes etc., and as far as I remember, she did! How does Zander like Alington, the young ones here say he was very good as an undermaster, though his nickname was appalling. So glad Zander is going to be a Green Jacket nicer than the S.L.I. I think. Though the latter are so good.

Lags July 22 – glad he saw our little red rover, nice, fat and throws his tongue well. Bisham Abbey was a masterpiece of ideas, also I know none of the co-takers. Remember me to Miss Honor Leigh if you see her, I am so sorry about her and G.S., she could have done nothing else and for Lady A. to make a fuss and say H. L. treated G. badly is too wicked, for 20 years Lady A. did not seem to know she had a son even and that anyone but herself existed – certainly not her fault that G.S. is such a good fellow. My love to Christopher, I am longing to meet him as a Coldstreamer. I agree re mess, "tea any day" always meant no day for me too.

Uncle R. July 25 – seems to work too hard, don't cut out all holidays. Friend Metclaf was a good riddance for us evidently. I suppose you are again busy as Ex since Stephen Burton's death, what a tragic end to the family, 3 sons killed.

Aunt C. July 8 and 22 – I do indeed remember Weston Super Mare after measles, but had forgotten the details.

Billy, May 14, July 7, 18, 27 and Ruby July 10 – so glad he has got Cooper back by no matter what means. My love to Mrs. Tabor, I am so very sorry about Denis T's maladie, such a good fellow. That leaves Teddy T of C.G's heir, unless S. J. T. gets a son, unlikely now. I wonder if Judy remembered her old haunts at Aldershot, she promenaded a lot with Draper. That's the lot, and parcels of much more recent dates, all my gratitude for all.

I wonder so much if my list, and subsequent additions to it, of clothes etc. wanted in Holland will have arrived. If it did and if the things were sent to *Mees* and *Loosen* as I suggested (though quite likely it was impossible) they will be there before me, which I little thought possible when I first wrote, when I was under the impression we were off at once. Other additions now are rather difficult to think of. I seem to have mentioned most things. My typewriter would be very useful in Holland – it is in a leather case in my room at 22, Belgrave Square, in fact it will be <u>very</u> useful there, so please include it.

I know its keyboard more or less and should have to relearn another. Also my Golf clubs – you notice I want to try and enjoy life again. For books, I want the complete series of English history, where each period is called "England under the Stuarts", "England under the Tudors" etc etc. All new and old novels dealing with present day which are really good. The last Volume of Disraeli's life, when published. Complete series of "Makers of 19th Century", except A.

Lincoln, which Edith Gibbs sent me. Hatchard's latest catalogue of books – an order at Mudie's for 4 or 6 books a month. That's all.

I <u>hope</u> to get a house there with Captain Wavell Paxton and possibly 1 other, but I don't know if it will be possible – also spare rooms. Bless you, dear heart, and for all of you my only blessing for so well caring for your pinioned relative. I am reading up Falconry a new sport to me.

My love to all.

Your very loving

Evelyn

October 13th 1917

My dear Nancy

Thank you for your very nice letter. I can see you all rosy with joy at having Staff safe with you. I am <u>delighted</u> he has resigned Bishopsthorpe he is destined for something so much bigger. How I envy Cosmo and Aidan! No better form of spat than going after anything – but not in Passchendael the importance of which Staff will no doubt explain. It's a fine race with winter whether we get it or not.

I hope to get a holiday when operations do stop, middle or end of November; not been to England since May. The two <u>real</u> signs of German deterioration are –

1st that it is necessary to have what they call 'Welfare' Officers to preach propaganda to their soldiers in the trenches!

2nd that each speech of Michaelis or Kuhlemann gives away a <u>little</u> and they fix on Alsace Lorraine now as a Never Never Land. It used to be Antwerp or Brussels.

I agree with every syllable of Asquith's speech at Liverpool, Times of 12th. Pity Lloyd George can't speak like that – so much more convincing in a Prime Minister than "We'll give 'em Hell" and such like droopings.

The jolly old Guard have again most gloriously distinguished themselves. October 9, they advanced very nearly 2 miles – took 2 Field Guns, 26 Machine Guns and 1000 prisoners – then 3rd Brigade on 12th enlarged the gains and made the left of the Army secure. Now they come out to rest and real billets away, away back and my heart is sore at losing them but rejoicing in their glory. I feel quite sure though that Sir D. H. will join us up again somehow someday.

Weather is indescribably awful and the chief is making big decisions today as to future policy. Second Army are near to the mobilisation level.

Tell Staff I can't help feeling cocky that again the old XIV Cups is out beyond the other hounds just as we were after Langemarck. I told Inez and I meant it – that it is chiefly because I ask God for <u>exactly</u> what I want and sing loud Te Deums to Him when I get it! He may think it queer and odd but it is sincere.

Then I'm blessed with the best Staff in the world by ruthlessly drafting the weaklings.

Forgive this ebullition but I always was a bit cocky and I'm in glorious form just now and let my pen run with my spirits.

If you never loose the curb you'll sour the temper.

Yours ever

Cavan

Absender:
Captain Gibbs
Room 50
Offiziergefangenenlager Freiburg, Baden

November 15th 1917

Darling Nan

You see I have changed camp once more, and have returned to Baden. I am comfortable here, in a small room, 5 of us, which is a Godsend as most of the rooms are *heated* luckily. I am one of the seniors here, my companions are ---- (he and I have been together all the time) Murray (who was at Reg Dawes) Craig (M.P. and friend of George Gibbs) and one other. We were moved from Holzminden at short notice.

It is an excellent exchange for us. Here it is peaceful and the minimum of worry. There it was all the reverse. The houses at Holzminden were better in that they were new and modern but cooking our food was made as difficult as possible. The servants were taken away from us at all hours and were locked up is a separate building from 6 p.m. to 8 a.m.

Here the building is the old University, a jolly old place round a miniature Quadrangle. Very thick walls and old beams, rather dark, gas lighting and good stoves on each landing for cooking, very convenient.

We have long walks twice a week, and two short ones, which go on while the young play football on a very good grass field outside the town – so one gets out 4 times a day into the country, which is very pretty, the fields and first row of woods are low ---- and going off. What pleased me most about ---- coming here was that I knew that Tollemeche was here (although only that he was at Freiburg) and so I have got pretty recent news of many at home and am delighted to see him also (he has jumped over me as he is a Lt. Col. now).

Altogether I am very glad to be here, all the Coldstream officers, except Christie Mella came with us and we also left Jack Coke and one Gough.

Send messages to W. Davenport from me. I hear he is much better, but do not know if he is recovering from a wound or disease?

Also do not let him miss anything or want anything that I could supply.

Love to Draper and Wood also. Will you send me two Hymn books with the music in – not too heavy or thick, but the music is the important – I want to catch my tenor and bass.

Evelyn

On November 24th 1917, Major Lancelot Merivale Gibbs returned to France.

November 24th. Left Belgrave Square at 10:30 a.m. for Waterloo – Georgie, Via and Blanche coming to see me off – train did not leave till 11:55 a.m. Special for Officers only. Got to Southampton at 2:30 p.m. Took a long time to report and take my bags round to S.S."Marguerite", which was a perfectly filthy boat; no cabins and very much a transport; walked into town and sent postcards to friends ! "High Tea" at 5:15 p.m. in South Western Hotel and went on board after 6 p.m. and got a seat to lie on. Left quay at 8:30 p.m. and anchored off Netley until 11 p.m., when they put out. Kept at it for one hour and then found it too rough and came back into Southampton and anchored about 2 a.m.

November 25th. We landed about 7:30 a.m. and had a bath and breakfast in the Hotel. Rang up on the telephone. Met Ralph Webber and walked up to Rest Camp of American Troops with him, of which he is Inspector. About 2 miles out. Back to Southampton and found we were due to start out again to-night. Reported at 4 p.m. and was on board at 5 p.m. we put out at 5 past 6 p.m., anchoring off "Needles" until 11:30 p.m., when we faced the "raging deep" and had a very rough crossing.

November 26th. Got into LE HAVRE at 5 a.m. and landed at 7:30 a.m.: breakfast in rather dirty café and out to the Base depot; found about 10 Officers there. Commanding Officer Major Royds, Adjutant Boyd Rochfort V.C. Met Lewinsky who used to be at Miss Evans' with me.

November 27th. A quiet morning and into LE HAVRE in afternoon to shop.

November 28th. A quiet fine day. No news of my going up. Guards Division appear to have been in very hot place at BOURLON WOOD.

November 29th. Nothing to do; went with Boyd Rochfort into Bazaar at Le Havre. Had to buy numerous tickets for raffles: met a Mrs. Neville, friend of Blanche's. Watched boxing, dull except for 2 blacks (West Indies) who fought well.

November 30th. Lewinsky left for England having been transferred from the Royal West Kents to the Scots Guards.

December 1st. Codrington (Coldstream Guards) and draft of 20 arrived. Watched a bad football match. Much colder ending in rain. Feeling very depressed as I get no letters here and have written about 30 during the week. Rumour that 1st Coldstream have been badly knocked about.

December 2nd. Went to Early Service in Church Hut. Very cold, rain and sleet. Pearson (son of St Dunstan's – P) came in and saw me and we walked through HARFLEUR and back. Read whole evening.

December 3rd. Irish Guards Band arrived and Officer conducting "Livingston-Learmouth". Colder than ever. Dined with Pearson (RPA) in LE HAVRE and got back about 9:30 p.m.

December 4th. Irish Guards went up and still no news of my going up. Heard some news of attack near CAMBRAI, which was not too good.

December 5th. Very cold; spent entire day trying to get warm.

December 6th. (Founder's Day) Froze hard. Got orders to go up to-night. Was made O.C. Train, so had to march down whole party, about 800. Some difficulty about entraining some Australians who had 'had a couple'. Had 2 other fellows in my carriage. Slept little.

December 7th. Got to ROUEN about 7:30 a.m. Went up to Hôtel de la Poste for shave and breakfast: reported again at 9:30 a.m. and got orders to go on at 10:30 p.m. Lunched and dined at Hôtel de la Poste, met Arthur Llewellyn who is commanding a base section, and talked until I left. Made O.C. Train again with one other Officer.

December 8th. First real stop, ALBERT, about 8:30 a.m., then on to ACHIET-LE-GRAND and then BOISLEUX where I got out. Got a lift in an A.S.C. car to BEAUMETZ, when I walked about 4 - 5 miles to 2nd Guards' Brigade Headquarters where I found Budget Lloyd and Colonel Ardee. Budget rather depressed over the loss of his brother, who was killed last week. Guards Division sent a car for me. Went to see Gilly and Edwin at 2nd Coldstream for tea. Back to BEAUMETZ to pick up my luggage and servant (Nutall). Thence to FOSSIEUX to Headquarters Guards Division, where I stay until 4th Coldstream return on Monday.

December 9th. Becky and I went to Church in YMCA hut. Raining hard. Took a walk before lunch and again before tea.

December 10th. Went round billets of 4th Coldstream with Acland-Hood (for DAA and QMG Guards Division) and Blacker, billeting Officer of 4th Battalion. Went in car with Becky and Billy Wynne-Finch to 1st Guards Brigade in BERNEVILLE. Went and saw Longueville and Bingham of our 3rd Battalion. After that on to 2nd Battalion Grenadiers and saw Guy Rasch and Bailey, also Brigadier General De Crespigny (GOC 1st Guards Brigade) on to lunch with 2nd Coldstream with Gilly and Edwin Brassey. After lunch I looked up Breirly; Firbank; St Leger; Fellows and others. Tea and then home to Guards Division on my old "wholer" pony that I had when with 1st Guards Brigade and chose at Remount Camp at ABBÉVILLE in October 1916. Dined with Guards Division Major General (Feilding) just returned from PARIS. Returned to billets about 11 p.m. Battalion got in about ¼ to 1 a.m., having marched from BEAUMETZ and so to bed.

December 11th. Very cold night. Huts not too good for men and as transport had not arrived, men were very cold. Colonel and self rode over to SIMENCOURT to see 1st Coldstream. I lunched with Barny O'Brien (2nd Irish Guards). Came in for conference of Officers Commanding all Coldstream Battalions for redistribution of Officers and N.C.O's. Digby rode back with us to FOSSEUX. Early dinner. Got 30 letters and good many parcels which took most of the evening to read.

December 12th. After breakfast I rode over to BARLY to look for better billets, which I found there, huts with stoves for the men and houses for Officers' Messes. Returned to lunch and the Battalion marched over in the afternoon. A small Château for Headquarters Mess. Ralph Cavendish came over in the afternoon to see me. Very cold and my billet is a mile from the mess.

December 13th. Went round billets with Commanding Officer. Men fairly comfortable, mostly in huts. Rode over to AVESNES, a moderate town. Cold and rain.

December 14th. After going round billets. I rode over to BERNEVILLE and lunched with Francis Longueville – 3rd Coldstream. Went round and saw Gilly and Crawley de Crespigny at Headquarters 1st Guards Brigade. Latter rather depressed as his month's leave is not too certain. Spent evening marking names of fellows in Guards Division on the Staff who get a Mention in Dispatches, of which there are a good many.

December 15th. Round billets and Companies drilling. Took a short walk alone after lunch. My "Bath Night"! Colonel (late Brigadier General) Wright, this area Commandant, came to dinner and talked hard.

December 16th. Frosty and cold. Head (Senior Chaplain of the Division) came over about 5 p.m. and gave rather a good voluntary service in the hut behind the "Corps Officers Rest Station" Château. He dined after.

December 17th. Snowing hard so Battalion could not shoot, nor start the Inter-Platoon football matches. This weather seems to have quieted down the gunnery a bit.

December 18th. A hard frost during the night had made the roads very bad. A very large mail was anticipated which turned out to be very moderate, at least as far as I was Concerned. Furze (Captain of No: 4) returned from a Course. A very cold night and my "Bath Night"!

December 19th. Woke up with swollen 'glands' and felt rather seedy. However started with Colonel round the Companies and billets, practising for GOC Division's Inspection on Friday. Cold enough to freeze one's Breath on the moustache. Went to bed fairly early.

December 20th. Face more swollen so stayed in bed all day. Doctor Raffle brought another man in to see me, but they were not sure of my disease.

December 21st. Diagnosed 'Mumps', and Ambulance sent for. Scott returned but I could not take him to Hospital. Got off about 2 p.m., roads covered with ice. Changed cars at No: 4 Field Ambulance at AVESNES-LE-COMPTE, and on to ST. POL to No: 12 Stationary Hospital for Isolated Cases. My ward was a tent with a bad stove and one Stable Companion with the same ailment.

December 22nd. There are two aged Nurses and 3 very dirty Orderlies and a Medical Officer, a Captain Attley (a Doctor at Eton College). A very cold place a tent, and food also very chilly as it has to come so far.

December 23rd. My 28th Birthday passed without any Incident except that heard Merton Beckwith-Smith was engaged to Honor Leigh, but this was not new to me. Still very cold. A big Air Raid on BOULOGNE with 'some' results I hear. I don't think the Mumps Ward are going to spend a very happy Christmas.

December 24th. My right swelling going down a bit and weather looks like breaking. But more snow came instead quite covering all the paths outside.

December 25th. Christmas Day. As deadly a Christmas Day as anyone could hope for. The Colonel and Matron came round. I got a Red Cross Stocking, consisting of sticky sweets and a nice packet of Woodbines. A letter from Barbie which cheered me up a hit. A bit of Turkey for dinner with 3 bottle of Akermann Lawrence 'Royal Dry' Army Champagne!!

December 26th. Colder than ever. A new Mump patient came in during the night – not a bright specimen.

December 27th. Got up after lunch and went to "Mumps Officers Hut". Very chilly spot. Pascal (2nd Lt. Royal Garrison Artillery) came too –

feeling too depressed to talk much. Got about 6 letters.

December 28th. Up again after lunch and to the hut. Colder than ever, got 4 letters and wrote as many.

December 29th. Froze about 22°F during the night and kept it up fairly hard during the day.

December 30th. Took a walk up the road for about an hour North of ST. POL. Had rather a bad headache and felt very depressed. Got 9 letters and wrote 5. A new sort of coal having arrived the hut is warmer.

December 31st. A little more snow otherwise an ordinary day. A short walk. Did not stay up to see the New Year come in.

1918

January 1st. Warmer. Took a walk in the morning and afternoon.

January 2nd. A thaw and some rain. Some excitement in the Hospital as many Nurses had received orders to go up to POPERINGHE which looks like "something". Took two walks.

January 3rd. Hard frost. Took two walks.

January 4th. Lovely day. Had a long talk to Lt. Colonel Burk RAMC, who runs this Hospital. Walks as usual accompanied by 2nd Lieutenant Turner of 9th Suffolks (late Cashier London County and Westminster Bank Brighton) who has had Mumps too.

January 5th. A slight thaw. Got three Pheasants from Via.

January 6th. No Church. Fine day.

January 7th. Up a little earlier. Walked with Turner. We bought 2 eggs and cooked them on the stove for tea when the Nurse was not looking. Stove smoked a little. Big thaw with rain, snow almost gone.

January 8th. Usual walks. Thaw.

January 9th. Snowing hard but went down to ST. POL and found out about trains. Very small and dirty town. Finished "Tale of Two Cities" in evening and proceeded to dream about it.

January 10th. Packed hard and got an Ambulance to take self and luggage to ST. POL Station. Met B.G. Chief Engineer XIVth Corps in street and asked for a lift to ARRAS, found him perfectly charming. We went and fetched my luggage and coat and went on to Corps

Headquarters. From there he sent me on alone to ARRAS. Went to Town Commandant Colonel C. W. Trotter, who gave me a very good lunch. Guards Division gave me a car afterwards which took me onto the 4th Battalion, who were in a quite good Nissen Hut Camp about 2 miles East. Found Battalion very comfortable. Had to go with 7 others including Commanding Officer to dine with 9th Battalion Gordon Highlanders (Pioneer Battalion to 15th Scottish Division). Dinner of 45 in wonderful mess they had built in their camp. Pipers played after and we danced eightsomes and reels till 1:30 a.m.

January 11th. Got up feeling very "thick". Walked with Piggott up to line we (4th Battalion) are making – about 1½ hours walk in rain, some through trenches, and sometimes in open in view of Huns at about 1,200 yards. But being a misty day they could see little. Drenched through and very tired, this being my first proper walk, I went into lunch with Gillie Follett, who is temporally commanding 1st Guards Brigade, who was in great form as he was just off on a month's leave. Guy Darell came in after lunch, so I took his car back to our camp while he walked round. An early bed!

January 12th. Rode down to Transport with Furze and walked round it then on to ARRAS. Went and saw Tuppi Headlam and then to Divisional Headquarters for lunch. Talked to General "Boy" Brooke (Temporary GOC Division) about my chances of getting a Coldstream Battalion, which he promised to put before the Major General on his return from leave. He motored me back after. Much colder.

January 13th. Service in a Nissen Hut at 11:15 a.m. by Hubbard. About 2:00 p.m. I rode off to ARRAS Station and caught the Passenger train at 4 p.m. to AMIENS. Guy Westmacott came in same carriage en route for 7 days in PARIS. Got to AMIENS about 8 p.m., took a room at the Hôtel du Rhin and had a large dinner at Godbert's.

January 14th. Train left at 6:57 a.m. Had to carry a coat, rug, and bag to Station. Got to Gare du Nord ROUEN at 12 noon. Went to "Hôtel de la Pôste" with a Major Trench (Worcesters). Took a large room with a bathroom etc. Lunch and a tram out to R.E. Training School, about 3 miles in the Champs. Looked round trenches till about 4 p.m. Quite a good School, all different sorts of revetments; deep mined dug outs; "Cut and Cover" dug outs; Machine Gun and Trench Mortar emplacements. Returned to town and toured shops. Early dinner and bed.

January 15th. Went out to School in a Taxi and heard a lecture on mined dug outs, walked round after. Lunch in R.E. Instructors Mess followed by demonstration in Drill single apron barbed wire entanglement, quite good. A short lecture on levelling and surveying. Back to ROUEN. Went up and saw Arthur Llewellyn in his house.

January 16th. Rained hard but we walked round and round. "Students" were making a "Slab" road. Went back to ROUEN about 3 p.m. Found 4th Battalion 3rd Echelon. Talked to Sergeants Fallen and Mascorde. Arthur Llewellyn came to dinner at Hôtel de la Poste and we talked hard and late.

January 17th. Went up to School about 9:30 a.m. Got my movement order and back to ROUEN for lunch. Caught 4:40 p.m. at Gare du Nord, arriving AMIENS at 10:15 p.m. Walked round town till 11:45 p.m. trying to find a room with man carrying my 2 bags. Got in at last at Hôtel de la Paix.

January 18th. Went in and saw Rudolph de Trafford who told me where the Xth Royal Hussars were. Just caught PARIS-CALAIS Express at Gare St Roche by getting in wrong side of train without a ticket. Got to PICQUIGNY 20 minutes later. Got a fellow in 2nd Life Guards to give me a lift and found Willie about 12 mid-day. Stopped to luncheon. Hailed a Flying Corps car and got a lift back to AMIENS. Caught 5:52 p.m. Passenger train to ARRAS, arriving about 9 p.m. and so to Rifle Camp where the Battalion still were.

January 19th. With the thaw has come a deluge of sticky mud and universal falling in of trenches, and so all our work has been changed and parties are split up into every available communication trench. A lovely day and lots of flying activity.

January 20th. Stuffy day but fine. I started off with Morrais and we walked via ATHIES and road North of SCARPE, through FAMPOUX up to some trenches his Company were clearing. Very muddy but quiet walk. Stayed and lunched with 2nd Coldstream Battalion Headquarters, who were holding left front sector of Right Brigade. Jimmy Coats and Edwin Brassey being there, thence home by same road which was lucky as 5.9"s began falling on road South of SCARPE the whole way down as I walked. Got very hot as I was wearing my short mackintosh and mackintosh trousers. Paid bills all the evening. Trenches in bad condition owing to thaw and rain.

January 21st. Went up to left side with Orderly. Walked up 'Camel Avenue' and found some of our men working, but lost my way and later found myself at 3rd Battalion Grenadier Headquarters. Took a drink off Ralph Cavendish and then back to 'Hyderabad Switch' across the open. Went in to lunch with Francis Longueville 3rd Coldstream as I was so tired, and on home. Bertie Whaley arrived to join Battalion and dined at Headquarters. We talked "Cottesmore Shop".

January 22nd. Felt too tired to go up the line and so made a map for myself instead. Rode over to inspect the Transport. Came over rather queer about 6 p.m. and so went to bed and drank Rum and hot water.

January 23rd. Did not go up the line as still felt rather seedy. Rode into ARRAS with Wilbraham and bought several things including Wall paper for my hut (white with hunting pictures on it!). Tea at L'Hôtel L'Universe which has just re-opened. Town placarded with notices of our 3rd Battalion Troupe 'The Lillywhites' (Dance, Drivel, Drama) which is going on in St. Georges' Hall. Nearly had a nasty accident with my horse who shied at Motor Lorry and crashed into side of it, but luckily I managed to slip off.

January 24th. Walked up line with Bertie Whaley, first to Headquarters 3rd Battalion Coldstream, then on to several trenches No: 1 were cleaning off mud. Then back to Headquarters 3rd Battalion to have a glass of Port. Home via Canal Tow Path from FAMPOUX. We went for the Launch down the Canal but found it didn't start for ½ hour so it wasn't worth waiting. Took no further exercise.

January 25th. Wrote most of morning. About 12:30 p.m. a nose cap of an Anti-Aircraft shell came through the top of my hut going in-between my arm and head, through the writing table onto my knee, where it raised a good bruise, a near shave for my head. After lunch Furze and I walked into ARRAS, self limping rather. Tea with 2nd Battalion and so home. Army had intercepted German wireless saying they are going to have a gas bombardment to-day, and so causing a good deal of excitement which entailed sending up to warn our working parties and doubling sentries. Sure enough it started at 9:30 p.m., but did not come much West of FAMPOUX (about 3 miles from here) but would have caught the working parties.

January 26th. Did not go up line, wrote letters instead. Knee still rather sore.

January 27th. Rode up with Furze to FAMPOUX. Misty so we walked up 'Stafford Lane' and got into 'Hyderabad Switch'. Work much improved. Walked back with Piggot and Blocker. Service at 2 p.m. in "Clyde" hut by Reverend Head. Wrote hard whole evening for subscriptions to Regimental Wedding Present for Beckwith-Smith.

January 28th. Continued writing and stayed indoors. Walked into ARRAS and went to the "Lillywhites", the 3rd Battalion show - very good. Two men in the troupe have excellent voices. Lutyens runs it. Went to dine at Headquarters mess 2nd Coldstream; Edwin Brassey and Jimmy Coats etc. Division lent me a GOC's car to come back in, which made it far more comfortable.

January 29th. Walked up to left side and over to extreme left. 'Hyderabad Switch' going well, deepening to 8ft and putting in 'A' frames on expanded metal revetment. Got back very tired. Walked over to transport with Furze and Bootle-Wilbraham and went for a ride over ARRAS racecourse, jumped one small fence. Huns put down lot of gas shells in and around FAMPOUX during the night.

January 30th. Started on a Field General Court-Martial as President at "College Communal" Headquarters of 3rd Coldstream, and Perry and King (Coldstream) as Members at 9:30 a.m. Had an hour for lunch and finished at 6:30 p.m. Very long day. Dined with Francis Longueville as it was so late and so missed our own dinner to Gordon Highlanders, which was very good. Rode back after with Francis who was going up the line to see his Battalion who were on fatigue.

January 31st. Walked up to see some wire we are putting up near the Chemical Works East of FAMPOUX. Met "Bulgey" Thorne who asked after Evelyn. Valley up SCARPE smelt very strong of gas bombardment by the Hun the night before. Wrote letters whole of afternoon.

February 1st. Went up with Roger Edge to 'Lemon' trench and went down 4 mined dug outs. Very interesting to see the way the men worked. Then on up to 'Clyde Avenue' and so home. A very misty and so quiet morning. Rather tired so did not move in afternoon.

February 2nd. Did not go up the line. Went into ARRAS about 5 p.m. and to 3rd Coldstream troupe. Not quite so good. Dined with Francis Longtail and slept there. We sang up till about 1:30 a.m.

February 3rd. Breakfast with 3rd Battalion and then went and saw General as to my future (Boy Brooke). Rode back and got in rather late for Voluntary Service at 10:30 a.m. at Rifle Camp. Dined with No: 2 Company.

February 4th. Rode up North road, walked through FAMPOUX and up 'Stafford Lane' to 'Hyderabad Switch' and new support line. Very clear day and so had to keep to trenches. Could see MONCHY very clearly towering over all the hills around, certainly a very important point to have taken inspite of the losses to the Xth Royal Hussars and others as our whole present line would be untenable without it. Met Boy Brooke in 'Hudson trench' on the way home, also Little and Bingham (Lord) of 1st Battalion. Met my horse and rode home. A lovely day for a walk.

February 5th. Walked into ARRAS with Bertie Whaley. Met Guy Darrell at Divisional Headquarters and went to our Divisional Cinema and Irish Guards Band. Band good – Cinema moderate. Had dinner at Hôtel l'Universe after, quite good but slow. Motored back to Rifle Camp.

February 6th. A sore heel I have, had begun to swell and so I did not go up line. Spent day in Camp in slippers.

February 7th. Remained in Camp again. Walked into ARRAS about 4 p.m. Had tea with 3rd Battalion and went on to see their troupe for their last performance. After we had a large dinner at the Hôtel l'Universe. Major General Torquil Matheson came, a farewell dinner to the 3rd Battalion who leave this Division tomorrow and go with 4th Battalion Grenadiers and 2nd Battalion Irish Guards as the 4th Guards Brigade under Brigadier General Lord Ardee to the 31st Division. Up till this date the 4 Battalions of the 1st Guards Brigade had been together since August 1914 and so everyone was very sorry at the break up of what we always considered the finest Brigade in the B.E.F.

85 Officers came but unfortunately only 77 could sit down. Dinner went off well. Torquil Matheson at the end proposed the health of the 3rd Battalion and Francis Longueville answered with a very lame speech. A motor bus had been chartered to take the 4th Battalion Officers home. This was the first occasion that all 4 Battalions had been able to have a dinner together since the War.

February 8th. Rode up with Bertie Whaley to the line. Went and saw some mined dug outs. Started in the Southern Sector, also some wire round the Railway Embankment. A few 'Woolley Bears' on the North road made me keep to the trench longer than usual

February 9th. Rode up to North end of Work and met Piggott. A few 5.9"s made us leave the road and go down a trench up to North end of 'Hyderabad Switch' very nearly finished – so home. Met Kenneth Digby on the way. Battalion got a wire to say Drill Sergeant Black had been found 20 miles from here, having committed suicide in a wood. No reason found for it. Cannot understand it, as he was such an excellent man and never in trouble.

February 10th. Voluntary Service in 'Clyde' hut at 9:30 a.m. by Head. Few of our fellows but mostly Scots Guards who have taken over the Gordon's Camp. Misty day. Did not go up line. Rode with Wilbraham up to race course and jumped some small fences. Saw Francis L. at Headquarters 2nd Coldstream.

February 11th. Went round gathering details of Drill Sergeant Black's death. Got a car from Division in which Wilbraham and I went first to several supply columns then to AGNEZ-LES-DUISANS where the Guards Division Re-inforcement Battalion is. Thence to WORLOY (Third Army Musketry School) about 40 miles. Saw Myles Hardy of this Battalion but found out little. Dark and with moderate lights we went home via ALBERT and BAPAUME, about 35 miles.

February 12th. Wrote round to Battalions for news of Black's movements, went in and saw Gunston (APM Guards Division) and had lunch in "B" mess. A car with Raffle-Park and Gunston and self to ESTRÉE-CAUCHIE where body of Black is. Gathered little more and so home. Several large guns drawn by Tractors going past our camp on the way 'up'.

February 13th. Went up to look at some wire on South side of Railway Embankment. Got very wet.

February 14th. Telephone message to say GOC Division wanted to see me. Walked in and saw him at Headquarters. Promised me GSO 3 of Division and to go on quickly as Brigade Major outside the Division. Lunched with Toby Bailey (2nd Grenadiers) and rode out to Artillery jumps after with Wilbraham. Could not get either of our horses to jump. Went in to Boxing match at theatre in ARRAS. Our fellow "Spugden" beat the 74th Battalion RFA man in 10 round contest. Also Smith (Coldstream Guards) beat a Scots Guards fellow. Guy Darell, Wilbraham, and self dined at Hôtel l'Universe and Division lent us a car to go home in. Met Ralph Stobart who made himself known to me.

February 15th. Prepared to go off. Bertie, W, and self went and looked at a Platoon Shooting Competition of 15th Division. Not very good!

February 16th. Car came at 9 a.m and took Wilbraham, Sergeant Lynham and self over to ESTRÉE-CAUCHIE for Court of Enquiry on how Drill Sergeant Black committed suicide or was killed. Witnesses took a long time. W. and self got an omelette and some "chips" from a farmer's wife for luncheon and we got back to Rifle Camp about 4 p.m. Think the Court must bring in "Suicide".

February 17th. Went up to look at some wire put out near the Railway. Lunched with Toby Bailey on the way back.

February 18th. Came into "G" office, Guards Division in morning. Found Aubrey-Fletcher – GSO 2; W. Laing – Intelligence Officer; J. Buchanan – as learner. Am to be GSO 3 in place of Olaf Hambro. Found there was a great deal to learn.

February 19th. Started work about 9 a.m. Mostly looking through Maps. Went up the line in a car to see some Company Commanders. Lunched with Kennie Digby (13 Coldstream) and back about 3 p.m. Slept in office on duty for night.

February 20th. Very little of interest going through. Digby came in to make arrangements about his "stunt". Started to rain about 4 p.m. Commanding Officer DA Column came to dinner (Watkins). All front very quiet.

February 21st. Was alone in office most of the morning. Four prisoners were captured during night of which one died. They showed a new Division in the line but could not give much information, but we found out a good deal which was useful. Boyd Rochfort (late 21st Lancers) gave a lecture on tanks which was interesting. Charles Trotter dined.

February 22nd. The C-in-C visited Division Headquarters but only saw GOC; GSO 1; and CRA. He brought no news except that Cavan has got Command of British Forces in Italy. Went for a walk to Citadel in ARRAS and looked round.

February 23rd. Two more prisoners captured by 3rd Guards Brigade during night. Laing and self drove up to right Brigade and he interviewed prisoners while I walked round line with Calverly Bewicke and looked at RŒUX. Lunched at 3rd Guards Brigade Headquarters (General Seymour) and back to ARRAS. Becky came in to "G" office and saw us. Slept the night in "G" office.

February 24th. Very quiet night – much warmer and muggy. GSO 1 and Buchanan went up line and had a most unpleasant walk, the Bosch shelled the Batteries considerably. Went to Service at YMCA hut by Schramm Barracks. Dined with Charles Trotter. Arranged about Leave.

February 25th. Fletcher went up line. Got a car at 2 p.m., drove to AUBIGNY. Thence by train to BOULOGNE to Folkestone Hotel. Slept night.

February 26th. Boat sailed at 9:30 a.m. Smooth crossing and in London by 3:30 p.m. George and Via in Belgrave Square. Tea with Curzon's.

Wednesday February 27th – Thursday March 7th, LEAVE

March 7th. Having had a wire Monday 4th morning recalling me – a second wire cancelling my recall, a third wire morning 5th recalling me again on 7th – lunched with George, Via, and Blanche at Ritz and caught Staff train at Charing Cross 1:40 p.m. Travelled with Aubrey Tennyson and Reggie Wilson. Rather choppy sea. Stayed at Folkestone Hotel BOULOGNE.

March 8th. Caught 10:07 a.m. Travelled with Forrester and Walpole. Train stopped an hour at TANQUES so had tea with 3rd Coldstream who happened to be billeted there. Division sympathetic at my recall, found all very quiet but Corps and Army had thought an attack by Huns was imminent and so all General Staff Officers were recalled.

March 9th. A raid by 15th Division South of SCARPE unsuccessful but 56th Division North of us had a good one and got 4 prisoners. Lovely day. Quiet, a few gas shells along SCARPE. Slept in office. Summer time comes in.

March 10th. XVIIth Corps Heavies rang up about 1:30 a.m. to synchronize their time again, so I had to ring up 3rd Guards Brigade to make sure. At 5 a.m. a raiding party of about 30 from 1st Battalion Welsh Guards went at German line just North of R. SCARPE. They found trenches empty but Huns returned while they were there but were kept off with bombs, an identification was obtained which unfortunately escaped before he could be got back. Party returned with few casualties having done in a good many Huns. Fletcher and self went up South side and walked round back trenches. Lovely day and very quiet. Lunched with General Boy Brooke at 2nd Guards Brigade and then back to ARRAS. A redistribution will probably take place tomorrow to strengthen the front line held for which I spent most of the evening writing out orders. RFC telephoned to say they think they have spotted some tanks, but these were eventually decided to be trucks.

March 11th. Orders received to take up Battle position, entailing much telephoning. Corps Commander came round to see Division Headquarters and intimated the Germans must start attacking very soon. Walked over to tea with 4th Coldstream, all very quiet and very lovely day.

March 12th. Went up line with GSO 1 (McClintock). Lovely day and quiet walk, looked at Machine Gun positions, back by 2 p.m. Went to Band (Welsh) and Cinema show at Theatre with Guy Darell. Considerable nervousness at Corps. Slept in the office, rung up twice by Division on our left during night. Tomorrow is said to be the day for the German attack.

March 13th. A very quiet morning and no sign of attack. Had to remain in office until relieved. After lunch went round Brigade Headquarters to make up distribution map and returned with General de Crespigny. Very hot day.

March 14th. Very quiet morning, a few gas shells. 1 Officer in 1st Coldstream wounded and 2 others in Division yesterday. Billy Darell (Brigadier General DA & QMG IVth Corps) came to tea. Went for ride on Merton Beckwith-Smith's horse so as to celebrate his wedding day.

March 15th. Very quiet night except for a few gas shells. Went up with Intelligence Officer and went down whole support line to Second System from top to RŒUX. Motored to 'Stirling' Camp and lunched with 2nd Coldstream, thence back to office. Very quiet morning. Slept in office.

March 16th. Very quiet night. Lovely day. Excitement about German attack dying down. Went to Divisional Movies and Band and dined with Gillie and Jimmy Coats at Hôtel l'Universe after.

March 17th. 56th Division made a raid near OPPY which unfortunately was not successful in its object to get an identification. Service in Divisional Recreation room at 11 a.m. Went up to 1st and 2nd Guards Brigade's Observation posts. Wonderfully clear day. Trains and transport could be seen moving behind German line. Ballantyne-Dykes went off to take over job on Railways GHQ and Calverly Bewicke takes his place. Guy Darell becomes DAAG and Calverly Bewicke DAQMG. Very mild day.

March 18th. Deserter captured by 15th Division, otherwise very quiet. Went for ride in evening.

March 19th. Raining hard. Start of Division's relief, 2nd Guards Brigade come to ARRAS and 3rd Guards Brigade to WARLUS. Relief went off very quietly.

March 20th. Still raining. Quiet day. Went over to 4th Division Headquarters and handed over map.

March 21st. Woken up about 5 a.m. by ARRAS being shelled by long range Naval gun. Bombardment of front line and rear lines continued. Walked down to office and found it was really the VIth Corps front (South of us) who were getting it. Still a good deal of noise about 9 a.m. An unfortunate shell in our little Square killed John Balfour (Scots Guards] also a Signalling Officer, wounding badly Boycott (4th Coldstream) and Williams (Scots Guards). Reports showed attack launched around BULLECOURT on right of VIth and left of Vth Corps. Line penetrated in 3 places. ARRAS shelled intermittently the whole morning with High Explosive. Shelling slackened in afternoon. Right of VIth and left of IVth Corps penetrated to depth of about 2 miles. 59th Division got most of the attack and lost heavily in guns and men, otherwise losses not so heavy, IVth Corps front remains more or less as it was. About 4 p.m. 2nd Guards Brigade ordered to move to MERCATEL in support. Slept in office, more or less quiet night.

March 22nd. Orders for 2nd Guards Brigade to move up in Support behind HÉNIN as Germans pressing on through there. Went down in car handed over orders personally to General Brooke, 1st Coldstream, and 1st Scots Guards on left and right on RVC line of 3rd System, 3rd Grenadiers in support. 3rd Guards Brigade ordered to move up to MERCATEL. Went for a walk with Jack Stirling, came back to find Division had suddenly been put under orders of HQ Corps, and Fletcher had gone over to Corps Headquarters. Orders to move came in about 9:30 p.m. GSO 1 & 2 wrote orders and people buzzed about generally. Division Headquarters move to BRETENCOURT. 1st Guards Brigade to BOIRY ST. MARTIN. The other two Brigades already being at MERCATEL. They were ordered to take over 3rd System. Situation roughly, Huns have got HÉNIN HILL also ST. LÉGER, line on our right very vague, on our left 3rd Division, on our right 31st Division. A difficult side slip relief was effected during night. GSO l and self left ARRAS at 11:30 p.m.

March 23rd. Went out at 1 a.m. in a car to find the Headquarters of the 2nd and 3rd Guards Brigade. Road blocked with traffic, found them fairly happy we have 3 Battalions in line and some details of 31st Division. Saw 1st Guards Brigade who had just come in and were digging on 'Army' line. Got back 7 a.m. – to bed for 3 hours. About 12 noon message came that Huns were massing on HÉNIN HILL. All guns put on and Infantry warned. Hun was seen walking in small parties down the roads on the Western edge of HÉHIN HILL. 'Paddy' Beaumont-Nesbitt arrived from England and took over Brigade Major of 3rd Guards Brigade. Afternoon continued quiet and our men continued digging in. Fletcher slept in office and had a moderately quiet night.

March 24th. Morning spent fairly lively'ly and the Hun came down the western slopes of HÉNIN HEIGHTS in small parties getting into HÉNIN and eventually having a 'go' at the 3rd Division right, but was "seen off". All guns available got onto him and must have fairly knocked them. Several new RA Brigades attached to this Division and situation generally clearer. Another attack on HÉNIN trenches which was repulsed. Bosche collected behind ST. LÉGER to have a go at 31st Division. Guns got on to them and dispersed them well. Aeroplane reported they were running in every direction. 5 tanks have been sent up to help the join between us and the 3rd Division on our left in case of heavy attack. Enemy reported massing due East from BOYELLES at about 7:30 p.m. news came in that COMBLES, MORVAL & LES BŒUFS have fallen which is bad. Strong patrols go out from all Brigades. Artillery S.O.S adjusted accordingly. C-in-C sent an inspiring message to the Armies. About 11:30 p.m. we heard that Huns had got ERVILLERS and were making for GOMLECOURT which means that the right of the 31st Division must have given way and so endangering our right. A hasty conference was held at Divisional Headquarters of CRE; BG-GDA & GOC to decide line of retirement. Transport is to be brought back and the "Purple Line" worked on by all available. Brigade were warned of the possible retirement.

March 25th. At about 2 a.m. we heard that Huns had got across the ARRAS BAPAUME road South of SAPIGNIES but wire to Corps so bad on account of them continually moving that it is very hard to hear. 2nd Guards Brigade were ordered to form a defensive flank to South East at 2:30 a.m. About 7:30 a.m. the S.O.S. went up from the left Brigade of the 31st Division (on our right), but nothing much happened. Enemy tried to get through the 3rd Division's wire but got seen off. Morning passed fairly comfortably. The 31st Division Headquarters, who had left their Headquarters rather hurriedly, had by this time returned but the wire to them was very bad and it is difficult to find out the situation, which is wanted about every hour. Luckily the 3rd Division are in this Village.

Boy Brooke having been gassed and gone sick, Gillie Follett is made Brigadier General Commanding 2nd Guards Brigade. An aeroplane dropped message to say Enemy in BIHUCOURT and pushing on to SAPIGNIES. Some 400 dead Huns were counted in front of Machine Gun position in 3rd Division front. Some 60 pounders and 6" Howitzers attached to the Division. About 5 p.m. the 31st Division decided to go back to their Switch line, our right Brigade must conform to this. About 6:00 p.m. the 31st rang through on priority wire saying Huns had taken GOMLECOURT and were moving on COURCELLES asking for immediate help. Corps was rung up and told how serious the situation was and asked if we all could retire to "Purple Line". 2nd Grenadiers were sent down to form a further defensive flank facing South, making our line about 8,000 yards long. At this moment the Corps shifted its Headquarters making further telephoning impossible. 31st Division have a large gap on their right, but they think they can hold COURCELLES. Retirement ordered about 8 p.m. onto an intermediate line. 31st Division to start at 9:15 p.m. and Guards Division at 10:00 p.m. Retirement to be covered by small covering parties.

March 26th. Withdrawal was completed, but touch was not gained with 31st Division. About 8 a.m. an S.O.S. went up on 3rd Division front – part of 31st Division. Gun 500 yards in front of HAMELINCOURT and our Royal Artillery shooting short (Received by Pigeon from front line). This information was sent by Special Despatch Rider to 31st Division as telephone communication no good (9:15 a.m.). Prisoners report that another attack by 26th Reserve Division is unlikely owing to casualties. It appears that the 2 left Battalions of 31st Division never received the orders to retire last night, which is reason why no touch has been gained with them. They did so at 10:15 a.m. in daylight. A report came in that enemy were massing in BOYELLES about 11:15 a.m. All available guns turned on. At 1 p.m. an aeroplane reported that the 31st Division were retiring to "Purple Line" (i.e. behind us). GSO 2 went to 31st Division to have it stopped, as all lines to them were down. Report that enemy were through SOUASTRE, and Corps Headquarters moving North: result that another period of non-communication with the Corps occured. Position very serious. 4th Guards Brigade (31st Division) being unable to gain touch with Headquarters 31st Division asked if they could come under orders of Guards Division, which was granted by us as no higher authority could be got. (They returned soon after to command of 31st Division). Pioneer Battalion was sent up to be ready to hold "Purple Line" about 1:30 p.m. 1st Guards Brigade reported that left Battalions of 31st Division had been ordered to go back to the "Purple Line" and "be damned quick about it" which afterwards proved to have been an order sent by a Staff Officer who had gone off his head. Touch was gained about 4 p.m. and VIth Corps sent a message to say this line must be held at all costs. The gap on our right and 31st Division's left was ordered to be filled at 4:30 p.m.; we extended to the right a bit. Later information received that Huns had brought Field Guns onto the open on ridge opposite us. Most of our Heavies for counter battery work had been withdrawn, but a strong letter was written for them to be brought back at once as, (said by an eminent General) they might just as well be in England for all the good they were doing us even if a few are captured. An attack from MOYENNEVILLE is expected tomorrow morning. All Artillery will shell it heavily before dawn tomorrow.

March 27th. Corps Headquarters move forward again and communications again cut off for a bit. At 12 noon right of 31st Division heavily attacked and had to fall back, but Battalions on our right holding on. About 12:30 p.m. an attack developed on our right (1st Guards Brigade), all guns were turned on. Priority wire from 31st Division soon after 1 p.m. to say whole of their front is coming back and they are very short of gun and rifle ammunition. Can we help? We do to a certain extent as we have a good deal up. 31st Division said to be East of AYETTE, but even this is much further back than we are. About 3:30 p.m. a wire came in to say our 2 right Companies had been heavily attacked but the enemy had been beaten off with heavy casualties. In the evening an aeroplane with British Markings flew over our lines and dropped bombs.

March 28th. 97th Infantry Brigade attached to Division which will be a great stand by. They went off to ADINFER. Gillie Follet made Brigadier to command 2nd Guards Brigade. S.O.S. went up somewhere on 31st Division front at 3:00 a.m. 4th Guards Brigade appears to be holding most of the 31st Divisional front. Casualties in the Division up to date not very heavy. Bosche attack fairly heavily from South and East of MOYENNEVILLE got in but was pushed out by counter attack. Enemy has got into AYETTE but was pushed back. Large quantity of Germans reported all along our front massing in roads etc. About 5:30 p.m. Huns had another go at 1st Guards Brigade but were "seen off". At 7 p.m. S.O.S. went up at AYETTE. 31st Division almost done, Corps ordered us to send 97th Brigade to help them. Staff Officer of 31st Division will guide them up. He didn't arrive however, but they got there without him. 3rd Division on our left were being attacked most of the morning. Thank goodness 2 Brigades, 2nd Canadian Division, arrived behind 3rd Division who were very tired. Heavy Guns have now moved up and are taking on the Bosche Batteries.

March 29th. At 12:30 a.m. Enemy got a footing in NEUVILLE VITASSE (3rd Division front). Seven of our guns have been hit. All available labour is being put onto this "Purple Line", our flanks in it altered which entailed further work. By this time all Brigade

Headquarters had come back to BLAIRVILLE as BOIRY STE RICTRUDE was too unhealthy. Heavy Counter Battery work in progress. A much quieter day as I think the Bosche had had a pretty good knock here.

March 30th. A quiet night. Several of our guns still shooting short. Enemy had another half-hearted "go" at the right Brigade (1st) but was kept off. 2nd Canadian Division have taken over from 3rd Division. A real good lot. 3rd Division had done most awfully well and had been very often heavily attacked, but were terribly weak. Very heavy Barrage on our left Brigade and Canadian front extended back for 2,000 yards. This lasted from 8 a.m. to 11 a.m. at which time the 1st Battalion Grenadiers and parts of the 2nd Battalion Scots Guards were attacked by 3 Hun Battalions. Storm troops in front. A regularly planned attack. They had a splendid shoot and the Hun only got in in one place near a sunken road from which he was bombed out and caught by a machine gun as he ran back. They estimated they killed 400 in the one Battalion. The 2nd Grenadiers were also partially attacked but our guns got onto the enemy before he could get out of HAMELINCOURT and MOYENNEVILLE and it never developed. (2nd Grenadier Guards much disappointed!) 2nd Canadian Division have taken over a bit of our front. Congratulatory message from Corps Commander (General Haldane).

March 31st. Easter Sunday. BGGS (Kearsley) came round and discussed the line. A very quiet day. A prisoner captured yesterday stated that the attack was to have taken BOISLEUX ST MARC and then swung South to get High Ground.

April 1st. Enemy aeroplanes dropped many bombs during the night but no damage done. An S.O.S. was sent up on the Canadian front, which caused considerable excitement. Upon the Divisional Headquarters being rung up, they were found very calm and said "It is only one of the 'Stunts' of the boys in the front!" 31st Division relieved by the 32nd, which makes our right much safer.

April 2nd. Considerable shooting was heard early in the morning, but it was found to be up North. Major General and self rode up to BOISLEUX ST MARC. Not too pleasant a ride. I looked at the grave of Edward Gibbs (*The grandson of the Rev. Joseph Gibbs, William Gibbs of Tyntesfield's brother; see letter page 193*) who had been killed near there about 3 days before. We went to Battalion Headquarters of 1st Battalion Irish Guards and 2nd Battalion Scots Guards. Our road considerably shelled on way home. Major General and self walked 100 yards apart to avoid being hit by same shell. One burst about 20 yards from us. 2 Canadians captured on 29th re-entered our lines and gave some valuable information. Another Machine Gun Company put at our disposal. All our men very tired but no sign of relief yet.

April 3rd. At 2:00 a.m. 32nd Division attacked AYETTE being very successful and getting through and out behind it except for one machine gun post, taking 5 Officers and 150 Other Ranks prisoners. Very good attack which all goes to strengthen our right. Headquarters 1st Guards Brigade had a narrow shave last Night, a shell taking half the hut away and most of General "Crawley's" kit. George Paynter, (R) Ward, and Billy Wynne-Finch came to tea. A fairly quiet day, roads very much shelled. An S.O.S. went up in front of AYETTE about 9:30 p.m., which caused considerable shooting. It turned out to be the 32nd Division taking a bit of trench and green lights were sent up by the Germans. S.O.S. stopped. In the meantime a 6" had been shooting short over 2nd Coldstream but no damage done. Heavy Artillery tried to find out which gun it was. Grigg returned from Corps with the depressing news that there is no hope of relief yet. Division has had 14 days fighting and been continuously in trenches since January 1st 1918.

April 4th. A quiet night and rather wet, no attempt by the Bosche to retake AYETTE. Major General and Grigg had conference of Brigadiers at 8:30 a.m. with a view to shortening the line as we now look like staying here for some time. Norman Orr Ewing has taken over Command of 3rd Guards Brigade, Copper Seymour having gone home. Guy Darell and self went up to Brigade Headquarters, also explored the underground passages under BLAIRVILLE which were made by the Germans 2 years ago before their retreat. Tea with 3rd Guards Brigade and so home. Divisional Conference on a new method of holding the line so as to save men. Rained most of the day.

April 5th. A heavy attack on the French and British East of AMIENS was kept off, but another expected up here to relieve it. Night very wet, simply poured. 1st Guards Brigade captured a prisoner, but he had no news. Heavy barrage on Centre Brigade (1st) about 7 a.m. which died down. Later it started on the Canadians by MERCATEL. A raid by the Hun was repulsed in front of the Canadians. The heavy attack on the French East of AMIENS got about 2,000 yards of ground but did not make the French use any reserves. The Hun used 12 Divisions, 8 of which were fresh ones. Fletcher and self walked up to Battalion Headquarters of 1st Battalion Coldstream and 1st Scots Guards. Not a very pleasant walk. Officer Commanding No: 7 Tank Battalion came in to see us, also 2 Corps Officers. "Tiny" Buchanan came to join "G" office Divisional Headquarters. I sleep in office.

April 6th. 3 prisoners captured during night, 2 coming from fresh Division caused considerable telephoning. 32nd Division did a raid last night South of AYETTE to get a length of trench. German garrison was too strong to hold it, but they killed a lot and had very few casualties themselves. Tiny and self went up to Brigade Headquarters to get their dispositions on a map. Found the 1st Guards Brigade Headquarters had moved owing to several shells falling on their old Headquarters. Went off with Grigg to Headquarters 32nd Division (South of us) hoping to see Joe Gibbs (Brigade Major Divisional Royal Artillery) but he was out. Looked at 32nd Division dispositions and back home. Had a long letter from Evelyn to Blanche.

April 7th. A quiet night. Two RAMC orderlies escaped from Germans and came in. Colder day. Several low flying aeroplanes came over BGGS to say considerable movement behind Bosche lines which might indicate a big attack in these parts. RAMC orderlies stated that prisoners were very hard worked and fed worse by the Bosche. Our Artillery had done much damage in back areas. German morale is low. Bosche estimated casualties for 1st day of their advance – 70,000.

April 8th. Quiet night except for gas shells into BOIRY ST MARC most of night but few casualties. Raining hard. Fletcher and self went up to "Purple Line" near ADINFER WOOD where 2 Companies of 1st Battalion Scots Guards are. Found them very wet and miserable, tried to get them into Village of ADINFER. Went to 3rd Brigade Headquarters and so home very wet. Men of Division get too dreadfully tired, exhausted and considerable sick wastage. Strong representations sent to Corps and Army that if not relieved soon they will take months to recover.

April 9th. Having slept in office, very quiet night, some gas shelling in BOIRY ST. MARTIN early. Ellison and self rode over to RANSART, looked at new Brigade Headquarters and tracks back west of RANSART back across country. Very little sign of relief. Heavy mist all day. (Heard that I had sold car for £300!).

April 10th. Some more gas shelling during the night. Canadian R.E. Officer from Third Army blew the white Arch Bridge at BOISLEUX-AU-MONT during night without any reference to Division or Brigades; result he nearly killed 10 men. He was taken for a spy and very roughly handled by 2nd Scots Guards and sent down under arrest. It appears he was ordered direct by Army. Strong protests sent up. News came in Line in front of LAVENTIE held by Portuguese attacked and bent back to ESTAIRES. PLOEGSTEERT and MESSINE RIDGE fallen which is bad. Fletcher and self motored to BOISLEUX and went round all Battalion Headquarters of Battalions in Line and in Reserve (9), long walk but very quiet. Fairly cheered but very tired. Tea with "Bulgey" Thorne, O.C. 3rd Grenadiers. Went into each Brigade Headquarters and so home to hear 19th Division (Major Jeffries) had retaken MESSINE, that 11 new German Divisions had been used opposite ESTAIRES, that German casualties opposite Third Army alone estimated at 280.000. All good news. Our relief looks no nearer.

April 11th. Small signs of relief by 2nd Division. General Pereira and his GSO 1 came in and talked over it for an hour. Much warmer and in consequence much more aeroplane activity. "G" office took on "Q" office at football and beat them 4 - 2. The 2nd Canadian Division were attacked twice today but repulsed both.

April 12th. General Pereira and his GSO 1 arrived to go round "Purple Line". Lovely day very clear and in consequence considerable Enemy Aircraft and Artillery activity. Gunstan-Whitall and self rode over to RANSART to select place for prisoners cage, and to look at rear Brigade Headquarters under construction. Corps Commander came but could say nothing definite about relief of us by 2nd Division. News from the North about the same. MERVILLE reported lost. General de Crespigny to tea. Much quieter in front. Enemy reported fairly thick on our front and that of 32nd Division, by aeroplane. Everything seems to point to an early attack on the Third Army front probably just South of us. Arrangements being made for relief of this Division by 2nd Division tomorrow and Sunday, but no orders received.

April 13th. A dull morning and consequently a quiet morning. Ellison and self walked up to Brigade Headquarters. Some shelling round BLAIRVILLE. 'Rusty' Eastwood (from New Zealand Division) came in also one Wallace (Highland Light Infantry) from Army (IIIrd) but not much news. Order for relief arrived from Corps about 4:30 p.m. Order eventually came in about 6 p.m. and relief continued.

April 14th. Relief of 1st Guards Brigade by 5th Infantry Brigade (2nd Division) complete 2 a.m. Morning spent packing. 4 British soldiers captured March 21st came into our lines during night. On interrogation they gave very cheering account of the Huns who are in a very bad way as regards food and material etc. 5th Infantry Brigade got one German who walked into their lines having lost his way. A quiet day. Staff of 2nd Division arrived in batches all day. Calverly-Whitall and I eventually left about 7 p.m. and drove over to BAVIRCOURT. Very crowded in the Château as 1st Guards Brigade Headquarters are there too. Dined with 1st Guards Brigade.

April 15th. Very cold. 2nd & 3rd Guards Brigades got out well last night and now everyone is back except 2 Machine Gun Companies. GOC. GSO 1 & 2 came over about 10:30 p.m. Château very full. Drove round Brigade Headquarters with Head (Senior Chaplain). Played football after tea.

April 16th. Major General and Brigadiers went out to do reconnaisances of "Red" and "Purple" lines down South. Bosche got into short bit of trench left of 2nd Division (our old sector) where 2nd Canadian Division joins. Went over to 4th Battalion Machine Gun Guards, also 1st Battalion

Coldstream. French General came in to look at our maps. Very strenuous game of football versus 2nd Grenadiers. 2nd Division regained small length of trench and line is now intact. ALBERT shelled and Leaning Virgin brought down, otherwise no change on British front. Dined with 2nd Battalion Coldstream.

April 17th. Warmer. Very bad news from 4th Guards Brigade. Our 3rd Battalion has 15 Officer casualties of which Christopher Gurney is among the missing. 4th Battalion Grenadiers and 2nd Battalion Irish Guards had equally bad time. Major General wrote privately asking for them to be disbanded (the 4th Guards Brigade) as it will be impossible to make them up without robbing this Division. CRA of 39th Division Artillery came in. His Groups are temporarily attached to this Division for Counter Attack work if necessary. W. Laing returned to take over his Intelligence Work again. News of YPRES salient to be reduced. Attacks around MERVILLE and BAILLEUL by Bosche unsuccessful.

April 18th. Very quiet on Corps front. Very cold and raining. Official list shows Christopher is not among missing, which is good. Division Headquarters played 2nd Battalion Coldstream at football. Cut my finger badly and had to retire. Heavy attacks on FESTUBERT front beaten off by 1st & 4th Divisions.

April 19th. Fletcher and self went up to "Purple Line" on Canadian Front and looked round. Very cold with snow. Went over to tea with 2nd Grenadiers and walked back with Crawley de C. No news. Edwin (now Lt. Colonel commanding 2nd Coldstream) and Jimmy Coats to dinner.

April 20th. Considerable activity around FESTUBERT over which the 1st Division were again successful and took an enemy post. Liason Officer from GHQ said that 4th Guards Brigade had been put in a gap North of MERVILLE and successfully held the Bosche up, although some of themselves being surrounded, while an Australian Division detrained at HAZEBROUCK and came up just in time to help them out. Division played 1st Coldstream at football and were beaten. I did not take part. Very cold again. Dined with 1st Guards Brigade Headquarters.

April 21st. Went to Service in Divisional Club tent. Rode over to Headquarters 3rd Guards Brigade and lunched with 4th Coldstream. News of further unsuccessful attacks near FESTUBERT. Played football Divisional Headquarters beating Combined Ambulances of Guards Division Officers.

April 22nd. Warning order for Guards Division to relieve 32nd Division in the Right Sector of VIth Corps front. North and South of AYETTE on nights of 24th/25th and 25th/26th April. Grigg went over to see GSO 1 32nd Division. Day fine.

April 23rd. Preparations for relief continued and Officers went up to line. Played football versus the 1st Coldstream and got beat.

April 24th. Order for relief eventually arrived from Corps. I was warned to go as Brigade Major to 140th Brigade, 47th Division. 1st Guards Brigade to line.

April 25th. Divisional Headquarters left, and I left in car from Train for Headquarters Xth Corps. Arrived about 5 p.m. and they sent me on in one of their cars to CANCHY Headquarters of 47th Division. Had tea with Walter Batten Pool and then on to 140th Brigade Headquarters at LE TITRE (about 5 miles North of ABBÉVILLE). Found Brigadier General Kennedy (KRR): Staff Captain Deveral (Post Office Rifles); Stickland (Learner); Carter (Intelligence Officer); Boughton (Signals).

April 26th. Went into ABBEVILLE and brought several things in car lent by the owner of our Château. Dined with 21st London Regiment (Lt. Colonel Dawes – South Staffordshires).

April 27th. Rode round Battalions and watched training. Drove into ABBÉVILLE. Met Willie O. G. (*Otter Gibbs*) on way in and arranged to lunch with him tomorrow.

April 28th. Orders for a move on Monday 29th arrived and warning order sent out to Units. We are to be lent by Third Army to Fourth Army to withdraw 2nd Australian Division. Dined Divisional Headquarters and met General Sir George Gorringe. Orders for move tomorrow by Bus up to Sector in front of ALBERT.

April 29th. Brigade moved in Buses and Lorries up to WARLOY. Orders very vague. Brigade put under 2nd Australian Division who seemed to take very little trouble. Went up in Divisional car with Deveral, Boughton (Signals), and Coeux (Intelligence). Called at 2nd Australian Division; got our locations. Staff Captain went off and billeted. I found 38th Division and so called on Bobby Pratt Barlow for lunch. Buses arrived about 5:30 p.m. Brigadier and self met them. Lt. Colonels and General McDowall came to dine.

April 30th. Brigadier and self went up to 6th Australian Brigade Headquarters at HÉNENCOURT. Brigadier went round line. I took over all papers from Brigade Major (Bridges). After lunch we returned and held Brigade Conference in evening. Dined Headquarters 38th Division, sat next to B. P. Barlow. Wrote orders for relief.

May 1st. Spent most morning packing up. Merton Beckwith-Smith to lunch. Went over to 47th Division for tea and then up to HÉNENCOURT Château. 15th London Regiment on Right, 17th London Regiment on Left, 21st London Regiment in Support in LAVIÉVILLE. Relief complete at 12:30 a.m.

May 2nd. Brigadier and self went round line, up to 17th London Regiment first – Left Battalion about 1,000 yards from Huns. Trenches very shallow and narrow and not through in some places. Shelling on ALBERT-AMIENS road rather heavy and so we cut our visit to 15th London Regiment rather short. Very good view of ALBERT. Lots of papers keep coming in.

May 3rd. Major General proposed coming up, so I went up alone about 9:30 a.m. right round front, got back at 2 p.m. Good deal of work had been put in. Found General Birdwood with Brigadier on my return. News that Huns may attack between ALBERT-ARRAS on May 8th.

May 4th. Brigadier and Major General went round whole line from 5 a.m. – 12 noon. Quiet day. Went round line of Reserve Battalion with Lt. Colonel Dawes.

May 5th. Went off at 10:30 a.m. with Laird (O.C. R.E. Company) and chose Battalion Headquarters in MILLENCOURT as we now have taken over extra bit of line North and hand over South. Then up to 15th London Regiment and round their right bit of line South of ALBERT road. Walked over the open most of the way, which seemed dangerous but was all right. Found not a great deal of work done and trenches very shallow. Home by 2 p.m. wet to the skin by rain and heat of day. Went round to 142nd (General McDowall) and tried to arrange relief but did not get very far.

May 6th. Representatives from 54th Infantry Brigade (Sadler Jackson) arrived and went up to respective Battalion fronts which they take over tonight. Brigade Major came and fixed up details. We are side slipping one Battalion frontage to the North. Went round HÉNENCOURT defences and met Major General Montgomerie (MGGS IVth Army). About dinner time it started to pour and continued all night delaying the relief. About 8:30 p.m. a wire from Division to say Anti-tank craters were to be made on our front involving carrying parties and covering parties being left behind for a bit and interfering with relief.

May 7th. Relief complete at 5:30 a.m. Still raining very hard. Brigadier and Staff Captain went up to Battalion Headquarters. Wire from Army saying whole Mackensen's Army from Romania in front of us, which is jolly. 3rd Cavalry Division behind us, also a French Army. Dined with Lt. Colonel Dawes (2nd London Regiment) and went up to his front line. Walked most of it, very slippery and muddy but quiet. Got back about 1:00 a.m.

May 8th. General went up line. Lots of visitors including Feilding, 6th Cavalry Brigade, various Tank Officers, came in. Went round to Tanks and went all over a "male" tank. Quiet. Walked to Headquarters Trench Mortar Battery, round all Machine Gun Batteries, then on to 17th

Battalion line. Walked from 3:00 – 7:30 p.m. Had large bottle of Champagne as was very tired.

May 9th. Lovely day. Heavy barrage put down 3:30 a.m. by Bosche and our Château shelled, which turned out to be a raid on Brigade North of us, where the Huns got into a small piece of trench, and the first counter attack failed to eject them.

May 10th. Our front quiet. A "biff" during the night got the Huns out of the 142nd Brigade trenches. Went up round the Machine Guns and right Battalion front. Merton Beckwith-Smith came over but I did not see him. General Archie Seymour came in, also Mark Feilding. 15th Battalion London Regiment relieve 17th Battalion in right sub-sector.

May 11th. Quiet morning, went up to 2nd Battalion Headquarters in MILLENCOURT, on leaving 21st Battalion was hurried out by six 5.9"s dropping rather close. Went round rear defences and back to lunch. Few shells into bottom of HÉNENCOURT in the evening.

May 12th. Service by Brown-Wilkinson at 8:45 a.m. A quiet day.

May 13th. Some shelling of back area, mostly brought on by Cavalry working parties coming up too early in the evening. Ralph Gibbs (*sixth son of Henry Martin Gibbs of Barrow Court*) came in about 11 a.m. Very wet as it poured the whole day. Arranged for relief for 14th, which had to be cancelled owing to Brigade relief on 15th.

May 14th. Fine day. Brigadier went up with Major General at 6 a.m. round line. Several people came in about relief by 174th Infantry Brigade on night of 15th/16th. Wrote relief orders. Several messages that Huns are detraining at ALBERT, also several Bus loads of men seen.

May 15th. A message about 1 a.m. to say Division on our right (18th) was being heavily gassed. Morning very quiet. Company Commanders of 174th Infantry Brigade came and looked round sector. Brigade Major and Brigadier came and looked round back trenches with self. Arthur Moon, Intelligence Officer, came up to dinner. Relief started well.

May 16th. Relief complete 1:10 a.m. About 2 a.m. left Battalion rang up to say they heard Tanks. Counter preparation put on and nothing happened. Brigadier, self, and "Signals" went out in Brigadier General Archie Seymour's car, lent for morning. Lunched with Headquarters 60 Car Brigade. Went over in a car to MOLLIENS AU BOIS to arrange with 58th Division as to our stopping in CONTAY. Stayed one night at the Château with Headquarters 3rd Cavalry Division. Ralph Gibbs to dinner.

May 17th. Turned out of Château by Headquarters 58th Division and found small House in CONTAY Village. Very hot again. Merton Beckwith-Smith came to lunch. Rode out to look at WORLOY ranges and Battalions. Lt. Colonel Davies (GSO 1) and Alexander (DAAC's) came to dinner.

May 18th. Very hot and stuffy. After lunch it started to fairly pour with rain and thunder. One of our Aeroplanes got caught in an air pocket and fluttered down near our Village, both occupants being killed.

May 19th. A very noisy night owing to Australians taking VILLE-SUR-ANCRE. Brigadier and self went to Service by 15th Battalion. Conference of Commanding Officers after lunch as to our Counter Attack if HÉNENCOURT or LAVIÉVILLE are taken. Later Brigadier and self went up in Officer Commanding "B" Company 1st Tank Battalion's car to look at HÉNENCOURT RIDGE.

May 20th. Expected attack did not come off. Very hot again. General Turner to lunch and Kirkpatrick (GHQ) came in after, but not much news. German attack expected tomorrow 21st. Brigadier and self went over to tea with O.C. "B" Company Tank Battalion and then back to 17th Battalion Londons and watched "Follies".

May 21st. No attack. Went up with O.C. Tanks and looked at dug outs and came back via Battalions. John Hugh Smith came in and saw me for a few minutes. Division Conference. Ralph Stobart to dinner. Many German aeroplanes over the Village.

May 22nd. Brigadier and self met most of the Officers of the Brigade just North of HÉNENCOURT WOOD and we went over the ground for a Counter Attack. Got back to lunch very hot. Went in Divisional car to DOULLENS. Met young Codrington also Watkins (Coldstream). 21st Battalion London Regiment shifted their Camp owing to shelling this morning. CONTAY bombed by a good many aeroplanes. (About 50 bombs).

May 23rd. Several bombs fell close here. Casualties caused, including 6 horses of Northumberland Hussars which I saw. Started at 5 a.m. and rode up to 55th Infantry Brigade Headquarters, meeting Adjutant of 17th Battalion London Regiment (Martin) en route. Breakfasted there at BAIZIEUX. Rode out to see their Battalions, one being forward on AMIENS-ALBERT road near LAVIÉVILLE, and other two back. 55th are Brigade in Reserve. (GOC Wood) and (B/M Chell). A good wind which will stop any bombing tonight. Much cooler.

May 24th. Rained whole morning. Brigadier and self and Carden Roe and Alexander from Division went to find 15th Battalion London Regiment another site for their Camp. Four or five 6" Howitzers and about 6" guns and 60 pounders having come into the old place and made it untenable. Not very successful.

May 25th. 17th in LAVIÉVILLE line. 15th & 21st Battalions in Valley by ST LAUVENT FARM. Brigadier and self rode up to our new Headquarters at BAIZIEUX and took over. Rode down to 15th & 21st, and after lunch to 17th now in BRESLE. Fine day but dull.

May 26th. Intercepted wireless message of Germans, which foreshadowed a Gas concentration between 9 – 11 p.m. and 5 – 7 a.m., that did not come off. Brigadier and self went to Voluntary Service of 15th Battalion and I stayed to Holy Communion after (where there were 60 Communicants from the one Battalion and Trench Mortar Battery). After lunch Brigadier, Deverel, and self rode down to near FRANVILLERS to look at camping ground. O.C "B" Company 2nd Tank Battalion to dinner and 21st Battalion Band played. BAIZIEUX rather heavily bombed by aeroplanes about 11 p.m. and onwards.

May 27th. Thundery day. Went down towards FRANVILLERS and saw armoured car. Ralph Gibbs came round and saw me. Tank demonstration at 8:45 p.m., not very successful.

May 28th. A few bombs from aeroplanes at 2:30 a.m., no damage. Went out at 6:30 a.m. up to LAVIÉVILLE line Battalion, cool and quiet. Had breakfast with Pargiter (15th Battalion London Regiment) after. Few H.V. shells into Village – one unlucky one into the Machine Gunners. Eastwood (Divisional Q) to lunch. Heard rumours of big attack down near SOISSONS. Enemy said to have penetrated 12 miles and to be well over the AISNE.

May 29th. Brigadier and self went to watch the 17th Battalion training. Met Major General there. Ralph Gibbs to lunch.

May 30th. Went up to 142nd Infantry Brigade Headquarters and round line. Line fair, some shelling by "Wizz-Bangs". While looking from an O.P. the Hun spotted us and put over about 6 quickly, which luckily missed the trench by 20 or 30 yards. Quiet afternoon. Some bombing at night.

May 31st. Having moved back to ÉBARTS FARM BEAUCOURT yesterday, we are comfortably installed in the Château where the Caretaker has opened the "Dining Hall" (built 1909 imitation 16th Century). H.V Gun shelled over our heads most of the day towards BEAUCOURT Château (47th Division Headquarters). Bad news from SOISSONS, the Hun having got to CHÂTEAU THEIRRY, but the French seem calm. Corps Commander (Butler IIIrd Corps) came in to see us. He appears very nervous of this front and is convinced the Hun will attack shortly. Corps keep on asking if everything is ready. Wyndham Portal arrived to take over 47th Machine Gun Battalion from Davies. 6th Cavalry Brigade have come up.

June 1st. Quiet day. 35th Division had a rather unsuccessful show at AVELUY WOOD. Rode up to see 15th & 17th Battalions. Archie Seymour (Brigadier General) and Algy Howard dined. String Band of "Follies" played for dinner. 15th Battalion went in on right of right sector. 17th Battalion on left and 21st into support.

June 2nd. Brigadier "Swanky" and self motored up to Brigade Headquarters at 8 a.m. Brigade Headquarters consist of dug outs in the side of the hill about ½ mile North of RIBEMONT. Front line is about 1,700 yards long from just South of ALBERT-AMIENS road to 5 mile West of DERNANCOURT. Trenches are good but not deep enough. The 142nd Infantry, who we took over from, had walked about in the open far too much and so there is a good deal of shelling. Lt. Colonel Segrave to lunch. Lt. Colonels Davies and Turner (GSO I & III) and self went to O.P. on South side of Valley through MERICOURT Station. I looked at old haunts of Xmas and January 1917 with 2nd Coldstream. Had dinner in deep dug out. Went to bed early.

June 3rd. Got up at 5 a.m. and went round trenches at 6 a.m. to get the cool and quiet. Got the former but not the latter, as some trench mortaring on right by the "C.C.S." and on entering the front line they put 2 x 4.2"s about 15 yards and so "went round the other way". 17th Battalion had 7 men killed during the night. Trench Mortar Battery and Officer and 3 NCO's wounded.

June 4th. Quiet day. Several visitors including Becky-Smith, who had been round the line. News from SOISSONS that German advance had been stopped. Colonel Segrave and self went up to Battalion Headquarters. He stayed the night at Brigade Headquarters and we had a large dinner party to celebrate General Kennedy's "C.M.G".

June 5th. Brigadier went up line to arrange about a raid by our right Battalion. C.E. of IIIrd Corps came in (Brigadier General Rolands). Colonels Segrave and Stickland went on leave. Went up to right Battalion front. News that we shall probably be here 24 days instead of 16 as things are quieting down. Raid put off for time being.

June 6th. Hot and quiet. Went up to left Battalion and round the line with Lt. Colonel Dawes for about 4 hours. Called in on Colonel Parish (Poplar and Stepney Rifles) on way back. American Officer attached. R.A.F. Pilot crashed near Brigade Headquarters and came into dinner, sleeping the night. S.D.R. from Division stating impending attack imminent, perhaps on our front. Result of Derby:- Corporal of our Brigade Headquarters won £100.

June 7th. Brigadier and Major General went round line. About 25 more Americans attached. John Hugh Smith came up and we went up to O.P. on Australian front. On my return I found 5 American Officers and about

20 Other Ranks to be attached. They were successfully disposed of.

June 8th. Took one of the American Officers attached to Brigade Headquarters up the line. Brigadier General of 6th Australian Brigade (on our right) to lunch also C.R.A. and Bridgeman his Brigade Major to discuss plans for their raid on 10th/11th. Very quiet day.

June 9th. Considerable shelling during night including some Gas round Brigade Headquarters, but it did not affect us. Big show South of MONTDIDIER where the Hun was unsuccessful. Went down to Brigade Headquarters of 6th Australian Brigade in HEILLY after tea to see about their big raid. American Captain attached to us unfortunately killed last night.

June 10th. Quiet and cold. John Hugh Smith (Coldstream) joined Brigade as a learner of Brigade Major duties for a month. A great addition. Big attack by 7th Australian Brigade on our right (just South of ANCRE}, quite successful. 500 yards taken on 2,500 yards front. One small raid by 6th Australian Brigade on our immediate right successful and identifications obtained, a second one not so successful. Two American Colonels to stay with us for night.

June 11th. Took John Hugh Smith up right side of line. All Americans left and new lot arrived and sent up to Battalions. Various raids on either side arranged but afterwards cancelled.

June 12th. Went up with General and American Major round line and got back at 2:15 p.m. Quiet day. Two raids by 54th & 55th Infantry Brigades on our left.

June 13th. Brigadier went round with Major General. Lovely day. Went up to 21st Battalion (right) to dine, and after Hutchence and self went out into "No man's lands" and sited positions for Camouflaged Saps (Russian Saps) to go to. Very quiet and only one burst of Machine Gun fire anywhere near us.

June 14th. A good deal of "wind" accumulated as to a Bosche attack on our front tonight and a "Bosche Snaffling" patrol was organized, meanwhile the 6th Australian Brigade on our right arranged a larger raid. The Brigade on our left to let off Gas and the 18th Division North of them to make two raids. About 9 p.m. several Gunners came in saying that they had been ordered by the IIIrd Corps to man O.P's all night etc. to be ready. Very considerable harassing fire was put over by all available Guns.

June 15th. On account of excessive shelling our patrol could not find any Bosche. The Australians got a few and 2 Machine Guns, and the 18th Division raids did not come off, nor did the expected attack. Day much cooler. Brigadier went up to try and arrange another raid. A "Snatching party" went out but was unsuccessful.

June 16th. Corps and Army Commanders visited Brigade, former still windy. Brigade Major Arthur Moon and another from 174th Infantry Brigade came to lunch and arranged relief for 18th June. Quiet day. Lot of orders came in from Units on either side as to raids. 15th Australian Brigade were going to let off Gas etc.

June 17th. Heard during the night that this Brigade were to go out to very good billets West of AMIENS, which hopes however were dashed to the ground about 11 a.m. by a wire which cancelled the whole thing and detailed the Division to go out around MOLLIENS-AU-BOIS. Complicated orders for embussing and de-bussing the Brigade were now unnecessary. Major General and Major General of 58th Division, which is relieving us came round line. Hectic message from Corps calling them to a conference at Spa had to be specially sent up. Lovely day.

June 18th. Parties of NCO's and Officers to go up the line from 174th Infantry Brigade came up 10 a.m. A quiet day. Relieving Units passed through about 10 p.m. Started to rain later which made the going very bad. Relieving Staff General Higgins, Brigade Major Barrington-Ward. Everything went off quietly.

June 19th. Relief complete at 2 a.m. when General, Signals, and self motored down to MONTIGNY Château shared with IIIrd Corps Heavy Gunners. After breakfast a H.V Gun sent over several shells. Lunched at Division Headquarters and afterwards motored on to MOLLIENS-AU-BOIS. The Battalions being in tents in the wood. Raining which made tent-life unpleasant for them. Fairbrother, the new Chaplain arrived and stayed at Brigade Headquarters.

June 20th. Waited most of the day for orders to move on Friday. Went in Flying Corps tender to DOULLENS and back. Orders for embussing 21st.

June 21st. John Hugh Smith went down to embussing point at 10 a.m. and superintended. Brigadier "Swanky", Signals Officer, and self motored down to new area west of AMIENS, lunching at PICQUIGNY, then on to BOVELLES Château. 15th Battalion at GUIGNEMICOURT; 17th Battalion at SAISSEVAL; and 21st at FERRIÈRES. Trench Mortar Battery at BOVELLES. Very nice country and good billets. Battalions got in about 5 p.m.

June 22nd. Day spent in cleaning up and looking round. Divisional Conference at 6 p.m. attended by Brigadier Generals and Brigade Majors; all Commanding Officers etc.

June 23rd. A Service at 9:45 a.m. Very cold. Brigadier, John Hugh Smith, and Carter motored to TRÉPORT. I rode round the area to get to know it. Stickland returned off leave.

June 24th. Rode round the Battalions with the Brigadier and watched training. Going a little sticky at first. Met Major General at 17th. Motored over to play Polo, but found no one there. Very cold wind. Arranged about the ARA platoon competition, also started to prepare at Brigade exercise.

June 25th. Brigadier and self rode round and saw Battalions training. Brigadier and self met Corps Commander and Division Commander and went round Battalions who were doing "Recreational Training". (Corps Commander Lt. General Butler with Douglas Legge, Coldstream ADC.). Day warmer.

June 26th. Brigadier Deverell and self motored off to reconnoitre route to re-inforce VILLERS BRETONNEUX if required. Observed from BOVES CHÂTEAU. After lunch we went and played Polo with the 6th Cavalry Brigade at a ground near CAVILLON. Very amusing afternoon. So home weary and sore.

June 27th. John Hugh Smith and self went down early to ARA platoon competition range. Platoons arrived also most of Divisional Staff; went well; 17th Battalion London Regiment winning it. After lunch Merton Beckwith-Smith arrived and I went with him to GHQ, staying with him at his Château.

June 28th. Got up late after a big dinner the night before with most of the O.A. Staff headed by Major General Davidson. Merton and self motored down to see some Whippet Tanks, where I met Willie (*Gibbs*) and went back to lunch with him. Found Phil Gregory and Jack Leslie there. Merton returned and after dropping him at his office, went on to Greys who were about 3 miles out, George Rodney, T. Holland-Hibbert, Archie Melville, and others, former two returned with me to MONTRIEUL, and we four (including Merton) dined at Officers Club. Most amusing dinner for some months. Slept in MONTRIEUL.

June 29th. Returned with Merton during morning to BOVELLES, finding Brigadier Deverell and Carter just off to PARIS PLAGE for weekend. John Hugh Smith having gone off yesterday as acting Brigade Major to 141st Infantry Brigade vice (*in place of*) Mann who goes to England, to have his toe cut off (!). Motored over to 6th Cavalry Brigade Polo ground where I had 6 very good Chukkas on two of my Brigadier's ponies and one of Babington's, and so home with C.R.E. who gave me a lift.

June 30th. Lovely day at last. Short Service by Fairbrother in garden. Rode over to ground where taped trenches for 17th's and 21st's "stunt" were being prepared by Laird (R.E.); Dawes (21st.): and Maynard (17th.). Lunched with 21st and had to drink Champagne. Rode back to BOVELLES and went to sleep in garden. Much hotter day.

July 1st. Army Commander (General Rawlinson) visited Brigade and saw 17th and 21st training. He appeared pleased in spite of being sent to the wrong rendez-vous. Lovely day.

July 2nd. Walter Dalkeith arrived in a car about 10:30 p.m. and we went up to 1st Guards Brigade Race Meeting held near HUMBER CAMP. Very amusing day, about 200 Officers there and lots of friends, lost on most races running. Got back at 7:30 p.m. Dined with Wyndham Portal, large party, played Baccarat after until about 12 midnight.

July 3rd. No training. Got an RAF tender to take us over to lunch with 141st Infantry Brigade. General Mildren and John Hugh Smith. We afterwards all went over to Water Carnival on SOMME at PICQUIGNY. Quite good show. Early dinner and on to Cinema of French Flying Squadron. My French taxed to limits with flying and cinema technical expressions!

July 4th. Major General Gorringe went round Battalions and presented Medal Ribbons and made a speech to each Battalion. After lunch we all played tennis with French Flying Officers and some French Ladies, amongst whom was one of the Ladies who lived at SELINCOURT when 3rd Coldstream were there in October 1916. 15th's Band played whole afternoon.

July 5th. Went round 15th Battalion to watch training. My first flight in an Aeroplane with a French Pilot in a SPAD with Lieutenant/Pilote Bérard of the French Cavalry. Went over to AMIENS and back. Very nice too. Rather high wind. Was up for 20 minutes and up to rather over 2,000 feet. Dined with 44th Escadrille of French Flying Corps. Very amusing dinner, played poker after and lost 150 francs. Thence home about 1 a.m. a sadder and wiser man; i.e. – not to play poker under French rules when you only understand ¼ of what they say.

July 6th. Rode round Battalions training. Paddy Parish and Hutchence to lunch, after which these two, Stickland and self motored via MONTRIEUL to LE TOUQUET and PARIS PLAGE, staying at Hôtel Britannique. Walked round to see Miss de Trafford at the Duchess of Westminster's Hospital. Dined at Cigal Restaurant and after went round to Madame de Sirer's house and danced. Found Misses Russell and Wineyton there. So to bed about 12 midnight.

July 7th. After a late breakfast Paddy and self motored over to MERLIEMONT where we found Billy Trewman and Willie, the latter returning to lunch at PARIS PLAGE to meet all the Ladies of last night at the Hôtel Continental. A large bathing parade followed after which Paddy and self went to tea with the Misses de Trafford and Hestor Stevens at the Nurses house near the Casino. Dinner at 7 p.m. and so back to BOVELLES after a very amusing weekend.

July 8th. Euan Wallace came over to see me and rode some of the way back. Watched some of the 17th Battalion London march past. A very hot and close day. Got a car from the French Aviators and went over to dine with Euan Wallace at LE MEUSE.

July 9th. Rode round to 15th and 17th Battalions to watch training. Staff Officer from GHQ lectured to Division on the war in French Hanger near BOVELLES. Rather interesting. Some rain which did good. 5 French Aviator Officers to dine, after which we played "Chemin de Fer" (leaving Gibbs a richer man by 400 francs!). To bed at 1 a.m.

July 10th. Some more rain. Rode over to 17th Battalion and watched final exercise over taped Course. Brigadier etc: went to XXIInd Corps race meeting. Stayed and started on Operation Orders for move on Saturday. Lloyd from MT Column to dinner.

July 11th. Went by car to MOLLIENS AU BOIS and WARLOY to see Brigade we take over from (54th), made arrangements. Brigade moving Friday instead of Saturday caused much alteration.

July 12th. Went with the French Commandant of the Flying Corps to ABANCOURT, missed 9:15 a.m. but caught 1:10 p.m. and got to PARIS at 7 p.m. Went to Ritz where I found Scott who had gone on ahead. Dined there and met Ian Bullough and Lily Elsie.

July 13th. Met George Rivière, who introduced me to Mrs. Hine and Mrs. Morrison.

July 14th. Raining hard. Tried to see Independence Day Fête, but too big a crowd.

July 15th. Changed to Crillon Hotel.

July 16th.   *PARIS*
Had a large dinner party, bade a fond farewell to Franny and Lena and caught the 10:15 p.m. at Gare du Nord, a 'Wagon Lit'.

July 21st. Returned from leave.

July 22nd. Got to ABBÉVILLE at 5:30 p.m. Caught a train to AILLY-SUR-SOMME and thence per car borrowed from 6th Cavalry Brigade to CONTAY and up to HÉNENCOURT WOOD to dug outs.

July 23rd. Found a large accumulation of papers to read. Waited in most of the day to see Commanding Officer etc. of the 1st Battalion 131st American Regiment, who only arrived about 9 p.m. Stayed up writing and answering letters until 3:45 a.m., when the 22nd Battalion went through our right Battalion and raided the Enemy Trenches on that front with considerable Artillery box barrage. Result good; two prisoners and one Machine Gun got, who were from the 450th Regiment (Prussians). Got to bed at 6 a.m.

July 24th. Wrote most of morning. Went round with Cutts, bicycling to 17th Battalion Headquarters over a very rough country track. A long walk and back at 7:45 p.m. Paddy Parish to dinner on his way to England. Wrote most of morning.

July 25th. Humphrey Gilkes returned to Brigade as Intelligence Officer. 58th Division did a daylight raid at 10:00 a.m. by 1 Battalion about AMIENS-ALBERT road, successful in getting 20 Bosche prisoners and inflicting casualties, but caused English some casualties. Went up about 7:00 p.m. to arrange side slip South for tomorrow. Got back about 10 p.m. after going round Americans and 21st Battalion. Worked till after 1 a.m. with the orders for the side slip for 26th/27th.

July 26th. Went round line and arranged further for side slip. Stickland went up and helped Americans to do the relief, which took up till 2 a.m.

July 27th. Arranging most of the day for Americans to go off. Relieved by 17th Battalion, 15th Battalion came into support. Rained hard all day.

July 28th. Brigadier General Wolfe of 66th American Brigade and Officer Commanding 131st American Regiment came and went up with me round the whole front. They got very tired; very hot.

Mesopotamia

July 28, 1918

My dearest Nancy,
    Best thanks for letter. It was very sad poor Ruby collapsing and having to give up Burnham. I was afraid all along of the move. I hope you still like Rumsey and that Stafford is really better by now. Ruby said he was to have 2 or 3 months rest. It is the only cure I am sure for nervous strain. This is a hot country and a dusty uninteresting camp. There are a few of the old officers still in the regiment and one gets through the time somehow. The early mornings and evenings we train the men. Perhaps we may get on the move about September. I wonder if Germany will produce a decent peace offer in the Autumn.
    I have had many bathes in the Euphrates, which is a muddy river and is here about as broad as the Thames in London. We had a man drowned in it last night. The country is very flat and very little cultivated hereabouts, and away from the river it is pure sandy desert. The inhabitants are very sturdy Arabs. Very primitive and fearful thieves. They are quite friendly to meet and we employ many thousands of them.

Baghdad is a miserable place but pretty big, as towns go out here. Very glad Aunt E's relative said Evelyn looked young and well. We live in tents, the floors of which are dug down to 3½ feet for coolness. The rest of our brigade are mostly black men (Indian troops).

Best love to Staff and the family.

Your loving Billy

July 29th. Brigadier went up line with Major General. Brigade Major of 66th Infantry Brigade came up and went round with Stickland and John Hugh Smith. A quiet day and fairly hot, some shelling East of SENLIS. Showed American Brigade Major how the Office was run. Brigadier returned about 5 p.m. very tired.

July 30th. At 9 a.m. the British opened a hurricane bombardment along the whole Vth Corps front, which just fringed on us in the North. It lasted 20 minutes and was a sham raid. Very little retaliation (and what a waste of ammunition). Very hot day. Spent morning preparing for relief. Relief arrived about 4:30 p.m. and we went off. John Hugh Smith still Acting/Brigade Major of the 141st. Went to the "Follies" which I did not enjoy much as I had a sore throat. Dined with Wyndham Portal.

July 31st. Woke up feeling much worse, after working a bit, General and I rode over to Divisional Headquarters, where we stopped to lunch. Sat next to Lt. Colonel Montgomerie the new GSO 1, was not much taken with him, rather abrupt and pompous!! "The Orange" (Major General) rather sad. I think they must have told him that he is not going to get a Corps. Went into 6th Field Ambulance on way home, who said I had got Tonsillitis and must go to the IIIrd Corps Rest Station. After making a few arrangements went off in Ambulance to FLESSELLES, the Château. Same Château as Headquarters 1st Guards Brigade came to on way to SOMME early in September, owned by Marquis de Sévigné.

August 1st. Throat pronounced rather bad, and so stopped in bed. General Kennedy and few others came and saw me in evening.

August 2nd. Still in bed. Raining hard. Good news from the South: Salient between SOISSONS and REIMS almost straightened out.

August 3rd. Still in bed. News continued good.

August 4th. The start to the 5th year of the war. I got up after lunch. Carter came in the evening having been to BOULOGNE with General Kennedy.

August 5th. Up, but raining hard. Got some letters.

August 6th. Walked a bit. Went to tea with Tom Gurney, the 2nd Life Guards Machine Gun Battalion being in the Village.

August 7th. Band played in Gardens. Bosche back on the AISNE. Dined with 2nd Life Guards. Very cheery dinner: Tom Gurney; Archie Sinclair: Miles Graham etc: also their Band.

August 8th. Lunched and dined with 2nd Life Guards.

August 9th. Dined with 2nd Life Guards.

August 10th. The Big attack on the Salient towards AMIENS having gone very well. The 47th Division thought they would be "for it". So General Kennedy was recalled off leave, and so I came out of the Rest Station and went back to the Brigade who were in the Quarry between LAVIÉVILLE and HÉNENCOURT. My arrival was greeted with a salvo of 8" shells from the Bosche, one hitting our Mess Kitchen and smashing every single thing we had to eat with or off. Lt. Colonel Friend of 24th Battalion London Regiment commanding Brigade in absence of General Kennedy and Lt. Colonel Segrave having gone to command the 152nd Infantry Brigade. Gunners kindly fed us for night.

August 11th. General Barber of 53rd Infantry Brigade arrived to arrange about night's relief. Brigade relieved by 53rd Infantry Brigade and went into BAIZIEUX.

August 12th. Orders received for Brigade to relieve 142nd Infantry Brigade in trenches (Old British) west of MORLANCOURT. Stickland and self rode over and saw Brigade Major. This was cancelled and Brigade remained at BAIZIEUX for the night. Brigadier returned with Lionel Gibbs to go as ADC to General Gorringe.

August 13th. Moved in the afternoon. Went to Division for tea at HEILLY. Battalions came up to new area which is the old British trenches South west of MORLANCOURT. The 175th Infantry Brigade having gone away early, some confusion was caused as to where Battalions were to go to. Brigade Headquarters in a Bank just above MÉRETTE WOOD near MÉRICOURT.

August 14th. Went round 21st Battalion's trenches. Headquarters Brigade moved down onto the SOMME about 1,000 yards west of VAUX-SUR-SOMME in tents and "lean-to's". Major General and Lionel came over.

August 15th. Brigadier and self rode up to 142nd Brigade Headquarters at MENIN COPSE to arrange about relief, back again by 1:30 p.m. Wrote orders. John Hugh Smith came up to tea. No news.

August 16th. Went up to Battalions, lunching with Colonel Dawes (21st Londons). Very hot day. Walked up via our new Brigade Headquarters across to Headquarters in MENIN COPSE, taking over from 142nd

Infantry Brigade. Bosche active on the BRAY-CORBIE road. 15th Battalion went up to right front: 21st to left; 17th Support. A noisy relief, the 21st Battalion getting a direct hit on a limber and another partial one on a water cart throwing it into a shell hole. Bad luck after their losing 20 horses from a bomb 3 nights ago. Relief complete at 2:30 p.m. after a very difficult relief.

August 17th. Brigadier, Humphrey Gilkes. Lt. Colonel Johnston [Group Commander 250th R.F.A. Brigade), and self started up the line at 6 a.m. Fairly quiet, went to front line on left and right, having to go over the top most of the time. "Terrible" lot of bodies still about and most of them very old now. Bosche still active on BRAY-CORBIE road. Corps Commander (Godley) came up and saw us, also our Major General and Lionel. Major General rang up to say we were to advance our posts on the right. Wrote orders and arranged with Artillery and Machine Guns to push their "S.O.S." Barrages further East. Zero hour 10 p.m. 15th Battalion to do their "Stunt". Four parties went out to try and establish themselves on the East side of the ÉTINEHEM-MÉAULTE road. Right post got in and stayed. Next post started to consolidate but got shelled out, the left two posts never got across the road owing to Machine Guns firing down the road. Net result only one post established.

August 18th. 15th Battalion Londons had a good many casualties in last night's show and the shelling that went with it, 40 in all. Went up round 17th Battalion (Support) lines and to Battalion Headquarters of front Battalions. Priestman and another from the Army came round but had no news. General saw Bates (15th) personally and explained how the posts were to be advanced tonight. Orders for future operations arrived after dinner. Patrols went out at 10:30 p.m. No:b2 post was established, but owing to a misunderstanding the other two patrols went the wrong way and could not get across the road, digging themselves in on the west side of it. The Machine Guns were again active. Aeroplane dropped 8 bombs about 200 yards from Brigade Headquarters.

August 19th. General and Humphrey Gilkes went off to investigate the night's doings. Lt. Colonel R. C. Feilding (S. R. Coldstream) arrived to take over Command of 15th Battalion London Regiment. Stayed at Battalion Headquarters. Major General came round with Lionel and confided in me date of big attacks. Further instructions for offensive arrived.

August 20th. Quiet night. Lt. Colonel Johnston B.F.A. came and saw Brigadier and we discussed Advanced Guard. Kit went off at 3 p.m. and the Staff of the 141st Infantry Brigade relieving us arrived at 5 p.m. The General and I rode back to dug-outs just North of MARETT WOOD by MÉRICOURT. All 3 Battalion Headquarters in Bank.

August 21st. Up fairly early. General and I went to Division Headquarters, where we heard all the latest news of attack to take place on 22nd. A Commanding Officers' Conference on our return, where the Brigadier explained all about the attack to Commanding Officers. Spent whole afternoon writing orders and reading other peoples. Large quantity of visitors. Good news of French attack West of SOISSONS - 10,000 prisoners. Also IIIrd Army attack going well. Watches synchronized at 7:00 p.m. by Lewis (GSO IInd Division). Lt. Colonel Kaye (KOYLI) arrived to take over 17th Battalion London Regiment, and came to dinner.

August 22nd. Battalions marched off to their assembly areas at 6 a.m. Brigade Headquarters at 7 a.m. Assembly areas being just west of TAILLES WOOD. The hour for the attack by the 141st Infantry Brigade was 4:45 a.m. The 142nd Infantry Brigade was formed up in rear. The "Brown" line was reached about 7 a.m., and the 142nd Brigade went through to the "Green line", which they got to meeting a fair resistance. Little news came through until lunch time, when a Counter attack had started after the 2 Squadrons of the Northumberlands had tried to get through and been shelled off. This shook the left and they began to come away. A telephone message came through from the 19th Battalion (141st) to ask for help saying they could not get through to their own Brigade. The 17th Battalion was sent up to the Left and the 15th Battalion to the right, with the help of the remnants of the 141st Brigade they took up a line just west of the ALBERT-BRAY road and so stopped the ruck. The whole of the forward troops were now put under General Kennedy and the 142nd Brigade withdrawn. The line was straightened out during the night.

August 23rd. Nothing particular happened during the night. About 7 a.m. I went up to see Lt. Colonel Furgusson (19th) to try and find out the dispositions, but found everything very uncertain and so with the help of Lt. Colonel Neely (18th Battalion) we crawled up to near front line and examined it. Bosche snipers very active, also TAILLES WOOD heavily shelled all day with occasionally one or two near Brigade Headquarters. Orders were received that the 140th Brigade (on left) and 175th (58th Division on right) would attack the "Green line" again on the 24th and the front must be reorganized to do this. The 141st Brigade were to arrange the assembly posts. The 21st Battalion (on left) and 17th Battalion (on right) were in position by about 12 midnight. The 15th Battalion remained down where it originally went so that after the advance they could mop up "HAPPY VALLEY".

August 24th. The hour for the attack was 1 a.m. and was started with a heavy barrage. The "Green line" was taken and some 300 prisoners were taken in HAPPY VALLEY. The Bosche who had been expecting these attacks put down a very heavy barrage at once on the ALBERT-BRAY road and also on the "Green line". A small pocket of Machine Guns and Trench Mortars remained on the 21st Battalion's left and stopped the 12th Division on our left coming up. These started to hammer the 21st Battalion causing considerable casualties and the situation looked serious, their left being quite in the air. The 15th Battalion therefore went up and formed a defensive flank. I went up and discovered the situation much better than expected. Going right up to the left I found the Trench Mortar gone but the Machine Guns still active. Otherwise the Brigade front was intact and in touch on the right. The front was reorganized after dark, the 15th Battalion coming up on the right and taking over partly from the right Brigade and a bit from the 17th Battalion. The 17th Battalion in the centre with the 21st Battalion, now weak on the left.

Awarded Bar to the Military Cross. (*See C.V. at the end*).

August 25th. The attack started at 2:30 a.m. and met with very little opposition, the Battalions going forward under the barrage up to their objectives on the East side of BRONFAY FARM and digging in almost untouched. I got up there about 9 a.m. having ridden most of the way. Some Machine Guns were now worrying a bit, also they started to shell rather heavily but wildly. All the men now very tired but very pleased with themselves. Relief arranged the 173rd Brigade having gone through us to BILLON WOOD. Battalions came back to the "Green line" in the evening and Battalion Headquarters were established back at Brigade Headquarters. Brigade Headquarters went to dug outs near VILLE. I spent the whole night on a horse arranging where Battalions were to go.

August 26th. After "filthy" night we moved to shelters just South of VILLE-SUR-ANCRE. Battalions returned to old British trenches west of MORLANCOURT by 12 noon after relief in "Green line" by 142nd Brigade. Rest of day spent in rest.

August 27th. A long rest. Rode up to Battalions. IIIrd Corps Commander came to see us.

August 28th. Brigadier and self rode up to Battalions at 11 a.m. and the Brigadier told them all the congratulatory messages. To Division Headquarters for lunch and back to Battalions, where Divisional Commander spoke to all Officers and told them about the Future. Rained hard.

August 29th. Brigade moved up to CARNOY area and took over from 37rd Infantry Brigade. 141st and 142nd Brigades going to MAUREPAS.

August 30th. At 6 a.m. Brigade started to move forward in order 15th Battalion; 21st Battalion; "A" Company; 47th Machine Gun Battalion; 17th Battalion. "Rendez-vous" BRIQUETPRIE South West of BERNAFAY WOOD in column of route @200 yards interval between Companies. Brigade Headquarters moved to MAUREPAS RAVINE and stayed there all day. Men of Brigade getting into shelters west of Ravine. Brigade Headquarters returned to CARNOY for night. During day 141st and 142nd got on fairly well.

August 31st. Brigade Headquarters moved up at about 10 a.m., Battalion having remained in their Bivouacs during the night. Brigade Conference at 3 p.m., Brigadier explained operations for next day for 140th Brigade. A fairly quiet day. 141st and 142nd had got on and established a line West of PRIEZ FARM. Brigade Headquarters established in MAUREPAS RAVINE. Battalions moved up during night to positions of Assembly which entailed them moving all night as it was very dark.

September 1st. Attack started at 5:30 a.m. 15th Battalion on left; 21st on right; and 17th in Support and to mop up RANCOURT. About 6:30 a.m. an urgent wire from the 17th Battalion to say their Doctor had been badly hit, however luckily they captured a complete German Ambulance in RANCOURT and kept the Doctors. PRIEZ FARM caused a great difficulty on the left, 37th Infantry Brigade were unable to keep, the 17th Battalion left was reported in the air at 7 a.m. Prisoners taken from 53rd and 16th German Regiments reported their orders were to retire on ST. PIERRE VAAST WOOD. 7:30 a.m. PRIEZ FARM reported to have been taken. Prisoners from 11 different Regiments taken. At 8 a.m. RANCOURT reported mopped up and 15th Battalion going on well to objective (ST. PIERRE VAAST WOOD Western Edge) which they reached at 9 a.m. At 10 a.m. PRIEZ FARM still reported held by enemy. 21st Battalion not very happy on the right, 17th Battalion sent up a Company to help. A gap of 500 yards between 15th and 21st which was serious as it is probable line of Counter Attack, but (at present) Huns are walking about aimlessly in the wood. Major Hutchence 21st Battalion wounded in head so news of 21st Battalion rather sketchy and Bosche filtering down a bit and sniping heavily. Orders were received at 6:30 p.m. to withdraw the Brigade and to go in behind 74th Division South West of BOUCHAVESNES. No time to write them so orders explained to me and I went up on Motor Bicycle and told each Commanding Officer personally. Men all very tired and a very difficult operation owing to the Huns being in forward posts and the 15th Battalion more or less behind them. Hot meals were got up to troops on main RANCOURT-PERONNE road in spite of its proximity to Enemy and Battalions were moving all night down to new positions, arriving shortly before dawn. 21st Battalion much reduced in numbers.

September 2nd. In the orders received over night the Brigade were to follow behind the 74th Division (230 Brigade) and mop up MOISLAINS. At 2:30 a.m. the order for mopping up MOISLAINS was changed and the 230th Brigade were going to do it owing to a "misunderstanding" between the Divisions! This involved our orders having to be entirely changed about 3 hours before the attack was due to start. Gilkes took these orders up. Brigade Headquarters established 3 mile East of LEFOREST (near MAUREPAS). Soon after our arrival the General's Black Mare and Groom also both my horses were killed by a shell outside our Headquarters. Bombs were asked for and Stickland took a load up in a Divisional car about 5 p.m. The news all day was sketchy but it appeared the 230th Brigade did not get on or take MOISLAINS. The 17th Battalion on the right were much exposed. MOISLAINS was not taken and some enemy got through a gap on the western side, thus getting behind part of the 15th Battalion, they however held on. The 230th Brigade and part of 229th Brigade got across the Canal South of MOISLAINS but Machine Gun fire from East of it caused many casualties to troops of 15th and 21st on South side of the BOUCHAVESNES-MOISLAINS road. Very few of 74th Division could be found and the 140th Brigade who should have been in Support found themselves holding a front line all along our front. Enemy guns firing over open sights from Ridge East MOISLAINS reported at 12 noon. All the above information was sent down by Gilkes who was at Advance Brigade Headquarters and made continual reconnaissance personally. 142nd got on fairly well on our left but a small gap existed. The 140th Brigade however was by now so weak, we had to have all our men on our front and could not close it. Pioneer Battalion sent up to clear up ST. PIERRE VAAST WOOD. The evening became quieter and the Bosche was thought to be retiring. 140th Brigade withdrawn a little to rear and 21st Battalion back to MAUREPAS RAVINE.

September 3rd. Brigade about 665 Rifles strong and started to refit.

September 4th. Brigadier and self went up and saw Battalions who are round about trenches West of ST. PIERRE VAAST WOOD now fairly quiet. The 21st Battalion had been amalgamated with the 15th Battalion, and Lt. Colonel Dawes returned to his Transport lines.

September 5th. 142nd Infantry Brigade to go on with attack. 141st to go through as an advance guard and the 140th to be ready to exploit success. At 9 a.m. Gilkes from position North west of MOISLAINS reported Bosche seen retiring on NURLU-PÉRONNE road and asked for Artillery. Heavy Machine Gun fire from ÉPINETTE WOOD. Attack held up on right and 17th Battalion ordered to form a defensive flank facing South on East side of CANAL DU NORD. Cause of failure of attack appears to be that 74th Division did not start on right owing to some "misunderstanding" in their orders. A very unpleasant situation. A conference between all GOC Brigades and a second attack arranged at 7:00 p.m. behind a small barrage. The 74th Division on right and 12th Division on left conforming, the objective being the very high ridge of NURLU-PÉRONNE road approached by an absolute glacié. Attack launched successfully and 17th Battalion filtrated through ÉPINETTE WOOD to the East side to make a jumping off line for tomorrow. Rations for 17th Battalion went wrong and did not get up till 5 a.m. (6th).

September 6th. Attack continued by 15th Battalion at 5 a.m. with very little opposition. I got up just in time to see 15th Battalion take the ridge South of LIÉRAMONT, which they did in excellent formation getting shelled a bit on the East side. The 141st Brigade were rather long coming up on the left, but eventually took LIÉRAMONT easily. A quiet day, Brigade relieved by 175th Infantry Brigade (SBE Division) and withdrew to ground East of MOISLAINS.

September 7th. Brigade was carried in Buses to HEILLY, which took a long time owing to congestion on road. Battalions very moth-eaten and tired, but "full of beans".

September 8th. Spent refitting, washing, and resting.

September 9th. Battalion started to entrain for CHOCQUES, which took some 36 hours.

September 10th. Brigade arrived in driblets and was billeted in CHOCQUES. Not very comfortable owing to Village being deserted. Brigadier and self motored up.

September 11th. Started off on leave to England in Signals car. Slept BOULOGNE.

September 12th. Crossed at 9 a.m. Victoria 4 p.m. where I met Blanche.

Leave until 27th.

September 28th. Caught 9 a.m. train to BOULOGNE – up to ANVIN. Jumped a car ST. POL to ST. MICHEL where I found the 140th Infantry Brigade. Lt. Colonel Dawes commanding as Brigadier Kennedy was on leave. Found them all preparing to go to Italy, but no definite orders yet.

September 29th. To Parade Service with 21st Battalion. Rained most of the day. Lt. Colonel Montgomerie (GSO 1) to dinner.

September 30th. Major General returned with gloomy prospects of going to Italy. Lt. Colonel Dawes and self rode up to 17th Battalion at BRYAS. Dined with 15th Battalion, Knox sang, quite excellent voice (USA Medical Officer). Also another fellow, quite good and very good pianist. They also sang one duet.

October 1st. Orders came in about 1 a.m. that transport would probably be moving today. This was confirmed at 8:30 a.m., a great hurry ensued as it had to be clear of the main ST. POL-ARRAS road by 10:30 a.m.

They were in consequence late getting off. Orders came in very sketchily. 141st Brigade went off up to take over from part of 59th Division.

Station: Bourton-on-the-Water
Telephone: 6 Bourton-on-the-Water: Telegrams: Upper Slaughter
Copse Hil
Lower Slaughter
Gloucestershire

September 30th 1918

Dearest Nancy

I thought you would be pleased to know that Billy has got Command of the 7th. I had a cable from him on Friday. He will be so delighted and it is the job he would like better than anything else. I only hope he will keep fit. I have just had some letters from him dated July 20th and 27th. He said it was very hot there, but I dare say by now it is cooler again. It is too splendid that he has got the Command.

I wonder if you have heard from Stafford yet, and hope he is all right. I hear that Lags is home and hear that he gave a dance in London!

Please give him my love if you see him. Awful weather here and continuous rain.

With love

Yours affectionately

Ruby (Gibbs)

October 2nd. After waiting about all day, the Brigade went off in 2 trains from ST. POL at 20:19 & 21:19. Lt. Colonel Dawes and self went up in R.A.F. tenders to MERVILLE, then to LESTREM, and so to LE PETIT MARAIS where the Brigade Headquarters were.

October 3rd. Brigade temporally under 59th Division were ordered to be ready to move at 8:30 a.m., which was communicated to Battalions with difficulty. A few hours sleep and 47th Division rang up to say they had taken over and we should not move till after lunch. 141st started an Advanced Guard at 7:00 a.m. Rode round Battalions and Division Headquarters. Brigade moved at 2:00 p.m. to RUE TILLELOY area, Brigade Headquarters near LA FLINQUE cross roads. Heard news that Gilly Follett has been killed. Very sad after so long and gallant a career. Orders to continue advance tomorrow received at 20:00 o'clock.

October 4th. The Brigade continued the advance at 8 a.m. in column of route being in reserve. Marching in order 21st; 17th; and 16th. The 140th

Trench Mortar Battery; "A" Company Machine Gun Battalion to take up position near LE MAISNIL-EN-WEPPES. Road much blocked by traffic owing to nearly every cross road having been mined and blown up by the Huns which made progress slow. In position at 11 a.m. Brigade Headquarters established for day at HAYEM with Advanced Division Headquarters. Very uncomfortable. Later we moved to an old Prisoner of war Camp in LE MAISNIL. 141st Infantry Brigade met considerable opposition at Railway Embankment East of RADINGHAM and so Advance stopped. Orders received that no move would be made tomorrow. A chilly night.

October 5th. Orders sent out for 140th to relieve 141st in Left Sector tonight. Colonel Dawes and self went round line and found a gap of 1,000 yards in between front two Battalions, which I don't think 141 Brigade Staff knew anything about. Very wet line and rather unsatisfactorily held. Relief started at 6:30 p.m. and finished at 11 p.m. During the day 140th Brigade Headquarters was moved back to a Pill Box near HAYEM, from which 10 Bosche mines had been removed. We hope there are no more!

October 6th. The 21st Battalion were now on the right with the 17th Battalion on the left and 15th in Support. During the afternoon the 21st Battalion tried to get onto the embankment and through a door in a Culvert, this woke up the Bosche who had a Machine Gun sitting right on top of it. He got onto the embankment and our Lewis Gun accounted for 8 Bosche for certain and the Machine Gun out of action. Our casualties being 1 killed and 2 very slightly wounded – good show! 17th Battalion were not so lucky when pushing South down the embankment to try and join up, meeting a Machine Gun they had 20 casualties including an Officer killed and were unable to stay there. The Hun shelled considerably more during the night and especially round the 21st Battalion Headquarters on road running North from RADINGHAM, including a good sprinkling of gas.

October 7th. The 21st Battalion shifted their Headquarters into RADINGHAM. Otherwise a quiet day. Some "Pine-apple" trench mortaring in Copse on 21st Battalion front. 60 pounders and 6" howitzers were got onto it, which temporarily stopped it. 17th Battalion did not get all their dead back and they think the Hun got the Officer's body which is very unfortunate. Front to be re-organized, 142nd to have internal reliefs and 141st to relieve us on 9th/10th night. Heard various Peace Rumours. That Germans are trying President Wilson. Also Austria is prepared to accept President Wilson's 14 points. Several Honours and Rewards for the SOMME show came in including a Bar to Military Cross for self.

October 8th. A quiet night. 17th unable to get any bodies in. Major General (+Lionel Gibbs) came round full of congratulations and went on up the line altering most of the dispositions. Issued orders for the relief after seeing Douglas (Brigade Major 141st Brigade). Much colder. Some of our attached Sappers in trying to clear a gassed Pill Box up forward, got themselves gassed while doing it.

October 9th. Bosche seem to be very quiet on our front. Went up to 21st Battalion on right. Brigade relieved by 141st Infantry Brigade and came back into Support in FROMELLES-LE-MAISNIL. Relief complete about 22:00 o'clock. Brigade Headquarters at RUE TILLELOY LAVANTIE-SEC.

October 10th. General Birdwood commanding Fifth Army in which we are in came to Brigade Headquarters at 12:00. News continues excellent. CAMBRAI having been captured yesterday. Brigadier General Kennedy and Carlton returned off leave. Colonel Dawes stopped the night with the Brigade.

October 11th. Brigadier and self went up to Battalion Headquarters in a car. Raid carried out by 142nd Brigade; not altogether a success as no Bosche found, but no casualties to our side. Brigadier and self went up to Battalions. News that British are well East of LE CATEAU, which is splendid. Hassal (DAAG IXth Corps) came round and took away D.Young en route for PARIS.

October 12th. Muggy day. Court Martial of yesterday continued. Rode up to 141st Infantry Brigade to lunch with them and arrange relief for tomorrow, which was subsequently 'washed out' as news received that 47th Division are going to Italy. probably on 18th and would be relieved in this sector on 14th by 57th Division. Various orders received during the evening. Some Portuguese Officers for attachment did not turn up.

October 13th. Cold and bleak. Deverell went off to find billets in ESTAIRES for the Brigade also CALONNE. News continues excellent and many rumours current as to German reply to President Wilson's answer. Prisoner taken on next Division front stated Germans are going back behind LILLE tomorrow, (which I hope is not true as it will somewhat impede our departure to Italy!). Major General and Lionel G. came round and saw us. Orders from 47th Division arrived about 17:00. Orders sent out to Units by SDR. Division very excited as possibility of Hun retirement tomorrow morning.

October 14th. 142nd Infantry Brigade had "a go" at the Railway Embankment in front of RADINGHAM which was not a success as strongly held, no prisoners taken. 172nd Infantry Brigade started to arrive about 12:30 p.m. Mark Maitland commanding that Brigade temporally. Battalions to ESTAIRES. Brigade Headquarters to Convent ST. VENANT where we arrived about 4 p.m.

October 15th. ROULERS has been taken and Belgians are going on well.

Brigadier and self rode out to watch Battalions march in. Came in very well. 15th Battalion London Regiment. 140th Trench Mortar Battalion, and 4th Field Ambulance to ST. VENANT. 17th Battalion, 21st Battalion, 517th Field Company RE, and No: 2 Company Train to ST. FLORIS. Much colder. 142nd Infantry Brigade got on a bit and took ENNENTIERS.

October 16th. Battalions spent the day cleaning up. Played football for Brigade Headquarters at 3 p.m. versus Battalion Headquarters of 15th Battalion and got "beat". Very stiff in consequence. Orders arrived for move to ST. HILAIRE area tomorrow.

October 17th. Brigade marched over to ST. HILAIRE area using FONTES and ROMBLY as well, arriving about 1 p.m. Went into AIRE for lunch; found it very much knocked about. 57th Division, who relieved us very near or into LILLE, the 142nd having driven the Huns out of the LILLE defences.

October 18th. OSTEND and ZEBBRUGGE-DONAI and all LILLE taken. Fine day. Went round and saw 17th and 21st Battalions. Major General came round to see Brigade Headquarters. Rode over to FONTES to see 15th Battalion and Division at NORRENTES-FONTES. Italy seems rather far off. BRUGES taken.

October 19th. Much colder day but fine. Went out with Montgomerie (GSO 1) to reconnoitre for Training ground and Ranges. Divisional "Follies" show at 8 p.m. Major General dined with us first also Lionel.

October 20th. Rained all night. Church parade on football ground had to be put off after all had assembled. A short service and Medal Ribbon giving in the YMCA hut. Lunched with 15th Battalion in FONTES and rode over training ground with Lt. Colonel Feilding to arrange a Brigade exercise. Motored over to Machine Gun Battalion and had tea with Wyndham Portal. Brigadier and Swankey spent afternoon in LILLE. Started 140th Brigade Sweepstake Cambridgeshire.

October 21st. Rode up to rifle range and watched 21st Battalion shooting. Conference at 47th Division Headquarters when Divisional General explained programme of training and also told us *we* should be moving up to west of LILLE on Saturday, brushing up Sunday and taking part in the triumphal entry on Monday 28th October. Dined with 142nd Infantry Brigade.

October 22nd. A platoon from 15th Battalion to practice with an Officer from the Irish Guards Training Battalion to show during the afternoon. Brigadier, self, Colonel Feilding, and Portal rode round training area. Platoon demonstration by Lt. Fowles HAC, quite good. Wyndham Portal, Dickie Dill, Lionel, and self dined at Restaurant in AIRE.

October 23rd. Cold and fine. Brigade exercise carried out by 15th Battalion and witnessed by all the "Knobs" including Major General CRA etc: quite successful and over by 12:00. A quiet afternoon. Old woman in my billet got bad toothache so I gave her 10 gr. of Phenecitin, but feared afterwards it was too big a dose and would kill her.

October 24th. Old Lady still alive and had a very good night – great relief. Exercise by 21st Battalion London Regiment over the same ground as yesterday. Quite well done. Lionel and Major General there; the former told me Willie had been badly wounded.

October 25th. Major General presented medals to winning Platoon in Army Rifle Association Competition of 17th Battalion. Staff Captain took billeting party from Brigade to LOMME, East of LILLE. Transports marched off to stage at ESTAIRES en route for LOMME. Orders for move by train tomorrow issued.

October 26th. Lorries with kit and troops started about 10:00 a.m. Managed to get a tender from Flying Corps and motored up with General to LILLE. Walked about town and had excellent lunch at Hôtel de L'Europe. All inhabitants appear absolutely delighted at deliverance and most windows have "Glory be to our Deliverers". Whole streets are bedecked with flags. Met Prince of Wales and Claud Hamilton in street and walked about most of the afternoon with them. Back to dinner in beautiful Château in LOMME where we live.

October 27th. Conference with Commanding Officers, as to march through LILLE TOMORROW. at 11:15. Cold and Bleak. Went into LILLE and listened to the Band. Colonels Feilding and Kaye to dinner. (Had a head and felt very depressed!).

October 28th. From 9:00 a.m. onwards troops were marching past our Headquarters to the starting point at CANTELAU BRIDGE. At 11:15 a.m. we formed up and moved off ¼ hour ahead of time. Battalions, Field Company RE, and Ambulance all very well cleaned up. Long crowds lined the streets and clapped, many women having been reduced to tears at a very early hour. We marched through about 3 miles of streets, eventually coming to the Grand Place of LILLE, where stands had been erected and bunting hung. A Dais in the corner where General Birdwood had given his Penion to the Mayor and from where they watched the March Past. The Column consisted only of the 47th Division complete and took nearly 3 hours to pass the Saluting Point. 140th Infantry Brigade was given top marks for marching. Lunched in LILLE afterwards and then on to our new billets in FIVES (about 1½ miles out) where we are billeted in a splendid house inhabited at present only by an English Governess (Miss Mault) who had been there the whole Seige – she joined our Mess. Went into LILLE in an Ambulance to see the "Cordites" (XIth Corps Troupe) at the Theatre – bad show.

October 29th. A holiday for all. I finished off the Cambridgeshire Sweepstake. In the evening we gave a dance in our Château, the 3 (very pretty!!) daughters of the sub-mayor of LILLE coming. Music by 2 out of the Orchestra in our "Follies" Troupe. Kept it up till 1 a.m.

October 30th. General, having had a wire to say his Mother had been knocked over by a motor, went off to England on Special Leave at 5:30 a.m. Battalions moved up into Reserve area preparatory to taking over from 172nd Infantry Brigade (57th Division). Colonel Dawes and self motored up and went round Battalion Headquarters.

October 31st. Walked into LILLE and back before lunch. About 3:30 p.m. we started up to Brigade Headquarters at CATEAU to take over Battalions moving into the line. Relief complete about 8 p.m. Line fairly quiet.

November 1st. Colonel Dawes and self rode up at 10 a.m. to Headquarters 15th Battalion at FROYENNES, lunched and went up to right part of line and looked round. Very odd line all through houses and out of windows etc. 17th Battalion in HONNEVAIN shelled.

November 2nd. Waited a long time for Major General and eventually rode up and met him at 17th Battalion's Headquarters. He looked round Reserve Positions only and up to 15th Battalion Headquarters.

November 3rd. Everyone at Brigade Headquarters feeling very ill and several went down with Flue. Went round left front of 15th Battalion. Convent somewhat heavily shelled but not very near us. Went to bed before dinner (Note: - these were the last shells I saw fall in the War.)

November 4th. Stayed in bed as feeling worse and temperature up to 102.6° about lunchtime. Taken off to Hospital about 9 p.m. eventually getting to the Girls School off the Boulevard de la Liberté, LILLE about 12 midnight.

November 5th to 10th

IN HOSPITAL.

November 11th. Got up be'times. Got a lift off a GHQ Supply Column car right up to LA TOMBE just North of TOURNAI to which place I found the Brigade had just returned. Still felt very weak. Had a large dinner and drank to the Armistice.

Chapter Six

The Armistice and Versailles

November 11th ARMISTICE from 11:00 a.m. onwards.

November 12th. Divisional Conference 10 a.m. Division Commander thanked everyone for all they had done and went on to talk of Education and Employment of Men after the war. Rode up to MONT ST. AUBERT and looked at view. Very good.

November 13th. Frost but sunny. Brigadier and Deverell went off to billet the Brigade along the Railway running East from TOURNAI. Walked down to Machine Gun Battalion Headquarters and had a long talk to Lt. Colonel Portal on work after the war. Walked into TOURNAI with Colonel Feilding and looked round the Cathedral.

November 14th. Rode over to see Portuguese Battalion and 21st Battalion along Railway, East of TOURNAI. Germans have broken up that Railway most effectively. Every rail is cut and craters of 6ft and more blown every 50 yards going for miles and miles. It must have taken months to do.

November 15th. We are now transferred to First Army (Horne), but remain in XIth Corps (Haking). General and self rode and jumped cars to 15th Battalion London Regiment some 12 miles off. Main TOURNAI road crowded with returned Refugees going to LILLE.

November 16th. At 9:30 a.m. Brigadier General Hordern (BGGS Ist Corps) picked General Kennedy and self up and we went to ZEEBRUGGE via COURTRAI and BRUGES. Most interesting though cold drive. The "Vindictive" and "Thetis" and one other ship still lying in the mouth, and the hole in the Mole still open. We lunched at BRUGES on the way back and looked at the Cathedral. Naylor (141st Brigade Headquarters) stayed the night on his return from leave.

Head Quarters
140th Infantry Brigade
British Expeditionary Force

November 16th 1918

Darling Nancy
    Finished! It is really rather wonderful to feel that one has not got to go under any more shells or gas; and that the war is <u>really</u> over. After

4¼ years one does not know what it is to be without War. Out here it was all taken very calmly. We were attacking on the 10th November and we received a very simple message sent just the same way as 20 others one might receive every day; saying "Hostilities will cease at 11.00 and all troops will stand fast where they are"; and so ended one of the greatest wars in the world's history.

Now we are starting extensive Educational Schemes also an Employment Bureau; my General is in charge of the latter.

The road we are on Brussels – Tournai is one long stream of refugees (who have been freed by the Bosch) who are returning to Tournai, Lille etc, pushing their few belongings on barrow with them, also many English soldiers – prisoners who have got away. A large depot has been put up at Tournai for the soldiers to feed and clothe them and arrange to send them on to England.

We have not been selected as one of the Divisions to go to the Rhineland, many are sorry, personally I am not as I think by staying back here one will get far more leave, and probably (eventually) get back to England sooner. Anyhow I think it will be many months before anyone gets back.

Tomorrow I <u>hope</u> to go to Zeebrugge, which will be very interesting if it comes off.

I'm bound to say I agree with you, I should love to have been in London on the 11th, although those who were say it was not <u>really</u> very exciting and the papers made much more of it than really happened. I am delighted to see what a lot the King and Queen have been doing and how they will have been received. You ask if the army were sick at not getting to Germany – No! I think everyone was so delighted at the thing being over, they did not really mind and also the average Private Soldier is not really very vindictive, not nearly enough so. They forget so easily. It would have taken such a lot more fighting at the pace we were going to get right into Germany and the terms of the Armistice are sufficiently strong to compensate for most things.

Poor Albinia, I hope she does not have a very bad time and that he really does her some good.

I hope someone will tell me when Evelyn arrives. I fear I shall not get leave to England before January but I hope to get to Paris for a week in December.

Your loving

Lags

P.S. I have got over my Flu now, but for days after coming out of Hospital I felt like "nothing on earth". I haven't felt so bad for years. It made one so weak.

November 17th. After lunch went into LILLE for tea, rather dull.

November 18th. Brigade moved to WILLEMS, less 15th Battalion who stage at LA TOMBE. Snowing hard and very slippery, turning to rain. Billets bad.

November 19th. Cold bleak and unpleasant. 15th Battalion arrived in WILLEMS.

November 20th. Brigadier and 2 others motored to BRUSSELS and received a most enthusiastic welcome as no troops had yet got there. Lunched and dined with 21st Battalion.

November 21st. Worked at Employment Bureau.

November 22nd. Sunny and fine. Conference of Commanding Officers at Brigade Headquarters at 10:30 a.m. on Education Scheme. 'Car jumped' into LILLE, had tea with XIth Corps (Pickering and Martin Alexander) and so home.

November 23rd. General went to BRUSSELS. I stayed at home.

November 24th. Brigade Parade Thanksgiving Service of all denominations. Colonel Feilding returned from BRUSSELS saying Evelyn was there. Watched some football.

November 25th. Dashed off to BRUSSELS in car with Lewis and Turner (of Division) to see Evelyn. Got there about 12:30 p.m. Went to Dutch and British Embassy also to Baron Lambert's house but could not find him, and so came to the conclusion he had returned to THE HAGUE. Dined at Savoy and danced after, leaving at 9:15 p.m., arriving WILLEMS 1:30 a.m.

November 26th. Brigade started its long march to AUCHEL area. Marched to HAREBOURDIN together with 47th Machine Gun Battalion. General and self lunched in LILLE.

November 27th. Brigade started about 8 a.m. Fine day. General and self started about 9:30 a.m. and caught up Brigade. Men marching well. Some Battalions had 21 miles to go. Got back to BÉTHUNE about 5 p.m. Went round outside area on motor bicycle.

November 28th. On again at 10 a.m. to AUCHEL area, 15th Battalion (CSR) to FERFAY. 17th Battalion to CAUCHY. Swankey and Signals returned. Rained hard – filthy day. We are billeted with Madame Crossart. Dined at Division.

November 29th. General and self rode over to FERFAY and CAUCHY to see Battalions.

November 30th. Continued on Education and Employment Committee all day, very little else to do. Meeting of Educational Officers of Brigade at 5 p.m.

December 1st. Church at 10:15 a.m. Rode over to 15th Battalion Dentist and got a tooth stopped. Lecture by Sir Francis Younghusband on Central India

December 2nd. Rode round 15th, 17th, and 21st Battalions. Sent in application for self to go to PARIS.

December 3rd. Went to C.S. Rifles Dentist in morning; spent most of afternoon trying to get a car to go to AMIENS en route for PARIS.

December 4th. Off to PARIS. By Ambulance to ST. POL, thence to PARIS where we arrived at midnight.

PARIS UNTIL

December 15th. Left PARIS 9:30 a.m. via AMIENS and got to PERNES at 7 p.m. Dined there and thence by Ambulance to AUCHEL.

December 16th. Raining and unpleasant day. Sent out 100 Christmas Cards. Dined with 15th Battalion London Regiment on the opening night of their Battalion Mess.

December 17th. Rode up to 15th Battalion and back by 17th. After lunch up to see tie of Divisional Football Match between 21st Battalion and 140th Trench Mortar Battery.

December 18th. Lecture by Colonel Dowding on Reinstatement, quite interesting.

December 19th. Rode round to 17th Battalion and home. Played football without any disastrous results. Dined with 21st Battalion.

December 20th. Feeling rather stiff still. Went over to see 15th Battalion Dentist, who hurt rather. Took over the Demobilization part of Brigade.

December 21st. Paid another visit to Dentist. Rained most of the day.

December 22nd. Church with 21st Battalion. Aeroplane made a forced landing on our Aerodrome and came into Office to wire his Squadron.

December 23rd. A red letter day in so far as my Birthday is concerned, otherwise it poured with rain all day.

December 24th. A conference of Commanding Officers over latest orders as to Men on leave getting demobilized, after which Kaye, Young, and Jones (TMB) stayed to lunch. Rain and sleet most of the day.

December 25th. Christmas Day.
Went round in an Ambulance to the Service at each Battalion. Went to NCO's Dinners at 2:30 p.m. and stopped there till 5 p.m., varying one's drinks from Beer to Crème de Menthe to somewhat sweet Champagne! Home to sleep till dinner, after which an early bed, but was soon woken up (about 12:30 a.m.) by NCO's coming to General's window and demanding a speech, followed by the Officers of the Trench Mortar Battery coming at 1:30 a.m. and singing Carols for half an hour.

December 26th. Snowed a bit. Walked (nearly!) to Charlie Chaplin (Camblain-Châtelan) with 'Sigs'. Went into Men's Christmas Dinners and drank a glass of beer with them.

December 27th. Rain the whole day. Dined with Wyndham Portal, Dickie D. etc: took 30 Francs off them at Roulette!

December 28th. Rain again!

December 29th. Major General came to 15th Battalion's Service and presented Medal to Private Young from "Ministrie de Marine de France" (sort of Albert Medal). Rained the whole day. Walked over to Division for tea.

December 30th. (Rain!) Rode over to 15th Battalion and back by 17th Battalion.

December 31st. (Rain!) Watched football.

1919

January 1st. Went over to 57th Division Race Meeting at ARRAS Race Course. Backed George Paynter and won a bit, met Ian Leslie Melville among others. A very cold drive. Dined at "Cosy Corner" AUCHEL

January 2nd. Rode over to 15th Battalion to see Young as they had had some trouble in one of their Companies. Dined with Dickie Dill at his Headquarters. Wyndham Portal came in after and we played Roulette. (I won!).

January 3rd. Very busy morning with Demobilization. Went to show of 'Follies' rehearsal in Khaki only.

January 4th. Brigadier went over and talked to the 15th Battalion on Parade. "Follies" had a full dress rehearsal and a full house to watch.

January 5th. Church with 21st Battalion.

January 6th. A ride to FLORINGHAM to see Company of 17th Battalion London Regiment making the Camp there. A letter from Georgie to say Evelyn had got back to England. Wired and wrote to him.

January 7th. Rode over to 15th Battalion with Walford. Men who were to have been demobilized today have been stopped, presumably because of the Mutinies they have been having at Folkestone and Dover.

January 8th. Went over to 15th Battalion where we had an Inspection by an old man who had been knocked down 2 nights ago and had 1,300frs taken off him, to try and identify the man who did it, but failed. General Segrave came to lunch.

January 9th – 11th. Nothing of importance happened. About 80 men left for Demobilization.

January 12th – 19th. Football and Demobilization. Brigade has lost about 300 men this last week.

January 20th – 26th. Football and Demobilization. Brigade has sent off 420 men this last week.

January 27th – 29th. Motored down to BOULOGNE and stayed Hôtel Folkestone.

January 30th. Crossed on leave by early boat, arriving in London about 1:30 p.m. where I met Evelyn.

LEAVE.

February 10th. Crossed back off leave with General Kennedy, having been recalled, as appointed a GSO 2 to Supreme War Council VERSAILLES.

February 11th. Came up in car from BOULOGNE.

February 12th. Spent day saying " Good Byes" to all the remainder of the Brigade, which now numbers 350 only.

February 13th. Left the 140th Infantry Brigade with a tremendous "Send Off" and Caught the 1:30 p.m. at BÉTHUNE for PARIS. In PARIS by 7.00 p.m.

February 14th. Drove across PARIS (took 2 Taxis for my kit!) and caught the Electro to VERSAILLES. Reported to Bertie Studd and arranged to live at his house with Brigadier General Thomson, Colonel Bell, and Currie at 61 Boulevard St. Antoine.

British War Council.

Peace Commission.

VERSAILLES.

February 15th. Started work at the Office which is in the Trianon Hôtel. A nice room to myself on the 4th Floor. In "A" Branch under Brigadier General Thomson, my section being under Lt. Colonel Lister R.F.A. and I work with one Major Rolls. Work consists of compiling records, Political and Military about German France – Belgium – Holland – Denmark and Switzerland. It is mostly Political and Germany occupies most of one's attention. My room is fitted up with every conceivable necessity for an Office, and any maps that are wanted.

February 16th. The House and Mess are quite nice, especially the latter. The conversation is somewhat political, but I presume instructive. I do most of the listening. Lunched with Humphrey de Trafford, wife and Bell, also Crankshaw (one arm) at Ritz.

February 17th. Others in my branch very busy owing to a paper on the political situation in Southern Russia, having been asked by the C.I.G.S. (General H. Wilson) for the meeting of the S.W. Council tomorrow.

February 18th and 19th. My side of branch were asked for the situation of our troops in the Trans-Caucasus, the need, if any, of reinforcements. However luckily this did not come under one of my Countries.

February 20th. A "quiet" day. So read up a lot of back "stuff" on German political situation since the Armistice and her internal troubles.

February 21st. A few notes on reconstruction of German Army and present location of Corps Districts came in. Motored in with Currie etc: dined with Lady Hood and danced at "Salle Hoche".

February 22nd. Some information from French Section ref: new German Army. Affairs in North of Caucasus not too bright. Denekin's Army short of everything and to re-inforce it, is a doubtful policy. Dined at a small Restaurant in Montmartre called "L'Auberge du Clou". Quite good meal and cheap. Attended British Embassy Reception for Prince of Wales, who talked to all, then to dance at Majestic with Fraser-Tytler, Rolls etc: Met a Miss Boyle who claims Nancy as a distant connection. Got back to VERSAILLES at 3:15 a.m. with heavy cold.

February 23rd. Lovely day. Did not feel very bright! Not much news.

Good deal of scrapping in German Towns. Most of Bavarian Ministry seemed to have been wounded or killed. Dined with Bertie Studd and family at Ritz.

February 24th. Cyril Daubeny came down to lunch and seemed exactly the same as ever. Went off to PARIS about 5 p.m. and after a haircut, dined with Mrs. Paleret and danced at 61 Avenue de Victor Hugo given by "?". No news in. German Government seems more or less established into National Assembly and Committee of States.

February 25th. Raining, and nothing much doing.

February 26th. Question of a Neutral States between Romania and Austria discussed by S.W.C. Some very long-winded Romanian delegates attended.

February 27th. Went for a ride round the lake in front of Château, as there was "nothing doing" in the Office. Dined with Humphrey de T, wife, and Reggie Pembroke at Ritz. Went on with Rolls later to very Bohemian flat in an attic of a house got up like the last scene in La Bohême, where we danced to a gramophone for ½ hour, thence home.

February 28th. Suggestion put forward that the Territory on North West Corner of Germany from LÜBECK to Holland to include BREMEN, should be made a Neutral State. Quite impracticable, so a letter was written to that effect but I don't know what the result will be. Object is to stop Germany having any Naval Base on the open sea, which she is not likely to agree to.

March 1st. Lovely morning and very little to do. Dined with Butler-Stoney at Hôtel Majestic and went on to dance there. Very good dance. Home 4 a.m. (Having lost an hour's sleep by the clocks going onto Summer Time.)

March 2nd. Just finishing about 12 noon when a paper on the advisability of helping the Germans at LIBAU 'v' the BOLSHEVIKS was asked for. Colonel Lister, General Thomson, Rolls, and self had to "fairly get down to it", as it was required for the SNC meeting Monday at 9 a.m. I drew a large map as all the Clerks had gone off duty, while others wrote feverishly from the German file. We finished at 6 p.m.; upon which jumped into a car in which was Buzzard, Fraser-Tytler, and Miss Sharpe (his fiancée) and went to dine with the Duke De Massa. A very rowdy evening. We played "Bears" in her Drawing-Room.

March 3rd. After all our efforts, the paper was not looked at this morning. Spent a quiet day. Heard about poor little Peter's death. Wrote long letter to Albinia.

March 4th. Papers on the Schleswig question came in but did not contain much fresh information. Went to a "Thé Dansant" given by Madame du Prés. Only French Ladies there which was rather alarming. Dined with Holmes, Valentine Williams (Daily Mail) and Benoy at Inter Allied Club and on to General Spiers' dance.

March 5th. We seem to be getting less and less news in. A paper wrote on Schleswig and put in the Daily Summary was not quite approved of by the Brigadier General! Dined at "Le Chien qui fume" VERSAILLES and went back to No: 12, where Lister and Buzzard played and sang. On duty at the Trianon all night.

March 6th. Nothing of any importance in. The arrival of the Duke of Connaught, Lloyd-George, and the C.I.G.S. in PARIS last night may bring us more to do. Dined at Henri's with Antrobus, also Mrs. Tufton and a Miss P..?, and onto "Pasteur" which I understood with the help of Mrs. Tufton who translated for me in between the Scenes. A short dance to the gramophone at the Majestic with Rolls, Holmes, Misses Sharpe and Hope of 20 minutes, and so home!

March 7th. Lovely day again. Continued my study of Schleswig Question, also a resumé of the German Forces on the Eastern Frontier came in from the war Office. Dined with Holmes, Misses Boyle and Hope. Went downstairs at Majestic and danced till 11:30 p.m.

March 8th. Papers on allowing the Germans to re-inforce the front at LIBAU returned, as leave not granted by S.W.C. Considerable complications over car for "Majestic" Ball tonight, arrangements took most of the afternoon! Dined with Palerets at Majestic and then went on to the dance below, which was excellent. Home at ¼ to 4 a.m.

March 9th. Meeting in M.R's room attended by us all on Military aspect of the League of Nations. Very interesting, the chief argument centred round the feasibility of having a Military Commission in each Country always to superintend the Training and Armaments. It was more or less agreed that to do away with the Secret Service would be to lose all real knowledge as the Commission would find out nothing the Country in which they lived did not want it to find out. Dined with Duchesse De Massa. A quieter evening than last Sunday.

March 10th. An interrupted morning. Lunched at Ritz with Miss Sedgewick (USA), and Lady Doreen Knatchbull-Hugessen and Husband. Met Stafford and brought him back to VERSAILLES, where we went over the Palace and Trianon's.

March 11th. Stafford left for England. Started to Précis a long screed on "Germany's future policy". Dined with Cranborne at La Rue's and danced at Majestic to a piano till 12 o'clock.

March 12th. Finished précis I started last night. A young German journalist, Grabousky by name, puts the view very clearly, emphasizing a Commercial and Democratic future instead of a Military Bureaucratic one. He also acknowledges the need for Great Britain to be a strong Naval Power. On reading the minutes of the Military terms for Germany's future Army discussion, I noticed an amendment was adopted which I suggested when we had them here before they went up! Went into PARIS. Dined at Majestic with Holmes, the Misses Hope, Carnegie, and Cockrane, and on to the Opera "Madame Butterfly". Home with Holmes and Fraser-Tytler, the latter very depressed as his engagement with Miss Sharpe had just been broken off.

N.B. Miss Bell, Mrs. and Miss Studd lunched. Miss Bell is an expert on Trans-Caucasian and Persian matters and has been with the Army out there (paid as a GSO 1.) on the Intelligence side.

March 13th. The troubles in BERLIN appear to be increasing. Lunched at Allied Press Club, 80 Champs Elysees, with Valentine Williams (Daily Mail) and Holmes. Most extraordinary house built by D...?, local Selfridge! Hair cut and home, dined in.

March 14th. Mr. Wilson having returned the SWC should get right on with the Peace Terms. Some friction seems to be going on as to the Future Mandatory of such places as SMERNA and NORTHERN SYRIA. The French and Italians being especially active. Played Golf (10 holes) at La Boulie with Rolls. Stopped rather late at the Office and returned to dine alone at "61".

March 15th. Rolls having gone on leave, I have added his 12 Countries to my 6. Several papers on Germany's internal troubles. Went to French Section and saw Lestapis (who talks fairly slowly and so is easy to follow!) to try and get something on the Baltic Provinces, but he had little. Dined at La Rue's with Tiger Denniston, MacReady, and Neil Fraser-Tytler and on to the Majestic where we danced till 2:30 a.m.

March 16th. Lovely day. Morning spent in arranging dance for Monday night at No: 12 Rue Reservoir. Large luncheon party Villa Romano (General Sackville-West being away!) and onto PARIS. Dined with Duchesse De Massa, as usual 8 of us from VERSAILLES there. Neil left for England.

March 17th. The "Western and General Report" contained a long screed on the Internal Affairs of Germany, but reports are most conflicting. Large dinner party of 20 at No: 61, followed by a very good dance at No: 12 (VERSAILLES) given mostly by Holmes, and Currie. Bed at 3:30 a.m.

March 18th. Visit from two of the Italian Section who are enquiring about Switzerland's Army and all about it, but I could not help them. Most of the day spent in arranging to go away on Thursday next as had to cancel dinner party on Saturday. A quiet dinner at VERSAILLES.

March 19th. Wrote a long "brochure" on the "Trans-Caucasian Rivalries" (but came to the conclusion I know very little about it). Dined with Holmes, Misses Bevan and Wyndgate at Majestic, and had table next to General Allenby, Wilson etc: Had lunch with M. Representative to meet Willingdon's.

March 20th. Lovely day. Went into PARIS at 10:30 a.m.; Holmes, (Scott) and self. Caught the 12 midday train arriving BOULOGNE 4 p.m. Quiet crossing and in London by 8 p.m.

March 21st. Evelyn came up. Went to Regimental Orderly Room to enquire about Saturday's March, but got little news. Eventually arranged to go as Staff Captain to 1st Guards Brigade (Brigadier General de Crespigny). Dined with George and Ruby at Carlton and on to Ball at Chesterfield House given by Lady Burton. Bed 20 Minutes to 6 a.m.!

March 22nd. Went round to see George Crighton who offered me the Adjutancy of 2nd or 3rd Battalions. Lunched at Chelsea Barracks and paraded at 1 p.m. for the Triumphal March of the Guards Division through London. Very good reception. Home by 5 p.m. Dined with Blanche and John Hugh Smith at the Ritz.

March 23rd. A late morning. Lunch Ritz and then round to 40 Lowndes Street, where we stayed some time. Tea with Deverell and dine "On Guard" with Francis Longueville, Lloyd, Towers-Clark, John Hugh Smith and others.

March 24th. Motored down to Hendon hoping to fly back to France, but weather too bad. Caught the 12:57 p.m. at Victoria. Many people going back after Saturday's show. A rough crossing, but got a cabin with the help of Crisp. The night train to PARIS.

March 25th. Got in at 6:45 a.m. and motored out to VERSAILLES. Found a good accumulation of work, mostly notes on Meeting of Armistice Commission. Much amusement in our Branch caused by Bell and Currie getting the "OBE"! Cole arrived and joined our house.

March 26th. "Terrible" lot to read, but of no great interest. Communications between the Armistice Commission at SPA and the German delegates come in in Précis form. A great many small troubles seem to be occurring notably between our men and the Germans in the Streets and elsewhere. Also, Germans appear to be always asking for small concessions that are contrary to the Armistice Conditions. Dined with Holmes, Misses Hope and Carnegie, and danced until 12 midnight.

March 27th. Further copies of "Pour Parlers" with S.P.A. Commission came in. Dined with Cole and Rolls at Beaugé (Rue St. Mark) and went on to President's Box at Théatre Français. Found a French Colonel and 2 others, also 2 American Officers there. Danced Salle Hoche.

March 28th. Cold but fine. A few revelations as to the state of Germany in COURLAND which showed that the "Iron Division" is still in being. Dined with Bowes Butler-Stoney at Majestic.

March 29th. Worked up a short paper on German Army. Went in and saw Boyan (who was a prisoner with Evelyn at HEIDELBERG). Changed at Majestic and went to Fouquet's Bar (Champs Élysées) where I gave dinner party: Cranbornes, 3 Nickersons, Misses Hope and Carnegie, Benoy Holmes, and Bodleys, and so on to Majestic Ball.

March 30th. Lunched at "61". Miss Bell, General Bliss (American M.R.), Sir Eyre Cros, and others to PARIS and dined with De Massa's. Home early with Tiger Denniston.

March 31st. Map on Schleswig question required and supplied. Lunched Trianon Palace to meet Monseigneur ...? of "Jockey Club". Dined Crankshaw at Inter Allied Club and on to the Opera "Thais" in Madame de Neuflisse's Box.

April 1st. Frost but fine. By way of enlivening the Office played a few "1st April" jokes, which were not altogether appreciated by the older members! (but they will learn!!). Worked up till 7 p.m., then dined at "Chien qui Fume" VERSAILLES with Bowes and Miss Butler-Stoney, Miss Hope, Buzz and Cuthbert. Sang at No: 12 till 11 p.m.

April 2nd. General Lockeridge (USA. Chief of Staff) came to lunch, also one 'Pomerol', who had just returned from HUNGARY and was most interesting. Dined with Lady Hood in PARIS and danced till 2 a.m.

April 3rd. Took over two more Countries, in Spain and Portugal, which does not entail much extra. Lunched Trianon and went to La Boulé with Rolls. Played 9 holes of Golf. Dined with Holmes, Philippa, and Miss Boyle at Baugé's and on to "Bourgeois Gentilhomme". Very good and most amusing. Night duty at Trianon.

April 4th. Still very cold. Long paper on Spanish Government troubles in. Dined with Humphrey at La Rue's and 7 others. Sat next to a Russian who is Military Attaché in PARIS. Most interesting fellow. He seemed to think Russia would eventually come round.

April 5th. Just as I was getting ready to go, a paper on the advisability of provisioning the Germans at LIBAU and the sending of an Allied Commander-in-Chief was asked for. This did not really affect me, and so after leaving them all the information I had on the subject, I went to PARIS with General Studd. Lunched with Cyril Daubeny, Rex Benson,

Skeffington-Smyth (9th Lancers) and Charles Hunter (4th Dragoon Guards) at Ritz, and from there back with Cyril to LA MORLAYE, where he lived. Same party dined and Cyril sang after dinner!

April 6th. Rode over to CHANTILLY Training Ground. Lovely day and most interesting magnificent Training Ground. Played Golf at CHANTILLY Golf Course. Charles Hunter and self beat Cyril and Skeffington-Smyth. Home via CHANTILLY Château.

April 7th. Started in Cyril's car at 8 a.m. and picked up a S.W.C. car at Ritz PARIS and back to VERSAILLES. Opinion on Saturday's paper strongly suggested that the Allies should define their policy in the Baltic, deprecated any supply of troops, vetoed an Allied Commander-in-Chief as the Germans (our enemies) would not stand for it (to become an Ally there) and suggested that if the Army was to be raised from the Letts, a number of Instructors would be necessary and a great quantity of money and material. Was it justified?! Mrs. Halsey and Diana Leigh dined with me at Ritz also Crankshaw and Holmes. Somewhat surprised the old Ritz clients by dancing along the corridor after dinner!

April 8th. Played 10 holes of golf during luncheon interval and beat Rolls! Went into PARIS and saw "Mr. Robins" of Toronto who gave very cheering accounts of that place. Dined with Philippa and Irene Boyle, also a Colonel Grant (US Army) and danced to gramophone at Majestic.

April 9th. Lovely day again, but trees have only just started to come out. Lunched and dined in.

April 10th. Some interesting notes from Armistice Commission at SPA, including Protocol of DANZIG question and Annexe. All of which has now been settled and General Haller should start shortly. Went to Dentist and on to dine with Mrs. Thyers followed by a very 'American' dance at the American Embassy. Have heavy cold.

April 11th. Lovely day. Charles Grant and Lady Sybil, General Sackville-West and Leggatt to lunch. Went for a walk round Château Gardens. Dined at home.

April 12th. Raining hard. However played 16 holes of Golf. Finding that Leggett would take on my duty for the evening, dined with Butler-Stoney and danced at Majestic.

April 13th. A small luncheon party consisting of Captain and Mrs. Greenfield. Misses Boyle, Carnegie, and Butler-Stoney, Holmes, Bowes, Currie and self, followed by a walk in the VERSAILLES Park and dinner at the "Flottie".

April 14th. Preparations for the arrival of the Germans and the making room in our Offices for more of our Peace delegates to come here. A dinner party of Butler-Stoney's followed by a dance at Ralph Lambton's flat given by Crankshaw for Duchess of Sutherland and others on their way through PARIS. Slept at Crankshaw's flat.

April 15th. Breakfast at 7:30 a.m. after which Bowes and Miss Butler-Stoney, Holmes, Leggett and self (and Scott) set out in a "Lancia" open car and "Vauxhall" shut car for the SOMME Battlefields. Got to COMPIÈGNE at 11 a.m. where we lunched, thence to COUCHY-LE-CHÂTEAU, which the Germans blew up before their retreat. A lovely Château in a most commanding position. We then tried to go to GOBAIN where a lovely view of the surrounding country is obtained, but after going 5 miles we got badly stuck in a bit of "No man's lands". Half an hour's struggle in torrents of rain effected a removal of the car and back we went heading for HAM which we passed about 5 p.m. Thence North until we struck the VILLERS-BRETONNEUX road at BRIE. Proceeding along it westwards following the line of the retirement of the Fifth Army in March/April 1918. The lateness of the hour and the inclemency of the weather prevented us stopping at VILLERS-BRETONNEUX to see where the Australians effectually stopped the German advance, but even under the motor-hood one could see the extreme importance of the Village and immediately on debouching on the western side, AMIENS and all the surrounding country. The PARIS railway in particular came under view. AMIENS was reached about 7:30 p.m. and an extremely expensive and rather moderate dinner and rooms obtained at the Hôtel de L'Universe, the Hôtel du Rhin being full.

April 16th. The only place to get petrol being on the ABBÉVILLE road, our departure was delayed until 11 a.m. Taking the CORBIE road as being one of more interest in view of the advance in August/September 1918, we passed MÉRICOURT, VILLE-SUR-ANCRE and stopped for a few moments in MÉAULTE, being the Village the 1st Guards Brigade rested in prior to the attack 15th September 1916. The shells of houses being all that remains, identification of houses occupied at that date was almost impossible. Bowes and Holmes, however were fully convinced that they found their respective resting places, and the journey was continued via MAMETZ to GINCHY WOOD. Here we all got out and walked over the famous attack of 15th September 1916, visiting many of the Graves such as Vaughan's, Tufnell's etc: Rain prevented us from spending more time here and we returned to GINCHY WOOD for a small lunch which Scott had prepared in a hut. Later we proceeded to LES BŒUFS – LE TRANSLOY – SAILLY-SAILLISEL and on to COMBLES, where Miss Butler-Stoney and self went down the Catacombs necessitating considerable scrambling and crawling. A return was made via BAPAUME-HAVRINCOURT to CAMBRAI. Here the Chef de Ville had promised to find us rooms, but he had unfortunately mistaken the day. After much searching in the rain, a room was secured in one of the few houses left standing for Miss Butler-Stoney and we other four got 4 beds in a long dormitory at the E.F. Officers Club; all by this time very wet.

April 17th. Getting away soon after 10 a.m., we made for GOUZEAUCOURT, the pace had to be very slow as we were going down the line of "No man's land" and the roads were awful. The Lancia's springs were also very weak. After going through NURLU and PÉRONNE we struck East to try and get to BELLENGLISE as Leggatt had fought there, but just before reaching VERMAND, one of the most deserted parts we had yet been through, a front spring in the Vauxhall broke over an extra bad hole. Prospects of getting home looked "blue" being then 12:30 p.m., so we decided to have lunch in a mine crater and let the Chauffeurs do their best. About an hour later we found the Vauxhall ready to go on. The driver of the Lancia car having made a very good job of it by binding a tyre lever across, which eventually held until we got home. Any idea of further sight-seeing had now to be abandoned as it appeared doubtful that we should get home and the leave of three of us expired that night. We continued through HAM – NOYON – COMPIÈGNE – SENLIS to PARIS, where we arrived at 8:30 p.m., after a most interesting although perhaps rather too hurried trip. If going again one would take more provision for sleeping in destroyed places and not rely on finding anything. CAMBRAI was far less destroyed than most of those places, but we were very lucky to get what we did. The thing that struck one most was the vast extent of absolute "abomination of desolation". One can almost say that from the time we left AMIENS until we got to COMPIÈGNE via BAPAUME and CAMBRAI there was hardly a complete house. A distance of considerably over 200 miles, and of Village after Village we passed there was not a brick to mark it's original existence. The complete absence of troops, the presence of dejected looking German prisoners, and, which was far worse, the pitiable sight of the returned inhabitants trying to start their homes again, living in Shanties consisting of wooden erections put up against the one remaining wall of their old house and covered with bits of corrugated iron, made one realize far more than the last 4½ years have done, what the European War has been. To enter a town like PARIS only 1½ hours after leaving the last destroyed Village; PARIS aglow with lights, shops, and gaiety but yet so close to all this misery. It is a huge contrast with so short an interval between (i.e. 1½ hours is about 40 miles).

April 18th. On arriving at the Office, I found it was a Holiday and so went off to play golf. Returned after to read up what I had missed these last three days away. Dined with Butler-Stoneys.

April 19th. Went to the Office in the morning. Golf with the Pro and an early dinner and bed.

April 20th. About 10:00 a.m. Bowesy, Cim, Leggett, and self went to FONTAINEBLEAU by CHEVREUSE, lovely drive, went round the Château then on to MORET and home for dinner.

April 21st. Lunch party consisting of Studd family after which we motored to ST. GERMAINE and MAISON LAFITTE. A picnic tea and home. Dined Ritz with Mrs. Birkbeck, Reynolds, and Crank. Thence to Hôtel Majestic Dance till about 3 a.m.

April 22nd. Found my Office full of "Stuff" to read, mostly notes from Armistice Commission Meetings. Great preparations being made for arrival of Bosches.

April 23rd. Played Tennis for the first time in courts of Trianon Palace Hôtel with Beadon, Buzzard, and Leggett. Dined "Chez Moi".

April 24th. A letter on Bolshevism by Haking which was quite good. Emphasizing raising the Blockade without delay if Germany and possibly France too, are to be saved. Also a memo on the Referendum in Luxemburg came in. Leggett dined with me at "61". Italian split at Peace Conference and Italian Prime Minister (Orlando) and others left for ROME during afternoon. Everyone is wondering what is the next step!

April 25th. Advanced party of Germans arrived very quietly at VERSAILLES. Lunched Cole and Mrs. Cole in their tiny flat in VERSAILLES. Tennis with Beadon, Buzzard and Leggett, thence to PARIS where Mrs. Birkbeck and Reynolds, Holmes, Prince Obolenski and I dined at Fouquet's and went to Majestic dance.

April 26th. Very wet. Lady Cranborne came down to lunch with me at "61". Unfortunately I waited for her at Trianon Palace and the car took her straight to "61". Result she had to walk in alone to meet 8 people she did not know! To PARIS after lunch. Tea at Astoria and on to see Lena Morrison. Dinner with Jean, Richard and Kay at Ritz, on to Théatre Capucines ("some" show!). Met General Kennedy and wife who had just arrived from COLOGNE.

April 27th. Jean, Richard, Kay, and Crankey came out to lunch at "61". After a short walk round the Trianon, Crank and self motored off to HARRISON near FONTAINEBLEAU where we found Mrs. Birkbeck and Reynolds. As it was raining hard we stayed in and played poker until 11:30 p.m. Thence back to VERSAILLES.

April 28th. Snowing hard. Long War Office Summary on reconstruction of German Army. The new REICHSWEHR and its construction. More Germans arrive. Dined with Admiral Hope and on to dance given by

Thyers – moderate! Home by 1 a.m.

April 29th. Raining and very cold. Remainder of Germans arrive tonight. Dined with General Kennedy, his wife, Jack Wilson and wife, R.H. Carter and Tiger Denniston at Ritz and then on to "Follies Bergères".

April 30th. Raining and continued the whole day. Gendarmes and Sentry are now met at every corner and VERSAILLES is in a ferment of excitement. Went into PARIS EARLY and tea with Lena. Met General Kennedy there. Dined Inter Allied Club and danced at Majestic till 12 midnight.

May 1st. Rain. Almost snowed under with papers. Armistice Commission notes, results of Peace Conferences. American Section had a secret paper on Hindenberg's Army, which I had to try and get diplomatically. They would only allow me to take notes, (however I copied most of it!). Holmes and self motored to PARIS expecting to meet many strikers, but found all quiet. Dined at Inter Allié Club and danced a short time at Majestic, thence for about an hour at Princesse du Murat's.

May 2nd. Several Germans from the Economic Commission came to 'Trianon Palace' for a meeting. My notes of Hindenberg's Army caused much excitement and they were sent to be typed. Lunched with Freeman-Thomas at Villa Romane to meet Ivo Grenfell who was passing through. Dined at home and read.

May 3rd. Fine morning and so went for a ride. Played Golf till 4 p.m. and then to PARIS. Dined with Ben and Mrs. Birkbeck, and Mrs. Reynolds. To the Follies Bergères and then the dance at Hôtel Majestic.

May 4th. Golf before and after lunch. Sat in Avenue Bois de Boulogne till 8 p.m., when Philippa, Cuthbert, and self dined at the "Piccadilly" in Avenue Victor Hugo.

May 5th. Several "Astoria Daily Bulletins" came round. Played Tennis with Leggatt, thence to PARIS where I dined with Lena (Morrison) and with Dick Hennesy and Hazel Kelly, we went to "Palace".

May 6th. Lovely day. Very few papers in; a few Secret boxes circulated containing minutes of Economic Council Meetings. Played Tennis with Beadon, Buzzard, and ...? (Lt. Colonel Australian Contingency). Dined with Betty and Bobbety (also Holmes,) at 51 Avenue Montaigne and on to the "Taming of the Shrew" in French at the Theatre Antoine. Very nice piece. Back to dance 'chez' Lady Hood, where I met 2 Russian Ladies, friends of "Buzz", and so home.

May 7th. One of the greatest days in one's life "The Presentation of the Peace Terms". All the morning the whole of the Trianon Palace Hôtel was in a ferment of excitement. The dining room had had a large table erected going the whole way round the room. The Allies sitting on three sides, the Germans occupying the 4th. I looked round about 12 midday and saw where each was going to sit. Each place being named according to the Country of the Delegate. After a hurried lunch, Bell and I went back to the Hôtel, the Officers of the 4 Sections taking up their places in the Hall. From 2 p.m. onwards Delegates started to arrive together with learned looking Secretaries and large boxes of papers. Each Head Delegate and General was saluted by us all. Lloyd George arrived last full of smiles. By 3 p.m. they were seated. About 5 minutes past 3 p.m. a sudden hush fell on the Hall and we saw 3 cars draw up out of which got the 6 German Delegates, accompanied by Colonels Lister and Henri. They filed through the Hall looking very self-conscious, but determined, considering they were about to face Delegates from the whole world. The British Section were the only Officers who saluted the German Delegates as they passed through. Managed to get close up to the door (glass) and so watched the Germans the whole of the sitting. Saw Baron Rantzau make the whole of his speech. He looked very ill and I was not surprised that he did not stand up. After 1½ hours the Meeting broke up and Germans took the Peace Terms away. Huge crowd in VERSAILLES.

May 8th. Very little doing. Had dinner party consisting of Duc and Duchesse De Massa, de Bontray, Betty and Bobbety Cranborne, and Miss Cimmie Curzon, Kathleen Carnegie, Holmes, Nickerson, and on to a moderate Concert given by the R.A. Band at the Trocadero.

May 9th. Except for a strenuous game of Tennis I did very little.

May 10th. After a short morning's work, Rolls and self went to LA BOULIE and played Golf till 5 p.m. After a hurried change I dined at Laurent's with "Niggs", Lady Curzon, Cimmie, Miss Dickson-Poynder, Holmes, etc: thence to Majestic dance.

May 11th. Lunched Cranbornes, and we went a party of 6 to LONGCHAMPS. Rain rather spoilt the Meeting. Applied for as Adjutant 3rd Battalion Coldstream Guards.

May 12th. Lunched with General Sackville-West and met Cimmie and Miss Dickson-Poynder. To Jockey Club where I met Boutillier and was taken round and introduced to all Members. Dined there. A very formal dinner.

Joan Dickson-Poynder was a VAD Ambulance Driver. After the war she married Edward Grigg (later Lord Altrincham). Her two friends Ursula and Cecilia Lawley were VAD nurses in France during the First World War. The Lawley sisters were mentioned in despatches and awarded the Royal Red Cross. Ursula in due course married George Abraham Gibbs of Tyntesfield. On New Years Day 1918, Geoffrey Dawson wrote in his dairy,

"Both the Lawley girls appear in the Gazette tonight with the Royal Red Cross, and richly deserve it. They have been nursing in France with hardly a break from the beginning, doing almost inconceivable hours at a stretch and living in great discomfort. I only wish these great outpourings of honours could be limited to people of their kind." [xxiii]

Three of the patients nursed by Sister Ursula Lawley were soldiers with one leg due to be amputated. In each case Ursula argued vehemently with the surgeon insisting that the leg could be saved. Each of the surgeons eventually conceded but said that their patients would need a great deal of intensive nursing care. Ursula immediately volunteered to take personal care of each of the gravely injured soldiers. In due course their legs were saved and they recovered. Ursula called them "her knee boys". [xxiv]

Figure 59. Ursula Lawley, later Lady Wraxall, served as a VAD nurse during the First World War.

May 13th. Found my box very full of papers, but of very little interest. Dined at Jockey Club, large Inter-allied dinner. Stayed with Cranbornes.

May 14th. Dentist at 10 a.m. A successful visit. To VERSAILLES for lunch. Played Tennis with "Buzz, Beed", and Holmes at 4 p.m. Dined with Hennesey, Mrs. Morrison and Kelly and on to "Phi Phi", a very hot night.

May 15th. Some Armistice Commission papers, otherwise nothing. Got to LONGCHAMPS about 2:30 p.m. Had very bad luck over one horse which won at about 12-1, but was disqualified by "Insensible". Dined Cranborne's at Armonenville's and on to Goldsmith's dance in 55 Avenue Bois de Boulogne, where I met some very "famous" people!

May 16th. A muggy morning. Betty came down to play Golf at LA BOULIE, (Bobbety could not come at last moment) but we eventually walked in the wood and dined at Hôtel de France.

May 17th. Lunched at 51 Avenue Montaigne, after which Nickersons, B, and self went to "Tiv au Pigeon" and played Tennis. Dined with Lister at Drouants and on to President's Box for "Castor and Pollox". To the Majestic. Stayed Avenue Montaigne.

May 18th. Slept late. Lunched with Bobbety and Betty at "La Cascade" and on to LONGCHAMPS. Lovely day, but lost money! Gibson, Walters came to dine at Avenue Montaigne, after which the former sang. Lovely voice. He sang in the Opera in DRESDEN before the War.

May 19th. Caught 8:30 a.m. at 'Les Invalides'. No sooner at VERSAILLES than I had to dash into the Astoria, PARIS, to try and find out the strengths of the Police, Gendarmeries, and Custom Officials of all the Countries in Europe before the war. "Astoria" and War Office know nothing. Back to VERSAILLES after lunching at Jockey Club. To come in again at 6 p.m. Tea at Avenue Montaigne and change, and on to dine

with Greenfield's near Palais Royale, to General Spiers' dance till 3 a.m.!

May 20th. Lovely day. Had to try and find out more about the German Army report I got off the American Section. This required considerable care so as not to give away what I was getting at. Dined at "Auberge du Clou" in MONTMATRE with Cranborne's after which we went to Cinema and thence to Hood's dance.

May 21st. Having caught a chill on Tuesday cancelled all PARIS arrangements and went for a ride.

May 22nd. Hot again. Went into Dentist and afterwards to tea at Avenue Montaigne. Dinner with Miss Harding, Betty, and Bobbety at the "Ambassadors" and afterwards to Lady Hood's dance. To bed at 3 a.m., sleeping at Avenue Montaigne.

May 23rd. Caught 8:30 a.m. at Les Invalides. Nothing to do at the Office. Lunched at the Trianon, walked about the Park and eventually dined at "La Flotte" with Betty and Bobbety.

May 24th. Spent most of the morning telephoning to arrange weekend. After lunch I motored to 20 Rue de Chalgrin where I met Betty, and at 3:30 p.m. she, Miss Dudgeon and self motored down to BARBIZON near FONTAINBLEAU in Lord Robert Cecil's car. After tea we walked in the Forest and eventually Bobbety, Walters, Bakers, Butler, Forbes-Adams joined us. Stayed at Hôtel de l'Exposition. We all slept in the annexe. Lovely evening.

May 25th. After a Breakfast Party in Betty and Bobbety's room, we got up and wandered into the Forest. Lunch in the open, then 5 of us motored to FONTAINBLEAU going round the Château. Had to catch the 4:50 p.m. and dined with La Duchesse De Massa in PARIS, and so on to a dance given in a magnificent house in Rue de la Faisanderie by Madame Hayes. Bed at 3 a.m.

May 26th. Rather an influx of work which however was got over by 5 p.m. Tea at 20 Rue Chalgrin. Dined at the Majestic with Lord Robert Cecil, Cranbornes, and Miss Hope, and thence to Madame Mallaville's dance. Lovely garden leading down to the river, otherwise a moderate dance!

May 27th. Most of the day spent in arranging the dinner etc. At about 7:15 p.m. the "guests" started to arrive. 39 in all. We then all walked round to the Hôtel de France in the "Place de l'Armée", VERSAILLES for dinner. Had Betty Cranborne on my right and Miss Studd on my left. 5 tables of 8 each. After dinner we went back to No: 12 Rue de Resevoir and Mademoiselle Henry played about 6 pieces on the Violin. She was about the best I have ever heard. Gibson also sang 3 songs very well. We then danced for 1½ hours, most of which time I played. Bed about 2 p.m.

May 28th. Very hot. Afghan question assuming rather serious proportions and many papers and wires coming about it. Played Tennis with Beadon, Buzz, and Holmes. Thence to dine at Inter Allied Club and dance at the Majestic.

May 29th. A whole Holiday being Ascension Day. Rode early and then went to PARIS. Went out shopping with Betty Cranborne, but found them all shut. Lunched at Jockey Club. Picked up Betty Cranborne at Arthur Balfour's flat and went to LONGCHAMPS. Hot and crowded. Tea at "Les Deux Lacs" and back to dine at "Gauliers" (Rue St. Marc) and on to "La Presidente" with Cranborne's.

May 30th. Hotter than ever. Long talk with Fuller (American Section) over Germany's future. General von Kluck seems to be lost and they think he may be scheming in accordance with this new concentration. To

PARIS about 6 p.m. was to have dined with Crankshaw, but as he did not turn up, I joined the Cranborne's in the Majestic. Went to 'Movies' in Champs Elysées. Back to Majestic to find my car had gone off without me. So Cranborne very kindly put me up in his dressing room.

May 31st. Car picked me up at 9 a.m. Raining hard. Spent the morning preparing to hand over. A quick lunch at "61" and into PARIS. Found Bobbety and Betty just starting lunch and so had a second with them! Did several purchases for Blanche. Dined at Majestic and on to the dance and from there to a dance at Ralph Lambton's flat, which was great fun.

June 1st. Slept till 10 a.m. and then breakfasts in dressing-gowns. We tried to go to Church at 12, but were too late. Lunched with MacIndoe's, Cranborne's at Majestic and on to LONGCHAMPS, where made a little money. Back to tea with Lady Edward Cecil. Dined with Massa's, very French dinner party. Had a long talk on racing with Baron de Varenne after, and bade them a fond farewell.

June 2nd. Lovely day. Prepared for my parting. Dined at "Laurents" with Crank, Buzzard, and Holmes.

June 3rd. Came into PARIS at 10 a.m. Picked up Cranbornes at Maison and got to Gare du Nord. Train left at 12 mid-day. Bet and I had lunch on board. Crossing the Chanel very comfortably in a cabin and got onto first train to Victoria, arriving 9 p.m. All out at Belgrave Square, and so dined with Bet and her Sister at Portman Square. This day is great day for me, as it signals the finish of Active Service and also the papers publish my getting a "DSO".

So Ends the War.

VENI -VIDI -VICI !

Victoria de Burgh Gibbs and the Red Cross during the First World War.

When the Marchioness of Bath started the Somerset Branch of the Red Cross in 1910, Mrs Victoria de Burgh Gibbs (Via) was invited to be one of the Vice Presidents. Via encouraged local doctors to teach the elements of First Aid and Nursing to volunteers and persuaded the Matron of Bristol General Hospital to allow a number of V.A.D. (Voluntary Aid Detachment) volunteers to attend the hospital for a fortnight to learn something about nursing in hospitals. Only three months after the War began, voluntary hospitals were asked for in North Somerset, and Clevedon started with a hospital for Belgians in November 1914. Mrs Gibbs made regular visits to the Headquarters of the Red Cross in London to interview nurses.

Figure 60. Oaklands House - a Red Cross Hospital at Clevedon during the First World War (once the home of John Lomax Gibbs, William Gibbs' nephew).

In December 1914 she equipped a large part of the empty Flax Bourton Workhouse as hospital wards, supplying much of the necessary equipment and furniture from Tyntesfield. When the Flax Bourton provision was deemed inadequate, she got Portishead and Foye House Hospitals accepted instead and moved the equipment and furniture there. Foye House opened on 4th May 1915 with 30 beds and by Christmas 1917 there were 145 beds with an annexe added at Bannerleigh. Vegetables, eggs, fruit and flowers were supplied by Tyntesfield. By 1916, Via was responsible for three hospitals and she worked tirelessly to ensure their smooth running and success. Early in 1917 a hospital for officers was needed and Via persuaded Mrs Smyth of Ashton Court, where the house was empty, to offer Ashton Court as a hospital. Mrs Smyth generously donated £1,000 to help equip and run the hospital. At the same time she had taken on another house at Clevedon, and a further house to accommodate staff from Foye House and Bannerleigh at Leigh Woods.

In June 1917, Via organised a large Fete and Sale with musical and dramatic performances, sports, a military band, dancing and festivities in the Park at Long Ashton with Mrs Smyth's support. £730 was raised for the Red Cross. Mrs Gibbs contributed £100, and Mrs Smyth £300. Via's father, Mr Walter Long contributed the use of a large motor omnibus. 1,232 patients had passed through the hospital by the end of the summer in 1919.

In 1918, the C.B.E. was conferred upon Via for her splendid services in the war. "I consider she gave her life for her country as truly as any man who died on the field," said one of her close friends.[xxv]

Nancy, Anstice Katharine Crawley, worked for the Red Cross in York.[xxvi]

Figure 61. Anstice Katharine Crawley.

LANCELOT MERIVALE GIBBS

7th Son and 10th Child of Antony and Janet Gibbs, (née Merivale), of Tyntesfield, Bristol.

Born December 23rd 1889.

Eton College 1902 to 1908.

Commissioned: - Somerset Light Infantry. 1908.

Commissioned: - Coldstream Guards. December, 1910.

Served First World War in France 1914-1919.
Adjutant 2nd Battalion 1915.
Commanded 2nd Battalion 1916-1917.
Staff Captain Guards Brigade 1918.
Brigade Major 140th Infantry Brigade 1918.
GSO (2) British war Council Versailles 1919.
Adjutant 3rd Battalion Coldstream Guards 1919.

Appointed ADC to Lord Rawlinson Commander-in-Chief India 1922.
Second in Command 2nd Battalion Coldstream Guards in Shanghai Defence Force 1927 – 1928.
Commanded British Troops in Paris for Marshal Foch's Funeral 1929.
Commanded 1st Battalion Coldstream Guards 1930 – Sudan and Cairo.
Lieutenant Colonel, December 1930.
Retired 1938.

Recalled as Brigadier in charge of Administration, London District 1939-1945.
Recalled again by war Office to arrange Victory March 1946.

Member of Gentlemen at Arms, Her Majesty's Bodyguard.

Died December 8th 1966.

HONOURS & DECORATIONS.

C.V.0	1937.	
D.S.0.	1919.	London Gazette 3rd June 1919
M.C.	1916	London Gazette 1st January 1917
Bar to M.C.	1918	London Gazette 11th January 1919

Mentioned in Despatches 4 times 1915-1919.

CAMPAIGN MEDALS.
1914 Star.
British War Medal.
Victory Medal.
Defence Medal.
North West Frontier Medal and one clasp in Waziristan Campaign, India.

OTHER AWARDS.

King George V Coronation.	1911.
King George V Jubilee.	1935.
King George VI Coronation.	1937.
Queen Elizabeth II Coronation.	1953.

CITATIONS
DISTINGUISHED SERVICE ORDER
For gallant and distinguished service in France.

Bar to the <u>MILITARY CROSS.</u>
Captain Lancelot Merivale Gibbs, M.C., Coldstream Guards, attached 140th Infantry Brigade, H.Q.

"For conspicuous gallantry and devotion to duty. When the position on the left flank was very obscure owing to the next Division failing to reach its objective, he made a daring reconnaissance to gain information and get in touch. He collected troops and organised the situation, and brought most valuable information to the Brigade. He was under intense fire from machine-guns and minenwerfer at close range."
(M.C. gazetted 1st January, 1917.)

<u>24th August 1918. Near Morlancourt</u>

Chapter Seven

Peace Returns

After the War the family returned to their normal lives. John Evelyn Gibbs married the Marquis of Cambridge's daughter Lady Helena Augusta Frances Cambridge. The Marquis was the Duke of Teck and Queen Mary's brother. Lady Helena's mother was Lady Margaret Grosvenor, daughter of the First Duke of Westminster. Evelyn had met Helena at Waterloo Station in 1914 when he was on his way to the Western Front. As the train left she tossed a little mascot of green jade to him in his railway carriage. When they met again at a Ball given for his regiment at Windsor Castle, he reminded her of the green jade "little lady", which she had not forgotten. He was astonished to discover that she was Queen Mary's niece. He told Helena all about his War Service, his experiences as a Prisoner of War, about big game hunting and his life in India. He shot tigers in India and the skins were displayed at 22 Belgrave Square. He was released in April 1918 from the German Prisoner of War Camp and went to The Hague, where he assisted after the Armistice in repatriating other prisoners of war. He was a great polo player and Captain of the Coldstream Guards' team. He had travelled extensively visiting Japan and America before the War. When he proposed to Lady Helena she accepted, and the King and her Father willingly gave their consent.[xxvii] The wedding was in St. George's Chapel, Windsor Castle, on Tuesday 2nd September 1919. The King and Queen were in Balmoral, but they placed Frogmore House at the disposal of the family for the Wedding Reception. They sent the message,

"We send bride and bridegroom affectionate good wishes for their happiness. We much regret not being present at the Wedding at Windsor today. Hope everything will go well. Our thoughts are with you all. George and Mary."

Members of the Royal Family who were present included Princess Christian and her daughter Princess Marie Louise, Princess Alice, Countess of Athlone and the Earl of Athlone, Lord Trematon and Lord Leopold Mountbatten. Major Lancelot Merivale Gibbs was the best man. George Abraham and Victoria Gibbs' daughter, Doreen, was one of the bridesmaids. The bride accompanied by her father drove from Frogmore Cottage in the Royal Landau drawn by a couple of greys to the West Door of St. George's Chapel. The officiating clergy included Bishop Carr Glyn, the Rev. Stafford Crawley, the Rev. J. S. Gibbs, the Dean of Windsor and the Canon of St. George's Chapel.

The bride and bridegroom left Frogmore House later in the afternoon in a car loaned by George Abraham Gibbs for Slough Station, whence they took the train for Tyntesfield.[xxviii]

Figure 62. The Wedding of Major John Evelyn Gibbs and Lady Helena Frances Augusta Cambridge at St. George's Chapel, Windsor on September 2nd 1919.

Figure 63. Tyntesfield, 6th July 1928. Seated the Duke of York, Lady Wraxall, and the Duchess of York. Standing from the left – Lady Helen Graham, Colonel John Evelyn Gibbs, M.C., Lord Erskine, Lady Helena Gibbs, Mr Patrick Hodgson C.M.G., C.V.O., the Hon. Doreen Gibbs, Lord Wraxall, Lady Marjorie Erskine.

On 29th March 1920, Victoria de Burgh Gibbs died. On March 18th, she had taken a leading part in a Women's Unionist Association Meeting in Bristol. The aim was to unite women of all classes against Bolshevism. Via had a cold and sore throat, which she did not take seriously, but insisted on going with a party of Bristol ladies to Cardiff to arouse enthusiasm for their cause in Wales. She probably caught the fatal influenza virus in the Hall in Cardiff, and possibly a chill in the train on her way home.

Next morning she came down for breakfast and spent most of the day with Doreen in the Nursery. Her husband went out hunting and when he returned was surprised to hear that Via had gone to bed, which was most unlike her. The influenza turned into septic pneumonia and pleurisy. A specialist came down twice from London and everything possible was done, but in the end her heart failed.

A friend and admirer wrote, "She was so full of radiant sunshine, and stood for all that was best in the world, that I feel the world is immeasurably poorer by her absence".

The funeral service was held on April 1st and Victoria de Burgh Gibbs was buried in the family vault at Wraxall Church.[xxix]

George Abraham Gibbs did not see active service abroad during the First World War, but he raised in 1914 and commanded until 1917 the Second Regiment of the North Somerset Yeomanry, formed to supply drafts to the First Regiment which was on active service in France. He was acting Brigadier General commanding his regiment's Brigade (then on bicycles) at Ipswich from October 1916 until 1917. From 1917 until 1928, he was in the Territorial Army Reserve. As a Member of Parliament for Bristol West from 1906 until 1928, he had other responsibilities during the war, and from 1917 to 1919 he was Parliamentary Secretary to Walter H. Long M.P., Secretary of State for the Colonies, who was also his father-in-law. Between 1917 and 1928, George Abraham Gibbs was a Conservative Whip in the House of Commons. He served as Treasurer to the Royal Household from 1921 until 1928, and became a Privy Councillor in 1923.

Seven years after the untimely death of his first wife, George Abraham married Ursula Mary Lawley, the eldest daughter of Sir Arthur Lawley, later the Sixth Lord Wenlock, and his wife Lady Annie Allen, daughter of Sir Edward Cunard. The wedding on July 21st 1927 was at St Margaret's, Westminster and was attended by the King and Queen. In January 1928 he was raised to the Peerage as Baron Wraxall of Clyst St George. They had two sons, the Hon. George Richard Lawley Gibbs born on the 16th May 1928 and the Hon. Eustace Hubert Beilby Gibbs, born on the 3rd July 1929.

Antony Hubert Gibbs was appointed Major in the North Somerset Yeomanry in 1912. In the Great War he served with his regiment in

France from the 2nd November 1914 until May 1915 as part of the Sixth Cavalry Brigade, which was part of the Third Cavalry Division under Major General Julian Byng. From May 1915 until March 1917, he commanded the 3rd North Somerset Yeomanry at Bath, and then was on the Quarter Master General's Staff of Southern Command at Salisbury from May 1917 until the end of the War. He then returned to his Directorships of the City Bank and the Exeter Bank in Devon and to his family home at Cyst St George.

Figure 64. The Wedding of George Abraham Gibbs and Ursula Mary Lawley.

William Gibbs of the 7th Hussars was the Brigade Major (as a Captain) of the Eastern Mounted Brigade from March 1913 until October 1916. He served in Gallipoli from October to December 1915, and then in Egypt from December 1915 until October 1916 as a Staff Officer in the Western Defence Force, being Brigade Major for the Coastal Area. From October to December 1917 he was in France as a Major in the 12th Battalion of the Yorkshire Regiment. From April 1918 until April 1919 he was in Mesopotamia with the 7th Hussars, which he commanded from September 1918. He was wounded at Shergat near Mosul on 28th October 1918. He was awarded the Croix de Guerre avec Plume by France and mentioned twice in dispatches in 1916 and 1919; he was promoted Lieutenant Colonel in 1919. After the War, he continued his military career and became one of the Exons of the King's Bodyguard of the Yeomen of the Guards. He returned to his family home at Admington Hall, Shipston on Stour, Warwickshire.

On July 10th 1929, Brigadier Lancelot Merivale Gibbs married the Hon. Marjorie Florence daughter of Sir Arthur Kenlis Maxwell, D.S.O., the 11th Baron Farnham of County Cavan, Ireland, at St Margaret's Westminster.

Figure 65. Tyntesfield. Lady Wraxall greets the Duchess of York.

Figure 66. Wedding of Lieutanant Colonel Lancelot Merivale Gibbs and the Hon. Marjorie Florence Maxwell at St Margaret's Westminster on July 10th 1929.

Lieutenant Richard Alexander Bennett, Albinia Rose's husband, served in the Gloucester Yeomanry (Territorial Force) in England and Ireland during the Great War. He was promoted to Captain in 1919 and after the war returned to the family home at Thornbury Park.

The Reverend Arthur Stafford Crawley, Anstice Katharine's husband, served as a Chaplain during the Great War, in France with the Guards Division and then the 8th Division from 1915 to 1917, and with the 48th Division in Italy from 1918 to 1919. He was awarded the Military Cross in 1916 for conspicuous gallantry and devotion to duty during an attack upon a hostile position. He displayed the greatest fearlessness and devotion throughout the day, never hesitating to expose himself that he might render assistance to the wounded, and making his way twice through an intense bombardment in order to fetch stretcher-bearers. His conduct afforded a splendid instance of gallantry and self-sacrifice.[xxx] In 1917 he was awarded a Bar to his Military Cross for rescuing wounded soldiers between the trenches while under fire. He became Canon of St. George's Chapel Windsor from 1933 until his death in 1948. In 1916, during the First World War, his wife, Anstice Katharine, worked at Nunthorpe Hospital, York, as a member of the Voluntary Aid Detachment of the Red Cross.

Captain William Otter Gibbs, Janet Blanche's husband, served in France and Belgium during the Great War. In 1914 he was attached to the Headquarters of the Third Cavalry Brigade and left for France on the 11th August. On the 3rd September he joined the 18th Hussars and then on the 10th October rejoined the 10th Hussars. In the First Battle of Ypres, he was wounded near Hooge on November 1st and was invalided home to England. He rejoined his regiment on the 12th March 1915 only to be wounded again in the Second Battle of Ypres near Potije. He returned to France on the 19th August 1915, where he remained until 1918, serving at various times as Acting Lieutenant Colonel of the 10th Hussars. On the 9th June 1918, he was seconded to the Tank Corps and was slightly wounded again on August 23rd, but remained on duty. His war service ended with a fourth wound on the 17th October 1918 near Vaud Audigny. He was mentioned in Despatches in the Gazette of May 1917, and awarded the 1914 Star, the British War Medal and the Allies Victory Medal. His wife, Janet Blanche, was Assistant Commandant of the Red Cross Hospital at Chippenham from 1917 to 1918.[xxxi]

The Rev. Francis Antony Woodard Gibbs, Chaplain with the First Hertfordshire Battalion, was awarded the Military Cross in 1918 for conspicuous gallantry and devotion to duty during a raid on the enemy's lines. He followed up the raid and brought in several wounded under very heavy fire. Later, hearing that some men were still missing, he went and searched for them, and brought two in from inside the enemy's wire. He behaved splendidly.[xxxii] Later that year he was awarded a Bar to add to his

Figure 67. The Reverend Arthur Stafford Crawley and his wife Anstice Katharine on the Terrace at 4, Canons Cloister, Windsor Castle.

Figure 68. The Duke of Norfolk, Cosmo Crawley and Lieutenant Colonel William Gibbs at the Funeral of King George V.

Military Cross for conspicuous gallantry on October 9th during the advance on Caudry. He bandaged the wounded in full view of the enemy and under heavy machine-gun and close-range artillery fire. Though hit by a machine-gun bullet, he continued to bandage the wounded and organise their evacuation for four hours afterwards. During the four days' fighting he was continually moving among the men and encouraging them on. He showed the highest devotion to duty.[xxxiii]

There were numerous casualties of War in the Parish of Wraxall and Failand, who were employed at or linked to Tyntesfield, Belmont and Charlton. The fatalities included:

Ball, Charles Edward: born 1881, son of William Ball, Agricultural Labourer of Belmont, Private C. E. Ball of the North Somerset Yeomanry died on 17 April 1917 and is buried in the Faubourg d'Amiens Cemetery at Arras, France.

Bane, Hubert W: born 1897, son of Rosina Nicholas and Henry James Bane, Agricultural Labourer of Summer House Lodge, Tyntesfield. Private H. Bane of the First Battalion of the Somerset Light Infantry died on 8 October 1917. He is buried in Mendinghem Military Cemetery. Medals – Regimental Number 25412: Victory Medal, and the British Medal.

Brice, James Job: born 1890, son of Elizabeth and Charles Brice, Carter of Moat House Cottage, Charlton, and latterly of Hales Farm Cottage Tickenham, Somerset. Private J. J. Brice of the First Battalion of the Grenadiers Guards died on 10 March 1915 and is remembered with honour at the Le Touret Memorial, France. Medals – Regimental Number 15646: Victory Medal, British Medal, and the 1914 Star, with Clasp, 8 November 1914.

Brimble, Sidney Howard: born 1896, Son of Sarah and Frederick Brimble, Carter of Old Smiths Farm Failand, and latterly of Jubilee Cottage, Wraxall. Private H. S. Brimble of the Eleventh Battalion of the Middlesex Regiment died on the 8th July 1916 and is remembered with honour at the Thiepval Memorial for the Battle of the Somme, France. Regimental Number 11138 Campaign Medals – Mrs Brimble made application for medals in respect of the services of her son on the 24th January 1920.

Butchers. Charles: born 1897, Son of Sarah and William Butchers, Gamekeeper, Tyntesfield. Private C. Butchers of the Gloucester Regiment died on the 16th March 1916 and is buried at the Sucrerie Military Cemetery in France. Medals –

Regimental Number 3051TE: Victory Medal, British Medal, and the 1914 Star.

Butchers, Joseph Thomas: born 1890, the Son of Sarah and William Butchers, Gamekeeper, Tyntesfield, Private in the First Battalion of the Grenadier Guards, who died on the 27th September 1918 and is buried at the Sanders Keep Military Cemetery, Graincourt les Havrincourt in France. Medals – Regimental Number 25889: Victory Medal.

Freeman. Walter: born 1889, son of William Freeman, Coachman of Rectory Cottage. Private Walter Freeman of the Grenadier Guards died on September 10th 1916 and is remembered with honour at the Thiepval Memorial for the Battle of the Somme, France. Medals – Regimental Number 11740: Victory Medal, British Medal, and the 1914 Star.

Gibbs, Eustace Lyle: born 1885, the son of Antony and Janet Gibbs of Tyntesfield. Captain Eustace Lyle Gibbs of the North Somerset Yeomanry died on the 11th February 1915 at Ypres and is buried in the Commonwealth War Graves Section of the Town Cemetery at Ypres. Medals – Victory Medal, British Medal and 1914 Star.

Gould, Richard Francis: born 1879, son of Mary and John Gould, Carter of Home Farm Cottages, Tyntesfield, and husband of Ada May Gould of 65 Worrall Road, Clifton, Bristol. Private R.F. Gould of the 36th Battalion Training Reserve, 599th Agricultural Company, Labour Corps is buried in All Saints Long Ashton Churchyard. Medals – Regimental Number: Norfolk Regiment 8098. Re-enlisted Norfolk Regiment 72301: Victory Medal, British Medal, and the 1914 Star: He first served in the Asiatic Theatre of War on the 15th November 1914.

Partridge, Albert Victor: born 1885, son of James Partridge, Carter near Ham Farm. Driver A.V. Partridge died on 24th May 1918 and is remembered with honour in All Saints Wraxall Churchyard. Regimental Number T4/262954: Victory Medal, and the British Medal.

Price, Ernest John: born 1896, son of Frances Price, Shopkeeper of The Grove. Rifleman E J. Stokes of the Seventh Battalion of the King's Royal Rifle Corps died on 15th September 1916 and is remembered with honour at the Thiepval Memorial for the Battle of the Somme, France.

Regimental Number 10964: Victory Medal, British Medal, and the 1914-15 Star (16th July 1915).

Stokes, Charles William Howard: born 1894 son of Charles and Sarah Ann Stokes of "Oaklands" Wraxall. Private C. W. H. Stokes of C Company of the Seventh Battalion of the Bedfordshire Regiment was killed in action on the 27th June 1916 and is buried in Carnoy Cemetery, France. Medals – Regimental Number 14819: Victory Medal, British Medal, and the 1914-15 Star (26th July 1915).

Stokes, Harold Ernest: born 1890, living with William Weeks, Wheelwright, listed as "son", was the husband of Ada Mary of Saw Mills, Wraxall. Lance Corporal H. E. Stokes of the Sixth Dragoons (Inniskilling), Household Cavalry and Cavalry of the Line was killed in action on the 1st December 1917. He is remembered with honour at the Cambrai Memorial, Louverval, France. Medals – Regimental Number: Private 3053, Corporal D/12212, Victory Medal, and the British Medal.

Vowles, George Joseph: born 1882, son of Joseph Vowles of Wraxall and Sophia Vowles, who died in 1894. Sergeant G. J. Vowles enlisted in the Royal Marines Light Infantry, Plymouth Division on the 21st March 1900 and died on the 6th April 1916. He is remembered with honour at All Saints Church Wraxall. Medals – Regimental Number: PLY/10259, Long Service and Good Conduct Medal.

Williams, Oscar: born 1874, son of Mary and David Williams gardener of Failand House, Bristol. Private Oscar Williams of the Second Battalion of the Welsh Regiment died on the 9th May 1915 and is remembered at Le Touret Memorial, France. Medals – Regimental Number 2354: Victory Medal, British Medal, and the 1914-15 Star.

Wyatt, Thomas William: born 1893, was the son of James Wyatt, Gardener of Stables House, Belmont. Private T. W. Wyatt of the Fifteenth Battalion of the Welsh Regiment was killed in action on the 26th August 1918. He is buried in Bulls Road cemetery, Flers near the Somme in France. Medals – Regimental Number 40140: Victory Medal, and the British Medal.[xxxiv]

Most of these sad losses are recorded on the War Memorial at All Saints Church, Wraxall and on the Brass Memorial Plaque inside the Church.

After the First World War, dramatic changes occurred due to the casualties and the cost of the titanic struggle. One million British dead and many more maimed and injured brought grief and sorrow to millions of families across the land. These sad losses also led to a shortage of manpower, which had serious consequences for the economy of the United Kingdom. Country houses no longer had the same number of servants, gardeners and agricultural workers. Families were less affluent and expenses had to be reduced.

Tyntesfield survived and had a brief Indian summer when George Abraham Gibbs married Ursula Lawley in July 1927, and in the New Year's Honours of 1928 was raised to the peerage as Baron Wraxall of Clyst St George. The birth of two sons – George Richard Lawley Gibbs and Eustace Hubert Beilby Gibbs – lifted the family's spirits. There was a Royal Visit to Tyntesfield in 1928, when the Duke and Duchess of York came to greet the first-born son, and then stayed overnight from July 6th to July 7th. [xxxv]

At the end of 1928, the family moved to their new London home at 81, Eaton Square. However the untimely death of Lord Wraxall on the 28th October 1931 left Ursula a widow with two little boys to bring up. She responded admirably to the challenge and aided by her brother in law, Geoffrey Dawson, Editor of the Times and Trustee for her two sons, she conserved Tyntesfield and kept the family together. Lady Wraxall had been a VAD nurse in the First World War and her father, Sir Arthur Lawley, had served as Red Cross Commissioner in France and Mesopotamia and had represented Britain at the founding of the International Red Cross. Lady Wraxall continued her close association with the Red Cross into the Second World War.

November 11th 1918 was more than the end of a ghastly and appalling war, for the English Country House as indeed for the Nation as a whole it was the end of an era.

ILLUSTRATIONS

Figure 1. Officers of the North Somerset Yeomanry in France, October 1914. ... 3
Figure 2. Four of Antony and Janet's children at Charlton – Nancy, Eustace, Albinia and Blanche. 8
Figure 3. Charlton House, North Somerset, now the Downs School. 9
Figure 4. Charlton Model Farm, now The Children's Hospice South West. 9
Figure 5. Pembroke Lodge School, near Bournemouth 10
Figure 6. Demonstration against Women's degrees at Cambridge in 1897. 13
Figure 7. House Group at Eton in 1891. No 1 = William Gibbs, No 2 = George Abraham Gibbs, No 3 = Antony Hubert Gibbs and No 4 = Richard Bennett. 14
Figure 8. The Gibbs boys at the front entrance to Tyntesfield in order of age from left to right, George Abraham, Antony Hubert, William, John Evelyn, Eustace Lyle and Lancelot Merivale. 15
Figure 9. Horse riding at Tyntesfield in 1897 - left to right - Richard Bennett, George Abraham, Anstice Katharine, Albinia Rose and John Evelyn Gibbs. 16
Figure 10. Cycling at Tyntesfield in 1896 - left to right - Janet Blanche, Antony, Albinia Rose, Francis, AL, WC, Anstice Katharine, ECG, WHG, and Lancelot Merivale Gibbs. 16
Figure 11. Antony Gibbs - Photograph taken in Cairo. 17
Figure 12. The Suez Canal opened in 1869 photographed by Antony Gibbs. 18
Figure 13. The eruption of Vesuvius in 1872 just before Antony's visit. 18
Figure 14. Il Duomo - the cathedral - in Milan. Gothic architecture loved by William and Antony Gibbs. 19
Figure 15. Antony, Janet, George Abraham and Albinia Rose on holiday in Venice. 19
Figure 16. George Abraham Gibbs (front left of centre) with the Christchurch Beagles in 1895. 21
Figure 17. George Abraham Gibbs (front row right) with the North Somerset Yeomanry. 21
Figure 18. Walking on the Mer de Glace, Chamonix, 1894. 22
Figure 19. Tyntesfield's Tilbury gig to take you to the Railway Station. 22
Figure 20. Anstice Katharine Gibbs, known as Nancy. 23
Figure 21. Albinia as Amy Robsart 1892. 25
Figure 22. George Abraham Gibbs' 21st Birthday - July 6th 1894. 44
Figure 23. The Gibbs family on a walk from Loch Kennard. 49
Figure 24. Antony Gibbs in his Deerstalker and the Gibbs family at Loch Kennard. 1896. From left to right – Anstice Katharine, Janet Louisa, Mrs. Llewellyn, Antony Gibbs, Albinia Rose, Winifred Elton, ---- , George Abraham Gibbs. In the hammock Lancelot to the left and William to the right. 53
Figure 25. Loch Kennard 1896. Left to right - Janet Blanche, Antony, Cyril Gurney, Janet Louisa, William, Albinia Rose, Margaret Evelyn Gurney, Cyril. Daubeny. Eustace Lyle, Anstice Katharine, Kathleen Elton, George Abraham, John Evelyn and Lancelot Merivale Gibbs. 54

Figure 26. Naish House, Wraxall. 59
Figure 27. Family group at the entrance to Tyntesfield. Left to right John Evelyn Gibbs, L.C., Charlotte Merivale, Anstice Katharine, William and George Abraham Gibbs, T.S.C., Antony Hubert and Albinia Rose Gibbs. 60
Figure 28. The Family at Tyntesfield, 1894. Front row L to R – Fraulein, Nancy (Anstice Katharine), Albinia, Antony and Janet Gibbs. Behind Nancy & Albinia – Janet Blanche and in the back row Lancelot Merivale and John Evelyn Gibbs... 61
Figure 29. English batsmen waiting their turn at Staten Island, New York. Richard Bennett is to the left of the padded batsman. 62
Figure 30. Wedding of Richard Bennett and Albinia Rose Gibbs at Wraxall. ... 63
Figure 31. Guests at Tyntesfield for Richard and Albinia's wedding................ 63
Figure 32. George Abraham Gibbs was in the Body Guard for Field Marshal Lord Roberts at the Entry into Pretoria on June 5th 1900. 65
Figure 33, John Evelyn Gibbs at Tyntesfield in the battle uniform of the Coldstream Guards with Lancelot behind playing at soldiers. 71
Figure 34. William Gibbs at Tyntesfield in the battle uniform of the 7th Hussars. 79
Figure 35. The ocean liner, which brought William Gibbs home..................... 100
Figure 36. George (centre rear) and Via (seated 2nd from left) at a party. 102
Figure 37. The Wedding of Victoria De Burgh Long and George Abraham Gibbs 102
Figure 38. George and Via at Milton Lodge, Dorset... 103
Figure 39. Fancy dress in the Conservatory at Tyntesfield. 104
Figure 40. Wedding of the Rev. Arthur Stafford Crawley and Anstice Katharine Gibbs at Tyntesfield on June 16th 1903. The bridesmaids left to right are Miss Katherine Spencer, Miss A.Pringle, Katherina Gibbs, Janet Blanche Gibbs, Beatrice Crawley, Alice Gurney, Miss Goodden, and Mary Gibbs. 105
Figure 41. Cricket Week 1904. Richard Bennett and Eustace Lyle Gibbs batting. 106
Figure 42, Cricket Week, Tyntesfield 1905. 107
Figure 43. Croquet at Tyntesfield.. 107
Figure 44. Fancy Dress in the Library, Christmas 1905. This photograph reflects the values and attitudes of the age. 108
Figure 45. Tyntesfield Cricketers - Front Row - centre George Abraham Gibbs far right Richard Bennett – Back Row from Left – Antony Hubert (2), John Evelyn (4), Eustace Lyle (5) and William Gibbs (6). 108
Figure 46, Winter Sports at St. Moritz, Switzerland, 1902. Anstice Katharine (Nancy) 109
Figure 47. Janet, Cosmo and Aidan Crawley - Gibbs Grandchildren............. 110
Figure 48. Antony Gibbs in old age. 111
Figure 49. Via Gibbs on one of the Nizam of Hyderabad's elephants, 1904. ... 114
Figure 50. John Evelyn Gibbs as A.D.C. to the Viceroy of India..................... 115
Figure 51. George Abraham Gibbs (front left) and Geoffrey Glynn (front centre) at North Somerset Infantry Camp in 1910... 125
Figure 52. North Somerset Infantry, Frome, 1913. Seated George Abraham Gibbs centre and Antony Hubert Gibbs 3rd from right with Eustace Lyle Gibbs standing at the end right. 125

Figure 53. Captain Eustace Lyle Gibbs, Commanding Officer with B Squadron, North Somerset Yeomanry, Christmas 1914. 128

Figure 54. This map of the Ypres region at the time of the First World War shows many of the places referred to in the Diary and Letters................ 131

Figure 55. Frederick Rudolph Lambart, the Tenth Earl of Cavan..................... 216

Figure 56. Jack Merivale as a boy... 232

Figure 57. The Somme where Captain Lancelot Merivale Gibbs' Brigade moved at the end of July 1916. 311

Figure 58. Brigadier General Walter Long, Victoria Gibbs' brother - Toby.... 336

Figure 59. Ursula Lawley, later Lady Wraxall, served 410

Figure 60. Oaklands House - a Red Cross Hospital at Clevedon during the First World War (once the home of John Lomax Gibbs, William Gibbs' nephew)... 414

Figure 61. Anstice Katharine Crawley 415

Figure 62. The Wedding of Major John Evelyn Gibbs and Lady Helena Frances Augusta Cambridge at St. George's Chapel, Windsor on September 2nd 1919. 419

Figure 63. Tyntesfield, 6th July 1928. Seated the Duke of York, Lady Wraxall, and the Duchess of York. Standing from the left – Lady Helen Graham, Colonel John Evelyn Gibbs, M.C., Lord Erskine, Lady Helena Gibbs, Mr Patrick Hodgson C.M.G., C.V.O., the Hon. Doreen Gibbs, Lord Wraxall, Lady Marjorie Erskine. 419

Figure 64. The Wedding of George Abraham Gibbs and Ursula Mary Lawley. 421

Figure 65. Tyntesfield. Lady Wraxall greets the Duchess of York................... 422

Figure 66. Wedding of Lieutanant Colonel Lancelot Merivale Gibbs and the Hon. Marjorie Florence Maxwell at St Margaret's Westminster on July 10th 1929. 422

Figure 67. The Reverend Arthur Stafford Crawley and his wife Anstice Katharine on the Terrace at 4, Canons Cloister, Windsor Castle. 424

Figure 68. The Duke of Norfolk, Cosmo Crawley and Lieutenant Colonel William Gibbs at the Funeral of King George V..................................... 424

COLOURED PLATES

Plate One. Lord Roberts of Kandahar, who led the British Army to Victory in the Boer War. A Portrait by Robertson at Tyntesfield, January 1901.................... 221

Plate Two. 22 Belgrave Square, George Abraham Gibbs' London home from 1911 to 1928, where Via was hostess until her death in 1920......................... 222

Plate Three. Via, Victoria de Burgh Gibbs by Albert Henry Collins, 1908..... 223

Plate Four. The Grave of Captain Eusatce Lyle Gibbs in the Town Cemetery at Ypres. He died on 11th February 1915. Flowers and photograph by the Author, 2008... 224

Plate Five. Captain Eustace Lyle Gibbs by Albert Henry Collins, a posthumous portrait.. 225

Plate Six. Eustace Lyle Gibbs as a boy by William Blake Richmond............. 226

INDEX

A

Abancourt, 376
Abbéville, 325, 326, 327, 346, 366, 376, 405
Abel-Smith, Desmond, 316
Aberfeldy, 47, 48, 49, 50, 51, 52, 53, 55
Achiet-Le-Grand, 345
Addington Manor, 109
Adinfer, 360, 363
Adinfer Wood, 363
Afghanistan, 412
Agnez-Les-Duisans, 353
Agra, 113, 117, 122
Ailly-sur-Somme, 376
Ainsworth, Jock, 143
Aire, 389
Aisne, 145, 150, 370, 379
Albert, 316, 345, 353, 365, 366, 367, 368, 369, 371, 377, 381
Aldenham, Lord, 7
Alexandria, 228, 229, 233, 236
Allenby, General E.H.H., 402
Allenby, Lieutenant Colonel E.H.H., 68, 94
Alma Wood, 294
Altrincham, Lord, 409
Amber Fort, 120
Ambian St Nazain, 237
Amiens, 130, 150, 315, 316, 317, 318, 325, 327, 328, 334, 335, 338, 349, 350, 362, 367, 369, 371, 373, 375, 377, 379, 395, 405, 406
Ancre, 372, 382, 405
Antony Gibbs and Sons, 225
Antrim, Lady, 117
Anvin, 385
Anzac, 229, 232, 233, 237
Arbuthnot, Lt. Gerald Archibald, 323
Ardee, Brigadier General Lord, 353
Argyle and Sutherland Highlanders, 66
Armadale Castle, Skye, 109
Armentières, 213
Armstrong, Pat, 138
Arques, 250, 297
Arras, 335, 348, 349, 350, 351, 352, 354, 355, 356, 357, 358, 367, 385, 396
Arthur, Sir George, 313

Assouan, 296
Assuit, 296, 300, 303
Athies, 350
Attley, Captain, 347
Aubigny, 355
Aubrey-Fletcher, 354, 355, 357
Auchel, 254, 394, 395, 396
Austria, 17, 124, 141, 387, 399
Authuille, 316
Aveluy Wood, 371
Avery, Eric, 293
Avesnes, 346
Avesnes-Le-Compte, 347
Ayette, 360, 362, 365

B

Baden, 105, 173, 183, 186, 206, 343
Baden, Grand Duke of, 299
Baghdad, 378
Bailey, Jonah, 307, 328
Bailey, Nanny, 7
Bailey, Toby, 354
Bailie, Bill, 306
Bailleul, 171, 173, 280, 365
Baily, W. R., 318
Baizieux, 369, 370, 379
Balfour, Arthur, 412
Balfour, John, 357
Ball Charles Edward, 425
Ballantyne-Dykes, 293, 357
Bane Hubert W, 425
Bapaume, 353, 358, 405, 406
Barber, General, 379
Barbizon, 412
Baring, Guy, 265, 270, 322
Baring, Mrs G., 183
Barly, 346
Baroda, 122
Barrington-Ward, Major, 373
Barrow Court, 7, 14, 20, 112, 247, 368
Barry, Gerald, 323
Barton Place, 30, 112
Bath, Marchioness of, 414
Batten Pool, Walter, 366
Bavircourt, 364
Baynes, "Judge", 295, 331, 333, 337
Beaucourt, 370
Beaufort West, 81
Beaumetz, 345, 346
Beaumont Hamel, 327
Beaumont-Nesbitt, Fred, 175

432

Beaumont-Nesbitt, Paddy, 145, 148, 171, 172, 176, 185, 277, 358
Beauval, 316
Beckwith
   Miss, 82
   William, 74, 83, 90
Beckwith-Smith, 195, 272, 306
   Cissie, 152, 247, 252, 253
   Merton, 152, 292, 306, 307, 308, 310, 312, 314, 315, 317, 318, 320, 322, 323, 325, 327, 328, 347, 351, 356, 366, 368, 374
Bedminster, 45
Belgrave Square, 124, 195, 222, 246, 271, 295, 327, 341, 344, 355, 413, 418, 431
Belgravia, 113, 123, 124
Bell, Colonel, 397
Bell, Gertrude, 401, 403
Belle Croix, 277
Bellenglise, 406
Belmont House, 14, 16, 425, 427
Benenden, Kent, 106, 109, 110
Bennett
   Albinia, 14, 67, 69, 88, 127, 141, 171, 172, 211, 247, 256, 282, 291, 299, 313, 340, 393, 423
   Alexander, 340, 341
   Rev. Alexander Sykes, 62
   Richard, 4, 14, 16, 29, 46, 62, 63, 64, 65, 67, 88, 104, 106, 247, 423
Benson, Rex, 403
Bentinck, Druce, 219, 244, 251, 258, 259, 271, 279, 281, 284, 285, 314
Bentinck, Roger, 137
Berck Plage, 250, 251
Berkely Johnson, Colonel, 176
Berlin, 134, 173, 276, 401
Bernafay Wood, 318, 319, 323, 382
Berneville, 346
Bertrancourt, 314, 315
Bethell, Colonel, 315
Béthune, 176, 178, 180, 181, 186, 189, 190, 195, 197, 199, 200, 203, 204, 205, 206, 210, 212, 213, 218, 219, 240, 241, 242, 243, 244, 246, 247, 248, 249, 250, 266, 267, 268, 269, 394, 397
Beuvry, 244, 245, 246
Bevan, Tom, 189
Bewicke-Copley, R, 135, 152, 155, 317, 331
Bihucourt, 359

Billon Camp, 335
Billon Farm, 336
Billon Wood, 337, 382
Bingham, Ralph, 244, 316, 317, 326, 337
Birdwood, General, 229, 367, 388, 390
Birdwood, Lady, 256
Bishopthorpe, York, 193
Black Mount, 15
Black Watch, 173, 214
Black, Drill Sergeant, 353, 354
Blair Atholl, 51
Blairville, 361, 362, 364
Blendecques, 297
Bliss, US General, 403
Bloemfontein, 97
Blomfield, Sir Arthur, 112
Boeschepe, 151, 289
Boiry St Marc, 363
Boiry St. Martin, 357
Bois de la Haie, 329, 330, 331
Bois Warnimont, 316
Boisleux, 345, 361, 363
Boisleux St Marc, 361
Boitron, 135
Bolsheviks, 399
Bonvalet, E St L, 261
Botha, General Louis, 67
Bouchavesnes, 383, 384
Boulogne, 89, 90, 171, 186, 195, 197, 209, 246, 253, 275, 282, 283, 295, 296, 327, 338, 347, 355, 378, 385, 397, 402, 408
Bouquemaison, 310
Bourlon Wood, 344
Bourton-on-the-Water, 386
Bovelles, 373, 374, 375, 376
Boves Château, 374
Boyd Rochfort, 345, 354
Boyd, Captain, 289
Boyelles, 358, 359
Boyle, Irene, 400, 404
Boyle, Philippa, 400, 403, 404, 408
Brabazon, Jerry, 179, 182, 219, 239, 240
Bramwell, Ralph, 175
Brassey, Edwin, 275, 281, 288, 346, 350, 351
Brassey, Ruby Mabel, 124
Bray, 327, 380, 381
Bremen, 399
Bretencourt, 357
Brice James Job, 425

Brie, 405
Brielen, 302
Brimble Sidney Howard, 425
Briqueterie, 334
Briquetprie, 382
Britstown, 74, 75, 76, 77, 78, 79, 81, 82, 83, 84, 90, 95
Bronfay, 331
Bronfay Farm, 382
Brook, George, 147
Brooke, Boy, 265, 279, 315, 349, 352, 356, 359
Brooke, General, 357
Brown, Dermot, 172, 200, 202, 248, 250
Brown, Father, 306
Browne, Eileen, 292
Bruges, 389, 392
Brussels, 38, 342, 393, 394
Buchanan, Tiny, 362
Buckingham, Emma, 80
Budget Lloyd, 152, 156, 172, 179, 182, 194, 198, 212, 214, 243, 244, 246, 248, 268, 269, 275, 282, 284, 285, 287, 302, 335, 337, 345
Bulkeley Johnson, Bigadier General, 174
Bullecourt, 357
Burk, Lt Colonel, 348
Burn, Hugh, 251, 255, 304, 321
Burrington, 62, 109
Burton, Lady, 402
Burton, Stephen, 338, 341
Burton, Steven, 190, 330
Butchers Charles, 425
Butchers Joseph Thomas, 426
Butler 2nd Lt. J. H. R., 321
Butler, Lt General, 374
Butler-Stoney, Bowes, 399, 403, 404, 405, 406, 407
Butler-Stoney, Miss, 403, 405
Byng, Major General Julian, 421

C

Café de Paris, 334
Cairo, 17, 113, 233, 234, 303, 313, 416
Calais, 151, 284, 350
Calcutta, 122
Calonne, 269, 270, 277, 278, 388
Calverly Bewicke, 355, 357
Camblain-Châtelan, 396
Cambrai, 345, 388, 405, 406
Cambridge, 6, 12, 13, 27, 42, 43

Cambridge University, 12, 13
Cambridge, Lady Helena, 418, 419
Cambridge, the Marquis of, 418
Cambrin, 239, 240, 241, 243, 244
Cameron Highlanders, 163, 214
Campbell, Colonel, 302
Campbell, Donald, 308, 309
Campbell, John, 244, 268, 274, 278, 289, 297, 307, 316, 320, 323, 324, 326, 327
Canada, 114
Canaples, 316
Canchy, 366
Cantelau Bridge, 390
Cape Colony, 64, 82
Cape Nebruisi, 232
Cape Town, 64, 76, 79, 89, 90, 92
Cardiff, 420
Carlton, 252, 271, 272, 283, 295, 388, 402
Carnegie, Kathleen, 401, 402, 403, 409
Carnes, Alan, 236
Carnoy, 317, 318, 319, 382, 383
Carrington, Lady A., 122
Cassel, 283, 284, 290
Cateau, 391
Cauchy, 394
Cavan, 10th Earl, 121, 140, 141, 142, 143, 146, 154, 162, 168, 179, 186, 188, 197, 199, 209, 215, 216, 217, 218, 237, 242, 250, 251, 257, 258, 259, 260, 261, 262, 263, 264, 265, 272, 273, 274, 275, 276, 289, 290, 296, 304, 306, 307, 308, 314, 322, 343, 355, 421
Cavendish, Ralph, 346, 350
Cavillon, 374
Cecil, Lord Robert, 412
Ceylon, 113
Champagne, 255, 259
Chantilly, 404
Charley, Major, 231
Charlton House, 5, 6, 7, 8, 10, 11, 12, 28, 38, 47, 58, 104, 126, 245, 425
Charly, 135
Chavonne, 141, 145
Cheltenham, 208
Chequers Court, 109
Chester Master, Margaret, 84
Chesterfield House, 402
Chevillon, 136
Chevreuse, 407
Chichester, General, 205

Chile, 225
Chitar, 120
Chocques, 244, 250, 269, 385
Chocques-Lillers, 250
Christchurch College Oxford, 13, 20, 21
Citadel, 327, 328
Clark, Francis, 324
Clark-Jervoise, 298
Clevedon, 24, 26, 27, 29, 30, 34, 35, 39, 40, 46, 99, 109, 414, 415
Clevedon Court, 59, 69
Clifton, 24, 27, 28, 29, 30, 31, 32, 33, 36, 40, 41, 45, 47, 56, 57, 58, 59, 61, 88, 113, 426
Clutterbuck, Rupert, 172, 280, 290
Clyst St George, 39, 104, 109, 112, 420, 428
Coats, Jimmy, 326, 328, 329, 350, 351, 356, 365
Coats, Lt Colonel Edwin, 365
Cobham, William, 43
Cockran, General, 298
Codrington, General, 298, 301
Coke, Hermione, 326
Coke, Jack, 344
Coldstream Guards, 64, 71, 124, 128, 129, 132, 142, 144, 147, 150, 158, 168, 170, 171, 172, 175, 176, 180, 185, 188, 190, 195, 196, 203, 206, 209, 210, 211, 212, 213, 214, 217, 218, 220, 227, 237, 238, 240, 241, 242, 244, 253, 254, 255, 262, 266, 267, 268, 269, 271, 273, 274, 275, 276, 277, 278, 279, 280, 281, 282, 284, 285, 286, 288, 289, 290, 292, 293, 295, 297, 298, 301, 302, 303, 304, 305, 306, 307, 308, 309, 310, 312, 314, 315, 316, 317, 318, 319, 320, 321, 322, 323, 324, 325, 326, 327, 328, 330, 331, 332, 333, 334, 336, 338, 344, 345, 346, 349, 350, 351, 352, 353, 354, 355, 356, 357, 362, 365, 366, 369, 371, 372, 374, 375, 380, 409, 416, 417, 418
Colenso, 97, 99
Colesburg, 80
Colincamps, 315
Cologne, 407
Combles, 324, 329, 330, 331, 332, 358, 405
Compiègne, 405, 406
Conroy's Commando, 85
Constantinople, 231, 233

Contay, 368, 369, 376
Cook Alston, 316, 325
Cook, Roger, 252
Cooper, Gladys, 300
Corbett, Rowland, 183
Corbie, 380, 405
Cordoba, 17
Corkran, Brigadier General, 246, 337
Corrie Fergis, 15
Cotterell-Dormer, 190
Couchy-Le-Château, 405
Couin, 315
Coulommiers, 134
Courcelles, 144, 315, 359
Courland, 403
Courtrai, 392
Couvrelle, 136
Coyecoues, 253
Crabbes' Column, 87
Cranborne, Betty, 408, 409, 411, 412, 413
Cranborne, Bobbety, 408, 409, 411, 412, 413
Cranborne, Lady, 403, 407, 409, 411, 412, 413
Cranborne, Lord, 400, 403, 409, 411, 412, 413
Crawford, Bunny, 270, 295, 297, 308, 310, 314, 316, 334, 338
Crawley
  Aidan, 342
  Anstice Katharine (Nancy), 5, 8, 23, 30, 39, 40, 61, 70, 72, 73, 74, 76, 77, 79, 80, 81, 82, 83, 84, 85, 88, 89, 90, 91, 92, 93, 94, 95, 96, 97, 98, 99, 100, 104, 109, 117, 123, 124, 126, 128, 139, 144, 145, 154, 157, 160, 162, 163, 167, 171, 172, 174, 175, 178, 180, 181, 184, 185, 187, 190, 191, 192, 193, 195, 196, 197, 199, 201, 203, 204, 209, 211, 212, 214, 215, 227, 238, 240, 241, 242, 244, 245, 247, 252, 253, 255, 258, 262, 266, 267, 271, 272, 273, 283, 294, 295, 296, 299, 303, 305, 309, 312, 338, 339, 342, 377, 386, 392, 398, 415, 424
  Beatrice, 84, 105, 106
  Cosmo, 110, 181, 272, 296, 342, 424
  Eustace, 116
  Fanny, 57

George Baden, 105
Janet, 207
Rev. Arthur Stafford, 4, 70, 99, 100, 105, 106, 109, 110, 116, 117, 118, 119, 123, 140, 144, 157, 163, 175, 186, 192, 195, 197, 204, 213, 252, 253, 254, 255, 256, 257, 258, 259, 260, 263, 265, 266, 267, 268, 269, 270, 271, 272, 273, 274, 275, 279, 280, 285, 287, 296, 297, 303, 305, 307, 308, 314, 318, 319, 325, 326, 332, 334, 337, 342, 343, 351, 377, 386, 400, 418, 423, 424

Crawley Boevey
Anne, 57
Cilla, 58
May, 43

Crichton, Harry, 187
Crighton, George, 402
Crooke Lawless, Lady, 206
Cros, Sir Eyre, 403
Crossley, Frank, 138
Cubitt, Harry, 247, 255, 257, 269, 306, 307, 322
Cuinchy, 189, 190, 191, 198, 199, 205, 213, 249, 255
Cunard, Sir Edward, 420
Curzon, Cimmie, 409
Curzon, Lady, 409
Cys, 136, 137, 141, 142, 143, 145, 150

D

Dalkeith, Walter, 375
Danzig, 404
Dardanelles, 260
Darell, Brigadier General Billy, 356
Darell, Colonel Guy, 277, 278, 279, 289, 349, 354, 356, 357, 362
Darell, Lt Colonel W., 290
Daubeny
Cyril, 24, 26, 46, 77, 93, 184, 186, 188, 270, 275, 327, 399, 403
Family, 34, 39, 57
Mabel, 46
Margery, 272
Mary, 92
Ralph, 83

Davidson, Major-General, 374
Davy, Jack, 168
Dawes, Colonel, 387, 388, 391

Dawes, Lt Colonel, 366, 367, 371, 379, 384, 385, 386
Dawson, Geoffrey, 409, 428
Dawson-Damer, George, 283
De Aar, 74, 76, 81
De Crespigny, Crawley, 171, 185, 242, 250, 297, 302, 307, 308, 316, 346, 356, 364, 365, 402
De Haviland, Brigadier, 206
De Massa, Duc, 399, 403, 409, 413
De Massa, Duchesse, 400, 401, 403, 409, 412, 413
De Sévigné, Marquis, 378
De Trafford, Humphrey, 199, 265, 270, 279, 292, 304, 314, 398, 399
De Trafford, Rudolph, 195, 335, 350
De Varenne, Baron, 413
Decaville, 336
Declaration of War, 126
Deelfontein, 80, 81
Delhi, 118
Denekin, Russian General, 398
Dennebroeucq, 253
Denniston, Tiger, 401, 403, 408
Dernancourt, 371
Deveral, Staff Captain, 366
Deverell, Brigadier, 374
Dickson-Poynder, Joan, 409
Dielfontein, 78
Digby, Kenneth, 353, 354
Dill, Dickie, 389, 396
Doullens, 310, 369, 373
Dove Leys, Staffordshire, 109
Dowding, Colonel, 395
Down Ampney, 87
Down Ampney House, 109
Downall Family, 45
Dresden, 411
Dressel, Herr, 41, 42, 43
Dromesnil, 325, 327
Drury
Family, 47
Isabel, 35
Du Murat, Princesse, 408
Du Prés, Madame, 400
Duchess of York, 419
Duke of Connaught, 327, 400
Dunkerque, 204
Durban, 97, 98, 99
Dyer, John, 316
Dykes, Captain, 316

E

Eastwood, Rusty (N.Z.), 364
Edinburgh, 55
Edmonstone, Lt. William George, 321
Ednam, Eric, 283
Egerton, Arthur, 250
Eglantine Hanbury, Miss, 206
Egypt, 17, 81, 103, 113, 183, 296, 303, 421
Eksternest, 155, 160, 163, 164
Elandsfontein, 94
Elliot, Esmee, 285
Elton
   Ambrose, 54
   Angela, 27
   Bernard, 35
   Family, 25, 29, 36, 40, 58
   Kathleen, 27, 28, 30, 31, 32, 33, 34, 35, 37, 38, 39, 40, 41, 42, 43, 44, 45, 46, 52, 53, 54, 60
   Lady, 54
   Laura Beatrice, 69
   Sir Arthur Hallam, 69
   Sir Edmund, 54
   Winifred, 31, 33, 34, 35, 39, 42, 53, 54, 55, 57, 292
Englebelmer, 315
English, Margaret, 152, 163
Ennentiers, 389
Épinette Wood, 384, 385
Ervillers, 358
Essars, 185, 188
Estaires, 275, 363, 388, 390
Estrée Blanche, 269
Estrée-Cauchie, 353, 354
Étinehem, 380
Eton College, 12, 13, 14, 20, 30, 45, 57, 62, 81, 82, 83, 87, 100, 206, 207, 225, 226, 238, 269, 279, 301, 313, 340, 347, 416
Euphrates, 377
Evans, Hilda, 27, 33, 40
Exeter College, Oxford, 112
Exwick, 112

F

Fampoux, 350, 351, 352
Farnham, George, 83
Fatehpur-Sikri, 117
Fauquembergues, 252
Feilding, Colonel Geoffrey, 145, 153, 194, 197, 210, 211, 242, 389, 392, 394
Feilding, General, 170, 185, 197, 206, 273, 277, 281, 289, 293, 298, 301, 306, 346, 367, 368, 380, 390
Ferfay, 394
Fergusson, Capt. Robert A. A., 321
Ferrieres, 373
Festubert, 215, 220, 239, 365
Fismes, 150
Fitzgerald, Desmond, 284
Flax Bourton, 28, 30, 31, 35, 46, 58, 112, 414
Flers, 320
Flesselles, 316, 378
Florence, 17, 106
Floringham, 397
Foch, Marshal, 416
Folkestone, 88, 295, 296, 355, 397
Follett, Gillie, 75, 88, 90, 139, 145, 164, 167, 168, 169, 170, 177, 178, 179, 195, 206, 207, 260, 265, 266, 267, 268, 269, 271, 273, 275, 278, 279, 281, 282, 283, 284, 286, 287, 288, 289, 297, 302, 306, 307, 308, 309, 325, 345, 346, 349, 356, 359, 360, 386
Follies Bergères, 408
Fontainebleau, 407, 412
Fontenay, 134
Fontes, 389
Forbes-Adams, Ronald, 412
Ford, Mr R. A., 25, 29, 36
Ford, Roger, 187
Forêt de Nieppe, 279
Fortnum and Mason, 138, 147, 161, 164, 169, 207
Fosseux, 346
Fouquereuil, 246, 247
Fouquières, 242
Franvillers, 370
Franz Ferdinand, Archduke, 124
Fraser-Tytler, 399
Fraser-Tytler, Neil, 398, 401
Freeman Walter, 426
Freeman, Violet, 43
Freiberg, 128
Freiburg, 343
Freman, Pierre, 30
French, General, 80, 101, 250
Frezenberg, 159, 161, 164
Frilsham House, Berks, 109
Frogmore House, 418

Fromelles-le-Maisnil, 388
Frost, Major C. G., 280
Froyennes, 391
Fruges, 251
Fry, Edward, 25
Fry, Elizabeth, 86
Furgusson, Lt Colonel, 381

G

Gage, Grubby, 333
Gallipoli, 128, 229, 230, 234, 237, 421
Gaythorne-Hardy, 213, 308
Geluveld, 304
Genoa, 113
Gheluvelt, 128, 156, 158, 163
Gibbs
    Albinia Rose, 4, 5, 6, 12, 13, 16, 23, 24, 25, 26, 27, 28, 29, 30, 31, 32, 33, 34, 36, 38, 39, 40, 41, 42, 45, 46, 47, 48, 49, 50, 51, 52, 53, 55, 56, 57, 58, 60, 62, 63, 64
    Alice, 44
    Anstice Katharine (Nancy), 4, 5, 7, 22, 23, 24, 64, 81, 99, 105, 126
    Antony, 110, 111
    Antony (Tyntesfield), 5, 24, 62
    Antony Edmund, 69
    Antony Hubert, 6, 8, 10, 13, 14, 15, 24, 26, 27, 34, 36, 38, 41, 42, 43, 45, 46, 47, 49, 52, 53, 55, 60, 62, 68, 77, 90, 100, 104, 109, 125, 147, 166, 167, 169, 170, 171, 174, 175, 176, 192, 196, 197, 204, 247, 253, 256, 271, 272, 291, 340, 420
    Beresford, 314
    Doreen, 150, 420
    Dorothea, 7, 35, 43, 52, 57
    Edith, 172, 342
    Edward, 193, 361
    Emily, 64, 291
    Ethel, 47, 49, 50, 51, 152, 300
    Eustace Hubert Beilby, 420
    Eustace Lyle, 5, 7, 8, 12, 14, 15, 23, 26, 29, 32, 33, 35, 36, 37, 38, 40, 41, 43, 48, 50, 52, 54, 55, 57, 59, 60, 70, 71, 87, 88, 106, 124, 125, 128, 147, 157, 166, 167, 168, 170, 171, 174, 176, 181, 184, 190, 192, 193, 208, 225, 226, 287, 294, 296, 297, 426, 431
    Francis Antony, 15, 20, 423
    George Abraham, 5, 6, 8, 10, 13, 14, 15, 16, 19, 21, 23, 24, 25, 26, 27, 29, 30, 31, 34, 35, 36, 37, 39, 40, 43, 44, 45, 52, 53, 54, 60, 62, 64, 65, 67, 68, 70, 75, 76, 77, 81, 88, 90, 95, 97, 101, 102, 103, 108, 111, 113, 114, 123, 124, 125, 129, 138, 139, 146, 148, 171, 172, 193, 195, 202, 207, 220, 222, 247, 252, 253, 271, 272, 282, 283, 292, 296, 299, 313, 327, 340, 343, 344, 355, 397, 402, 409, 418, 420, 421, 424, 428, 431
    George Antony, 114
    George Louis Monck, 69
    George Richard Lawley, 420, 428
    Guy Melvil, 15, 20, 165, 166, 167, 170, 176
    Henry Hucks, 7, 20, 172
    Henry Martin, 7, 14, 20, 64, 111, 112, 167, 291, 292, 368
    Jack, 41, 42, 269, 300, 322
    Janet, 62
    Janet Blanche, 4, 5, 7, 16, 38, 53, 54, 55, 60, 64, 70, 105, 106, 109, 127, 129, 138, 148, 149, 163, 171, 172, 173, 185, 191, 195, 206, 207, 208, 211, 247, 252, 253, 256, 266, 271, 272, 282, 295, 299, 312, 344, 355, 402, 423
    Janet Louisa, 4, 5, 6, 13, 24, 109, 111, 228, 416, 426
    John, 29, 35
    John Evelyn, 4, 7, 13, 15, 16, 23, 24, 26, 27, 28, 30, 33, 35, 36, 37, 38, 39, 46, 48, 49, 50, 51, 52, 53, 54, 56, 57, 58, 59, 60, 64, 65, 70, 71, 72, 73, 74, 75, 76, 78, 79, 80, 81, 82, 83, 85, 86, 87, 88, 89, 91, 92, 93, 94, 95, 96, 97, 98, 99, 100, 106, 114, 115, 116, 117, 118, 119, 121, 123, 124, 128, 134, 138, 142, 148, 155, 157, 158, 160, 161, 163, 166, 174, 184, 188, 192, 208, 257, 272, 292, 294, 296, 301, 303, 314, 339, 342,

344, 352, 363, 378, 393, 394, 397, 402, 403, 418, 419
John Lomax, 114, 414
Katherina, 105, 106
Lancelot Merivale, 4, 5, 7, 14, 15, 16, 29, 33, 37, 43, 52, 53, 54, 70, 77, 106, 124, 127, 128, 134, 140, 142, 145, 147, 154, 157, 161, 162, 165, 168, 172, 174, 176, 179, 180, 184, 186, 190, 192, 196, 197, 200, 202, 204, 207, 210, 211, 213, 215, 220, 226, 238, 240, 241, 242, 244, 245, 253, 260, 262, 266, 268, 273, 294, 296, 300, 303, 305, 309, 311, 313, 339, 340, 341, 344, 386, 393, 417, 418, 421, 422
Lionel Cyril, 15, 20, 133, 165, 167, 170, 192, 379, 380, 387, 388, 389, 390
Louis Merivale, 7
Major Joe, 363
Margot, 171, 172
Mary, 106
Mary Albinia, 15, 64
Mary Mercy, 62, 77, 104, 109, 164, 171, 172, 174, 188, 195, 247, 253, 271, 272, 340
Matilda Blanche, 6, 7, 106
May, 36
Noel, 292
Noel Martin, 15, 20
Ralph Crawley Boevey, 15, 20, 165, 167, 170, 368, 370
Robert Tyndall, 114
Roland Vicary, 15, 20
Ruby, 124, 161, 207, 247, 256, 271, 272, 282, 296, 299, 300, 303, 313, 341, 377, 386, 402
Stanley, 34, 36
Vicary, 35, 172, 184, 186, 187, 195, 200, 202, 257
Victoria de Burgh, 90, 95, 103, 113, 114, 129, 133, 149, 152, 178, 183, 195, 207, 246, 247, 253, 257, 282, 283, 299, 313, 335, 344, 348, 355, 414, 420, 449
William, 7, 23, 26, 27, 28, 34, 35, 36, 37, 38, 43, 46, 49, 50, 51, 53, 57, 59, 62, 64, 65, 67, 73, 75, 76, 77, 81, 85, 88, 89, 92, 93, 94, 95, 98, 124, 127, 128, 138, 186, 195, 247, 252, 256, 277, 296, 300, 303, 305, 313, 327, 341, 375, 378, 386, 421, 424
William Otter, 15, 20, 38, 81, 114, 138, 152, 154, 171, 195, 207, 209, 247, 251, 256, 265, 266, 269, 291, 366, 374, 375, 423

Gilkes, Humphrey, 377, 380, 384
Gillibecke, 303
Ginchy, 317, 318, 319, 320, 405
Ginchy Wood, 405
Givenchy, 188, 196, 199, 201, 209, 210, 212, 220, 246, 247, 248, 255
Glenfeshie, 15
Glynn, Geoffrey, 125, 193, 335
Gobain, 405
Gomlecourt, 358, 359
Goodenough, Maudina, 88
Gordon Highlanders, 349, 352
Gordon-Lennox, Amy, 327
Gordon-Lennox, Doris, 172, 195
Gore Langton, Captain, 263
Gore Langton, Monty, 262
Gore-Langton, Francis, 156, 157, 158
Gorringe, General Sir George, 366, 375, 379
Gort, Major, 206, 217, 273, 278, 279, 280, 289, 293, 294, 295, 298, 302, 304, 305, 314, 315
Gosfield Park, 313
Gough, Eric, 152
Gough, Hugo, 138
Gough, Sergeant, 255
Gould Richard Francis, 426
Gouzeaucourt, 406
Graaff Reinet, 70, 72, 73, 75, 78, 79, 82, 95, 96, 97, 99
Graham, Miles, 379
Grant, Charles, 404
Grant, US Colonel, 404
Grantully Castle, 50
Grantully Hill, 51
Graves-Sawle, 160
Greenwood, Chick, 306
Gregory, Phil, 374
Grenadier Guards, 89, 132, 138, 143, 145, 148, 150, 158, 159, 167, 171, 176, 177, 179, 185, 188, 193, 194, 200, 201, 202, 214, 215, 216, 217, 218, 227, 237, 239, 242, 251, 253, 255, 260, 262, 263, 268, 269, 270, 271, 273, 274, 278, 279, 280, 282,

284, 287, 294, 297, 298, 306, 307, 310, 312, 314, 315, 316, 317, 318, 319, 320, 321, 322, 323, 324, 325, 326, 328, 330, 346, 350, 353, 354, 357, 359, 361, 363, 365, 425, 426
Grenfell, Ivo, 408
Greville, Charles, 292
Grigg, Edward William M., 290, 304, 308, 322, 362, 363, 365, 409
Grosvenor, Hugh, 187
Grosvenor, Lady Margaret, 418
Grosvenor, Ned, 292
Gueudecourt, 324, 325
Guignemicourt, 373
Guillemont, 317, 319
Gunstan-Whitall, 364
Gurney
   Alice, 64, 106, 247
   Christopher, 365
   Cyril, 23, 45, 46, 54, 57, 61, 85, 89, 184, 247
   Eric, 309
   Evie, 207, 247, 257, 291
   Ginger, 28
   Thomas, 207, 379
   William, 24, 31, 35, 47
Guthrie, Charles, 137
Gwalior, 121, 122
Gwynne, Father, 263

H

Haig, General Sir Douglas, 250, 265
Haig, Major Douglas, 67, 79
Haking, General, 189, 265, 273, 274, 277, 392, 407
Haldane, General, 361
Hall, Lieutenant, 289
Haller, General, 404
Halte, 159, 167
Ham, 405, 406
Hambro, Olaf, 354
Hamelincourt, 359, 361
Hamilton, Angus, 264
Hammersley, Violet, 272
Hanover, 339
Happy Valley, 381
Harcourt-Vernon, 137
Hardie, Rev. John, 12
Harfleur, 345
Hargreaves Brown, 256
Harmon Hodge, 290
Harrison, 407
Harrison, Major, 281

Havrincourt, 405
Hay, Arthur, 129, 130, 132, 142
Hay, Bache, 135
Hayem, 387
Hayes, Madame, 412
Hayworth, General, 274, 292
Hazebrouck, 151, 154, 181, 195, 295, 301, 365
Headlam, Cuthbert, 250, 252, 259, 268, 290
Headlam, Tuppi, 349
Heath, Baron John Benjamin, 6
Heath, Frances Rose, 6
Heberden
   Evelyn, 36
   Family, 36
   Mr and Miss, 34
Hebuterne, 335
Heidelberg, 94, 128, 173, 183, 184, 186, 206, 208, 291, 299, 312, 340, 403
Heilly, 372, 379, 385
Hendon airfield, 402
Hénencourt, 366, 367, 368, 369, 379
Hénencourt Wood, 369, 376
Hénin Hill, 357, 358
Hennesy, Dick, 408
Hertford Street, 13, 103
Hertfordshires, 176, 188, 194, 209, 211, 212, 215, 217, 227, 247, 248, 249
Herzeele, 285, 309, 310
Hesdigneul, 268
Hesdin, 298
Heywood, Guffin, 297, 298, 315, 337
Heywood, Sergeant, 304
Heywood, Sir Arthur, 109
Higgins, General, 373
Hill, Phyllis, 46
Hindenberg, 408
Hinges, 203, 269
Hodgson, Maureen, 207
Hodgson, Mick, 87, 207
Hodgson, Patrick, 419
Hoge, 155, 161, 302, 304, 306
Hohenzollern redoubt, 258, 259, 265, 266
Holland-Hibbert, T, 374
Hollyhead, Sergeant, 289
Holmes, Benoy, 400, 401, 402, 403, 404, 405, 407, 408, 409, 411, 412, 413
Holyrood, 55
Holzminden, 128, 343

Honnevain, 391
Hood, Lady, 398, 403, 408, 411
Hooge, 423
Hope Barton, 49
Hope, Arthur, 304, 330
Hopwood, Byng, 152, 171, 173, 177, 183, 186, 190, 191, 200, 201, 248, 250, 265, 269, 270, 278, 314, 329
Hordern, Brigadier General, 392
Horlick, Jimmy, 171, 190
Hormhout, 302
Hornoy, 325, 326
Hôtel de Paris, 189, 338
Houldsworth, Dorothy, 247
Houtkerque, 285, 309, 310
Howard, Algy, 371
Hughes, Jack, 189
Hungary, 403
Hunlock, Philip, 274
Hunter, Charles, 404
Hutton, 26, 36
Hyde Park Gardens, 5, 6, 7, 22, 70, 100, 109, 113
Hyderabad,, 113

I

Imperial Yeomanry, 64, 65, 67, 72
India, 6, 20, 83, 113, 114, 115, 116, 117, 118, 119, 120, 121, 122, 123, 124, 395, 416, 417, 418
Indian Corps, 198
International Red Cross, 428
Invergeldie, 74
Irish Guards, 129, 138, 142, 152, 159, 178, 185, 188, 190, 194, 195, 197, 215, 217, 239, 249, 252, 259, 260, 262, 265, 266, 267, 277, 279, 280, 282, 285, 289, 293, 298, 301, 305, 306, 307, 310, 314, 319, 320, 322, 325, 326, 328, 337, 345, 346, 352, 353, 361, 365, 389
Irving, Private James, 323

J

Jaipur, 113, 119, 120
James, Lt Colonel, 307
Japan, 418
Jeffreys, Lt Colonel, 273, 277, 278
Jeffries, General George, 333
Johannesburg, 64, 93, 97, 98
Johnston, Lt Colonel, 380

K

Kaye, Lt Colonel, 381
Keble College, Oxford, 111, 112
Kelly, Hazel, 408
Kenmare, 52
Kennedy, General, 366, 371, 378, 379, 381, 388, 392, 397, 407, 408
Kew Gardens, 41
Khartoum, 103, 113
Khartoum, Bishop of, 290, 317
Kilberry, Argyleshire, 109
Kimberley, 94, 97, 101
King George V, 268, 314
King, Charles, 256, 300, 313
King's Liverpool Regiment, 179
Kitchener, General Lord, 80, 103, 124, 242, 257, 264, 300
Knatchbull-Hugessen, Lord and Lady, 400

L

L'Abeele, 286
La Bassée, 243, 254, 279
La Boulie, 409, 411
La Brique, 286, 307
La Celle, 134
La Couronne, 170
La Couture, 182
La Flinque, 282, 386
La Gorgue, 270, 271, 274, 275, 277, 280, 282
La Morlaye, 404
La Tombe, 391, 394
La Tretoire, 135
La Viéville, 379
Labassée, 267
Lacon, 185
Ladysmith, 97, 99
Lambton, General Billy, 309
Lambton, Major, 213
Lambton, Ralph, 335, 405, 413
Lane Fox, Father, 326
Lane, George, 172, 274, 277, 280, 315, 316, 326
Lane, Joe, 247, 282
Lang
  Cosmo, Archbishop of York, 171, 178, 180, 301
  Cosmo, Bishop of Stepney, 105
Langemarck, 343
Langford, 34, 62, 198
Lansdowne, 119

Laon, 142
Lapugnoy, 219, 237
Lascelles, Viscount, 314, 315, 316
Lavantie-Sec, 388
Laventie, 273, 274, 277, 279, 280, 363
Laviéville, 366, 369, 370
Lawley, Cecilia, 409
Lawley, Lady Annie, 420
Lawley, Sir Arthur, 299, 420, 428
Lawley, Ursula Mary, 299, 409, 410, 420, 421, 428
Lawrence, Capt. Michael, 203, 290, 292, 322
Le Cateau, 388
Le Havre, 129, 130, 271, 272, 344, 345
Le Maisnil, 387
Le Mans, 132
Le Petit Marais, 386
Le Plantin, 247, 248, 249
Le Préol, 210, 212, 214, 219
Le Quesnoy, 198, 200, 203, 208, 210, 211, 212, 245, 247, 248, 249
Le Rutoire, 254
Le Sart, 280
Le Titre, 366
Le Touquet, 375
Le Touret, 200
Le Transloy, 405
Le Treport, 327
League of Nations, 400
Lear, Charlton bailiff, 10
Lear, Edith, 38
Ledringhem, 285
Leforest, 384
Leger Glyn, 280
Legge, Douglas, 374
Legge, Walter, 280
Legge-Bourke, Lt. Nigel, 158, 160
Legh, Joe, 290
Leigh, Diana, 404
Leigh, Honor, 341, 347
Leigh-Bennett, Pro, 144, 145, 152, 160, 164, 183, 185, 189, 194, 198, 202, 203, 215, 217, 219, 239, 241, 242, 250, 251, 258, 259, 262
Les Boeufs, 320, 322, 323, 324, 325, 358, 405
Les Glaumes, 218
Les Lauriers, 278, 279, 280
Leslie, Jack, 374
Lestrem, 386
Leuze Wood, 332
Libau, 399, 400, 403
Liebert, Frederick, 168

Liéramont, 385
Lille, 195, 206, 210, 388, 389, 390, 391, 392, 393, 394
Lillers, 268, 269, 271, 273
Lister, Lt Colonel, 398, 399
Llewellyn
   Arthur, 345, 349, 350
   Evan Henry, 10, 34, 50, 51, 52, 62
   Mary Mercy, 62
   Thomas, 46
   Wynn, 154, 161, 309
Lloyd George, David, 342, 400, 409
Loch Katrine, 53
Loch Kennard, 15, 47, 49, 53, 54, 55, 96, 97
Loch Lomond, 53
Loch Tay, 53
Lockeridge, US General, 403
Locon, 180, 182, 185, 202, 203, 209, 270
Loddington, 272
Lomme, 390
London Regiment, 366, 367, 368, 369, 370, 374, 379, 380, 381, 389, 390, 392, 395, 397
Long
   Lady Dorothy Blanche, 103
   Rt. Hon. Walter Hume, 103, 415, 420
   Toby, 144
   Victoria de Burgh, 75, 101, 102, 103
   Walter (Toby), 101, 335, 336
Longchamps, 409, 411, 412, 413
Longueness, 297, 298
Longueville, Francis, 210, 257, 269, 308, 333, 346, 350, 352, 353, 402
Lord Salisbury, 20
Louvencourt, 315
Loveband, Molly, 174
Lubeck, 399
Luck, Sergeant, 286
Lude House, 15
Lumbres, 250, 251
Luxemburg, 407
Luzerne, 106, 299

M

MacArthur, Captain, 236
MacCormack, Sir William, 101
MacDonald Ronald Monkton, 106
Macdonell, Madie, 247
MacGregor, Colonel, 251, 269

MacGregor, Lt. John Atholl, 324
MacGregor, Major, 177, 178, 191,
    192, 198, 199, 203, 213, 214, 215,
    217, 218, 227, 237, 239, 246
Mackenzie, Eric, 172
Mackinnon, Margaret, 34, 52
Madden, Colonel, 263
Madrid, 17, 114
Mafeking, 101
Magaliesberg, 68
Magdalen College Oxford, 13, 14, 20,
    225, 226
Maillot, 31, 41
Maison Lafitte, 407
Maitland, Mark, 388
Mallaville, Madame, 412
Mallet, Hugh, 30
Mallett, Hugo, 86
Malta, 115, 229
Maltzhorn, 329
Mametz, 405
Marett Wood, 380
Maricourt, 335
Markham, Tony, 155, 285
Marne, 135
Marshall, Freddy, 201
Maurepas, 337, 338, 382, 383, 384
Maxim's, 334
Mazingarbe, 237, 255
McBride, 183, 185, 189, 190, 191, 194
McCalmont, Colonel, 308
McDowall, General, 366, 367
McLean, Douglas, 67
Méaulte, 316, 317, 318, 325, 328, 333,
    380, 405
Medley, Rev. John, 12, 30, 31, 33, 47,
    57, 76, 105
Melksham, 109
Melville, Archie, 374
Menin, 155, 287, 294, 379
Menin Gate, 226
Menzies, Sir Robert, 48
Mercatel, 357, 362
Mérette Wood, 379
Méricourt, 334, 371, 379, 380, 405
Merivale
    Agnes, 28
    Catherine, 6, 11, 30, 31, 45, 57,
        211, 235, 245, 313
    George, 85, 96, 255, 267
    Herman, 46
    Janet Louisa, 6
    John (Jack), 128, 228, 230, 231,
        232, 233, 236, 237
    John Lewis, 6, 111
    Louis, 28
    Molly, 255, 262, 266, 267
    Reginald, 6, 11, 40, 41, 49, 149,
        171, 172, 184, 234, 247, 271,
        282, 283, 291, 295
    Sophie, 48
Merliemont, 375
Merville, 269, 270, 271, 274, 279, 280,
    364, 365, 386
Mesopotamia, 377, 421, 428
Messine Ridge, 363
Meteren, 170, 171, 172, 173, 174
Methuen, Lord, 89, 101
Milan, 17, 19, 113
Mildren, General, 375
Military Cross, 308, 325, 333, 382,
    387, 417, 423
Millencourt, 367, 368
Millichope Park, 109
Milton Lodge, 103
Minto
    Countess of, 116
    Earl of, 114
Moislains, 383, 384, 385
Molinghem, 250
Molliens au Bois, 368, 373, 376
Monck, Charles, 153
Moncrieffe, 100
Moncrieffe House, 15, 99
Mont St. Aubert, 392
Montdidier, 372
Montgomerie, Lt Colonel, 378, 385
Montgomerie, Major General, 367
Montmartre, 411
Montrieul, 251, 374, 375
Moon, Brigade Major Arthur, 373
Mordaunt
    Family, 32, 40
    Harry, 36
    Milly, 32
Morehouse
    George, 25
    Mr G.T., 29, 30, 35, 37, 38, 40, 58
Moret, 407
Morlancourt, 325, 379, 382
Morrison, Lena, 408
Morteldje, 308
Morval, 324, 358
Moulle, 250
Moyenneville, 360, 361
Muirhouse, George, 69
Munro, General, 58, 143, 151

443

Murray Threipland, Colonel, 288, 289
Murray, Lady, 327
Musgrave, Thomas, 190

N

Naish House, 28, 29, 30, 34, 35, 36, 37, 41, 55, 56, 57, 58, 59, 61
Nansham, Rosabelle, 300
Naples, 17, 106, 113
Napoleon V, 297
Nedonchel, 253
Neely, Lt Colonel, 381
Neuve Chapelle, 197, 199
Neuville Vitasse, 360
Neuvillette, 310
New York, 64, 114, 226
Nichols, James - bailiff, 10
Nieuwpoort, 70
Noeux Les Mines, 227, 238, 243, 254
North Somerset Yeomanry, 20, 21, 64, 112, 128, 157, 167, 170, 171, 174, 225, 420, 425, 426
Northcote, Lord, 94
Northland, Fatty, 171, 182, 189
Notre Dame de Lorette, 214, 215
Noyelles, 260
Noyon, 406
Nurlu, 384, 406
Nurlu-Péronne, 384

O

O'Brien, Barny, 338, 346
Oakham, 272
Oblinghem, 211, 218
Obolenski, Prince, 407
Ogsdon, Lt Colonel, 314
Olivier, R. Ernest, 29, 46, 47
Omdurman, Battle of 1898, 103
Onslow, George, 234
Oppy, 356
Orange River Colony, 64, 66
Orlando, Italian Prime Minister, 407
Orr Ewing, Norman, 337, 362
Ostend, 389
Oudeberg, 72
Ouderdom, 170
Ouichy Le Château, 136
Ouve Wirquin, 250

P

Paddington, 6, 112, 209
Pakenham, Byng, 325
Paris, 17, 127, 150, 249, 270, 292, 307, 308, 317, 334, 346, 349, 350, 376, 388, 393, 395, 397, 399, 400, 401, 402, 403, 404, 405, 406, 407, 408, 411, 412, 413, 416
Paris Plage, 374, 375
Parish, Colonel, 371
Parish, Paddy, 375, 377
Parnell, The Hon. Lt. William Alastair D., 323
Partridge Albert Victor, 426
Pascal, Lieutenant, 347
Pau, Pyrenees, 106
Paynter, George, 362, 396
Pembroke Lodge, 10, 12
Pembroke, Reggie, 399
Pendel Court, 43
Pereira, Brigadier, 330
Pereira, Colonel, 97, 146, 178, 180, 200, 293, 315
Pereira, General George, 278, 293, 317, 364
Pernes, 395
Péronne, 337, 383, 406
Perth, 252, 253
Philadelphia, 64
Picquigny, 350, 373, 375
Pietermaritzburg, 99
Pitlochry, 53
Ploegsteert, 363
Pole Carew, General, 206
Pollock, Freddy, 184
Ponsonby, General J., 304
Ponsonby, John, 237, 265, 279, 307, 315, 322
Ponsonby, Maurice, 240, 241, 247, 250, 251, 275, 280, 283, 290, 293, 294
Pont du Hem, 271, 277, 280, 281
Pont Fixe, 198, 199, 200, 209, 210, 212
Pont Tournant, 185
Pont Tournant Locon, 214
Ponting, Herbert, 293
Poperinghe, 151, 283, 285, 286, 289, 290, 293, 294, 295, 296, 302, 304, 310, 348
Port Elizabeth, 82, 86, 97, 98, 99
Port Elliot House, 109
Portal, Lt Colonel, 392
Portishead, 8, 414

Portugal, 17, 403
Potijze, 294
Pratt Barlow, Bobby, 295, 366
President Wilson, 387, 388
Presles, 150
Pretoria, 64, 65, 66, 67, 97, 99
Price Jones, Victoria, 256
Price, Ernest John, 426
Priez, 337
Priez Farm, 335, 337, 383
Primrose League, 45
Prince Arthur of Connaught, 174, 176
Prince of Wales, 114, 171, 196, 218, 220, 273, 274, 276, 308, 314, 317, 318, 322, 325, 328, 390, 398
Princip, Gavrilo, 124
Pringle (formerly Crawley) Inez, 105
Pringle, Miss A, 106
Proven, 309, 310
Pytte, 109

Q

Queen Mary, 196, 418
Queen Victoria, 62, 126
Quelmes, 297
Quesnoy, 197
Quinchy, 246

R

Radingham, 387, 388
Radley College, 112
Rajputana, 118, 121
Rambures Château, 326
Rancourt, 383
Rankin, Charlie, 67
Ransart, 363, 364
Rantzau, Baron, 409
Rasche, Guy, 304
Ravensworth Castle, 109
Rawal Pindi, 114
Rawlinson, General, 317, 326, 375
Raymond, Colonel, 208
Rebais, 135
Red Cross, 134, 164, 187, 347, 414, 415, 423, 428
Reims, 378
Renescure, 250
Rhodes, Cecil John, 94
Ribemont, 371
Richardson, Stewart, 296, 297

Richebourg St Vaast, 181, 182, 206, 214, 215
Riddel, Walter, 256
Rimington's Tigers, 68
Riviera, George, 283
Rivière, George, 376
Robeqc, 278
Roberts, Lord Roberts of Kandahar, 8, 64, 65, 67, 168, 221, 431
Robson, Company Sergeant Major, 254
Rodney, George, 250, 374
Roeux, 355, 356
Rolands, Brigadier-General, 371
Rolls Royce, 132, 151, 171
Romania, 367, 399
Rombly, 389
Rome, 17, 90, 106, 113, 407
Rouen, 130, 132, 133, 345, 349, 350
Rouge Croix, 280
Roulers, 388
Rowley, Dick, 132
Royal Welsh Fusiliers, 273, 275
Russo-Japanese War, 113
Ruthven, Lt Colonel, 253, 277
Rutledge, Tom, 234

S

S.M.S. Blucher, 188
Sackville-West, General, 401, 404
Saillisel, 329, 337, 405
Sailly, 329
Sailly Labourse, 238, 239, 240, 241, 242, 266
Sailly-Saillisel Château, 329, 330
Saisseval, 373
Salonica, 260, 264
Sandhurst, 13, 20, 64, 74, 82, 87, 256
Sarajevo, 124
Sarton, 312, 314
Savigny, Marquis de, 316
Saxmundham, 252
Scarpe, 350, 352, 355, 356
Schleswig, 399, 400, 403
Schmincke
    Fraulein Anna, 12, 24, 26, 27, 28, 29, 30, 31, 32, 33, 35, 36, 37, 38, 39, 40, 41, 42, 43, 46, 55, 58, 60, 61, 126, 127
Schoombie, 88, 91, 92
Schwarmstadt, 339
Scots Guards, 68, 156, 173, 201, 266, 270, 293, 305, 306, 320, 328, 329,

331, 333, 337, 339, 345, 353, 354, 357, 361, 362, 363
Scott, Eileen, 207, 313
Scott, Francis, 116, 140, 150, 207
Sedan, 215
Seely, Jack, Brigadier General, 274
Segrave, General, 397
Segrave, Lt Colonel, 371, 379
Selincourt, 375
Selincourt Château, 326, 327
Senhouse, Oscar, 219, 227, 239, 240
Senlis, 378, 406
Sergisson-Brooke, Pru, 282
Seville, 17
Seymour Brigadier General Archie, 355, 368, 371
Seymour, Brigadier-General Lord H., 329
Seymour, Copper, 239, 362
Shanghai, 416
Shaw-Stewart, Guy, 151, 152, 195, 206, 208, 212, 220, 242, 247, 251, 270, 275, 279, 285, 295, 307, 315
Simencourt, 346
Simla, 115, 116, 117, 118
Sinclair, Archie, 379
Skeffington-Smyth, Colonel, 280, 404
Smerna, 401
Smith
  A. H., 227, 250, 252
  A. J. H.., 290
  Arthur, 129, 130, 132, 196, 210, 270
  Colonel Wilfred, 217, 218
  Grenville, 187
  Hugh Abbot, 300
  John Hugh, 269, 284, 369, 371, 372, 373, 374, 375, 378, 379, 402
  Miss D., 56
Smithmasters
  Monica, 46
  Mr and Mrs, 46
Soissons, 370, 371, 378, 381
Sokoloff, Leonide, 173
Somme, 306, 375, 378, 379, 387, 405
Somme Battle, 317
Souastre, 359
Soupir, 137, 138, 140, 142, 143, 144, 145, 150
Southampton, 98, 129, 272, 344
Spa, Belgium, 402, 404
Spaignies, 358, 359

Spain, 11, 17, 403
Spencer
  Eric, 27, 38, 83
  Evelyn, 28, 31, 33, 39, 40, 45, 46, 56
  Family, 35
  Katherine, 106
  Kathleen, 23, 24, 28, 55
  Mrs, 28, 29, 31, 32, 36, 37, 39
Spiers, General, 400, 411
St. Andrews, 55
St. Floris, 389
St. George's Chapel, Windsor, 4, 5, 418, 419, 423
St. Germaine, 407
St. Hilaire, 389
St. Jan, 286, 287, 288
St. Jean, 153
St. Juliaan, 153, 304
St. Léger, 357, 358
St. Mard, 142, 144, 145, 150
St. Martin, 297, 363
St. Michel, 385
St. Moritz, 17, 106, 109
St. Omer, 151, 168, 195, 250, 252, 297, 298, 301
St. Petersburg, 17
St. Pierre Vaast Wood, 383, 384
St. Pol, 310, 347, 348, 385, 386, 395
St. Simeon, 135
St. Venant, 269, 388, 389
Staple, 301
Ste. Marie Capell, 301
Steele, Graham, 240
Steele, Julian, Colonel, 209, 215, 219, 227, 241, 243
Steenvoorde, 283, 286
Stellenbosch, 80
Stevens, Hestor, 375
Stewart, Geoffrey, 208
Stewart, Lady, 50, 54
Stewart, Mrs G., 183
Steynsburg, 86, 87
Stickland, Colonel, 366, 371, 373, 375, 377, 378, 379, 384
Stobart, Ralph, 354, 369
Stokes, Charles William Howard, 427
Stokes, Harold Ernest, 427
Stormberg, 90
Stowe the Nine Churches, 112
Stralsund, 128, 173
Stratton Firs, 81
Studd, Bertie, 397, 399
Studd, General, 403

446

Studley, 46
Sutton Nelthorpe, 331
Sutton Veny, 109
Switzerland, 17, 106, 109, 113, 257, 291, 299, 301, 313, 398, 401
Sydney, 229, 235, 237, 255, 267
Syria, 401

T

Tailles Wood, 381
Tanques, 355
Tatinghem, 298
Tempest-Hicks, Colonel, 275
Tennant, Edward, 153, 171
Tennant, Mark, 283
Tennyson, Aubrey, 355
Tennyson, Lionel, 133
The Hague, 394
Thebus, 85, 86, 87, 89, 90, 91
Thiembronne, 251, 252
Thompson, Sir William, 66
Thomson, Brigadier General, 397, 398, 399
Thornbury, 327
Thorne, Bulgey, 285, 315, 363
Thurso, 15
Thyers, 408
Torquil Matheson, Major General, 353
Touquin, 135
Tournai, 391, 392, 393
Towers-Clark, 170, 217, 219, 239, 240, 241, 247, 293, 402
Transvaal, 64, 93, 97
Trefusis, Jack, 193
Trench, Major, 349
Treport, 373
Trianon Palace, 398, 400, 403, 407, 408, 412
Trinity Hall Cambridge, 13
Tritton, Alan, 177
Triumph H.M.S., 231
Trones, 331
Trones Wood, 319, 322, 323, 329, 330, 331, 332, 333
Trossachs, 53
Trots Tours, 310
Trotter, Archie, 159, 175, 179
Trotter, Charles, 354, 355
Tufnell, C. E., 321, 322, 405
Tulloch Castle, 109
Turks, 228, 229, 232, 233
Turner, 2nd Lt., 348

Turner, General, 369
Tyntesfield, 4, 5, 6, 7, 8, 10, 11, 12, 14, 15, 16, 17, 22, 41, 43, 55, 60, 62, 63, 64, 69, 71, 72, 73, 77, 79, 82, 86, 88, 91, 92, 97, 104, 105, 106, 107, 110, 111, 112, 113, 114, 123, 124, 126, 167, 169, 184, 187, 221, 244, 245, 247, 272, 327, 361, 409, 414, 416, 418, 419, 422, 425, 426, 428, 431

U

Udaipur, 120, 121

V

Vailly, 142, 143, 144, 148
Valentine Williams, 400
Vancouver, 114
Vauchelles, 312
Vaud Audigny, 423
Vaudricourt, 269
Vaughan, Little Man, 137, 173, 185, 188, 206, 210, 213, 219, 243, 245, 247, 249, 282, 295, 297, 316, 322
Vaughan, Rev. Edward, 11
Vaughan, Rev. Henry, 105
Vaux-sur-Somme, 379
Vendin les Béthune, 249
Venice, 17, 19, 106, 113
Verchocq, 250, 251, 252, 253
Verdun, 286
Vereeniging
    Treaty of, 31 May 1902, 101
Verelst, Hal, 324
Vermand, 406
Vermelles, 237, 254, 258, 259, 261, 265, 267, 268
Verquin, 264
Versailles, 397, 398, 400, 401, 402, 403, 404, 407, 408, 409, 411, 412
Versturme Bunbury, 78
Vesey Dawson, General, 204
Ville, 333, 334, 382, 405
Villers Bretonneux, 374, 405
Villers sur Marne, 135
Ville-sur-Ancre, 369
Vitermont, 314, 315
Vlamertinge, 289, 295, 302
Von Haiking, Baron, 173
Von Kluck, General, 412
Von Mackensen, General August, 367
Vowles George Joseph, 427

W

Wagget, Father, 182
Walker Bout, Sir R., 203
Walker, Lieutenant T. K., 293
Wallace, Euan, 376
Walrond, Victor, 283
Walsh, Emily, 313
Walton, Colonel, 208
Warde-Aldam, 156
Wardrecques, 250
Warloy, 366, 376
Warlus, 357
Warner
   Lee, 58
   Plum, 64
Waterloo, 271, 272, 344
Waterloo Station, 418
Waterlot Farm, 319, 323
Watman, 43, 46, 68
Watman, Arthur, 66
Watou, 283, 285, 302
Watson Smyth, 270
Watts Russell, 256
Wavell Paxton, Captain, 342
Webber, Ralph, 340
Webster, Mary Ann, 6
Wellington Barracks, 129
Wells, 56
Wells Cathedral, 226
Welsh Fusiliers, 214, 274
Weltje, 304, 307
Wenlock, Lord, 420
West Indies, 64, 81, 345
Westmacott, Colonel, 160
Westmacott, Guy, 349
Westminster, Duke of, 418
Weston Super Mare, 31, 39, 40, 341
Whaley, Bertie, 350, 351, 352, 353
Whitaker, Jack, 275
White, Lucia, 207
Wieltje, 154, 286, 293
Willems, 394
Williams, Oscar, 427
Williams, Valentine, 401
Willoughby, Claud, 200
Wills, Honey, 40
Wilson, General H., 398
Wilson, President, 402
Wilson, Reggie, 355
Wimereux, 192, 209
Winchester, 277, 278, 280, 282, 313
Windsor, 41
Wing, General, 261
Wolfe, Brigadier-General, 377
Woodyer, Henry, 5, 7, 12
Worloy, 353, 368
Wormhout, 284, 285, 293, 309
Woyen, Drill Sergeant, 288
Wraxall, 64, 225
Wraxall, First Lord
   George Abraham, 428
Wraxall, Second Lord
   George Richard Lawley, 110
Wraxall, Third Lord
   Eustace Hubert Beilby, 110
Wright, Colonel, 346
Wyatt Thomas William, 427
Wynburg, 83, 85
Wyndham Portal, 370, 375, 378, 389, 396
Wynne-Finch, Billy, 346, 362
Wynne-Finch, John, 195, 241, 243, 246, 300
Wynne-Finch, Maisie, 247
Wynne-Finch, Mrs, 292, 300

Y

Yatton, 73
York, 62, 124, 147, 154, 162, 193, 197, 204, 208, 296, 338, 340, 423
York, Duchess of, 422, 428
York, Duke of, 419, 428
Young, Bella, 171, 195, 197
Ypres, 20, 131, 151, 152, 153, 155, 158, 159, 160, 161, 162, 169, 192, 210, 212, 213, 218, 224, 226, 263, 286, 287, 293, 294, 295, 296, 297, 303, 304, 306, 365, 423, 426, 431

Z

Zeebrugge, 389, 392, 393
Zegers-Cappel, 284, 285
Zillebeke, 155, 167
Zonnebeke, 161, 287

References

[i] Will of Matilda Blanche Gibbs, London Metropolitan Archive.
[ii] Family Memorials, Anna Merivale, Thomas Upward, Exeter, 1884.
[iii] Pedigree of the Merivale Family.
[iv] Pedigree of the Family of Gibbs, Rachel Gibbs, Kingprint Ltd. 1981. Chart XVIII.
[v] Pedigree of the Family of Gibbs, Rachel Gibbs, Kingprint Ltd. 1981. Charts XVIII and XXIV.
[vi] Sheila Hanlon, April 16, 2011, and Dr Alan Baker of Emmanuel College Cambridge, January 28, 2011.
[vii] Pedigree of the Family of Gibbs, Rachel Gibbs, Kingprint Ltd. 1981. Chart XXIV.
[viii] Photo albums of Anstice Kathereine and Janet Blanche Gibbs, and trophies at Tyntesfield.
[ix] Photo albums of Antony Gibbs (Tyntesfield), and of Anstice Katharine and Janet Blanche Gibbs.
[x] Diary of Henry Hucks Gibbs for 1873, courtesy of Lord Aldenham.
[xi] Pedigree of the Family of Gibbs, Rachel Gibbs, Kingprint Ltd. 1981. Chart XXIV.
[xii] Long Family Archive, Wiltshire County Archives, Chippenham.
[xiii] Via Gibbs, A Memoir by Madeline Alston, 1921 Constable, London.
[xiv] Photo Album of George and Via's visit to Egypt and the Sudan, 1902, Tyntesfield.
[xv] Bristol Newspaper – Press cutting June 17th 1903.
[xvi] Photo Albums of Albinia Rose and Janet Blanche Gibbs.
[xvii] Photo Albums of Albinia Rose, Anstice Katharine & Janet Blanche Gibbs.
[xviii] Doreen Bathurst Norman, née Gibbs, in conversation.
[xix] Via Gibbs, A Memoir by Madeline Alston, 1921 Constable, London.
[xx] Pedigree of the Family of Gibbs, Rachel Gibbs, Kingprint Ltd. 1981. Charts XXIV and XIVA.
[xxi] Pedigree of the Family of Gibbs, Rachel Gibbs, Kingprint Ltd. 1981. Chart XVIII.
[xxii] Pedigree of the Family of Gibbs, Rachel Gibbs, Kingprint Ltd. 1981. Chart XXXVII (8)
[xxiii] British Red Cross Records. Letter of 13th August 2004.
Geoffrey Dawson Diaries. Bodleian Library. Oxford.
[xxiv] Eustace, Lord Wraxall in conversation February 27th 2007.
[xxv] Via Gibbs, A Memoir by Madeline Alston, 1921 Constable, London.
[xxvi] Pedigree of the Family of Gibbs, Rachel Gibbs, Kingprint Ltd. 1981. Chart XXIII(1)
[xxvii] Daily Sketch, July 19th 1919, Romance of Queen's Niece, Page 3.
[xxviii] From contemporary press cutting.
[xxix] Via Gibbs, A Memoir by Madeline Alston, 1921 Constable, London.
[xxx] M.C. gazetted 14th November, 1916.
[xxxi] Pedigree of the Family of Gibbs, Rachel Gibbs, Kingprint Ltd. 1981. Chart XXIV(4)
[xxxii] M.C. gazetted 15th October, 1918.
[xxxiii] Bar to M.C. gazetted 30th July, 1919.
[xxxiv] Commonwealth War Graves Commission, and War Memorial at the Church of All Saints, Wraxall.
[xxxv] The Times. July 7th 1928, The Duke and Duchess of York, page 8.